# A Living Tree

# A Living Tree

THE ROOTS AND GROWTH OF JEWISH LAW

ELLIOT N. DORFF and ARTHUR ROSETT

A Centennial Publication of
The Jewish Theological Seminary of America

STATE UNIVERSITY OF NEW YORK PRESS

Published by
State University of New York Press, Albany

For information, address State University of New York Press,
90 State Street, Suite 700, Albany, NY 12207

**Library of Congress Cataloging-in-Publication Data**

Dorff, Elliot N.
   A living tree.

   Includes index.
   1. Jewish law—History.  2. Personal injuries (Jewish
law)  3. Marriage (Jewish law)  4. Conflict of laws
(Jewish law)  I. Rosett, Arthur I., 1934-
II. Title.
LAW                    340.5'8'089924          86-14581
ISBN 0-88706-459-0
ISBN 0-88706-460-4 (pbk)

10  9  8  7  6  5  4  3  2

*In honor of our children,*

Tammy, Michael, Havi, and Jonathan Dorff
David, Martha, and Daniel Rosett

Rabbi Meir said: When the Israelites came to receive the Torah, God said to them: "Bring to Me guarantors that you will observe it." They answered: "Our ancestors will vouch for us." God answered: "Your guarantors would need guarantors themselves for I have found fault with them." The Israelites answered: "Then our Prophets will vouch for us." God replied: "I have found fault with them also." Then the Israelites said: "Let our children be our guarantors." This was acceptable, and God then gave the Torah to Israel.

*Song of Songs Rabbah* on verse 1:4

# Contents

vii

# Preface

This book grew out of the course which we have taught together since 1974 at the School of Law of the University of California, Los Angeles. Rabbis Ben Zion Bergman and David Gordis taught with us during that first year, and they have given us invaluable help as we have carried our thinking further. Drs. Joel Rembaum and Elieser Slomovic of the University of Judaism and Dr. Israel Francis of the Jewish Theological Seminary of America have reviewed and commented on earlier versions of our manuscript or sections of it. Judith Wilson Ross reviewed and edited the manuscript for us. We are sincerely grateful for the constructive criticism which these teachers and colleagues have given us. None of them is responsible for the deficiencies in our work, but all deserve credit and thanks for their contributions and insights. We also thank Leslie Evans for his professional help with production and indexing.

"Rabbi Hanina said: Much have I learned from my teachers, more from my friends, and most of all from my students" (Ta'anit 7a). Our students throughout the years have contributed immeasurably to this volume. It has been a real joy to see these materials through their eyes. In the process we have, indeed, learned a great deal from them.

We would like to thank our secretaries over the years who have patiently typed and retyped the many previous versions of this manuscript. Their patient skill and good humor have been invaluable in creating this book. They include: Dorothe Brehove, Genevieve Gilbert-Rolfe, Sophie Gross, Irene Jensen, and Phyllis Weiner. We would also like to thank the University of Judaism and the School of Law of U.C.L.A. for making them available to us.

Ms. Edith Judith Nelson has given a generous grant to help insure the proper production and the wide distribution of this volume. Her constant enthusiasm for this project has been a source of strength and joy for us. We thank her for her financial and moral support, her patience, her unflagging interest, and her grace.

And finally, we would like to thank our families. At times they surely must have thought that we were engaged in a never-ending project that was taking an inordinate amount of our time and effort, but they proved willing to bear us and bear with us through the long period of this book's gestation. We thank them for their patience, their prodding, their good will, and their love.

Elliot N. Dorff

Arthur Rosett

# Acknowledgments

We acknowledge the following publishers who granted us permission to quote from their works:

**The Jewish Publication Society**

Excerpts from The Torah, The Prophets, and The Writings. Jacob Lauterbach (trans. 1935, 1973) Mekhilta, Nezikin, Ch. VI and VIII, Vol. III.
Solomon Freehof, A Treasury of Responsa, 1963.
All of the above copyrighted by and used through the courtesy of The Jewish Publication Society.

**Doubleday**

Excerpts from *The Jerusalem Bible*, copyright © 1966 by Darton, Longman & Todd, Ltd. and Doubleday & Company, Inc. Reprinted by permission of the publisher.

**Hebrew Union College Press**

Excerpts from Solomon Freehof, *Reform Responsa for Our Time*, Ch. 11, 1977. Reprinted by permission of the publisher.

**Jewish Theological Seminary of America**

Louis Finklestein, *Jewish Self-Government in the Middle Ages*. Reprinted by permission of the publisher.

**Little, Brown, and Company**

Karl N. Llewellyn, *The Common Law Tradition*, Appendix C. Reprinted by permission of the publisher.

**Oxford University Press**

Psalm 19 from *The New English Bible*. Copyright © The Delegates of the Oxford University Press and The Syndic of the Cambridge University Press, 1961, 1970. Reprinted by permission.

**Union of American Hebrew Congregations**

Excerpts from Solomon Freehof, *Reform Jewish Practice*, 1944. Reprinted with the permission of the Union of American Hebrew Congregations, New York, NY.

**Hebrew Publishing Company**

Excerpts from Birnbaum, *The Daily Prayerbook*. Reprinted by permission of the Publishers, Hebrew Publishing Company, copyright © 1949. All rights reserved.

**Princeton University Press**

Excerpts from James B. Pritchard, *The Ancient Near East in Pictures Relating to the Old Testament*, 2nd. ed. with supplement. Copyright 1954, © 1969 by Princeton University Press. Reprinted by permission of Princeton University Press.

**Commercial Law Journal**

Excerpts from C. Rothschild, "A New Deal on Costs," 39 Commercial Law Journal 43 (1934). Reprinted by permission of the publisher.

**Mercer Law Review**

Excerpts from Douglas Sturm, "American Legal Realism and the Covenantal Myth" 31 Mercer Law Review (1980). Reprinted by permission of the publisher.

**The Rabbinical Assembly**

Excerpts from Proceedings of the Rabbinical Assembly, 1968, "T'nai B'Kiddushin." Reprinted by permission of the publisher.

**Vanderbilt Law Review**

Excerpts from Karl N. Llewellyn, "Remarks on the Theory of Appellate Decision and the Rules or Canons About How Statutes are To Be Construed." 3 Vanderbilt Law Review 395 (1950). Reprinted by permission of the publisher.

**West Publishing Co.**

Excerpts from California Jury Instructions Civil (BAJI), 7th ed., 1986. Reprinted with permission of the publisher.

## Fred B. Rothman & Co.

Excerpts from Blumberg, "Cohabitation without Marriage," 28 UCLA Law Review, 1981. Reprinted by permission of the publisher.

## The American Law Institute

Excerpts from Restatement, Second, Conflict of Laws. Copyright 1971 by The American Law Institute. Reprinted with the permission of The American Law Institute.

## The New Yorker

"Notes and Comment," from The Talk of the Town, The New Yorker, August 30, 1976. Reprinted by permission of the publisher.

## Time

Excerpts from "The Hazards of Homemade Vows" and "The Ties That Bind." Copyright 1975, 1983, Time Inc. All rights reserved. Reprinted by permission from TIME.

# PART I

## *The Literature and Methods of Jewish Law*

# Introduction

This book traces the development of a legal system that has operated for more than three millenia in a variety of cultural, political, and economic environments around the world. The system has held together so long because the individuals subject to it, the Jews, see themselves as a single people, with a common history and destiny. Most important for our purposes, the Jews have been sustained by a shared body of law. Every human group that survives for a substantial period of time develops rules and norms to govern its members' relations and activities, but few civilizations have been so preoccupied with law as have the Jews.

The Jews have wandered over most of the earth, absorbing parts of many different cultures. Within Jewish communities diverse patterns of life have flourished. Despite these variations, the identity of the Jews has been sustained throughout their history by their allegiance to their people and to their law. That allegiance to law is the theme of this book. We believe it will be of interest to those nonlawyer Jews who wish better to understand their tradition and to non-Jewish lawyers who wish better to understand their calling.

## A. The Origins and Aims of This Book

This book grew out of a course in Jewish law at the UCLA School of Law. That course was originally designed to provide a professional tool for young lawyers working in legal service programs in Jewish neighborhoods in Los Angeles. From the first time the course was offered in 1974, the instructors, who then included Rabbis Ben Zion Bergman and David Gordis, were surprised and pleased to note that most of the students were seeking answers to larger questions than mere professional concerns. We have been reinforced in our personal commitment to discover that non-Jewish and nonreligious students are both drawn to these issues and feel rewarded and enriched by studying them.

Jewish law makes a number of assumptions that are at variance with those of American law. American law is seen as positivistic, skeptical, realist, democratic, mutable, functional, and instrumental. People make laws to get a job done, and when the law does not serve the perceived needs of the majority, it is to be changed. As the Declaration of Independence puts it: "To secure these rights, governments are instituted among men." Yet many Americans today long for intrinsic values that can claim to be true now and forever and certain beyond doubt. Jewish law grows out of a tradition that affirms these elements of life and tries to incorporate them in its institutions.

It is not our goal to provide readers with the truths of religion nor to convert them to observance of religious law. We are not salesmen for a system of religious law: its virtues sell themselves, and the limitations on its application in the modern world are apparent. Rather, we are interested in explaining two legal traditions to each other so that those committed to each may learn from the strengths of the other.

In the course of this study, those acquainted with the Jewish tradition will see familiar materials in a new perspective. Traditional Jews will find that texts they have studied from a religious perspective are even more meaningful when seen as legal materials responsive to the professional concerns of lawyers and judges. The legal perspective does not supplant the religious; it adds another kind of meaning. Religious readers may learn more about the assumptions of their tradition by contrasting them with those of another legal tradition, namely American law. Their identities as Jews and people of the modern age may be clarified by this examination of the two civilizations to which they belong.

Readers familiar with American law will find themselves addressing questions rarely asked in law school. Why is it important to have a legal system in the first place? When is it appropriate for officers of the law to change it? Why should anyone obey the law? What is the relationship of law to morality? Such questions are fundamental to any legal system, and American law is based on a specific way of answering them. Americans are often unaware of the assumptions embodied in American law, and they commonly think that the American way of handling issues is the only way to do so. Exposure to another system will help students of American law understand and evaluate its distinctive viewpoint and methodology. Jewish law is especially useful for this purpose because in some ways it is strikingly different from American law, and in other ways remarkably similar.

It is difficult to find any modern reader who is conversant with all of the pieces of this puzzle. Those who have been assiduous students of the rabbinic tradition are likely not to be familiar with the mind cast of the professional lawyer. There are many talented American-Jewish lawyers who slept through, or avoided, Hebrew school. In our eight years of teaching this material to Jewish and gentile law students, we have been frustrated by the need to explain material to one part of our audience that seems elementary to another part. Our universal experience, however, is that whatever part of the audience thought that a particular point was old hat would be likely to find some equally basic point novel. Since our aim is to contribute to explaining two great traditions to each other, we are likely to expend more time on basics than any single reader will find necessary. We also will look at some familiar material from a perspective that many readers may find surprising, even suspect. It may trouble some readers that we take a critical stance even when dealing with a divine text. Our skepticism is based on a deep respect for the material we examine and our confidence that this material will bear that scrutiny.

## B. THE STRUCTURE AND METHODS OF THIS BOOK

No one book can hope to encompass the richness, complexity, and coherence of the Jewish tradition over time, but we must dip in somewhere to sample the flavor. This book is divided into two units, which will introduce the reader to the tradition from somewhat different perspectives.

The first unit attempts to provide a historical and literary conspectus of the whole. In it the reader is introduced to a variety of legal forms, including codes, judicial opinions and rulings, legislation, scholarly treatises, and custom. The unit follows a chronological sequence, tracing the development of the law of personal injury through the ages. A chronological approach is used because most of the forms of law are associated with a particular historical period, although some, particularly judicial precedents and customs, are created in every age.

Legal form cannot be appreciated without an appreciation of substance. The law of personal injury is of course very important for its own sake, but it is not our primary concern. Personal injury is used as the example for Part I to demonstrate the breadth of Jewish law. While large bodies of Jewish law are devoted to the ritual and family concerns that Americans usually consider part of the domain of religions, Jewish law encompasses all of the topics included in secular legal systems, such as criminal law, civil law (contracts, property, credit and security, landlord-tenant relations), court procedures, medical law, and public law (those governing the operation of the state). The study of Jewish law therefore provides an opportunity to examine the relationship between religion and law in the context of a tradition that sees life as suffused with both. There are several other jurisprudential issues that will be considered when introducing the literature and methodology of Jewish law in Part I. These include basic questions about the functions and authority of law and its practitioners. At different points the tradition seems to see the law as a mysterious, Divine command engraved in stone, the indeterminate outcome of an argument among experts, the substance of a wise man's opinion, the provision of a human statute enacted by a representative legislature, one section of a comprehensive code of law, or a reflection of the community's customary practice. Sometimes it sees law as all of these. Judges can be seen as instruments for implementing long-established law, but they are also political leaders who manipulate the law to accomplish social ends, autocratic authorities who act by whim as much as by rules, or agents of God who reinforce old worlds and create new ones by mediating God's revelation to the human world. These jurisprudential inquiries into the nature of law, its operation, and authority may be the most fascinating aspect of this book for many readers.

Another major objective of the first unit is to examine the methodology of law in general and Jewish law in particular. Since the history of Jewish law spans close to 4,000 years, Jews have often been faced with the task of implementing law that has been received in forms and words that they found strange but that they believed nonetheless to be Divine in origin and authority. Such law could not be ignored, although it required great skill to interpret and apply it in a different setting. This is a perfect opportunity to examine the preoccupation with interpretive method and authority that marks lawyers of every age and culture.

The second unit examines the institution of marriage, in part because its structure provides an interesting contrast with contemporary secular attitudes toward intimate family relations. In addition, marriage illustrates how Jewish law has reacted to the existence of conflicting legal systems. During two millenia of exile Jewish law has been forced to recognize that the authorities of the land claimed jurisdiction over the Jews who lived within its borders. Since the eighteenth-century Enlightenment, the secular state has asserted regulatory authority over marriage, divorce, and family concerns. This second unit thus will be a study in the conflict of laws, how Jewish law has responded to secular law, and how secular authorities have responded to Jewish law.

To appreciate this legal tradition one must read the texts that embody it; it is not enough to read *about* the law. Jewish legal texts place heavy demands on the reader. The readings given here in translation are heavily edited, and the reader is thrown into them without the lengthy preparation students of the tradition receive. The conventions of language and reasoning are difficult to convey in translation, and texts that are many centuries old are not easy reading even when one knows the language. These problems should not be understated. They can be overcome, however, and the effort to do so will be rewarded by a sense of the dynamic operation of the system that cannot be achieved by a narrative description of what the text says.

Many texts would be needed to provide a comprehensive view of the law and to support all the assertions made in introductory notes, but it is important that the materials be kept to manageable length. Crucial texts are therefore included in the body of materials, but no attempt is made to adduce every relevant source on any topic.

In addition to the texts and introductory notes, the materials contain readings from Anglo-American law to provide a contrast for the texts from the Jewish tradition. It would be facile to suggest that one can make direct comparisons from scraps of text drawn from distinct traditions separated by thousands of miles and years. Nonetheless, many aspects of each system have analogies in the other, and some awareness of how other lawyers deal with a problem will increase the reader's understanding and appreciation of both systems.

## C. Who Are the Jews?

To understand Jewish law, it is important to have a rudimentary knowledge of the whereabouts and activities of the Jews during the major epochs of their past. The Jewish tradition has its own system for numbering years from the date of the creation of the world, under which the first half of 1987 falls in the year 5747. For most secular purposes Jews conform to the system of years used by their Christian neighbors. Those years before Christ (B.C.) are referred to as years Before the Common Era (B.C.E.), and those after Christ (A.D.) are referred to as years of the Common Era (C.E.).

The following provides an overview. Other relevant historical information is included throughout the book to help the reader understand the legal developments of a period. Reference to a globe or map of Europe and the Middle East will make the following overview more understandable and memorable.

1. *The Biblical Period* (c. 1700 B.C.E–150 B.C.E)

a. *The Patriarchal Period* (c. 1700–c. 1600 B.C.E.) The biblical stories of Abraham, Isaac, and Jacob reflect a time when the ancestors of the Jews, called the Hebrews, moved from Mesopotamia (modern Iraq and Iran) to Canaan (Palestine), where they gained the name "Israelites" (meaning Children of Israel, Israel being another name for Jacob).

b. *Egypt and the Exodus* (c. 1600–1290 B.C.E.) The Israelites lived in Egypt, first as a favored group and then as slaves. They left Egypt about 1290 B.C.E. and wandered in the wilderness stopping at Mount Sinai, where God's will was revealed in the most important theophany of the Jewish faith.

c. *The Conquest of the Land: Joshua, the Judges, Saul, David, and Solomon* (1290–922 B.C.E.) The Israelites wandered through the Sinai and trans-Jordan, crossing into Canaan at Jericho. During the next three centuries they gradually gained possession of all of modern-day Israel and a section of modern Jordan. There were intermittent periods of unity and disunity, war and peace. Under King David (c. 1000–961 B.C.E.) and King Solomon (c. 961–922 B.C.E.) their territory expanded considerably, from the Euphrates River in modern Syria to the Brook of Egypt in the northwestern corner of the Sinai Peninsula, incluing modern Israel, Jordan, and Gaza, and parts of Lebanon, Syria, and Egypt.

d. *The First Temple Period* (c. 922–586 B.C.E.) King Solomon built the First Temple, which was not only a place of worship, but the center of government and commerce for his whole realm. After his death, however, Solomon's heirs fought over the right of succession, and from c. 922 B.C.E. until 722 B.C.E the Israelites were split into two kingdoms, a northern kingdom (Israel or Efraim) consisting of ten of the twelve tribes, and a southern kingdom (Judah) consisting of two tribes. In 722 the Assyrians, from the northern Tigris River valley, conquered Samaria, the capital of the northern kingdom, and its population was dispersed. From then on, the ten northern tribes lost their identity and became, as they were later known, "the Ten Lost Tribes." The Assyrians continued south and beseiged Jerusalem, capital of the southern kingdom, but did not destroy it. The Jews (that is, citizens of the Kingdom of Judah) continued on as a vassal territory subject to Assyria from 722 to 612, when the Babylonians (from the southern Tigris and Euphrates River valleys) conquered the Assyrian capital of Nineveh. The Babylonians took over Judah (despite an attempt led by Egypt to prevent them from doing so) and ruled it until 586, when they destroyed the Temple (and, with it, the First Commonwealth) in response to a revolt. The First Temple Period was the age of the prophets and kings, including Elijah, Elisha, and King Ahab (mid-ninth century), Amos (c. 750) and Isaiah of Jerusalem (or First Isaiah, c. 742–701 B.C.E.), and King Josiah and Jeremiah (c. 622–586 B.C.E.)

   e. *The Babylonian Exile* (586–516 B.C.E.) The Babylonians took most of the inhabitants of Jerusalem to Babylonia. There the Jews dreamed of returning to Israel, and prophets like Ezekiel and Second Isaiah assured the people that they would return. The Persians (from modern Iran) conquered the Babylonians in 539. They permitted the Jews to return to Jerusalem, and in 516 some did under the leadership of Haggai and Zekhariah. They rebuilt the Temple and founded the Second Jewish Commonwealth in Israel. Many Jews remained in Persia because they were treated well there. In fact, from 586 B.C.E. to about 1050 C.E., a period of over 1600 years, a Jewish community thrived in that area of the world.

2. *The Second Temple Period* (516 B.C.E.–70 C.E.) (also known as the Inter-Testamental Period)

   In this period Jews lived primarily in Israel and Persia, although there were Jewish communities throughout the Mediterranean Basin and the Middle East from this point in history to the present. A second attempt to bring significant numbers of Jews back to Israel was organized under Ezra and Nehemiah in the middle of the fifth century B.C.E. Ezra is credited with establishing the official version of the Torah and appointing a group of elders to be its official interpreters. This body, known at different periods as the Great Assembly, the Gerousia, and the Sanhedrin, served as the supreme judicial authority for the Jewish people. Its decisions were handed down orally from one generation to the next. From the fifth through the second centuries B.C.E. Hellenistic influence was very strong as Israel was alternately ruled by the Seleucids (Syrian Greeks) and the Ptolemies (Egyptian Greeks). This is reflected in some of the Wisdom literature that makes up the last part of the Hebrew Bible (Proverbs, Job, Ecclesiastes), and even more strongly in some of the books of the Apocrypha (the outside books), which Jews produced but which were not ultimately accepted as part of the Jewish Bible. The Apocrypha also includes the books of Maccabees, which tell the tale of the Jewish revolt against Greek rule in 165 B.C.E. (the Hanukkah story) and the resultant reign of Jewish kings in Israel for close to a century. After that time, the Romans gained control of Israel. That is the regime reflected in the New Testament. In response to a revolt (66–70 C.E.), the Romans destroyed the Second Temple in 70, bringing this period to a close. During this time there were a number of Jewish sects, with varying interpretations and practices;

only in the next period did Judaism become fixed in roughly the form that it is now known.

### 3. The Mishnaic (Tannaitic) Period (70–220 C.E.)

The destruction of the Second Temple was a traumatic event for the Jewish people, for the center of Jewish political and religious life was demolished. A series of political and religious persecutions, coupled with difficult economic conditions, made life even worse for the Jews during the next century and a half. Consequently, during the second century a significant number of Jews migrated from Israel to Persia, where they joined a relatively well-off Jewish community. The difficult conditions also prompted the rabbis to organize and consolidate the oral traditions. The most important collection is the Mishnah, which gained authority second only to the Torah almost as soon as it was published (c. 220 C.E.).

### 4. The Talmudic (Amoraic) Period (220–500 C.E.)

During this period a large group of Jews lived in Persia and a significant number continued to live in Israel. When Rome became Christian in the fourth century, increasing legal restrictions were placed upon the Jews in Israel living under Roman and Byzantine rule. Consequently, by about 400 the Israeli rabbis consolidated and edited their traditions in what became known as the Palestinian (or Jerusalem, or Western) Talmud. In Persia the Jews enjoyed relative religious freedom and autonomy during most of this period. Jewish legal and cultural institutions flourished. Following a period of persecutions between 455 and 475, however, the rabbis in Persia felt the need to edit their interpretations and applications of the Mishnah in what became known as the Babylonian Talmud. The Babylonians ruled the Jews for only a brief period of Jewish history—605–539 B.C.E.—but it was they who brought Jews in exile to the Tigris-Euphrates basin. Consequently from then on Jews commonly called that area of the world "Babylonia," no matter who ruled it. Hence the name is "Babylonian Talmud," even though the text was produced between 200 and 500 C.E., when the Babylonians were long gone.

### 5. The Period of the Saboraim (500–650 C.E.)

During this period the sages living in Persia added comments and notes to the text of the Babylonian Talmud as Jews continued to live in a relatively stable and tolerant environment. Jews living in Israel were under the rule of the Byzantines, and the legal restrictions against them grew increasingly harsh throughout the fifth and sixth centuries, culminating in a series of anti-Jewish riots between 550 and 650. There are virtually no remains of Israeli legal activity from this time, possibly as a result of the suppression of studying the Mishnah that began with the decree of Emperor Justinian I in 553.

## 6. *The Geonic Period* (650–1050)

Jews living in southern Europe and Asia Minor during this period were under the often intolerant rule of Christian kings and clerics, but most Jews lived in the Muslim Arab realm, including those in Israel, North Africa, and Babylonia. Although there were periods and places in which Jews suffered persecution, especially toward the end of this period, by and large Jewish communal and cultural life flourished under Arab rule. The universally recognized centers of Jewish life at this time were the Jewish law schools in Sura and Pumbeditha in Babylonia. The heads of those law schools, called Geonim, were consulted by Jews throughout the world on matters of Jewish law. They answered in responsa—that is, responses to the questions they were asked. That genre of legal literature became the primary vehicle for the operation of Jewish law from that time to today. The official head of the Jewish community was a man appointed by the government, known as the Exilarch (head of the community in exile from Israel) as it had been during Persian times. The Israeli community attempted to reassert its authority during the ninth century by reviving the system of fixing the calendar through sightings of the moon taken in Jerusalem, but the Geonim successfully asserted the preeminence of their own authority over that of the Israeli leaders. A longer and harder battle had to be waged against the Karaites, especially during the ninth and tenth centuries. The Karaites denied the authority of rabbinic interpretations of the Torah from the time of Ezra to their own; they claimed instead that Jews should live by the written Torah alone. Rabbinic Judaism ultimately emerged triumphant, but only after a long, hard fight. Interest among Jews in the Hebrew language flourished during this period, when a number of Hebrew grammars and a large body of Hebrew liturgical poetry were produced.

## 7. *The Period of Posekim and Rishonim* (1000–1550)

The capital of the Umayyid Caliphate (661–750) was in Damascus, and its successor, the Abbasid Caliphate (750–1258), ruled from Baghdad. As a result, the cultural and economic center during the first centuries of Muslim rule was indisputably in the east, and the Jewish communities of Iraq (Babylonia) were the center of the Jewish world too. Even so, the wave of Muslim conquest across North Africa and on into Spain in the seventh, eighth, and ninth centuries brought with it the migration of some Jews to the western Mediterranean, where they took advantage of the new economic opportunities the unified realm provided.

By the eleventh century, however, it appears that most of the world's Jews lived in the Muslim and Christian lands of the west. Increasing political strife and civil disorder in Iraq began in the late ninth century. This increased the flow of Jews to the west. The Fatimid counter-Caliphate (909–1171) in North Africa and their successors, the Ayyubids (1171–1250), ignored the Koran's discriminatory tariffs against nonbelievers and even permitted Jews to hold high political office. These regimes were open and aggressive in their economic activities. They fostered a tolerant, humanistic culture. Under such conditions Jewish communities flourished. The Jewish community of Qayrawan (in modern Tunisia) was especially well known for its scholarship, and its counterpart in Fustat, Egypt, gained prominence in size, wealth, and political influence. Jews in Muslim, and later Christian, Spain of the tenth and eleventh centuries enjoyed a vertible golden age, combining economic and political security with rich cultural creativity.

Parallel developments in Christian western Europe promoted Jewish migration there. Beginning with Charles the Great (Charlemagne, crowned in 800) and his dynasty, and continuing with the Capetian and Ottonian dynasties, Christian emperors in France and Germany ignored the rules of the Church and extended liberal economic charters to Jewish tradesmen, granting them freedom of worship and economic advantages if they would help establish the commercial structure of their empires. The number of Jews in most European communities would reach only several dozen families, in comparison to the tens of thousands of persons in the largest Jewish communities under the Muslims, but the cultural productivity of the Europeans earned them a place in Jewish memory far beyond what their numbers would warrant.

From the eleventh through the fourteenth centuries, then, most Jews lived in the western Mediterranean basin and in western Europe under the feudal systems prevailing in both the Muslim and Christian countries. The Jews had been scattered before, but now, with the decline of both the Muslim and Jewish centers of power in Iraq, there was no single place in the world which was the recognized center for Jewish learning and the authoritative forum for decisions on matters of Jewish practice. Consequently, rabbis recognized the need for written commentaries on the Torah and Talmud and for codes summarizing the requirements of Jewish law so that Jews living in far-flung communities could continue the tradition. The commentary of Rashi (Rabbi Shlomo Yitzhaki, 1040–1105) and the codes of Maimonides (1135–1204, the *Mishneh Torah*) and Jacob ben Asher (1270–1343, the *Tur*) became especially popular. Because there was no central authority, various community customs became more important during this period and ultimately entered the codes and precedents that were produced by rabbis all over the world. A number of Jewish communities also issued *takkanot*, that is, legislative enactments designed to regulate the practices of the members of those communities. This period ended with the writing of the *Shulhan Arukh*, a code that gained more authority than any other because it recorded the practices of Jews living in the Mediterranean Basin and the Middle East (the *Sepharadim*) and also included notes indicating the different practices of Jews living in France and Germany (the *Ashkenazim*). Jews were not allowed to own land or engage in agriculture in many Christian countries, and so most earned a living through business and international trade, leading to the stereotypes that pervade Christian literature during the last thousand years. This was the period of the Crusades and the Inquisition, during which Jews were murdered in pogroms, forced to engage in staged disputations with Christian authorities, and ultimately expelled from most of the countries of Western Europe.

## 8. The Period of the Aharonim (1550–present)

Expelled from Western Europe, Jews moved east to the central and eastern sections of Europe and the Mediterranean Basin. There they found themselves in the uncomfortable position of being middlemen between the landowners and the peasants, and they often were the objects of the ire of the latter group toward the former. The *Shulhan Arukh* was generally accepted as the standard of Jewish practice, but the many commentaries and glosses written about it effectively continued the diversity in Jewish practice in communities throughout the world. In the nineteenth and twentieth centuries Jews living in Western and Central Europe and in America were strongly influenced by the ideologies and politics of the Enlightenment. Yet, until World War II, most Jews lived under authoritarian regimes in Eastern Europe and Muslim countries, where conditions remained virtually the same as in medieval times. The decimation of European Jewry by Nazi Germany, the emergence of the American Jewish community as the largest in the world, and the establishment of the State of Israel have radically changed Jewish cultural, political, and religious life in the second half of the twentieth century.

Those who would delve into Jewish history deeper will find the following books helpful: Robert M. Seltzer, *Jewish People, Jewish Thought: The Jewish Experience in History* (New York: Macmillan, 1980)—a readable, clearly written treatment with considerable attention to Jewish intellectual history as well as Jewish social history, with chronological tables and maps; Haim Hillel Ben-Sasson, ed., *A History of the Jewish People* (Cambridge: Harvard University Press, 1976)—a compilation of extensive, thorough monographs on Jewish social history; Leo W. Schwarz, ed., *Great Ages and Ideas of the Jewish People* (New York: Modern Library, 1956)—six essays by distinguished historians on the ideational development of the major periods of Jewish history; and Louis Finkelstein, ed., *The Jews: Their History, Culture, and Religion,* 4th ed. (New York: Schocken, 1949, 1970)—a rich collection of essays on many aspects of Jewish history, culture, and religion.

### D. COMMON MISCONCEPTIONS ABOUT JEWISH LAW

Jews and Christians often labor under a number of misconceptions about Jewish law, and it is important to dispel some of the more common ones at the very beginning.

Contemporary Jews come into contact with Jewish law primarily in ritual and family matters. They know, for example, that there are laws concerning diet (the rules of kosher food), the Sabbaths and festivals, and life-cycle events, including birth, adolescence (Bar or Bat Mitzvah), marriage, divorce, and death. As important as those rules are, Jewish law is not limited to them. Rabbinic courts throughout the ages have also dealt with the whole range of civil and criminal matters, including contracts, bailments, landlord-tenant disputes, land law, inheritance, bankruptcy, fraud, theft, assault, and murder. Consequently, when rabbis describe Judaism as a way of life, they are not just engaging in poetic flourish; they are accurately describing a system that embraces all of life. As already indicated, remedies for personal injuries has been chosen as the topic for the first unit to emphasize this point, but it is only one example of the topics that Jewish law treats.

Misunderstandings about the content of Jewish law are fairly easy to correct, but the misconceptions that Jews and Christians have about its methodology and effectiveness are much harder to uproot. Jewish law is *not* equivalent to biblical law, and it did *not* end with the close of the biblical period or the advent of Jesus. It is based on the Bible, but it has developed continuously since then through interpretation, legislation, and custom, and for most of Jewish history it has been the major, if not the exclusive, governing authority for Jews. Jewish law is thus a prime example of how law develops. Methods to apply and adapt the law were built into its corpus from the time of the Bible on. The rabbis of the classical tradition claimed that their interpretations were the new form of God's revelation, replacing visions and voices. Those features of Jewish law proclaim loudly that it is intended to be a law for all generations, and so Jews have lived it.

The fact that legal interpretation represents the primary form of God's revelation available in our time means that studying the law is a holy act. Even God, according to the Jewish tradition, spends a quarter of each day studying Jewish law, and He spends another quarter instructing school children (*Avodah Zarah* 3b). A legend relates that when Moses visited God in His heavenly abode, he found Him lovingly placing elaborate crowns on the Hebrew letters of the Torah so that later generations, including Akiba and his rabbinic colleagues, would be able to "expound upon each dot heaps and heaps of laws" (*Menahot* 29b). For the Jewish tradition, the law is not just a convenient mechanism for running society. It is the word and occupation of God Himself, and it embraces all that is valuable and worthwhile in life. Studying law is to be prized over many other important pursuits, for it encompasses them all.

> *Shabbat* 127a
> Performance of these commands brings an immediate reward as well as bliss in the time to come: honoring one's parents; deeds of loving kindness; prompt attendance, morning and evening, at the house of study; hospitality to strangers; visiting the sick; dowering the needy bride; caring for the dead; devotion in prayer; and making peace among people. But the study of Torah is equivalent to them all.

Jewish law is therefore not narrowly ritualistic, and it is not archaic either. On the contrary, Jewish tradition compares Jewish law to a living tree. As the Torah, the sacred scroll of the Five Books of Moses, is returned to the ark after being read in synagogue services, the liturgy quotes from the biblical book of Proverbs (4:2, 3:18, 17):

> I give you good instruction; never forsake My Torah.
> It is a tree of life for those who hold fast to it, and those who uphold it are happy.
> Its ways are pleasant, and all its paths are peace.

The tree of Jewish law certainly has many tangled branches—so many that one sometimes wonders how they can all be part of the same organism. Some parts of the tree of tradition thin out over time, while others flourish and broaden to suit the needs at hand. Some readers may doubt whether the twisted shapes, bent by time and the diversity of human husbandry, still possess the regenerative power of a living tree. The doubters should look hard at the tips of the branches, for there they will see new fruit just now forming.

# Topic One: Biblical Law

Biblical materials are a natural starting place for any discussion of Jewish law. The biblical books contain the basic legal norms the tradition holds to be part of the covenant between God and Israel. The legal content of the Bible comes to be regarded in later periods as a constitutional body of doctrine that is of unique authority because of its Divine authorship. This material thus forms the literary core upon which later Jewish law is built.

The study of biblical law is concerned primarily with the extensive collection of codes, commandments, and cases reported in four of the books of the Pentateuch (the five books of Moses). These materials are explicitly legal in style and content. Before turning our attention to these codes, however, it is worth noting that the descriptions of the earlier patriarchal period in the first book of the Pentateuch, the Book of Genesis, also contain clear evidence that the society of those early times had developed sophisticated legal institutions.

Throughout this book, biblical translations without further reference will be from the Jewish Publication Society editions: *The Torah* (1962); *The Prophets* (1978); and *The Writings* (1982). At a number of points a substitute translation from a Catholic publication, *The Jerusalem Bible* (1966), or from a Protestant translation, *The New English Bible* (1961) has been used. When one of the latter two translations is used, it is indicated in the citation.

## A. The Biblical World

The Book of Genesis is in part a sacred family history and in part a collection of long-remembered tales to be told around the fire. It traces the tale of the clan of Abraham from the beginning of Creation. Whatever its sources may be, there is little reason to doubt the essential authenticity of the tales or that they were carefully preserved for many generations before being reduced to their present, written form. Modern archaeology has provided ample evidence that these stories contain a kernel of historic truth that their transmitters may not have always understood. For our purposes, the most important kernels of history are the signs of a fairly sophisticated legal system that operated in the patriarchal period.

The Bible describes Abraham and his kinsmen as "ēv'rim" coming from the root meaning "to pass"—in this instance, to wander along the Fertile Crescent of Mesopotamia, which is located in what today is part of Syria and Iraq. Some of the ēv'rim or "Habiru," kept flocks of sheep and herds of cattle, as Abraham did. Others were skilled craftsmen. Still others hired themselves out as workers or warriors. Often they made sudden raids on caravans and on weak, outlying communities. When successful, they settled down permanently in the areas they had conquered; when unsuccessful, they became prisoners of war and slaves of their conquerors. Eventually, those who lost in war were absorbed by the settled communities in which they were enslaved, and the conquering nomads adopted names associated with the territories they had acquired. Hence the Moabites, Ammonites, and Edomites. (Consequently, beginning with Jacob, the Bible no longer uses the term "Hebrews," but "Children of Israel.")

It is this nomadic raider's life that is described in the story of the war in chapter 14 of Genesis, for at that time the land of Canaan was well suited to such free movement. In Abraham's time, the land was held under loose Egyptian control. Because the lowlands had the best soil and water supply, the cities of Canaan were located along the Mediterranean coastal plain and in the valleys of Jezreel and the Jordan. Central Canaan, the hilly region between the Jordan Valley and the coastal plain, was not good farming land and was sparsely settled. The high country was able to support the grazing of sheep and cattle, however, and nomadic newcomers would not have to compete with a firmly settled people to use the land for that purpose. The hilly country of Canaan thus was especially inviting to wanderers. It was there and in the even emptier and drier Negev valley below that Abraham and his family settled. In the hill country, Abraham, Isaac, and Jacob settled in such places as Mamre, Bethel, Shekhem, and Dothan. Archaeologists have unearthed the last three places and have found tangible evidence of what the Bible reports. In the Negev, Beersheva was the strategic center then, as it has remained ever since. In Abraham's time, Sodom and Gemorah and other towns flourished at the southern end of the Dead Sea. Recent excavations have supplied support for the biblical story of their catastrophic end.

Abraham and his family, including his nephew, Lot, lived a semi-nomadic life that required a clear and simple chain of command within

the community. The basic social unit in this patriarchal society was
the clan. In the nomadic tribes the elders of each clan ruled their families within a larger unit that consisted of a loose council. The common
pattern was for the elders to sit together in camp, or, when settled, in
the gate of the city and supervise the community's affairs. In time of
crisis, an ad hoc leader, often referred to as a "judge," might be given
temporary power to rule. From time to time a charismatic leader
would appear to unite the scattered clans for some great effort. But the
residual and crucial social unit remained the extended family, united
by common descent and loving allegiance to a ruling elder.

As communities became more settled, the practice of electing a
temporary ruler or king led to permanent royal government. Eventually the idea of a dynasty took hold, in which the right of succession
passed by descent from father to son with little residual power in the
clan elders to deny ratification, no matter how untalented the heir
might be. By 2000 B.C.E. the royal laws of the kingdoms of Mesopotamia were embodied in law codes, but the Israelites were not governed
by a permanent monarchy until a thousand years later.

The documents from those early times that survive in Genesis include several that appear to have been designed to serve primarily a legal function by a draftsman whose mindset would be familiar to anyone who knows how lawyers draft documents that create and protect
interests in land. Chapter 23 of Genesis records Abraham's purchase of
real property, the cave of Makhpelah, which is the traditional burial
place of the Hebrew patriarchs near the present-day city of Hebron.
The concerns of the author of the ancient text are apparent and would
be quite understandable to a modern real estate lawyer. He is interested in establishing a record that will place his client's title to the
burial caves beyond all cloud or conceivable adverse claim. As you read
the text, note, for example, (a) Abraham's refusal to take the caves as
a gift and his insistence that he provide consideration and purchase
them; (b) the repeated recitals in the text of the presence of witnesses
to the transaction, especially for two vital steps—the naming of the
price by the seller and the payment by the buyer; (c) the careful description of the precise boundaries of the parcel sold—not just the
cave, but the adjacent field and the trees as well; (d) the mention that
the transaction occurred in the town gate, the appropriate location for
public business; and (e) the careful preservation of the chapter itself as
a sort of closing memorandum stuffed in the file. What follows is the
chapter itself, without its context. It has been placed in the Bible without obvious connection to the material that immediately precedes or
follows it.

*Genesis 23:*
Sarah's lifetime—the span of Sarah's life—came to one hundred and twenty-seven years. Sarah died in Kiriath-arba—now Hebron—in the land of Canaan; and Abraham proceeded to mourn for Sarah and to bewail her. Then Abraham rose from beside his dead and spoke to the children of Heth, saying, "I am a resident alien among you; sell me a burial site among you, that I may remove my dead for burial." And the children of Heth replied to Abraham, saying to him, "Hear us, my lord: you are the elect of God among us. Bury your dead in the choicest of our burial places; none of us will withhold his burial place from you for burying your dead." Thereupon Abraham bowed low to the people of the land, the children of Heth, and he said to them, "If it is your wish that I remove my dead for burial, you must agree to intercede for me with Ephron, the son of Zohar. Let him sell me the cave of Makhpelah which he owns, which is at the edge of his land. Let him sell it to me in your presence, at the full price, for a burial site."

Ephron was present among the children of Heth; so Ephron the Hittite answered Abraham in the hearing of the children of Heth, all who sat in the gate of the city, saying, "No, my lord, hear me:

I give you the field and I give you the cave that is in it; I give it to you in the presence of my people. Bury your dead." Then Abraham bowed low before the people of the land, and spoke to Ephron in the hearing of the people of the land, saying, "If only you would hear me out! Let me pay the price of the land; accept it from me, that I may bury my dead there." And Ephron replied to Abraham, saying to him, "My lord, do hear me! A piece of land worth four hundred shekels of silver—what is that between you and me? Go and bury your dead." Abraham accepted Ephron's terms. Abraham paid out to Ephron the money that he had named in the hearing of the children of Heth—four hundred shekels of silver at the going merchants' rate.

So Ephron's land in Makhpelah, facing Mamre—the field with its cave and all the trees anywhere within the confines of that field—passed to Abraham as his possession, in the presence of the children of Heth, of all who sat on the council of his town. And then Abraham buried his wife Sarah in the cave of the field of Makhpelah, facing Mamre—now Hebron—in the land of Canaan. Thus the field with its cave passed from the children of Heth to Abraham, as a burial site.

The Book of Genesis contains other artifacts of legal concerns in patriarchal society, including:

- The tale of Esau's sale of his birthright suggests a fixed system of succession on death, with preference for primogeni-

ture and recognition that the expectation of the firstborn is
alienable (Gen. 27);

- Laws against marriage out of the clan (Gen. 24; 26:34–35;
27:46–28:9);

- Obligations of levirate marriage, the obligation of a brother
to marry a childless brother's widow (Gen. 38); and

- Ritual matters—such as, not eating blood (Gen. 9:4), circumcision (Gen. 17:10–14), not eating the sciatic nerve
(Gen. 32:32).

## B. Fundamentalist and Historical Approaches to the Bible

There are two general approaches to understanding biblical texts.
One, the fundamentalist view, is held by many Orthodox Jews, some
Protestant Christians, and almost all Moslems. It contends that the
whole Pentateuch was given by God to Moses at Sinai and that the remaining books of the Hebrew Bible are the direct word of God to the
prophets or sages whose names are attached to them. The other, historical view, is held by the great majority of the Conservative and Reform
Movements in contemporary American Judaism, much of Christendom, and most biblical scholars. It is that the Bible consists of a number of texts, composed by a variety of people in a number of places and
times and later compiled in written form by a redactor.

The fundamentalist approach has the distinct advantage of imparting divine certainty and authority to the ideas and norms of the Bible. If you believe that the Bible is literally the word of God, its power
to shape your thought and action is inescapable. Those who follow the
historical approach must explain the Bible's authority in some other
ways—if they attribute any authority at all to the words of the text.

On the other hand, the historical approach has several strengths.
One is its ability to provide a plausible explanation for the apparent in-
consistencies in biblical narratives, laws, and philosophies. Some such
discrepancies may be readily resolved, for the texts in question may apply to different circumstances. In other cases, the texts are not easily
reconciled and almost certainly say contradictory things about the
same subject. Since fundamentalists believe that God is consistent and
that the Torah (the first five books of the Bible) is the inerrant record of
God's word given at one time, they must find some way to apply such
texts, even if they must distort the texts' plain meaning. Those who
take an historical view of the Bible need not do that. They can point to

the differing times and places in which inconsistent texts were written and can marshal internal and external evidence suggesting that one text should be assigned to one time period and the conflicting text to another. Available evidence indicates that the Torah includes materials written from the eleventh century B.C.E. to the sixth century. It is not surprising, then, that the Torah reflects changes occurring during that length of time, although ancient societies probably changed much more slowly than our own does. Assigning inconsistent texts to different time periods often makes for a more straightforward, and probably more accurate, understanding of the discrepancies.

The historical method also explains why biblical stories and institutions often parallel those of neighboring cultures. Archaeological digs in the Middle East during the last hundred years have revealed sizable quantities of written texts that had long lain buried in the sand. Stories and laws similar to those of the Bible have been found. These finds undermine the fundamentalists' belief that the biblical text is a unique document given by God to Moses at Sinai discontinuous with the ideas and institutions of the surrounding peoples. Biblical laws and stories differ from those discovered in the ruins of the ancient Near East, but the differences are those one would expect to find among neighboring cultures, not the discontinuities that separate completely different patterns of thought and practice. The similarities between the civilization of the Israelites and that of their neighbors, then, also argue for understanding the Bible as the product of an historical context.

This book uses the historical method based on textual criticism to understand the Jewish tradition because of the advantages described above and because we believe that that is the appropriate way for historians and social scientists to study any culture. Like any such scholars, we seek to describe and understand the culture we are studying and to reconcile the conflicting evidence regarding the operation of that legal system as plausibly as possible. At the same time, this book will indicate where fundamentalists offer different interpretations of specific legal phenomena. It will also describe many sources of authority which Jews have attached to their tradition throughout the ages so that it can fairly present the passion and commitment which this tradition has engendered among its adherents.

## C. THE STRUCTURE AND CONTENTS OF THE BIBLE

The name "Bible" was first used by the Jews of Alexandria, whose language was Greek. *Biblia* was the Greek equivalent of "The Books," from *biblos,* "book" or "paper," which, in turn, derives from Byblos, a Phoenician city noted for the manufacture and sale of paper. In the Book of Daniel (9:2), the Bible is referred to as "The Books." This is the oldest name known to us for what we today call "The Bible." The word *canon* has also come to mean "The Bible." This word comes from the Greek word *Kanon* meaning measuring rod, and perhaps ultimately from the same root as the Hebrew word *Kanne,* meaning rod. The standard version of the official text of the Greek classics was called the "canon." The early Christian Church Fathers applied the same term to the official version of the Bible.

In the Jewish tradition the Bible is commonly known in Hebrew as the *Tanakh,* which is an acronym composed of the first consonants of the three major divisions of the work—Torah, Nevi'im and Ketuvim.

Hebrew letters are not all easily noted in English characters, and there are several systems for transliterating them. When we introduce the reader to a Hebrew term, we use the form of transliteration used in the *Encyclopedia Judaica,* in both our text and translations, but when we quote materials by other translators, we reproduce their transliterations. So, for example, we have written *get* for the Aramaic word for a writ of divorce, but one of the authors we cite writes this word *Get* and a British court opinion uses *gett.* There are not many Hebrew or Aramaic words that the reader will have to learn in this book, however, and so we trust that the variant transliterations will not cause problems.

## 1. *Torah*

The term, "Torah," carries a number of connotations, including law or instruction in general. Its primary meaning, however, is to describe the Pentateuch, consisting of the five books of Moses, traditionally believed to have been delivered by God to Moses at Mount Sinai. These books, known in English as Genesis (Gen.), Exodus (Ex.), Leviticus (Lev.), Numbers (Num.), and Deuteronomy (Deut.), trace the story of the Jews from the period of the patriarchs, through their enslavement and deliverance from Egypt, to the point when they were about to reenter the Promised Land. These books also contain several extensive law codes consisting of civil, criminal, and cultic rules, as well as ethical imperatives.

Over the centuries, beginning probably as early as 2000 or 1700 Before the Common Era (B.C.E.), a body of legends, stories, and accounts of historical events began to develop among the Hebrew tribes. Some grew from their shared experiences and adventures. Some they borrowed from the cultures of other peoples among whom they lived, reshaping them to better fit their own world view.

This material was passed down orally for centuries. It is not at all certain when parts of it were first written down, but judging from the details of the patriarchal narratives (the accuracy of which has been demonstrated by recent archaeological discoveries), much of it was committed to writing at a very early date.

Beginning with the time of the establishment of the first Jewish monarchy, about the year 1000 B.C.E., these writings began to be systematically collected and edited by various schools of scholars and editors. By about 400 B.C.E., the Torah as we know it, an interweaving of the efforts of these schools, had come to be recognized by the Jewish people as a complete, unique, and holy text. This date is based on the description in the Book of Nehemiah (Neh. 8:13–18) of a public reading of the Torah which included how to celebrate the festival of Sukkot, a practice the text indicates the people did not know before. The date is also confirmed by the fact that the Samaritans, who were excluded from the Jewish community around 450 B.C.E. and have remained outside the Jewish community ever since, accept the Torah as it was written at that time as holy text.

## 2. Prophets

During the period of the kingdoms of Judah and Israel and the first exile to Babylon (1000–444 B.C.E.), the institution of prophecy flourished. Divinely inspired persons were a major source of religious, moral, and, to a lesser degree, legal and political instruction. The second division of the Tanakh is made up of books from the prophetic era. Six books recount the history of the period—Joshua, Judges, I Samuel, II Samuel, I Kings, and II Kings. Together these books are called "Former Prophets." They are "former" not in a chronological, historical sense, but only in the sense that these books come before the books of the literary prophets in the traditional, Jewish ordering of the Hebrew Bible. Following these historic books is a collection known as "Latter Prophets." This collection consists of fifteen books which contain the words of the literary prophets: Isaiah, Jeremiah, Ezekiel, and the twelve minor prophets (minor primarily in the sense that their books are shorter).

The writing and compiling of the prophetic books took place over a very long period of time. Some portions, such as Joshua and Judges, may be as old as some of the material included in the Torah itself, while other parts were probably written as late as 300 B.C.E. Some claim that the prophetic canon was closed by the end of Persian hegemony (323 B.C.E.) because prophetic literature lacks Greek words and any reference to the downfall of the Persian empire and the transition to Greek rule. All agree, however, that the latest possible closing date for this section is about 200 B.C.E.

This date has come to be the cut-off date for two major reasons. First, the Book of Daniel is clearly a prophetic book in style and content but was excluded from this section. The Book of Daniel was written in about 170 B.C.E. and is likely to have been excluded because the public recognized the completeness of the prophetic section and therefore felt it could not be opened to include another prophet. Second, in the Book of Ecclesiasticus, written around 180 B.C.E., the writer, a Jewish teacher named Ben Sira, refers to the Torah and lists the books of the former and latter prophets as we know them today, indicating these as two complete entities—Torah and Prophets.

One of the reasons Palestinian Jews did not accept Jesus as a prophet was that they believed prophecy was closed. In fact, Zekhariah 13:2–5 reports that prophecy fell into discredit after the return from the Exile in the late sixth century B.C.E.

## 3. Writings

The third major division of the Tanakh, the Ketuvim, or "Writings," consists of historical books tracing the history of the people from the death of Moses to the restoration after the Babylonian exile. The Ketuvim also includes poetic and wisdom literature—Psalms, Proverbs, Song of Songs, Lamentations, Ecclesiastes (Kohelet), Job, Jonah, and Esther.

For a number of generations, books were added and dropped from the collection of sacred texts before it took final shape. We know of other popular books, such as Tobit, Judith, Maccabees, and Ecclesiasticus (The Wisdom of Ben Sira) that circulated among the people at the same time as books that were later included in the Ketuvim section. In Ecclesiasticus, for instance, Ben Sira refers to the Books of Psalms, Proverbs, Ezra, Nehemiah, and Job, and so it is clear that these books were widely read by 180 B.C.E.

By the year 132 B.C.E., Ben Sira's nephew records the existence of three sections of sacred writings, but none with a specific name. The Book of Maccabees, written in approximately 125 B.C.E., recognizes three sections with only the third section lacking a specific name. The Mishnah reports that the rabbis debated the inclusion of Ben Sira, Esther, Song of Songs, and Ecclesiastes in the Bible during the first and early second centuries C.E.

4. *The Closing*

The Bible as a complete set of documents was probably closed by about the year 125 C.E. The sacredness of the Torah and Prophetic sections had been accepted long before that. Most of the decisions concerning the Ketuvim were made by the Council of Yavneh (Jamnia) in 90 C.E.

In addition to the Hebrew Bible, the Christian Bible has, of course, incorporated the four Gospels containing accounts of the life of Jesus, the Book of Acts, the Epistles, and the apocalyptic Book of Revelation. Since Jews do not accept Jesus as Messiah, these books were left out of the Hebrew canon. There were other books, however, where the decision was considerably tougher. The losers, known generally as the Apocrypha, are not included in the Hebrew Bible, although they are found in some Christian Bibles. The Apocrypha includes the books of I and II Esdras, Tobit, Judith, Additions to Esther, The Wisdom of Solomon, Ben Sira (Ecclesiasticus), Barukh, The Letter of Jeremiah, The Prayer of Azariah, Susanna, Bel and the Dragon, The Prayer of Manesseh, and I and II Maccabees. Those books were included in the Greek translation of the Bible known as the Septuagint, and the Catholic Church therefore considers them canonical. Protestants do not accept them as part of their canon, however; neither do Jews.

A list of the books of the Hebrew Bible in the traditional, Jewish ordering appears in Appendix I.

D. The Biblical Law Codes

Three major law codes are found in the Torah: Exodus 19–24, Leviticus 1–26, and Deuteronomy 4–26. As an example of early biblical law, this topic will examine the Exodus law code in some detail.

The Exodus code is often called "The Book of the Covenant," and it is believed to be the oldest of the three biblical codes. You will find it helpful to read this text over at least once to gain a sense of its sweep and content. It is presented here in a modern, American English translation from Hebrew. This reduces some of the textual problems you would have were you to attempt to read the original. There punctuation and spacing of words is often uncertain, and the breakdown of the text into verses and chapters does not exist since that is of relatively recent origin. Many of the words are known to us only through the text itself, and thus there are numerous instances in which it is not clear what the words themselves mean. Over time, scribal errors and some variations in the text have obscured its meaning. In addition, because the text is very ancient, the usage and grammar are unfamiliar, and a modern reader inevitably will have the same sorts of problems with the text that he or she would have with a text from Chaucer or the Magna Carta. The important point is that these difficulties are not uniquely those of the modern reader. As you ponder the meaning of what follows, be aware that the scholars of the classic, rabbinic period two millenia ago were confronted with similar, although by no means identical, problems with this text. For them, too, it was an ancient text written in an archaic language and an unfamiliar literary form.

Many readers of this text may have the converse problem in dealing with it freshly. For thousands of years Western civilization assumed that every cultured person knew this very familiar story. Nothing is so hard to read as a text to which one has been exposed since childhood. We know the story so well that we are likely to see in it just what we expect to see. "Here comes Mount Sinai and the Ten Commandments again!" Such readers will find it helpful to read this text as if they had never read it before. In particular, note the places where you do not understand the words (or where the translators indicate there is doubt regarding the meaning of the text) and those places where you do not see the connection between one statement and those preceding or following. The crucial point is that the rabbinic tradition took this text seriously as an authoritative legal code. We ask you to do the same so that you can understand the problems the keepers of the tradition have had and their responses to those difficulties.

In reading this text you will be exposed to a central problem with which this book will be concerned. The tradition we are studying holds that what the biblical text says is *the* authoritative guide for human behavior, and yet what the text means is persistently unclear. In other words, the starting point for Jewish law is the legitimacy of the text, which precedes its intrinsic clarity or persuasiveness. This text is the *law*, and its authority is not a function of our ability to understand it.

Of course, what has just been described is familiar terrain for lawyers in every age faced with positive law. The parallels between biblical interpretation and constitutional interpretation should be obvious. Similar techniques are used to discover the meaning of the cryptic, centuries old text of the United States Constitution. But the parallel is equally analogous to the position of a traffic court judge who must apply a traffic ordinance that the judge is not free to question. The starting point of any such enterprise is to read the text itself and seek to derive its meaning directly. Go through the text now any way you can. It will be referred back to it again and again as we see how several millenia of interpreters have approached it in an effort to find the eternal meaning they were confident could be found in it.

Notice the variety and diversity of the subjects treated in the Exodus text. It is concerned with correct social behavior, the penalties for wrongdoing, the treatment of slaves and animals, and the relationships of individuals in a family. What does it tell you about the society in which it was adopted? Here are a few assertions about that society you should test as you read the text: (a) it was a stratified society with distinct social classes; (b) the status of women and slaves was inferior, but both groups were seen as possessing human dignity; (c) the economy was primarily agricultural, although the pastoral keeping of herds existed alongside the raising of crops; (d) people lived in houses rather than tents; and (e) there was a strong sense of group responsibility and interdependence, but at the same time the group did not live in isolation and expected to have outsiders living with them.

The text also contains a variety of legal forms. Is it a single, coherent document or a series of quite different pieces? Compare the text of chapters 19 and 20 with chapters 21 through 23. Note how the text goes from the sublime, all-encompassing mandates of the Ten Commandments to very specific, almost mundane matters.

Two distinct styles of legal expression are presented in the code, apodictic and casuistic. Apodictic law is in the imperative form, "thou shalt" and "thou shalt not." The casuistic form begins with the words "If . . ." or "When . . ." It appears to be the report of a specific situation followed by a ruling. Part of the Exodus code, particularly the Ten Commandments in chapter 20, is in apodictic form, while much of the rest of the code is in casuistic form. These differences in form may tell us something about the sources of these laws. Apodictic law suggests a general command given by an authority, while the casuistic form, particularly when the circumstances become very specific, suggests that the law is the report of an actual case and indicates that the rule has grown from the accumulation of practice rather than a single legislative act. This distinction might be thought of in terms of the distinction between statutory legislation and the organic processes of case decision in a common law system. At the very least, the form tells something about the place of general principle, concept, and rule as opposed to the importance of instance, example, precedent, and particular circumstance in the legal consciousness of the society.

The text suggests a variety of reasons for observance of the law. The message of chapters 19 and 20 is unmistakable: "Obey this law because you promised the Almighty you would obey it. Moreover, God is impassioned, punishing those who disobey and fail to keep their prom-

ises." Chapters 21 through 23 are quite different. The sanctions here
are human and social, the aim is a just and peaceful community. We
should all act this way because that is the right way for people to treat
each other. Toward the end of chapter 22 the tone shifts again. Now
the fair and compassionate treatment of strangers, widows, orphans,
and debtors is no longer based solely on the fear of Divine anger. Instead the major appeal is to the moral quality of compassion, the memory of our own suffering that leads us not to cause others to suffer. Finally, in chapter 24 yet another tone becomes dominant. Now the
covenantal act is described in ceremonial terms resembling a treaty between the elders of the tribes of Israel and God. The pact is sealed in an
epiphanal meal and with sacrifices, much as a treaty between desert
chiefs might be concluded.

Remember while reading the Exodus code that it was probably
transmitted orally for centuries before being committed to writing.
This affected its form since the rememberer needs memory jogging devices as a transition from one verse to the next to help him keep his
place and preserve the text. Consequently the order is based on associations that one makes from one law to another. This feature differenti-
ates the biblical code from a modern secular code, which is likely to be
ordered much more strictly by topic or principle. Nevertheless, you
should be on the lookout for organizational logic that suggests the connections between successive points.

The code should not be seen as merely secular law in the modern
sense, and the text will not permit you to read it that way. Many
important religious tenets are contained in the code, not the least of
which is the principle of law observance itself. The source of the law is
not an earthly being, a king or prophet, but God Himself, who reveals
law directly. Stemming from this belief in God's law are notions that
justice is an all-encompassing principle. The obligation of just dealing
insisted on in the code is not limited to the male members of the clan,
but extends to women, slaves, strangers, and animals. Exodus demonstrates that from its beginnings Jewish law combined the secular and
the religious. The codifier was not impressed with the distinction. To
him, both aspects of law are simply parts of an integrated and homoge-
neous system by which God rules the world.

Exodus

Chapter 19:
    On the third new moon after the Israelites had gone forth from the
land of Egypt, on that very day, they entered the wilderness of Sinai.
[2] Having journeyed from Rephidim, they entered the wilderness of

Sinai and encamped in the wilderness. Israel encamped there in front of the mountain, [3] and Moses went up to God. The LORD called to him from the mountain, saying, "Thus shall you say to the house of Jacob and declare to the children of Israel: [4] 'You have seen what I did to the Egyptians, how I bore you on eagles' wings and brought you to Me. [5] Now then, if you will obey Me faithfully and keep My convenant, you shall be My treasured possession among all the peoples. Indeed, all the earth is Mine, [6] but you shall be to Me as a kingdom of priests and a holy nation.' These are the words that you shall speak to the children of Israel."

[7] Moses came and summoned the elders of the people and put before them all the words that the LORD had commanded him. [8] All the people answered as one, saying, "All that the LORD has spoken we will do!" And Moses brought back the people's words to the LORD. [9] And the LORD said to Moses, "I will come to you in a thick cloud, in order that the people may hear when I speak with you and so trust you thereafter." Then Moses reported the people's words to the LORD, [10] and the LORD said to Moses, "Go to the people and warn them to stay pure [see v. 15] today and tomorrow. Let them wash their clothes. [11] Let them be ready for the third day; for on the third day the LORD will come down, in the sight of all the people, on Mount Sinai. [12] You shall set bounds for the people round about, saying, 'Beware of going up the mountain or touching the border of it. Whoever touches the mountain shall be put to death: [13] no hand shall touch him, but he shall be either stoned or pierced through; beast or man, he shall not live,' When the ram's horn sounds a long blast [meaning of Hebrew uncertain], they shall come up onto the mountain."

[14] Moses came down from the mountain to the people and warned the people to stay pure, and they washed their clothes. [15] And he said to the people, "Be ready for the third day: do not go near a woman."

[16] On the third day, as morning dawned, there was thunder, and lightning, and a dense cloud upon the mountain, and a very loud blast of the horn; and all the people who were in the camp trembled. [17] Moses led the people out of the camp toward God, and they took their places at the foot of the mountain.

[18] Now Mount Sinai was all in smoke, for the LORD had come down upon it in fire; the smoke rose like the smoke of a kiln, and the whole mountain [some Hebrew manuscripts and the Greek, "all the people"] trembled violently. [19] The blare of the horn grew louder and louder. As Moses spoke, God answered him in thunder. [20] The LORD came down upon Mount Sinai, on the top of the mountain, and the LORD called Moses to the top of the mountain and Moses went

up. [21] The LORD said to Moses, "Go down, warn the people not to break through to the LORD to gaze, lest many of them perish. [22] The priests also, who come near the LORD, must purify themselves, lest the LORD break out against them." [23] But Moses said to the LORD, "The people cannot come up to Mount Sinai, for You warned us saying, 'Set bounds about the mountain and sanctify it.'" [24] So the LORD said to him, "Go down, and come back together with Aaron; but let not the priests or the people break through to come up to the LORD, lest He break out against them." [25] And Moses went down to the people and spoke to them.

*Chapter 20:*
God spoke all these words [Tradition varies as to the division of the commandments in vss. 2–14, and as to the numbering of the verses from 13 on.] saying:

[2] I the LORD am your God who brought you out of the land of Egypt, the house of bondage: [3] You shall have no other gods beside Me.

[4] You shall not make for yourself a sculptured image, or any likeness of what is in the heavens above, or on the earth below, or in the waters under the earth. [5] You shall not bow down to them or serve them. For I the LORD your God am an impassioned God, visiting the guilt of the fathers upon the children, upon the third and upon the fourth generations of those who reject Me, but showing kindness to the thousandth generation of those who love Me and keep My commandments.

[7] You shall not swear falsely by [others, "take in vain"] the name of the LORD your God; for the LORD will not clear one who swears falsely by His name.

[8] Remember the sabbath day and keep it holy. [9] Six days you shall labor and do all your work, [10] but the seventh day is a sabbath of the LORD your God: you shall not do any work—you, your son or daughter, your male or female slave, or your cattle, or the stranger who is within your settlements. [11] For in six days the LORD made heaven and earth and sea, and all that is in them, and He rested on the seventh day; therefore the LORD blessed the sabbath day and hallowed it.

[12] Honor your father and your mother, that you may long endure on the land which the LORD your God is giving you.

[13] You shall not murder.

You shall not commit adultery.

You shall not steal.

You shall not bear false witness against your neighbor.

[14] You shall not covet your neighbor's house: you shall not covet your neighbor's wife, or his male or female slave, or his ox or his ass, or anything that is your neighbor's.

[15] All the people witnessed the thunder and lightning, the blare of the horn and the mountain smoking; and when the people saw it, they fell back and stood at a distance. [16] "You speak to us," they said to Moses, "and we will obey; but let not God speak to us, lest we die." [17] Moses answered the people, "Be not afraid; for God has come only in order to test you, and in order that the fear of Him may be ever with you, so that you do not go astray." [18] So the people remained at a distance, while Moses approached the thick cloud where God was.

[19] The LORD said to Moses:

Thus shall you say to the Israelites: You yourselves saw that I spoke to you from the very heavens: [20] With Me, therefore, you shall not make any gods of silver, nor shall you make for yourselves any gods of gold. [21] Make for Me an altar of earth and sacrifice on it your burnt offerings and your sacrifices of well-being [others, "peace-offering." Exact meaning of shelamim uncertain.], your sheep and your oxen; in every place where I cause My name to be mentioned I will come to you and bless you. [22] But if you make for Me an altar of stones, do not build it of hewn stones; for by wielding your tool upon them you have profaned them. [23] Do not ascend My altar by steps, that your nakedness may not be exposed upon it.

*Chapter* 21:
These are the norms that you shall set before them:

[2] When you acquire a Hebrew slave, he shall serve six years; in the seventh year he shall be freed, without payment. [3] If he came single, he shall leave single; if he had a wife, his wife shall leave with him. [4] If his master gave him a wife, and she has borne him children, the wife and her children shall belong to the master, and he shall leave alone. [5] But if the slave declares, "I love my master, and my wife and children: I do not wish to be freed," [6] his master shall take him before God [others, "to the judges."]. He shall be brought to the door of the doorpost, and his master shall pierce his ear with an awl; and he shall then remain his slave for life.

[7] When a man sells his daughter as a slave, she shall not be freed as male slaves are. [8] If she proves to be displeasing to her master, who had designated her for himself, he must let her be redeemed; he shall not have the right to sell her to outsiders, since he broke faith with her. [9] And if he designated her for his son, he shall deal with her as is the practice with free maidens. [10] If he marries another, he must not

withhold from this one her food, her clothing, or her conjugal rights
[or "ointments"]. [11] If he fails her in these three ways, she shall be
freed, without payment.

[12] He who fatally strikes a man shall be put to death. [13] If he did
not do it by design, but it came about by an act of God, I will assign
you a place to which he can flee.

[14] When a man schemes against another and kills him treacher-
ously, you shall take him from My very altar to be put to death.

[15] He who strikes his father or his mother shall be put to death.

[16] He who kidnaps a man—whether he has sold him or is still
holding him—shall be put to death.

[17] He who repudiates [or "reviles"] his father or his mother shall
be put to death.

[18] When men quarrel and one strikes the other with stone or fist,
and he does not die but has to take to his bed—[19] if he then gets up
and walks outdoors upon his staff, the assailant shall go unpunished,
except that he must pay for his idleness and his cure.

[20] When a man strikes his slave, male or female, with a rod,
and he dies there and then [literally, "under his hand"], he must be
avenged. [21] But if he survives a day or two, he is not to be avenged,
since he is the other's property.

[22] When men fight, and one of them pushes a pregnant woman
and a miscarriage results, but no other misfortune ensues, the one responsible [Hebrew, "he"] shall be fined according as the woman's husband may exact from him, the payment to be based on reckoning [i.e.,
the age of the embryo; others, "as the judges determine"]. [23] But if
other misfortune ensues, the penalty shall be life for life, [24] eye for
eye, tooth for tooth, hand for hand, foot for foot, [25] burn for burn,
wound for wound, bruise for bruise.

[26] When a man strikes the eye of his slave, male or female, and destroys it, he shall let him go free on account of his eye. [27] If he
knocks out the tooth of his slave, male or female, he shall let him go
free on account of his tooth.

[28] When an ox gores a man or a woman to death, the ox shall be
stoned and its flesh shall not be eaten, but the owner of the ox is not
to be punished. [29] If, however, that ox has long been a gorer, and its
owner, though warned, has failed to guard it, and it kills a man or a
woman—the ox shall be stoned and its owner, too, shall be put to
death. [30] If ransom is laid upon him, he must pay whatever is laid
upon him to redeem his life. [31] So, too, if it gores a minor, male or female, [the owner] shall be dealt with according to the same norm. [32]

But if the ox gores a slave, male or female, he shall pay thirty shekels of silver to the master, and the ox shall be stoned.

[33] When a man opens a pit—or when he has dug a pit but has not covered it—and an ox or an ass falls into it, [34] the one responsible for the pit must make restitution; he shall pay the price to the owner, but shall keep the dead animal.

[35] When a man's ox injures his neighbor's ox and it dies, they shall sell the live ox and divide its price; they shall also divide the dead animal. [36] If, however, the ox has long been known as a gorer, and its owner has failed to guard it, he must restore ox for ox, but shall keep the dead animal.

[37] When a man steals an ox or a sheep, and slaughters it or sells it, he shall pay five oxen for the ox, and four sheep for the sheep. [This constitutes chap. 22:1 in some editions.]

Chapter 22:
If the thief is seized while tunneling [i.e., under a wall for housebreaking], and he is beaten to death, there is no bloodguilt in his case. [2] If the sun has risen on him, there is bloodguilt in that case.—He must make restitution; if he lacks the means, he shall be sold for his theft. [3] But if what he stole—whether ox or ass or sheep—is found alive in his possession, he shall pay double.

[4] When a man lets his livestock loose to graze in another's land, and so allows a field or a vineyard to be grazed bare, he must make restitution according to the top yield from that field or vineyard.

[5] When a fire is started and spreads to thorns, so that stacked, standing, or growing [literally, "field"] grain is consumed, he who started the fire must make restitution.

[6] When a man gives money or goods to another for safekeeping, and they are stolen from the man's house—if the thief is caught, he shall pay double; [7] if the thief is not caught, the owner of the house shall depose before God [see note on 21:6] that he has not laid hands on his neighbor's property. [8] In all charges of misappropriation—pertaining to an ox, an ass, a sheep, a garment, or any other loss, whereof one party alleges, "This is it"—the case of both parties shall come before God: he whom God declares guilty shall pay double to the other.

[9] When a man gives to another an ass, an ox, a sheep or any other animal to guard, and it dies of injuries [or "dies or is injured"] or is carried off, with no witness about, [10] an oath before the LORD shall decide between the two of them that the one has not laid hands on the property of the other; the owner must acquiesce, and no restitution shall be made. [11] But if [the animal] was stolen from him, he shall

make restitution to its owner. [12] If it was torn by beasts, he shall bring it as evidence; he need not replace what has been torn by beasts.

[13] When a man borrows [an animal] from another and it dies of injuries [or "is injured or dies"; see note on v. 9], its owner not being with it, he must make restitution. [14] If its owner was with it, no restitution need be made; but if it was hired, he is still entitled to the hiring fee.

[15] If a man seduces a virgin who has not been spoken for, and lies with her, he must make her his wife by payment of a bride price. [16] If her father refuses to give her to him, he must still weigh out silver in proportion to the bride price for virgins.

[17] You shall not tolerate [literally, "let live"] a sorceress.

[18] Whoever lies with a beast shall be put to death.

[19] Whoever sacrifices to a god other than the LORD alone shall be proscribed [see Lev. 27:29].

[20] You shall not wrong a stranger or oppress him, for you were strangers in the land of Egypt.

[21] You shall not mistreat any widow or orphan. [22] If you do mistreat them, I will heed their outcry as soon as they cry out to Me, [23] and My anger shall blaze forth and I will put you to the sword, and your own wives shall become widows and your children orphans.

[24] If you lend money to My people, to the poor who is in your power, do not act toward him as a creditor: exact no interest from him. [25] If you take your neighbor's garment in pledge, you must return it to him before the sun sets; [26] it is his only clothing, the sole covering for his skin. In what else shall he sleep? Therefore, if he cries out to Me, I will pay heed, for I am compassionate.

[27] You shall not offend God, nor put a curse upon a chieftain among your people.

[28] You shall not put off the skimming of the first yield of your vats [meaning of Hebrew is uncertain]. You shall give Me the first-born among your sons. [29] You shall do the same with your cattle and your flocks: seven days it [i.e., the male first-born] shall remain with its mother; on the eighth day you shall give it to Me.

[30] You shall be men holy to Me: you must not eat flesh torn by beasts in the field; you shall cast it to the dogs.

Chapter 23:
You must not carry false rumors; you shall not join hands with the guilty to act as an unjust witness. [2] Do not side with the mighty

[others, "multitude"] to do wrong, and do not give perverse testimony in a dispute by leaning toward the mighty; [3] nor must you show deference to a poor man in his dispute.

[4] When you encounter your enemy's ox or ass wandering, you must take it back to him.

[5] When you see the ass of your enemy prostrate under its burden and would refrain from raising [For this use of the verb 'zb see Neh. 3:8, 34. For the whole verse see Deut. 22:4.] it, you must nevertheless raise it with him.

[6] You shall not subvert the rights of your needy in their disputes. [7] Keep far from a false charge; do not bring death on the innocent and the righteous, for I will not acquit the wrongdoer. [8] Do not take bribes, for bribes blind the clear-sighted and upset the pleas of the just.

[9] You shall not oppress a stranger, for you know the feelings of the stranger, having yourselves been strangers in the land of Egypt.

[10] Six years you shall sow your land and gather in its yield; [11] but in the seventh you shall let it rest and lie fallow. Let the needy among your people eat of it, and what they leave let the wild beasts eat. You shall do the same with your vineyards and your olive groves.

[12] Six days you shall do your work, but on the seventh day you shall cease from labor, in order that your ox and your ass may rest, and that your bondman and the stranger may be refreshed.

[13] Be on guard concerning all that I have told you. Make no mention of the names of other gods; they shall not be heard on your lips.

[14] Three times a year you shall hold a festival for Me: [15] You shall observe the Feast of Unleavened Bread—eating unleavened bread for seven days as I have commanded you—at the set time in the month of Abib, for in it you went forth from Egypt; and none shall appear before Me empty-handed; [16] and the Feast of the Harvest, of the first fruits of your work, of what you sow in the field; and the Feast of Ingathering at the end of the year, when you gather in the results of your work from the field. [17] Three times a year all your males shall appear before the Sovereign, the LORD.

[18] You shall not offer the blood of My sacrifice with anything leavened; and the fat of My festal offering shall not be left lying until morning.

[19] The choice first fruits of your soil you shall bring to the house of the LORD your God.

You shall not boil a kid in its mother's milk.

[20] I am sending an angel before you to guard you on the way and to bring you to the place which I have made ready. [21] Pay heed to him and obey him; do not defy him, for he will not pardon your offenses, since My Name is in him. [22] But if you obey him and do all that I say, I will be an enemy to your enemies and a foe to your foes.

[23] When My angel goes before you and brings you to the Amorites, the Hittites, the Perizzites, the Canaanites, the Hivites, and the Jebusites, and I annihilate them, [24] you shall not bow down to their gods in worship or follow their practices, but shall tear them down and smash their pillars to bits. [25] You shall serve the LORD your God, and He will bless your bread and your water. And I will remove sickness from your midst. [26] No woman in your land shall miscarry or be barren. I will let you enjoy the full count of your days.

[27] I will send forth My terror before you, and I will throw into panic all the people among whom you come, and I will make all your enemies turn tail [literally, "back"] before you. [28] I will send a plague [others, "hornet"; Hebrew uncertain] ahead of you, and it shall drive out before you the Hivites, the Canaanites, and the Hittites. [29] I will not drive them out before you in a single year, lest the land become desolate and the wild beasts multiply to your hurt. [30] I will drive them out before you little by little, until you have increased and possess the land. [31] I will set your borders from the Sea of Reeds to the Sea of Philistines, and from the wilderness to the Euphrates; for I will deliver the inhabitants of the land into your power, and you will drive them out before you. [32] You shall make no covenant with them and their gods. [33] They shall not remain in your land—lest they make you sin against Me by serving their gods—for this would be a snare to you.

*Chapter 24:*
Then He said to Moses, "Come up to the Lord, you and Aaron, Nadab and Abihu, and seventy elders of Israel, and bow low from afar. [2] Only Moses shall come near the LORD, but they shall not come near; and the people shall not come up with him at all."

[3] Moses went and repeated to the people all the commands of the LORD and all the norms; and all the people answered with one voice, saying, "All the things that the LORD has commanded we will do!" [4] Moses then wrote down all the commands of the LORD.

Early in the morning, he set up an altar at the foot of the mountain, with twelve pillars for the twelve tribes of Israel. [5] He delegated young men among the Israelites, and they offered burnt offerings and sacrificed bulls as offerings of well-being to the LORD. [6] Moses took one part of the blood and put it in basins, and the other part of the blood he dashed against the altar. [7] Then he took the record of the covenant and read it aloud to the people. And they said, "All that the

LORD has spoken we will faithfully do [literally, "we will do and obey"]!" [8] Moses took the blood and dashed it on the people and said, "This is the blood of the covenant which the LORD now makes with you concerning all these commands."

[9] Then Moses and Aaron, Nadab and Abihu, and seventy elders of Israel ascended; [10] and they saw the God of Israel: under His feet there was the likeness of a pavement of sapphire, like the very sky for purity. [11] Yet He did not raise His hand against the leaders [Meaning of Hebrew 'asilim uncertain.] of the Israelites; they beheld God, and they ate and drank.

[12] The LORD said to Moses, "Come up to Me on the mountain and wait there, and I will give you the stone tablets with the teachings and commandments which I have inscribed to instruct them." [13] So Moses and his attendant Joshua arose, and Moses ascended the mountain of God. [14] To the elders he had said, "Wait here for us until we return to you. You have Aaron and Hur with you; let anyone who has a legal matter approach them."

[15] When Moses had ascended the mountain, the cloud covered the mountain. [16] The Presence of the LORD abode on Mount Sinai, and the cloud hid it for six days. On the seventh day He called to Moses from the midst of the cloud. [17] Now the Presence of the LORD appeared in the sight of the Israelites as a consuming fire on the top of the mountain. [18] Moses went inside the cloud and ascended the mountain; and Moses remained on the mountain forty days and forty nights.

# Topic Two: The Biblical Law of Injury

## A. The Covenant Code's Treatment of Personal Injury

The social responses to personal injury are so deeply imbedded in cultural experience that it is difficult to think about the matter freshly. The consequences of one person injuring another is a universal concern of every legal system. Personal injury is a timeless social phenomenon, and a community's resolution of the issue tells a great deal about the social, cultural, and moral attitudes of that community. The definition of consequences and remedies for losses of one person attributable to another person's behavior must be matched with definition of the kinds of losses that are legally cognizable. The Exodus text makes distinctions between the consequences of actions that cause death (Ex. 21:12); assaults that cause disability but not death (Ex. 21:18–19); and personal injuries to humans caused by the failure of a person to control his animals (Ex. 21:28). Moreover, the text in Ex. 21.13 appears to be on the point of recognizing that even as to life-destroying behavior there may be grades and categories and that death by design may have one set of consequences while death that came about by an act of God is treated in a different manner. To clarify the biblical approach to personal injury, this unit will provide some legal materials from cultures that are near in time and space to that of the Covenant Code. Before going back to those unfamiliar cultures, it may be helpful to examine in very general terms modern attitudes on these issues. Anglo-American law refers to the rules of injury as the law of torts.

The legal consequences of personal injury are likely to depend on whether one focuses attention on the behavior of the person whose acts cause the injury, on the consequences of the injury to the victim, or on the impact of the event on the community. One common legal approach emphasizes the injuring party's aggressiveness as the crucial element and seeks ways to treat the actor so as to preclude repetition of the undesirable behavior. That treatment might be highly punitive: death, mutilation, exile, or incarceration. It might seek to exorcise the evil influence believed to be dwelling in the actor and causing the injury to the victim. In a more modern perspective, the treatment might be educational or therapeutic, seeing the injurious behavior as a symptom of pathology or the need for training. Consider the situation of Peter, who is injured when struck by a car driven by Robert. The car was going down a residential street at night at 55 MPH with no headlights. Society might associate Robert's behavior with his drug or alcohol abuse and see his accident causing proclivity as a medical problem. Or it might decide that someone who drives that way needs to be sent to driving school. Or it might be decided that Robert is a callous and reckless person who should be punished. Or it might be decided that the best thing to do is to isolate Robert from the dangerous situation by taking away his driver's license or locking him up in the county jail for a year so he will not be driving around hurting other people. Still focussing on Robert, society might decide to raise his consciousness of his behavior's inherent dangerousness by causing him to associate this behavior with pain. Punishment will deter him from engaging in this behavior in the future by causing him to remember the discomfort he was subjected to because of his past behavior. Taking a somewhat different tack, the emphasis might be on obliging Robert to repair the separation and disturbance the events have caused. Robert might then assume the burdens of the person he injured or compensate Peter for his pain and suffering. Or Robert might be given an opportunity, by performing useful labor, to demonstrate that he is a worthy member of society. Alternatively, Robert might be required to offer public lectures on the danger of alcohol abuse or reckless driving. Finally, Robert could be looked at as an economic animal, rather than as a moral being, and it could be determined whether his behavior is wrongful in terms of its costs in comparison to the costs of avoiding it. Along these lines, a famous American judge defined negligence as injury causing behavior that produces a greater loss to the victim than the burden of prevention and avoidance to the actor times the probability of the accident occurring.

Emphasis on the actor in personal injury law, whether the concern is motivated by moral or therapeutically instrumental considerations, is likely to focus attention on one's mental state, particularly the intention with which the actor committed the hurtful act. The Covenant Code recognizes this in Exodus 21:13, where a distinction is made between homicide that is the result of intentional lying in wait and accidental deadly behavior that is seen as the act of God. To return to the accident between Robert and Peter, the legal assessment of Robert's liability may well be influenced by a judgment that he was morally at fault and acted intentionally or wrongfully to injure Peter. Suppose, for example, that the reason Robert was careening down the hill so fast with no headlights on was that his car had been hit by lightning at the top of the hill, the electrical system put out of order by the bolt, and the car's controls frozen in a running position so that Robert could not stop. Should Robert nonetheless be liable for Peter's injuries? Should the extent of the legal consequences be different because of the circumstances? The kinds of circumstances that constitute a legal excuse vary markedly over time and also depend on the kind of legal consequence that is being contemplated. It might well be decided that Robert should not be criminally liable because of the accident that followed the lightning bolt, but he may nonetheless be held liable for the property damages and personal injury. Or it may be decided that the whole accident was an act of God and leave the burden of loss on Peter.

When the focus shifts from the actor to the victim, the emphasis in consequences for injury changes. The suffering of the injured is not easily converted into any other currency. Those who cause suffering should be made to suffer themselves. These may be troubling notions, but they are also quite universally acknowledged. The first thought is to inflict comparable injury on the actor. Robert's car is likely to have been wrecked in the accident, but if he can walk it may give Peter some satisfaction to kick Robert's car or better yet, roll it over a cliff. Giving Robert a punch in the nose might also set Peter on the road to a speedier recovery. On a somewhat different level, Robert may be required to give of his time and property until it hurts as much as the injury did.

Notice that the discussion has just gone over a watershed from retaliation as an afflictive sanction on the actor that vindicates the victim's sense of injury to compensation that repays the victim for his losses or promotes his recovery from the injury. The line is an indistinct one, and even in ancient texts it is often uncertain when one passes over it since the same legal consequence can serve more than one end. Most societies recognize a distinction between explicitly punitive consequences of injury and those that seek to compensate or restore the victim. This is one way to describe the distinction that is drawn between the criminal law and the civil law of torts. Even today the dividing line between the two may not be sharp and perhaps should not be. A common and plausible criticism of American criminal procedure, for example, is that it rarely provides a place for the victim and is generally not concerned with repairing the victim's injury. Other modern legal systems, for instance French law, give the victim a place in the criminal trial and allow punishment and compensation to the victim to be awarded as part of one process. The Covenant Code appears to treat homicide as an occasion for punishment, but to limit the consequences of assault to compensation (compare Ex. 21:12 with

21:18–19). Similarly, theft of farm animals has consequences that are partly restorative and partly punitive (Ex. 21:37) while housebreaking has clearly afflictive consequences (Ex. 21:1).

Once the watershed between retaliatory punishment and compensation to the victim is passed, a whole new set of questions opens up. Now it becomes necessary to find some way to put a compensatory measure on injuries that are not easily quantified. It is easy enough to see that Robert should pay Peter's hospital and doctor bills and that he should also pay for the earnings on the job that Peter was deprived of because he was in the hospital. It is also easy to see that Robert should pay for the loss of Peter's car, although already there may be tricky questions of value (it was an old car, but Peter only drove it 34,000 miles, he took beautiful care of it, loved it, and had just put on new tires and installed a tape deck). It probably is not too hard to see that Robert should be required to pay some compensation for Peter's pain and suffering, but here the problems of measurement become very troubling.

Lawyers have wrestled with such problems since Exodus with only partial success. The accident may have had other consequences, however, that are neither clearly compensable nor easily measured. Peter's mother fainted when she heard the crash of the cars and struck her head as she fell. She still cries a lot and has difficulty sleeping because she is haunted by her memories of the accident. Peter has lost his nerve and finds himself shy with his girlfriend. He is very troubled by the fear that others think he is not a competent driver and believes that the accident is the reason his boss took him off the job of driving the delivery truck and left him with a job that pays the same but offers fewer career opportunities.

The compensatory basis for injury is easy to see when the harm is direct and physical, but as the loss becomes less tangible and the chain of causation from act to hurt is extended, the grounds for compensation weaken until many legal systems declare them too remote and speculative and beyond the scope of protection. Suppose that instead of hitting him with his car Robert merely said that Peter was a jerk and a lousy driver, causing Peter to feel terrible and lose his job. Would the same consequences follow? Suppose Robert was Peter's boss and the injury was that he decided to hire someone else for the new position that became available, causing Peter great pain and loss of opportunity.

The law may place limits not only on the length to which the chain of causation can be extended to produce liability, but to the persons entitled to assert that a legal duty owed them has been breached. Peter may be able to go quite far in relating injuries he later suffers to the cause of the accident. He may be allowed to recover for losses that are remote in time and connection. A more stringent test may be applied to the claims of his mother or his girlfriend who were less directly involved in the accident, and recovery may be denied the person who drives past the scene the day after the accident and is so shocked by what he sees that he is nervous for the rest of the day and cannot enjoy his dinner that night.

It is apparent from the face of the text of Exodus that its author was familiar with these linedrawing problems and that the legal culture in which he operated had gained substantial sophistication in making these sorts of distinctions between injuries and consequences.

A third perspective from which a legal system might perceive the consequences of a personal injury must be examined at least briefly before leaving Peter and Robert. That accident affected the entire neighborhood, and its social implications must be considered in assigning consequences. Perhaps Robert should be prevented from driving or isolated or required to move away to reduce the chances that he will recklessly injure other neighbors. Alternatively, a 25 MPH speed limit might be placed on the street to reduce the likelihood of people coming down the hill too fast to see cars pulling out of driveways. On a broader, community level, a law might be enacted requiring all cars to carry a device that makes it impossible to put the car in gear in the dark without turning the lights on. A community campaign for driver training, a crackdown on drunk drivers, or better street lighting might also be instituted. The community interest might also lead the county counsel to sue Robert for the public funds expended to clean up the accident or for the welfare paid Peter and his family during his disability. Some of these steps may be punitive or compensatory, but others are primarily restorative, they seek to relieve the entire community of the damaging consequences of the accident. These consequences may include mistrust of neighbors, or a constricting fear of being victimized that limits the free movement of the community and restricts opportunities for social interaction. There is also a sense in which the accident is likely to have separated both Robert and Peter from the community. Robert has lost status and is no longer seen as a fine fellow. People are also likely to be uncomfortable around Peter, who hobbles around in obvious discomfort on his crutches. By declaring the rights and wrongs of the situation, giving Robert a chance to make up for his misbehavior and relieving their anxiety about Peter by vindicating his rights with social force, the community may speed the healing process.

All of this is by way of introduction to the approach taken toward personal injury in the Covenant Code, which is the major biblical statement on the subject. The text may not be perfectly or obviously consistent regarding the consequences of different kinds of injury, but then again many critics would suggest that neither is modern American law. The underlying legal maxim in the biblical text is "an eye for an eye." Interpreting this maxim has presented a major problem for each successive generation, for it is unclear whether the rule is meant to provide retaliation, punishment, or compensation, and if all three, in what combination and measure. Some scholars argue that an eye for an eye has always been meant as a guide for compensation, originating at a time when a slave market provided a basis for computing damages for personal injury. Others see the maxim as purely retaliatory and interpret it quite literally to command the infliction on the actor of the injury suffered by the victim. In its context, an "eye for an eye" might suggest that there is a set of supplementary remedies available in addition to the specific provisions of the other verses in the chapter which, to some extent, seem to overlap.

This may be a good time to read Exodus 21, verses 12–25 a second time, seeking in it a coherent approach to the legal consequences of various kinds of personal injury. Compare verses 18–19 with verses 22–25. Does the general statement of verse 23–25 apply only in situations not covered by the more specific provisions that precede it, or does it summarize the rules applicable in all cases? You may want to list the interpretative problems you find in the text and compare it to the problems that bothered readers of later historical periods. For example, do the remedies apply to women when they cause injury or are victims? To understand the text of Exodus, it may help to examine the two other biblical texts that contain the same maxim. Compare Exodus 21:23–24 with Leviticus 24:17–23 and Deuteronomy 19:15–21. Are they consistent? If so, what do they suggest regarding the meaning of an eye for an eye?

*Leviticus 24:17–22:*
[17] If a man kills any human being, he shall be put to death. [18] One who kills a beast shall make restitution for it: life for life. [19] If anyone maims his fellow, as he has done so shall it be done to him: [20] fracture for fracture, eye for eye, tooth for tooth. The injury he inflicted on another shall be inflicted on him. [21] He who kills a beast shall make restitution for it; but he who kills a human being shall be put to death. [22] You shall have one standard for stranger and citizen alike: for I the Lord am your God.

*Deuteronomy 19:15–21:*
[15] A single witness may not validate against a person any guilt or blame for any offense that may be committed; a case can be valid only on the testimony of two witnesses or more. [16] If a man appears against another to testify maliciously and gives false testimony

against him, [17] the two parties to the dispute shall appear before the Lord, before the priests or magistrates in authority at the time, [18] and the magistrates shall make a thorough investigation. If the man who testified is a false witness, if he has testified falsely against his fellow man, [19] you shall do to him as he schemed to do to his fellow. Thus you will sweep out evil from your midst; [20] others will hear and be afraid, and such evil things will not again be done in your midst. [21] Nor must you show pity: life for life, eye for eye, tooth for tooth, hand for hand, foot for foot.

## B. The Code of Hammurabi

The approach to personal injury taken by the Covenant Code of Exodus may be better understood when it is contrasted with the legal codes of contemporaneous neighboring countries. A wealth of archaeological evidence testifies to the sophistication of these other cultures and to their similarities to the Hebrews. Although there is no direct evidence of contact between the biblical and Mesopotamian legal codes, they are close in time and space, and the patriarchs of the Bible undoubtedly had Mesopotamian cultural contacts. The high point of the legal tradition was the Code of the Babylonian King, Hammurabi, which combines older Sumerian traditions and Semitic Akkadian elements.

The following excerpts from the Code of Hammurabi will give some idea of its law of injuries.

> The Code of Hammurabi: 195–214 (ca 1728–1686 B.C.E.) From James B. Pritchard, *Ancient Near Eastern Texts Relating to the Old Testament*, 2nd ed. (Princeton, NJ: Princeton University Press, 1955), 175–76.

195: If a son has struck his father, they shall cut off his hand.

196: If a seignior has destroyed the eye of a member of the aristocracy, they shall destroy his eye.

197: If he has broken a(nother) seignior's bone, they shall break his bone.

198: If he has destroyed the eye of a commoner or broken the bone of a commoner, he shall pay one mina of silver.

199: If he has destroyed the eye of a seignior's slave or broken the bone of a seignior's slave, he shall pay one-half his value.

200: If a seignior has knocked out a tooth of a seignior of his own rank, they shall knock out his tooth.

201: If he has knocked out a commoner's tooth, he shall pay one-third mina of silver.

202: If a seignior has struck the cheek of a seignior who is superior to him, he shall be beaten sixty (times) with an oxtail whip in the assembly.

203: If a member of the aristocracy has struck the cheek of a(nother) member of the aristocracy who is of the same rank as himself, he shall pay one mina of silver.

204: If a commoner has struck the cheek of a(nother) commoner, he shall pay ten shekels of silver.

205: If a seignior's slave has struck the cheek of a member of the aristocracy, they shall cut off his ear.

206: If a seignior has struck a(nother) seignior in a brawl and has inflicted an injury on him, that seignior shall swear, "I did not strike him deliberately"; and he shall also pay for the physician.

207: If he has died because of his blow, he shall swear (as before), and if it was a member of the aristocracy, he shall pay one-half mina of silver.

208: If it was a member of the commonalty, he shall pay one-third mina of silver.

209: If a seignior struck a(nother) seignior's daughter and has caused her to have a miscarriage, he shall pay ten shekels of silver for her fetus.

210: If that woman has died, they shall put his daughter to death.

211: If by a blow he has caused a commoner's daughter to have a miscarriage, he shall pay five shekels of silver.

212: If that woman has died, he shall pay one-half mina of silver.

213: If he struck a seignior's female slave and has caused her to have a miscarriage, he shall pay two shekels of silver.

214: If that female slave has died, he shall pay one-third mina of silver.

Note that as in Exodus, the emphasis is on the proportionality between the injury and its legal consequences. In the Hammurabi code the class (seignior, aristocrat, commoner, slave) and the sex of the parties plays a greater role. The compensation due an upper-class victim appears greater than that due a lower-class victim with similar injury. This may merely suggest a more rigid class system, or it may indicate a sense that people in different social positions suffer disproportionate losses and therefore must be compensated differently for the same physical injury. Except for slaves, the Bible does not recognize these class distinctions, but as shall be seen, later rabbinic law will, at least as to the element of disgrace invoked in injury.

Also notice the variety of means that are used to even the score between the aggressor and the injured party, including monetary compensation, physical retaliation, the taking of hostages, cure, and simple punishment. What sense do you detect in the classifications of injuries that are compensated exclusively by monetary payment and those that result in retaliatory physical injury? Note that injuries offending the social order and the authority structure of parents and the aristocracy also seem to call for punitive retaliation.

Verse 210 presents special problems. Here the compensatory injury is to another, presumably innocent person. This provision does not respect the personhood of the daughter of the assaulting seignior, but it does preserve the principle of proportionality in terms of the losses suffered by the two aristocratic clans. Vicarious punitive liability of this sort was recognized through most of history and was a sufficiently serious possibility for the framers of the United States Constitution in 1789 that article III, section 3:2 of the Constitution specifically provides that "attainder of treason shall not work corruption of blood." Centuries before this, the Bible wrestled with these problems and sought to preclude the punishment of children for the sins of their parents (Deut. 24:16).

## C. THE HITTITE LAWS

The Hittites were an Indo-European people who settled in western Asia Minor (modern Turkey and Syria). By the fourteenth century B.C.E. they had become dominant in that area and conquered Babylon. The stories of the Patriarchs in Genesis testify to extensive contacts between the Hittites and the Hebrews around the time that the Hittite law codes were current. The purchase of the cave of Makhpelah, described in Genesis 23, is a good example of that. Note that the elements of compensation and cure in a framework of proportionality between injury and consequences are clearer in these codes than in Hammurabi's.

> *The Hittite Laws*, Tablet I, sections 1–18 (ca 15th–13th century B.C.E.), from Pritchard, *Ancient Near Eastern Texts*, 189–90.

> 1: If anyone kills a man or a woman in a quarrel, he has to make amends for him/her. He shall give four persons, man or woman, and pledge his estate as security.

2: If anyone kills a male or a female slave in a quarrel, he has to make amends for him/her. He shall give two persons, man or woman, and pledge his estate as security.

3: If anyone strikes a free man or woman and he/she dies, (only) his hand doing wrong, he has to make amends for him/her. He shall give two persons and pledge his estate as security.

4: If anyone strikes a male or a female slave and he/she dies, (only) his hand doing wrong, he has to make amends for him/her. He shall give one person and pledge his estate as security.

5: If anyone kills a Hittite merchant, he shall give 100 minas of silver and pledge his estate as security. If (it happens) in the country of Luwiya or in the country of Pala, he shall give 100 minas of silver and replace his goods; if (it happens) in the Hatti land, he has (also) to make amends for the merchant himself.

7: If anyone blinds a free man or knocks out his teeth, they would formerly give 1 mina of silver, now he shall give 20 shekels of silver and pledge his estate as security.

8: If anyone blinds a male or female slave or knocks out his/her teeth, he shall give 10 shekels of silver and pledge his estate as security.

9: If anyone batters a man's head, they would formerly give 6 shekels of silver; he who was battered would receive 3 shekels of silver, and they would receive 3 shekels of silver for the palace. Now the king has abolished the (share) of the palace and only he who was battered receives 3 shekels of silver.

10: If anyone batters a man so that he falls ill, he shall take care of him. He shall give a man in his stead who can look after his house until he recovers. When he recovers, he shall give him 6 shekels of silver, and he shall also pay the physician's fee.

13: If anyone bites off a free man's nose, he shall give 1 mina of silver and pledge his estate as security.

15: If anyone mutilates a free man's ear, he shall give 15 shekels of silver and pledge his estate as security.

16: If anyone mutilates the ear of a male or female slave, he shall give 6 shekels of silver.

17: If anyone causes a free woman to miscarry—if (it is) the 10th month, he shall give 10 shekels of silver and pledge his estate as security.

18: If anyone causes a slave-woman to miscarry, if (it is) the 10th month, he shall give 5 shekels of silver.

The Hittite code begins with a situation in which one person kills another in the heat of a quarrel and verse 3 seems to have in mind homicides that result from incidents in which the intent of the actor was to strike but not to kill. In both cases the killer is not himself killed. Instead he must restore to the family of the victim compensatory workers to make up for the economic loss suffered. It is not clear why the compensation is fourfold or twofold, but presumably the intention was to compensate with laborers for the losses of social status, pain, suffering, and disgrace incident to the killing of a clan member. The scheme certainly seems strange if the primary intent was to punish wrongdoers rather than to compensate the injured. In contrast, Exodus 21 does not see homicide as an economic matter at all. Indeed in interpreting these biblical texts later generations of rabbis will preclude the recovery of any damages for assaults if the victim later dies. Along the same lines Numbers 35:31−32 forbids accepting monetary ransom instead of capital punishment of the killer. For the Bible homicide is unmistakably a crime against God as well as humans.

Verse 9 of the Hittite text suggests that a tension was recognized between compensatory payment to the victim and a fine paid by the assaulter to the king for the offense against the community. The king gave up his share, and the reduced payment thereafter was wholly compensatory.

The Bible also treats assault in a purely compensatory context, in contrast to American law, which emphasizes the criminal aspects of assault and is unlikely to fully compensate the victim.

It is noteworthy that Exodus, Hammurabi, and the Hittite laws all treat the loss of a fetus after an assault as a compensable injury. The unborn child's loss is considered as something less than homicide. The fetus is valued by the Hittites at less than the value of a nose or an ear.

# Topic Three: Biblical Jurisprudence

## A. LAW AND WORLD VIEW

This topic examines salient aspects of the biblical view of law, particularly the biblical understanding of where the law comes from, why it is important to obey it, how the law changes over the course of time and changing circumstance, and how community institutions of justice are to be organized and operated in the face of conflicting values.

These questions are worth investigating because to say that law suggests a world view is to say that law is a statement of values. All legal systems suggest a world view. Law tells us what is right and how things ought to be. Even in the most whimsical and arbitrary tyranny, law has its reasons and its connections to larger ends. Law indicates what the lawmaker thinks is important about the order or disorder of experience.

The Bible makes these values very explicit and accessible. It expresses a world view based on certain values that suffused and transformed the primitive, tribal organization of the Israelites into an organized legal system. Most notable among these values are notions of authority, continuity, justice, community, truth, responsibility, order, and contact with the Divine.

But every legal system incorporates a view, whether explicitly or implicitly, and that determines how it deals with a number of important philosophical issues which all legal systems face. Among these are the following:

*Legitimacy and Authority.* Every legal system makes a claim for allegiance on those it seeks to bind. Modern secular statutes rarely spell out why one should obey the law. Instead, the law demands obedience to its commands; it does not exhort compliance. Dominant schools of American legal philosophy share this perspective. They are skeptical and positivistic. To borrow the example provided by one of the leading expositors of this approach to law, Oliver Wendell Holmes, Jr., American law looks at the question of obedience from the perspective of the bad man who asks: "What will happen to me if I do not obey?" Such a person will comply only if the risks of disobedience in terms of pain or loss are greater than the potential rewards of defiance. This view of law leads to an emphasis on the chain of enforcement that can be invoked to ensure compliance. In American society this chain links the judge to the sheriff and ultimately to the *posse commitas*, which is now the United States Army. Those who contemplate defying the law must consider the possibility of having ultimately to deal with the 82nd Airborne Division, as the defiant school board of Little Rock, Arkansas, learned in 1958, when they disobeyed orders to racially desegregate their schools.

No extended analysis is needed to realize that the law cannot hope to gain effective compliance only by command and threat of punishment. It would require enough policemen to have one at every person's elbow at all times, and then there would have to be policemen to check on the policemen. The most authoritarian modern societies recognize that they can function only if the vast majority of citizens accept and obey the law on their own.

Modern secular society tends to swallow its reasons for obeying the law, although in fact it is very dependent on values and the commitments they engender. Because American law puts so much weight on the positivistic bases for law, its perspective often appears excessively materialistic, atomistic, mechanical, and individualistic. It is uncomfortable asserting moral values that have a universal claim for obedience. It is uncomfortable insisting that individuals have relationships to others that give rise to claims superior to the individual's preferences. So, for example, modern law is unwilling to accept a system of contract law that enforces agreements because people should keep their promises. Instead, it has struggled for centuries to find a secular, morally neutral basis for contract enforcement. Most notably, American law appeals to the morally neutral doctrine of consideration that bases the enforcement of promises on the elements of bargain and exchange (the promise must be kept because the promisor has been paid to keep it). However, the results have never provided a complete or satisfying explanation for what the social expectations of promise making have been all along.

Often modern secular law seems to distinguish between being law abiding and being good. To some extent this may reflect our culture's roots in the Christian tradition, which sometimes saw obedience to law as inconsistent with living in a holy spirit. In any event, modern law often seems to say that a person must go beyond the law to be good. At best, the law will only tell a person how to stay out of jail.

The problem of authority is especially urgent for the Jewish legal system. Modern American legal philosophy stresses the authority of the law to command obedience and to enforce that command with state power. Jews, however, for more than two millennia have not lived in a single state, and most often they were subjects of non-Jewish rulers who governed by rules other than Jewish law. The familiar geographical supports for national legal authority are consequently unavailable as a jurisdictional base for Jewish law. It has nevertheless survived as an effective legal system until recent times because, from its biblical roots, its authority has been derived from another powerful source, the commandment of God.

This strong link between the legal and the Divine has led the Jewish mind to see the world as organized by law. The profound order of creation is revealed not only through the laws of nature, but also by the cultic, ritual, and ethical laws that govern mankind. Everyday community customs and regulations take on a new meaning when seen in this light: they are part of a grand scheme that connects and holds the universe together. In Psalm 19, which will be read later in this topic (Section D:3), the Psalmist provides a vision of a world filled and ordered by law. This may seem strange to the citizen of a modern secular society, in which the authority of the law stems from political power or majoritarian consent, but it enables Jewish law to base its authority on a much broader ground than that available to secular law. As shall be seen, for Jews the law is not merely a way to avoid punishment; the law, obedience to it and study of it, are vital links to God, who uses law to bring people to human fulfillment.

*Continuity and Change.* A second, pervasive problem for legal systems is the tension between continuity and change. Law must accommodate the need for continuity and stability as well as have a capacity to meet changing circumstances. Each generation is linked to those before it but has an undeniable interest in reconsidering and expressing its own values. Oliver Wendell Holmes, Jr., the renowned American judge and legal philosopher of the realist school, has expressed this conflict well (O. W. Holmes, Jr., "The Path of the Law," 10 *Harvard L. Rev.* 457.47 [1897]):

> At present, in very many cases, if we want to know why a rule of law has taken its particular shape, and more or less if we want to know why it exists at all, we go to tradition. . . . The rational study of law is still to a large extent the study of history. History must be a part of the study, because without it we cannot know the precise scope of rules which it is our business to know. It is a part of the rational study, because it is the first step toward an enlightened skepticism, that is, towards a deliberate reconsideration of the worth of those rules. When you get the dragon out of his cave to the plain and

in the daylight, you can count his teeth and claws, and see just what is his strength. But to get him out is only the first step. The next is either to kill him, or to tame him and make him a useful animal. For the rational study of the law the black-letter man may be the man of the present, but the man of the future is the man of statistics and the master of economics. It is revolting to have no better reason for a rule of law than that so it was laid down in the time of Henry IV. It is still more revolting if the grounds upon which it was laid down have vanished long since, and the rule simply persists from blind imitation of the past.

The continuity of Jewish legal thought, though, is unique in human experience. The traditional Jew considers the body of law he obeys to have been revealed by God to Moses at Mount Sinai. Scholars extend the continuity of the tradition even further; they point out that many biblical laws have Mesopotamian antecedents and are closely connected with other Middle Eastern legal systems. The fact that Jewish law has endured for so long makes it an unusual specimen for the study of how a legal system can maintain continuity.

But it is not only the long history of Jewish law that makes it instructive on the issue of continuity and change: it is also the way it institutes and justifies change. Jewish law claims to be based on a single act of revelation that endures for all time. All subsequent decisions must be rooted in the constitutional authority of that revelation and of those who have the power to interpret it.

As shall be seen in section F, biblical literature recognized the possibility of legal change through new revelation or prophecy but was also concerned with maintaining the permanence of the law. Legal systems that base their authority on power or consent find it relatively easy to change the law, either by changing the ruler or by amending the law with majority approval. In a religious legal system, however, the need to return for further revelation may be strongly felt, but the possibility to do so is always uncertain. We may be very sure of the authenticity of the inspiration behind the visions and trances of ancient prophets, but we are likely to be more skeptical of contemporary seers. Like the Catholic Church, the Jewish tradition has been notably cautious in recognizing recent recipients of revelation. The tradition has changed, however, and the methods by which it has done so while maintaining its coherence are interesting features of this study.

*Belief and Action.* The traditional emphasis on law in Judaism has resulted in an emphasis on action rather than faith. Matters of belief are discussed thoroughly within the classical Jewish sources, and it is possible to describe a mainstream Jewish position on many issues. But as long as the Jew continues to observe the law, considerable freedom is allowed for the individual to decide the particular form of belief to adopt. In effect, Jewish law says "do not steal," leaving to the individual the choice of obeying because God so commanded at Sinai, or because God's will, as explained by the judges, would be best fulfilled by an orderly society that punishes stealing, or for some other reason. Since the source of authority is Divine and there is no single, authoritative, human lawgiver, there is little agreement on dogma and relatively great tolerance for divergent opinion. Even in matters of practice there is disagreement, although the degree of variation, at least until the past two centuries, has been considerably less than the variation in ideology.

*Rules and Spirit.* The emphasis on law and external behavior within the Jewish tradition has never been to the exclusion of other human values. On the contrary, from its biblical roots Judaism has attempted to make these human values concrete and effective through law. This attitude should be contrasted to that of modern secular law, which tends to see the content of intimate and affective relationships as largely beyond the reach of the law. It should also be contrasted to Christianity, which tends to see law as an obstacle to relations based on love.

For many Jewish thinkers the link between the law of God and the love of God is the intention of the actor. A person's obedience in action fulfills the law, but obedience can also illuminate his or her actions with meaning when accompanied by a loving intention. A system that emphasizes the primacy of action must recognize the different moral qualities that apparently identical acts can assume. One may obey the rules and not steal out of fear of being punished, or out of love for one's fellows, or out of a desire not to deprive others of what is rightfully theirs. One may punish another human being out of loving concern for him, or from hatred, envy, or misplaced sanctimonious superiority. Daily acts may be done in simple obedience to the physical laws of our animal bodies or be transformed by a transcendent intention into a celebration of our unity with all creation. Particularly in the later Jewish mystical tradition known as Hasidism, this emphasis on the saving quality of intention, which has roots in biblical thought, counterbalances the traditional insistence on the primacy of lawful action.

But lawyers of every tradition know that emphasis on intention can cause more problems than it solves. Part of the problem is evidentiary: How does one prove an actor's intention? The excerpt from Numbers 35 dealing with homicide (in section B:4c) indicates an early attempt to differentiate among different actions that produce death apparently on the basis of the likely intention of the actor. Beyond questions of proof, intention is a slippery concept, for often our intentions are unclear, inconsistent, or misguided. To be significant the intention must be conscious, but all legal doctrine that emphasizes human consciousness is limited by its ephemeral and problematic nature. Moreover, emphasis on intention can become a competitor to the law, as the history of Christianity shows. It is easy enough to see how loving intention enriches a lawful act and how it can make an ambiguous act a fulfillment of the law. But can good intentions justify the unlawful? When, if ever, can higher goals provide sufficient reason to steal, murder, or violate the holy? Can the loving ends justify the unlawful means?

We shall return to these themes, for they are the common work of all lawyers and the everyday concern of religious persons. Most members of modern Western civilization hold attitudes toward these profound matters that are traceable directly to the biblical attitudes to be described in this topic.

## B. BIBLICAL METHODS OF RESOLVING DISPUTES

### 1. *Trial by Judge: Types of Judges*

Information on how biblical societies resolved disputes and judged claims is limited to that provided by the Bible itself. While these data are not as complete as a student of procedure and jurisdiction might hope for, they do indicate the existence from the earliest biblical periods of formal methods for the resolution of disputes by a judicial process. Various jurisdictional bases for judicial authority are indicated in the biblical text.

These texts are helpful in clarifying who judges are and what they do. When the modern reader thinks of a judge, what is likely to come to mind is a professional official with specialized training and carefully differentiated official functions who is charged with resolving disputes and declaring legal rights. The judges described in the Bible have some of these characteristics, but there appears to have been a more intimate tie between political power in general and the power to judge. The importance the biblical world view attached to justice explains why judging is seen as an essential social function. Both judging and justice are dimensions of the human community required and ordained by God. Like God, men are not to resolve disputes by recourse to naked power, but through appeals to justice. The very placement of the text of Exodus 18:13–27 suggests this. The appointment of magistrates and the creation of courts immediately precedes the revelation at Sinai in chapters 19–24 in Exodus, the text read in Topic Two. Judges and courts come first, and then the content of the law is given to the people. The Exodus 18 text and its parallel in Deuteronomy 1:9–18 (in section 2a) also are noteworthy for their description of the pragmatic and human origins of the judicial institution. The advice to appoint judges comes from Moses' father-in-law as a way to conserve Moses' energy by choosing helpers to relieve him of the caseload. Note that this institution is not described in terms of a Divine command, nor as a longstanding group custom, but as an innovation by the human leaders to meet an emergent situation.

It is uncertain whether during the biblical period there was a group of specially trained persons whose major work was to decide disputes and lawsuits. Several of the following texts appear to contemplate the appointment of judges, but it is dangerous to apply modern categories to ancient societies. In particular it is unlikely that a distinction was clearly drawn between judicial and other administrative or executive officials. It is also not clear whether the functions described in the Bible for the various kinds of judges all existed simultaneously in a well-differentiated organization of judicial assignments, or whether the Bible rather reflects the variety of judicial institutions that existed at different times during the biblical period.

A second problem in understanding the nature and functions of biblical judges is that the connotations of some words that apparently refer to official positions are not known. This problem has been mentioned in reference to "judges," but it also applies to another group of officials, *elohim*. Most scholars assume that they were judges despite the fact that the term literally means "gods." They explain the use of that term in several ways. Umberto Cassuto, for example, points out that in the courts of other ancient peoples there were idols (*elohim*) denoting the gods, and the Israelites used the term as a stereotyped expression signifying the place of the court. (U. Cassuto, *A Commentary on the Book of Exodus* [Jerusalem: Magnes Press, 1967], 267.) J. H. Hertz, in his popular commentary used in many synagogues, follows Abraham ibn Ezra (1092–1167 C.E.) and Nahmanides (c. 1195–c. 1270 C.E.) in suggesting that the judges are called gods because they pronounce sentence in the name of God according to Deuteronomy 1:17, "for judgment is from God." (J. H. Hertz, *Pentateuch and Haftorahs* [London: Soncino Press, 1961], 307.) *The Jerusalem Bible* ultimately remains noncommittal as to whether *elohim* means judges at all. It translates the relevant passages in Exodus 22 as "the owner of the house must swear *before God*" (22:7), "the person whom *God* pronounces guilty" (22:8).

Another barrier to clear understanding is the tendency to construe the ancient texts according to the interpretations they later were given by the rabbis. This is a particular problem with Deuteronomy 17 (see section 2e), which rabbis interpreted many centuries after it was written as a broad charter for vigorous and extended judicial activity. How it was understood by its author's contemporaries is much less certain.

It is quite clear, despite these uncertainties, that judges did function in biblical times, that they decided interpretive questions of law as well as issues of fact, and that they recognized an obligation to follow past precedents and practices from earlier cases as well as to apply written rules in deciding cases. Moreover, even though positions were probably not as strictly defined in the ancient world as they are now, we can discern the following types of judges:

a. *Leader of the Nation.* Judicial authority is an aspect of general political power. Gradually in the European experience, for example, the term "King's Court" comes to carry two distinct connotations, one the personal entourage of the king and the other the official place for the hearing of litigated complaints and claims. Originally the two functions were fused. Similarly, the Hebrew root for "judge," *shfot,* connotes "judge," "rules," and "military commander," indicating that persons in this position in the ancient Near East exercised military and political, as well as judicial, authority. Adjudication of claims fell into the domain of these individuals, the judges, but unlike the American judiciary, biblical judges additionally carried out the many functions associated with a head of state. It was only over a period of time that the function of being a judge took on a distinct meaning.

The biblical combination of military, judicial, and political powers is not an arrangement confined to ancient times. The royal government established in England after the Norman Conquest possessed many aspects of a military occupation, with broad political and judicial authority delegated by the king to the local military lords (dukes, earls, marquis, and barons) in the countryside. The royal Commissioners in Eyre, beginning in the twelfth century, combined judicial and general administrative authority, and only at comparatively late stages in their historical development became limited exclusively to presiding as judges in the courts held throughout England. Even in the United States, with its constitutional doctrine of separation of powers, examples of such combinations exist. In many instances the sheriff in the American West during the nineteenth century functioned in this way, and military commanders still do. The sharply defined role of judges in modern America is, in fact, a relatively new phenomenon in human legal history.

The individuals in the following excerpts view the job of judge in different ways. In Exodus, the tribal chieftains act as judicial functionaries appointed by the highest judge, Moses. In the Book of Judges, the judges seem to spend little time hearing disputes; they are primarily military leaders. In fact, Deborah is the only one in the book who is specifically depicted as judging cases. This is ironic since women were barred from acting as judges in later Jewish tradition. The passage from II Samuel shows that individuals seeking political power saw the role of judge as one avenue to that power. By exercising the judicial function while his father David was still alive, Absalom asserted royal power. It was David's failure to provide justice that is described as the basis for this attempted revolution. This would suggest a royal monopoly on judicial activity at this time. The excerpt from I Kings serves as a reminder that the head of state is the one who makes decisions in cases and who acts as decision maker; there is no separate judiciary.

> *Exodus* 18:13–27:
> Next day, Moses sat as magistrate among the people, while the people stood about Moses from morning until evening. But when Moses' father-in-law saw how much he had to do for the people, he said, "What is this thing that you have undertaken for the people? Why do you act alone, while all the people stand about you from morning until evening?" Moses replied to his father-in-law, "It is because the people come to me to inquire of God. When they have a dispute, it comes before me, and I arbitrate between a man and his neighbor, and I make known the laws and teachings of God."
>
> But Moses' father-in-law said to him, "The thing you are doing is not right; you will surely wear yourself out, you as well as this people. For the task is too heavy for you; you cannot do it alone. Now listen to me. I will give you counsel, and God be with you! You represent the people before God: you bring the disputes before God, and enjoin upon them the laws and the teachings, and make known to them the way they are to go and the practices they are to follow. You shall also seek out from among all the people capable men who fear God, trustworthy men who spurn ill-gotten gain; and set these over them as chiefs of thousands, hundreds, fifties, and tens. Let them exercise authority over the people at all times; let them bring every major dispute to you, but decide every minor dispute themselves. Make it easier for yourself, and let them share the burden with you. If you do this—and God so commands you—you will be able to bear up; and all these people will go home content."
>
> Moses heeded his father-in-law and did just as he had said. Moses chose capable men out of all Israel, and appointed them heads over the people—chiefs of thousands, hundreds, fifties, and tens. And they exercised authority over the people at all times: the difficult matters they would bring to Moses, and all the minor matters they would de-

cide themselves. Then Moses bade his father-in-law farewell, and he
went his way to his own land.

*Judges* 4:4–7 (Jerusalem Bible):
   At this time Deborah was judge in Israel, a prophetess, the wife of
Lappidoth. She used to sit under Deborah's Palm between Ramah and
Bethel in the highlands of Ephraim, and the Israelites would come to
her to have their disputes decided. She sent for Barak son of Abinoam
from Kedesh in Naphtali. She said to him, "This is the order of Yahweh, the God of Israel: 'March to Mount Tabor and take with you ten
thousand men from the sons of Naphtali and the sons of Zebulun. I
will entice Sisera, the commander of Jabin's army, to encounter you at
the wadi Kishon with his chariots and troops; and I will put him into
your power.'"

*II Samuel* 15:1–6 (Jerusalem Bible):
   After this, Absalom procured a chariot and horses, with fifty men
to run ahead of him. He would rise early and stand beside the road
leading to the gate; and whenever a man with some lawsuit had to
come before the king's court, Absalom would call out to him and ask,
"What town are you from?" He would answer, "Your servant is from
one of the tribes in Israel." Then Absalom would say, "Look, your
case is sound and just, but there is not one deputy of the king's who
will listen to you." Absalom would go on to say, "Oh, who will appoint me judge in the land? Then anyone with a lawsuit or a plea
could come to me and I would see he had justice." And whenever anyone came up to do homage to him, he would stretch out his hand and
take him and kiss him. Absalom acted in this way with all the Israelites who came to the king for justice, and so Absalom seduced the
hearts of the men of Israel.

*I Kings* 3:16–28 (Jerusalem Bible):
   Then two prostitutes came to the king and stood before him. "If it
please you, my lord," one of the women said, "this woman and I live
in the same house, and while she was in the house I gave birth to a
child. Now it happened on the third day after my delivery that this
woman also gave birth to a child. We were alone together; there was
no one else in the house with us; just the two of us in the house. Now
one night this woman's son died; she overlaid him. And in the middle
of the night she got up and took my son from beside me while your
servant was asleep; she put him to her breast and put her own dead
son to mine. When I got up to suckle my child, there he was, dead. But
in the morning I looked at him carefully, and he was not the child I
had borne at all." Then the other woman spoke. "That is not true!
Your son is the dead one, mine is the live one." And so they wrangled

before the king. "This one says," the king observed, " 'My son is the one who is alive; your son is dead,' while the other says, 'That is not true! Your son is the dead one, mine is the live one.' Bring me a sword," said the king; and a sword was brought into the king's presence. "Cut the living child in two," the king said, "and give half to one, half to the other." At this the woman who was the mother of the living child addressed the king, for she burned with pity for her son. "If it please you, my lord," she said, "let them give her the child; only do not let them think of killing it!" But the other said, "He shall belong to neither of us. Cut him up." Then the king gave his decision. "Give the child to the first woman," he said, "and do not kill him. She is his mother." All Israel came to hear of the judgment the king had pronounced, and held the king in awe, recognizing that he possessed divine wisdom for dispensing justice.

b. *The Elders of the Community.* The clan, tribe, or city served as the source of government for some biblical communities rather than a king or military leader. In such a setting, judicial authority appears to have been shared among the heads of families or elders of the community. The trials described are quite formal and the role of the elders is perhaps closer to that of an official witness to the formal declarations and proofs of the parties than it is to trial of contested factual and legal questions. The selections from Deuteronomy show that the elders not only judged but carried out their judgments in three different ways: in the case of the blood feud, they hand the offender over to the avenger for punishment; in the case of the defiant son, they authorize the men of the town to inflict the punishment; and in the case of the fraudulent charges against a woman's virginity, they execute the punishment themselves. In the last passage they have a different role altogether, that of official witness, as well as persuaders or mediators.

Justice is an aspect of community life, and the leadership group of any community is likely to participate actively in resolving disputes. This is particularly likely in the early and simple stages of community organization, when public business is less likely to be seen as a specialized political function. Courts of suitors, in which the concerned members of the community leadership participated with litigants in the hearing and disposition of claims, were a common feature of Anglo-Saxon courts before the Norman Conquest. As was suggested in the last section of this topic, only gradually did the English Curia Regis, Court of the King, come to denote an institution in which legal specialists judged lawsuits. Before that time "the Court" referred generally to the entourage of the king, where the leaders of the land congregated and participated with the sovereign in dealing with the administration of the kingdom, the making of laws, and the judging of disputes brought by suitors to the king's attention with a claim that the king do justice.

Similarly, during much of the medieval period the king's courts were quite limited in their jurisdiction. Many important disputes were within the primary competence of local courts of towns and the specialized courts in which commercial and maritime traders applied the law merchant, the "pie powder courts" of fairs, as well as feudal courts of local magnates. Such courts often operated as courts of suitors at which the regional notables or masters of trade would gather at regular times of the year both to press their own claims and to participate in the resolution of claims of other members of the group. Such meetings also were the occasion to announce rules and ordinances established by the local authority and to formally witness and authenticate important transactions.

In both biblical and English law, then, the elders of the community functioned in a variety of legal capacities to insure that justice was done in their communities.

*Deuteronomy* 19:11–13:
If, however, a man who is his neighbor's enemy lies in wait for him and sets upon him and strikes him a fatal blow and then flees to one of these towns, the elders of his town shall have him brought back from there and shall hand him over to the blood-avenger to be put to death; you must show him no pity. Thus you will purge Israel of the blood of the innocent, and it will go well with you.

*Deuteronomy* 21:18–21:
If a man has a disloyal and defiant son, who does not heed his father or mother and does not obey them even after they discipline him, his father and mother shall take hold of him and bring him out to the elders of his town at the public place of his community. They shall say to the elders of his town, "This son of ours is disloyal and defiant; he does not heed us. He is a wastrel and a drunkard." Thereupon the men of his town shall stone him to death. Thus you will sweep out evil from your midst: all Israel will hear and be afraid.

*Deuteronomy* 22:13–19:
A man marries a woman and cohabits with her. Then he takes an aversion to her and makes up charges against her and defames her, saying, "I married this woman; but when I approached her, I found that she was not a virgin." In such a case, the girl's father and mother shall produce the evidence of the girl's virginity before the elders of the town at the gate. And the girl's father shall say to the elders, "I gave this man my daughter to wife, but he has taken an aversion to

her; so he has made up charges, saying, 'I did not find your daughter a virgin.' But here is the evidence of my daughter's virginity!" And they shall spread out the cloth before the elders of the town. The elders of that town shall then take the man and flog him, and they shall fine him a hundred [shekels of] silver and give it to the girl's father; for the man has defamed a virgin in Israel. Moreover, she shall remain his wife; he shall never have the right to divorce her.

*Deuteronomy 25:5–10:*
When brothers dwell together and one of them dies and leaves no son, the wife of the deceased shall not be married to a stranger, outside the family. Her husband's brother shall unite with her and take her as his wife, performing the levir's duty. The first son that she bears shall be accounted to the dead brother, that his name may not be blotted out in Israel. But if the man does not want to marry his brother's widow, his brother's widow shall appear before the elders in the gate and declare, "My husband's brother refuses to establish a name in Israel for his brother; he will not perform the duty of a levir." The elders of his town shall then summon him and talk to him. If he insists, saying, "I do not choose to marry her," his brother's widow shall go up to him in the presence of the elders, pull the sandal off his foot, spit in his face, and make this declaration: Thus shall be done to the man who will not build up his brother's house! And he shall go in Israel by the name of "the family of the unsandaled one."

c. *The Whole Community as Judges.* The description of the treatment of the manslayer in Deuteronomy 19 (in section b) suggests that it is the elders of the town that decide whether the accused is to be granted sanctuary or turned over to the avenger for execution. The version of these laws in Numbers is somewhat variant and appears to vest decisional power in a broader segment of the community. The passage is also remarkable for the detail with which it tells of the specifics of the procedure.

*Numbers 35:22–29:*
But if he pushed him without malice aforethought or hurled any object at him unintentionally, or inadvertently dropped upon him any deadly object of stone, and death resulted—though he was not an enemy of his and did not seek his harm—in such cases the assembly shall decide between the slayer and the blood-avenger. The assembly shall protect the manslayer from the blood-avenger, and the assembly shall restore him to the city of refuge to which he fled, and there he shall remain until the death of the high priest who was anointed with the sacred oil. But if the manslayer ever goes outside the limits of the city of refuge to which he has fled, and the blood-avenger comes upon him outside the limits of his city of refuge, and the blood-avenger kills

the manslayer, there is no bloodguilt on his account. For he must remain inside his city of refuge until the death of the high priest; after the death of the high priest, the manslayer may return to his land holding.

Such shall be your law of procedure throughout the generations in all your settlements.

  d. *Priests as Judges.* The word "priest" in English conjures up images of Roman Catholic priests, but biblical priests were considerably different. Any Roman Catholic male may become a priest, but the biblical priesthood was restricted to the male descendants of Aaron (Numbers 3:10). One becomes a Roman Catholic priest through a process of learning and acceptance of commitments, but one is born into the biblical priesthood as a descendant of Aaron. Biblical priests were similar to Catholic priests in one respect, however: they were responsible for the cult. With that as a base, in some historic periods they constituted an independent political force in society, as for example when they allied with the monarchy against the prophets.

  As an outgrowth of their cultic responsibilities, biblical priests functioned as judges in specific areas, especially regarding maintenance of the Temple, sacrifices, and determination of purity and impurity. Some legal wrongs that a modern person might consider secular may be sinful as well as wrong. Righting the situation may then require repentance and sacrifice as well as compensation. Breach of an oath, failure to keep a promise, untruth, and even the failure to come forward and speak the truth as a witness all fall into this category. The next two excerpts outline the judicial mandate of the priests; the third (from Haggai) is an example of priestly adjudication in a cultic matter; the fourth (from Leviticus 19) indicates the priestly role in cases of sexual misbehavior with a betrothed female slave; and the fifth (from Leviticus 5) spells out the priests' jurisdiction in civil and procedural matters.

  *Leviticus* 10:8–11:
  And the Lord spoke to Aaron, saying: Drink no wine or ale, you or your sons with you, when you enter the Tent of Meeting, that you may not die—it is a law for all time throughout your generations—for you must distinguish between the sacred and the profane, and between the unclean and the clean. And you must teach the Israelites all the laws which the Lord has imparted to you through Moses. [See Deut. 21:5, in section 4a.]

*Ezekiel* 44:15, 23–25 (Jerusalem Bible):
As regards the levitical priests, the sons of Zadok, who did their duty to me in the sanctuary when the Israelites strayed far from me, they may still approach me to serve me; they may stand in my presence to offer me the fat and blood—it is the Lord Yahweh who speaks.

They are to teach my people the difference between what is sacred and what is profane and make them understand the difference between what is clean and what is unclean. They are to be judges in disputes; they must judge in the spirit of my statutes; they must follow my laws and ordinances at all my feasts and keep my sabbaths holy. They are not to go near a dead man, in case they become unclean, except in these permissible cases, that is, for father, mother, daughter, son, brother or unmarried sister.

*Haggai* 2:11–14 (Jerusalem Bible):
On the twenty-fourth day of the ninth month, in the second year of Darius, the word of Yahweh was addressed to the prophet Haggai as follows, "Yahweh Sabaoth says this: Ask the priests for a decision on this question, 'If a man carries consecrated meat in the fold of his gown and with this fold touches bread, broth, wine, or food of any kind, does such food become holy?'" The priests answered, "No, it does not." Haggai then said, "If a man made unclean by contact with a corpse touches any of this, does it become unclean?" The priests answered, "Yes, it does." Haggai then spoke out. "It is the same with this people," he said, "the same with this nation as I see it—it is Yahweh who speaks—the same with everything they turn their hands to; and what they offer here is unclean."

*Leviticus* 19:20–21:
If a man has carnal relations with a woman who is a slave and has been designated for another man, but has not been redeemed or given her freedom, there shall be an indemnity; they shall not, however, be put to death, since she has not been freed. But he must bring to the entrance of the Tent of Meeting, as his guilt offering to the Lord, a ram of guilt offering.

*Leviticus* 5:1–13, 20–26:
If a person incurs guilt:

When he has heard a public imprecation and—although able to testify as one who has either seen or learned of the matter—he does not give information, so that he is subject to punishment;

Or when a person touches any unclean thing—be it the carcass of an unclean beast or the carcass of unclean cattle or the carcass of an unclean creeping thing—and the fact has escaped him, and then, being unclean, he finds himself culpable;

Or when he touches human uncleanness—any such uncleanness whereby one becomes unclean—and, though he has known it, the fact has escaped him, but later he finds himself culpable;

Or when a person utters an oath to bad or good purpose—whatever a man may utter in an oath—and, though he has known it, the fact has escaped him, but later he finds himself culpable in any of these matters—when he realizes his guilt in any of these matters, he shall confess that wherein he has sinned. And he shall bring as his penalty to the Lord, for the sin of which he is guilty, a female from the flock, sheep or goat, as a sin offering; and the priest shall make expiation on his behalf for his sin.

But if his means do not suffice for a sheep, he shall bring to the Lord, as his penalty for that of which he is guilty, two turtledoves or two pigeons, one for a sin offering and the other for a burnt offering. . . .

And if his means do not suffice for two turtledoves or two pigeons, he shall bring as his offering for that of which he is guilty a tenth of an *ephah* of choice flour for a sin offering. . . . Thus the priest shall make expiation on his behalf for whichever of these sins he is guilty, and he shall be forgiven. . . .

The Lord spoke to Moses, saying: When a person sins and commits a trespass against the Lord by dealing deceitfully with his fellow in the matter of a deposit or an investment, or through robbery; or if he has intimidated his fellow; or if he has found something lost and lied about it and sworn falsely—any one of the various things that one may do and sin thereby—when one has thus sinned and, realizing his guilt, would restore that which he got through robbery or intimidation, or the deposit that was entrusted to him, or the lost thing that he found, or anything about which he swore falsely, he shall repay the principal amount and add a fifth part to it. He shall pay it to its owner when he realizes his guilt. Then he shall bring to the priest, as his penalty to the Lord, a ram without blemish from the flock, or the equivalent, as a guilt offering. The priest shall make expiation on his behalf before the Lord, and he shall be forgiven for whatever he may have done to draw blame thereby.

## 2. Trial by Judge: Jurisdictions of Judges

Over the course of the biblical era the tribes of Israel settled the land, built cities, and formed a national state. The jurisdictional basis of the judiciary inevitably was influenced by these changes. The following texts trace the stages of that development and the modifications in the role played by judges in the community as these changes occurred.

To make our point we have tried to differentiate and separate the strands of community organization as best we can. The data from biblical texts is too limited to do this with great confidence, just as it is difficult to make such distinctions with confidence in Anglo-American court jurisdictions. The basic unit of court organization in most American states remains the county, although some states have created multicounty district or circuit courts and a few retain municipal courts for urban areas. Americans today correctly think of the county as a purely geographic subdivision, typically based on early patterns of settlement and the compromise adjustments of political power among local forces within the state. Yet as more levels of history are peeled away, the medieval origins of the English counties can be seen as units of royal military power after the Norman Conquest of England in 1066. The heads of these units bore titles that have clear military as well as feudal connotations: counts, earls, lords lieutenant, sheriffs. When we probe still further back, we find that many of the older English counties or shires are the residual shells of distinct political and ethnic communities. They bear witness to the waves of Celtic, Germanic, and Danish tribes that invaded England over the centuries.

It is difficult from the biblical text to fit the centralized royal and priestly courts together with local and community courts. Perhaps the two existed side by side, perhaps our texts are drawn from different historical periods when local or central national powers were variously dominant. It may be useful to remember that these difficulties are also presented by familiar secular court systems. By Tudor times in England, the county and other local authorities had become subordinate to a national royal government, and the judges and other officials increasingly became the king's men sent into the local community. English local authorities today remain an arm of central administration primarily responsible to a minister at Westminster.

The American experience has been quite different in most states. Here counties are traditional bastions of local power, locally elected, funded from local taxes, and staffed by officials drawn from the community in which they serve. Only in the past two generations have broad-based sales and income taxation in the hands of the state and national governments displaced local property taxes as the primary revenue source for education, public welfare, police, and courts. As these functions of local government have increasingly become dependent on central government subventions, local control over these matters has been drastically diminished. Yet in almost every state the local judges, police chiefs, county administrators, and prosecutors are drawn exclusively from the community itself. Outsiders need not apply! Even in the federal courts, where judges are appointed by the president on a national basis, one will have to look hard to find a federal judge who is not drawn from the district in which he or she will serve. In those states divided into more than one federal district court, the local quality of the personnel is still strictly maintained. The tension between local and central government remains, and the dominance of one over the other appears to oscillate in response to larger political and social events. It seems plausible that the divergences apparent in the biblical treatments of these matters reflect comparable tensions.

a. *Chiefs of Thousands, Hundreds, Fifties and Tens:* judges organized on a tribal, military basis. (See section 1a, Exodus 18:13–27.)

Two biblical texts describe a judiciary organized on a tribal, military basis. Both Exodus 18:13–27, cited in Section 1a above, and Deuteronomy 1:9–18, which follows, refer to the time in Israel's history when it was travelling from Egypt to Canaan. The lack of a permanent land and the military goals of the people at that time made it appropriate to organize the judiciary according to numbers of people. It is hard to know how long that form of organization persisted once the people settled in Canaan.

> *Deuteronomy 1:9–18:*
> Thereupon I said to you, "I cannot bear the burden of you by myself. The Lord your God has multiplied you until you are today as numerous as the stars in the sky. May the Lord, the God of your fathers, increase your numbers a thousandfold, and bless you as He promised you. How can I alone bear the trouble of you, and the burden, and the bickering! Pick from each of your tribes men who are wise, discerning, and experienced, and I will appoint them as your heads." You answered me and said, "What you propose to do is good." So I took your tribal leaders, wise and experienced men, and appointed them heads over you: chiefs of thousands, chiefs of hundreds, chiefs of fifties, and chiefs of tens, and officials for your tribes. I further charged your magistrates as follows, "Hear out your fellow men, and decide justly between any man and a fellow Israelite or a stranger. You shall not be partial in judgment: hear out low and high alike. Fear no man, for judgment is God's. And any matter that is too difficult for you, you shall bring to me and I will hear it." Thus I instructed you, at that time, about the various things that you should do.

b. *Magistrates for Tribal Settlements:* judges organized on a territorial basis.

Deuteronomy 16 assumes a settled community and bases judicial organization on geographic regions. Later, rabbinic texts assume that both the organization by numbers mentioned in the texts above and the regional pattern of organization of Deuteronomy 16 were everlastingly relevant for the Jews in the Promised Land; the resulting rule was then that there had to be a specific number of judges for each region and a greater number of judges for areas with large populations (B.T. *Makkot* 7a). That tradition, practical as it is, may well reflect the reality in First Temple times too.

> *Deuteronomy* 16:18–20:
> You shall appoint magistrates and clerks for your tribes, in all the settlements that the Lord your God is giving you, and they shall govern the people with due justice. You shall not judge unfairly: you shall show no partiality; you shall not take bribes, for bribes blind the eyes of the discerning and upset the plea of the just. Justice, justice shall you pursue, that you may thrive and occupy the land that the Lord your God is giving you.

c. *A Centralized Judiciary of Magistrates and Priests:* judges organized on a national basis.

Deuteronomy 17 describes a judiciary organized on a national basis, with a central, supreme court in the Temple in Jerusalem, "the place which the Lord chose." This clearly refers to a time after King David conquered Jerusalem (c. 1000 B.C.E.), and it may well derive from the period after the destruction of the Northern Kingdom (722 B.C.E.) since only then would there be no opposition from that quarter to centralizing authority in Jerusalem. It may even come from a period as late as King Josiah, who concentrated the cult in Jerusalem (c. 622 B.C.E.) and presumably the judiciary along with it. II Chronicles attaches the institution of a centralized judiciary to a much earlier period, that of King Jehoshaphat (873–849 B.C.E.), but II Chronicles itself probably reflects a late tradition. However the dating question is resolved, a centralized judiciary, as required by Deuteronomy, became part of the sacred scriptures of the Jewish people, and so the later tradition assumes the existence and authority of a supreme court in the Holy City. Jerusalem, then, was the natural place to which the exiles would return under Ezra and establish mechanisms to administer justice.

> *Deuteronomy* 17:8–15:
> If a case is too baffling for you to decide, be it a controversy over homicide, civil law, or assault—matters of dispute in your courts—you shall promptly repair to the place which the Lord your God has chosen, and appear before the levitical priests, or the magistrate in charge at the time, and present your problem. When they have announced to

you the verdict in the case, you shall carry out the verdict that is announced to you from that place which the Lord chose, observing scrupulously all their instructions to you.

You shall act in accordance with the instructions given you and the ruling handed down to you; you must not deviate from the verdict that they announce to you either to the right or to the left. Should a man act presumptuously and disregard the priest charged with serving there the Lord your God, or the magistrate, that man shall die. Thus you will sweep out evil from Israel: all the people will hear and be afraid and will not act presumptuously again.

*II Chronicles* 19:4–11 (Jerusalem Bible):

After a stay in Jerusalem, Jehoshaphat made another progress through his people, from Beersheba to the highlands of Ephraim, to bring them back to Yahweh, the God of their ancestors. He appointed judges in the country in every one of all the fortified towns of Judah. He said to these judges, "Give due thought to your duties, since you are not judging in the name of men but in the name of Yahweh, who is with you whenever you pronounce sentence. May the fear of Yahweh now be on you. Keep the Law, apply it, for Yahweh our God has no part in fraud or partiality or the taking of bribes."

In addition, Jehoshaphat appointed priests, Levites and heads of Israelite families in Jerusalem to pronounce the verdicts of Yahweh and to judge disputed cases. They lived in Jerusalem and Jehoshaphat gave them the following instructions, "You are to perform these duties in the fear of Yahweh, faithfully and with all your heart. Whatever dispute comes before you from your brothers living in their towns: a question of blood vengeance, of the Law, of some commandment, of statute, or of ordinance, you are to clarify these matters for them so that they do not incur guilt before Yahweh, whose wrath will otherwise come on you and your brothers. Do this and you will incur no guilt.

"Amariah, the chief priest, will preside over you in all religious matters, and Zebadiah son of Ishmael, controller of the House of Judah, in all matters affecting the king. The Levites will serve as your scribes. Be resolute, carry out these instructions, and Yahweh will be there to bring success."

*Ezra* 7:11–16, 25–26 (Jerusalem Bible):

This is a copy of the document which King Artaxerxes handed to Ezra, the priest-scribe, the scribe who was especially learned in the text of Yahweh's commandments and his laws relating to Israel:

"Artaxerxes, king of kings, to the priest Ezra, scribe of the Law of the God of heaven, perfect peace.

"Here then are my orders: Anyone in my kingdom who is of the people of Israel, of their priests or their Levites and who freely chooses to go to Jerusalem, may go with you. For you are sent by the king and his seven counselors to make an inspection of Judah and Jerusalem according to the Law of your God, which is in your possession, and also to carry the silver and gold which the king and his counselors have voluntarily offered to the God of Israel who dwells in Jerusalem, as well as all the silver and gold you find in the whole province of Babylonia, together with those voluntary offerings given by the people and the priests for the Temple of their God in Jerusalem.

"And you, Ezra, by virtue of the wisdom of your God, which is in your possession, you are to appoint scribes and judges to administer justice for the whole people of Transeuphrates, that is, for all who know the Law of your God. You must teach those who do not know it. If anyone does not obey the Law of your God—which is the law of the king—let judgment be strictly executed on him: death, banishment, confiscation or imprisonment."

### 3. Trial by Judge: Biblical Judicial Procedures

The description of judicial procedure in the Bible is at best incomplete. In places the scriptures seem to be describing variant systems, perhaps at different historical periods of development. And yet, several key elements are carefully described. Truth speaking is the central value upon which cases are to be decided. The system is one of judicial decision based on a testimonial trial, the discovery of the truth by judgment. Witnesses not only testify as to what they have seen or heard (percipient testimony) but may also confirm the worthiness of a party's oath (formal act of compurgation). The rules of truth speaking and honest judgment are strict and central to the value of the process. Heavy sanctions are provided against failure to testify, false testimony, and judicial corruption or bribery.

#### a. Two Witness Rules

For the Bible, testimony has legal effect if, and only if, it comes from two witnesses. While Deuteronomy 17 applies this rule specifically to capital cases, Deuteronomy 19 requires two witnesses regarding "any offense that may be committed."

> *Deuteronomy 17:6:*
> A person shall be put to death only on the testimony of two or more witnesses; he must not be put to death on the testimony of a single witness.

*Deuteronomy 19:15:*
A single witness may not validate against a person any guilt or
blame for any offense that may be committed; a case can be valid only
on the testimony of two witnesses or more.

### b. *Withholding Testimony as a Sin*
People are often reluctant to come forward and testify regarding
crimes they have witnessed. There are many sources of this reluctance: a desire to protect wrongdoing neighbors from a potentially
harsh system of punishment; the fear of revenge by the wrongdoer for
testifying against him; or the desire to avoid attracting official attention to oneself. The Federal Penal Code still contains the remnant of
the shadowy common-law offense of misprision of felony. It is not
clear how this offense was understood long ago, and it has been virtually a dead letter for a century, although it survives in the code in the
following form:

*Title 18, United States Code § 4.*
Whoever, having knowledge of the actual commission of a felony
cognizable by a court of the United States, conceals and does not as
soon as possible make known the same to some judge or other person
in civil or military authority under the United States, shall be fined
not more than $500 or imprisoned not more than three years, or both.

The biblical description of the obligation to testify is not perfectly
clear either. It does strongly suggest, however, that a person who failed
to respond to an official call for information was subject to punishment and in addition was guilty of a sin requiring confession and sacrifice.

*Leviticus 5:1, 5–6:*
If a person incurs guilt:

When he has heard a public imprecation and—although able to testify as one who has either seen or learned of the matter—he does not
give information, so that he is subject to punishment; . . . when he realizes his guilt in any of these matters, he shall confess that wherein
he has sinned. And he shall bring as his penalty to the LORD, for the
sin of which he is guilty, a female from the flock, sheep or goat, as a
sin offering; and the priest shall make expiation on his behalf for his
sin.

### c. *Punishment and Expiation for False Testimony*
The justice of biblical courts depended not only on the availability, but the veracity of witnesses. This was so important that the com-

mand that people avoid bearing false witness was included in the Ten Commandments. Punishment for violating that commandment was also prescribed, although Leviticus 5 and Deuteronomy 19 describe different remedies for false testimony. Recognizing this, the rabbis applied Leviticus 5 to cases in which the content of the testimony was false (that is, the witnesses say that X happened when they know that it did not), and they used Deuteronomy 19 to refer to plotting witnesses (*adim zomemim,* based on the Hebrew for "scheme" in verse 19), that is, witnesses whose testimony may in fact be correct, but who were not at the scene at the time and therefore cannot legitimately serve as witnesses. Their very desire to do so is an indication of the scheme that they are plotting. While that is a clever differentiation of the two texts and has some textual warrant, the biblical passages themselves do not draw that distinction. The two treatments of false testimony probably stem from different periods in biblical history. In any case, it is clear that perjury was considered a serious crime, one in which both God and man were offended.

*Exodus* 20:13 (from the Ten Commandments):
You shall not bear false witness against your neighbor.

*Leviticus* 5:20–26:
The LORD spoke to Moses, saying: When a person sins and commits a trespass against the LORD by dealing deceitfully with his fellow in the matter of a deposit or an investment, or through robbery; or if he has intimidated his fellow; or if he has found something lost and lied about it and sworn falsely—any one of the various things that one may do and sin thereby—when one has thus sinned and, realizing his guilt, would restore that which he got through robbery or intimidation, or the deposit that was entrusted to him, or the lost thing that he found, or anything about which he swore falsely, he shall repay the principal amount and add a fifth part to it. He shall pay it to its owner when he realizes his guilt. Then he shall bring to the priest, as his penalty to the LORD, a ram without blemish from the flock, or the equivalent, as a guilt offering. The priest shall make expiation on his behalf before the LORD, and he shall be forgiven for whatever he may have done to draw blame thereby.

*Deuteronomy* 19:16–21:
If a man appears against another to testify maliciously and gives false testimony against him, the two parties to the dispute shall appear before the LORD, before the priests or magistrates in authority at the time, and the magistrates shall make a thorough investigation. If the man who testified is a false witness, if he has testified falsely against his fellow man, you shall do to him as he schemed to do to his

fellows. Thus you will sweep out evil from your midst; others will hear and be afraid, and such evil things will not again be done in your midst. Nor must you show pity: life for life, eye for eye, tooth for tooth, hand for hand, foot for foot.

#### d. Warnings to Judges

Since there were no juries in ancient biblical courts, all power rested in the hands of judges. The Bible therefore carefully delineates rules of judicial ethics. Of special concern in these texts is that judges avoid being influenced by the wealth or power of some litigants and the poverty of others. That the Torah should warn against judicial favoring of the rich and influential seems both necessary and proper, but its admonitions against favoring the poor and powerless may be surprising. Biblical law requires society to help poor people survive honorably (see Leviticus 25:35–55), but in legal disputes justice must be the sole criterion of judgment.

> *Exodus* 23:1–9:
> You must not carry false rumors; you shall not join hands with the guilty to act as an unjust witness. Do not side with the mighty to do wrong, and do not give perverse testimony in a dispute by leaning toward the mighty; nor must you show deference to a poor man in his dispute. . . .
>
> You shall not subvert the rights of your needy in their disputes. Keep far from a false charge; do not bring death on the innocent and the righteous, for I will not acquit the wrongdoer. Do not take bribes, for bribes blind the clear-sighted and upset the pleas of the just.
>
> You shall not oppress a stranger, for you know the feelings of the stranger, having yourselves been strangers in the land of Egypt.

> *Leviticus* 19:15–16:
> You shall not render an unfair decision: do not favor the poor or show deference to the rich; judge your neighbor fairly. Do not deal basely with your fellows. Do not profit by the blood of your neighbor: I am the LORD. [See also Deut. 1:16–17; 16:18–20; and 27:19, 25.]

#### 4. Resolving Disputes Through Mechanisms Other Than Judges

Despite its emphasis on judicial decisions based on a rational assessment of testimonial witnesses, biblical law retained other means of resolving factually indeterminate questions. Some of these ceremonial trials bore heavy magical and cultic overtones. Since the whole world is connected by a single order, its secrets may be discovered in various places. Questions that cannot be reliably decided by a testimonial trial may be answered by looking at another part of the unitary fabric.

Moderns may dismiss these as atavistic remnants, but we should recognize that most legal systems, including the common law, have depended for much of their history on procedures other than testimonial trial for the resolution of disputed facts. It took many centuries for the common law to establish a relatively rational system of trial by evidence before a judge and jury. Trials by physical ordeal with participation of a priest were forbidden by the church in the thirteenth century. While older forms of trial by oath and ordeal passed out of common use, the possibility of some forms of nontestimonial trial at law remained until the early nineteenth century. It was not until the reform acts of 1832 abolished forms of action at common law that the possibility of trial by compurgation or appeal of felony, resolved by battle of champions, finally passed out of the law.

Today's law theoretically is left only with rational means to resolve disputes. The claim of rationality is only theoretical because lawyers' fictions often continue to distort or supplant existential reality in the modern court process. The lawyer's insistence that all testimony be in question and answer form, and subject to the lawyer's rules of what is an appropriate question and answer often distorts the truth and leaves the truthful witness at the mercy of the lawyer's insinuations. Legal rules of evidence frequently refuse to admit evidence of probabilities and inferences intelligent people rightly use in making important decisions in everyday life. Moreover, the contemporary system of litigation can hope to resolve only those disputes that produce evidence capable of being addressed in court under the lawyers' rules.

The simple fact is that there is no ultimately reliable way for judges to reconstruct the past with confidence. The American system caters to our predilection for rationality, but it often violates modern standards of factfinding and psychology. It is hard to imagine that if we were to start today to design a system to arrive at the highest probability of truth we would end up with one that looks much like our contemporary system, which excludes much scientific evidence and often prefers the highly unreliable recollections of eyewitnesses. Statistical inferences and evidence recorded outside of court are excluded in favor of fading and fleeting memories.

The ancient devices described in this section indisputably held out other virtues to those who used them. In this respect, they may suggest serious shortcomings with the modern court process, which too often is not only inaccurate, but fails to satisfy the emotional and social needs of those who use it. Note the emphasis in the ceremonies described on the restoration of the integrity of the community and the land after the violent incident. The concern is not so much for accurate reconstruction of the past, but rather a felt need to restore the balance of the world. Shed blood must be compensated for by blood one way or the other, in this case by the blood of a young animal. This notion survived the biblical period at least as late as the time of the Mishnah (second century C.E.), for in Mishnah *Sotah* 9:2 it states that the ceremony is not required when the corpse is found hanging from a tree. If the earth has not been polluted by absorbing the blood, then the calculus does not require payment by blood to cleanse the earth.

a. *Resolving an Unsolved Murder: Proximity as the Measure.* What happens today when the situation described in Deuteronomy 21 arises? The area is photographed and dusted for fingerprints, and a police report is completed. Most homicides are the work of relatives and social acquaintances. A few killers are caught at the scene. But if neither of these circumstances is present, the likely reality is that the police investigation will produce no suspects. Eventually a coroner's jury or a medical examiner holds an inquest and finds that the victim died by the hands of persons unknown. The matter is closed with a modern ceremony that is no more determinate than the ancient ceremony and is not noticeably more satisfying. The stain of violence lingers on until the incident is forgotten.

*Deuteronomy* 21:1–9:
    If, in the land that the LORD your God is giving you to possess, someone slain is found lying in the open, the identity of the slayer not being known, your elders and officials shall go out and measure the distances from the corpse to the nearby towns. The elders of the town nearest to the corpse shall then take a heifer which has never been worked, which has never pulled in a yoke; and the elders of that town shall bring the heifer down to a watered wadi, which is not tilled or sown. There, in the wadi, they shall break the heifer's neck. The priests, sons of Levi, shall come forward; for the LORD your God has chosen them to minister to Him and to pronounce blessing in the name of the LORD, and every disputed case of assault is subject to their ruling. Then all the elders of the town nearest to the corpse shall wash their hands over the heifer whose neck was broken in the wadi. And they shall pronounce this declaration: "Our hands did not shed this blood, nor did our eyes see it done. Absolve, O LORD, Your people Israel whom You redeemed, and do not let guilt for the blood of the innocent remain among Your people Israel." And they will be absolved of bloodguilt. Thus you will remove from your midst guilt for the blood of the innocent, for you will be doing what is right in the sight of the LORD.

b. *Trial by Water.* The problem of sexual jealousy between spouses, described in Numbers 5, is found in every society, including our own, and is never easily resolved. The issues involve questions of fact, but more importantly concern matters of family and status and raise highly charged emotions to public view. Many societies use procedures in this situation that accentuate the unequal positions of men and women. For example, in some cultures the husband is authorized to kill the wife suspected of infidelity. The procedures described in Numbers manifest some of these elements. The ceremony does provide a way to allay unjustified accusations and in all cases is designed to resolve the matter, although the marital relationship for the vindicated wife probably could not be made whole. There is no penalty for the falsely accusing husband. Modern legal procedures are not obviously superior to ancient ones when dealing with indeterminate situations in which the past cannot be reconstructed reliably by available evidence. What every community needs in such a situation is a satisfying ceremony to formally relieve all concerned of the overhanging anxiety the situation has created.

> *Numbers* 5:11–31:
> The LORD spoke to Moses, saying: Speak to the Israelite people and say to them:
>
>> If any man's wife has gone astray and broken faith with him in that a man has had carnal relations with her unbeknown to her husband, and she keeps secret the fact that she has defiled herself without being forced, and there is no witness against her—but a fit of jealousy comes over him and he is wrought up about the wife who has defiled herself; or if a fit of jealousy comes over one and he is wrought up about his wife although she has not defiled herself—the man shall bring his wife to the priest. And he shall bring as an offering for her one-tenth of an ephah of barley flour. No oil shall be poured upon it and no frankincense shall be laid on it, for it is a meal offering of jealousy, a meal offering of remembrance which recalls wrongdoing.
>
>> The priest shall bring her forward and have her stand before the LORD. The priest shall take sacral water in an earthen vessel and, taking some of the earth that is on the floor of the Tabernacle, the priest shall put it into the water. After he has made the woman stand before the LORD, the priest shall loosen the hair of the woman's head and place upon her hands the meal offering of remembrance, which is a meal offering of jealousy. And in the priest's hands shall be the water of bitterness that induces the spell. The priest shall adjure the woman, saying to her, "If no man has lain with you, if you have not gone astray in defilement while married to your husband, be immune to harm from this water of bitterness that induces the spell. But if you

have gone astray while married to your husband and have defiled yourself, if a man other than your husband has had carnal relations with you"—here the priest shall administer the curse of adjuration to the woman, as the priest goes on to say to the woman—"may the LORD make you a curse and an imprecation among your people, as the LORD causes your thigh to sag and your belly to distend; may this water that induces the spell enter your body, causing the belly to distend and the thigh to sag." And the woman shall say, "Amen, amen!"

The priest shall put these curses down in writing and rub it off into the water of bitterness. He is to make the woman drink the water of bitterness that induces the spell, so that the spell-inducing water may enter into her to bring on bitterness. Then the priest shall take from the woman's hand the meal offering of jealousy, wave the meal offering before the LORD, and present it on the altar. The priest shall scoop out of the meal offering a token part of it and turn it into smoke on the altar. Lastly, he shall make the woman drink the water.

Once he has made her drink the water—if she has defiled herself by breaking faith with her husband, the spell-inducing water shall enter into her to bring on bitterness, so that her belly shall distend and her thigh shall sag; and the woman shall become a curse among her people. But if the woman has not defiled herself and is pure, she shall be unharmed and able to retain seed.

This is the ritual in cases of jealousy, when a woman goes astray while married to her husband and defiles herself, or when a fit of jealousy comes over a man and he is wrought up over his wife: the woman shall be made to stand before the LORD and the priest shall carry out all this ritual with her. The man shall be clear of guilt; but that woman shall suffer for her guilt.

c. *The Blood Avenger.* The blood avenger is a surviving family member with legally recognized status to enforce without recourse to the judiciary the family's private remedy against the murderer of one of the family. Originally, private revenge was legitimate not only for homicide but also for mayhem (Gen. 4:23–24) and rape (Gen. 34:25–31), but, as Numbers 35:16–21 and Deuteronomy 19:11–13 make clear, it was later restricted to murder with malice aforethought or committed with a murderous instrument. There are biblical instances of a father (II Sam. 13:31–38), a son (II Kings 14:5–6), brothers (Judges 8:4–21; II Sam. 2:22–23; 3:26–30), and also the king (I Kings 2:29–34) as avengers, and later Jewish law allowed any next of kin, male or female, who were entitled to inherit the deceased party's estate to act as the avenger (see Maimonides, *Mishneh Torah*, Laws of Murder, 1:2,3).

Once the murder had been avenged, no further acts of vendetta were condoned. The situation could, of course, get out of hand and become a family or clan feud, but the legal recognition of blood vengeance was an attempt to confine the vengeance to one person. As Jewish law developed, the mechanism of vengeance was controlled further. This selection already indicates that the unintentional manslayer is entitled to refuge from the avenger (vv. 12, 15; see also Deut. 19:4–6), and later Jewish law restricted the avenger's rights to cases in which there had been a prior judicial conviction of the murderer (see Num. 35:12). That the avenger had a role in court seems probable from verse 24, "the assembly shall decide between the slayer and the blood-avenger." Later commentators differed as to the nature of that role. Some held that he initiated the proceedings by searching for the manslayer and bringing him to court for trial; some thought that he functioned as the prosecutor in the trial; and others depicted him as the executioner with the right and responsibility to carry out the capital verdict decreed by the court. Whichever interpretation we adopt, the intervention of a court trial makes the Bible's blood avenger considerably less atavistic and offensive than it seems on the first reading.

The Bible describes a time when Jewish law was not yet willing to abandon blood vengeance. Those who are surprised by this biblical institution should recognize that blood feuds were common in nineteenth-century America and continue in a number of nations today. The appeal of felony, in which the complaint was settled by trial by battle between the victim or his representative and the accused, was recognized in English law until 1832.

*Numbers 35:9–32:*
The LORD spoke further to Moses: Speak to the Israelite people and say to them: When you cross the Jordan into the land of Canaan, you shall provide yourselves with places to serve you as cities of refuge to which a manslayer who has killed a person unintentionally may flee. The cities shall serve you as a refuge from the avenger, so that the manslayer may not die unless he has stood trial before the assembly.

The towns that you thus assign shall be six cities of refuge in all. Three cities shall be set aside beyond the Jordan, and the other three shall be set aside in the land of Canaan: they shall serve as cities of refuge. These six cities shall serve the Israelites and the resident aliens among them for refuge, so that anyone who kills a person unintentionally may flee there.

Anyone, however, who strikes another with an iron object so that death results is a murderer; the murderer must be put to death. If he struck him with a stone tool that could cause death, and death resulted, he is a murderer; the murderer must be put to death. Similarly, if the object with which he struck him was a wooden tool that could cause death, and death resulted, he is a murderer; the murderer must be put to death. The blood-avenger himself shall put the murderer to death upon encounter; it is he who shall put him to death. So, too, if he pushed him in hate or hurled something at him on purpose and death resulted, or if he struck him with his hand in enmity and death resulted, the assailant shall be put to death; he is a murderer. The blood-avenger shall put the murderer to death upon encounter.

But if he pushed him without malice aforethought or hurled any object at him unintentionally, or inadvertently dropped upon him any deadly object of stone, and death resulted—though he was not an enemy of his and did not seek his harm—in such cases the assembly shall decide between the slayer and the blood-avenger. The assembly shall protect the manslayer from the blood-avenger, and the assembly shall restore him to the city of refuge to which he fled, and there he shall remain until the death of the high priest who was anointed with the sacred oil. But if the manslayer ever goes outside the limits of the city of refuge to which he has fled, and the blood-avenger kills the manslayer, there is no bloodguilt on his account. For he must remain inside his city of refuge until the death of the high priest; after the death of the high priest, the manslayer may return to his land holding.

Such shall be your law of procedure throughout the generations in all your settlements.

If anyone kills a person, the manslayer may be executed only on the evidence of witnesses; the testimony of a single witness against a person shall not suffice for a sentence of death. You may not accept a ransom for the life of a murderer who is guilty of a capital crime; he must be put to death. Nor may you accept ransom in lieu of flight to a city of refuge, enabling one to return to live on his land before the death of the priest.

   d. *Cultic Mechanisms to Restore the Guilty and to Provide Restitution to Injured Persons.* Modern law treats crime in a very matter-of-fact way: breaking a law requires penalties and, in some cases, restitution to the aggrieved party. Biblical law recognizes a wholly different element in the transgression of law. Since the law comes from God and is as much a part of nature as a physical law, transgression is an affront against God and nature. A taint is produced by sin, a disturbance of the natural order. Punishment of the wrongdoer or even restitution will not set things right: the contamination must be cleansed, the world put back in order. To do that the Bible prescribes cultic mechanisms, especially sacrifices. Blood is the sign of life in the Bible (see Deut. 12:23), probably because it moves more than any other part of the body. Sprinkling blood can therefore symbolically bring life back to a part of the world that has been deadened by the transgression. Moreover the sacrifice is a compensatory balance; something is given up as an equivalent to offset the wrong. Through these symbols the Bible expiates guilt, compensates for the breach of the natural order, reconciles the sinner and society to each other, and restores the integrity of the world.

As the following selections indicate, the cult was used for both individual and social transgressions. Especially because the rite of the scapegoat has been so widely misunderstood, note that these cultic acts were used in addition to restitution and penalties: they did not replace the human remedies. They did, however, address those aspects of dispute resolution that courts and police officers cannot treat, that is, the violation of society and nature that is involved in a violent criminal act, the guilt associated with that, and the restoration of both the individual and the society to a state of completeness.

*Numbers* 5:5–10:
The LORD spoke to Moses, saying: Speak to the Israelites: When a man or woman commits any wrong toward a fellow man, thus breaking faith with the LORD, and that person realizes his guilt, he shall confess the wrong that he has done. He shall make restitution in the principal amount and add one-fifth to it, giving it to him toward whom he is guilty. If the man has no kinsman to whom restitution can be made, the amount repaid shall go to the LORD for the priest —in addition to the ram of expiation with which expiation is made on his behalf. So, too, any gift among the sacred donations that the Israelites offer shall be the priest's. And each shall retain his sacred donations: each priest shall keep what is given to him. [See also Lev. 5:20–26 in section B:1d.]

*Leviticus* 16:2, 5–10, 15–18:
The LORD said to Moses:

Tell your brother Aaron that . . . from the Israelite community he shall take two he-goats for a sin offering and a ram for a burnt offering.

Aaron is to offer his own bull of sin offering, to make expiation for himself and for his household. Aaron shall take the two he-goats and let them stand before the LORD at the entrance of the Tent of Meeting; and he shall place lots upon the two goats, one marked for the LORD and the other marked for Azazel. Aaron shall bring forward the goat designated by lot for the LORD, which he is to offer as a sin offering; while the goat designated by lot for Azazel shall be left standing alive before the LORD, to make expiation with it and to send it off to the wilderness for Azazel.

He shall then slaughter the people's goat of sin offering, bring its blood behind the curtain, and do with its blood as he has done with the blood of the bull: he shall sprinkle it over the cover and in front of the cover. Thus he shall purge the Shrine of the uncleanness and transgression of the Israelites, whatever their sins; and he shall do the same for the Tent of Meeting, which abides with them in the midst of their uncleanness. . . .

When he has made expiation for himself and his household, and for the whole congregation of Israel, he shall go out to the altar that is before the LORD and purge it.

## 5. Ultimate Judgment by God, the Judge and Executor of the Law

The biblical texts do not present a unanimous view of the role God plays in His position as final judge and executor of the law. Sometimes the statements portray God as an active agent intervening directly to punish wrongdoers, while at other times God's role seems to be limited to legislation: it is a human task to enforce the law. The difference is demonstrated by the pronouncements that are said to come from God: some are commandments urging people to act in the image of their Maker while others seem to be predictions of the fearful consequences of wrongful behavior. All of God's actions are divine and all are built into a world that God created, but the course of His action is uncertain.

How will His justice be effected?

In the following excerpts, God's execution of justice takes many forms. When He acts, sometimes it is as arbitrator, peacemaker, or judge of last resort, and sometimes as avenger. Contrary to the Mesopotamian and Greek gods, He does not take bribes. While God is just, He has a special concern for the unfortunate as a model for human beings. God balances justice with mercy, but He will exact the demands of justice. There is thus a transcendent factor in judgment, and those who execute human justice do God's work.

Genesis 9:1–6:
God blessed Noah and his sons, and said to them. "Be fertile and increase, and fill the earth. The fear and the dread of you shall be upon all the beasts of the earth and upon all the birds of the sky—everything with which the earth is astir—and upon all the fish fo the sea; they are given into your hand. Every creature that lives shall be yours to eat; as with the green grasses, I give you all these. You must not, however, eat flesh with its life-blood in it. For your life-blood, too, I will require a reckoning: of every beast will I require it; of man, too, will I require a reckoning for human life, of every man for that of his fellow man!

Whoever sheds the blood of man,
By man shall his blood be shed;
For in the image of God
Was man created."

*Exodus* 22:20–26:
You shall not wrong a stranger or oppress him, for you were strangers in the land of Egypt.

You shall not mistreat any widow or orphan. If you do mistreat them, I will heed their outcry as soon as they cry out to Me, and My anger shall blaze forth and I will put you to the sword, and your own wives shall become widows and your children orphans.

If you lend money to My people, to the poor who is in your power, do not act toward him as a creditor: exact no interest from him. If you take your neighbor's garment in pledge, you must return it to him before the sun sets; it is his only clothing, the sole covering for his skin. In what else shall he sleep? Therefore, if he cries out to Me, I will pay heed, for I am compassionate.

*Exodus* 34:4–7:
So Moses carved two tablets of stone like the first, and early in the morning he went up on Mount Sinai, as the LORD had commanded him, taking the two stone tablets with him. The LORD came down in a cloud; He stood with him there, and proclaimed the name LORD. The LORD passed before him and proclaimed: "The LORD! the LORD! a God compassionate and gracious, slow to anger, rich in steadfast kindness, extending kindness to the thousandth generation, forgiving iniquity, transgression, and sin; yet He does not remit all punishment, but visits the iniquity of fathers upon children and children's children, upon the third and fourth generations."

*Deuteronomy* 10:17–18:
For the LORD your God is God supreme and LORD supreme, the great, the mighty, and the awesome God, who shows no favor and takes no bribe, but upholds the cause of the fatherless and the widow, and befriends the stranger, providing him with food and clothing.

*Deuteronomy* 24:10–15:
When you make a loan of any sort to your neighbor, you must not enter his house to seize his pledge. You must remain outside, while the man to whom you made the loan brings the pledge out to you. If he is a needy man, you shall not go to sleep in his pledge; you must return the pledge to him at sundown, that he may sleep in his cloth and bless you; and it will be to your merit before the LORD your God.

You shall not abuse a needy and destitute laborer, whether a fellow countryman or a non-citizen in your communities. You must pay him his wages on the same day, before the sun sets, for he is needy and urgently depends on it; else he will cry to the LORD against you and you will incur guilt.

## C. The Source of the Law and Legal Obedience: The Covenant

The connection between God, the people of the Bible, and obedience to law is most apparent in the exchange of promises between God and man.

It is significant to note that the law codes of the ancient Hebrews are cast within the framework of the covenant. In the Torah, the laws are placed within the context of the formation or the reformation of a covenanted people. Laws about crime, property, torts, family relations, judicial procedure, as well as laws about sacred days, priests, and religious rituals, are all located within the structure of the covenant. Thus the meaning of the laws derives from the covenant. They are interpreted in light of the covenant. Their violation is understood as a betrayal of the covenant. They are changed and amended as the covenanted people discern the shifting needs of changing times. What remains constant as the overarching reality and demand is the covenant itself and its qualities and obligations.

Curiously, a covenant is honored even in its breach, for a broken covenant is just that, a broken covenant. The covenantal qualities and obligations—liberation, faithfulness, justice, peace—persist as the basis for interpreting and judging the people's condition. A rift in a relationship does not totally destroy the relationship, otherwise it could not be rendered as a rift. Under the conditions of a broken covenant, a people stands in contradiction to itself. Its identity is a judgment against its existence.

The myth of the covenant is not merely a story about times past. . . . [It] is a communication about the real world, the world of human existence. It is a statement of ontological and anthropological significance. The claim of a myth is that it divulges important truths about our own reality, truths that we should understand if we would be indeed realistic. The myth of the covenant is cast in narrative form. It has the appearance of historical description. But it is more than historical description of a unique set of events that occurred in past times. It is, in addition, a paradigmatic statement. The narrative should be comprehended as a presentation about the structure and dynamics, the meaning and import of the world. It is a world view.

What is the alleged truth symbolized in and conveyed through the myth of the covenant? Negatively, it is a rejection of both individualism and corporativism as understandings of human association. That is, according to the myth of the covenant, we are not and cannot adequately understand ourselves as essentially isolated individuals who may make and break social relations at will. Rather we are and should understand ourselves as responsible participants in a whole host of relationships—natural, social, political, economic. On the one hand, these relationships constitute the given context of our individuality. On the other hand, these relationships bear the imprint of our personal creativity. Life is a constant give and take. We receive and we give. How we receive and how we give make all the difference in the world. Some ways of receiving and giving enhance life. Other ways of receiving and giving degrade, delimit, and destroy. That is the narrative of human life. That is the narrative of a covenantal way of looking at and living in the world. If in our receiving and in our giving we are constituted by the qualities of liberation, faithfulness, justice, and peace, then life is enhanced. If, on the contrary, in our receiving and in our giving we are constituted by the qualities of oppression, disloyalty, injustice and alienation, the result is the destructiveness and degradation of life. (Douglas Sturm, "American Legal Realism and the Covenantal Myth: World Views in the Practice of Law," 31 *Mercer L. Rev.* 502–503 [1980])

A striking theme throughout biblical writing is that the law and commandments are binding because obedience has been promised. The rules of behavior are seen as part of a mutual exchange, a contract or covenant between God and humanity. The excerpts that follow exemplify different aspects of this notion of covenant. In the early excerpts it is not clear whether the promises of God and the people are really mutual and dependent, or whether what is described is a promise of bounty and a commandment—two unilateral acts of God in which the humans are passive recipients.

Note that in at least the first two examples only God makes the promises, but nonetheless the promisees somehow become bound thereby. In the later excerpts the element of mutual exchange is more clearly delineated.

This sequence is consistent with the familiar pattern in the development of the contract as a legal institution. In many cultures the early emphasis is on the formal binding quality of promises themselves. Only later does mutuality become an important aspect of the binding promise. A crucial step in that development is the recognition that receiving a promise creates some obligation in the promisee. This is one root of the Anglo-American doctrine of consideration, which holds that a person is bound by his own promise because he has received the value of the other person's reciprocal undertaking.

It is difficult to tell from the Noah and Abraham texts in just what way God is bound by his promise. If Noah's descendants eat living creatures in violation of Genesis 9:4, is God released from His promise in Genesis 9:8–11 not to destroy the world?

In reading these excerpts also note that while God's role in the covenants is apparently constant, the identity of the party of the second part shifts from Noah and his offspring and all living creatures to the clan of Abraham, to part of that clan, to the tribes of Israel. In the same way, the substance of the Divine promise becomes more specific and complex in each successive story. Noah is simply promised that the world will not be destroyed, while Abraham is promised offspring and the land, and the people at Sinai are promised a specific and ongoing relationship to their Divine sovereign. The social, even governmental, aspects of the covenant are clearest in the historic record, seen in Nehemiah, of the covenant dated Tishri 24, 444 B.C.E. Here the obligations are highly specific; the people are fully informed and given time to consider before each person, individually, takes the oath before witnesses.

Finally, these excerpts provide a rather complete catalogue of the sorts of formalities or solemnities that mark the especially binding promise. The rainbow in the sky is the formal token that reminds both parties of the covenant with Noah. The covenant of pieces in Genesis 15 follows ancient Near Eastern ceremonial practice, which, in turn, contains strong elements of sympathetic magic. As the parties to the promise pass between the severed pieces of the sacrificed animals, they invoke a similar fate upon themselves should they prove to be promise breakers. The extraordinary solemnity of the promise is reinforced further because it is not part of a mundane conversation, but is experienced by Abraham while in an ecstatic trance. In Genesis 17, two new formal elements are added. Abraham and his wife both take new names (and with them new identities) in token of the promise they have received. Similarly, in feudal law the king and his chief vassals assumed new titles upon the exchange of promises of fealty and homage. The second new token of promise is circumcision. The physical altering of Abraham's body and that of his sons through the ages is a seal of the covenant to mark its permanence. We use seals to change the shape of documents whose contents we want to confirm permanently. The covenant with God is everlasting and inescapable, and hence the seal is even more personal and indelible, but the thinking is the same: the mark on the flesh signifies the promise and serves as an ever-present reminder.

In Exodus 19:8 the revelation by God and the reciprocal public declaration by the people is marked by the ceremonial publication of the covenant. In chapter 24 a variant ceremonial form is described in which the tribal elders, not the whole community, participate in the formalities. Public readings, declarations, sacrifices, sprinkling of blood, a shared meal of food and drink between God and the elders, and finally, of course, the stone tablets all record the promises and the seriousness with which their obligations were undertaken.

A modern lawyer of skeptical bent may have trouble with these supernatural extravaganzas but will have no trouble identifying with the contract formalities described in Nehemiah. Here there is no revelation, no wondrous sign, no epiphanic meal. Instead, the communal authorities, the scribes, the priests, the governor appointed by the secular king, and the heads of families all gather at the Water Gate with the rest of the people. There they recite the "whereas" clauses of their shared history. They read and give a plain sense explanation of the covenant and affirm its promises. These formalities are written, witnessed, sealed, and finally sworn to and acknowledged by all the people individually, including women and those children capable of understanding.

> *Genesis 9:*
> God blessed Noah and his sons, and said to them, "Be fertile and increase, and fill the earth. The fear and the dread of you shall be upon all the beasts of the earth and upon all the birds of the sky—everything with which the earth is astir—and upon all the fish of the sea; they are given into your hand. Every creature that lives shall be yours to eat; as with the green grasses, I give you all these. You must not, however, eat flesh with its life-blood in it. For your life-blood, too, I will require a reckoning: of every beast will I require it; of man, too, will I require a reckoning for human life, of every man for that of his fellow man!
>
> Whoever sheds the blood of man,
> By man shall his blood be shed;
> For in the image of God
> Was man created.
>
> Be fertile, then, and increase; abound on the earth and increase in it."

> And God said to Noah and to his sons with him, "I now establish My covenant with you and your offspring to come, and with every living thing that is with you—birds, cattle, and every wild beast as well—all that have come out of the ark, every living thing on earth. I will maintain My covenant with you: never again shall all flesh be cut off by the waters of a flood, and never again shall there be a flood to destroy the earth."

God further said, "This is the sign of the covenant that I set between Me and you, and every living creature with you, for all ages to come. I have set My bow in the clouds, and it shall serve as a sign of the covenant between Me and the earth. When I bring clouds over the earth, and the bow appears in the clouds, I will remember My covenant between Me and you and every living creature among all flesh, so that the waters shall never again become a flood to destroy all flesh. When the bow is in the clouds, I will see it and remember the everlasting covenant between God and all living creatures, all flesh that is on earth. That," God said to Noah, "shall be the sign of the covenant that I have established between Me and all flesh that is on earth."

*Genesis* 15:
Some time later, the word of the LORD came to Abram in a vision, saying,

"Fear not, Abram,
I am a shield to you;
Your reward shall be very great."

But Abram said, "O Lord GOD, what can You give me, seeing that I continue childless, and the one in charge of my household is Dammesek Eliezer!" Abram said further, "Since You have granted me no offspring, one of my household will be my heir." The word of the LORD came to him in reply, "That one shall not be your heir; none but your very own issue shall be your heir." He took him outside and said, "Look toward heaven and count the stars, if you are able to count them." And He added, "So shall your offspring be." And because he put his trust in the LORD, He reckoned it to his merit.

Then He said to him, "I am the LORD who brought you out from Ur of the Chaldeans to give you this land as a possession." And he said, "O Lord GOD, how shall I know that I am to possess it?" He answered, "Bring Me a three-year-old heifer, a three-year-old she-goat, a three-year-old ram, a turtledove, and a young bird." He brought Him all these and cut them in two, placing each half opposite the other; but he did not cut up the birds. Birds of prey came down upon the carcasses, and Abram drove them away. As the sun was about to set, a trance fell upon Abram, and a deep dark dread descended upon him. And He said to Abram, "Know well that your offspring shall be strangers in a land not theirs, and they shall be enslaved and oppressed four hundred years; but I will pass judgment on the nation they shall serve, and in the end they shall go free with great wealth. As for you,

You shall go to your fathers in peace;
You shall be buried at a ripe old age.

And they shall return here in the fourth generation, for the iniquity of the Amorites will not be fulfilled until then."

When the sun set and it was very dark, there appeared a smoking oven, and a flaming torch which passed between those pieces. On that day the LORD made a covenant with Abram, saying, "To your offspring I give this land, from the river of Egypt to the great river, the river Euphrates: the Kenites, the Kenizzites, the Kadmonites, the Hittites, the Perizzites, the Rephaim, the Amorites, the Canaanites, the Girgashites, and the Jebusites."

*Genesis* 17:

When Abram was ninety-nine years old, the LORD appeared to Abram and said to him, "I am El Shaddai. Walk in My ways and be blameless. I will establish My covenant between Me and you, and I will make you exceedingly numerous."

Abram threw himself on his face, as God continued speaking to him, "As for Me, this is My covenant with you: You shall be the father of a multitude of nations. I will make you exceedingly fertile, and make nations of you; and kings shall come forth from you. I will maintain My covenant between Me and you, and your offspring to come, as an everlasting covenant throughout the ages, to be God to you and to your offspring to come. I give the land you sojourn in to you and your offspring to come, all the land of Canaan, as an everlasting possession. I will be their God."

God further said to Abraham, "As for you, you shall keep My covenant, you and your offspring to come, throughout the ages. Such shall be the covenant, which you shall keep, between Me and you and your offspring to follow: every male among you shall be circumcised. You shall circumcise the flesh of your foreskin, and that shall be the sign of the covenant between Me and you. At the age of eight days, every male among you throughout the generations shall be circumcised, even the homeborn slave and the one bought from an outsider who is not of your seed.—The slave that is born in your household or bought with your money must be circumcised!—Thus shall My covenant be marked in your flesh as an everlasting pact. An uncircumcised male who does not circumcise the flesh of his foreskin—such a person shall be cut off from his kin; he has broken My covenant."

And God said to Abraham, "As for your wife Sarai, you shall not call her Sarai, but her name shall be Sarah. I will bless her; indeed, I will give you a son by her. I will bless her so that she shall give rise to nations; rulers of peoples shall issue from her." Abraham threw himself on his face and laughed, as he said to himself, "Can a child be born to a man a hundred years old, or can Sarah bear a child at ninety?" And Abraham said to God, "Oh that Ishmael might live by Your favor!" God said, "Nevertheless, Sarah your wife shall bear you a son, and you shall name him Isaac; and I will maintain My covenant with him as an everlasting covenant for his offspring to come. As for Ishmael, I have heeded you. I hereby bless him. I will make him fertile and exceedingly numerous. He shall be the father of twelve chieftains, and I will make of him a great nation. But My covenant I will maintain with Isaac, whom Sarah shall bear to you at this season next year." And when He was done speaking with him, God was gone from Abraham.

Then Abraham took his son Ishmael, and all his homeborn slaves and all those he had bought, every male among Abraham's retainers, and he circumcised the flesh of their foreskins on that very day, as God had spoken to him. Abraham was ninety-nine years old when he circumcised the flesh of his foreskin and his son Ishmael was thirteen years old when he was circumcised in the flesh of his foreskin. Thus Abraham and his son Ishmael were circumcised on that very day; and all his retainers, his homeborn slaves and those that had been bought from outsiders, were circumcised with him.

[See Exodus 19:1–21;24 in Topic One above.]

*Nehemiah* 8:1–10:39 (Jerusalem Bible):

### Chapter 8
When the seventh month came, all the people gathered as one man on the square before the Water Gate. They asked Ezra the scribe to bring the Book of the Law of Moses which Yahweh had prescribed for Israel. Accordingly Ezra the priest brought the Law before the assembly, consisting of men, women, and children old enough to understand. This was the first day of the seventh month. On the square before the Water Gate, in the presence of the men and women, and children old enough to understand, he read from the book from early morning till noon; all the people listened attentively to the Book of the Law.

Ezra the scribe stood on a wooden dais erected for the purpose; beside him stood, on his right, Mattithiah, Shema, Anaiah, Uriah, Hilkiah and Maaseiah; on his left, Pedaiah, Mishael, Malchijah, Hashum, Hashbaddanah, Zechariah, and Meshullam. In full view of all the people—since he stood higher than all the people—Ezra opened the book; and when he opened it all the people stood up. Then Ezra blessed Yahweh the great God, and all the people raised their hands and answered, "Amen! Amen!"; then they bowed down and, face to the ground, prostrated themselves before Yahweh. (Jeshua, Bank, Sherebiah, Jamin, Akkub, Shabbethai, Hodiah, Maaseiah, Kelita, Azariah, Jozabab, Hanan, Pelaiah, who were Levites, explained the

Law to the people while the people remained standing.) And Ezra read
from the Law of God, translating and giving the sense, so that the people understood what was read.

Then (Nehemiah—His Excellency—and) Ezra, priest and scribe
(and the Levites who were instructing the people) said to all the people, "This day is sacred to Yahweh your God. Do not be mournful, do
not weep." For the people were all in tears as they listened to the
words of the Law.

He then said, "Go, eat the fat, drink the sweet wine, and send a portion to the man who has nothing prepared ready. For this day is sacred
to our Lord. Do not be sad: the joy of Yahweh is your stronghold."
And the Levites calmed all the people, saying, "Be at ease; this is a sacred day. Do not be sad." And all the people went off to eat and drink
and give shares away and begin to enjoy themselves since they had
understood the meaning of what had been proclaimed to them.

Each day, from the first day to the last, Ezra read from the Book
of the Law of God. They celebrated the feast for seven days; on the
eighth day, as prescribed, there was a solemn assembly.


Chapter 9
On the twenty-fourth day of this month the Israelites, in sackcloth
and with dust on their heads, assembled for a fast. Those of Israelite
stock separated themselves from all those of foreign origin; they stood
confessing their sins and the transgressions of their ancestors. (Standing, each man in his right position, they read from the Book of the
Law of Yahweh their God for one quarter of the day; for another they
confessed their sins and prostrated themselves before Yahweh their
God.)

Blessed be you, Yahweh our God,
from everlasting to everlasting.
And blessed be your name of glory
that surpasses all blessing and praise.
Yahweh, you are the only one.
You made the heavens, the heaven of heavens, with all their array,
the earth and all it bears,
the seas and all they hold.
To all of these you give life
and the array of the heavens bows down before you.

Yahweh, you are the God
who chose Abram,
brought him out from Ur in Chaldaea,
and gave him the name of Abraham.

Finding him faithful of heart before you,
you made a covenant with him,
to give him the land of the Canaanite,
of the Hittite and Amorite,
of the Perizzite, Jebusite, Girgashite,
to him and his posterity
And you kept your promise
because you are just.

You saw the distress of our fathers in Egypt,
you heard their cry by the Sea of Reeds.
You worked portents and miracles against Pharaoh,
against his servants and all the people of his land;
for you knew how they treated them with arrogance.
You won a reputation which you keep to this day.
Now therefore, our God,
great and mighty God who must be feared,
maintaining your covenant and your kindness,
count as no small thing this misery
that has happened to us, our kings, our leaders,
our priests, our prophets, and all your people
from the time of the kings of Assyria
to the present day.
You have been just
in all that has happened to us,
for you have shown your faithfulness,
we our wickedness:
our kings, our leaders, our priests and our fathers
have not kept your Law.
they have been unmindful of your commandments and the warnings
that you gave them.

While they were in their kingdom
with the good things you lavished on them,
in the wide and fertile land
that you had set before them,
they did not renounce their evil deeds.
Here are we now, enslaved;
here in the land you gave our fathers
to enjoy its fruits and its good things,
we are slaves.
Its rich fruits swell the profit of the kings
whom for our sins you have set over us,
who dispose as they please of our bodies and our cattle.
Such the distress we endure!

Chapter 10

... As a result of all this we make a firm agreement, in writing. Our leaders, our Levites, and our priests have put their names to the document under seal. ...

But also the rest of the people, priests, and Levites—gatekeepers, cantors, oblates—in short, all who have broken with the natives of the countries to adhere to the Law of God: as also their wives, sons and daughters, all those who are old enough to understand, join with their kinsmen and leaders and undertake, under curse and oath, to walk according to the Law of God given through Moses, the servant of God, and to observe and practice all the commandments of Yahweh our Lord, his customs and his laws.

In particular: we will not give our daughters to the natives of the land nor take their daughters for our sons.

If the natives of the land bring goods or any foodstuff whatever to sell on the sabbath day, we will buy nothing from them on sabbath or holy day.

We will forgo the fruits of the soil in the seventh year, and all debts.

We recognize the following obligations:

to give one third of a shekel yearly for the liturgical requirements of the Temple of our God: for the loaves set out, for the perpetual oblation, for the perpetual holocaust, for the sacrifices on sabbaths, on New Moon feasts and on solemnities, for sacred foods, for sacrifices for sin to atone for Israel; in short, for all the services of the Temple of our God;

and further, to bring yearly to the Temple of our God the first fruits of our soil and the first fruits of every fruit of every tree, also the firstborn of our sons and of our cattle, as is written in the Law—those first-born of our herds and flocks taken to the Temple of our God being intended for the priests officiating in the Temple of our God. Furthermore, we will bring to the priests, to the chambers of the Temple of our God, the best of our meal, the fruit of every tree, new wine and oil; and to the Levites the tithe on our soil—the Levites themselves will collect the tithes from all our agricultural towns; a priest, a son of Aaron, is to accompany the Levites when they collect the tithes, and the Levites will pay a tenth part of the tithes into the Temple of our God, into the treasury offices; since these rooms are where the Israelites and the Levites bring the contributions of corn, wine and oil, and where the supplies are kept for the sanctuary, the officiating priests, the gatekeepers and cantors.

Furthermore, as regards deliveries of wood for burning on the altar of our God as is written in the Law, we have arranged, by drawing lots

among the priests, Levites and people, that these deliveries are to be
made at the Temple of our God by each family in turn at stated times
every year.

We will no longer neglect the Temple of our God.

The biblical passages go from the very poetic to the very concrete.
What is clear throughout, however, is that the essential nature of the
tie between God and the Jewish people is covenantal.

For Americans schooled on Locke and Montesquieu, the covenantal basis of American government comes immediately to mind.
There are several similarities between the American and Jewish covenants. Both compacts are based on agreements between the covenanting parties, and both societies honor the events in which the agreement was initiated. Each covenant binds all of the descendants of the
covenanting parties, even when they are outside its territorial limits.
And both the Jewish and American compacts use human courts to enforce the terms of the covenant.

On the other hand, some dissimilarities are immediately apparent.
Human beings continue to determine the content of the American
covenant, whereas God determined the content of the Jewish covenant, at least initially, and, in theory, from then on. God is the ultimate enforcer of the Jewish covenant, and there is no appeal against
His justice (although there may be complaints). God has no such role
in American law. All members of the American covenant can enforce
the terms of the covenant on all other members, including governmental officials; but the terms of the Jewish covenant cannot be enforced
on one of its parties, namely, God.

The American covenant is initiated with the complete free will
of the people signing the document. The Bible clearly records Israel's
agreement to the covenant both at Sinai (Exodus 19:8; 24:3,7) and during the reaffirmation in Ezra's time, and it asserts that the covenant
was made with the people Israel for all generations (Deuteronomy 5:3;
29:13–14, 28), who presumably agreed to it. The Bible also speaks,
however, of God commanding the clauses of the Torah amidst thunder
and lightning; it describes the people's fear at the time (Deuteronomy
5:19ff); it expresses God's wish that the people fear Him enough to
obey the commandments (for example, Deuteronomy 5:26); and it
confirms the covenant in a ceremony which is designed to inspire awe
and fear (Deuteronomy 11:26–32; 27:11–26). All of that certainly does
not sound like voluntary acceptance of the covenant! Later Jewish tradition articulates the biblical ambiguity on this point by telling two
stories. According to one, the Israelites accepted the covenant freely after all other nations refused to accept it (*Sifre Deuteronomy*, par. 343;

*Numbers Rabbah* 14:10). According to the other, God overturned Mount Sinai on the Israelites present and said that He would bury them there unless they accepted the covenant (*Shabbat* 88a; *Avodah Zarah* 2b). Even the former story, however, pictures Israel accepting the covenant without knowing its terms. The dominant theme in both the Bible and rabbinic literature is thus that the initiators had little choice in the matter, and whatever choice they did have was both coerced and uninformed.

The descendants of the parties to the American covenant can theoretically dissolve it, and individuals can give up their American citizenship and thereby renounce their obligations as well as their privileges in American law. Jews can never be freed of their obligations under the covenant, either collectively or individually, even if they convert to another religion.

Thus the term "covenant" to describe the agreement between God and Israel is only partially parallel to its use in American law and legal theory. Biblical scholars point out that the model for it is probably ancient suzerainty treaties between a king and his subjects rather than the contract between equals that we are used to.

Nevertheless, the term does help to explain a number of features of biblical and later rabbinic law. Since the Bible proclaims that God rules over all mankind, one might expect that God's law would apply to everyone. Both the obligations and privileges of Jewish law, however, are restricted to the people Israel (for example, Exodus 19:5–6; 34:10; Leviticus 20:22–26; 25:39–46; and so on). The covenant model makes this restriction understandable since a covenant binds only the covenanting parties. One might also expect Divine law to be beyond human legal categories, but the Bible provides for ongoing interpretation by judges. The covenant terminology explains this, for it articulates the terms of the relationship which are then open to interpretation and new application through legal methods. The very fact that God relates to Israel in covenantal terms makes the relationship between them one of honor and love. This explains a feature of Jewish law that we shall explore in the next section, that is, that adherence to Jewish law is motivated by many factors beyond reward and punishment. Thus even if the Jewish use of covenantal terminology is not completely consonant with its later use in secular law, it does serve to explicate some of its most important characteristics.

## D. Reasons for Obeying the Law

The selections that follow will consider some of the reasons the Bible gives for obeying the law. The elements on the list overlap and are incomplete. Several of the grounds for obedience appear inconsistent with others. Obedience out of prudence, for example, seems to preclude obedience out of love of God. Principled reasons do not sit comfortably with the pragmatic goals of earning reward and avoiding punishment.

One may question the inner consistency of the Bible in giving such divergent reasons for obedience, but this inconsistency is amply compensated for by the breadth of concerns the Bible brings out. The biblical approach emphasizes law as an aspect of the whole of life, rather than as a detached enterprise concerned only with maintaining the social order. Life is not neatly and consistently played out on only one plane. Inconsistency may be a price that must be paid for a view of the law that reflects how it actually operates in experience. Modern Western jurisprudence emphasizes the ways in which law is a reflection of a unique society with unique instrumental goals and policies that indicate its situation in a particular time and place. The Bible, in contrast, tends to emphasize aspects of law and obedience that are personal, universal, and transcendent.

Biblical concerns are not all transcendent and philosophical; the familiar social reasons for obedience to law also are recognized as important. In the Covenant Code, for instance, the early verses of chapter 22 deal with the law as a necessary precondition for a peaceful human community. Compensation and restitution must be paid for injury to one's fellows. Serious crime carries afflictive punishment. Burglars may be beaten to death on the spot if caught redhanded. Formal court process appears required for such offenses as sorcery and bestiality (vv. 17–18). Remedies are sought that will allow expression of hurt and pain before it erupts in social conflict. An extreme aspect of the social dimensions of legal obedience is the threat to cut the offender off from human society, either by capital punishment or by the excommunication provided as the punishment for idolatry (see v. 19). Obedience is demanded on pain of being shunned by the rest of the community and expelled from the group. Finally, wrongdoing is constrained by shame and the fear of failure to meet group expectations. For example, verses 24–26 suggest that the laws of lending must be obeyed because to act otherwise is simply not a decent way for human beings to behave toward each other.

In addition to these social reasons for obeying the law, the biblical text suggests a number of other, very different, affirmative bases for law. Aesthetic grounds for obedience, covenant as a basis for compliance, and law as grounded on love are especially significant because they shape the institutional and formal structures of biblical law and help us understand why those structures took on the forms they did.

Legal structures reflect the reasons why the law exists. Form follows function. If law is all obedience to avoid punishment, it is likely to have a very authoritarian structure. If law is based on covenantal love, it is likely to take corresponding operational forms in the community. Those readers familiar with the tradition will find our discussion of the grounds for love elementary, but they may find the treatment useful in explaining the institutions of biblical law in part E of this topic.

In secular legal systems one must search hard to find expressions of positive feelings for the law. Positive motivations for creating government under law are recited in the American Declaration of Independence and in the Preamble to the United States Constitution, but such considerations are provided as justifications for the existence of government, not as reasons for the individual to obey the law. Modern citizens are rarely told to obey the law because it is human nature to live this way and they will be happier if they live in consonance with themselves. Consider a lawgiver who says, "I don't care whether you obey or not. I'm telling you what the law is and what is good for you so you can better choose and understand the world and yourself." Or imagine a legislator saying, "I love you; love me in return and obey my law, for it tells you how to be like me."

Yet American culture does try to motivate obedience to the law by means other than the threat of punishment. American citizens believe they ought to obey the law because they have participated in the democratic process of making these laws. They have committed themselves to support the legal system by taking a role in its formulation, however theoretical or passive that role may be. Moreover, they have reaped the benefits of a free, secure society and therefore owe it the duties of responsible citizenship. Beyond these moral and pragmatic factors, there is the emotional one, the allegiance and patriotism engendered in American children and adults through education, communal activity, and patriotic, ceremonial song. How are these factors similar to those that will be described which motivate obedience to biblical law, and how are they different?

## 1. *Divine Rewards and Punishments as a Ground for Obedience*

At the root of many biblical exhortations to obey law is the positivistic demand for compliance with God's command and the threat of severe punishment for those who deviate from His rules. The vision of the jealous God of the Bible has disturbed sensitive people for millennia and threatens to obscure and distort the broader and more affirmative view of legal observance of which it is only a part.

The following excerpt from Leviticus is quoted at length to indi-

cate some of the ideas that are intertwined with the strongest statements of threatened punishment and promised reward. Most fundamental is the assumption underlying this passage that human behavior
has consequences in the world. The impact of right behavior and
wrongdoing are felt in society, in the physical world, and in the moral
order of God. In short, what people do matters, and human existence is
important to the world and to God. This strongly suggests that there is
an order to things which is all encompassing and persistent, but in a
very real sense it is also fragile. By their acts people have the capacity
to reinforce or to disturb that order, to pollute or to beautify the world
physically and morally, to destroy life or to cultivate it. By obedience
to the demands of the world's order, people bring upon themselves and
others either good or evil consequences. Implicit in this primitive-
appearing ideology, therefore, are affirmations of world order, the consequential importance of human action, and the reality of human
choices for good or evil.

But something else lies behind this vision of the jealous God. The
very choice of the word "jealous" suggests the underlying love that
leads to the threats and promises. Love is neither disinterested nor dis-
passionate. We shall return to this theme later in this topic, but here it
will suffice to ask the reader to listen carefully to the rumbling voice of
the threatening God and catch in it the tone of the fretful and implor-
ing lover. The authors of this text heard in the threats and cajoling the
ultimate promise of everlasting love. The worst consequences are
threatened if the people disobey, but this God is not evil or cruel by nature, and even the worst threats have limits. "I will not reject them or
spurn them so as to destroy them, annulling My covenant with them."
God's loving remembrance of the people and the vows they have exchanged will endure and in the end will lead them back together. After
all their disasters, the people will atone in the end for their mistakes
and return to loving obedience of the law.

The themes of covenant, love, *imitatio dei*, and owing God obedience share a common aspect. They all express the conviction that humans are intimately connected to the essential order of things and to
God's purpose for the universe. God cares about people, and He cares
that people care about Him. The world is essentially sympathetic to
humanity, and the world is therefore not inherently hostile or evil. Life
is good. The subsection that follows attempts to separate out these
themes for purposes of analysis, but in reality they are intertwined and
fused into an optimistic faith in reality and in life.

*Leviticus* 26:3–46:
   If you follow My laws and faithfully observe My commandments, I
will grant your rains in their season, so that the earth shall yield its

produce and the trees of the field their fruit. Your threshing shall overtake the vintage, and your vintage shall overtake the sowing; you shall eat your fill of bread and dwell securely in your land.

I will grant peace in the land, and you shall lie down untroubled by anyone; I will give the land respite from vicious beasts, and no sword shall cross your land. You shall give chase to your enemies, and they shall fall before you by the sword. Five of you shall give chase to a hundred, and a hundred of you shall give chase to ten thousand; your enemies shall fall before you by the sword.

I will look with favor upon you, and make you fertile and multiply you; and I will maintain My covenant with you. You shall eat old grain long stored, and you shall have to clear out the old to make room for the new.

I will establish My abode in your midst, and I will not spurn you. I will be ever present in your midst: I will be your God, and you shall be My people. I the LORD am your God who brought you out from the land of the Egyptians to be their slaves no more, who broke the bars of your yoke and made you walk erect.

But if you do not obey Me and do not observe all these commandments, if you reject My laws and spurn My norms, so that you do not observe all My commandments and you break My covenant, I in turn will do this to you: I will wreak misery upon you—consumption and fever, which cause the eyes to pine and the body to languish; you shall sow your seed to no purpose, for your enemies shall eat it. I will set My face against you: you shall be routed by your enemies, and your foes shall dominate you. You shall flee though none pursues.

And if, for all that, you do not obey Me, I will go on to discipline you sevenfold for your sins, and I will break your proud glory. I will make your skies like iron and your earth like copper, so that your strength shall be spent to no purpose. Your land shall not yield its produce, nor shall the trees of the land yield their fruit.

And if you remain hostile toward Me and refuse to obey Me, I will go smiting you sevenfold for your sins. I will loose wild beasts against you, and they shall bereave you of your children and wipe out your cattle. They shall decimate you, and your roads shall be deserted.

And if these things fail to discipline you for Me, and you remain hostile to Me, I too will remain hostile to you: I in turn will smite you sevenfold for your sins. I will bring a sword against you to wreak vengeance for the covenant; and if you withdraw into your cities, I will send pestilence among you, and you shall be delivered into enemy hands. When I break your staff of bread, ten women shall bake your bread in a single oven; they shall dole out your bread by weight, and though you eat, you shall not be satisfied.

But if, despite this, you disobey Me and remain hostile to Me, I will act against you in wrathful hostility; I, for My part, will discipline you sevenfold for your sins. You shall eat the flesh of your sons and the flesh of your daughters. I will destroy your cult places and cut down your incense stands, and I will heap your carcasses upon your lifeless fetishes.

I will spurn you. I will lay your cities to ruin and make your sanctuaries desolate, and I will not savor your pleasing odors. I will make the land desolate, so that your enemies who settle in it shall be appalled by it. And you I will scatter among the nations, and I will unsheath the sword against you. Your land shall become a desolation and your cities a ruin.

Then shall the land make up for its sabbath years throughout the time that it is desolate and you are in the land of your enemies; then shall the land rest and make up for its sabbath years. Throughout the time that it is desolate, it shall observe the rest that it did not observe in your sabbath years while you were dwelling upon it. As for those of you who survive, I will cast a faintness into their hearts in the land of their enemies. The sound of a driven leaf shall put them to flight. Fleeing as though from the sword, they shall fall though none pursues. With no one pursuing, they shall stumble over one another as before the sword. You shall not be able to stand your ground before your enemies, but shall perish among the nations; and the land of your enemies shall consume you.

Those of you who survive shall be heartsick over their iniquity in the land of your enemies; more, they shall be heartsick over the iniquities of their fathers; and they shall confess their iniquity and the iniquity of their fathers, in that they trespassed against Me, yea, were hostile to Me. When I, in turn, have been hostile to them and have removed them into the land of their enemies, then at last shall their obdurate heart humble itself, and they shall atone for their iniquity. Then will I remember My covenant with Jacob; I will remember also My covenant with Isaac, and also My covenant with Abraham; and I will remember the land.

For the land shall be forsaken of them, making up for its sabbath years by being desolate of them, while they atone for their iniquity; for the abundant reason that they rejected My norms and spurned My laws. Yet, even then, when they are in the land of their enemies, I will not reject them or spurn them so as to destroy them, annulling My covenant with them: for I the LORD am their God. I will remember in their favor the covenant with the ancients, whom I freed from the land of Egypt in the sight of the nations to be their God: I the LORD.

To a secular lawyer these forms of retribution raise important questions regarding the nature of the covenant. In contract law terms, what is the consequence of breach by the people on the continued existence of the covenant? The agreement itself describes the consequences of some breaches; they lead to the imposition of penalties by God but do not dissolve the relationship. Those who transgress negative commands or fail to fulfill positive commands are in breach and may be penalized, even to the point of paying for their derelictions in serious cases with their lives. The basic obligations and the subsisting relationship between God and the People of Israel continue, however, after such breaches. When retribution goes beyond punishment of the breaching party, when it extends from the destruction of the sinner to the annihilation of the whole people, it suggests that the forbidden behavior was a material breach that terminates the relationship and excuses the other side (God) from the promises to the people of land and offspring that underlie the agreement. As early as the time of Moses, God was seen as threatening the whole people with annihilation (Exodus 32:9–10; Numbers 14:11–38), although in prophetic literature this threat was tempered with the promise that a remnant of the people would survive and ultimately be revived. Throughout history the threat of annihilation and genocide has been repeated; but however bad things became, the tradition has insisted that the covenant persists and that it places an outer limit on divine punishment.

## 2. The Presence of God as a Reward; Excommunication from God as a Punishment

The greatest of rewards is that God sees humanity as fit to live with. One heavy price for disobedience is excommunication, the removal of the Divine contact which provides knowledge and guidance to people. God agrees to abide with His Chosen People, and the Temple in Jerusalem is the sign of that presence. This is described in the following excerpt from Exodus. The people of the early biblical era assumed that once God made that agreement, God would never abandon them, no matter what. Jeremiah makes clear that their trust in the Temple to keep God among them is ill-founded: God's willingness to dwell among the Israelites is conditional on their obedience, and He is perfectly willing to destroy His Temple if necessary. That would be one clear sign of God's abandonment of the Israelites. Another is a cessation of communication from God, in which the prophets are struck dumb, as Amos and Ezekiel indicate.

*Exodus 25:1–9:*
The LORD spoke to Moses, saying: Tell the Israelite people to bring Me gifts; you shall accept gifts for Me from every person whose heart so moves him. And these are the gifts that you shall accept from

them: gold, silver, and copper; blue, purple, and crimson yarns, fine linen, goats' hair; tanned ram skins, dolphin skins, and acacia wood; oil for lighting, spices for the anointing oil and for the aromatic incense; lapis lazuli and other stones for setting, for the ephod and for the breastpiece. And let them make Me a sanctuary that I may dwell among them. Exactly as I show you—the pattern of the Tabernacle and the pattern of all its furnishings—so shall you make it.

*Jeremiah* 7:1–15:

The word which came to Jeremiah from the Lord: Stand at the gate of the House of the LORD, and there proclaim this word: Hear the word of the LORD, all you of Judah who enter these gates to worship the LORD!

Thus said the LORD of Hosts, the God of Israel: Mend your ways and your actions, and I will let you dwell in this place. Don't put your trust in illusions and say, "The Temple of the LORD, the Temple of the LORD, the Temple of the LORD are these buildings." No, if you really mend your ways and your actions; if you execute justice between one man and another; if you do not oppress the stranger, the orphan, and the widow; if you do not shed the blood of the innocent in this place; if you do not follow other gods, to your own hurt—then only will I let you dwell in this place, in the land which I gave to your fathers for all time. See, you are relying on illusions that are of no avail. Will you steal and murder and commit adultery and swear falsely, and sacrifice to Baal, and follow other gods whom you have not experienced, and then come and stand before Me in this House which bears My name and say, "We are safe"?—Safe to do all these abhorrent things! Do you consider this House, which bears My name, to be a den of thieves? As for Me, I have been watching—declares the LORD.

Just go to My place at Shiloh, where I had established My name formerly, and see what I did to it because of the wickedness of My people Israel. And now, because you do all these things—declares the LORD—and though I spoke to you persistently, you would not listen; and though I called to you, you would not respond—therefore I will do to the House which bears My name, on which you rely, and to the place which I gave you and your fathers just what I did to Shiloh. And I will cast you out of My presence as I cast out your brothers, the whole brood of Ephraim.

*Amos* 8:11–12:

A time is coming—declares my LORD GOD—when I will send a famine upon the land: not a hunger for bread or a thirst for water, but for hearing the words of the LORD. Men shall wander from sea to sea and from north to east to seek the word of the LORD, but they shall not find it.

*Ezekiel* 7:23–27:
Forge the chain, for the land is full of bloody crimes, and the city is full of lawlessness. I will bring in the worst of the nations to take possession of their houses; so shall I turn to naught the pride of the powerful, and their sanctuaries shall be defiled.

Horror comes, and they shall seek safety, but there shall be none. Calamity shall follow calamity, and rumor follow rumor. Then they shall seek vision from the prophet in vain; instruction shall perish from the priest, and counsel from the elders. The king shall mourn, the prince shall clothe himself with desolation, and the hands of the people of the land shall tremble. I will treat them in accordance with their own ways and judge them according to their deserts. And they shall know that I am the LORD.

Isaiah 29:10, Hosea 3:4, 5:6, Micah 3:6–7, and Lamentations 2:9 all announce similar punishments of being cut off from God's word if the Children of Israel fail to obey His commandments.

Another, slightly different, biblical notion is that disobedience pollutes the land and thus makes it impossible for God to continue to dwell among His people because of the impurity of their habitat.

*Numbers* 35:29–34:
Such shall be your law of procedure throughout the generations in all your settlements.

If anyone kills a person, the manslayer may be executed only on the evidence of witnesses; the testimony of a single witness against a person shall not suffice for a sentence of death. You may not accept a ransom for the life of a murderer who is guilty of a capital crime; he must be put to death. Nor may you accept ransom in lieu of flight to a city of refuge, enabling one to return to live on his land before the death of the priest. You shall not pollute the land in which you live; for blood pollutes the land, and the land can have no expiation for blood that is shed on it, except by the blood of him who shed it. You shall not defile the land in which you live, in which I Myself abide, for I the LORD abide among the Israelite people.

## 3. Aesthetic Reasons for Obedience to the Law: Preserving the Order and Harmony of the Universe

Aesthetic notions of what is beautiful and seemly blend into other ideas of the harmonious order of the world and the loving attachment that connects its parts. The biblical mind is sensitive to what is beautiful and what is disgusting in human behavior. Biblical law demands seemly behavior, and one reason given in the law itself for not engaging in forbidden practices is that the proscribed behavior is disgusting, ugly, unseemly, revolting. Sometimes the disgust belongs to God: He is offended by such acts. But often the disgust is the earth's: the world itself is so offended by this behavior that it will literally vomit out those who engage in it. At times the disgust is other peoples' and is marked by a concern with what the nations will say of those who engage in this behavior. One thinks of the Nuremburg trials, where "crimes against humanity" expressed the judges' utter revulsion at the acts of the Nazi defendants rather than a carefully honed legal category. The religious basis of biblical law attaches these ultimate values to nature and God as well as all humanity.

Disgust may also describe an imbalance or disproportion between the people's special role as a holy people, set apart for great things, and the demeaning quality of the behavior. The behavior is inappropriate because it makes the beautiful and the holy people ugly and disgusting, through cultic, carnal, or dietary offenses.

> *Leviticus* 18:2–5, 17–30:
> Speak to the Israelite people and say to them:
>
> I the LORD am your God. You shall not copy the practices of the land of Egypt where you dwelt, or of the land of Canaan to which I am taking you; nor shall you follow their laws. My rules alone shall you observe, and faithfully follow My laws: I the LORD am your God.
>
> You shall keep My laws and My rules, by the pursuit of which man shall live: I am the LORD. . . .
>
> Do not uncover the nakedness of a woman and her daughter; nor shall you marry her son's daughter or her daughter's daughter and uncover her nakedness: they are kindred; it is depravity.
>
> Do not marry a woman as a rival to her sister and uncover her nakedness in the other's lifetime.
>
> Do not come near a woman during her period of uncleanness to uncover her nakedness.
>
> Do not have carnal relations with your neighbor's wife and defile yourself with her.
>
> Do not allow any of your offspring to be offered up to Molech, and do not profane the name of your God: I am the LORD.
>
> Do not lie with a male as one lies with a woman; it is an abhorrence.
>
> Do not defile yourselves in any of those ways, for it is by such that the nations which I am casting out before you defiled themselves. Thus the land became defiled; and I called it to account for its iniq-

uity, and the land spewed out its inhabitants. But you must keep My laws and My norms; and you must not do any of those abhorrent things, neither the citizen nor the stranger who resides among you; for all those abhorrent things were done by the people who were in the land before you and the land became defiled. So let not the land spew you out for defiling it, as it spewed out the nation that came before you. All who do any of those abhorrent things—such persons shall be cut off from their people. You shall keep My charge not to engage in any of the abhorrent practices that were carried on before you, lest you defile yourselves through them: I the LORD am your God.

*Leviticus* 11:43–45:
You shall not draw abomination upon yourselves through anything that swarms; you shall not make yourselves unclean therewith and thus become unclean. For I the LORD am your God: you shall sanctify yourselves and be holy, for I am holy. You shall not make yourselves unclean through any swarming thing that moves upon the earth. For I the LORD am He who brought you up from the land of Egypt to be your God. You shall be holy, for I am holy.

On the other hand, obeying the law is an inherently wise thing to do—so much so that even the other nations will acknowledge its wisdom, as Deuteronomy says. That is because the law is perfect, precisely fitted to the order of the universe. Thus in Psalm 19, the biblical mind identifies God's justice and law with a larger harmony of all creation. Just as God introduces order into the physical world by the work of creation, so He creates order in the inner world of man's moral concerns by His law, as the psalmist's juxtaposition of those two themes makes clear.

*Deuteronomy 4:5–8:*
See, I have imparted to you laws and norms, as the LORD my God has commanded me, for you to abide by in the land which you are about to invade and occupy. Observe them faithfully, for that will be proof of your wisdom and discernment to other peoples, who on hearing of all these laws will say, "Surely, that is a great nation of wise and discerning people." For what great nation is there that has a god so close at hand as is the LORD our God whenever we call upon Him? Or what great nation has laws and norms as perfect as all this Teaching that I set before you this day?

*Psalms* 19 (New English Bible):

The heavens tell out the glory of God
the vault of heaven reveals his
    handiwork.

One day speaks to another,
night with night shares its knowledge,
  and this without speech or
    language
  or sound of any voice.
Their music goes out through all
    the earth,
  their words reach to the end of
    the world.
In them a tent is fixed for the sun,
who comes out like a bridegroom
    from his wedding canopy,
rejoicing like a strong man to run
    his race.
  His rising is at one end of the
    heavens,
  his circuit touches their farthest
    ends;
  and nothing is hidden from his
    heat.

The law of the LORD is perfect and
    revives the soul.
  The LORD's instruction never fails,
  and makes the simple wise.
The precepts of the LORD are right
    and rejoice the heart.
The commandment of the LORD
    shines clear
  and gives light to the eyes.
The fear of the LORD is pure and
    abides for ever.
The LORD's decrees are true and
    righteous every one,
more to be desired than gold, pure
    gold in plenty,
  sweeter than syrup or honey from
    the comb.
  It is these that give your servant
    warning,
  and he who keeps them wins a
    great reward.
. . . . . . . . . . . . . . . . . . . . . . . . . . . . . . . . .

## 4. *Owing God*

The Children of God owe Him obedience in return for the favors that He has done for them and their ancestors. Indeed, God could have done no more for Israel than He has; hence disobedience is ingratitude and deserves to be punished. But this motivation to obey the law does not collapse to simple reward and punishment. It is not even that both parties have specified obligations which they have promised each other contractually. It is rather that during their history together God has done a number of favors for Israel, and hence Israel has incurred obligations of gratitude. This is not the morality of promise keeping or the fear of punishment; it is the recognition of a debt owed for a favor done.

> *Deuteronomy* 4:32–40:
> You have but to inquire about bygone ages that came before you, ever since God created man on earth, from one end of heaven to the other: has anything as grand as this ever happened, or has its like ever been known? Has any people heard the voice of a god speaking from out of a fire, as you have, and survived? Or has any god ventured to go and take for himself one nation from the midst of another by prodigious acts, by signs and portents, by war, by a mighty hand and outstretched arm and awesome power, as the LORD your God did for you in Egypt before your very eyes? It has been clearly demonstrated to you that the LORD alone is God; there is none beside Him. From the heavens He let you hear His voice to discipline you; on earth He let you see His great fire; and from amidst that fire you heard His words. And because He loved your fathers, He chose their offspring after them; He Himself, in His great might, led you out of Egypt, to drive from your path nations greater and more populous than you, to take you into their land and give it to you as a heritage, as is now the case. Know therefore this day and keep in mind that the LORD alone is God in heaven above and on earth below; there is no other. Observe His laws and commandments, which I enjoin upon you this day, that it may go well with you and your children after you, and that you may long remain in the land that the LORD your God is giving you for all time.

> *Isaiah* 5:1–7:
>
> Let me sing for my beloved
> A song of my lover about his vineyard.
>
> My beloved had a vineyard
> On a fruitful hill.
> He broke the ground, cleared it of stones,
> And planted it with choice vines.
> He built a watchtower inside it,
> He even hewed a wine press in it;
> For he hoped it would yield grapes.
> Instead, it yielded wild grapes.

"Now, then,
Dweller of Jerusalem
And men of Judah,
You be the judges
Between Me and My vineyard:
What more could have been done for My vineyard
That I failed to do in it?
Why, when I hoped it would yield grapes,
Did it yield wild grapes?

"Now I am going to tell you
What I will do to My vineyard:
I will remove its hedge,
That it may be ravaged;
I will break down its wall,
That it may be trampled.
And I will make it a desolation;
It shall not be pruned or hoed,
And it shall be overgrown with briers and thistles.
And I will command the clouds to drop no rain on it."
For the vineyard of the LORD of Hosts
Is the House of Israel,
And the seedlings he lovingly tended
Are the men of Judah.
And He hoped for justice,
But behold, injustice;
For equity,
But behold, iniquity!

## 5. *Imitatio Dei*

In other cultures of the ancient Near East, the gods were powerful, but not good. For the Hebrews, God is not only powerful, but compassionate and holy. That change in theology led to a rather revolutionary change in the relationship between God and humanity. God not only governs mankind, but He wants people to be like Him. As modern moral philosophers have recognized, this provides a totally different quality of motivation for action. One obeys not because one wants to receive reward or avoid punishment, but rather because one aspires to be a person of esteem, a saint, or a hero. For the Bible the path to imitating God is to follow His law, which embodies His essence. This includes norms in all areas of life, as the following, famous passage makes clear:

*Leviticus* 19:1–4, 17–18, 26–37:
The LORD spoke to Moses, saying: Speak to the whole Israelite community and say to them:

You shall be holy, for I, the LORD your God, am holy.

You shall each revere his mother and his father, and keep My sabbaths: I the LORD am your God.

Do not turn to idols or make molten gods for yourselves: I the LORD am your God. . . .

You shall not hate your kinsman in your heart. Reprove your neighbor, but incur no guilt because of him. You shall not take vengeance or bear a grudge against your kinsfolk. Love your neighbor as yourself: I am the LORD. . . .

You shall not eat anything with its blood. You shall not practice divination or soothsaying. You shall not round off the side-growth on your head, or destroy the side-growth of your beard. You shall not make gashes in your flesh for the dead, or incise any marks on yourselves: I am the LORD.

Do not degrade your daughter, making her a harlot, lest the land fall into harlotry and the land be filled with depravity. You shall keep My sabbaths and venerate My sanctuary: I am the LORD.

Do not turn to ghosts and do not inquire of familiar spirits, to be defiled by them: I the LORD am your God.

You shall rise before the aged and show deference to the old; you shall fear your God: I am the LORD.

When a stranger resides with you in your land, you shall not wrong him. The stranger who resides with you shall be to you as one of your citizens; you shall love him as yourself, for you were strangers in the land of Egypt: I the LORD am your God.

You shall not falsify measures of length, weight, or capacity.

You shall have an honest balance, honest weights, an honest ephah, and an honest hin.

I the LORD am your God who brought you out from the land of Egypt. You shall faithfully observe all My laws and all My norms: I am the LORD.

## 6. Love

In biblical thought the covenantal dimension of the law is transformed into that most binding of commitments, love. The embodiment of that love is the promises made, which are symbolized not by a band of gold, but by the tablets of the law—although later biblical authors and the rabbis described the relationship between God and Israel in terms of wedding bands as well, and the observant Jew recites the following verses as he wraps himself with the leather straps of the *tefillin* each morning in preparation for prayer:

> I will betroth you to Myself forever,
> betroth you with integrity and justice,
>      with tenderness and love,
> I will betroth you to Myself with faithfulness,
> and you will come to know Yahweh (Hosea 2:21–22).

It is clear that love and emulation are important to God. The Bible never explains the reasons behind God's feelings, but it declares forcefully and repeatedly that God's love for man and man's reciprocation of love and fidelity to God are at the heart of human existence. They are at the heart of God's existence too: that God commands love suggests that God has needs, and this is amplified by those parts of the Bible that describe God as jealous when people pay attention to other gods.

In the end the bond between God and Israel, like all love, is essentially mysterious, but the following texts provide some insights into its qualities. First and most importantly, the transformation of legal commitment into loving commitment requires that each individual participate in, and become bound by, the covenant made at Sinai. Hence the text of Deuteronomy 5. The elements and benefits of God's love are enumerated in Deuteronomy 7, which also includes the specific announcement that God's love is not motivated by any of the physical attributes that might form the basis of human love. The seriousness and mutuality of the love relationships are articulated in the selections from Deuteronomy 10 and 6, the latter of which is used as the first paragraph of one of the central prayers in Jewish liturgy, the *Shema*. At least in form, Deuteronomy 6 is imperative: People must love God. This is persistently problematic, for it is hard to see how love can be commanded. An element of uncertainty remains, yet the link seems to be an expected connection between love and action. Obedience and proper action are acts of love. What could, in the end, be simpler than the exhortation of Deuteronomy 11?

> *Deuteronomy 5:1–3:*
> Moses summoned all the Israelites and said to them: Hear, O Israel, the laws and norms that I proclaim to you this day! Study them and observe them faithfully!
>
> The LORD our God made a covenant with us at Horeb. It was not with our fathers that the LORD made this covenant, but with us, the living, every one of us who is here today.

> *Deuteronomy 7:6–15:*
> For you are a people consecrated to the LORD your God: of all the peoples on earth the LORD your God chose you to be His treasured

people. It is not because you are the most numerous of peoples that the LORD set His heart on you and chose you—indeed, you are the smallest of peoples; but it was because the LORD loved you and kept the oath He made to your fathers that the LORD freed you with a mighty hand and rescued you from the house of bondage, from the power of Pharaoh king of Egypt.

Know, therefore, that only the LORD your God is God, the steadfast God who keeps His gracious covenant to the thousandth generation of those who love Him and keep His commandments, but who instantly requites with destruction those who reject Him—never slow with those who reject Him, but requiting them instantly. Therefore, observe faithfully the Instruction, the laws, and the norms, with which I charge you today.

If, then, you obey these norms and observe them faithfully, the LORD your God will keep with you the gracious covenant that He made on oath with your fathers: He will love you and bless you and multiply you; He will bless the issue of your womb and the produce of your soil, your new grain and wine and oil, the calving of your herd and the lambing of your flock, in the land that He swore to your fathers to give you. You shall be blessed above all other peoples: there shall be no sterile male or female among you or among your livestock. The LORD will ward off from you all sickness; He will not bring upon you any of the dreadful diseases of Egypt, about which you know, but will inflict them upon all your enemies.

*Deuteronomy* 10:12–16:
Mark, the heavens to their uttermost reaches belong to the LORD your God, the earth and all that is on it! Yet it was to your fathers that the LORD was drawn in His love for them, so that He chose you, their lineal descendants, from among all peoples—as is now the case. Cut away, therefore, the thickening about your hearts and stiffen your necks no more.

*Deuteronomy* 6:4–9:
Hear, O Israel! The LORD is our God, the LORD alone. You must love the LORD your God with all your heart and with all your soul and with all your might. Take to heart these words with which I charge you this day. Impress them upon your children. Recite them when you stay at home and when you are away, when you lie down and when you get up. Bind them as a sign on your hand and let them serve as a symbol on your forehead; inscribe them on the doorposts of your house and on your gates.

*Deuteronomy* 11:1:
Love, therefore, the LORD your God, and always keep His charge, His laws, His norms, and His commandments.

E. LAW AND JUSTICE IN THE BIBLE: THE RELATIONSHIP BETWEEN MORAL NORMS AND GOD'S WORD

God became identified with justice and morality as these concepts grew during the biblical period. This identification is certainly one of the Bible's great contributions to civilization, for in most other ancient societies the gods were understood to be powerful, but capricious. Associating justice with God makes it a core element in the nature of the world.

The tie between God and justice begins in the earliest patriarchal stories. Abraham's rhetorical question of the Almighty in the following excerpt was truly revolutionary. It also is a wonderful example of the lawyer's rhetorical techniques. Distinguishing cases, making an opponent take a position and draw a line (which is inevitably artificial because it is taken only in self-defense), and then using salami tactics —slicing away piece by piece at the chosen position—are legal skills that have persisted from early times until the present. Note how each of these maneuvers appears in Genesis 18.

*Genesis* 18:16–32:
The men set out from there and looked down toward Sodom, Abraham walking with them to see them off. Now the LORD had said, "Shall I hide from Abraham what I am about to do, since Abraham is to become a great and populous nation and all the nations of the earth are to bless themselves by him? For I have singled him out, that he may instruct his children and his posterity to keep the way of the LORD by doing what is just and right, in order that the LORD may bring about for Abraham what He has promised him." Then the LORD said, "The outrage of Sodom and Gomorrah is so great, and their sin so grave! I will go down to see whether they have acted altogether according to the outcry that has come to Me; if not, I will know."

The men went on from there to Sodom, while Abraham remained standing before the LORD. Abraham came forward and said, "Will You sweep away the innocent along with the guilty? What if there should be fifty innocent within the city; will You then wipe out the place and not forgive it for the sake of the innocent fifty who are in it? Far be it from You to do such a thing, to bring death upon the innocent as well as the guilty, so that innocent and guilty fare alike. Far be it from You! Shall not the Judge of all the earth deal justly?" And the LORD answered, "If I find within the city of Sodom fifty innocent ones, I will forgive the whole place for their sake." Abraham spoke up saying "Here I venture to speak to the LORD, I who am but dust and ashes: What if the fifty innocent should lack five? Will You destroy the whole city for want of the five?" And He answered, "I will not destroy if I find forty-five there." But he spoke to Him again, and said, "What if forty should be found there?" And He answered, "I will not do it, for the sake of the forty." And he said, "Let not the LORD be angry if I go on: What if thirty should be found there?" And He answered, "I will not do it if I find thirty there." And he said, "I venture again to speak to the LORD: What if twenty should be found there?" And He answered, "I will not destroy, for the sake of the twenty." And he said, "Let not the LORD be angry if I speak but this last time: What if ten should be found there?" And He answered, "I will not destroy, for the sake of the ten."

Linguistic evidence suggests that the Song of Moses is very ancient. This song states the theme relating to God and justice emphatically.

*Deuteronomy 32:3–4:*

For the name of the LORD I proclaim;
Give glory to our God!
The Rock!—His deeds are perfect,
Yea, all His ways are just;
A faithful God, never false,
True and upright is He.

In the ancient Near East the holiness of a god denotes the divinity's overawing power, that which makes the god special. In contrast to Greek myths where gods often used this holy power capriciously or ruthlessly, the prophet Isaiah, in the eighth century B.C.E., connected God's holiness to His justice, a truly groundbreaking idea.

*Isaiah 5:15–16 (our translation):*

See how man is bowed,
And mortal brought low.
The pride of the haughty is brought lower
And the LORD of Hosts is exalted by judgment.
The Holy God is proved holy by righteousness.

Although the association of God with justice is a fundamental biblical doctrine, it was not an easy tenet to adopt. The other peoples of biblical times, after all, did not believe that the gods were just, and in our own life experience the powerful are often not just, and vice versa. Consequently, we should not be surprised to find a number of instances in the Bible in which the commands or acts of God are morally questionable, and the text frequently does not even record discomfort with the act or command.

For example:

- The binding of Isaac (Genesis 22);

- God's hardening of Pharoah's heart (Exodus 12);

- The permission to enslave Gentiles (Leviticus 25:35–46);

- The vicarious punishment inflicted on Moses (Deuteronomy 4:20–22);

- The fate of the seven Canaanite nations (Deuteronomy 20: 10–18; see also Exodus 34:11–16; Deuteronomy 7:1–6); and

- The incident of Saul's mercy and God's anger (I Samuel 15).

God even sends the prophet Isaiah with a specific mandate to set a snare, to lead the people astray.

> *Isaiah 6:8–13:*
>
> Then I heard the voice of my Lord saying,
> "Whom shall I send? Who will go for us?" And
> I said, "Here am I; send me." And He said, "Go,
> say to that people:
>
> 'Hear, indeed, but do not understand;
> See, indeed, but do not grasp.
> Dull that people's mind,
> Stop its ears,
> And seal its eyes—
> Lest, seeing with its eyes
> And hearing with its ears,
> It also grasp with its mind,
> And repent and save itself."
>
> I asked, "How long, my Lord?" And He replied:
> "Till towns lie waste without inhabitants
> And houses without people,
> And the ground lies waste and desolate—
> For the LORD will banish the population—
> And deserted sites are many
> In the midst of the land.

But while a tenth part yet remains in it, it shall repent. It shall be ravaged, like the terebinth and the oak of which stumps are left even when they are felled: its stump shall be a holy seed."

The biblical text insists on God's justice; at the same time, it does not deny the injustices of the world, and it affirms God's role in these injustices. The paradox of holding both of these views simultaneously becomes more apparent when God's unity is strongly asserted, most famously in the Deuteronomic verse (6:4) known as the *Shema*, "Hear, O Israel, the Lord is our God, the Lord is one." Since there is only one god, and since that god rules over everything, evil must be attributed to Him. By hypothesis, there is no other god, and no human being can act without God's acquiescence. This problem (known as "the problem of evil") became even more acutely apparent during the Second Temple period, when Jews came into direct contact with the Persians and Greeks. Exposure to those cultures encouraged the Jews to begin thinking of each person as an autonomous individual and not just as a member of a group. Consequently, the suffering of apparently innocent persons could no longer be written off as simply part of the *group's* balance of payments, as it were, with God; now a just God was expected to judge, reward, and punish *each person* individually. The unfortunate fact, however, is that the innocent and good sometimes suffer while the guilty and evil prosper.

It is difficult to date precisely the following texts from Isaiah and Job. Scholars assume that chapters 40 to 66 of the Book of Isaiah were written by a different person than the first 39 chapters, since the later chapters are addressed to the community exiled to Babylonia after the destruction of the First Temple in 586 B.C.E., while the earlier chapters are connected to the fall of the Northern Kingdom in 722 B.C.E. The Book of Job is even harder to date because it lacks clear references to historical events, but most scholars believe it was written around 400 B.C.E. Consequently, these two excerpts represent an awareness of the injustice of God's world as seen at a late point in the development of biblical text.

*Job* 9:1–35 (Jerusalem Bible):

Job spoke next. He said:
Indeed, I know it is as you say:
   how can man be in the right against God?
If any were so rash as to challenge him for reasons,
   one in a thousand would be more than they could answer.

His heart is wise, and his strength is great:
  who then can successfully defy him?
He moves the mountains, though they do not know it;
  he throws them down when he is angry.
He shakes the earth, and moves it from its place,
  making all its pillars tremble.

The sun, at his command, forbears to rise,
  and on the stars he sets a seal.
He and no other stretched out the skies,
  and trampled the Sea's tall waves.
The Bear, Orion too, are of his making,
  the Pleiades and the Mansions of the South.
His works are great, beyond all reckoning,
  his marvels, past all counting.
Were he to pass me, I should not see him,
  nor detect his stealthy movement.
Were he to snatch a prize, who could prevent him,
  or dare to say, "What are you doing?"
God never goes back on his anger,
  Rahab's minions still lie at his feet.
How dare I plead my cause, then,
  or choose arguments against him?
Suppose I am in the right, what use is my defense?
  For he whom I must sue is judge as well.
If he deigned to answer my citation,
  could I be sure that he would listen to my voice?
He, who for one hair crushes me,
  who, for no reason, wounds and wounds again,
leaving me not a moment to draw breath,
  with so much bitterness he fills me.
Shall I try force? Look how strong he is!
  Or go to court? But who will summon him?
Though I think myself right, his mouth may condemn me;
  though I count myself innocent, it may declare me a hypocrite.
But am I innocent after all? Not even I know that,
  and, as for my life, I find it hateful.
It is all one, and this I dare to say:
  innocent and guilty, he destroys all alike.
When a sudden deadly scourge descends,
  he laughs at the plight of the innocent.

When a country falls into a tyrant's hand,
  it is he who blindfolds the judges.
  Or if not he, who else?

My days run hurrying by,
  seeing no happiness in their flight,
skimming along like a reed canoe,
  or the flight of an eagle after its prey.
If I resolve to stifle my moans,
  change countenance, and wear a smiling face,
fear comes over me, at the thought of all I suffer,
  for such, I know, is not your treatment of the innocent.
And if I am guilty,
  why should I put myself to useless trouble?
No use to wash myself with snow,
  or bleach my hands pure white;
for you will plunge me in dung
  until my very clothes recoil from me.
Yes, I am man, and he is not; and so no argument,
  no suit between the two of us is possible.

There is no arbiter between us,
  to lay his hand on both,
to stay his rod from me,
  or keep away his daunting terrors.
Nonetheless, I shall speak, not fearing him:
  I do not see myself like that at all.


*Isaiah* 45:5–7 (our translation):

I am the Lord and there is none else;
Beside Me, there is no god.
I arm you, though you have not known Me,
So that they may know, from east to west,
That there is none but Me.
I am the Lord and there is none else,
I form light and create darkness,
I make good and create evil—
I, the Lord, do all these things.

The Bible could hold paradoxically that God is just and good despite the evils of life because the biblical traditions placed less emphasis on logical consistency in matters of belief than did the Greek philosophers who greatly influenced Western thought. The Hebrews preferred to describe life as they experienced it, even if what they say did not fit into a neat, logical pattern. Moreover, when their eyes saw great injustice, the people of the Bible nonetheless expressed their hope that God ultimately would set things right.

*Psalms* 94:1–13, 20–23 (Jerusalem Bible):

Yahweh, God of revenge,
God of revenge, appear!
Rise, judge of the world,
give the proud their deserts!

Yahweh, how much longer are the wicked,
how much longer are the wicked to triumph?
Are these evil men to remain unsilenced,
boasting and asserting themselves?

Yahweh, they crush your people,
they oppress your hereditary people,
murdering and massacring
widows, orphans and guests.

"Yahweh sees nothing," they say,
"the God of Jacob takes no notice."
You most stupid of men, you fools,
think this over and learn some sense.

Is the inventor of the ear unable to hear?
The creator of the eye unable to see?
The punisher of the pagans unable to punish?
Yahweh the teacher of mankind
knows exactly how men think,
how their thoughts are a puff of wind.

Yahweh, happy the man whom you instruct,
the man whom you teach through your law;
his mind is at peace though times are bad,
while a pit is being dug for the wicked.

.   .   .

You never consent to that corrupt tribunal
that imposes disorder as law,
that takes the life of the virtuous
and condemns the innocent to death.

No! Yahweh is still my citadel,
my God is a rock where I take shelter;
he will pay them back for all their sins,
he will silence their wickedness,
Yahweh our God will silence them.

The implications of God's justice for man's life are clear. Despite the injustice of the world and the ambiguity of God's connection to it, God demands that people act with justice, morality, and love.

*Deuteronomy* 6:17–19:
Be sure to keep the commandments, exhortations, and laws which the LORD your God has enjoined upon you. Do what is right and good in the sight of the LORD, that it may go well with you and that you may be able to occupy the good land which the LORD your God promised on oath to your fathers, and that your enemy may be driven out before you, as the LORD has spoken.

*Micah* 6:6–9:

With what shall I approach the LORD,
Do homage to God on high?
Shall I approach Him with burnt offerings.
With calves a year old?
Would the LORD be pleased with thousands of rams,
With myriads of streams of oil?
Shall I give my firstborn for my transgression,
The fruit of my body for my sins?

"He has told you, O man, what is good,
And what the LORD requires of you:
Only to do justice
And to love goodness.
And to walk modestly with your God;
Then will your name achieve wisdom."

Consistent with this Divine demand for justice is the command that judges are to punish only individuals who commit crimes and not attaint their families—an idea that was novel in human culture. As noted earlier, it was not until about 1830 that the possibility of attaint, under which descendants would suffer for their ancestors' treason, was abolished. Corruption of blood and attaints or forfeitures that extend beyond the life of the criminal were banned by article 3, section 3 of the United States Constitution in 1789. The Bible was already sensitive to this aspect of justice.

*Deuteronomy* 24:16:
Parents shall not be put to death for children, nor children be put to death for parents: a person shall be put to death only for his own crime.

There is one aspect of the relationship of God to justice in biblical theology which moderns would find troubling. Despite these demands of justice on human beings, God is described in the Bible as punishing children for the sins of parents.

> *Exodus* 34:6–7:
> The LORD passed before him [Moses] and proclaimed: "The LORD! The LORD! a God compassionate and gracious, slow to anger, rich in steadfast kindness, extending kindness to the thousandth generation, forgiving iniquity, transgression, and sin; yet He does not remit all punishment, but visits the iniquity of fathers upon children and children's children, upon the third and fourth generations."

> *Numbers* 14:18–19:
> "'The LORD! slow to anger and abounding in kindness; forgiving iniquity and transgression; yet not remitting all punishment, but visiting the iniquity of fathers upon children, upon the third and fourth generations.' Pardon, I pray, the iniquity of this people according to Your great kindness, as You have forgiven this people ever since Egypt."

This doctrine is known as "vertical retribution," in that punishment is transferred not horizontally to the other members of one's generation, but vertically in time to those of the generations to come. In its positive form, the rabbis later refer to it as "the merit of the ancestors," which suggests that children prosper as a result of their ancestors' righteous deeds. As Jacob Milgrom has pointed out, in the previous passages cited Moses is not asking for forgiveness from God but rather reconciliation and His continued commitment to the covenant after He executes His punishment. "Moses is quite content to invoke the dreaded doctrine of vertical retribution, provided that *salah* will also be dispensed, justice will be tempered by mercy, and God will continue as Israel's God and fulfill the promise of His covenant" (*Conservative Judaism* 34:3 [Jan./Feb., 1981], 16). Moses does not question the propriety of punishing the children for the parents as long as God does not destroy and abandon Israel, as He threatened to do (Exodus 32:10; Numbers 14:12). Thus the doctrine of retribution "legalizes the divine right not to be bound by the individual retribution which prevails in human justice (Deuteronomy 24:16) but to punish the innocent along with the guilty" (*ibid.*, 14–15).

But how can that be? How can God require human judges to punish only the individuals who are guilty when He Himself does not? The Bible itself felt the problem. One strand of biblical literature, associated by scholars with the Deuteronomic tradition, sought to solve it by claiming that God only punishes the children *when they themselves are guilty* because they continue in the transgression of their parents. Thus the two renditions of the Ten Commandments in the Torah describe God using the same language as the passages cited, but they add identical crucial phrases that modify the theology to preserve God's justice in this way:

> *Exodus* 20:4–6 and *Deuteronomy* 5:8–10:
> You shall not make for yourself a sculptured image or any likeness of what is in the heavens above, or on the earth below, or in the waters under the earth. You shall not bow down to them or serve them. For I the Lord your God am an impassioned God, visiting the guilt of the fathers upon the children, upon the third and upon the fourth generations *of those who reject Me*, but showing kindness to the thousandth generation *of those who love Me and keep My commandments* [emphasis added].

This means of resolving the problem apparently entered into the consciousness of the masses since it is also articulated in the Book of Psalms, which was used in liturgical contexts.

> *Psalms* 103:17–18:
> But the LORD's steadfast love is for all eternity toward those who fear Him, and His beneficence is for the children's children *of those who keep His covenant and remember to observe His precepts* [emphasis added].

This modification, however, only mitigated the moral problem; it did not resolve it. For according to this revised theory, if the children continue in the path of their parents, they prosper or suffer not only for their own actions, but also for those of their ancestors. They now suffer in part for their own sins, but they still suffer for their parents' sins as well.

Another biblical tradition understood the doctrine of vertical retribution as an aspect of God's mercy. In some ways this is similar to the mentality that moderns have about credit cards: we consider it a favor not to have to pay now even though we know that the day of reckoning will ultimately come. In some passages the Bible similarly considers God's willingness to delay punishment a manifestation of His mercy. God does this only if the sinner shows contrition and therefore merits the postponement. Thus, when King David has Uriah, the Hittite, killed in battle so that he could take Bathsheba as his wife, he admits his sin when confronted by the prophet Nathan, and thereby gains a reprieve. Nathan tells David, however, that his son would die for his sin

(II Samuel 12:13–14). King Ahab's punishment is also postponed, and there the wording of the rationale and the consequences is explicit.

> *I Kings* 21:29:
> Since he [Ahab] has humbled himself before Me, I will not bring disaster in his days; I will bring the disaster down on his house in the days of his son.

Speaking in the name of God, the prophetess Huldah applies the same theory to Josiah.

> *II Kings* 22:19–20:
> Because your heart was softened and you humbled yourself before the LORD when you heard what I decreed against this place and its inhabitants—that it will become a desolation and a curse—and because you rent your clothes and wept before Me, I for My part have listened, declares the LORD. Assuredly, I will gather you to your fathers, and you will be laid in your tomb in peace. Your eyes shall not see all the disaster which I will bring upon this place.

And the generation of the spies was told that "your children [will] roam the wilderness for forty years, *suffering for your faithlessness*, until the last of your carcasses is down in the wilderness" (Numbers 14:33; emphasis added).

While this theory is understandable on some levels, on others it simply compounds the problem. Parents who have any compassion whatsoever for their children will never want them to suffer, and certainly not for the parents' own sins. In light of these difficulties, one can understand why the prophets look forward to a world in which children will no longer suffer for their forebears.

> *Jeremiah* 31:27–30:
> See, a time is coming—declares the LORD—when I will sow the House of Israel and the House of Judah with seed of men and seed of cattle; and just as I was watchful over them to uproot and to pull down, to overthrow and to destroy and to bring disaster, so I will be watchful over them to build and to plant—declares the LORD. In those days, they shall no longer say, "Fathers have eaten sour grapes and children's teeth are blunted." But everyone shall die for his own sins: whosoever eats sour grapes, his teeth shall be blunted.

> *Ezekiel* 18:1–20:
> The word of the LORD came to me: What do you mean by quoting this proverb upon the soil of Israel, "Fathers eat sour grapes and their children's teeth are blunted"? As I live—declares the LORD God—

this proverb shall no longer be current among you in Israel. Consider, all lives are Mine; the life of the father and the life of the son are both Mine. The person who sins, only he shall die.

Thus, if a man is righteous and does what is just and right: If he has not eaten on the mountains or raised his eyes to the fetishes of the House of Israel; if he has not defiled his neighbor's wife or approached a menstruous woman; if he has not wronged anyone; if he has returned the debtor's pledge to him and has taken nothing by robbery; if he has given bread to the hungry and clothed the naked; if he has not lent at advance interest or exacted accrued interest; if he has abstained from wrongdoing and executed true justice between man and man; if he has followed My laws and kept My rules and acted honestly—he is righteous. Such a man shall live—declares the LORD God.

Suppose, now, that he has begotten a son who is a ruffian, a shedder of blood, who does any of these things, whereas he himself did none of these things. That is [the son] has eaten on the mountains, has defiled his neighbor's wife, has wronged the poor and the needy, has taken by robbery, has not returned a pledge, has raised his eyes to the fetishes, has committed abomination, has lent at advance interest, or exacted accrued interest—shall he live? He shall not live! If he has committed any of these abominations, he shall die; he has forfeited his life.

Now suppose that he, in turn, has begotten a son who has seen all the sins that his father committed, but has taken heed and has not imitated them: He has not eaten on the mountains or raised his eyes to the fetishes of the House of Israel; he has not defiled his neighbor's wife; he has not wronged anyone; he has not seized a pledge or taken anything by robbery; he has given his bread to the hungry and clothed the naked; he has refrained from oppressing the poor; he has not exacted advance or accrued interest; he has obeyed My rules and followed My laws—he shall not die for the iniquity of his father, but shall live. To be sure, his father, because he practiced fraud, robbed his brother, and acted wickedly among his kin, did die for his iniquity; and now you ask, "Why has not the son shared the burden of his father's guilt?" But the son has done what is right and just, and has carefully kept all My laws: he shall live!

The person who sins, he alone shall die. A son shall not share the burden of a father's guilt, nor shall a father share the burden of a son's guilt; the righteousness of the righteous shall be accounted to him alone, and the wickedness of the wicked shall be accounted to him alone.

While this may appeal to our moral sensitivities, Robert Gordis has pointed out that vertical retribution may be more true to fact. For while morally we might like it to be a world in which each individual receives what is due him, that is not the way it happens. We suffer from the foibles and weaknesses of our parents and their generation, as we are all too well aware, and we also benefit from their merits and strengths, a fact we often ignore. Thus vertical retribution, for all its moral problems, is part of the reality of life, a reality in which God Himself shares.

> A murderer who pays the supreme penalty visits punishment upon his innocent mother, upon his young children, upon all who are stained by the shame of his wrongdoing. Virtually no man is so thoroughly alone in the world that he can suffer without involving others with him. This law of human existence constitutes part of the existential tragedy of man. To be sure, the doctrine of interdependence of mankind is often professed, but all too rarely taken seriously, but that is the measure of the sin of our age and of its consequences. The physical and moral peril of modern man flows from the fact that he is a citizen of the world and does not know it. . . . The consequences of the act, be they good or ill, do not necessarily fall upon the individual himself, but upon other members of society, who share an ineluctable unity of life and destiny with him. That vicarious suffering, which is a law of life, includes God himself, is one of the deepest insights of the Judeo-Christian tradition. It is expressed in the Rabbinic interpretation of a passage in Isaiah [63:9]: "In all their troubles, He shares their pain;" and in the Talmudic utterance: "When Israel suffered exile, the Divine Presence went forth into exile with them" [Sifre Numbers on Numbers 35:34]. In Christianity, it was extended to the doctrine of vicarious atonement. Thus from their individual vantage points, both traditions underscored the truth of the interdependence of mankind, as well as the cosmic interrelationship of God and man (Gordis, A Faith for Moderns [New York: Bloch, 1960], 181–82).

Another way of handling the problem is very different from all that has been discussed. The ancient Semites knew how to curse well. At the end of their covenants they invoked blessings on those who would obey its terms and heaped a multitude of curses on those who would break them. There are examples of that in the Torah itself (Leviticus 26; Deuteronomy 28). The curse of knowing that your children will suffer is perhaps most painful of all, especially if it is for your sins. If Exodus 34 and Numbers 14 are read in that light, two possibilities emerge. One is that God did not ever intend to punish the children for their parents' sins since His justice would not permit that, but He uses that as the ultimate threat in order to deter people from sinning. Another possibility is that God fully intends to carry out the threat, and

He (or the authors of those passages) thought that it was worth preventing people from transgressing God's will even if that required tainting God's reputation for justice.

The doctrine of vertical retribution, however it is interpreted, is part of the Bible's understanding of the relationship of God to morality. The picture that we obtain by pulling together all of the biblical strands on this issue is a mixed one. There are evils in the world, and since there is only one God, He must take part in their creation (Isaiah 45:7). He even punishes children for their parents' sins—a true depiction of the world, but a morally troubling one nonetheless. The dominant message that the Bible proclaims, however, is that God is just and that He demands justice through His law. He demands, in fact, even more: He requires purity in heart as well as in deed.

*Psalm* 24:3–5 (Jerusalem Bible):

Who has the right to climb the mountain of Yahweh,
who the right to stand in his holy place?
He whose hands are clean, whose heart is pure,
whose soul does not pay homage to worthless things
and who never swears to a lie.

The blessing of Yahweh is his,
and vindications from God his savior.

Thus observing God's law became increasingly identified with the good. Plato divided the two (*Euthyphro* 9ff.), and since then the relationship between God's laws and the good (or, more broadly, between religion and morality) has troubled Western philosophers. Jews from the late biblical period until at least the Middle Ages, however, would have had difficulty even understanding the question because for them goodness was simply and unequivocally defined in terms of observing God's commands. Topic Six will examine how the later rabbinic tradition understood and applied this biblical conviction.

## F. Biblical Law and Change: Adapting Divine Law to New Circumstances

The biblical world view posits an intimate connection between God and the world of which the laws God has given people are an important link. Moreover, the biblical perspective was timeless, its attention was fixed on what seemed eternal rather than on what appears mutable. These characteristics lead to a low value being placed on the capacity of the law to change. The basic assumption is that the law is just and perfect because the legislator is an Eternal God. Inevitably, of course, some allowance had to be made for new situations and changed circumstances. The biblical text appears to contain more than one set of expectations regarding the finality of the law. For example, divergent viewpoints are found virtually side by side in Deuteronomy. The text repeatedly states that the law is final and complete and needs only to be obeyed, but at other points recognizes various ways to clarify, apply, and expand the law in unanticipated situations. The tension can be stated in terms of two differing perspectives; one emphasizes that the law is given by God, so the job of humans is to obey and observe. The other perspective emphasizes that each person in every generation must rediscover the law for himself and stand anew at Sinai with those who have gone before and those who will follow in successive generations. Every individual is an active participant in this process, by learning, discovering, observing, and teaching.

Law seen as the unilateral gift of God brings hard problems into close focus. The omniscient and all-powerful lawgiver can be expected to operate on a transcendent plane, unlimited by the particularities of time and place or the vagaries of communication through symbolic language. His perfect law is good everywhere and forever. When this aspect of Divine law is emphasized, legal change can be legitimate only when the modification comes from a source equally as exalted as the original. How can humans modify God's law? Yet how can humans encourage or demand that the Divine lawgiver supplement or amend the code when they feel the need or cannot find guidance in what was previously received?

The biblical answers to these concerns vary and are not always perfectly compatible with each other. The view that seems to emerge from the Bible is that the law is final and complete when it is correctly expanded and applied by judicial interpretation and occasional further revelation.

1. *The Law Is Final and Complete, and Humans Have the Ability to Understand and Obey It.*

> *Deuteronomy* 4:1–2:
> And now, O Israel, give heed to the laws and norms which I am instructing you to observe, so that you may thrive and be able to occupy the land that the LORD, the God of your fathers, is giving you. You shall not add anything to what I command you or take anything away from it, but keep the commandments of the LORD your God that I enjoin upon you.

*Deuteronomy* 13:1:
Be careful to observe only that which I enjoin upon you: neither add to it nor take away from it.

*Deuteronomy* 30:11–14:
Surely, this Instruction which I enjoin upon you this day is not too baffling for you, nor is it beyond reach. It is not in the heavens, that you should say, "Who among us can go up to the heavens and get it for us and impart it to us, that we may observe it?" Neither is it beyond the sea, that you should say, "Who among us can cross to the other side of the sea and get it for us and impart it to us, that we may observe it?" No, the thing is very close to you, in your mouth and in your heart, to observe it.

## 2. *Continuing Revelation Is Possible.*

The biblical text does not exclude the possibility of new revelations to prophets or oracles, although it recognizes the difficulty in establishing the authenticity of prophecy.

Each of the excerpts that follows contains the report of a concrete legal case that is resolved by consultation with a divine oracle. The modern reader may be put off by this, for we are conditioned to expect that revelation will be a dramatically ultramundane experience, while in contrast we expect the decision of a lawsuit to be as close to rational as we can make it. In playing out the ceremonies of the law we fancy ourselves as reasoning creatures, who follow well-established procedures dispassionately and apply rules almost mechanically. Of course, our rationality often turns out to be rationalization, and many of our most important personal and legal choices are made arationally, if not irrationally. Nonetheless the legal rules lend a semblance of orderliness to decisions reached by other means.

Even when we accept human limits on our capacity to be rational, we are likely to be uncomfortable with the converse proposition: our brilliantly reasoned decisions, our insightful perceptions, our courageous choices are all inspired. They are the revelation of a larger order and are points of connection between our experience and the reality of God. They are rational precisely to the degree that they are consonant with the larger logic of existence. We are more ready to see the divine revelation in the enthusiastic poetry of the prophet than we are to see the same inspiration in a wise judicial decision. These excerpts present rather mundane disputes, the resolution of which is stated to be an act of revelation. This may remind us that the processes of reason, wisdom, and inspiration overlap and can be continuous.

The implications of this insight for familiar secular experiences may be troubling. If revelation need not be ultramundane, accompanied by thunder, fire, and signs, then the still small voice of brilliant insight is a form of revelation. Take three important, novel, and brilliant decisions of the Supreme Court of the United States. In *Marbury* v. *Madison*, decided in 1803, the Court used the occasion of a rather mundane dispute concerning Mr. Marbury's right to his commission as Justice of the Peace for the District of Columbia as the launching point for a seminal exposition of the power of the Court to declare invalid legislation that the Court finds inconsistent with the Constitution. In *Brown* v. *Board of Education*, decided in 1954, the Supreme Court declared that the long-established practice of racial segregation in public schools violated the Constitution. That decision set this country on a long journey along a new path. In *Miranda* v. *Arizona*, decided in 1966, the Court invalidated the process by which a confession was obtained by the police from a criminal suspect and set forth in its decision a detailed and radical new set of standards for police behavior, which the Court understood to be required by the Constitution. Each of these decisions was an insightful and inspired new departure from what had gone before. Were they revelations? What would it imply in terms of their authority, their mutability, and their rationality if we believed these court decisions to be revealed? Are all court decisions that are inspired, revealed? How about the Supreme Court's ground breaking decision in *United States* v. *Brown Shoe Co.*, regarding the appropriate scope of the antimerger regulations provided in the amendment to section 7 of the Clayton Act? That decision is crucial to the social and political fabric of the American community, but it is also very technical and mundane. Does God inspire humans only through wonders and poetry, or may His word sometimes come in technical and dry regulations? In short, is the *Brown Shoe* decision the revealed will of God—or just old shoe?

Here are some biblical instances of revelation after Sinai in which new laws were announced.

> *Leviticus* 24:10–23:
> There came out among the Israelites one whose mother was Israelite and whose father was Egyptian. And a fight broke out in the camp between that half Israelite and a certain Israelite. The son of the Israelite woman pronounced the Name in blasphemy, and he was brought to Moses—now his mother's name was Shelomith daughter of Dibri of the tribe of Dan—and he was placed in custody, until the decision of the LORD should be made clear to them.
>
> And the LORD spoke to Moses, saying: Take the blasphemer outside the camp; and let all who were within hearing lay their hands upon his head, and let the whole community stone him.

And to the Israelite people speak thus: Anyone who blasphemes his God shall bear his guilt; but if he pronounces the name Lord, he shall be put to death. The whole community shall stone him; stranger or citizen, if he has thus pronounced the Name, he shall be put to death.

If a man kills any human being, he shall be put to death. One who kills a beast shall make restitution for it: life for life. If anyone maims his fellow, as he has done so shall it be done to him: fracture for fracture, eye for eye, tooth for tooth. The injury he inflicted in another shall be inflicted on him. He who kills a beast shall make restitution for it; but he who kills a human being shall be put to death. You shall have one standard for stranger and citizen alike: for I the LORD am your God.

Moses spoke thus to the Israelites. And they took the blasphemer outside the camp and pelted him with stones. The Israelites did as the Lord had commanded Moses.

*Numbers* 15:32–36:
Once, when the Israelites were in the wilderness, they came upon a man gathering wood on the sabbath day. Those who found him as he was gathering wood brought him before Moses, Aaron, and the whole community. He was placed in custody, for it had not been specified what should be done to him. Then the LORD said to Moses, "The man shall be put to death: the whole community shall pelt him with stones outside the camp." So the whole community took him outside the camp and stoned him to death—as the LORD had commanded Moses.

*Numbers* 27:1–11:
The daughters of Zelophehad, of Manassite family—son of Hepher son of Gilead son of Machir son of Manasseh son of Joseph—came forward. The names of the daughters were Mahlah, Noah, Hoglah, Milcah, and Tirzah. They stood before Moses, Eleazar the priest, the chieftains, and the whole assembly, at the entrance of the Tent of Meeting, and they said, "Our father died in the wilderness. He was not one of the faction, Korah's faction, which banded together against the LORD, but died for his own sin; and he has left no sons. Let not our father's name be lost to his clan just because he had no son! Give us a holding among our father's kinsmen!"

Moses brought their case before the LORD.

And the LORD said to Moses, "The plea of Zelophehad's daughters is just: you should give them a hereditary holding among their father's kinsmen; transfer their father's share to them.

"Further, speak to the Israelite people as follows: 'If a man dies without leaving a son, you shall transfer his property to his daughter. If he has no daughter, you shall assign his property to his brothers. If he has no brothers, you shall assign his property to his father's brothers. If his father had no brothers, you shall assign his property to his nearest relative in his own clan, and he shall inherit it.' This shall be the law of procedure for the Israelites, in accordance with the LORD's command to Moses.''

Revelation was also used to expand and interpret Pentateuchal laws or to announce and give divine support to practices that had become customary although not part of Pentateuchal law. For example, Jeremiah indicates that carrying objects within the public domain or from private property to public property constitutes a violation of the Sabbath, and Isaiah and Nehemiah (10:32, 13:15ff.) declare that doing business is not allowed on the Sabbath. Both of those rules are not explicitly legislated in the Pentateuch.

*Jeremiah 17:19–27:*
Thus said the LORD to me: Go and stand in the People's Gate, by which the kings of Judah enter and by which they go forth, and in all the gates of Jerusalem, and say to them: Hear the word of the LORD, O kings of Judah, and all Judah, and all the inhabitants of Jerusalem who enter by these gates!

Thus said the LORD: Guard yourselves for your own sake against carrying burdens on the sabbath day, and bringing them through the gates of Jerusalem. Nor shall you carry out burdens from your houses on the sabbath day, or do any work, but you shall hallow the sabbath day, as I commanded your fathers. (But they would not listen or turn their ear; they stiffened their necks and would not pay heed or accept discipline.) If you obey Me—declares the LORD—and do not bring in burdens through the gates of this city on the sabbath day, but hallow the sabbath day and do no work on it, then through the gates of this city shall enter kings who sit upon the throne of David, with their officers—riding on chariots and horses, they and their officers—and the men of Judah and the inhabitants of Jerusalem. And this city shall be inhabited for all time. And people shall come from the towns of Judah and from the environs of Jerusalem, and from the land of Benjamin, and from the Shephelah, and from the hill country, and from the Negeb, bringing burnt offerings and sacrifices, meal offerings and frankincense, and bringing offerings of thanksgiving to the House of the LORD. But if you do not obey My command to hallow the sabbath day and to carry in no burdens through the gates of Jerusalem on the sabbath day, then I will set fire to its gates; it shall consume the fortresses of Jerusalem and it shall not be extinguished.

*Isaiah 58:13–14:*
If you refrain from trampling the sabbath,
From pursuing your affairs on My holy day;

If you call the sabbath "delight,"
The LORD's holy day "honored";
And if you honor it and go not your ways
Nor look to your affairs, nor strike bargains—
Then you can seek the favor of the LORD.
I will set you astride the heights of the earth,
And let you enjoy the heritage of your father Jacob—
For the mouth of the LORD has spoken.

Similarly the last two sections of the Bible (the Prophets and Writings) add these other rules to the corpus of Pentateuchal law: a prohibition against working on the New Moon (Isaiah 1:13; I Samuel 20:18–19); the requirements of three prayer services per day (Daniel 6:11; Psalms 55:18); the form and instruments of sale (Ruth 4:7–12; Jeremiah 32: 6–15, 42–44); and the rites for mourning (Ezekiel 24:15–18; Job 1: 18–20; II Samuel 1:11–12, 13:30–31, 14:1–2; Jeremiah 9:16–17).

## 3. *Ultimately Prophecy Ceased to Have Any Legal Authority*

The rabbis declared that legitimate prophecy ceased shortly after the destruction of the First Temple. The following selection from the biblical Book of Zekhariah is difficult to date. It probably comes from either the time of the prophet Zekhariah (520–516 B.C.E.) or in the centuries thereafter. In any case, its message is clear: prophecy is a bad thing, something which should make the putative prophet feel embarrassed. Thus the rabbinic hostility to prophecy has biblical precedent.

> *Zekhariah 13:2–4 (Jerusalem Bible):*
> In that day, too—declares the Lord of Hosts—I will erase the very names of the idols from the land; they shall not be uttered anymore. And I will also make the "prophets" and the unclean spirit vanish from the land. If anyone "prophesies" thereafter, his own father and mother, who brought him into the world, will say to him, "You shall die, for you have lied in the name of the Lord"; and his own father and mother, who brought him into the world, will put him to death when he "prophesies." In that day, every "prophet" will be ashamed of the "visions" [he had] when he "prophesied."

Why did prophecy cease to carry authority among the Jewish people? The trauma of the destruction of the First Temple was certainly part of the reason. The accepted prophets had claimed that Israel's sinfulness would be punished not only by the destruction of the Temple, but also by the cessation of prophecy (Amos 8:11–12; Micah 3:4, 6, 7; Jeremiah 18:18, 23:29–40; Ezekiel 7:26). The people undoubtedly thought that since the destruction had occurred, genuine prophecy must also have ceased. Only in the eschatological future would prophecy be renewed (Isaiah 11:2, 61:1; Joel 3:1–2; Malachi 3:23)—and indeed apocalyptic literature abounded in the intertestamental period.

Theoretical objections to prophecy surely played a role in its demise. There never was a good way of distinguishing a true prophet from a false one. Deuteronomy tried twice, suggesting first that a false prophet was to be identified by the heretical content of his message and then by the failure of his predictions.

*Deuteronomy 13:2–6:*
If there appears among you a prophet or a dream-diviner and he gives you a sign or a portent, saying, "Let us follow and worship another god"—whom you have not experienced—and the sign or portent that he named to you comes true: do not heed the words of that prophet or that dream-diviner. For the LORD your God is testing you to see whether you really love the LORD your God with all your heart and soul. Follow none but the LORD your God, and revere none but Him; observe His commandments alone, and heed only His orders; worship none but Him, and hold fast to Him. As for that prophet or dream-diviner, he shall be put to death; for he uttered falsehood about the LORD your God—who freed you from the land of Egypt and who redeemed you from the house of bondage—to make you stray from the path that the LORD your God commanded you to follow. Thus you will sweep out evil from your midst.

*Deuteronomy 18:9–22:*
When you enter the land that the LORD your God is giving you, you shall not learn to imitate the abhorrent practices of those nations. Let no one be found among you who consigns his son or daughter to the fire, or who is an augur, a soothsayer, a diviner, a sorcerer, one who casts spells, or one who inquires of the dead. For anyone who does such things is abhorrent to the Lord, and it is because of these abhorrent things that the LORD your God is dispossessing them before you. You must be wholehearted with the LORD your God. These nations that you are about to dispossess do indeed resort to soothsayers and augurs; to you, however, the LORD your God has not assigned the like.

The LORD your God will raise up for you a prophet from among your own people, like myself; him you shall heed. This is just what you asked of the LORD your God at Horeb, on the day of the Assembly, saying, "let me not hear the voice of the LORD my God any longer or see this wondrous fire any more, lest I die." Whereupon the LORD said to me, "They have done well in speaking thus. I will raise up a prophet for them from among their own people, like yourself: I will put my words in his mouth and he will speak to them all that I command him; and if anybody fails to heed the words he speaks in My name, I Myself will call him to account. But any prophet who presumes to speak in My name an oracle which I did not command him to utter, or who speaks in the name of other gods—that prophet shall die." And should you ask yourself, "How can we know that the oracle was not spoken by the Lord?"—if the prophet speaks in the name of the LORD and the word does not come true, that word was not spoken by the LORD; the prophet has uttered it presumptuously: do not stand in dread of him.

But we have seen in section (2) of this topic that there were new rules announced by several of the accepted prophets (although not the abrogation of previous rules), and there were a number of oracles delivered by recognized prophets which did not come true. For example, Jeremiah predicted an ignominious end for King Jehoiakim (Jer. 22:19), but II Kings belies that. Ezekiel predicted the destruction of Tyre by Nebuchadnezzar (Ezek. 26:7–14), but he himself later acknowledges that the king's seige of the city was unsuccessful (Ezek. 29:17–20). Both Haggai's (2:21–23) and Zekhariah's (4:6–7) glorious anticipations and designs for Zerubbabel never materialized. To make matters worse, a true prophet might be misled by a false one (I Kings 13), and false prophecy might even be inspired by God to deceive and entice Israel (I Kings 22:21ff.). God might even seduce a true prophet to deliver a false message (Ezekiel 14:9–11). Consequently it is not surprising that there were many "false prophets," and some of those accepted as true complain bitterly about the imposters (for example, Jer. 6:13–15; 14:4; 23:23–40; 27:9–18; 28:1–17; 29:21–32). Even if a true prophet could be recognized, he could not be given legal authority for practical reasons. For if the law were subject to change through prophecy, then God conceivably could announce completely new rules through a prophet at any time—or a prophet could claim that He had—and that spells legal chaos.

The combination, then, of the people's expectations of God's punishment and the problems inherent in working with prophecy led to the rabbinic doctrine that it had ceased, with its foreshadowing in the doctrines of the Bible.

## 4. God's Law Can Be Made Applicable to New Circumstances Through the Judiciary.

Throughout the biblical period, even during the heyday of prophecy from the ninth through the sixth centuries B.C.E., judges applied the law in new cases. The biblical record of Moses appointing judges in Exodus 18 (see section B1a) attests to the antiquity of the Israelite judiciary, and the paragraph in Deuteronomy 17:8–15 (see section B2c) clearly indicates that judges not only had power to decide cases in which the issue was one of fact but also those in which the law itself was in question: the Supreme Court in Jerusalem was to rule in cases which were "too baffling for you to decide, whether in a matter of homicide, civil law, or assault" (Deut. 17:8). The rabbis later drew far-reaching consequences from this mandate for human, judicial interpretation and application of God's law, but the seeds were planted in the theory and practice of the Bible.

# Topic Four: Rabbinic Law of Injuries

The next major periods of Jewish history are the Second Temple period (from 539 B.C.E. to 70 C.E.) and the rabbinic period (from 70 C.E. to approximately 500 C.E.). During the Second Temple period some of the prophetic books of the Bible and many of the books of the Hagiographa (*Ketuvim*, or Writings) were written. At the same time, the Torah was interpreted and applied to new situations, and a body of precedents and customs developed. Through recent archaeological digs and other research we are learning that this was a period in which many forms of Judaism flourished. Thus the process by which later Judaism became identified with rabbinic Judaism was by no means a direct one; other denominations existed, although ultimately rabbinic Judaism became the norm and the other denominations were branded as sects. The rabbinic period is generally divided into the periods of two groups of rabbis, the *Tanna'im* (70 to 220 C.E.) and the *Amora'im* (220 to 500 C.E.).

During these centuries, Jewish religious and legal thought changed radically. The period of prophecy and revelation ended, and a basic scriptural canon became relatively fixed in written form. The responsibility for legal development passed from king and tribal leader, prophet and priest, to the rabbis, a specifically trained group of teachers familiar with scripture and the oral interpretative traditions surrounding it.

The shift in community power from kings, priests, and prophets to rabbis took centuries and influenced the substance of Judaism in a number of profound ways. The transformation established a pattern that has supported Jewish community life in an extreme range of circumstances for almost two thousand years. The major dimensions of this complex transformation can be outlined in simplified form:

   a. a seminomadic, pastoral, and farming society became urbanized to include artisans and merchants, as well as a large proletariat;

   b. the cultural patterns of the Israelites and Judeans, which had been influenced by exposure to Mesopotamian, Egyp-

133

tian, and Babylonian culture and by desert wandering, confronted and responded to Greek and Roman civilization, and in the process became a coherent world civilization;

c. a small tribal hegemony that had developed into an unstable monarchy lost political power and became the permanent satellite of larger world powers;

d. tribal, royal, and priestly ruling groups were overthrown, and their community leadership passed to a rather open-ended meritocracy of scholars and scribes, the rabbis;

e. biblical religion, with its strong grounding in agriculture and a sacrificial cult presided over by hereditary priests, shifted emphasis and became rabbinic Judaism, a faith stressing the importance of communal study, prayer, and action; and

f. a traditional body of group myths, laws, customs, and half-remembered history was formed by the rabbis into a comprehensive legal framework adaptable to different social settings, resistant to repression, and supportive of group identity.

The point should not be overstated. Many important elements of biblical religion were retained, including the beliefs that God had commanded eternal laws, that those laws included a significant ethical component as well as rituals, that God would enforce His laws, and that the People Israel had a special obligation to be exemplary in their conduct (or, in religious terms, "holy") because they had been given God's special gift of the Torah. But much was built upon these fundamentals, and the task of this unit is to introduce the institutions and processes through which the changes described came about.

There were primarily two methods by which the received biblical text was expanded and applied: exegesis, and judicial decisions based on and contributing to the oral tradition. We shall examine each of these methods in turn, but first we must catch up on a little history.

## A. An Overview of the History and Literature of the Second Temple and Rabbinic Periods

### 1. The Second Temple Period (539 b.c.e. – 70 c.e.)

The priests had been the least influential element in the First Temple triumvirate of king, prophet, and priest. The Bible reports little about the activities of specific priests compared to its reports of the activities of famous kings and prophets. By the beginning of the Second Temple period, however, following the return from Babylonian exile in 516 B.C.E., the Jews no longer had kings or prophets, and priests came to the center of power. This trend became more pronounced during the last half of the Second Temple period, when Jewish political leaders were either priests themselves (the Maccabees) or consciously linked themselves with the priesthood (Herod).

During the same period a new group of leaders emerged. These were the scribes, teachers, and judges. There had been judges among the Israelites at least since the time of Moses, but their functioning was specifically reaffirmed early in the Second Temple period when the Persian king gave Ezra a mandate to appoint interpreters and judges of the Torah (Ezra 7:25–26).

Their authority was not linked to Temple office or family lineage in the priesthood, nor was it based on wealth. In part it was a result of governmental authorization, but it was at least as much a function of the people's esteem for the knowledge and good character of the judges. The people respected the judges' knowledge of the scriptures and traditions and treated their words as those of God Himself. The center of their activity was the synagogue, where they read and interpreted the Torah. (Jesus attacks both the chief priests and the Pharisees, a group of scholars and judges, in the Temple [Matthew 21:23, 45], the seat of priestly authority; but he also debates with the Pharisees specifically in synagogues [Luke 6:6–11], he attacks them for seeking "the chief seats in synagogues" [Matthew 23:6], and to win followers he adopts the Pharisaic practice of reading and interpreting the Bible there [Luke 4:16–30].)

The early part of the Second Temple period coincided with accelerating cultural and political change in the Mediterranean world. In the sixth century B.C.E., Greek culture flowered, and the city-states stopped the expansion of Persian influence into Europe. In the fourth century, under Alexander the Great, a more self-confident Greek power conquered the known world, creating a vast empire and the first world culture. From then on, to be civilized meant to be Greek.

According to legends preserved in the writings of Josephus (*Antiquities* 11:329ff.) and in the Talmud (*Tamid* 31b–32b), Alexander was welcomed into Jerusalem by its priestly and secular leaders, and he conversed with them on a series of philosophical topics. The probable reality behind the legends is that the relationship between Alexander and the Jews was good. Alexander had forcefully put down the Samaritans in the Galilee twice, in the years 322 and 321, and the Jews of Jerusalem went out of their way to insure that he understood that they would accept his rule even though their Samaritan cousins and enemies had not. During the first century after Alexander's death, Judea was part of the Ptolemaic Empire centered in Egypt. Judaic and Hellenistic cultures lived together relatively peacefully, and Greek cities were founded in Judea as elsewhere in the Eastern Mediterranean area. Greek culture and technology were absorbed, particularly by the urban and aristocratic classes, and relative cultural tolerance seems to have been the rule.

Jews were an important minority in Egypt, constituting perhaps 40 percent of the population of Alexandria. The intellectual and moral sensitivities of the Jews were attractive to the Greek world. The invisible, transcendent, and universal God of the Jews appealed to philosophical and spiritual gentiles. Many became proselytes. Jewish traders settled throughout the civilized world and spread their religious and moral ideas, at the same time absorbing the cultures in which they lived. In the fruits of this cross-pollination were the seeds of rabbinic Judaism and Hellenistic Christianity.

In 198 B.C.E., the situation changed radically when the Seleucid successors to Alexander, centered in Syria, took Judea from the Ptolemies, centered in Egypt. The new rulers brought a more assertive, more missionary, and less tolerant brand of Hellenism to Palestine. The Syrian Greeks increasingly pushed aside the Hebraic cult with the help of the Jewish aristocrats and most of the priestly class, who had been heavily influenced by Hellenistic attitudes. Assimilation became more forceful and obnoxious to the pietistic traditionalists among the Jews. Rebellion broke out under the leadership of the Maccabees, a dissident priestly family. In 165, the rebels retook Jerusalem and the Temple from the Hellenists (the Hanukkah story).

For several generations Judea remained a more or less independent commonwealth, but in time Roman rule spread over the world. The centuries of Roman domination were hard for the Jews. The Romans admired the Jews' vigor, rationalism, and universalism, but reacted harshly to their insistence on religious and cultural uniqueness and to their resistance to encroachment by the alien state. Constant war and long-term economic depression led to moral decadence and political collapse. That contributed to the apocalyptic view of the world that was common in those centuries and is much in evidence in the Christian Bible. Roman tolerance disintegrated in the face of political insubordination and religious movements that threatened state security. Ultimately the Romans destroyed the Temple in Jerusalem in 70 C.E. in an effort to quell a Jewish rebellion. Since the Temple was not only the center of worship but also the political and economic center of the Jewish people, the destruction of the Temple amounted to the destruction of the Second Jewish Commonwealth. Jews did not govern themselves in their own country again until 1948.

The precise structures and procedure of the judges of the Second Temple period remain somewhat of a mystery. Sources in the Apocrypha, the New Testament, Josephus, and rabbinic literature speak about three institutions—a Great Assembly, a Gerousia, and a Sanhedrin. The Great Assembly was probably a national assembly which met occasionally to decide constitutional issues beginning in the time of Ezra (see Nehemiah 5:7; Ezra 10:1, 7, 12–14; I Maccabees 14:27–29; Berakhot 33a). The Gerousia was apparently a local council of elders of Jerusalem during Hellenistic times (from 323–168 B.C.E.).

The identity of the Sanhedrin during the Second Temple period is hard to pin down, although the term clearly refers to a court with great jurisdiction. There are significant variations in the accounts from this period regarding the person who had the authority to convene the body, the identity of its members, the issues which it decided, and the procedures which it used. Rabbinic literature and the New Testament differ on these issues, and neither is internally consistent on these points. It is clear, however, that the Sanhedrin met infrequently during Second Temple times, that it had to be convened by someone, and that it had judicial powers of some sort.

## 2. The Literature of the Second Temple Period (539 B.C.E.–70 C.E.)

From the perspective of the rabbinic tradition, revelation ceased after the First Temple was destroyed and was replaced by interpretation of the authoritative text of revelation, the Torah. One can see the political reasons why the rabbis would hold this, for acceptance of new revelations would limit the rabbis' own power, which was based on their ability to interpret and apply the Torah. There were also other ideological and emotional reasons for the refusal to accept new revelations, and we shall examine all of these rationales in Topic Five.

Despite this later rabbinic view, we now know that the Second Temple period produced many and varied Jewish writings. The Torah itself achieved its final form during this period, first through the process of editing together its various strands during the time of Ezra, and then through the careful textual work of the scribes during the later centuries of this period. Some of the books of the second part of the Hebrew Bible, the Prophets, may well have been written after the Second Temple had been constructed (for example, Malakhi), and probably much of the third section of the Hebrew Bible, the Writings, was written then.

Since the rabbis regarded revelations after the First Temple period as either inferior to the Torah or totally false, they tried to justify those books that they accepted as part of the Bible, but which gave evidence of being written after 586 B.C.E., as the work of First Temple authors. In fact, one book they liked very much, The Wisdom of Ben Sira (also known as Ecclesiasticus), was not included in the biblical canon precisely because it announces too clearly that it was written during the Second Temple period. The rabbis certainly knew and honored the writings of their scholarly and judicial predecessors during this period, but they asserted that these writings were part of the oral tradition that did not achieve authoritative form until after the Second Temple was destroyed.

Other books which were not included in the biblical canon were preserved by Christianity in the form of the Apocrypha (a Greek term meaning "the outside books" since they were outside the Hebrew Bible) and the Pseudepigrapha (literally, "books of fraudulent ascription"). The Apocrypha became part of the Catholic canon because its books appear in the early Greek and Latin translations even though they are not in the Hebrew Bible, but Protestants have rejected their canonical authority. The books of the Pseudepigrapha were not accepted as canonical by the Roman Catholic or Protestant churches despite their claims to be part of God's revelation, but they were accepted in part in the canon of the Ethiopic church.

In some cases there is very little in the content of these books to suggest why the rabbis did not include them in the canon. That is true, for example, of the apocryphal books of Tobit, Judith, and Susannah, and it is certainly true of The Wisdom of Ben Sira, which they quote in the Talmud, and the two books of Maccabees, which are the basis of the holiday of Hanukkah. We have to assume that the rabbis suspected that those books were written after the First Temple period, and they excluded them on that basis. Some of the apocryphal and pseudepigraphal books include specific Christian references, but scholars assume that even those books were originally written by Jews and that the Christian material was added later.

The major reason for this assumption is the archaeological evidence unearthed in the twentieth century. The Dead Sea Scrolls, discovered in 1948 in the caves of Qumran on the northwestern edge of the Dead Sea, revealed an ascetic group of Jews who lived by a strict regimen and had apocalyptic beliefs about the Messiah. That made contemporary scholars realize that the books of the Apocrypha and Pseudepigrapha, which describe practices and beliefs at variance with rabbinic Judaism, may nevertheless be the work of Jews, and they now assume that Judaism during the Second Temple period was extremely rich and varied.

## 3. The Advent of Rabbinic Authority (70–220 C.E.)

The Jews underwent a catastrophic series of rebellions, defeats, and persecutions in the Roman world during the first and second centuries. These included the destruction of the Temple in 70, the siege and suicide of the Zealots in Masada in 73, the rebellions of the Jews in Parthia (Babylonia), Cyprus, Egypt, and Cyrene (modern Libya) between 115 and 117, and the second Judean rebellion (the Bar Kokhba revolt) between 132 and 135, followed by the Hadrianic persecutions. Although the restrictions against study and observance of Jewish law imposed by Hadrian were ultimately lifted (about 150 C.E.), one permanent result of the Bar Kokhba revolt and its aftermath was the loss of Jewish population in Palestine, especially Judea. Those who survived fled from Roman persecution to other parts of the world, especially to the Parthian kingdom situated in ancient Babylonia, where there had been a sizeable Jewish community from the time of the Babylonian exile in 586 B.C.E. The leadership of Jewish life gradually passed from Palestine to Babylonia, although the Babylonians themselves continued to recognize the hegemony of the Israeli judges well into the fourth century C.E..

After the destruction of the Second Temple in 70 C.E., rabbinic institutions became formalized. It was then that the process of ordination and the title "Rabbi" appeared to designate someone who was authorized to serve as a judge, and the rabbinic group began to constrain its members to bow to the will of the majority. Some sources mention a president during the Second Temple period from the time of Hillel on (that is, from 30 B.C.E.), but the descriptions of his activities indicate that this title then denoted the head of the Pharisaic party of the rabbis, not the national, political leader that the president became after the destruction of the Temple. Moreover, in the decades immediately following the destruction there are reports of several instances when the Sanhedrin and its president asserted their authority forcefully against individual rabbis who exercised the autonomy they previously had enjoyed. (See Mishnah *Eduyot* 5:6; *Rosh Hashanah* 24b–25a; and *Bava Metzia* 59b, all of which appear in Topic Five.)

These changes were timely because the demise of the Second Commonwealth spelled the end of power for the priests and the Herodians. The rich aristocracy of Jerusalem was no more. The only type of leader left to the scattered and powerless remnant of Israel was the judge, now in the form of the ordained, rabbinic sage. After 70 C.E., and for the first time, rabbis represent the Jewish community in Roman courts, both locally and in Rome. In order to handle their new responsibilities in the community, the judges of old had to reorganize.

In the course of this reorganization, the composition of the Sanhedrin, its presidency, and its membership procedures changed. Before 70, there had been a number of groups within the Sanhedrin, none of them particularly dominant. The primary parties were the Sadducees, who represented the priestly and landed families, and the Pharisees, who were legal scholars and scribes drawn largely from peasants and urban artisans. Another important party was the Essenes, who were ascetic in orientation (if the Dead Sea Scrolls reflect the views of the Essenes), and may have been the group to which Jesus belonged. A fourth party was the Zealots, who pushed for the insurrection against Rome and who fled to Masada for their famous last stand there between 70 and 73 C.E.

After the destruction of the Temple, the Pharisees emerged as the clearly dominant party: the Zealots' cause had been lost; the Essenes ceased to have recognizable legal interest or effect; and the Sadducees' base of power (the Temple) had been destroyed. A number of members of the priestly families joined Pharisaic ranks after 70.

The masses accepted Pharisaic leadership both because its interpretations were based on the Bible, recognized as the word of God, and because their rulings were generally more lenient and showed more concern for the common man than those of the aristocratic Sadducees—so much so that Josephus says that in public life the Sadducees of his time submitted to Pharisaic law "because the multitude would not otherwise bear them" (*Antiquities* XVIII. i.4; see also B.T. *Niddah* 33b).

That certainly does not sound like the description of the Pharisees found in the New Testament, where they are portrayed as harsh and legalistic. The New Testament records the reactions of the Pharisees' opponents, who were trying to create an identity distinct from the Pharisaic tradition. Those who remained Jews, however, had a very different view of the Pharisees, reflected in Talmudic literature and by Josephus, who twice says that the Pharisees were simply "nicer" than the Sadducees (*Wars* 2:166; *Ant.* 18:17). That perception induced most people to follow Pharisaic leadership.

Even before the destruction of the Second Temple, the presidency of the Sanhedrin became hereditary. After 70, it took on increasingly political dimensions, almost as though the presidency was supplanting the Jewish monarchy. The presidency of Hillel (30 B.C.E.–10 C.E.) was devoid of sovereign power or monarchic connotations. The president was simply the leader of the Pharisaic party. By the end of the second century, however, Judah the President is repeatedly tied in lineage not only to Hillel, but also to King David, a hint of past glory and of Messianic hopes for a future Jewish national revival.

In a sense, the rabbinic institution during these centuries went full circle, as a group respected for its intellectual merit gradually acquired political power. Scholarly, pedagogical, and judicial leadership originally open to wise men from all social strata became hereditary. Ultimately, the rabbis, as the last leaders of a scattered people, came to be identified with the long defunct monarchy.

## 4. The Literature of the Tanna'im (70–220 c.e.)

For a variety of reasons that shall be discussed, much of Jewish law was kept in oral form. Some of it found written expression in the biblical codes, but the bulk of judicial decisions and customs that governed the people was passed down orally from one generation to another. Eventually the task of remembering and transmitting the oral traditions became professionalized. There was a group of professional rememberers known as the *Tanna'im* (singular *Tanna*), who were specifically chosen for their ability to remember, not analyze. Their function was to accurately transmit to their successors what they had received from their predecessors. The job of making the rulings that were to be passed on was the work of a different group of men, the judges.

The rebellions, defeats, and persecutions of the first two centuries c.e. threatened to destroy the oral tradition as those who carried it in Israel were either slaughtered or dispersed. This threat was a powerful incentive for the Pharisees to organize and edit their decisions. There were several stages in the process of editing the oral tradition. Rabbis Joshua b. Hananiah and Eliezer b. Hyrcanus produced collections of laws between 90 and 120 c.e., but Rabbi Akiba is known as the principal instigator of the editorial process. His students, including Rabbis Meir, Jose, Judah, Simeon, Eleazar, and others, continued the task of collecting, organizing, and editing the oral teachings of the tradition, basing themselves primarily on the content and organizational pattern of Rabbi Akiba's collection, but introducing some of the teachings of other Tanna'im as well. None of these collections is extant, however, because the collection of Rabbi Judah Ha-Nasi (the president of the Sanhedrin) incorporated most of their materials and became the indisputably authoritative one. That collection, edited around 220 c.e., is called the *Mishnah*, the term stemming from the root meaning "to repeat," "to study," and "to teach." While the tradition affirms that Rabbi Judah Ha-Nasi embodied in his work most of the traditions of the past (*Bava Metzia* 33b), there is evidence that he also changed some of their content, combined various sources, added to them, and decided which of several conflicting opinions would be authoritative. Because of the immediate authority which his collection enjoyed, he is known simply as "Rabbi" without attaching his proper name to his title, that is, rabbi par excellence.

Another collection of Tannaitic materials which gained some degree of authority is called the *Tosefta* ("the additions"). Edited by R. Hiyya and R. Hoshiah, it contains rulings by the same rabbis who appear in the Mishnah, and it is organized along similar lines. Some of the rulings in the two collections are the same, some have different wording, and some appear in one collection but not in the other.

Some decisions that do not appear in either the Mishnah or the Tosefta are mentioned in the discussions of them in the centuries following their compilation. Those decisions are called *Baraitot* (literally, "the outside ones," because they are outside the Mishnah).

The Mishnah is organized according to subject matter. A list of the subsections, the *S'darim* (orders) and *Massekhtot* (tractates or books), together with a brief description of the content of each appears in the appendix.

Another type of literature from this period is *Midrash Halakhah*, the interpretation (*Midrash*) of the legal sections (*Halakhah*) of the Torah. Each book is arranged according to the order of the Bible, so that the comment on Exodus 21:11, for example, is followed immediately by the comment on Exodus 21:12, even though the two verses speak about totally different matters.

That example is typical: the laws of the Bible are not organized by topic, and thus laws on a particular subject may appear in several places. Since Midrash Halakhah is a line-by-line interpretation of the legal sections of the Bible, it is not arranged by topic either, and that makes it rather cumbersome for a judge to use. Moreover, the Midrash Halakhah often records several different possible interpretations of a verse without coming to a decision as to which one of them is the law. It should not be surprising, then, that the Mishnah almost immediately superseded the Midrash Halakhah in its authority: since the Mishnah is arranged by topic and records decisions, judges could easily use it in deciding the cases before them; and since it carries the name and authority of Rabbi Judah, the president of the Sanhedrin, there were political as well as practical reasons for its influence.

On the other hand, the Mishnah rarely supplies the reasons for its decisions. Consequently the Midrash Halakhah has often been used by later rabbis who need to know the rationale behind a law to apply it in a new or difficult case. In the same way, an American judge who has an immediate need to know the law turns first to the statutes and codes, but when the same judge settles down to consider a difficult case, the judge will turn to contextual sources, legislative history, and other aids to determine the intent of Congress in passing the legislation.

## 5. *The Period of the Amora'im and the Gemara* (220–500 c.e.)

With the decline of the Palestinian Jewish community, leadership passed to Babylonian Jewry. Many Jews had lived in Babylonia since the destruction of the First Temple, and only a small percentage of them had returned to Israel with Ezra. Between 200 and 500 c.e., the Babylonian community lived rather securely under Persian rule. Great law schools developed there (especially in the cities of Sura and Pumbeditha) where the Mishnah was discussed and applied by the scholars, known as the *Amora'im*. These scholars not only interpreted the Mishnah; through judicial precedents they also created many laws not found in tannaitic literature in order to deal with the new situations that they confronted. As long as their rulings only added to the tannaitic corpus and did not contradict it, they found no theological problem in this creative activity.

The legal discussions of these scholars were at first kept in oral form, but political and economic conditions at the end of this period again forced the reduction to written form. Increasing pressure on Jews by radical Zoroastrian rulers in Persia endangered the chain of tradition and convinced the rabbis that their discussions must be organized and edited if they were not to be lost. The record of those discussions is called the *Gemara*, from the Aramaic word that means "to learn," or *Talmud*, from the Hebrew word meaning the same thing. Both names indicate that the material records how the Amora'im interpreted the Mishnah.

The Jews who remained in Israel under Roman rule were not allowed to teach or practice their religion during much of this period. They did succeed in establishing one academy in Tiberias, far from the centers of Roman power in Palestine. The rabbis often had to meet in hiding, but they managed to carry on discussions of the Mishnah in which they applied the law to cases. As the Roman Empire became more and more thoroughly Christianized, the restrictions against the Jews grew harsher and harsher, and consequently the Palestinian rabbis felt the need to record their discussions in their own Gemara or Talmud lest they be lost.

Thus there are two Gemarot, or two Talmuds: the Babylonian and the Palestinian. The Palestinian Talmud is sometimes called "The Western Talmud" (*Talmud Hamaravi*) or, more commonly, "The Jerusalem Talmud" (*Talmud Jerushalmi*) even though the discussions it records did not take place in Jerusalem. Because the Babylonian community was closer to the center of Arab power and trade routes in the next major period of Jewish history, the Babylonian Talmud spread to many more Jewish communities than the Palestinian Talmud and became more authoritative. Consequently, a reference to "The Talmud" is to the Babylonian Talmud.

Since the discussions in the two Talmuds were based on the Mishnah, they follow the same order and divisions of the earlier work. The Gemara for some tractates of the Mishnah, however, is missing in either or both Talmuds.

One other type of rabbinic literature that was produced in this time period (although most of it was not compiled until later) is the *Midrash Aggadah*, the interpretation (*Midrash*) of the nonlegal sections of the Bible (*Aggadah*). Since there is much more Midrash Aggadah than Midrash Halakhah, the Midrash Aggadah is often called simply "The Midrash." The purpose of the rabbinic comments was to stimulate the intellect and enhance commitment, not to decide legal issues. In rabbinic terminology, the Aggadah was intended "to draw the heart of a person" (*Shabbat* 87a, *Yoma* 75a, *Hagigah* 14a).

### 6. A Note on Citation Form

References to biblical books traditionally are cited by book, chapter, and verse (for example, Exodus 12:2). References to the major collection of Midrash Aggadah, known as *Midrash Rabbah*, can easily be confused with biblical references, because they also are to book, chapter, and verse. The letter R is added to indicate a reference to the Midrash Rabbah (for example, *Ex.R.* 28:6). References to the Mishnah are by tractate, chapter, and law (for example, *Bava Kamma* 4:2).

References to the Babylonian Talmud follow the same tractate scheme, but can be distinguished from the Mishnah because folio pages bearing the letters a or b are used in lieu of chapter and law (for example, *Bava Kamma* 83b). Fortunately, the page numbering of the Bomberg edition of the Babylonian Talmud, the first complete printing of the Talmud (1520–1523), has been universally accepted, and sections are always cited according to that numbering. Since the Babylonian Talmud is the more authoritative one, its contents are usually cited by tractate and page exclusively, although B. T. (Babylonian Talmud) or T.B. (Talmud Bavli) are appended to the citation when many different sources are being cited. Citations from the Palestinian Talmud are usually preceded by "P.T." (Palestinian Talmud) or "T.J." (Talmud Jerushalmi). Sections of the Palestinian Talmud are either cited by chapter and law (for example, P.T. *Peah* 4:1), indicating that the passage occurs in the discussion of that Mishnah in the Palestinian Gemara, or they are cited by the page number and column in the common, one-volume Venice edition of the Palestinian Talmud (for example, P.T. *Peah* 17d).

## B. MIDRASH HALAKHAH

After the Torah became recognized as the primary law of the Jewish people, judges who were required to rule according to the law had to interpret it in order to apply it. This process of interpretation began very early. As the text of the Torah became fixed and the process of interpretation was regularized, hermeneutic rules were formulated to summarize standards of interpretation and to distinguish good legal reasoning from bad.

The process of interpretation starts with what seems to be the simple task of assigning meaning to the words and symbols of the text. The process soon goes beyond this, however, and becomes an open-ended search for meaning and connotations in the text. Reading an ancient Hebrew text in translation may not give the reader an adequate sense of the difficulty of the interpretive task. Even at the initial, simple level of attaching meaning to words, formidable stumbling blocks confront the text reader. A number of Hebrew words are known only from their use in the Bible so that their precise meaning cannot be determined from external sources. Sometimes such words appear in only one or two passages of the Bible, or in obscure passages, and then affixing a meaning to the words may be sheer guesswork based on whatever clues the context provides. Many words refer to objects that are not familiar today, and often the references were already uncertain by the rabbinic period.

Problems of voice and style abound, an inevitable result of reading a literary document in a different historical and cultural period. By the time of the rabbis the language in which the Bible was written had become archaic and was no longer generally spoken. Hebrew texts are usually written without vowels. The reader is expected to supply the correct vocalization contextually, but there frequently are alternative possible vocalizations that modify meaning. Moreover, ancient texts tend to be very spare with punctuation; words, sentences, and paragraphs are not clearly delineated and often run together. The familiar chapter and verse numbers of modern biblical texts and translations were added in medieval times; they did not exist during the rabbinic period. In short, opportunities abound for obscure texts and legitimate, variant readings of those texts.

This topic examines the law of personal injury in the three major legal works of the classic rabbinic period: Midrash Halakhah, Mishnah, and Gemara. The Midrash Halakhah provides verse by verse commentary on the legal sections of the Bible, organized in the order of the biblical text rather than by subject matter. There are extant books of Midrash Halakhah on four books of the Bible, namely, the *Mekhilta* on the legal materials in Exodus; the *Sifra* on Leviticus; and the *Sifre* on Numbers and Deuteronomy. We actually have two books of Midrash Halakhah on Exodus, the *Mekhilta of Rabbi Ishmael* and the *Mekhilta of Rabbi Akiba.* Since the latter was discovered only recently, the title "Mekhilta" without modification refers to the one which has long been known, the one of Rabbi Ishmael. There is no extant book of Midrash Halakhah on Genesis because there are only a few explicit laws in Genesis.

The Midrash Halakhah was transmitted orally for many centuries and finally written down when political and economic conditions endangered its continued existence in oral form. Some claim that it was written at the end of the second century, contemporaneously with the redaction of the Mishnah; others claim that its written form was produced much later, around 500 C.E. The material in the Midrash Halakhah, however, probably includes some of the earliest rabbinic material extant. Predominantly it records the views of the disciples of Rabbi Akiba and those of their second-century disputants, the school of Rabbi Ishmael.

A comment in Midrash Halakhah typically begins with a verse and then either simply records one interpretation or discusses two or more possible interpretations. When it does the latter, it usually begins with one possible interpretation and then says, "You say that? Perhaps it could be this." At that point there is usually an explanation of why the second alternative is problematic so that the first construction of the biblical law is preferable. The deliberation may stop there or may continue several steps further. The style suggests that a debate is taking place in which one person is proposing one interpretation and another person argues for a different reading. That may or may not be the case: the argumentation could be simply the work of one person thinking through the various possible readings of the biblical verse.

In any case, the reader should be aware that the text of the Midrash Halakhah does not generally alert us to a shift from the analysis of one interpretation to a consideration of the other by some obvious device like naming or numbering the various interpretations and inserting the name or number before a passage in support of that interpretation. The Hebrew text does not have punctuation marks to guide us either. Instead, we must determine that such a shift has taken place by figuring out which interpretation would be supported by the argument that is being presented. It is not as difficult as it sounds, however, because there are clue words that effectively function as punctuation marks. By paying attention to those, one learns after a while to identify the position that is being defended with reasonable ease.

The *Mekhilta* excerpt that follows contains segments of the interpretation of Exodus, chapter 21, verses 18–25, the Covenant Code laws on personal injuries. As you read the *Mekhilta*, do not expect to understand all of the references or the details of its analysis. Note the argumentative flavor of the text. This is certainly not a tradition that accepts statements passively; it thrives on debate. Try also to identify the questions that are raised about the biblical text and the answers proposed. Earlier it was suggested that you make a list of the interpretive questions that the text of chapter 21 of Exodus presents to a modern mind. Before reading the *Mekhilta* excerpt that follows, you may wish to refresh your recollection of that list. Our experience has been that modern and ancient lists share much in common.

The section starts off with a question, asking why Exodus 21:18–19 is necessary at all since the rules it announces might be thought to be subsumed in verse 25, which states the general principle of "eye for eye." The question proceeds from the rabbinic assumption that each word of God's law has a distinct function and is designed to teach something unique. Verses 18–19 must therefore come to teach something distinct from verse 25. This rather cryptic first paragraph lays the foundation for the view, detailed in the Mishnah reading later in this chapter, that the basic compensatory measure of damages for personal injury (eye for eye) includes a number of distinct elements, in this instance a specific indemnity for loss of time and expense of healing. As we shall see, other verses are relied on as the basis for finding a total of five distinct elements of compensation.

From this initial question, the debate in the *Mekhilta* passage shifts without apparent pause or bridge to a familiar and modern problem of defining the word "men." Does the word in the text denote all members of the human species, or is it limited to males, excluding women? This linguistic point is more problematic in Hebrew than in English because the male form is used in both nouns and verbs to describe both male groups and mixed groups of males and females.

The next point of interpretation is similar: does the reference in Exodus to injuries caused by stones or fists delimit an exclusive group of weapons that are to be treated specially, or is it indicative of a broader class of weapons causing injury (for example, any implement capable of producing death)?

We hope these few paragraphs have succeeded in introducing you to the genre of Midrash Halakhah and giving you a taste of its methodology and verve. While you may not understand every detail of the remaining passages below, try to plumb them as well as you can, for nothing can replace your own personal experience of wrestling with these texts to demonstrate to you the flavor of generations of rabbinic scholarship. This is a tradition in which the mind was constantly chal-

lenged and everything was open to question. You will see even more of
that later on when we study some selections from the Gemara, but the
Midrash Halakhah is the first example we have of this lively interaction with the text. Note: in the following translation, "R." stands for
"Rabbi."

MEKHILTA, NEZIKIN, CHAPTERS VI AND VIII (LAUTERBACH, TRANS.
1949)

*Chapter VI (Ex.* 21:18–19):
*And if Men Contend.* Why is this section set forth? Because it says
only: "Eye for eye"; but we have not heard about the indemnity for
the loss of time and for the expenses of healing. Therefore it says here:
"And if men contend . . . if he rise again and walk abroad . . . and shall
cause him to be thoroughly healed," etc. (vv. 18–19). Scripture thus
comes to teach about this subject those regulations that were missing.

*And if Men Contend.* I thus know only about men. How about
women? R. Ishmael used to say: All the laws about damages found in
the Torah are not explicit on this point. But since in the case of one of
them Scripture explicitly states (Num. 5:6) that women are to be regarded like men, it has thus made it explicit in regard to all the laws
about damages found in the Torah that women are to be regarded like
men. R. Josiah says: "A man or a woman" (Num., ibid.). Why is this
said? Because it says: "And if a man shall open a pit" (v. 33), from
which I know only about a man. But how about a woman? Therefore
it says: "A man or a woman." Scripture thus comes to declare man
and woman alike in regard to all the laws about damages found in the
Torah. R. Jonathan says: There is no need of this scriptural proof. Has
it not been said: "The owner of the pit shall make it good" (v. 34);
"The one that kindled the fire shall surely make restitution" (Ex.
22.5)? Hence, what purpose is there in saying: "A man or a woman?"
It comes for a special teaching of its own.

*And One Smite the Other with a Stone or with His Fist.* This is to
declare that one is guilty if he smites with either one of them. *With a
Stone or with His Fist.* This is to tell that a stone and the fist are
merely types of instruments capable of producing death. You say it
comes to teach this. Perhaps however it only comes to teach that if he
smite him with a stone or with his fist he is guilty, but if he smite him
with any other thing he is not guilty? It says however: "And if he
smote him with a stone in the hand, whereby a man may die, and he
died, he is a murderer," etc. (Num. 35:17). This expressly tells that he
is not guilty unless he struck him with a thing that is capable of producing death. And how do we know that he is not guilty unless he
struck him on a part of the body where such a blow could produce
death? It says: "And lie in wait for him and rise up against him, and

smite him mortally that he die" (Deut. 19:11). This tells that he is not guilty unless he struck him with a thing that is capable of producing death and on a part of the body where such a blow could produce death. R. Nathan says: This is to declare that a stone must be like the fist, and the fist must be like a stone. Just as the stone is something that can produce death, so also the fist must be such as to be capable of producing death. And just as the fist is something that can be identified, so also the stone must be such as can be identified. Thus, if the stone with which he struck him became mixed with other stones, the assailant is free.

*And He Die Not but Keep His Bed.* This [the fact that the Bible contemplates the possibility that assault can lead to death] intimates that bad temper may lead to death.

*And He Die Not but Keep His Bed.* But if he struck a blow strong enough to produce death, he is free from paying indemnity for the loss of time and for the expenses of healing (since he is subject to the death penalty and that cancels lesser penalties).

*If He Rise Again and Walk.* I might understand this to mean within the house, but it says: "Abroad." But even when it says: "Abroad," I might still understand it to mean even if he is falling away. Therefore it says: "If he rise again, and walk abroad upon his support," that means, restored to his health. This is one of the three expressions in the Torah which R. Ishmael used to interpret as being figurative. Similarly: "If the sun be risen upon him" (Ex. 22:2). But does the sun rise upon him alone? Does it not rise upon the whole world? It simply means this: What does the sun signify to the world? — Peace. So, then, if it is known that this burglar would have left the owner in peace, and yet the latter killed him, he is guilty of murder. Similarly: "They shall spread the sheet" (Deut. 22:17). They should make the matter clear as a white sheet. Also here you interpret "Upon his support" to mean, restored to his health.

*Then Shall He That Smote Be Quit.* I might understand that he can offer surety and in the meantime walk around in the streets free. But Scripture says: "If he rise again and walk abroad." This tells that they keep the assailant imprisoned until the victim is restored to health. *Then Shall He That Smote Be Quit.* Of the death penalty. I might understand it to mean also free from paying indemnities for the loss of time and for curing expenses. But Scripture says: "Only he shall pay for the loss of his time and shall cause him to be thoroughly healed." Aside from compensation for injury to limb, he is paid for his loss of time and the expenses of his cure.

*Only He Shall Pay for the Loss of His Time.* I might understand this to mean, for an unlimited time. But it also says: "And shall cause him to be thoroughly healed." Just as in regard to the curing expenses he

pays only for the cure of ailments resulting from the injury, so also in
regard to the loss of time he is to pay only for such loss of time as resulted from the injury.

*And Shall Cause Him to Be Thoroughly Healed.* If it gets healed
and then gets sore again, gets healed and gets sore again, and even if
this happens four or five times, he is still obliged to pay for curing it. It
is to teach us this that Scripture says: "And shall cause him to be
thoroughly healed." Suppose ulcers grow on his body around the
wound. If they are results of the wound he is obliged to pay for curing
them, but if they are not results of the wound he is not obliged to pay
for curing them. For, when the Torah says: "Only he shall pay for the
loss of his time, and shall cause him to be thoroughly healed," it indicates that just as he pays for the loss of time only when it is the result
of the injury, so also when he is to pay for the healing he is to pay only
for the healing of ailments resulting from the injury.

Another Interpretation: This passage suggests that you can learn
proper conduct from the Torah. "Only he shall pay for the loss of his
time, and shall cause him to be thoroughly healed."

> *Chapter VIII (Ex. 21:22–25):*
> *And if Men Strive Together,* etc. Why is this section set forth? [i.e.,
what do we learn from it which we do not already know from the previous verses]? Because of this. It says: "And if a man come presumptuously upon his neighbour," etc. (v. 14). From this we have heard only
that one who aims to kill his enemy and actually kills him is to be
punished by death. But we have not heard about one who, aiming to
kill his enemy, kills his friend. Therefore it says here: "And if men
strive together. . . . But if any harm follow," etc. (vv. 22–23). Scripture
thus comes to teach you about one who, aiming to kill his enemy,
kills his friend, (and it tells you that) such a one is likewise to be punished by death. For this purpose this section is set forth. Rabbi says: If
one who aims to kill an enemy of his but kills another person who is
likewise his enemy is free, it is but logical that one who aims to kill
his enemy but kills his friend should surely be free. Scripture here
merely comes to teach you that the compensation for injuries to a
wife is to be paid to her husband, and compensation for causing a miscarriage also belongs to the husband; and that one who incurs the penalty of death is exempt from making monetary compensation. R. Isaac
says: Even if one aims to kill and kills, he is free unless he has expressly said: I am going to kill this man. For it is said: "And lie in wait
for him, and rise up against him and smite him mortally" (Deut.
19:11). What then is the purpose of saying: "And if men strive together?" Because it says: "And he that smiteth anybody mortally"
(Lev. 24:17), which I might understand to mean even if he kills a child
born after only eight months of pregnancy. Therefore it says: "And if

men strive together," thereby telling us that one is not guilty of death unless he kills a viable child.

. . .

*Then Thou Shalt Give Life for Life.* It is with life that he must pay for life. He cannot pay for life with money. Another Interpretation: *Then Thou Shalt Give Life,* etc. With life only shall he pay, but he is not to pay for a life with life and with money. Rabbi says: *Then Thou Shalt Give Life for Life.* This means, monetary compensation. You interpret it to mean monetary compensation. Perhaps this is not so, but it means death? Behold, you reason thus: Here the expression "laying upon" is used and there (v. 30) the expression "laying upon" is used. Just as the expression "laying upon" used there implies only monetary compensation, so also here it implies only monetary compensation.

*Eye for Eye.* This means, monetary compensation for an eye. You interpret it to mean money for an eye. Perhaps this is not so, but it means an eye literally? R. Ishmael used to say: Behold it says: "And he that killeth a beast shall make it good and he that killeth a man shall be put to death" (Lev. 24:21). Scripture thus declares cases of injuries inflicted upon man to be like cases of injury inflicted upon beasts, and vice versa. Just as cases of injuries inflicted upon beasts are subject only to payment of indemnity, so also cases of injuries inflicted upon man are subject only to payment of indemnity. R. Isaac says: Behold it says: "If there be laid on him a ransom," etc. (v. 30). Now then, by using the method of *kal vahomer* you reason thus: If even in a case where the penalty of death is imposed only a monetary compensation is exacted, it is but logical that in this case, where no death penalty is imposed, surely no more than a monetary compensation should be exacted. R. Eliezer says: "Eye for Eye, etc." I might understand that whether one injures intentionally or unintentionally one is to pay only an indemnity. But behold Scripture singles out the one who inflicts an injury intentionally, declaring that he is not to pay money but is actually to suffer a similar injury. It is said: "And if a man maim his neighbor, as he hath done so shall it be done to him" (Lev. 24:19). This is a general statement. "Eye for eye" (Lev. 24:20) is a specific statement. Now, a general statement followed by a specific statement cannot include more than the specific statement. When it says however: "As he hath maimed a man," etc. (ibid.), it again makes a general statement. But perhaps the second general statement is to be considered identical with the first general statement? You must say: No! This is a general statement followed by a specific statement and by another general statement, all of which must be interpreted as including only things similar to those mentioned in the specific statement. Now, in this case the specific statement specifies that for injuries resulting in a permanent defect and affecting chief organs and visible, though inflicted intentionally, one is subject only to payment of indemnity. Hence, for any injuries resulting in a permanent defect and affecting chief organs and visible, though inflicted intentionally, one is subject only to payment of indemnity. Thus Scripture says: "As he hath maimed a man"—that is, if he has intentionally inflicted an injury.

> *Burning for Burning.* If you interpret it to mean that he wounded him thereby and drew blood from him—has it not already been said: "Stripe for stripe"? What need then is there of saying: "Burning for burning"? Simply this: Suppose he burned him on the sole of his foot without producing a visible mark, or he put a load of stones upon him, thereby causing him pain, or put snow upon his head and made him suffer from cold; behold, in such cases he has to pay him indemnity for the pain. But suppose he was tender and delicate and reared with indulgence so that his pain is double? This sort of pain too is referred to in the Torah when it says: "Burning for burning."

## C. Mishnah

The Midrash Halakhah adheres closely to the biblical text and deals with the immediate problems that it raises. Its emphasis on text makes it cumbersome as a tool for judges because it discusses a topic in widely scattered places, just as the Bible does. When political and social conditions in the second century c.e. made it imperative to put the oral tradition in writing, editors tried to organize it by subject matter for easy judicial use. As we have seen, the Mishnah and the Tosefta are the principal collections that were produced, but both were based on earlier attempts to organize the oral tradition by topic, primarily by Rabbi Akiba and his students. As Rabbi Judah Ha-Nasi, editor of the Mishnah, said:

> To whom can Rabbi Akiba be compared? To a worker who took his basket and went outside. He found wheat which he put in it, he found barley which he put in it, he found spelt which he put in it, he found beans which he put in it, and he found lentils which he put in it. When he returned to his house, he separated the wheat by itself, the barley by itself, the spelt by itself, the beans by themselves, and the lentils by themselves. In that way Rabbi Akiba arranged the entire Torah according to the nature of each part (*Avot d'Rabbi Nathan* 18:1).

The fact that the collections that resulted were designed for judicial use is evident not only in their organization but also in their style. The decisions are given in direct, simple terms that lay out the rules.

Sometimes a minority opinion is mentioned, but the rationales behind the decisions almost never appear: the historical conditions under which these codes were written did not allow for such details, and the primary concern was to preserve the decisions themselves.

The mishnaic excerpt that follows is concerned with giving practical content to the concept of compensatory damages for personal injury, which the rabbis now understood to be the intent of the command of "an eye for an eye." Ancient law codes like that of Hammurabi assigned a fixed monetary value to a particular injury of a person possessing a given social status inflicted by a person of a given class. In the Mishnah a more sophisticated and individual approach is taken to these problems. Instead of assigning a rather arbitrary, fixed value to a general group of injuries, the damages in each case are to be calculated by the judge on the basis of the circumstances. The total recovery to which the injured person is entitled is understood to be the sum of five distinct factors:

a. *Damage.* This is the lost capital value caused by the injury. Each person's body represents an asset which loses value from injury.

b. *Pain.* The injury causes pain and suffering for which the injured person should be compensated.

c. *Healing.* Even in an age of simple medical techniques, payment must be made for the doctor's bills and costs of medicine, and this is clearly the responsibility of the wrongdoer.

d. *Maintenance.* A seriously injured person will not be able to work and will lose the economic value of lost earnings for the period of disability, for which the injuring party must pay.

e. *Insult.* Injury is degrading. A person loses status both because of the humiliating circumstances of the injury itself and the lowered social position he now occupies because of his disfigurement or other handicap.

Each of these elements is computed in its own way. Moreover, in some cases the injuring party may be liable for some but not all of the elements. The approach used to compute damages also reflects the emphasis placed on ethical and religious values in deciding legal issues. The distinct specialness of each individual, the dignity to which all humans are entitled, the importance of kindness, and the need for forgiveness all find their way into the discussion of damages. Such elements can be found in the Covenant Code of Exodus, but it is important to note how they have developed alongside the more technical legal rules that they feed.

Chapter eight of *Bava Kamma* is the primary section of the Mishnah in which personal injuries are treated. The distinctions between the Mishnah and the Midrash Halakhah in style and order will be immediately apparent as you read the chapter.

This excerpt contains most of what the Mishnah has to say on this subject. How helpful is it in identifying the values that underlie the rabbinic law of injuries?

1. Consider, for example, matters of human equality and differentiated social status. The Mishnah distinguishes between the economic losses attendant upon injury and the psychic and social costs involved. Note that the three economic elements treat all people alike: that is, damages are measured by a person's value in the slave market as a unit of production; maintenance for loss of time is measured as if the injured person were the watchman over a cucumber patch and paid the minimum wage for menial labor; healing is measured objectively in light of experience and expenses actually incurred by the injured person. The measure suggested for pain is troubling since it assumes that the injured person would agree to suffer even agonizing and life threatening injury if only you paid him enough. (Consequently some manuscripts of the Mishnah insert a negative word so that the criterion is how much a person would require in order *not* to be so pained.) But the difficulties the rabbis had with the inevitable social status elements of indignity are greater and lead the text to record dissenting views.

2. The difficult problem of putting a price on insult and indignity also forced the rabbis to examine the significance of the intention of the injurer in computing damages. We are told in Mishnah 1 that unintentional injury, for instance, by a person falling off a roof and landing on someone below, creates liability for most of the elements, including damages, pain, healing, and loss of time. But the unintentional actor is not liable for indignity of insult inflicted on the victim. So long as we maintain our focus carefully on the injured party alone, we can see that being hurt intentionally may in some situations be more painful and cause loss of greater social status than being hurt accidentally. To paraphrase O. W. Holmes, "Even a dog knows the difference between being kicked and being tripped over." Nevertheless, once we emphasize the actor's intention, our focus is likely to slip from strict compensation for the injured party to matters of the moral fault and punishment of the actor. Certainly the citation of Deuteronomy 25:11 at the end of Mishnah 1 indicates this. The woman who intervenes in a fight between two men by grabbing one man by the genitals is being punished

when her hand is cut off. There is no element of compensation in that rule.

3. Mishnayot 6 and 7 appear to distinguish between self-inflicted injury, injury inflicted at the request of the injured party, and injury done at the request of the injured party accompanied by a promise of immunity from liability. These distinctions suggest the role of consent of the victim to the injury in assessing liability. Mishnah 7 emphasizes three factors: (a) whether the victim explicitly granted the actor immunity from liability when inviting the injury; (b) the seriousness of the injury; and (c) the liability of an agent who injures a third party at the request of and upon a promise of immunity from his principal. The third of those factors is the easiest to understand: the agent is not relieved of liability by his principal's promise of immunity.

We are not told in this text whether the principal also is liable to the victim or whether the agent may enforce the promise of immunity against the principal if the agent is found liable. The distinction between a simple invitation to injury and one accompanied by promises of immunity seems forced and formal. Might it be an attempt to discourage people from taking up ill-considered requests to inflict injury too quickly, by requiring that there be an explicit offer of immunity for the injury as well as the request?

The seriousness of the injury inflicted at request seems to be an overriding factor. Neither consent, nor an invitation, nor a promise of immunity relieves the actor from liability for serious bodily injuries, such as blinding an eye, cutting off a hand, or breaking a leg. The law is more permissive if the requested injury is to property, for instance breaking a pitcher or tearing a garment. The distinction is clear enough at the extremes, but the Mishnah sheds no light on the difficult intermediate positions. May one consent and invite any personal injury? Suppose a person invites a brawl and then is hurt more seriously than either party expected?

These specific issues should not obscure the primary legal point made in this chapter. No matter what the difficulties may be in reconciling the mishnaic rule with the Bible, the rule definitely is that the remedy for assault is monetary compensation, not retribution or punishment. This stands in sharp contrast to American law, where punishment is the primary response to assault and there may also be exemplary (deterrent) punitive damages to be paid. In Jewish law there is no criminal penalty for assault except if the offender does it repeatedly. Then the rabbis might impose stripes for upsetting the general order of the community. But there is no specific punishment prescribed in the law, and the penalty of lashes was generally not applied for one or two acts of assault.

In addition to these substantive matters, the reader should note a few organizational features of the selection. The first Mishnah appears to give a general and authoritative compendium of the rules of personal injury, and the mishnayot that follow add several specific rulings. This organizational plan of presenting the general rules first and the details afterward is common in the Mishnah, although this is an especially clear example of it.

The catalogue of the five elements and their modes of computation in Mishnah 1 ends with the fifth element, degradation. That Mishnah, however, does not end with the formula for computing degradation, as one would expect. Instead, after indicating that the amount awarded for degradation depends on the status of the perpetrator and the victim, it continues with some specific rules concerning the application of this remedy, that is, whether it applies to a naked person, a sleeping person, and so on. Only then does the Mishnah go back to the first element and discuss further details about it. This is an example of "associative reasoning" common to the Mishnah and later rabbinic literature, in which the discussion of one topic leads the editor to include other material on that topic or another subject related to it before continuing with the general organizational pattern of the section. Here the association is topical: after specifying the way of assessing monetary compensation for degradation, further rulings about it follow. Sometimes, however, the association is based on the fact that a particular rabbi handed down one ruling on the subject at hand, and that leads the editor to include other rulings of that rabbi, whether related to the topic or not. Another common form of association is verbal: a striking phrase is used in the formulation of a ruling relevant to the topic under discussion, and that leads to a citation of a number of other instances in which that phrase was used. Modern readers accustomed to tight, topical organization might find this disconcerting and perhaps even sloppy; but one must remember that the Mishnah's rulings were communicated orally, and in that context associative reasoning is an indispensable tool for remembering a vast amount of material.

Associative reasoning also explains the organization of the chapter as a whole. After the brief, associative excursion at the end of Mishnah 1, mishnayot 2 to 5 announce rulings about the categories of people liable for the five elements. The first five mishnayot are not clearly restricted to permanent injuries, as the later discussion in the Gemara makes clear, but Mishnah 6 seems to be specifically about temporary injuries. If the editor of the Mishnah understood the first five mishnayot to treat permanent injuries exclusively, it would make sense for him to shift from that to the related topic of temporary damages, which he announces by giving specific examples of what he has in mind at the beginning of Mishnah 6. The first clause specifies amounts that may be in payment for all five elements in a temporary injury or, on the basis of the two following clauses, for degradation only. In either case, Rabbi Akiba's story makes the point that for him no considerations of status are relevant to computing compensation for degradation, but it is also an example of degrading oneself, and that leads the editor to associate this discussion with a more general ruling about injuring oneself or one's property in any way. The last Mishnah stipulates that after the remedies have been paid, forgiveness must be sought and granted, and it also rules in cases where no forgiveness is necessary, that is, where the victim asked to be victimized. For someone used to organization by topic, this potpourri of subjects in this order would be perplexing, but one who understands associative reasoning would find the organization of this chapter understandable and even artistically elegant.

If one assumes, on the basis of the context provided by the following two clauses, that the opening clause of Mishnah 6 refers to degradation only, there are three methods specified for computing the compensation for degradation in Mishnah 6, only one of which conforms to the formula in Mishnah 1. Specifically, Mishnah 1 and the general principle in Mishnah 6 provide that the award depends on the social status of the individuals involved; the opening clause of Mishnah 6 stipulates specific amounts for specific injuries; and Rabbi Akiba argues against any consideration of social status in the computation. Because the opening clause of Mishnah 6 is not identified as the minority opinion of an individual, the later tradition, recorded in the Gemara's discussion of this Mishnah, sought to reconcile it with the general principle which immediately follows it by assuming that the specified amounts are awarded only to the most honored victim, but lesser people would get less according to the general principle. Since the Mishnah gives no hint that the first clause is about the most honored class, it would probably be more plausible to say that the amounts specified apply to the generality of mankind, but allowances must be made for unusually high or low social status, as according to the general principle. In either case, Rabbi Akiba then expresses his minority opinion that social status should not be considered in computing degradation.

The Mishnah which follows reiterates one important feature of Jewish law. There is no pause or demarcation between the Mishnah's stipulation of the remedies for personal injury and its requirement that the tortfeasor ask the victim's forgiveness. This is a further expression of themes we saw in biblical law, that is, the conviction that life is all of one piece and the consequent intertwining of law with morality and religion. Japanese law is similar: after making restitution, the assailant must apologize to the victim and the emperor for injuring both the individual and the social order.

Americans, especially those familiar with American law, might find the Mishnah's demand for asking forgiveness strange and inappropriate for a code of law. That is because Americans are used to separating church and state, and they object to legislating morality. These principles, deeply rooted in the American psyche, have some important advantages. They prevent the imposition of a specific form of piety or morality, thereby guaranteeing individual freedom and fostering religious and moral debate and interchange.

Isolating the law from religion and morality, however, is artificial: life is not lived in neatly divided compartments of law, religion, and morality. Consequently American legislators and jurists are constantly trying to provide for the religious and moral dimensions of life in an indirect way through cover of statute, precedent, or the general principle of equity. In contrast, religious legal systems have no qualms about addressing the religious and moral factors of a situation because they assume that life is a seamless whole. They therefore can go unobtrusively from legal remedies to moral and personal ones, as Mishnah 7 does, without worrying about overstepping their jurisdiction. This enables them to treat legal problems more adequately and fully than American law can.

*Mishnah, Bava Kamma, chap. 8:*

*Mishnah 1.* He who injures a person is liable on five counts: for damages, for pain, for healing, for loss of time, and for insult.

"For damages"—how is this assessed? If he blinded another's eye, cut off his hand, or crippled his leg, we consider the injured person as if he were a slave to be sold in the market and we estimate how much he was worth beforehand and how much he is worth now.

"For the pain"—if he burned him with a spit or a nail, even if he did so on his fingernail, where no wound is produced, we estimate how much a man of his type would demand to suffer such pain.

"For healing"—if he struck him, he must heal him. If ulcerations appear on the victim's body, the injurer is liable if the ulcerations are the result of the blow, but not otherwise. If the wound healed and then broke open, healed and broke open again, he continues to be responsible for healing him, but once the wound is completely healed, he is no longer responsible to heal him.

"For loss of time"—we consider the victim as if he were a guard of cucumber patches since the tortfeasor already gave him compensation for his hand or foot.

"For indignity"—everything depends upon the (social standing of the) offender and offended. If someone insults a naked man, a blind man, or a sleeping man, he is liable; a sleeping man who insults someone else is free of liability. If someone falls off a roof and causes injury and insult, he is liable for the damages but not for the insult, as it says, "And she puts forth her hand and grabs hold of his genitals" (Deuteronomy 25:11), implying that a person is liable for insult only if he acts with intent.

*Mishnah 2.* This is the additional liability of a human tortfeasor over an animal (literally, "an ox"): a person must pay compensation for damages, pain, healing, loss of time, and insult, and he must pay damages for causing a miscarriage, but an animal creates liability only for damages, and then not for miscarriages.

*Mishnah 3.* One who strikes his father or mother but does not wound them, and one who injures another person on the Day of Atonement, are liable on all counts. One who injures a Hebrew slave is liable on all counts, except for loss of time if the slave is his. One who injures a Canaanite slave belonging to someone else is liable on all counts. R. Judah says: slaves are not entitled to compensation for insult.

*Mishnah 4.* It is a bad thing to knock against a deaf-mute, a mentally defective person, or a minor, since one who injures any one of them is liable, but if any one of them wounds someone else, he is not liable. It is a bad thing to knock against a slave or a woman since one who injures either of them is liable, but if they wound others, they are not liable, except that they must pay compensation later if the woman is divorced or the slave freed.

*Mishnah 5.* One who strikes and wounds his father or mother, and one who injures another person on the Sabbath, are free of liability on all counts because such a person is subject to the death penalty. One who injures his own Canaanite slave is free of liability on all counts.

*Mishnah 6.* One who hits another person with his fist must pay him a *sela*. R. Judah says in the name of R. Jose the Galilean: a *maneh*. If he slapped him, he must pay two hundred *zuz*; if he hit him with the back of his hand, he must pay him four hundred *zuz*. If he pulled his ear, tore out his hair, spat at him and the spittle reached him, stripped his cloak from him, or bared the head of a woman in the market, he must pay four hundred *zuz*. This is the general principle: everything depends upon a person's dignity. R. Akiba said: we must consider even the poorest in Israel as if they were freemen who lost their estates, for they are the children of Abraham, Isaac, and Jacob.

There was a case where a man uncovered a woman's head in the marketplace. She came before R. Akiba, and he fined the man four hundred *zuz*. The defendant said: "Rabbi, grant me time (to pay)," and he gave him time. The defendant kept an eye out for her, and when she was standing at the entrance of her courtyard, he broke a cruse containing an *issar*'s worth of oil in front of her. She uncovered her head, scooped up the oil with her hand, and applied it to her hair. He had set up eyewitnesses against her, and he came before R. Akiba and said to him: "Rabbi, to one such as this I must pay four hundred *zuz*?" R. Akiba replied, "You have said nothing: a person is not permitted to injure himself, but if he does so, he is free of liability; if others injure him, they are liable. Similarly, a person is not permitted to cut off his own plants, but if he does so, he is free of liability, but if others cut down his plants, they are liable."

*Mishnah 7.* Even though the tortfeasor pays the victim, God does not forgive him until he asks the victim's forgiveness, as it is said, "Therefore, restore the man's wife and he will pray on your behalf" (Genesis 20:7). And how do we know that if the victim does not pardon him, he (the victim) is considered cruel? Because it says, "Abraham then prayed to God, and God healed Avimelekh, etc" (Genesis 20:17).

If a person says (to another), "Blind my eye," "Cut off my hand," or "Break my leg," he who does so is liable; even if he did it on condition that he would be held free of liability, he is still liable. If a person says (to another), "Tear my garment" or "Break my pitcher," he who does so is liable; but if he did it on condition that he would be free of liability, he is exempt. (If a person says to another), "Do such-and-such (an injury) to so-and-so on condition that you will be free of liability," he (the agent) is liable, whether the injuries are against the victim's person or his property.

## D. California Jury Instructions

The stylistic quality of the Mishnah, as well as its substantive brilliance, may be more obvious when it is compared to a contemporary document. Personal injury lawsuits in America may be tried by a jury of twelve laypersons, although in practice all but a small fraction of such disputes are settled without trial, or decided by a judge without a jury. When a jury trial is held, the professional lawyer-judge must instruct the jury as to the law it is to apply to the evidence.

In the past, judges' jury instructions often were given in a conversational manner by the judge, who would connect the applicable legal doctrine to the testimony and then give the jury his view of the evidence. The jury verdict precludes review of factual findings. Since jury instructions are matters of law, however, they are subject to review by an appeals court. With the more general use of stenographic court reporters to provide a verbatim transcript of the judge's instructions, appeals courts increasingly use supposed errors in those instructions to reverse jury verdicts they consider to be improper. As one might imagine, use of this legal pretext has multiplied the number of reversals on appeal and has encouraged disappointed litigants to appeal ever more frequently.

As judges' directives to juries have been subjected to full interpretive scrutiny, trial judges have become increasingly precise and cautious in what they say. They now often read their prepared instructions rather than orally discuss the case with the jury. The instructions themselves have become more technical, less spontaneous, and frequently more difficult for a lay person to understand. In the federal court system and in some states the formality of jury instruction has been further enhanced by the use of pattern or standard jury instructions which the judge is required to use in giving instructions on common points of law.

If we assume that the Mishnah represents the redaction of an oral tradition that was later reduced to writing to assist those who must decide specific cases, then the parallel to jury instructions is quite close. Note the similarities in voice and style between the Mishnah you have just read and the standard California Jury Instructions (BAJI) now used in personal injury cases.

Now put yourself in the position of an untutored judge or juror called on to decide the appropriate damages in a personal injury case in which the plaintiff has been permanently but partially disabled and suffers loss of income as well as medical costs, pain, and suffering. Which set of instructions (Mishnah or BAJI) tells you more clearly how to go about your task? Before deciding that lawyers have learned nothing in two thousand years, consider the respects in which the author of the Mishnah had advantages in determining some of the tricky elements of loss (such as the availability of a slave market to compute the lost capital value of an eye or an arm).

Superior Court, Los Angeles County, *California Jury Instructions Civil* (BAJI) (7th ed., 1986).
BAJI 14.00 (1975 Revision)
COMPENSATORY DAMAGES—PERSONAL INJURY
AND PROPERTY DAMAGE—
INTRODUCTORY

If, under the court's instructions, you find that plaintiff is entitled to a verdict against defendant, you must then award plaintiff damages in an amount that will reasonably compensate him for each of the following elements of claimed loss or harm (subject to being reduced, as you will be instructed, if you should find that the plaintiff was contributorily negligent), provided that you find that such harm or loss was (or will be) suffered by him and proximately caused by the act or omission upon which you base your finding of liability. The amount of such award shall include:

### BAJI 14.10 (1973 REVISION)
### MEASURE OF DAMAGES—PERSONAL INJURY—
### EXPENSES INCURRED

The reasonable value of medical (hospital and nursing) care, services and supplies reasonably required and actually given in the treatment of the plaintiff (and the present cash value of the reasonable value of similar items reasonably certain to be required and given in the future).

### BAJI 14.11
### MEASURE OF DAMAGES—PERSONAL INJURY—
### LOSS OF EARNINGS

The reasonable value of working time lost to date.

In determining this amount, you should consider evidence of plaintiff's earning capacity, his earnings, how he ordinarily occupied himself, and find what he was reasonably certain to have earned in the time lost if he had not been injured.

(A person's ability to work may have a monetary value even though he is not employed by another.)

(Also, the reasonable value of services performed by another in doing things for the plaintiff which, except for his injury, plaintiff would ordinarily do for himself.)

### BAJI 14.12
### MEASURE OF DAMAGES—PERSONAL INJURY—
### LOSS OF EARNING CAPACITY

The present cash value of earning capacity reasonably certain to be lost in the future as a result of the injury in question.

### BAJI 14.13
### MEASURE OF DAMAGES—PERSONAL INJURY—
### PAIN AND SUFFERING

Reasonable compensation for any pain, discomfort, fears, anxiety and other mental and emotional distress suffered by the plaintiff and of which his injury was a proximate cause (and for similar suffering reasonably certain to be experienced in the future from the same cause).

No definite standard (or method of calculation) is prescribed by law by which to fix reasonable compensation for pain and suffering. Nor is the opinion of any witness required as to the amount of such reasonable compensation. (Furthermore, the argument of counsel as to the amount of damages is not evidence of reasonable compensation.) In making an award for pain and suffering you shall exercise your authority with calm and reasonable judgment, and the damages you fix shall be just and reasonable in the light of the evidence.

### BAJI 14.65
### DAMAGES—AGGRAVATION OF PRE-EXISTING CONDITION

A person who has a condition or disability at the time of an injury is not entitled to recover damages therefor. However, he is entitled to recover damages for any aggravation of such pre-existing condition or disability proximately resulting from the injury.

This is true even if the person's condition or disability made him more susceptible to the possibility of ill effects than a normally healthy person would have been, and even if a normally healthy person probably would not have suffered any substantial injury.

Where a pre-existing condition or disability is so aggravated, the damages as to such condition or disability are limited to the additional injury caused by the aggravation.

### BAJI 14.66 (1977 Revision)
### DAMAGES—ADDITIONAL HARM RESULTING FROM ORIGINAL INJURY

If you find that the defendant is (liable) (subject to liability) for the original injury (if any) to the plaintiff, he is also (liable) (subject to liability):

(1) [For any disease which is contracted because of lowered vitality resulting from the original injury and which rendered the plaintiff peculiarly susceptible to such disease.]

(2) [For any aggravation of the original injury or additional injury caused by negligent medical or hospital treatment or care of the original injury.]

(3) [For any injury sustained in a subsequent accident which is a normal consequence of an impaired physical condition caused by the original injury and which would not have occurred had the plaintiff's physical condition not been impaired.]

### BAJI 14.50 (1977 Revision)
### MEASURE OF DAMAGES—DEATH OF ADULT

The heirs of _____, deceased, are (the real parties in interest in this action; they are) _____, the widow, (and _____, _____, the child(ren)) of the deceased.

If, under the court's instructions, you find that plaintiff(s) (is) (are) entitled to recover against the defendant, you will award as damages such sum as, under all the circumstances of the case, will be just compensation for the loss which each heir has suffered by reason of the death of _____ deceased.

In determining such loss, you may consider the financial support, if any, which each of said heirs would have received from the deceased except for his death, and the right to receive support, if any, which each of said heirs has lost by reason of his death.

(The right of one person to receive support from another is not destroyed by the fact that the former does not need the support, nor by the fact that the latter has not provided it.)

You may also consider:

1. The age of the deceased and of each heir;

2. The health of the deceased and each heir immediately prior to death;

3. The respective life expectancy of the deceased and of each heir;

4. Whether the deceased was kindly, affectionate or otherwise;

5. The disposition of the deceased to contribute financially to support said heirs;

6. The earning capacity of the deceased;

7. His habits of industry and thrift; and

8. Any other facts shown by the evidence indicating what benefits each heir might reasonably have been expected to receive from the deceased had he lived.

With respect to life expectancies, you will only be concerned with the shorter of two, that of an heir or that of the decedent, as one can derive a benefit from the life of another only so long as both are alive.

Also you will award reasonable compensation for the loss of love, companionship, comfort, affection, society, solace or moral support, (any loss of the enjoyment of sexual relations), (any loss of the physical assistance to a spouse in the operation or maintenance of the home).

In determining the loss which each heir has suffered, you are not to consider:

1. Any pain or suffering of the decedent;

2. Any grief or sorrow of his heirs; or

3. The poverty or wealth of any heir.

(Also, you shall include in your award an amount that will compensate for whatever reasonable expense was paid out or incurred for funeral services in memory of the decedent and (or) for burial (disposition) of the body. In determining that amount, you shall consider the decedent's station in life and the financial condition of his estate, as these circumstances have been shown by the evidence.)

## E. Gemara on Injuries: Bava Kamma 83b–84a, 85a–86a, 86b, 90b

The primary talmudic discussion of personal injuries is based on the Mishnah in the previous section. The Gemara's style, however, is quite different from that of the Mishnah, varying from a close, linguistic exegesis of a text to a discussion of various possible constructions of precedents to historical tidbits, homilies, and medical cures. Often a question is discussed, the possible resolutions are suggested, and then the matter is left undecided. Those stylistic features obviously caused major headaches for the later codifiers and judges who had to render decisions in cases before them, but they give the Talmud a great deal of life and interest. Simply to understand the Gemara, however, the reader must be aware of the following features of its reasoning and style:

### 1. *The Purpose of the Gemara*

The primary purpose of the Gemara is to explain the laws stated in the Mishnah. It typically concerns itself with the following issues:

a. The meaning of the law as stated in the Mishnah if it is unclear or open to several interpretations.

b. The source of authority for the law, whether in scripture, precedent, or in common reason.

c. The identity of the author of the law.

d. Apparent conflicts between this law and other laws in the code, other precedents, or other rulings by the author.

e. The scope and ambit of the rule announced in the Mishnah and how it is to be applied by analogy to new cases.

### 2. *The Style of the Gemara*

The style of the Gemara may be more understandable to the uninitiated reader if it is compared to a set of lecture notes, complete with the teacher's jokes and excursions. To this day in American law schools a good set of class notes will be cherished and passed on from one generation of students to the next, saving students the inconvenience of having to come or stay awake in class. Like the Gemara, such notes often go off on tangents, both legal and nonlegal, since human conversations are not rigidly organized by topic. The Gemara frequently includes discussion of topics which are suggested by association with the topic under discussion. We saw subjects strung together by association in the Covenant Code of Exodus and the Mishnah; the Gemara's use of this organizing principle is similar, but more extended.

### 3. Judicial Precedent in Jewish Law

The Jewish legal system relies heavily on judicial precedents. The Gemara indicates the source of a precedent by using one of a set of conventional, introductory phrases to the citation. Tannaitic precedents are indicated in the Gemara by phrases such as "Our rabbis taught," "Come and hear," or "A Tanna taught."

### 4. Legal Interpretation of a Verse

When a law derives from a biblical verse, judges will try to justify their decisions as a plausible rendering of that verse. That does not mean that they will always adhere to the original intent of the verse. In Jewish law, as in American law, the words of a law are often interpreted in ways that the original codifiers could not have imagined, let alone intended. Nevertheless, judges attempt to link their decisions to the text of the law to preserve a sense of continuity and to give their decisions authority. They often cite other laws in the same code to explain the law in question on the assumption that the code is consistent throughout in both style and substance. Hence the numerous cross-references in the Gemara, even to seemingly unrelated laws.

### 5. Changes of Position in the Gemara

The style of the Gemara is similar to that of the Midrash Halakhah in that the text often does not alert the reader to a shift from the analysis of one position to a consideration of another. If anything, that is an even greater problem in the extended discussions of the Gemara than it was in the relatively short arguments of the Midrash Halakhah. Like the Midrash Halakhah, the Gemara lacks punctuation marks, but it does have clue words that help to identify the steps in the argument. They are not always as helpful as one would hope, however, and sometimes determining how a given passage fits into the discussion can be open to lively debate.

The first part of the following selection is most of the Gemara's discussion of "eye for an eye." The Gemara interprets the Exodus verse to mean that monetary compensation is the remedy for personal injury rather than retribution. It provides ten separate proofs for that position. Do not worry about understanding the details of each proof; note only how elaborate and defensive the Gemara is in supporting its contention. When an interpretation is sound, one or two demonstrations of its reasonableness should be ample. That the rabbis adduced ten different proofs of the pecuniary interpretation of "eye for an eye" indicates that they recognized that the original text does not mean that at all. The Gemara itself records the opinion of Rabbi Eliezer that the verse is to be taken literally, and it reinterprets his remarks implausibly in order to make everyone seem to agree. We have here a clear instance of judges interpreting a law against its plain meaning. When originally promulgated, "eye for an eye" was a relatively humanitarian reform, for societies theretofore had inflicted the death penalty and other disproportionate remedies for permanent injuries. By the rabbinic period, civilization had moved on, and now the reform was morally unacceptable. Since the rabbis were convinced that God's law is good, they sought ways to adjust the received law to their understanding of morality, although the interpretive path that enabled them to do so was tortured.

This selection also illustrates several other general features of the Gemara. Proofs are presented to justify interpreting the Bible as requiring compensation instead of retaliation. In some instances the Gemara shows that a particular line of reasoning does not prove that compensation is the correct interpretation because the biblical passage in which it is based can equally tolerate an interpretation that would require retaliation. That does not mean, however, that retaliation has now been proven to be the correct interpretation; it only means that a particular proof for compensation can be refuted because the verse which serves as its basis can be read differently. One must distinguish three logical possibilities: refuting a proof, refuting a position, and establishing a contradictory position.

The Gemara treats a number of issues which the Mishnah does not even mention, including the privilege of the victim to refuse the free medical services of a doctor suggested by the offender and remedies for illegal incarceration. The Gemara supports its rulings on these points in a variety of ways: the refusal of proffered medical services is rationalized by the aphorism that "a physician who heals for nothing is worth nothing"; the remedy for incarceration is based on linguistic elements in the Torah text regarding "wound for wound" and "he shall surely heal" in Exodus 21:25 and 21:19 which are taken to be unusual (even though they are not unusual at all). Precedent also plays a major role, even to the extent of motivating an implausible reading of a text. So, for example, in this selection the Amoraim assume that the Mishnah is only about permanent injuries, despite its clauses about spitting and healing. The Gemara records that the disposition of cases of temporary injuries was a matter of dispute to the fourth century, when Rava ultimately decides one way and Abbaye another. These sources of the law—common experience, interpretation of a statute, and precedent—are familiar to students of other legal systems.

The Gemara selection is typical in seeking to establish the author of the position announced in the Mishnah. The Gemara is interested in finding out whether a statement reported anonymously is the opinion of the majority or merely the opinion of one rabbi whose name was dropped in the course of oral transmission. The answer to that question determines the degree of authority to be attributed to the precedent. Our case is one example of another reason why the Gemara often seeks to identify an anonymous author: people usually make specific decisions in consonance with their general principles, and therefore knowing the identity of the author may help later judges apply his decision correctly to new cases. The instance before us is a particularly interesting one because it articulates completely different views of the nature of human dignity.

The Babylonian Amoraim continually faced the basic problem of determing what precisely were the objects to which the words of the Mishnah referred. Although the case in our selection is settled rather easily, there are times when the Gemara spends pages on such issues. In our own day, even with fast, transcontinental transportation and considerable international trade, citizens of one country may yet be unfamiliar with many of the objects that one encounters in everyday life in another country. The Babylonian Amoraim were unfamiliar with the names and functions of objects in common use in Israel in their own time, not to mention those in use centuries before.

The last paragraph of the selection is a good example of how the Gemara moves by association from the discussion of one topic to another. To identify the coin to which the Mishnah refers, the Gemara cites a precedent that answers the question but also addresses a completely different question, the eligibility of witnesses to act as judges. The apparently extraneous discussion lasts for only a paragraph, but in other instances the Gemara can go on for pages. This can make life difficult for a judge or codifier who needs to know the Gemara's total discussion on any given topic. Most of the Gemara on a topic probably will be found in the tractate and chapter where the Mishnah treats the issue, but crucial elements may be located in completely different places, where the topic is raised tangentially. The only way to know any subject, at least before helpful codes and indices were developed, was to know the whole Gemara!

The selections of Talmud are based on the cited sections of the Mishnah on personal injuries. The talmudic comments follow the order of the Mishnah, and so the reader may want to review the Mishnah to understand the context and order of these talmudic passages.

Note: "Rabbi" is the title of a tannaitic rabbi; "Rav" is the title of a Babylonian, amoraic rabbi, although some amoraic rabbis are referred to only by name (for example, Abbaye, Rava). As we shall see, the distinction in titles is due to the conviction that only rabbis ordained in Israel in the chain of tradition had full judicial authority. In the Middle Ages and thereafter, when the chain of ordination had been broken, the titles are no longer sharply differentiated. "Rabbi" by itself denotes Rabbi Judah, the president of the Sanhedrin in the late second and early third centuries C.E.; as editor of the Mishnah, he is rabbi par excellence, and hence the honorific of referring to him by his title alone.

*Bava Kamma* 83b–84a:
[Proof #1] Why is it compensation that the Mishnah requires? God said, "eye for an eye," and presumably that means actually putting out the eye of the offender.—Do not let that interpretation enter your mind, for it has been taught in a Baraita: You might think that where someone blinded another person's eye, the offender's own eye should be blinded, or where someone cuts off another person's hand, the offender's own hand should be cut off, or if someone broke another person's leg, the offender's own leg should be broken, but the Torah says, "He that smites a man. . . . He that smites an animal . . .": the fact that both appear in the same context indicates that just as compenstion is to be paid in the case of smiting an animal, so too compensation is to be paid in the case of smiting a man.

[Proof #2] And if you want an alternative proof, notice that God says, "You may not accept a ransom for the life of a murderer who is guilty of a capital crime" (Numbers 35:31), implying that it is only for the life of a murderer that you do not take a ransom, but you do take a ransom for the destruction of bodily parts that do not grow back.

As for the first proof, to what verse regarding smiting does it refer? If it is referring to the verse, "Whoever smites an animal shall pay for it, and whoever smites a man shall be put to death" (Lev. 24:21), that verse refers to a case where someone smites and kills (and not where one only wounds). Consequently the quotation must be from this text: "Whoever smites an animal mortally shall pay for it: life for life"

(Lev. 24:18), and close by it is the verse, "When a man maims his neighbor, as he did so shall it be done to him (Lev. 24:19).—But that text does not mention the word "smite"!—We speak of the effects of smiting implied in both texts to tell us that just as compensation is to be paid in the case of smiting an animal, so too compensation is to be paid in the case of smiting a man.—But is it not written, "One who smites anyone mortally shall surely be put to death" (Lev. 24:17) (and "fracture for fracture, eye for eye" appears in the same context; consequently Lev. 24:17 must refer to infliction of injury rather than murder, and yet retaliation is mandated)?—Even that verse refers to payment of pecuniary compensation.—How do you know that it refers to monetary compensation? Why not say that it really means capital punishment?—Do not let that enter your mind, for first, it is juxtaposed with the verse, "Whoever smites an animal shall pay for it," and moreover, after that verse (Lev. 24:17) is the verse, "When a man maims his neighbor, as he did so shall it be done to him" (Lev. 24:19), thus proving that it means monetary compensation. . . .

But since it is written, "You may not accept a ransom for the life of a murderer who is guilty of a capital crime" (implying the law of pecuniary compensation in the case of mere injury as according to Proof #2), why do I need the analogy made between smiting a man and smiting an animal (in Proof #1)?—It may be answered that if the law had been derived only from that verse, I might have said that the offender has the option of paying with the loss of his eye or with money equal to the value of his eye; we are therefore told that the inference is also from the case of the animal: just as one who smites an animal must pay with money, so too one who smites a man must pay with money.

[Proof #3] It was taught: Rabbi Dostai b. Judah says: "Eye for an eye" means pecuniary compensation.—You say pecuniary compensation, but perhaps it refers to actual retaliation by putting out the eye of the offender.—What then will you say when the eye of one was big and the eye of the other was little? In such a case how can I effectuate the parity which is clearly intended by "Eye for an eye"? And if you were to say that in all cases such as that take from him pecuniary compensation, the Torah says, "You shall have one standard" (Lev. 24:22), implying that the standard should be the same in all cases!—I might rejoin: what is the difficulty in such a case? Why not say that he deprived the victim of his eyesight and we will deprive him of his eyesight (without considering the sizes of the respective eyes)? For if you do not say this, [84a] how will we ever execute a small man who murders a large man or a large man who murders a small man? The Torah says, "You shall have one standard," implying that the standard should be the same in all cases! Rather we must say that the murderer took the victim's life and we will take his life, and similarly the offender took the victim's eyesight and we will take his eyesight.

[Since that interpretation is possible, no proof for compensation can be based on this line of reasoning.]

[Proof #4] Another Baraita taught: Rabbi Simeon b. Yohai says: "Eye for an eye" means monetary compensation.—You say monetary compensation, but perhaps it refers to actual retaliation by putting out the eye of the offender.—What then will you say if a blind man put out the eye of a sighted man, or if a cripple cut off part of the body of a man who is not crippled in that way, or if a lame man breaks off the leg of one who is not? How can I apply "Eye for an eye"? After all, the Torah said, "You shall have one standard," implying that the standard should be the same in all cases!—I might rejoin: what is the difficulty in this case? Why not say that it is only where it is possible to carry out the principle of retaliation that it is to be carried out, but where it is impossible, it is impossible, and the offender will have to be released altogether? For if you do not say this, what could we do if a person with a fatal, organic disease kills a healthy person (in which case the murderer could not be convicted by the testimony of witnesses according to *Sanhedrin* 78a)? You must therefore admit that it is only where it is possible to carry out the law of retaliation that it is to be invoked, but where it is impossible, it is impossible, and the offender will have to be released. [Therefore no proof for the principle of compensation can be derived from this line of reasoning since the text can be construed in line with the principle of retaliation.]

[Proof #5] The School of Rabbi Ishmael taught: Scripture says (literally), "so shall it be given in him" (Lev. 24:20), and there is no "giving" except in monetary terms.—But does that mean that in the beginning of the verse, i.e., "Whoever gives a wound in (inflicts a wound on) his friend" (ibid.), the word "giving" also refers to money? [Clearly not.]—But rather, the School of Rabbi Ishmael based its interpretation on the existence of a superfluous verse: since it has already been written, "And if a man maim his neighbor, as he has done so shall it be done to him" (Lev. 24:19), why, in the next verse, do we need (literally) "so it shall be given in him"? Learn from this redundancy that the latter verse refers to pecuniary compensation. But then why do I need the equally superfluous phrase in that verse, "as he gives (a blow that causes) an injury in a man"?—Since it was necessary to write, "so shall it be given in him" (i.e., the last clause of that verse), the text also writes, "as he gives (a blow that causes) an injury in a man" (i.e., the first clause of the verse to set the context for the necessary, latter clause).

[Proof #6] The School of Rabbi Hiyya taught: Scripture says, "hand in (for) hand" (Deut. 19:21), implying an article which is given from one hand to another, and what is that? Money. [The Hebrew prefix translated "for" in that verse also commonly means "in."]—But could you interpret the next words, i.e. "foot in (for) foot," along the same lines? [Clearly not.]—It may be replied that at the School of Rabbi Hiyya this text was expounded as a superfluous verse, for it has been written, "and you shall do to him as he plotted to do to his brother" (Deut. 19:19). If you assume actual retaliation for injury, why do I need the words, "hand in hand" (two verses later)? The existence of that phrase indicates that monetary compensation (and not retaliation) is intended.—But then why the phrase, "foot in foot"?—Since He wrote "hand in hand," He also wrote "foot in foot." [That is, the phrase "hand in hand" earlier in the verse led to the use of the same literary style when the verse came to describe wounds to the foot, even though the preposition "in" there does not carry the full meaning of the earlier usage.]

[Proof #7] Abbaye said: The principle of pecuniary compensation can be derived from the teaching of the School of Hezekiah, for the School of Hezekiah taught: "Eye for eye, life for life" (Ex. 21:24), but not life and eye for eye. Now if you assume that actual retaliation is intended, it could sometimes happen that both eye and life would be taken for eye, as, for instance, if the offender dies as he is being blinded. [Therefore compensation must be intended.]—But what difficulty is there here? Perhaps what it means is that we have to estimate whether the offender is able to live through the blinding of his eye or not: if he can, we exact retaliation, and if he cannot, we do not. And if, after we estimate that he can survive that punishment, we exact retaliation and he dies, then let him die, for we have learned regarding lashes (Makkot 3:14) that if they estimated that he could withstand the lashes due him but he died, the officer of the court is free of all blame. [Therefore there is no proof for the principle of compensation from this line of reasoning.]

[Proof #8] Rav Zevid said in the name of Rabbah: Scripture says, "wound for wound" (Ex.21:25). This tells us that compensation is to be made for pain even when depreciation is separately compensated. Now if you assume that actual retaliation is intended, would it not be that just as the victim suffered pain through the wound, the offender too would suffer pain through the mere act of retaliation? [How, then, could there be extra compensation for the pain involved, as indicated by the verse?]—What is the difficulty here? Why not say that a delicate person suffers more pain than someone less delicate, so that the practical import of the verse would be that the offender must pay for the difference in pain sustained [after retaliation is exacted. Therefore no proof can be derived from this line of reasoning for the principle of compensation since the verse can also be interpreted in line with the principle of retaliation.]

[Proof #9] Rav Papa said in the name of Rava: Scripture says, "he shall cause him to be thoroughly healed" (Ex. 21:19): this means that compensation is to be paid for healing even where depreciation is compensated separately. Now, if you assume that retaliation is intended, would it not be that just as the victim needs medical attention, the offender would also need that due to the act of retaliation? [But that is not provided for in Scripture, indicating that retaliation is not intended.]—What is the difficulty here? Why not say that there are people whose flesh heals speedily while there are others whose flesh does not heal speedily, so that the practical import of the Scripture verse is to require payment for the difference in medical expenses [after retaliation is exacted. Therefore this verse can be interpreted in line with the principle of retaliation and does not prove the principle of compensation.]

[Proof #10] Rav Ashi said: The principle of pecuniary compensation can be derived from the analogy of the word "for" (*tahat*) occurring in connection with injuring a man and the word "for" (*tahat*) occurring in connection with injuring an ox. Here the text reads, "eye for an eye" (Ex. 21:24), and there it reads "he shall surely pay ox for ox" (Ex. 21:36): just as in the latter text monetary compensation is stipulated, so too in the former.—On what basis do you compare "for" here (in regard to injuring a man) with "for" in regard to injuring an ox? Let us instead link it with the "for" in the verse that speaks of the killing of a man, i.e., "and shall give life for life" (Ex. 21:23) so that, just as in the case of murdering a man actual retaliation is exacted, so too in the case of injuring a man.—It can be said that it is more logical to link one case of injury with another rather than a case of injury with a case of murder.—But why not say, on the contrary, that it is more logical to link two laws that deal with a man than it is to link a law about a man to a law about an ox?—Rav Ashi therefore retracted his suggestion to use Ex. 21:36 and instead suggested the following: the principle of compensation is derived from the verse, "for (*tahat*) he has humbled her" (Deut. 22:29), where one case dealing with a person is linked to another, and one case dealing with injury is linked to another.

It was taught: Rabbi Eliezer said: "Eye for an eye" refers literally to removing the eye of the offender.—Can you possibly think that the verse is to be taken literally? Could Rabbi Eliezer disagree with all of the rest of the Tannaim enumerated above?—Rabbah therefore said: He only meant to say that the injured person should not be valued as if he were a slave (in order to calculate the amount for depreciation).—Abbaye said to him: How else can he be valued? As a free man? Can the bodily value of a free man be ascertained?—Rav Ashi therefore said: He meant to say that the valuation should be made not on the basis of the eye of the victim but rather on the basis of the eye of the offender (since then pecuniary compensation will serve more directly as a substitute for retaliation).

*Bava Kamma* 85a–86a:

If the offender says to the injured person, "I can personally act as your healer (and therefore you do not need to consult a physician), the victim can refuse, saying, "You are in my eyes like a lurking lion" (i.e., I am not prepared to trust you). If the offender says to him, "I will bring you a physician who will heal you for nothing," the victim can respond, "A physician who heals for nothing is worth nothing." If the offender says to him, "I will bring you a physician from afar," the victim can refuse, saying, "If the physician is a long way off, the eye will be blind before he arrives." If, on the other hand, the victim says to the offender, "Give the money for medical expenses to me personally, and I will cure myself," the offender can refuse, saying, "You might neglect yourself and then exact more money from me for your cure." Even if the victim says to him, "Let us agree on a fixed sum for my medical expenses," the offender can object and say, "Under those circumstances there is all the more danger that you might neglect yourself (and remain a cripple), and I will consequently be called, 'an injuring ox.'"

A Tanna taught: all of the other four items (pain, healing, loss of time, and degradation) must be paid even if depreciation is paid. How is that ruling derived? (1) Rav Zevid said in the name of Rava: Scripture says, "wound for wound" (Ex. 21:25) to indicate the payment of damages for pain even where depreciation is paid.—But that verse is required [85b] to extend liability for depreciation to cases where the injury was inflicted inadvertently just as it exists where the injury was inflicted willfully, and to cases where the injury was inflicted under compulsion just as it exists where the injury was inflicted willingly.—If the verse was required only for such a rule, then Scripture would have said, "wound in the case of wound" (*petza b'petza*). Why does it say, "wound for wound" (*petza tahat petza*)? To teach us that both inferences are to be drawn from the phrase. (2) Rav Papa said in the name of Rava: Scripture says: "and he shall surely be healed" (Ex. 21:19, using an emphatic form), indicating that medical expenses must be paid even when depreciation is paid independently.—But that verse is necessary for the ruling that we have in the name of the School of Rabbi Ishmael, who taught that it is on the basis of this verse that we derive God's authorization for the physician to heal (instead of leaving that totally to God).—If that were the only ruling to be derived from this clause, then Scripture would have read, "and the physician shall cure him." The fact that it does not say that indicates that we can also derive the ruling from this clause that medical expenses must be paid even when depreciation is paid.—But still, is not the clause necessary, as we said above, to emphasize that the victim must be thoroughly healed?—If that were all that was intended, then Scripture would have written either "to heal and to heal" (i.e., a repetition of the infinitive) or "he shall heal, he shall heal" (i.e., a repetition of the finite form of the verb). Why say, "to heal, he shall heal" (i.e., the infinitive followed by the finite form, a construction commonly used in the Bible for emphasis) unless to prove also that medical expenses must be paid even when depreciation is paid. [Translator's note: The principle of independent payment for each of the elements is not proved for loss of time and degradation, but apparently the above two proofs with regard to pain and medical expenses are enough to establish that principle, and then it can be applied to all five elements.]

From this discussion it would appear that a case could arise where the other four elements would be paid even where no depreciation was caused. How could such cases arise? Regarding pain the case could be like the one described in our Mishnah: "Pain—if he burned him either with a spit or with a nail, even on his fingernail, i.e., a place where no bruise could be caused." Medical expenses could be required where someone was suffering from a wound which was in the process of healing, but the offender applied a very strong ointment on the wound which made the skin look unnaturally white so that other ointments had to be applied to restore the natural color of his skin (and the offender must pay for those as well). Loss of time (without depreciation) could occur where the offender wrongfully locked him up in a room and thereby kept him idle. Degradation (without depreciation) could occur where the offender spat in his face. . . .

Rabbah asked: What would be the law regarding payment for loss of time in a case where the injured person is less valuable for the time being (i.e., where the injury is not permanent)—for example, where the offender broke the victim's arm, but the victim will ultimately recover fully? And what about depreciation in such a case? Since the arm will ultimately be fully healed, should the offender pay the victim nothing for that, or should he be required to pay him since for the time being the offender has diminished the victim's value?—Come and hear (a Tannaitic ruling): (Capital punishment exempts a person and his estate from civil liability, but) "if someone strikes his father and mother but does not bruise them (so that he has not committed the capital offense of Ex. 21:15), or if he injures another person on the Day of Atonement (which also involves no capital punishment by a human court, according to the Rabbinic interpretation of Lev. 23:30), [86a] he is liable for all of the five elements." Now, how are we to picture no bruise being made in such a case? Does this not refer to a situation where, for example, he struck him on his arm which will ultimately recover (since no bruise was made), and it is nevertheless stated that "he is liable for all five elements (including depreciation)?—. . . No, it could be that we are dealing with a case where he smeared a depilatory on their heads so that no hair will ever grow there again (i.e., the Tannaitic source is not determinative since it may be dealing with a permanent injury). . . .

This matter that was doubtful to Rabbah was quite certain to (his students), Abbaye taking one view and Rava taking the other. For it was stated: If someone struck another on his arm and the arm was broken but he would ultimately recover completely, Abbaye said that the offender must pay for depreciation (literally, "general loss of time") plus particular loss of time, while Rava said that he need only pay him for his loss of time for each day until he recovers. . . .

"Degradation: all is to be estimated according to the status of the offender and the offended." According to whom is our Mishnah? Apparently it is neither according to Rabbi Meir nor according to Rabbi Judah, but it is rather according to Rabbi Simeon, for it was taught: "All injured people shall be considered as if they were free men who have been impoverished, for they are, after all, the children of Abraham, Isaac, and Jacob, according to Rabbi Meir; Rabbi Judah says that degradation in the case of the eminent man must be estimated in accordance with his eminence, while the insignificant man's degradation must be estimated in accordance with his insignificance; Rabbi Simeon says that we should consider wealthy persons as if they are free men who became impoverished (because if we consider them as the rich people they are, there will be no end to the money owing to them for their degradation), while degradation for the poor should be estimated for all of them at the level of the least among them." According to whom could our Mishnah be? If you try Rabbi Meir, our Mishnah states that all are to be estimated in accordance with the status of the offender and the offended, while Rabbi Meir treats all alike. If you try Rabbi Judah, our Mishnah subsequently (in its next clause on p. 86b) states that he who insults a blind person is liable, but Rabbi Judah says that payment for degradation does not apply to a blind person. Therefore the Mishnah must be according to Rabbi Simeon— You could even say that it is in accordance with Rabbi Judah, for when Rabbi Judah says that payment for degradation does not apply to a blind person, that only means that payment will not be exacted from him if he injures someone else, but if someone else injures him, he must be paid for the degradation he suffers.—But the concluding clause of the Mishnah states, "If he insulted a sleeping person, he is liable to pay for degradation, while a sleeping person who insulted others is exempt," and no similar statement is made in regard to a blind person such that a blind person who insults others would be exempt. This surely implies that, for the Mishnah, degradation applies to a blind person, whether he is the offender or the victim (in contradiction to Rabbi Judah). It is therefore clear that the Mishnaic statements are according to Rabbi Simeon.

*Bava Kamma* 86b:
Rav Abba b. Memel asked: What would be the law where the offender humiliated a person who was asleep and who died before wak-

ing?—What is the principle involved in this question?—Rav Zevid said: The principle involved is this: Is degradation paid because of the insult to the aggrieved party, and since the victim in this case died before waking, he was never insulted and so no payment should be made; or is it because of the public disgrace involved, and since there was public disgrace involved in this case (since the degrading words or actions were open to public witness), payment should be made to the heirs?—Come and hear: "Rabbi Meir says: A deaf-mute and a minor are eligible for degradation payments, but an idiot is not eligible for degradation payments." Now, if you say that degradation is paid because of the public disgrace, then no difficulty arises; it then makes sense for a minor to be paid for degradation. But if you say that degradation is paid because of the insult, is a minor capable of feeling insulted?—What then? You say that degradation is paid because of disgrace? If so, why should the same not apply in the case of an idiot?—Here it may be said that the idiot by himself constitutes a public disgrace that is second to none. But in any case, why not conclude from Rabbi Meir's statement that degradation is paid because of public disgrace, for if it were because of insult, can a minor feel insulted?—As Rav Papa stated in another connection, if a minor feels abashed when he is reminded of the insult, then degradation must be paid to him; so also here Rabbi Meir may be referring to a minor who feels abashed when reminded of the insult.

Rav Papa, however, said that the principle involved in Rav Abba's question was this: Is degradation paid because of personal insult, and since he did not suffer any insult in this case due to his death, nothing should be paid for degradation to his heirs, or is degradation paid because of the insult suffered by the family?—Come and hear: "A deaf-mute and a minor must be paid for degradation, but an idiot need not be." Now, if you say that degradation is paid because of the insult suffered by the family, no difficulty arises, for then it makes sense that a minor should be paid for degradation. But if you say that degradation is paid on account of personal insult, can a minor suffer personal insult?—What then? Do you say that degradation is paid because of the insult sustained by members of the family? Why then should the same not apply in the case of an idiot?—Perhaps because an idiot by himself constitutes an insult to them which is second to none. But in any case, why not conclude from that Tannaitic statement that degradation is paid because of the insult suffered by the family, for if it were because of personal insult, can a minor suffer personal insult?—Rav Papa said: Yes, if the minor feels insulted when the insult is mentioned to him, as we have learned: "Rabbi [Judah, the President] says: Degradation must be paid to a deaf-mute, but it need not be paid to an idiot, and with regard to a minor, sometimes it must be paid and sometimes not." The former case referred to in the last clause of Rabbi's statement must be one in which the minor would feel insulted if the insult were mentioned to him, and the latter must be a case where he would not feel insulted if reminded of the insult.

*Bava Kamma* 90b

It was asked: Is it a Tyrian *maneh* (a coin) of which the Mishnah speaks, or is it only a local *maneh* (which is only an eighth of a Tyrian *maneh*) which is referred to? — Come and hear: "A certain person boxed another's ear and the case was brought before Rabbi Judah, the President. He said to him: 'Here I am, and here is also Rabbi Yose, the Galilean, so that you have to pay the plaintiff a Tyrian *maneh.*'" Does this not show that it is a Tyrian *maneh* which the Mishnah refers to? — It does.

What is the meaning of, "Here I am, and here is also Rabbi Yose, the Galilean"? If you say he meant, "Here I am who witnessed you doing this, and here is also Rabbi Yose, the Galilean, who holds that the payment should be a Tyrian *maneh,*" would this not imply that a witness is eligible to act also as a judge (since Rabbi Yose would be acting as both)? But how can this be the case since it was taught, "If the members of the Sanhedrin saw one man killing another, some of them should act as witnesses and the others should act as judges, according to Rabbi Tarfon. Rabbi Akiba, on the other hand, says that all of them are considered witnesses, and a witness may not act as a judge" (*San.* 34b; *B.B.* 114a). Now, even Rabbi Tarfon only meant that part of them should act as witnesses and the others as judges, but did he ever say that a witness giving evidence should be able to act in the same trial as a judge? — The ruling there (in the case of the Sanhedrin witnessing a murder) refers only to a case where they saw the murder taking place at night, when they were barred from acting in a judicial capacity (since judgments could only be handed down during the daytime, according to *San.* 4:1, but that still leaves the possibility that if they saw the murder during the daytime they could immediately act in the dual capacity of judges and witnesses). Or, if you prefer, I may say that this is what Rabbi Judah, the president, said to the offender: Since I am here, and I concur with Rabbi Yose, the Galilean, who stated that a Tyrian *maneh* should be paid, and since there are here witnesses testifying against you, go and pay the plaintiff a Tyrian *maneh.*

Does Rabbi Akiba really maintain that a witness cannot simultaneously act as a judge? After all, this has been taught: "'And one smites another with a stone or with his fist:' Simeon the Temanite remarked that just as a fist is a concrete object that can be submitted for examination to the assembly of the judges and the witnesses, so also it is necessary that all other instruments should be available for submission to the assembly of the judges and the witnesses, which excludes cases where the murder weapon disappeared after the witnesses saw it. Rabbi Akiba said to him: (Even if the weapon was placed before the judges), did the actual killing take place before the judges of the court such that they should be expected to know how many times the murderer struck the victim or the part of the body upon which he struck

him, whether on his thigh or on the tip of his heart? Again, if the murderer threw a man down from the top of a roof or from the top of a
mansion and the victim died, would the court have to go to the mansion, or would the mansion have to go to the court? Again, if in the
meantime the mansion collapsed, would it be necessary to erect it
anew (for the court's inspection)? [Clearly not.] We must therefore say
that just as a fist is a definite object that was in sight of the witnesses
(when the murder was committed), so too it is necessary that all other
weapons should have been in sight of the witnesses, which excludes a
case where the weapon was not visible in the hand of the murderer,
who is therefore free." We see then that Rabbi Akiba said to him,
"Did the actual killing take place before the judges of the court such
that they should be expected to know how many times the murderer
struck the victim?" which would imply that if he had killed him in
their presence, they who were the witnesses would have been able to
act as judges!—He was arguing from the point of view of Rabbi Shimon the Temanite, but that was not his own opinion.

## F. Sectarian Laws of Injuries

At the outset of this topic it was noted briefly that there were
many groups of Jews during the Second Temple period, and it was only
the later tradition that determined that the Pharisaic tradition should
be normative and the others sectarian. The most important groups
aside from the Pharisees were the Sadducees, the Essenes, and the
Zealots (described in Section A3 of this topic); the Samaritans and the
Hebrew Christians (see Topic V, Section E4); and the Christians, whose
deviation from Pharisaic Judaism in its later, rabbinic form will be discussed in some detail in Topic V, Section E3. Some sources from the
Second Temple and rabbinic periods also mention the Bana'im (*Mik-
va'ot* 9:6) and the Hemerobaptists (*Tovelei Shaharit*)—"morning bath-
ers" (see *Tosefta, Yadaim,* end; *Berakhot* 22a), of whom John the Baptist was probably a member. Each of these groups had unique beliefs
and practices, and yet their histories, associations, and segments of
their religions make it clear that they were forms of Judaism. Consequently, one must view Palestinian Judaism in the last centuries of the
Second Temple period as a complex, fluid phenomenon, composed of
many elements and subject to the emergence of new ones at any time.
Moreover, Jewish groups outside of Israel developed their own laws,
customs, and beliefs, and that added yet further to the multifaceted nature of Judaism at this time.

Although most of the variations of these groups occurred in beliefs
and ritual laws, there are some differences in the laws of personal inju-

ries too. The Book of Jubilees, a book of the Pseudepigrapha written
during the second century B.C.E., does not accept the Pharisaic rendition of "eye for an eye" as monetary compensation. Rather, like Rabbi
Eliezer in the Talmud (see the end of the section cited from *Bava
Kamma* 84a), Jubilees apparently retains a literal interpretation of the
text:

> At the close of this jubilee Cain was killed after him (Adam) in the
> same year; for his house fell upon him and he died in the midst of his
> house, and he was killed by its stones; for with a stone he had killed
> Abel, and by a stone was he killed in righteous judgment. For this rea-
> son it was ordained on the heavenly tablets: "With the instrument
> with which a man kills his neighbor with the same shall he be killed;
> after the manner that he wounded him, in like manner shall they deal
> with him" (Jubilees 4:31–32).

Philo, of first century Alexandria, Egypt, indicates a totally different set of remedies from those of either the Torah or the Mishnah:

> Enough has been said for the present on the subject of poisoners, but
> we must not fail to observe that occasions often arise unsought in
> which a man commits murder without having come with this pur-
> pose in his mind or with any preparations, but has been carried away
> by anger, that intractable and malignant passion so highly injurious
> both to him who entertains it and to him against whom it is directed.
> Sometimes a man goes to the market-place through stress of business;
> he meets another of the more headstrong kind who sets about abusing
> or striking him, or it may be that he himself begins the quarrel; then
> when they have set to, he wishes to break off and escape quickly; he
> smites the other with his clenched fist or takes up a stone and throws
> it. Suppose that the blow strikes home, then if his opponent dies at
> once, the striker too must die and be treated as he has treated the
> other; but if that other is not killed on the spot by the blow, but is laid
> up with sickness and after keeping his bed and receiving the proper
> care gets up again and goes abroad, even though he is not sound on his
> feet and can only walk with the support of others or leaning on a staff,
> the striker must be fined twice over, first to make good the other's en-
> forced idleness and secondly to compensate for the cost of his cure.
> This payment will release him from the death penalty, even if the suf-
> ferer from the blow subsequently dies. For as he got better and walked
> abroad, his death may be due not to the blow but to other causes
> which often suddenly attack and put an end to persons whose bodily
> health is as sound as possible (Philo, *The Special Laws*, III, 104–107).

Philo restricts the enforcement of an eye for an eye to those cases in
which the injurer did his act maliciously (ibid., III, 195), and there he is
insistent that that is the appropriate penalty.

The legislators deserve censure who prescribe for malefactors punishments which do not resemble the crime, such as monetary fines for assaults, disenfranchisement for wounding or maiming another, expulsion from the country and perpetual banishment for willful murder, or imprisonment for theft. For inequality and unevenness is repugnant to the commonwealth which pursues truth. Our law exhorts us to equality when it ordains that the penalties inflicted on offenders should correspond to their actions, that their property should suffer if the wrongdoing affected their neighbor's property, and their bodies if the offence was a bodily injury, the penalty being determined according to the limb, part, or sense affected, while if his malice extended to taking another's life his own life should be forfeit. For to tolerate a system in which the crime and the punishment do not correspond, have no common ground, and belong to different categories is to subvert rather than uphold legality (ibid., III, 181–182).

Josephus, the first century Jewish general who was taken to Rome and wrote a history there, reflects an intermediary position between the literal interpretation of the Bible and its total substitution by monetary compensation in the literature of the rabbis.

He who maims a man shall undergo the same, being deprived of that limb whereof he deprived the other, unless indeed the maimed man be willing to accept money; for the law empowers the victim himself to assess the damage that has befallen him and makes this concession, unless he would show himself too severe (*Antiquities*, IV, 8.35.280).

And then, of course, there is the famous dictum of Jesus on this:

You have learned that they were told, "An eye for an eye, and a tooth for a tooth." But what I tell you is this: Do not set yourself against the man who wrongs you. If someone slaps you on the right cheek, turn and offer him your left (Matthew 5:38–39).

The words and the context indicate that this is advice to individuals; it is not clear that Jesus would organize a society on this basis. Nevertheless, this interpretation of eye for an eye has historically characterized Judaism for Christians in a negative light, for it has led them to believe that Jews and Jewish law are legalistic and vindictive in comparison to appropriate behavior for a Christian. They know little about the actual functioning of religious, Christian societies on this issue, and even less of the rabbinic understanding of the biblical statute.

The principle of an eye for an eye assumes that the court, or even the victim himself, executes the punishment, and it is in that form that the rabbis rejected its literal meaning. That *God* punishes in this way, however, was seen as a very positive phenomenon, indeed a mark of His justice. With regard to God, the principle is commonly referred to in rabbinic literature as "measure for measure," and the rabbis held that "all the judgments of the Holy One, blessed be He, are on the basis of measure for measure" (*Sanhedrin* 90a). Note that this is not simply the principle of fairness, that is, that the *degree* of punishment fit the crime. It is rather that the very *form* of punishment or reward is the same as that of the initial act.

Even before the rabbis, we have some examples of this principle in Second Temple Jewish literature. In the biblical book of Job, for example, Job's rewards of children and material goods in chapter 42 are directly—one is tempted to say, mechanically—parallel to his trials in chapters 1 and 2. Similarly, in Esther, Haman boasts, in 5:11, of his riches, the multitude of his children, and his rank at court, and these are precisely the three things in which he is smitten. The principle is also asserted in two books of the Apocrypha which were widely read and quoted by Jews. Chapter 11 of Wisdom of Solomon is almost entirely devoted to demonstrating the proposition that "One is punished by the very things by which he sins" (11:16), and the second century B.C.E. book, II Maccabees, approvingly gives historical examples of this doctrine.

> He (Jason) who had cast out many to lie unburied had no one to mourn for him; he had no funeral of any sort and no place in the tomb of his fathers (5:10).

> And this (the death of Menelaus) was eminently just: because he had committed many sins against the altar whose fire and ashes were holy, he met his death in ashes (13:8).

Rabbinic examples of the principle of measure for measure abound. To take one, in commenting on the drowning of the Egyptians in the Reed Sea, the rabbis note that this is parallel to Pharoah's plan to drown all of the Israelite first-born males.

> By the plan which the Egyptians devised to destroy Israel I judge them. They planned to destroy Israel by water, and I will punish them with nothing but water (*Mekhilta* to Exodus 14:26).

Similarly, "Samson went after his eyes, and therefore the Philistines plucked out his eyes; Absalom gloried in his hair, and therefore he was caught by his hair" (*Sotah* 1:8).

The same principle works in the opposite direction, for reward. "Joseph buried his father in Canaan and was therefore worthy that his bones be interred there" (*Sotah* 1:9). Commenting on the verse, "The Lord went before them by day in a pillar of cloud" (Exodus 13:21), the rabbis said:

> This is to teach that by the measure with which a man measures is it meted out to him. Abraham accompanied the ministering angels on their way (Genesis 18:16), and so the All-present accompanied his descendents in the wilderness forty years. With our father Abraham it is said, "I will fetch a morsel of bread" (Ibid. 5), and so the Holy One, blessed be He, caused manna to descend forty years. With Abraham it is said, "Let a little water be fetched" (Ibid. 4), and the Holy One, blessed be He, caused a well to ascend for his offspring in the wilderness (Numbers 21:17ff.). With Abraham it is said, "He ran to the herd (to fetch meat for his three angelic guests)" (Genesis 18:7), and the Holy One, blessed be He, drove along quails for his descendants (Numbers 11:31). With Abraham it is said, "Rest yourselves under a tree" (Genesis 18:4), and the Holy One, blessed be He, spread seven clouds of glory for his descendants, as it is said, "He spread a cloud for a covering, and fire to give light in the night" (Psalms 105:39). With Abraham it is written, "He stood by (literally, "over") them" (Genesis 18:8), and the Holy One, blessed be He, stood over his descendants to protect them in Egypt so that they would not be smitten by the plagues (*Mekhilta* on Exodus 13:21).

In this form, with reference to God, the principle was very popular in Second Temple literature of other Jewish sects too. Jubilees, for example, gives voice to the principle of retribution measure for measure in the exact same context as the rabbinic comment quoted:

> And all the peoples whom he (Pharoah) brought to pursue after Israel, the Lord our God cast them into the midst of the sea, into the depths of the abyss beneath the children of Israel, even as the people of Egypt had cast their (the Israelites') children into the river (48:14).

And retribution measure for measure is proclaimed in numerous passages of the New Testament. "He who does evil shall receive again the wrong that he has done," says Paul (Colossians 3:25), and such retribution is a favorite theme of the parables of Jesus. Thus the unforgiving debtor is refused forgiveness (Matthew 18:23–35); the slothful servant loses what he had (Matthew 25:14–30); he who will not use his affluence to help a brother's need will lose it for himself (Luke 12:15–21); and the man who refuses to part with an offending eye or hand will eventually lose his whole body in Gehenna (Matthew 5:29–30; Mark 9:43–48).

Therefore, even though there was considerable disagreement during Second Temple times about human retribution, there was remarkable agreement about the tenet that God works in a directly retributive way. With that theology one can understand why some Jewish sects were reluctant to abandon retribution in the human sphere. Nevertheless, the rabbis emphatically did.

These examples amply illustrate, however, that the rabbinic substitution of monetary compensation for retributive injury was not at all obvious to the Jews of the Second Temple period nor unanimously held by them, and that indeed it took a long time to come about. In later periods of Jewish history, when Jews were scattered and lacked a religious and legal center, they often longed for what they imagined to be the fixed and unambiguous law of Temple times, but, as we have seen, that law was neither fixed nor unambiguous. It was, instead, the evolving law of a living community, with all of the diversity, controversy, dynamism, and richness that that entails.

# Topic Five: The Oral Torah: Rabbinic Exegesis and Oral Traditions

The rabbinic amplification of the biblical law of injuries derives from two primary legal resources, specifically exegesis of the biblical text, and oral traditions. The laws that these two methodologies produced were eventually collected into what we now call rabbinic literature. That literature in all its forms—Mishnah, Tosefta, Baraitot, Midrash Halakhah, Midrash Aggadah, and Gemara—are together called "the Oral Torah" (or "the Oral Law"). This name reflects the rabbinic doctrine that God gave Moses at Sinai both a Written Torah (the Pentateuch) and an Oral Torah later recorded in rabbinic literature.

Orthodox Jews understand this to mean that two distinct bodies of material were transmitted to Moses, one written and one oral. Those who take a historical view of the tradition understand the doctrine of the Oral Law to mean that there was a common law tradition of interpretations, decisions, and customs dating back to Sinai, and even antedating it, which accompanied the development of the written law over the centuries.

In either case, the Oral Torah encompasses both of the primary ways in which the rabbis applied the Bible, that is, through exegesis and through judicial decisions based on precedents and traditions. Consequently they were concerned to explain and justify that doctrine in both of its aspects. We will explore their justification of biblical exegesis in section A, their use of it in section B, and their reasons for using precedents and traditions in section C. Section D will discuss the degree to which these procedures produced a legal system capable of both continuity and change, and section E will define the limits to which these methodologies could be stretched until those stretching them were no longer part of the Jewish community or legal system.

The fact of change seems inevitable in every tradition; the major issue that arises in interpretative traditions, including the rabbinic and the American constitutional tradition, is how to describe the legitimate methods and agencies of change through interpretation. Based on

185

their personal experience or aesthetic taste, some expositors in each of the traditions want such decisions to be made by a central authority, while others prefer that the procedure be decentralized, perhaps to the point that significant issues become matters of individual choice.

The American experience illustrates this tension. At the time the United States Constitution was adopted, written constitutions were not common in other nations. The new governmental system was created to deal with the excessive divisiveness of the independent states under the Articles of Confederation. There was very little experience with the division and separation of powers between state and nation and among the organs of the national government. All factions feared being dominated by the others. It took almost a generation of trust-building experience and the forceful genius of Chief Justice John Marshall to reach a point in which there could be general consensus on the need to have one institution that is to be an ultimate interpreter of the meaning of the constitutional document.

The tension has still not been finally resolved. Since the doctrine of judicial review became established in *Marbury* v. *Madison* (1803), ultimate interpretive authority is generally understood to be invested in judges, particularly those of the one, national Supreme Court. Yet whenever a difficult constitutional issues arises, there will be those who will again vigorously assert that the states are the coequals of the national government or that Congress and the president are equally invested with the Supreme Court with power under the Constitution to say what the clauses that concern their prerogatives mean.

In addition to ongoing debates about who has authority to decide, there are also continual debates about appropriate methods of interpretation. Some, most recently including the Attorney General of the United States, insist that the meaning of the Constitution is limited to what it always meant and that its provisions govern only the issues and connotations the framers had in mind. Others see hidden in the Constitution's folds the answers to many contemporary issues which the framers could not have even known, let alone decided.

In these debates the same preferences are repeated in both the American and Jewish legal traditions between central authority versus local and individual choice; between coherent executive decision-making by an authoritative leader versus a group process in which all voices are heard and consensus is reached by mutual accommodation; between firm rules that are clear and simple versus flexible standards that can meet the varying needs of situations; between unified, strong, and professional central administration and more human, small, and local units that can reflect the specialness and specificity of needs; and between a literal reading and application of the words of the text versus a more expansive reading in accordance with its spirit.

The rabbis' justifications for using both exegesis and oral traditions to effect change appear in a number of brief statements scattered throughout rabbinic literature. Their style is cursive and aphoristic when they treat matters of ideology. Jews formulated lists of their principles of belief only in the Middle Ages, under external pressure from Christians and Moslems, but none ever gained the kind of acceptance within the Jewish community that such catechisms received in Christendom and other religious communities.

The rabbis' aphoristic style may seem rather offhanded to twentieth-century readers used to structured, logical argumentation, but it does not indicate casualness on matters of substance. On the contrary, that style reflects the Jewish tradition's tendency not to be dogmatic in ideological matters. Central Jewish religious concepts, such as the unity of God and the election of Israel, are understood in ways that allow room for widely differing viewpoints. Instead of theological dogmas, Jews made their ideological assertions in interpretive embellishments of biblical verses, often consisting of a play on words, anecdote, or short homily, all part of the Midrash Aggadah. This format enabled them to treat major issues in a way that was vivid and yet consistent with tradition. It also enabled them to deal with all of the complexities of life, including those that do not fit into the neat, consistent patterns that rules and principles describe. And, most important, it stimulated discussion rather than stifled it: there were few clear-cut boundaries that one dared not cross. In a story or fable based on a text one could experiment with all kinds of ideas. Stories about Moses visiting Rabbi Akiba's academy, even though they lived 1400 years apart, or of Elijah, the prophet, telling Rabbi Nathan how God reacted to a decision of the Sanhedrin, were meant very seriously, but not literally. The midrashic form is at once an expression of ideological assertion and of cognitive modesty.

## A. Two Ways of Dealing with a Fixed Text I: Exegesis and its Justification

### 1. *The Primacy of the Revelation to Moses*

The rabbis determined Jewish law through exegesis of the Torah because they believed that this body of literature contained God's word more clearly and accurately than any other. The Torah itself recognizes the possibility of God's revealing His will to people other than Moses, but it declares that no revelation to others can claim authority over the revelation to Moses (Numbers 12:6–8; Deuteronomy 34:10). The rabbis emphasized this point.

*Lev. R.* 1:14:
What was the distinction between Moses and the other prophets?
The latter looked through nine lenses, whereas Moses looked only
through one. They looked through a cloudy lens, but Moses through
one that was clear.

*Ex. R.* 28:6, 42:8:
What the prophets were destined to prophesy in subsequent generations they received from Mount Sinai . . . Moses gave utterance to all
the words of the other prophets as well as his own, and whoever pro-
phesied only gave expression to the essence of Moses' prophecy.

## 2. The Cessation of Prophecy

No prophet could be more authoritative than Moses, but there
were true prophets in the First Temple Period. Shortly after the destruction of the First Temple, however, prophecy ceased entirely.

*Sanhedrin* 11a:
When the latter prophets, Haggai, Zekhariah, and Malakhi died, the
Holy Spirit departed from Israel.

*Num. R.* 14:4:
The Holy One, blessed be He, said, "Twenty-four books (of the Hebrew Bible) have I written for you; beware and make no addition to
them." For what reason? "Of making many books there is no end"
(Eccles. 12:12). He who reads a single verse which is not from the
twenty-four is as though he read in "the outside books." Beware of
making many books (to add to the Scriptures), for whoever does so
will have no portion in the World to Come."

## 3. The Substitution of Exegesis for Prophecy

If prophecy was going to be eliminated as a methodology in the ongoing application of Jewish law, something had to take its place. Ezra is
known in the tradition for interpreting the text of the Torah, and that
is the method which the rabbis adopted since the Torah was the one
text whose revelational authority was indubitable in their eyes. They
justified human interpretation of that text as a means to resolve the
ambiguities found when applying it. Moreover, only through interpretation, they claimed, could the Torah have the flexibility necessary to
meet new circumstances. Besides, God Himself requires interpretation
in chapter 17 of Deuteronomy. Not to interpret the law anew in each
generation would be to disobey God's Law. For all these reasons, then,
the rabbis abandoned new prophecies as a way of understanding and
applying the Torah and relied instead on interpretation as God's new
mode of revelation.

*Bava Batra* 12a:
R. Abdimi from Haifa said: Since the day when the Temple was destroyed, the prophetic gift was taken away from the prophets and given to the Sages.—Is then a Sage not also a prophet?—What he meant was this: although it has been taken from the prophets, it has not been taken from the Sages. Amemar said: A Sage is even superior to a prophet, as it says, "And a prophet has a heart of wisdom" (Ps. 90:12). Who is (usually) compared with whom? Is not the smaller compared with the greater?

*Deut. R., Nitzavim* 8:6:
It is written, "For this commandment . . . is not in heaven" (Deut. 30: 11, 12). Moses said to the Israelites, "Lest you should say, 'Another Moses is to arise to bring us another Law from heaven,' therefore I make it known to you now that it is not in heaven: nothing is left of it in heaven." R. Hanina said: "The Law and all the implements by which it is carried out have been given, namely, modesty, beneficence, uprightness and reward."

Even Elijah, the prophet who will herald the arrival of the messianic age, will not be the source of new legal instruction.

*Eduyot* 8:7:
R. Joshua said: I have received a tradition from Rabbi Johanon b. Zakkai, who heard it from his teacher, and his teacher from his teacher, as a law given to Moses from Sinai, that Elijah will not come to declare impure or pure, or who must be expelled (from the priestly families on the grounds of questionable descent) and who received, but only to expel such (ineligible ones) that were received through violence and to reinstate those who were removed by violence. . . . R. Simon says (Elijah will come) neither to expel nor to receive, but only to make peace in the world.

The rabbis go further still. God Himself cannot interfere in the ongoing process of rabbinic interpretation and application of the Torah. We have seen the problems that the rabbis had with new revelations, but even when everyone agreed about the authenticity of a revelation, it was discounted. God had begun a process at Sinai which even He could not alter.

*Bava Metzia* 59a–59b:
We learned elsewhere: If he cut it (the material for an oven) into separate tiles, placing sand between each tile, Rabbi Eliezer declared it pure, and the Sages declared it impure. On that day Rabbi Eliezer brought forward every imaginable argument, but they did not accept them. Said he to them: "If the law agrees with me, let the stream of water prove it," whereupon the stream of water flowed backwards.

"No proof can be brought from a stream of water," they rejoined. Again he urged: "If the law agrees with me, let the walls of the schoolhouse prove it," whereupon the walls inclined to fall. But Rabbi Joshua rebuked them saying: "When scholars are engaged in legal dispute, what right have you to interfere?" Hence they did not fall in honor of Rabbi Joshua, nor did they resume the upright position in honor of Rabbi Eliezer, and they are still standing thus inclined. Again he said to them, "If the law agrees with me, let it be proved in Heaven," whereupon a Heavenly Voice cried out: "Why do you dispute with Rabbi Eliezer, seeing that in all matters the law agrees with him?" But Rabbi Joshua arose and exclaimed: "It is not in Heaven" (Deut. 30:12). What did he mean by this? Rabbi Jeremiah said: "That the Torah had already been given at Mt. Sinai; therefore we pay no attention to a Heavenly Voice, because You have long since written in the Torah at Mt. Sinai, 'One must follow the majority'" (Ex.23.2).

Rabbi Nathan met Elijah (the prophet) and asked him: "What did the Holy One, Blessed be He, do in that hour?" "He laughed with joy," he replied, "and said, 'My children have defeated Me. My children have defeated Me.'"

In justifying the substitution of exegesis for prophecy, the rabbis pointed out that even the Torah, which accepted prophecy, considered exegesis to be superior.

> P. T. Berakhot 1:4:
> To what are a prophet and a Sage to be compared? To a king who sent two ambassadors to a state. For one of them he wrote, "If he does not show you my seal, do not believe him"; for the other he wrote, "Even if he does not show you my seal, believe him." Similarly, in regard to a prophet, it is written, "If he gives you a sign or portent" (Deut. 13:2), but here (in Deut. 17:11, concerning judges) it is written, "You shall act in accordance with the instruction which they shall give you" (even without a sign).

These ideological justifications for the cessation of prophecy and its replacement by rabbinic interpretation all have some degree of merit, but a political analyst would see them all as a rationale for asserting the exclusive power of the rabbis. If no prophet could announce a new, authoritative revelation, there could be no rival to the rabbinic mode of ascertaining God's will through interpretation. Both ideological and political factors were undoubtedly at work in prompting the rabbis to deny the authenticity of new revelations, and it is difficult to determine the extent to which each was operative.

The rabbinic notion that God, although fountainhead of the law, was no longer free to tamper with it once it was given to humans, is reminiscent of the development in Western secular thought of the relationship between the English king and the law. From its earliest stages English political theory recognized limits on the monarch's power. Nonetheless, royal rule was highly personal. Laws were made in the king's name (with the advice of a group of counsellors that later developed into Parliament) and judgments of law were made by the king's court, which only gradually became differentiated from the king's personal entourage. In any event, by the beginning of the seventeenth century medieval political theory had been supplanted by more absolutist concepts of a national state ruled by a sovereign monarch, who held power by Divine Right. Increasingly powerful Tudor monarchs relied for administrative and ideological support on a cadre of lawyers, who were developing their own professional ethos and an allegiance to transcendent legal values distinct from the political crown or the spiritual values embodied in the church. Absolutist monarchs paradoxically saw their personal perogative as unlimited by other legal constraints, at the same time that their personal rule was becoming increasingly dependent on the skills and administrative talents of a professional, law-trained bureaucracy. The twin ideas of law as an overarching value distinct from, and ultimately superior to, the political will of the king and the concept of law as the special craft of law-trained persons became central aspects of the revolutions of the Tudor and Stuart eras. These concepts produced the theory of a constitutional monarchy and laid the foundation for the American constitutional experience. By the time James I ascended the English throne in 1603, the idea of the law as separate and superior to the person of the king had gained such strength that the king's attempt to sit personally as a judge could be actively resisted by Lord Chief Justice Coke. The following excerpt, from the law reports, describes what happened when King James attempted to sit in judgment in person in his Court of Kings Bench.

*Prohibitions Del Roy*, 12 *Co. Rep* 63 (1603):
Note, upon Sunday the 10th of November in this same term, the King, upon complaint made to him by Bancroft, Archbishop of Canterbury, concerning prohibitions, the King was informed, that when the question was made of what matters the ecclesiastical Judges have cognizance, . . . the King himself may decide it in his royal person and that the Judges are but the delegates of the King, and that the King may take what causes he shall please to determine, from the determination of the Judges, and may determine them himself. And the Archbishop said, that this was clear in divinity, that such authority belongs to the King by the word of God in the Scripture. To which it was answered by me, in the presence, and with the clear consent of all the

Judges of England, and Barons of Exchequer, that the King in his own person cannot adjudge any case . . . but this ought to be determined and adjudged in some court of justice, according to the law and custom of England; . . . so that the Court gives the judgment: and the King hath his Court, *viz.* in the upper house of Parliament, in which he with his Lords is the supreme Judge over all other Judges for if error be in the Common Pleas, that may be reversed in the King's Bench: and if the Court of King's Bench err, that may be reversed in the upper house of Parliament, by the King, with the assent of the Lords spiritual and temporal, without the Commons: and in this respect the King is called the Chief Justice. . . : but the judgments are always given *per curiam* (by the court); and the Judges are sworn to execute justice according to law and the custom of England. . . . Then the king said that he thought the law was founded upon reason and that he and others had reason, as well as the Judges: to which it was answered by me, that true it was, that God had endowed his Majesty with excellent science, and great endowments of nature; but His Majesty was not learned in the laws of his realm of England, and causes which concern the life, or inheritance, or goods, or fortunes of his subjects, are not to be decided by natural reason but by the artificial reason and judgment of law, which law is an act which requires long study and experience, before that a man can attain to the cognizance of it: and that the law was the golden met-wand and measure to try the causes of the subjects; and which protected his Majesty in safety and peace: with which the King was greatly offended, and said, that then he should be under the law, which was treason to affirm, as he said; to which I said, that Bracton saith, *quod Rex non debet esse sub homine, sed sub Deo et lege* (The King should not be subject to humans, but is under God and law).

Bracton's full statement was even stronger than the version quoted by Lord Coke: "The king himself ought not to be subject to men, but to God and the law, because it is the law that makes him king."

There are, of course, dissimilarities between the story in *Bava Metzia* and this event in English history. For one thing, Lord Chief Justice Coke did not consider James I to be the source of the law. Moreover, for the rabbis God had committed Himself to the covenant, but its terms could not be enforced against Him (see Job), and He was known to act in ways contrary to its provisions (for instance, vertical retribution). Finally, Coke's actions were part of a wider and more protracted attempt to check the power of the monarch, and the rabbis never claimed that God's power needed to be checked for the good of society. These distinctions are occasioned by the difference between human and divine monarchs. Nevertheless both stories differentiate carefully between the law and the law giver, such that even God is challenged in His attempt to bypass normal legal procedures.

## 4. *Exegesis in the Service of Scriptural Clarity and Adaptability*

The authority of the tradition depends heavily on its ties to the biblical revelation of God's will. But how could Jews carry out God's will if they were not sure what the revelation meant? Moreover, new circumstances demanded new laws. How could Jewish law accommodate such needs if it was to retain its ties to the Torah? These are basic tensions in Jewish law. Exegesis was one way in which the rabbis resolved them.

Of course, there is a paradox involved in this. On the one hand, interpreting the Torah makes its directions clear and links innovations to the authoritative text, however weakly. On the other, exegesis simultaneously liberates the tradition from the limitations of time and a fixed text by clarifying what is unclear and extending it to situations that it never contemplated.

The rabbis recognized this paradox. They stated clearly that exegesis was legitimated, and even mandated, by God Himself:

> *Sifre Numbers* 134:
> "This shall be the law of procedure for the Israelites in accordance with the Lord's command to Moses." (Numbers 27:11). The Torah itself gave the Sages authority to interpret and to declare.

But they knew that interpreting a text puts one in tension with it, and they disagreed over exactly how far their authority to stretch the biblical text extends.

> *Sifre Deut., Shofetim,* #154:
> "According to the sentence . . . of the judges shall you act, you shall not incline . . . to the right or to the left" (Deut. 17:11). Even if they demonstrate that that which seems to you right is left, and that that which seems to you left is right, hearken to them.

> *P. T. Horayot* 1:1:
> "You must not deviate from the verdict that they announce to you either to the right or to the left" (Deut. 17:11). You might think that this means that if they tell you that right is left and left is right, you are to obey them; therefore the Torah tells you, "to the right or to the left" (to indicate that), when they tell you that right is right and left is left (you are to obey them, but not otherwise).

Whatever the difficulties in establishing proper limits for exegesis, there simply was no choice but to use it. Exegesis was necessary because the text of the Torah is unclear and ambiguous.

*Sanhedrin* 34a:
"Is not My word like a hammer that breaks a rock in many pieces?" (Jer. 23:29). As the hammer causes numerous sparks to flash forth, so is a Scriptural verse capable of many interpretations.

*Shabbat* 31a:
It happened that a heathen came before Shammai and asked him, "How many Torahs do you have?" He answered, "Two—the written and the oral." He said. "With respect to the written Torah I will believe you, but not with respect to the Oral Torah. Accept me as a convert on condition that you teach me the former only." Shammai rebuked him and drove him out with contempt. He came before Hillel with the same request, and he accepted him. The first day he taught him the alphabet in the correct order, but the next day he reversed it. The heathen said to him, "Yesterday you taught it to me differently!" Hillel replied, "Do you not have to depend upon me for the letters of the alphabet? So must you likewise depend upon me for the interpretation of the Torah."

*Num. R.* 14:4:
"The words of the wise are as goads. . . . They are given from one shepherd" (Eccles. 12:11), that is, the words of the Torah and the words of the Sages have been given from the same shepherd (Moses). "And furthermore, my son, be careful: of making many books there is no end" (Eccles. 12:12) means: more than to the words of the Torah pay attention to the words of the Scribes. In the same strain it says, "For your beloved ones are better than wine" (Song of Songs 1:2), means: the words of the beloved ones (the Rabbis) are better than the wine of the Torah. Why? Because one cannot give a proper decision from the words of the Torah, since the Torah is shut up (ambiguous) and consists entirely of headings. . . . From the words of the Sages, however, one can derive the proper law because they explain the Torah. And the reason why the words of the Sages are compared to goads (*darbanot*) is because they cause understanding to dwell (*medayerin binah*) in men.

Interpretation is also needed and desired by God to give the law flexible adaptability.

*P. T. Sanhedrin* 22a:
If the Torah had been given in a fixed form, the situation would have been intolerable. What is the meaning of the oft-recurring

phrase, "The Lord spoke to Moses"? Moses said before Him, "Sovereign of the Universe! Cause me to know what the final decision is on each matter of law." He replied, "The majority must be followed: when the majority declares a thing permitted, it is permissible; when the majority declares it forbidden, it is not allowed; so that the Torah may be capable of interpretation with forty-nine points for and forty-nine points against."

*Seder Eliyahu Zuta, chapter 2:*
A king had two slaves whom he loved intensely. He gave each one a measure of wheat and a bundle of flax. The intelligent one wove the flax into a cloth and made flour from the wheat, sifted it, ground it, kneaded it, baked it, and set it (the bread) on the table on the cloth he had made before the king returned. The stupid one did not do a thing (with the gifts the king had given him). After some time the king returned to his house and said to them: "My sons, bring me what I gave you." One brought out the table set with the bread on the tablecloth; the other brought out the wheat in a basket and the bundle of flax with it. What an embarrassment that was! Which do you think was the more beloved? . . . (Similarly) when the Holy One, blessed be He, gave the Torah to Israel, He gave it as wheat from which to make flour and flax from which to make clothing through the rules of interpretation.

In practice, the rabbis often adhered quite closely to the words and intent of the Bible, but sometimes they used their judicial authority to make the text say things rather far from its original meaning—much like the behavior of American judges when interpreting the Constitution. The tension persists; but, as the rabbis saw it, exegesis was required and legitimated by the Torah, and it was necessary to understand and apply the Bible properly.

## 5. The Continuity and Coherence of the Tradition Despite Varying Interpretations

Exegesis can lend clarity and flexibility to a tradition, but it can also lead to discontinuity with the past and a lack of cohesiveness. This is especially true when individual authorities are free to suggest their own interpretations and when there is no way of conclusively ruling in favor of one interpretation over others. The former factor has always characterized Jewish law, and the latter has been true of it during most of its history, beginning with the demise of the Sanhedrin in talmudic times. Nevertheless the rabbis claimed that both the continuity of the law and its coherence would be preserved by the firm rooting of the tradition in the Torah.

When, according to the following Midrash, Moses visits the academy of Rabbi Akiba, who in fact lived some 1400 years after Moses, he does not even understand what Rabbi Akiba is saying, let alone agree with it. Nevertheless Moses is comforted when Rabbi Akiba cites Moses as the authority for one of the new laws that he announces because that indicates that there is a felt connection between past and present, however much the tradition has developed in the interim.

> *Menahot* 29b:
> Rabbi Judah said in the name of Rav: When Moses ascended on high, he found the Holy One, blessed be He, engaged in fixing crowns (decorative markings) to the letters (of the Torah). Said Moses: "Lord of the Universe, who stays Your hand?" (i.e., is there anything lacking in the Torah so that additions are necessary?) He answered, "There will arise a man at the end of many generations, Akiba ben Joseph by name, who will expand upon each decorative marking heaps and heaps of laws." "Lord of the Universe," said Moses, "permit me to see him." He replied, "Turn around." Moses went and sat down behind eight rows (of R. Akiba's disciples and listened to their discussion of the law). Not being able to follow their arguments he was ill at ease, but when they came to a certain subject and the disciple said to the master, "From where do you know it?" and the latter replied, "It is a law given to Moses at Sinai," he (Moses) was comforted. Thereupon he returned to the Holy One, blessed be He, and said, "Lord of the Universe, You have such a man and You give the Torah by me?!"

Aside from the fact that exegesis was practiced in a context replete with emotional and psychological connections to the past, the very method of exegesis would preserve the tradition through constant reference to the text of the accepted revelation, the Torah. Since God gave the Torah and God could be presumed to be consistent, the tradition issuing from the interpretation of the Torah would be coherent, continuous, and authoritative, if only we are sufficiently skilled to hear the many things which the text is saying.

> *Numbers Rabbah* 14:4:
> Lest a man should say, "Since some scholars declare a thing impure and others declare it pure, some pronounce it to be permitted while others declare it forbidden, some disqualify an object while others uphold its fitness, how can I study Torah under such circumstances?" Scripture states, "They are given from one shepherd" (Eccles. 12:11): One God has given them, one leader (Moses) has uttered them at the command of the Lord of all creation, blessed be He, as it says, "And God spoke all these words" (Ex. 20:1). Do you then on your part make your ear like a grain funnel and acquire a heart that can understand

the words of the scholars who declare a thing impure as well as those who declare it pure, the words of those who declare a thing forbidden as well as those who pronounce it permitted, and the words of those who disqualify an object as well as those who uphold its fitness. . . . Although one scholar offers his view and another offers his, the words of both are all derived from what Moses, the shepherd, received from the One Lord of the Universe.

Conversely, if Jews do not study the text sufficiently, the Torah would seem like two Torahs:

> *Sotah* 47b:
> When the number of students of Shammai and Hillel who had not sufficiently served (studied with) their teachers increased, dissensions increased in Israel and the Torah became like two Torahs.

With adequate study, however, debate could go on unimpeded because God Himself oversaw the process and proclaimed that all of the varying interpretations were "the words of the living God."

> *Eruvin* 13b:
> Rabbi Abba stated in the name of Samuel: For three years there was a dispute between the School of Shammai and the School of Hillel, the former asserting, "The law is in agreement with our views," and the latter contending, "The law is in agreement with our views." Then a Heavenly Voice announced, "The utterances of both are the words of the living God, but the law is in agreement with the rulings of the School of Hillel." Since, however, "both are the words of the living God," what was it that entitled the School of Hillel to have the law fixed in accordance with their rulings? Because they were kind and modest, they studied their own rulings and those of the School of Shammai, and they were even so humble as to mention the opinions of the School of Shammai before theirs.

In light of the wide dispersion of Jews and the recurrent lack of a central legal authority, one would expect that coherence would be a great concern, militating against free-flowing debate. Consequently it is remarkable that Jewish law tolerated as much diversity of opinion as it did—more, in fact, than most other traditions. Part of the reason for that is historical: there simply was no way to force Jews living all over the world to conform to one mold. Another part of the reason, however, was theological: Judaism assumes that the tradition was given to the whole Jewish people and not just the elders, and hence every Jew has both a right and an obligation to study it and actively engage in its

development. This made questioning and lively debate an integral part
of the Jewish experience. Coherence and continuity were values, and
Jews assumed that the tradition's roots in the Torah would preserve
those values; but they also assumed that the tradition's coherence and
continuity would not be compromised by the vibrant and rigorous debate to which Jews have become accustomed.

## B. Two Ways of Dealing with a Fixed Text—I: The Methods and Use of Exegesis

The authority of the rabbis to declare the law was based on their
interpretive competence, their claim to be masters of the Book, skilled
in understanding and explaining the ancient texts. In this respect they
resemble modern American judges, who also lack authority to legislate
or political power to impose the rules they think wise, but nonetheless
often make law under the guise of interpretation.

A legal system that emphasizes interpretation as a lawmaking
method must start with a high degree of confidence in the authority of
the text. The American experience is grounded on a deep faith that the
text of the Constitution is a dependable source of guidance on fundamental issues. Those rulings that can be based, however tenuously, on
the often cryptic provisions of that text thereby gain a special legitimacy that places them in a position superior to solemn and specific
legislative acts.

Similarly, the rabbinic tradition of interpretation starts with supreme confidence that, however subtle the text may be, somewhere
within it correct guidance on every legal issue can be found. The text
itself may appear repetitive, obscure, incomplete, or inconsistent, but
all the seeming problems just show the need for explanation. The text
is authentic, complete and correct; it is just our ability to read and understand it that is limited.

Rabbinic interpretation of Scriptures takes many forms, but to a
considerable degree it relies on hermeneutics, the discipline of applying specific interpretive rules to make the meaning of the text clear.
The textual words themselves are manipulated in hermeneutic analysis, in contrast to other forms of interpretation that may seek the intent of the legislative speaker or trace the historical development of
the received text in search of its meaning. While the elaboration of hermeneutic rules can become quite subtle and complex, the intent is not
to befuddle but rather to spell out what speakers or writers mean by
what they say. Rabbinic hermeneutic rules, in fact, probably envolved
out of judicial practice as pragmatic guides to give meaning to vague or

ambiguous texts. Over time these paradigms hardened into conventional laws. In a similar way, common-law judges of the nineteenth century developed canons of construction for the interpretation of Anglo-American statutes, and, until very recently, American law students would have a concentrated course in "legal method" (that is, rules of interpreting legal texts) before they ever read a case. The rabbinic tradition takes exegetical rules very seriously because it believes that the true meaning of God's revelation in the Torah can be derived by applying such principles.

This is likely to puzzle a modern lawyer, for it seems obvious that the principles involved, while helpful as common sense ways to approach a text, rarely dictate one and only one correct meaning of the text. There are simply too many canons of construction, they lead in divergent and often conflicting directions, and typically more than one is applicable in a given situation. The canons provide a helpful introduction to the various ways a text *might* be read, but then the reader must judge which approach is most sound on some other basis. Hermeneutics gives no hint of that process of weighing various factors; if anything, it hides it, and that is dangerous. In time, the process can become mechanical as disciples struggle with the elaborate rules announced by earlier masters and, in doing so, fail to realize that the rules are often after the fact justifications for results reached for other reasons. Then the later interpreter may lose sight of those other crucial reasons and treat the problem of uncovering the meaning of the law as if it were a matter of doing one's sums correctly.

I once heard a very eminent judge say that he never let a decision go until he was absolutely sure that it was right. So judicial dissent often is blamed, as if it meant simply that one side or the other were not doing their sums right, and, if they would take more trouble, agreement inevitably would come.

This mode of thinking is entirely natural. The training of lawyers is a training in logic. The processes of analogy, discrimination, and deduction are those in which they are most at home. The language of judicial decision is mainly the language of logic. And the logical method and form flatter that longing for certainty and for repose which is in every human mind. But certainty generally is illusion, and repose is not the destiny of man. Behind the logical form lies a judgment as to the relative worth and importance of competing legislative grounds, often an inarticulate and unconscious judgment it is true, and yet the very root and nerve of the whole proceeding. You can give any conclusion a logical form. You always can imply a condition in a contract. But why do you imply it? It is because of some belief as to the practice of the community or of a class, or because of some opinion as to policy, or, in short, because of some attitude of yours upon a matter not capable of exact quantitative measurement, and therefore of founding exact logical conclusions. Such matters really are battle grounds where the means do not exist for determinations that shall be good for all time, and where the decision can do no more than embody the preference of a given body in a given time and place. We do not realize how large a part of our law is open to reconsideration upon a slight change in the habit of the public mind . . . (O. W. Holmes, Jr., "The Path of the Law," 10 *Harvard L. Rev.* 457 [1897].)

On the other hand, there are clear advantages to the use of hermeneutics. The formidable technique and jargon of hermeneutics lends supporting weight to judges' conclusions. Hermeneutic rules, when used wisely, can tie a ruling convincingly to the authoritative text and thereby give that text ongoing relevance. A ruling made this way is more obviously part of a stable and continuous legal system. Moreover, by providing a ready rationalization, hermeneutics can impart tremendous flexibility to the process of interpretation, leaving the interpreter secure in the knowledge that authority can be cited for almost any result that is reached. Thus while application of hermeneutic principles may look like a game at times, the game is a serious one since it is one way through which a legal system seeks to be both stable and contemporary.

The interpretive styles of the Midrash Halakhah, Mishnah, and Gemara, to which you were introduced in the last topic, share a set of assumptions regarding the text of the Torah that they were to interpret. A few of these assumptions should be clear to you already. They include the expectation that the correct answer to a current problem can be found in the text. Some less obvious assumptions include:

a. Nothing in the Torah is superfluous. If a verse seems repetitive or adds nothing to the rest of the text, there is some subtle point to be discovered that is different from that made elsewhere.

b. The Torah is all of a piece and therefore one verse can be used to illuminate others in other books.

c. The correct interpretation of the text is partly a matter of logical extrapolation and partly a matter of received tradition, but the accepted construction is not one based on logical necessity nor on a sense inevitably demanded by the plain meaning of the words. Subtle and hidden meanings may be correct.

d. The process of interpretation is essentially open-ended. Many competing interpretations are possible. Varying viewpoints are accepted by the tradition and dissents are often respectfully preserved. There are right answers and wrong answers, but in a number of cases no clear and binding decision is recorded as being reached.

The classic expression of the rules for interpreting the legal sections of the Bible is known as the *Baraita of Rabbi Ishmael,* a man who lived in the second century of the Common Era. These rules are part of the obligatory study of all Jews and incorporated into the morning prayers recited daily. They are presented here with the illuminating illustrations prepared by Dr. Phillip Birnbaum for *The Daily Prayerbook* (New York: Hebrew Publishing Co., 1949), 41–46. Modern scholars have noted the similarity between these rules and those of the Greek scholars in Alexandria who were interpreting Homer at about the same time, and there may well have been cross-cultural influences. The rules and illustrations are presented here in their entirety so that the reader can get an idea of their sophistication, but there is no need to study them in depth in order to understand the later sections of this book. The illustrations will, however, enable those interested in some keen mental gymnastics to see how they can be used to decipher the Bible. We can see how helpful these rules are in resolving our textual problems with Exodus 21 in Topic 2, Section A.

*Sifra,* Introduction, *The Baraita of Rabbi Ishmael:*
Rabbi Ishmael says: The Torah is interpreted by means of thirteen rules:

1. Inference is drawn from a minor premise to a major one, or from a major premise to a minor one.

2. From the similarity of words or phrases occuring in two passages it is inferred that what is expressed in the one applies also to the other.

3. A general principle, as contained in one or two biblical laws, is applicable to all related laws.

4. When a generalization is followed by a specification, only what is specified applies.

5. When a specification is followed by a generalization, all that is implied in the generalization applies.

6. If a generalization is followed by a specification and this in turn by a generalization, one must be guided by what the specification implies.

7. When, however, for the sake of clearness, a generalization necessarily requires a specification, or when a specification requires a generalization, rules 4 and 5 do not apply.

8. Whatever is first implied in a generalization and afterwards specified to teach us something new, is expressly stated not only for its

own sake, but to teach something additional concerning all the instances implied in the generalization.

9. Whatever is first implied in a general law and afterwards specified to add another provision similar to the general law, is specified in order to alleviate, and not to increase, the severity of that particular provision.

10. Whatever is first implied in a general law and afterwards specified to add another provision which is not similar to the general law, is specified in order to alleviate in some respects and in others to increase the severity of that particular provision.

11. Whatever is first implied in a general law and is afterwards specified to determine a new matter, the terms of the general law can no longer apply to it, unless Scripture expressly declares that they do apply.

12. A dubious word or passage is explained from its context or from a subsequent expression.

13. Similarly, if two biblical passages contradict each other, they can be harmonized only by a third passage.

*Illustrations:*

1. If, for example, a certain act is forbidden on an ordinary festival, it is so much the more forbidden on Yom Kippur (the most restrictive of days in the Jewish liturgical year); if a certain act is permissible on Yom Kippur, it is so much the more permissible on an ordinary festival.

2. The phrase "Hebrew slave" (Exodus 21:2) is ambiguous, for it may mean a heathen slave owned by a Hebrew, or else, a slave who is a Hebrew. That the latter is the correct meaning is proved by a reference to the phrase "your Hebrew brother" in Deuteronomy 15:12, where the same law is mentioned ("If your Hebrew brother is sold to you").

3. (a) From Deuteronomy 24:6 ("No one shall take a handmill or an upper millstone in pledge, for he would be taking a life in pledge") the rabbis concluded: "Everything which is used for preparing food is forbidden to be taken in pledge." (b) From Exodus 21:26–27 ("If a man strikes the eye of his slave . . . and destroys it, he must let him go free in compensation for his eye. If he knocks out the tooth of his slave . . . he must let him go free") the rabbis concluded that when any part of the slave's body is mutilated by the master, the slave shall be set free.

4. In Leviticus 18:6 the law reads: "None of you shall marry anyone related to him." This generalization is followed by a specification of forbidden marriages. Hence, this prohibition applies only to those expressly mentioned.

5. In Exodus 22:9 we read: "If a man gives to his neighbor an ass, or an ox, or a sheep, to keep, or any animal, and it dies." The general phrase "any animal," which follows the specification, includes in this law all kinds of animals.

6. In Exodus 22:8 we are told that an embezzler shall pay double to his neighbor "for anything embezzled (generalization), for ox, for ass, or sheep, or clothing (specification), or any article lost" (generalization). Since the specification includes only movable property, and objects of intrinsic value, the fine of double payment does not apply to embezzled real estate, nor to notes and bills, since the latter represent only a symbolic value.

7. In Leviticus 17:13 we read: "He shall pour out its blood, and *cover* it with *dust.*" The verb "to cover" is a general term, since there are various ways of covering a thing; "with dust" is specific. If we were to apply rule 4 to this passage, the law would be that the blood of the slaughtered animal must be covered with nothing except dust. Since, however, the general term "to cover" may also mean "to hide," our present passage necessarily requires the specific expression "with dust"; otherwise the law might be interpreted to mean that the blood is to be concealed in a closed vessel. On the other hand, the specification "with dust" without the general expression "to cover" would have been meaningless.

8. In Deuteronomy 22:1 we are told that the finder of lost property must return it to its owner. In the next verse the Torah adds: "You shall do the same . . . with his *garment* and with anything lost by your brother . . . which you have found." *Garment*, though included in the general expression "anything lost," is specifically mentioned in order to indicate that the duty to announce the finding of lost articles applies only to such objects which are likely to have an owner, and which have, as in the case of clothing, some marks by which they can be identified.

9. In Exodus 35:2–3 we read: "Whoever does any work on the Sabbath shall be put to death; you shall not light a fire on the sabbath day." The law against lighting a fire on the Sabbath, though already implied in "any work," is mentioned separately in order to indicate that the penalty for lighting a fire on the Sabbath is not as drastic.

10. According to Exodus 21:29–30, the proprietor of a vicious animal which has killed a man or woman must pay such compensation as may be imposed on him by the court. In a succeeding verse the Torah adds: "If the ox gores a slave, male or female, he must pay the master thirty shekels of silver." The case of a slave, though already included in the preceding general law of the slain man or woman, contains a different provision, the fixed amount of compensation, with the result that whether the slave was valued at more than thirty she-

kels, or less than thirty shekels, the proprietor of the animal must invariably pay thirty shekels.

11. The guilt-offering which a cured leper had to bring was unlike all other guilt-offerings in this, that some of its blood was sprinkled on the person who offered it (Leviticus 14:13–14). On account of this peculiarity none of the rules connected with other offerings would apply to that brought by a cured leper, had not the Torah expressly added: "As the sin-offering so is the guilt-offering."

12. (a) The noun *tinshemeth* occurs in Leviticus 11:18 among the unclean birds, and again (verse 30) among the reptiles. Hence, it becomes certain that *tinshemeth* is the name of a certain bird as well as of a certain reptile. (b) In Deuteronomy 19:6, with regard to the cities of refuge where the manslayer is to flee, we read: "So that the avenger of blood may not pursue the manslayer . . . and slay him, and he is not deserving of death." That the last clause refers to the slayer, and not to the blood avenger, is made clear by the subsequent clause: "inasmuch as he hated him not in time past."

13. In Exodus 13:6 we read: "Seven days you shall eat unleavened bread," and in Deuteronomy 16:8 we are told: "Six days you shall eat unleavened bread." The contradiction between these two passages is explained by reference to a third passage (Leviticus 23:14), where the use of the new produce is forbidden until the second day of Passover, after the offering of the Omer. If, therefore, the unleavened bread was prepared of the new grain, it could only be eaten six days of Passover. Hence, the passage in Exodus 13:6 must refer to unleavened bread prepared of the produce of a previous year.

Professor Karl Llewellyn (1893–1962) provides a modern commentary on the use of interpretative rules to learn the true meaning of legal case decisions and statutes. He criticizes the "Formal Style" of interpretation dominant in nineteenth century common law courts. Professor Llewellyn was no stranger to the problems of statutes. He was the principle draftsman of the Uniform Commercial Code, which is now embodied in the law of virtually every American state. His approach to statutory interpretation is marked by attitudes that might be quite alien to the rabbinic world, particularly his insistence that every statute is to be understood instrumentally, in light of a definable purpose for which the law exists. To the rabbis, the ancient laws of God also serve a purpose, but these ends are sometimes not knowable to humans and thus are not available as a guide to interpretation.

Karl N. Lewellyn, "Remarks on the Theory of Appellate Decision and the Rules or Canons About How Statutes Are to Be Construed," 3 *Vanderbilt Law Review* 395 [1950].

I

One does not progress far into legal life without learning that there is no single right and accurate way of reading one case, or of reading a bunch of cases. For

(1) Impeccable and correct doctrine makes clear that a case "holds" with authority only so much of what the opinion says as is absolutely necessary to sustain the judgment. Anything else is unnecessary and "distinguishable" and noncontrolling for the future. Indeed, if the judgment rests on two, three, or four rulings, any of them can be rightly and righteously knocked out, for the future, as being thus "unnecessary." Moreover, any distinction on the facts is rightly and righteously a reason for distinguishing and therefore disregarding the prior alleged hold. But

(2) Doctrine equally impeccable and correct makes clear that a case "holds" with authority the rule on which the court there chose to rest the judgment; more, that that rule covers, with full authority, cases which are plainly distinguishable on their acts and their issue, whenever the reason for the rule extends to cover them. Indeed it is unnecessary for a rule or principle to have led to the decision in the prior case, or even to have been phrased therein, in order to be seen as controlling in the new case: (a) "We there said . . ." (b) "That case necessarily decided . . ."

These divergent and indeed conflicting correct ways of handling or reading a single prior case as one "determines" what it authoritatively holds, have their counterparts in regard to the authority of a series or body of cases. Thus

(1) It is correct to see that "That rule is too well settled in this jurisdiction to be disturbed"; and so to apply it to a wholly novel circumstance.

(2) It is no less correct to see that "The rule has never been extended to a case like the present"; and so to refuse to apply it: "We here limit the rule." Again,

(3) It is no less correct to look over the prior "applications" of "the rule" and rework them into a wholly new formulation of "the true rule" or "true principle" which knocks out some of the prior cases as simply "misapplications" and then builds up the others.

In the work of a single opinion-day I have observed 26 different, describable ways in which one of our best state courts handled its own prior cases, repeatedly using three to six different ways within a single opinion.

What is important is that all 26 ways (plus a dozen others which happened not to be in use that day) are correct. They represent no "evasion," but sound use, application and development of precedent. They represent not "departure from," but sound continuation of, our system of precedent as it has come down to us. The major defect in that system is a mistaken idea which many lawyers have about it—to wit, the idea that the cases themselves and in themselves, plus the correct rules on how to handle cases, provide one single correct answer to a disputed issue of law. In fact the available correct answers are two, three, or ten. The question is: *Which* of the available correct answers will the court *select*—and *why*? For since there is always more than one available correct answer, the court always has to select.

True, the selection is frequently almost automatic. The type of distinction or expansion which is always *technically* available may be psychologically or sociologically unavailable. This may be because of (a) the current tradition of the court or because of (b) the current temper of the court or because of (c) the sense of the situation as the court sees that sense. (There are other possible reasons a-plenty, but these three are the most frequent and commonly the most weighty.)

The *current tradition* of the court is a matter of period-style in the craft of judging. In 1820–1850 our courts felt in general a freedom and duty to move in the manner typified in our thought by Mansfield and Marshall. "Precedent" guided, but "principle" controlled; and nothing was good "Principle" which did not look like wisdom-in-result for the welfare of All-of-us. In 1880–1910, on the other hand, our courts felt in general a prime duty to order within the law and a duty to resist any "outside" influence. "Precedent" was to control, not merely to guide: "Principle" was to be tested by whether it made for order in the law, not by whether it made wisdom-in-result. "Legal" Principle could not be subjected to "political" tests; even legislation was resisted as disturbing. Since 1920 the earlier style (the "Grand Style") has been working its way back into general use by our courts, though the language of the opinions moves still dominantly (though waningly) in the style (the "Formal Style") of the late 19th Century. In any particular court what needs study is how far along the process has gotten. The best material for study is the latest volume of reports, read in sequence from page 1 through to the end: the current mine-run of the work.

The *current temper* of the court is reflected in the same material, and represents the court's tradition as modified by its personnel. For it is plain that the two earlier period-styles represent also two eternal types of human being. There is the man who loves creativeness, who can without loss of sleep combine risk-taking with responsibility, who sees and feels institutions as things built and to be built to serve functions, and who sees the functions as vital and law as a tool to be eternally reoriented to justice and to general welfare. There is the other man who loves order, who finds risk uncomfortable and has seen so much irresponsible or unwise innovation that responsibility to him means caution, who sees and feels institutions as the tested, slow-built ways which for all their faults are man's sole safeguard against relapse into barbarism, and who regards reorientation of the law in our polity as essentially committed to the legislature. Commonly a man of such temper has also a craftsman's pride in clean craftsman's work, and commonly he does not view with too much sympathy any ill-done legislative job of attempted reorientation. Judges, like other men, range up and down the scale between the extremes of either type of temper, and in this aspect (as in the aspect of intellectual power and acumen or of personal force or persuasiveness) the constellation of the personnel on a particular bench at a particular time plays its important part in urging the court toward a more literal or a more creative selection among the available accepted and correct "ways" of handling precedent.

More vital, if possible, than either of the above is *the sense of the situation as seen by the court*. Thus in the very heyday of the formal period our courts moved into tremendous creative expansion of precedent in regard to the labor injunction and the due process clause.

. . .

On the case-law side, I repeat, we ought all thus to be familiar with the fact that the right doctrine and going practice of our highest courts leave them a very real leeway within which (a) to narrow or avoid what seem today to have been unfortunate prior phrasings or even rulings; or (b), on the other hand, to pick up, develop, expand what seem today to have been fortunate prior rulings or even phrasings.

It is silly, I repeat, to think of use of this leeway as involving "twisting" of precedent. The very phrase presupposes the thing which is not and which has never been. The phrase presupposes that there was in the precedent under consideration some one and single meaning. The whole experience of our case-law shows that that assumption is false. It is, instead, the business of the courts to use the precedents constantly to make the law always a little better, to correct old mistakes, to recorrect mistaken or ill-advised attempts at correction—but always within limits severly set not only by the precedents, but equally by the traditions of right conduct in judicial office.

What we need to see now is that all this is paralleled, in regard to statutes, because of (1) the power of the legislature both to choose policy and to select measures; and (2) the necessity that the legislature shall, in so doing, use language—language fixed in particular words; and (3) the continuing duty of the courts to make sense, under and within the law.

For just as prior courts can have been skillful or unskillful, clear or unclear, wise or unwise, so can legislatures. And just as prior courts have been looking at only a single piece of our whole law at a time, so have legislatures.

But a court must strive to make sense as a whole out of our law as a whole. It must, to use Frank's figure, take the music of any statute as written by the legislature; it must take the text of the play as written by the legislature. But there are many ways to play that music, to play that play, and a court's duty is to play it well, and in harmony with the other music of the legal system.

Hence, in the field of statutory construction also, there are "correct," unchallengeable rules of "how to read" which lead in happily variant directions.

This must be so until courts recognize that here, as in case-law, the real guide is Sense-for-All-of-Us. It must be so, so long as we and the courts pretend that there has been only one single correct answer possible. Until we give up that foolish pretense there must be a set of mutually contradictory correct rules on How to Construe Statutes: either set available as duty and sense may require.

Until then, also, the problem will recur in statutory construction as in the handling of case-law: Which of the technically correct answers (a) should be given; (b) will be given—and Why?

And everything said above about the temper of the court, the temper of the court's tradition, the sense of the situation and the case, applies here as well.

Thus in the period of the Grand Style of case-law statutes were construed "freely" to implement their purpose, the court commonly accepting the legislature's choice of policy and setting to work to implement it. (Criminal statutes and, to some extent, statutes on procedure, were exceptions.) Whereas in the Formal Period statutes tended to be limited or even eviscerated by wooden and literal reading, in a sort of long-drawn battle between a balky, stiff-necked, wrong-headed court and a legislature which had only words with which to drive that court. Today the courts have regained, in the main, a cheerful acceptance of legislative choice of policy, but they are still hampered to some extent in carrying such policies forward by the Formal Period's insistence on precise language.

II

One last thing is to be noted:

If a statute is to make sense, it must be read in the light of some assumed purpose. A statute merely declaring a rule, with no purpose or objective, is nonsense.

If a statute is to be merged into a going system of law, moreover, the court must do the merging, and must in so doing take account of the policy of the statute—or else substitute its own version of such policy. Creative reshaping of the net result is thus inevitable.

But the policy of a statute is of two wholly different kinds—each kind somewhat limited in effect by the statute's choice of measures, and by the statute's choice of fixed language. On the one hand there are the ideas consciously before the draftsmen, the committee, the legislature: a known evil to be cured, a known goal to be attained, a deliberate choice of one line of approach rather than another. Here talk of "intent" is reasonably realistic; committee reports, legislative debate, historical knowledge of contemporary thinking or campaigning which points up the evil or the goal can have significance.

But on the other hand—and increasingly as a statute gains in age—its language is called upon to deal with circumstances utterly uncontemplated at the time of its passage. Here the quest is not properly for the sense originally intended by the statute, for the sense sought originally to be *put into it*, but rather for the sense which *can be quarried out of it* in the light of the new situation. Broad purposes can indeed reach far beyond details known or knowable at the time of drafting. A "dangerous weapon" statute of 1840 can include tommy guns, tear gas or atomic bombs. "Vehicle," in a statute of 1840, can properly be read, when sense so suggests, to include an automobile, or a hydroplane that lacks wheels. But for all that, the sound quest does not run primarily in terms of historical intent. It runs in terms of what the words can be made to bear, in making sense in the light of the unforeseen.

3. In his *The Common Law Tradition*, Appendix C, Karl N. Llewellyn continues the discussion.

When it comes to presenting a proposed statutory construction in court, there is an accepted conventional vocabulary. As in argument over points of case-law, the accepted convention still, unhappily, requires discussion as if only one single correct meaning could exist. Hence there are two opposing canons on almost every point. An arranged selection is appended. Every lawyer must be familiar with them all: they are still needed tools of argument. At least as early as Fortescue the general picture was clear, on this, to any eye which would see.

Plainly, to make any canon take hold in a particular instance, the construction contended for must be sold, essentially, by means other than the use of the canon: The good sense of the situation and a *simple* construction of the available language to achieve that sense, *by tenable means, out of the statutory language.*

[Editors' note: In the original of this exposition, Professor Llewellyn cites copious cases and treatises for each thrust and parry. These references are omitted here, since they are longer than the text.]

| THRUST | BUT | PARRY |
|---|---|---|
| 1. A statute cannot go beyond its text. | | 1. To effect its purpose a statute may be implemented beyond its text. |
| 2. Statutes in derogation of the common law will not be extended by construction. | | 2. Such acts will be liberally construed if their nature is remedial. |
| 3. Statutes are to be read in the light of the common law and a statute affirming a common law rule is to be construed in accordance with the common law. | | 3. The common law gives way to a statute which is inconsistent with it and when a statute is designed as a revision of a whole body of law applicable to a given subject it supersedes the common law. |
| 4. Where a foreign statute which has received construction has been adopted, previous construction is adopted too. | | 4. It may be rejected where there is conflict with the obvious meaning of the statute or where the foreign decisions are unsatisfactory in reasoning or where the foreign interpretation is not in harmony with the spirit or policy of the adopting state. |
| 5. Where various states have already adopted the statute, the parent state is followed. | | 5. Where interpretation of other states are inharmonious, there is no such restraint. |
| 6. Statutes *in pari materia* must be construed together. | | 6. A statute is not *in pari materia* if its scope and aim are distinct or where a legislative design to depart from the general purpose or policy of previous enactments may be apparent. |
| 7. A statute imposing a new penalty or forfeiture, or a liability | | 7. Remedial statutes are to be liberally construed and |

| THRUST | BUT | PARRY |
|---|---|---|

or disability, or creating a new right of action will not be construed as having a retroactive effect.

if a retroactive interpretation will promote the ends of justice, they should receive such construction.

8. Where design has been distinctly stated no place is left for construction.

8. Courts have the power to inquire into real—as distinct from ostensible—purpose.

9. Definitions and rules of construction contained in an interpretation clause are part of the law and binding.

9. Definitions and rules of construction in a statute will not be extended beyond their necessary import nor allowed to defeat intention otherwise manifested.

10. A statutory provision requiring liberal construction does not mean disregard of unequivocal requirements of the statute.

10. Where a rule of construction is provided within the statute itself the rule should be applied.

11. Titles do not control meaning; preambles do not expand section scope; section headings do not change language.

11. The title may be consulted as a guide when there is doubt or obscurity in the body; preambles may be consulted to determine rationale, and thus the true construction of terms; section headings may be looked upon as part of the statute itself.

12. If language is plain and unambiguous it must be given effect.

12. Not when literal interpretation would lead to absurd or mischievous consequences or thwart manifest purpose.

13. Words and phrases which have received judicial construction before enactment are to be understood according to that construction.

13. Not if the statute clearly requires them to have a different meaning.

14. After enactment, judicial decision upon interpretation of particular terms and phrases controls.

14. Practical construction by executive officers is strong evidence of true meaning.

|  THRUST | BUT | PARRY |
|---|---|---|

15. Words are to be taken in their ordinary meaning unless they are technical words of art.

15. Popular words may bear a technical meaning and technical words may have a popular signification and they should be so construed as to agree with evident intention or to make the statute operative.

16. Every word and clause must be given effect.

16. If inadvertently inserted or if repugnant to the rest of the statute, they may be rejected as surplusage.

17. The same language used repeatedly in the same connection is presumed to bear the same meaning throughout the statute.

17. This presumption will be disregarded where it is necessary to assign different meanings to make the statute consistent.

18. Words are to be interpreted according to the proper grammatical effect of their arrangement within the statute.

18. Rules of grammar will be disregarded where strict adherence would defeat purpose.

19. Exceptions not made cannot be read in.

19. The letter is only the "bark." Whatever is within the reason of the law is within the law itself.

20. Expression of one thing excludes another.

20. The language may fairly comprehend many different cases where some only are expressly mentioned by way of example.

21. General terms are to receive a general construction.

21. They may be limited by specific terms with which they are associated or by the scope and purpose of the statute.

22. It is a general rule of construction that where general words follow an enumeration they are to be held as applying only to

22. General words must operate on something. Further, *ejusdem generis* is only an aid in getting the meaning and does not

| THRUST | BUT | PARRY |
|---|---|---|
| persons and things of the same general kind or class specifically mentioned (*ejusdem generis*). | | warrant confining the operations of a statute within narrower limits than were intended. |
| 23. Qualifying or limiting words or clauses are to be referred to the next preceding antecedent. | | 23. Not when evident sense and meaning require a different construction. |
| 24. Punctuation will govern when a statute is open to two constructions. | | 24. Punctuation marks will not control the plain and evident meaning of language. |
| 25. It must be assumed that language has been chosen with due regard to grammatical propriety and is not interchangeable on mere conjecture. | | 25. "And" and "or" may be read interchangeably whenever the change is necessary to give the statute sense and effect. |
| 26. There is a distinction between words of permission and words imparting command. | | 26. Words imparting permission may be read as mandatory and words imparting command may be read as permissive when such construction is made necessary by evident intention or by the rights of the public. |
| 27. A proviso qualifies the provision immediately preceding. | | 27. It may clearly be intended to have a wider scope. |
| 28. When the enacting clause is general, a proviso is construed strictly. | | 28. Not when it is necessary to extend the proviso to persons or cases which come within its equity. |

## C. Two Ways of Dealing with a Fixed Text—II: The Oral Tradition

### 1. *The Definition and Authority of the Oral Torah*

Sometimes the term "Oral Torah" includes rabbinic exegesis of the Bible and sometimes it does not. Those who exclude it consider such exegesis so closely tied to the Bible that it is virtually identical with the Bible itself. After all, the Bible cannot be understood without exegesis, and so some consider exegesis to be part and parcel of the original, biblical text. The laws derived through exegesis then have biblical authority, and it is only judicial decisions and the customs of the people that constitute the "Oral Torah," which has inferior, but binding, rabbinic authority. Others include exegesis (or at least some examples of it) in the term "Oral Torah."

In either case, the rabbis claimed that the Oral Torah has divine authority because it was given by God Himself at Sinai along with the Written Torah. The Written Torah is contained in the Pentateuch; the Oral Torah was ultimately written down in the books that constitute rabbinic literature. The Oral Torah is "oral" in the sense that it was transmitted orally from one generation to another until historical circumstances required its transcription. It was given at Sinai along with the Written Torah in two senses: some of its laws are as old as those in the Written Torah attributed to the Sinai event; and those that represent later developments of the Jewish tradition (even outright revisions) derive their authority from the written code, especially Deuteronomy 17, which authorizes judicial interpretation.

This last point is important because it means that the Oral Torah encompassed a broad spectrum of rabbinic legislation. Thus the Talmud (Berakhot 19b) says that "the Rabbis based the authority of all their rulings on the negative commandment of 'Do not deviate from what they (the judges in your time) tell you, to the right or to the left' (Deuteronomy 17:11)," and they emphasized that authority through the liturgical formula that they ordained to precede all acts that they demanded on their own authority.

> Shabbat 23a:
> The blessing over the Hanukkah lights is "Blessed are You, O Lord our God, King of the Universe, who sanctified us through His commandments and commanded us to light the Hanukkah candle." But where (in the Torah) did He command us to do this (since Hanukkah is never mentioned in the Torah, let alone specific laws regarding it)? Rav Aviva said, "Do not deviate, etc."

Maimonides later restricted the term "Oral Torah" to the traditions that had been received, but he claimed that Deuteronomy 17 authorizes not only such traditions but also rules that the rabbis derived through interpretations of the Bible and ordinances that they instituted on their own without explicit biblical backing.

> Mishneh Torah, Laws of Rebels 1:2:
> Whoever does not act in accordance with their (the Rabbis') instruction transgresses a negative commandment, as it says, "Do not devi-

ate ..." (Deuteronomy 17:11). Whether the direction given by them is
with regard to matters that they learned by tradition—matters that
form the contents of the Oral Law—or with regard to rulings deduced
by any of the hermeneutical rules by which the Torah is interpreted—
rulings which they approved—or with regard to measures devised by
them to serve as a hedge around the Law—measures designed to meet
the needs of the times, comprising decrees, ordinances, and customs:
with regard to any of these three categories, obedience to the direction
given by them is a positive command, and whoever disregards any of
these transgresses a negative command also. For Scripture says: "according to the law which they shall teach you" (Deut. 17:11): this refers to the ordinances, decrees, and customs which they promulgate
in public in order to strengthen religion and stabilize the social order.
"And according to the judgments which they shall teach you" (ibid.):
this refers to the rulings derived by means of any of the exegetical
principles by which the Scripture is expounded. "From the sentence
which they shall declare to you" (ibid.): this refers to traditional matters, transmitted to them by preceding generations in unbroken succession.

## 2. The Historicity of the Oral Torah

The immediate question is, of course, the historical one: was there
such an Oral Torah given at Sinai? The rabbis justified their claim
through a variety of exegetical maneuvers such as the following:

> Berakhot 5a:
> What is the meaning of the verse, "And I will give you the tablets of
> stone, and the law and the commandment, which I have written, that
> you may teach them"? (Ex. 24:12). "Tablets of stone," i.e., the Deca-
> logue; "law," i.e., the Pentateuch; "commandment," i.e., the Mish-
> nah; "which I have written," i.e., the Prophets and Hagiographa (Writ-
> ings); "that you may teach them" i.e., the Gemara. The verse teaches
> that all of them were given to Moses on Sinai.

> P. T. Peah 2:6, 17a and elsewhere:
> "And the Lord gave me (Moses) the two tablets of stone inscribed by
> the finger of God with all of the words that the Lord had addressed to
> you at the mountain out of the fire on the day of the assembly" (Deu-
> teronomy 9:10). Rabbi Joshua b. Meir said: ... ("All" indicates that)
> Torah, Mishnah, laws, additions, legends, and even what a learned
> student will say before his teacher in the future were already given to
> Moses at Sinai," as it says, "If there is a matter where one says that it
> is new," his friend should respond to him, "it already existed from
> eternity" (Ecclesiastes 1:10).

These interpretations are, frankly, forced. In one sense, the historical question is impossible to answer, since nobody but Moses was on
the mountain with God. Oral transmission is suggested, however, by

the existence of a number of laws and customs in biblical stories that are not found in the codes until later, if at all. The existence of such traditions is to be expected; after all, the Hebrew tribes must have had *some* rules to govern their interactions with each other, and the laws of the Bible are rather sparse. Hence the existence of an Oral Law from even before the time of Sinai is likely, and so the doctrine of the Oral Law in the modern, critical sense is certainly true.

On the other hand, the existence of Oral Law in the Orthodox sense is doubtful. The Bible makes no explicit mention of an oral accompaniment to the body of written law—not even in its historical sections—which is surprising if it indeed existed. The doctrine is often attributed specifically to the Pharisees on the basis of Josephus (and, later, Maimonides), but we have no evidence in rabbinic or Christian literature that the Pharisees affirmed it or that the Sadducees and others denied it. The earliest sources specifically to declare that the Oral Law had originated at Sinai are in the *Sifra* and *Sifre Deuteronomy*, both of which are usually attributed to Rabbi Akiba in the early second century C.E.

Why, then, did Rabbi Akiba and those who followed him insist that there had been such an Oral Torah at Sinai? Part of the motivation may well have been political: if God revealed an Oral Law at Sinai through which the Written Law was to be interpreted, then a great deal of power rests with those who know that law—that is, the rabbis themselves. Rabbi Akiba was known for the extent to which he stretched the meaning of the biblical text—even interpreting the crownlets that embellish some of the letters of the traditional Torah scroll (*Menahot* 29b). One can understand why he would be anxious to shore up the authority of such interpretations in the face of objections from his more conservative colleagues.

There were also other, nonpolitical motivations for the rabbinic doctrine. One was the historical fact that a body of rules and customs, unsupported by the written Torah, was observed by the Jewish community by tannaitic times. Since many of those traditions modified the written law substantially, some justification had to be found for abiding by them.

But the most important consideration that led to the doctrine of an Orah Torah was undoubtedly the commitment of the rabbis to an ongoing, vital tradition that could be effective in every time and place. This is especially evident in the rabbis' claims that their exegesis represents an ongoing fount of revelation.

*Numbers Rabbah* 19:6:
   Matters not revealed to Moses were revealed to Rabbi Akiba and his colleagues.

*Tanhuma Buber, Devarim,* 1a:
When God revealed His presence to the Israelites, He did not show forth all His goodness at once, because they could not have borne so much good; for had He revealed His goodness to them at one time they would have died. . . . Thus, when Joseph made himself known to his brothers, they were unable to answer him, because they were astounded by him (Gen. 45:3). If God were to reveal Himself all at once, how much more powerful would be the effect. So He shows Himself little by little.

## 3. *The Philosophical Grounding and Implications of the Oral Torah*

Beyond the historical issues raised by the theory of the Oral Torah, how is it philosophically possible? That is, how can it be that everything was revealed at Sinai and yet new things are revealed each day?

Actually, the situation is not as contradictory as it may seem, as those trained in the secular law will readily recognize. On the one hand, with the exception of the last sixteen amendments, the Constitution of the United States is the same document it was in 1791, when the Bill of Rights was ratified. Its meaning, however, has been extended far beyond the probable intentions of its framers, because judges, lawyers, and scholars have carefully examined its every phrase in applying it to new problems and circumstances. Its meaning has changed a number of times when the Supreme Court reversed itself or greatly narrowed the application of previous rulings. Yet, in an important sense, all of the later developments were inherent in the original Constitution because they are all derived from governmental bodies that it created and the general principles that it established.

Similarly, each time a Jewish court or judge decided to interpret the Torah or Talmud in one way and not another, the meaning of those texts changed. Through this process of interpretation, or "Midrash," the texts sometimes were given meanings they never before had. Sometimes several possible alternative lines of interpretation were cut off by this process. Whether the application of a given verse in the Torah was expanded or contracted, this process was possible only because the Torah established the ground rules and procedures of Jewish law. On the other hand, in every generation the Torah is given new meanings and applications, and in that sense "matters that had not been revealed to Moses were revealed to Rabbi Akiba and his colleagues." The authority of Jewish law does not diminish, then, as it is applied anew in every generation. The rabbis clearly recognized that it must be so interpreted and applied if it was to continue to live.

The doctrine of the Oral Torah therefore has a surprising consequence: while it justifies the ongoing authority of Jewish law as it develops, it also provides a strong foundation for individual initiative and creativity. Because of this doctrine, Judaism is unusually tolerant of divergent personal opinions and leaves ample room for individuals, through study, to be personally involved in the discovery of the law. Authority is present in the world; the law was received by humans at Sinai. Yet every person is commanded to study and teach and discuss the commandments daily as an act of love. The individual is not a passive recipient of a definitive guide to life, but instead each person is a crucial actor in the never-ending task of turning the law over and over like a crystal in the hand. Each person must continually probe it for new meaning, new plays of light in the stone's facets, for ultimately everything can be found in it: "Turn it, and turn it again, for everything is in it" (Avot 5:22).

### 4. The Oral Torah's Preeminence Over the Written Torah

The theory of the Oral Torah thus became a crucial philosophical underpinning for Jewish law. It gave it at once flexibility, historical roots, and divine authority for its continuing developments. No wonder that the rabbis valued it as highly as they did—even over the Written Torah:

> Gittin 60b:
> The Holy One (God) made a covenant with Israel only for the sake of that which was transmitted orally, as it says, "According to (or, because of) these words I have made a covenant with Israel" (Exodus 34:27).

> Pesikta Rabbati, chap. 3, (ed. Friedmann 7b):
> No man should say, "I will not observe the precepts of the elders" (i.e., the Oral Law), since they are not of Mosaic authority (lit., contained in the Torah). For God has said, "No, my son, but whatever they decree for you, perform," as it says "when you (i.e., the elders) decree a command, it shall be fulfilled for you" (i.e., by Me, God) (a playful interpretation of Job 22:28).

> Sanhedrin 11:3:
> Disregard of the enactments of the Scribes is more severely punished than disregard of the injunctions of the Torah. If one says, "(Not to wear) phylacteries (Exodus 13:9, 16; Deut. 6:8, 11:18) is not a transgression of the Torah," he is exempt. (If one teaches that in the phylacteries) there should be five partitions, thus adding to the words of the Scribes (who prescribed four), he is culpable.

Maimonides, reflecting the views of the rabbis of the Talmud, was later to classify those who deny the authenticity of the Oral Torah among those who deny the (written) Torah itself.

> *Mishneh Torah,* Laws of Repentance 3:6,8:
> The following have no portion in the world to come but are cut off and perish, for their great wickedness and sinfulness are condemned forever and ever: heretics, Epicureans, those who deny the Torah. . . . There are three classes of those who deny the Torah: he who says that the Torah is not of divine origin—even if he says of one verse, or of a single word, that Moses said it on his own authority—is a denier of the Torah; likewise, he who denies its interpretation, i.e., the Oral Torah, and repudiates its reporters, as Zadok and Boethus (founders of the Sadducees) did; and he who says that the Creater changed one commandment for another, and that this Torah, although of divine origin, is now obsolete, as the Nazarenes and Moslems assert. Everyone belonging to any of these classes is a denier of the Torah.

## 5. The Oral Form of the Tradition

In both the Jewish and the Anglo-American traditions there was strong resistance to writing down the tradition. In Jewish sources, the reasons for that reluctance include the following:

a. God specifically gave some laws orally, so how can we dare to change their form?

> *Temurrah* 14b:
> R. Abba the son of R. Hiyya reported in the name of R. Yohanan: Those who write the traditional teachings (are punished) like those who burn the Torah, and he who learns from them (i.e., the writings) receives no reward. R. Judah b. Nahman, the teaching assistant of Resh Lakish, gave the following (as the Scriptural basis for that ruling): The verse says, "Write these words" and then says, "For by means of (lit. "by the mouth of") these *words* I have *written* a covenant with you and Israel" (Exodus 34:27): (the distinction created in the verse between those words which you are supposed to write as against those which you are supposed to hear) teaches you that matters received as oral traditions you are not permitted to recite from writing, and that written things (i.e., biblical passages) you are not permitted to recite from memory. And the Tanna of the School of R. Ishmael taught: Scripture says, "Write these words," implying that *these* words you may write, but you may not write traditional laws.

b. If the laws were written down, people would forget their connection to the Torah. This would impair the authority of rabbinic interpretation and the sense that it represents continuation of biblical law.

The following source has the standard form of the Mishnah and Gemara, but it is not part of those works. *Megillat Ta'anit* is a list of thirty-six days on which there were significant victories and happy events in the history of the Jews during the time of the Second Temple, and the rabbis accordingly forbade fasting on them. The book received its present form in the late first or early second centuries C.E., and it may be a remnant of the rebel party against Rome at that time.

> *Megillat Ta'anit, Mishnah* 10 and *scholium ad locum:*
> *Mishnah:* On the fourth of Tammuz there was the Assembly of the Book of Decrees.
>
> *Gemara:* The Sadducees had a written, official book of decrees (prescribing) who was subject to death by stoning, who by fire, who by the sword, and who by strangulation. When they sat (as judges) and someone would ask (for the basis of their rulings) and they would show him (the relevant passage) in the book, and he would say to them: "How do you know that this person is liable for death by stoning, this person by fire, this one by sword, and this one by strangulation?"—they did not know how to bring proof from the Torah (for the rule). The Sages said to them, "Is it not written, 'According to the Torah which they shall teach you, etc.' (Deuteronomy 17:11)? That teaches that we do not write laws in a book (since the verse requires judges to rule from the Torah)." . . . (Therefore) the day that they nullified (the authority of) that book they made a holiday.

  c. God was afraid that if the laws were written, the gentiles would discover them and either steal them for themselves, thus weakening the uniqueness and identity of the Jewish people, or else misinterpret them and use them to undermine rabbinic authority.

> *Tanhuma Buber, Ki Tissa,* 34, 58b:
> When God had finished (teaching the Written and Orah Torahs to Moses), He said to Moses: "Go and teach it to My children." . . . Moses said, "Lord, write it down for them." God said, "I indeed wanted to give it all to them in writing, but it was revealed that the Gentiles in the future will have dominion over them and will claim the Torah as their own, and then My children would be like the Gentiles. Therefore give them the Scriptures in writing, and the Mishnah, Aggada, and Talmud orally, for it is the latter which separate Israel from the Gentiles.

> *Numbers, Rabbah, Naso* 14:10:
> God gave the Israelites the Oral Law to distinguish them from other nations. It was not given in writing so that the nations could not falsify it, as they have done with the Written Law, and say that they are the true Israel.

  d. It is simply impossible to write down all of the laws that constitute the Oral tradition.

*Numbers Rabbah, Naso,*14:4:

R. Abba of Serungaya said: If one should ask you why the words of the Scribes were not given in a written form in the same way as the words of the Torah were, tell him that it was because it is impossible to write down all their words. That is the implication of the text, "And more than of them (*Mehemah*), my son, be careful" (Eccles. 12:12). What is the signification of the expression "*mehemah*"? It means: Confusion (*mehumah*) will enter your mind if you come to write down the words of the Scribes. Why? Because if you attempt to write down their words, you will find the material for the making of books to be endless and unlimited. Hence it is written, "Of making of books there is no end" (ibid.). What then should a man do? He should labor strenuously in the study of the words of the Sages.

    e. Many of the laws are difficult to master and consequently seem strange. There is a much better chance of explaining the laws and encouraging people to observe them if they are taught in the context of an intimate, student-teacher relationship rather than from an impersonal, difficult scroll.

*Gittin* 60b:

R. Eleazer said, "The greater portion of the Torah is contained in the written law and only the smaller portion was transmitted orally, as it says, "Though I wrote the major portion of my law for him, it is considered a strange thing (Hosea 8:12). R. Yohanan, on the other hand, said that the greater part was transmitted orally and only the smaller part is contained in the Written Torah, for it says, "For by the mouth of (by means of) these words I have made a covenant with you and Israel" (Exodus 34:27). But then what does he (R. Yohanan) make of the words, "Though I wrote the major part of the law for him"? (He would answer that) that is a rhetorical question (as if to say): "Should I have written the major portion of My law for him? (Even now, when it is not written) does he not consider it a strange thing?" And how does the other (R. Eleazar) interpret the verse, "For by the mouth of these words"? (He would say that) that implies that they are difficult to master (and therefore must be taught "by mouth," i.e., orally.)

    f. Only if the Oral Law remains oral can Jewish law retain sufficient flexibility to be able to adapt to new situations, especially in light of the Torah's prohibition to change it legislatively (Deuteronomy 4:2 and 13:1):

*P. T. Sanhedrin* 4:2, 22a:

If the Torah had been given in a fixed form, the situation would have been intolerable. What is the meaning of the oft-recurring phrase, "The Lord *spoke* to Moses?" Moses said before Him, "Sover-

222

eign of the Universe! Cause me to know what the final decision is on each matter of law." He replied, "The majority must be followed: when the majority declares a thing permitted, it is permissible; when the majority declares it forbidden, it is not allowed; so that the Torah may be capable of interpretation with forty-nine points *pro* and forty-nine points *contra*.

The Anglo-American tradition displayed the same reluctance to record cases in writing. The complex history of English law reports from the medieval yearbooks to the present reflects changing attitudes toward legal education (case reports have apparently always been a major teaching tool for young lawyers) and differing attitudes of courts regarding the binding quality of judicial precedent. Reports of the decisions of the major common law courts (Kings Bench, Common Pleas, Exchequer) changed substantially in form, quality, and reliability over the generations, but there is a fairly continuous tradition of reporting. But in the Chancellor's Court of Equity it was uncertain well into the seventeenth century whether it was appropriate to report decisions and rely on precedent in doing equity. Holdsworth quotes Lombard, a master in Chancery, who wrote in 1635:

Whether it be meete that the Chancellour should appoint unto himself, and publish to others any certaine Rules and Limits of Equity, or no; about which men both godly and learned doe varie in opinion: For on the one part it is thought as hard a thing to prescribe to equity any certaine bounds, as it is to make any one generall law to bee a meet measure of justice in all particular cases. And on the other side it is sayd, that if it bee not knowne before hand in what cases the Chancellour will reach forth his helpe, and where not, then neither shall the Subject bee assured how, or when he may possesse his owne in peace, nor the practizer in Law be able to informe his Client what may become of his Action.

The House of Lords exercises both legislative and judicial authority. By the end of the seventeenth century it was increasingly recognized as the final court of appeal from courts of law and equity. Decisions took on a form more appropriate to case decision than legislation. Nonetheless, the lords resisted the publication of their decisions and in 1698 decreed such publication a breach of privilege, punishable by the house. This was enough to frighten off would-be reporters for almost a century. No more reports of the House of Lords' cases appeared until 1784.

In more modern settings, the oral form of legal traditions continues, but often for reasons of convenience rather than for theoretical principles. Appellate decisions were delivered orally and not officially reported in many English courts until World War II. California law requires written decisions, but most states do not. Thus the oral form of preserving a legal tradition is not as foreign or as ancient as many modern Americans believe.

## D. *Continuity and Change*

We have seen the rabbinic ideological and emotional foundations for the continuity of the law: all of the varying interpretations are ultimately based on the Torah; all were revealed at Sinai as one unit; and those who bear the tradition at any time are the heirs of its previous followers. Some concrete structures were built upon these theoretical underpinnings. The continuing authority of the Sanhedrin was asserted, and provision was made to insure the existence of the court system. The rabbis also took one crucial step to provide for continuity in the content, as well as the instructions, of Jewish law. The authority of precedent was forcefully established, as is shown in this incident:

> *Tosefta Ta'anit 2:5; B. T. Eruvin 41a:*
> After the death of Rabban Gamliel, Rabbi Joshua entered (the academy) to abrogate his ruling (on a specific issue), when Rabbi Yohanon ben Nuri stood up and exclaimed, "I submit that 'the body must follow the head' (a proverb): throughout the lifetime of Rabban Gamliel we laid down the law in agreement with his view and now you wish to abrogate it? Joshua, we shall not listen to you since the law has once been fixed in agreement with Rabban Gamliel." And there was not a single person who raised any objection whatsoever to that statement.

American political theorists acknowledge the practical truth that the Supreme Court reads the election returns. Jewish tradition has followed a more conservative pattern, less willing to change course to meet changing social attitudes. A rule of precedent, particularly one that does not provide easy ways for a new majority to overturn it, is a very conservative, if not reactionary, force. But a rule of precedent can also be a creative influence, leading those who must announce the law to find flexible links between past, present, and future. Because abrupt change is suspect, the new must be connected with what has gone before. Wise men know that they must be modest and cautious if what they declare to be the law cannot easily be changed and therefore must meet varied and changing circumstances. Dogmatism and extremism are not likely to be valued characteristics in such a system.

The real trick is to balance coherence and continuity with capacity to make needed changes. The rabbis claimed that God authorized exegesis in order to make the law malleable and flexible. In addition to those ideological statements, the Mishnah presents a specific procedure for outright changes in the law. It records a debate in which both Hillel and Shammai voice opinions but the ultimate law announced is not according to the views of either. It then asks:

> *Eduyot* 1:5–6:
> 5. And why do they preserve the opinion of an individual against that of the majority, seeing that the adopted legal ruling can only be in accordance with the opinion of the majority? That is so that if a court favors the view of the individual, it may depend upon him, for a court must not annul the view of another court unless it excels it in wisdom and in number; if it excels it in wisdom but not in number, or in number but not in wisdom, it cannot nullify its ruling, but (it can nullify a ruling) only if it exceeds it both in wisdom and in number.
>
> 6. R. Judah said, If so, why do they put on record the view of the individual against that of the majority seemingly to no purpose? It is recorded so that if a man shall say, "I hold such a tradition," another may reply to him, "You have only heard it as the view of so-and-so."

There are obviously problems in interpreting these mishnayot (for example, how do you measure wisdom? does "number" refer to judges? constituency? age?), and later commentators offer varying readings. The important thing to note is that the Tannaim *did* provide for alternate rulings, even though their major efforts were devoted to organizing and fixing the law according to received precedent.

Significant changes in Jewish law sometimes come through outright revisions, but more often they were produced by shifting the weight accorded to varying constructions of precedents. So, for example, the Bible requires capital punishment for a variety of offenses, but the rabbis created such demanding court procedures in capital cases that it became virtually impossible to obtain a capital conviction. They required that the culprit be warned by two witnesses immediately before he committed the unlawful act carrying the death penalty (after all, he may not know that the act is illegal or punished so severely, and how can you hold him liable for death for transgressing a law that he never knew?); that he respond, "Even so, I am going to do it" (because he may not have heard the warning); that he commit the act within three seconds after hearing the warning (for otherwise he might have forgotten the law that he just heard and therefore could not be held responsible); that the witnesses not be related to each other or to the culprit; and that there be at least one judge on the court who votes to acquit him (for otherwise the court might be prejudiced against him—which, by the way, is the exact opposite of the requirement in American law for a unanimous jury). Some of those requirements—and some of the other things the rabbis required—are clearly implausible extensions of principles that are reasonable in a different form, and the rabbis certainly knew that, but they had decided to outlaw the death penalty, despite the numerous times the Bible requires it, and they used court procedures to accomplish that. Put another way, they interpreted the death penalty out of existence, and they intended that result and realized the issues involved fully.

> *Makkot* 1:10:
> A court which has put a man to death once in a seven year period is called "a hanging court" (lit. a destructive court). Rabbi Elazar ben Azariah says, "Even once in seventy years." Rabbi Tarfon and Rabbi Akiba say, "Were we members of the court, no person would ever be put to death." Rabban Simeon ben Gamliel retorted: "If so, they would multiply the shedders of blood in Israel."

On the other hand, while they effectually nullified the death penalty, they created a whole structure of Sabbath laws far beyond those in the Bible such that they themselves said:

> *Hagigah* 1:8
> The laws of the Sabbath are like mountains hanging by a hair, for they consist of little Bible and many laws.

Thus the rabbis consciously changed Jewish law as evidenced both by what they said and what they did, adding a number of laws, dropping some, and changing the form of some.

The rabbis considered their actions authorized by God because *they* were the ones appointed by the Torah to interpret and apply it in every age. In Jewish law, as in American law, the constitution establishes some laws and also bodies to interpret and apply those laws. In both systems, the interpretations in later generations may vary widely from the original intention of the constitutional laws—even to the extent of nullifying them—but the new interpretations carry constitutional authority because they are made by the bodies that the constitution establishes. In both cases, it is the *forms* (institutions) established by the constitution that determine its meaning, even to the point of effectively canceling sections of its contents, and it is because the new rulings issue from the duly authorized bodies that they carry constitutional authority. So it is that the rabbis stressed the ongoing authority

of contemporary judges, even if they do not measure up to the stature
of their predecessors:

> *Tosefta, Rosh Hashanah* 1:18:
> Scripture says, "And Samuel said to the people, 'It is the Lord that
> made Moses and Aaron,'" and it also says (in the same context), "And
> the Lord sent Jerubbaal and Bedan and Jepthah and Samuel" (I Samuel
> 12:6, 11). . . . We see therefore that Scripture places three of the most
> reprehensible characters on the same level as three of the most esti-
> mable to show that Jerubbaal in his generation is like Moses in his,
> Bedan in his generation is like Aaron in his, and Jepthah in his genera-
> tion is like Samuel in his to teach you that the most worthless per-
> son, once he has been appointed a leader of the community, is to be
> counted like the mightiest of the mighty. Scripture also says: "And
> you shall come to the priests, the levites, and the judge that shall be in
> those days" (Deuteronomy 17:9). Can we imagine that a man should
> go to a judge who is not in his days? (Why, then, the need for the
> phrase "in those days"?) This shows that you must be content to go to
> the judge who is in your days. It also says, "Say not, how was it that
> the former days were better than these?" (Ecclesiastes 7:10).

> *Numbers R.* 14:4:
> "They are given from one shepherd" (Eccles. 12:11). Although one
> scholar offers his view and another scholar offers his, the words of
> both are all derived from what Moses, the shepherd, received from the
> "One" Lord of the universe. "The words of the wise are as goads"
> (*ibid.*). It was taught: How can we infer that if a man hears an exposi-
> tion from the mouth of the least in Israel, he should regard it as having
> been heard from the wisest man in Israel? Because Scripture states,
> "And it shall come to pass, if you will hearken *diligently* unto My
> commandments which I command you this day" (Deut. 11:13). Ay,
> and not only as having heard it from the mouth of one wise man, but
> as having heard it from the mouth of many wise men; for it says,
> "Those that are gathered (*ba'ale asufot*)," means the Sanhedrin, as is
> borne out by the text, "Gather (*esefah*) unto Me seventy men of the el-
> ders of Israel" (Num. 11:16). And not merely as having heard it from
> the mouth of the Sanhedrin, but as having heard it from the mouth of
> Moses, for it says, "They are given from one shepherd"; and it says,
> "Then his people remembered the days of the old, the days of Moses
> . . . Moses was a shepherd" (Ex. 3:1). And not merely as having heard
> it from Moses, but as having heard it from the mouth of the Holy One,
> blessed be He; for it says, "They are given from one Shepherd"; and
> "Shepherd" denotes the Holy One, blessed be He as it says, "Give Ear,
> O Shepherd of Israel" (Ps.80:2), and "one" also refers to God; as it
> says, "The Lord is one" (Deut. 6:4).

Rabbinic law may have been saved at crucial junctures from the reactionary tendency of precedent because the tradition legitimizes a great deal of argumentation and controversy. Tolerating this degree of vigorous disagreement was not common among the Church Fathers or, for that matter, the leaders of any society, ancient or modern, until the advent of the United States. The rabbis made dissent one of the distinguishing features of Jewish law and of Jewish ideology. There are outer limits to the positions that one can advocate in thought and practice and still remain a Jew, and Jewish sources do not sing the praises of the "losers." But Judaism tolerated diversity of opinion and practice and encouraged uninhibited, far-ranging discussion.

This tolerance and willingness to change the law should not be confused with indifference or lack of zeal. Despite the changes the rabbis instituted, they did not think that "anything goes," or that they could play fast and loose with the law. They believed in the law and took measures to insure its coherence, continuity, and authority. The rabbis dared to make the changes they did because they took the law seriously, honored it, cherished it, and deeply wanted it to govern the Jewish community for all time.

### E. *The Limits of the Flexibility of the Text and the Tradition: Opposition Movements in Jewish Legal History*

While Judaism tolerates and even encourages discussion and debate, it does have limits. Any tradition must draw the line somewhere or else it will cease to have a distinctive perspective—or even a coherent one. During the rabbinic period, the rabbis had to defend their assertion of authority and their interpretation of the tradition against a number of other groups.

1. *Internal Debates.* Even within the rabbis' own ranks the lines of authority had to be clearly drawn. Rabbi Johanan ben Zakkai and Rabbi Gamliel II were respectively the first and second presidents of the Sanhedrin when it moved to Yavneh after (or perhaps even a little before) the destruction of the Temple. Rabbi Johanan ben Zakkai instituted ten revisions in law to accomplish the adjustment to post-Temple times, but his most important act was a symbolic one. While the Temple stood, if Rosh Hashanah (the New Year) happened to fall on the Sabbath, the *shofar* (ram's horn) would be blown exclusively within the precincts of the Temple. The following, famous story relates how Rabbi Johanan ben Zakkai used that fact rather deviously to establish the authority of the Sanhedrin apart from its location on Temple grounds.

*Rosh Hashanah* 29b:
Our Rabbis taught: Once New Year fell on a Sabbath and all the
towns assembled (at Yavneh to hear the blowing of the *shofar* by representatives of the Sanhedrin), and Rabbi Johanan said to Bene Bateyra
(descendants of the leaders of the Sanhedrin who had resigned in favor
of Hillel, according to *Pesahim* 66a): "Let us blow the *shofar*." They
said to him: "Let us discuss the matter." He said to them: "Let us
blow and afterwards discuss." After they had blown, they said to him,
"Let us now discuss the question." He replied, "The horn has already
been heard in Yavneh, and what has been done is no longer open to
discussion."

As Rabbi Johanan ben Zakkai confirmed the continuing authority
of the Sanhedrin, so Rabbi Gamliel II established the authority of its
president. Until the fourth century C.E., there was no fixed Jewish calendar. Instead, witnesses would come to the Sanhedrin during the day
and testify that they had seen the first sliver of the new moon on the
previous night, and the president of the Sanhedrin would then declare
that day the first day of the new month. There were some special rules
to make sure that the calendar would never be too much out of tune
with the movements of the sun and the moon, but the fixing of the
dates of the calendar did depend to a large extent on the testimony
of witnesses. This was very important; if the first day of the Hebrew
month Tishre was declared to be on a Monday, then that day was Rosh
Hashanah, no work should be done, special services should be held,
and Yom Kippur (the Day of Atonement) would be ten days later, on
the Tuesday night and Wednesday of the following week. If, on the
other hand, the first day of the month was declared to be on Tuesday,
then both Rosh Hashanah and Yom Kippur would take place a day
later, and all of the special laws of the High Holy days (including fasting and refraining from business and travel on Yom Kippur) would be
observed then.

*Rosh Hashanah* 2:8–9:
On one occasion two witnesses came and said: "We saw the new
moon at its expected time (the night after the 29th day of the previous
month), but on the next night it could not be seen" (when it should
have been even larger and clearer). Yet Rabbi Gamliel (who was President of the Sanhedrin) accepted them as true witnesses (assuming that
they did not see the moon on the next night simply because clouds
covered it). Rabbi Dosa ben Harkinas said, "I maintain that they are
false witnesses," and Rabbi Joshua ben Hananiah said to him, "I see
the strength of your arguments." (Since Rabbi Joshua was Vice-Pres-
ident of the Sanhedrin) Rabbi Gamliel sent a message to Rabbi Joshua,

saying: "I order you to come to me with your staff and money on the day on which, according to your calculations, Yom Kippur falls." Rabbi Akiba went and found Rabbi Joshua in distress (since he would have to publicly violate the laws of Yom Kippur on the day which he thought to be Yom Kippur). Rabbi Akiba said to Rabbi Joshua: I can prove (from the Torah) that everything which Rabbi Gamliel has done, he has done correctly, for the Torah says, "These are the appointed seasons of the Lord, holy convocations, which you shall proclaim in their appointed season" (Lev. 23:4) (which means): whether they are proclaimed at their proper time or not, I have no other "appointed season" but these. Rabbi Joshua then went to Rabbi Dosa ben Harkinas (who had agreed with Rabbi Joshua that the witnesses were false but who nevertheless) said to him: "If we call into question the decisions of the Court of Rabbi Gamliel, we must call into question the decisions of every single court that has existed from the days of Moses to the present day . . ." So Rabbi Joshua took his staff and his money in his hand and went to Yavneh to Rabbi Gamliel on the day on which Yom Kippur fell according to his own calculation. Rabbi Gamliel stood up, kissed him on his head, and said to him, "Come in peace my teacher and my pupil"—my teacher in wisdom, and my pupil in that you have accepted my decisons."

Two other conflicts between Rabbi Gamliel and Rabbi Joshua are recorded in the Talmud (*Bekhorot* 36a, *Berakhot* 27b–28a; see also P.T. *Berakhot* 7c–7d), and the Mishnah tells us of yet another challenge to Rabbi Gamliel's authority by Rabbi Akiba—although both the Palestinian and Babylonian Talmuds maintain that it could not possibly have been Rabbi Akiba, Heaven forfend! (See Mishnah *Rosh Hashanah* 1:6; P.T. ibid. 57b; B.T. ibid. 22a.) The resentment against the authority that Rabbi Gamliel aggregated to himself actually led to his impeachment, but he continued to participate in the deliberations of the assembly under its new president, Rabbi Eleazar ben Azariah, and was ultimately reinstated as copresident with him (*Berakhot* 27b–28a). In any case, he succeeded in making the Sanhedrin and its president the supreme authorities in Jewish law, with power to review and abrogate other judges' decisions. This gave Jewish law legal coherence, and that is precisely what Rabbi Gamliel claimed for his goals in this prayer.

> *Bava Metzia* 59b:
> Sovereign of the Universe! You know full well that I have not acted for my own honor, nor for the honor of my paternal house, but for Yours, so that strife may not multiply in Israel!

But challenges to the coherence and authority of the rabbinic tradition did not come from within the Pharisaic group alone. Large groups of Jews refused to accept rabbinic leadership. They are known in talmudic times as *amei ha'aretz*, a term that originally referred to people not careful about the laws of purity but that, in the second century, designated the opponents of the Pharisees. The term later is used to refer simply to ignorant people because the opposition of the *amei ha'aretz* of the second century included rejection of the Pharisaic emphasis on studying the law.

Such opposition groups have existed throughout Jewish history. Many discussions of Jewish law ignore them because most of the sources in hand were written by the "winners"—that is, those whose policies and interpretations were ultimately adopted. Some forms of rabbinic literature, particularly Midrash Halakhah and Gemara, carefully report both sides of contested issues, but the perspective of the reporter skews the presentation. This is especially true after the rabbinic period since all of the victors have seen themselves as transmitters of the rabbinic tradition. Judaism was no longer simply the religion of the Hebrew Bible: it had become the religion of the Bible as the rabbis of each generation interpreted it.

2. *Korah.* The dominant influence of the winning position can, of course, be seen in the Bible itself. The Golden Calf incident is portrayed in terms that leave no room for doubt that Aaron and the people were wrong (Exodus 32–34), and the same can be said of the incident of the twelve spies (Numbers 13–14; Deuteronomy 1), but the arguments may not have been as obviously weighted as the text would make it seem. Perhaps the clearest example of bias in our sources is the dramatic, if problematic, biblical story of Korah. Try to read it from Korah's point of view, despite the fact that the author is certainly happy that Moses was victorious. Neither Moses nor Korah emerges completely untainted from their struggle for power, but play the defense attorney for Korah for a moment. Is the case so clearly against him? To what extent is the story simply a justification of Mosaic authority and the priestly taxes imposed on the Israelites?

> *Numbers* 16:1–35:
> Now Korah, son of Izhar son of Kohath son of Levi, betook himself, along with Dathan and Abiram, sons of Eliab, and On, son of Peleth —descendants of Reuben—to rise up against Moses, together with two hundred and fifty Israelites, chieftains of the community, elected in the assembly, men of repute. They combined against Moses and Aaron and said to them, "You have gone too far! For all the community are holy, all of them, and the Lord is in their midst. Why then do you raise yourselves above the Lord's congregation?"

When Moses heard this, he fell on his face. Then he spoke to Korah and all his company, saying, "Come morning, the Lord will make known who is His and who is holy, and will grant him access to Himself; He will grant access to the one He has chosen. Do this: You, Korah and all your band, take fire pans, and tomorrow put fire in them and lay incense on them before the Lord. Then the man whom the Lord chooses, he shall be the holy one. You have gone too far, sons of Levi!"

Moses said further to Korah, "Hear me, sons of Levi. Is it not enough for you that the God of Israel has set you apart from the community of Israel by giving access to Him, to perform the duties of the Lord's Tabernacle, and to minister to the community and serve them? Thus He has advanced you and all your fellow levites with you; yet you seek the priesthood too! Truly, it is against the Lord that you and all your company have banded together. For who is Aaron that you should rail against him?"

Moses sent for Dathan and Abiram, sons of Eliab; but they said, "We will not come! Is it not enough that you brought us from a land flowing with milk and honey to have us die in the wilderness, that you would also lord it over us? Even if you had brought us to a land flowing with milk and honey, and given us possession of fields and vineyards, should you gouge out those men's eyes? We will not come!" Moses was much aggrieved and he said to the Lord, "Pay no regard to their presentation. I have not taken the ass of any one of them, nor have I wronged any one of them."

And Moses said to Korah, "Tomorrow, you and all your company appear before the Lord, you and they and Aaron. Each of you take his fire pan and lay incense on it, and each of you bring his fire pan before the Lord, two hundred and fifty fire pans; you and Aaron also (bring) your fire pans." Each of them took his fire pan, put fire in it, laid incense on it, and took his place at the entrance of the Tent of Meeting. As for Moses and Aaron, Korah gathered the whole community against them at the entrance of the Tent of Meeting.

Then the Presence of the Lord appeared to the whole community, and the Lord spoke to Moses and Aaron, saying, "Stand back from this community that I may annihilate them in an instant!" But they fell on their faces and said, "O God, Source of the breath of all flesh! When one man sins, will You be wrathful with the whole community!"

The Lord spoke to Moses, saying, "Speak to the community and say: Withdraw from about the abodes of Korah, Dathan, and Abiram."

Moses rose and went to Dathan and Abiram, the elders of Israel following him. He addressed the community, saying, "Move away from the tents of these wicked men and touch nothing that belongs to them, lest you be wiped out for all their sins." So they withdrew from about the abodes of Korah, Dathan, and Abiram.

Now Dathan and Abiram had come out and they stood at the entrance of their tents, with their wives, their children, and their little ones. And Moses said, "By this you shall know that it was the Lord who sent me to do all these things, that they are not of my devising: if these men die as all men do, if their lot be the common fate of all mankind, it was not the Lord who sent me. But if the Lord brings about something unheard-of, so that the ground opens its mouth wide and swallows them up with all that belongs to them, and they go down alive into Sheol, you shall know that these men have spurned the Lord." Scarcely had he finished speaking all these words when the ground under them burst asunder, and the earth opened its mouth and swallowed them up with their households, all Korah's people and all their possessions. They went down alive in Sheol, with all that belonged to them; the earth closed over them and they vanished from the midst of the congregation. All Israel around them fled at their shrieks, for they said, "The earth might swallow us!"

And a fire went forth from the Lord and consumed the two hundred and fifty men offering the incense.

Consider this exposition of Albert George Butzer in *The Interpreter's Bible* (*The Interpreter's Bible, The Book of Numbers* [New York and Nashville: Abingdon Press, 1953], II; 221–23.)

From our present vantage point we certainly cannot be too severely critical of Korah, Dathan, and Abiram. Today we glory in their two main contentions, *viz.* ecclesiastical and political democracy as over against autocracy in both of these realms. In what then did the crime of Korah and his associates consist? Was it not that they failed to see that their timing was wrong? Fine as their ideas were, they would not understand that the people of Israel were not ready for them. Indeed, had the rebellion of Korah succeeded at that time the result would have been the worst kind of chaos, and God's plan for Israel would have been dealt a retardingly disastrous blow.... There is ... destructive power in an idea whose time has not come.

In contrast, Martin Buber does not see Korah as an ancient democrat, but rather as a dangerous autocrat. In fact, for Buber Korah and his followers are reminiscent of the antinomian Nazi "werewolves" and "leopards" who soon were to destroy the German community in which Buber lived. Their argument was the same: law runs counter to the spirit; it must and can be replaced by the rule of the spirit as dictated by an elite group. That view, however, mistakes the present moment in history for the eschaton, dangerously substituting what may be appropriate then for what is necessary now. The law must be reinvested with the spirit continually, but it must remain binding if we are to be governed by the will of God rather than the dictates of self-aggrandizing tyrants.

The historical Moses, as far as we are capable of perceiving him, does not differentiate between the spheres of religion and politics; and in him they are not separated. When "Korah and his band" revolt against Moses, it is not to be interpreted as meaning that they rise against his cult privileges as such; for these privileges as such are not stressed and might as well be non-existent.

Rather do they rise at first against the fact that one man leads the people in the name of God. But they go beyond this and revolt against the fact that this man decides in the name of God what is right and what is wrong. "The whole people, all of them, are holy," and therefore nobody can give orders or issue prohibitions to anybody else in respect of what the latter's own holiness suggests to him. Since the people are holy, commandments from without are no longer necessary.

It should not be supposed that later stages of development are introduced here into the words of Korah. The attitude which finds expression in these words is known to us from far more primitive stages. In many of those tribes which are labelled as primitive, such motives have contributed vastly to the establishment of secret societies. A chief or shaman, whose authority is supported by a superhuman power, can be combatted in two ways. One is to attempt to overthrow him, particularly by shaking faith in the assurance that he will receive that support, and to take his place, which is precisely what some suppose to have been the nucleus of the story of Korah, that is, a manifestation of the personal struggle for power known to us from all phases of human history, and one which in general leaves the structure of society unchanged. The second method is to cut off the main roots of the leader's power by establishing, within the tribe but external to the official tribal life, a secret society in which the actual, the true, the "holy" communal life is lived, free from the bonds of the "law"; a life of "leopards" or "werewolves" in which the wildest instincts reach their goal on the basis of mutual aid, but in holy action. . . .

It is easy to adduce analogies at higher levels of development particularly out of the history of antinomist sects and movements. The issue is always that of "divine freedom" against "divine law"; but at these higher levels it becomes even more clear than at the more primitive stages that isolated divine freedom abolishes itself. Naturally God rules through men who have been gripped and filled by His spirit, and who on occasion carry out His will not merely by means of instantaneous decisions but also through lasting justice and law. If their authority as the chosen ones is disputed and extended to all, then the actual dominion is taken away from God, for without law, that is, without any clear-cut and transmissible line of demarcation between that which is pleasing to God and that which is displeasing to Him, there can be no historical continuity of divine rule upon earth.

The *true* argument of the rebellion is that in the world of the law what has been inspired always becomes emptied of the spirit, but that in this state it continues to maintain its claim of full inspiration; or, in other words, that the living element always dies off but that thereafter what is left continues to rule over living men. And the *true* conclusion is that the law must again and again immerse itself in the consuming and purifying fire of the spirit, in order to renew itself and anew refine the genuine substance out of the dross of what has become false. This lies in the continuation of the line of that Mosaic principle of ever-recurrent renewal.

As against this comes the false argument of the rebels that the law as such displaces the spirit and the freedom, and the false conclusion that it ought to be replaced by them. The falsity of this concluson remains hidden and even ineffective as long as the "eschatological" expectation, the expectation of the coming of the direct and complete rule of God over all creatures, or more correctly of His presence in all creatures that no longer requires law and representation, is maintained unweakened. As soon as it slackens, it follows historically that God's rule is restricted to the "religious" sphere; everything that is left over is rendered unto Caesar; and the rift which runs through the whole being of the human world receives its sanction.

Indeed, the false would become true as soon as the presence of God comes to be fulfilled in all creatures. It is here that the greatness and the questionability are to be found in every genuine eschatology; its greatness in belief and its questionability *vis-à-vis* the realities of history. The "Mosaic" attitude facing this is to believe in the future of a "holy people" and to prepare for it within history. . . .

It was the hour of decision. Both Moses and Korah desired the people to be the people of YHVH, the holy people. But for Moses this was the goal. In order to reach it, generation after generation had to choose again and again between the roads, between the way of God and wrong paths of their own hearts; between "life" and "death." For this God had introduced Good and Evil, in order that men might find their own way to Him.

For Korah the people, as being the people of YHVH, were already holy. They had been chosen by God and He dwelt in their midst, so why should there be further need of ways and choice? The people was holy just as it was, and all those within it were holy just as they were;

all that needed to be done was to draw the conclusions from this, and everything would be found to be good. It is precisely this which Moses, in a parting speech placed in his mouth and which appears to be a development of one of his traditional utterances, calls Death, meaning the death of the people, as though they were swallowed up while still alive (Buber, *Moses* [New York: Harper, 1946, 1958], 186–190).

3. *Christianity.* While Korah caused serious political and ideological problems in his time, Christianity is historically the most significant opposition movement. It grew out of Judaism and has retained an ambivalent, love-hate, relationship with Judaism ever since. There are theological issues that divide the two religions, but messianic ideas similar to those of the early Christians existed among Jews at that time. The evolution of the followers of Jesus into a separate community with a distinct religion is largely a result of the Christians' abandonment of Jewish law.

The disciples of Jesus differed among themselves as to the legal implications of his coming. Some followed Peter, the Apostle to the Jews, who claimed that Jewish law remained in force for Christians: the impact of Jesus was primarily in the theological realm. Those who took this position were known as Hebrew Christians, a sect that continued in existence until the fifth century.

The mainstream Christian position, however, followed Paul, the Apostle to the Gentiles. In several of his letters to Christian communities, he developed a position that claimed Jesus had brought an end to the Mosaic covenant of law between God and Israel. Although the law itself was good (it was, after all, God-given), it did not fit mankind very well: men learned to sin from the law rather than to act in a godly way. Consequently, God in His mercy sent Jesus so that, through him, men could symbolically die, thus breaking the covenant's authority without incurring guilt—just as marriage bonds are broken without culpability when one of the partners dies. God could then institute the new dispensation, in which man was to be ruled by the spirit, not the law. This would fulfill the purposes of the law ("Jesus came to fulfill the Law, not to abrogate it") but would nullify its provisions. This understanding of the law ultimately led to the split between Judaism and Christianity. It delineates the outer boundary, the limit of change within the rabbinic position: many specific laws can be modified, set aside, or instituted, but commitment to the body of law in its evolving form must be maintained.

As you read the following selections from Paul's writings in the New Testament, consider the following points:

1. Paul, an Apostle to the Gentiles, was seeking to missionize

among people who would be unlikely to accept the law's burdens. At the same time, he wanted to convert the Jews; that required him to retain ties to the Jewish tradition and to the law that is so much a part of it. These conflicting political objectives required some deft theological theorizing. The political context of Paul's writing is made especially clear by the fact that Peter, the Apostle to the Jews, did not advocate changing Israel's commitment to the law at all even though he shared Paul's belief in Jesus as the Messiah, and the Hebrew Christian sect that he established continued to observe Jewish law until its demise. Thus while theology is one factor in Paul's thinking, it is not the only one; political considerations also play an important role.

2. The abrogation of marital bonds through the death of one of the spouses provides a nice analogy for Paul because the covenant of marriage is then dissolved by a fact, similar to the death of Jesus, rather than a decision of either party for which that party is morally responsible. This permits Paul to say three things that appear to be in conflict: the original covenant was good; breaking it now is no crime; and replacing it with a new covenant of the spirit is appropriate since the life situation of the two partners of the original covenant (God and Israel) has significantly changed. The marital model of God's relationship with Israel has strong roots in the Hebrew Bible, and that makes it especially apt for Paul's use. In the analogy, however, the surviving spouse is guiltless only on the presumption that he or she did not cause the partner's death, and in Paul's analogue God specifically sends Jesus to die for us. Moreover, God chooses to send Jesus because He has determined that the experiment of ruling people through law has not worked. The Bible's understanding of God's omniscience does not preclude a change of mind on His part (see Genesis 6:6; Exodus 32:7–14, Numbers 14:11–25; and elsewhere), but one wonders why an omniscient God would ever have given mankind such an ill-fitting law in the first place.

3. Many Christian theologians from the early Church Fathers to the present have denied that Paul wrote The Letter to the Hebrews, largely because it was unknown to the earliest collectors of the New Testament materials and also because Paul, who knew Jerusalem well, would not have made the mistake of saying that the altar was in the Holy of Holies. Nevertheless, as the third century Church Father, Origen, said, the ideas are Pauline even if the expression of those ideas in the book as we have it was written by somebody else (Eusebius, History, VI:25). The author, in line with Paul's thinking, claims that "the Law contains but a shadow, and not a true image, of the good things which were to come; it provides for the same sacrifices year after year, and with these it can never bring the worshippers to perfection for all

time." God therefore "annuls" the law. But note that the new dispensation has its price: "If we wilfully persist in sin after receiving the knowledge of the truth, no sacrifice (to atone) for sins remains: only a terrifying expectation of judgment and a fierce fire which will consume God's enemies." Echoing a theme that we have seen earlier, the law may make demands and may be open to legalism and abuse of its spirit; but, as this text amply demonstrates, living by the spirit alone removes the protections and modes of atonement that the law provides for those who stumble. The law may thus be more loving than the spirit after all.

4. Following the spirit was sufficiently clear to Paul and the Apostles since they were a close enough group to have a set of mutual understandings of what that entailed. For anyone outside the group, however, it was difficult to know what one who wanted to follow the spirit should do. As the selection on the function of the law indicates, Paul himself confronted this problem when he found that the Galatians had understood the maxim of following the spirit in a way radically different from his own. That prompted him to specify the behavioral expectations of living by the spirit. But what is the difference between doing that and observing rules? Indeed, the development of Roman Catholic canon law and Protestant codes of practice raises real questions about whether one can live by the spirit—any spirit—without some formulation of rules. The Jewish and Christian traditions after Paul have put significantly different degrees of emphasis on norms of practice, but the legal manifestations of Christianity and the recurrent calls for proper intention in Judaism suggest that spirit and law are not mutually exclusive, as Paul describes them, but rather are complementary.

5. The key to the whole theory, of course, is that the advent of Jesus really did introduce a new era in the relationship between God and mankind. It is that theological belief which motivates Paul to write, and it is that tenet which divides Christians and Jews in both their theologies and their legal theories.

*Romans 7:1–8:8; 9:30–33 (Jerusalem Bible):*

The Christian is not bound by the Law
Brothers, those of you who have studied law will know that laws affect a person only during his lifetime. A married woman, for instance, has legal obligations to her husband while he is alive, but all these obligations come to an end if the husband dies. So if she gives herself to another man while her husband is still alive, she is legally an adulteress; but after her husband is dead her legal obligations come to an end, and she can marry someone else without becoming an adulteress. That is why you, my brothers, who through the body of Christ are

now dead to the Law, can now give yourselves to another husband, to him who rose from the dead to make us productive for God. Before our conversion our sinful passions, quite unsubdued by the Law, fertilized our bodies to make them give birth to death. But now we are rid of the Law, freed by death from our imprisonment, free to serve in the new spiritual way and not the old way of a written law.

### The function of the Law

Does it follow that the Law itself is sin? Of course not. What I mean is that I should not have known what sin was except for the Law. I should not for instance have known what it means to covet if the Law had not said "You shall not covet." But it was this commandment that sin took advantage of to produce all kinds of covetousness in me, for when there is no Law, sin is dead.

Once, when there was no Law, I was alive; but when the command-ment came, sin came to life and I died: the commandment was meant to lead me to life but it turned out to mean death for me, because sin took advantage of the commandment to mislead me, and so sin, through that commandment, killed me.

The Law is sacred, and what it commands is sacred, just and good. Does that mean that something good killed me? Of course not. But sin, to show itself in its true colors, used that good thing to kill me; and thus sin, thanks to the commandment, was able to exercise all its sinful power.

### The inward struggle

The Law, of course, as we all know, is spiritual; but I am unspiri-tual; I have been sold as a slave to sin. I cannot understand my own behavior. I fail to carry out the things I want to do, and I find myself doing the very things I hate. When I act against my own will, that means I have a self that acknowledges that the Law is good, and so the thing behaving in that way is not my self but sin living in me. The fact is, I know of nothing good living in me—living, that is, in my unspiri-tual self—for though the will to do what is good is in me, the perfor-mance is not, with the result that instead of doing the good things I want to do, I carry out the sinful things I do not want. When I act against my will, then, it is not my true self doing it, but sin which lives in me.

In fact, this seems to be the rule, that every single time I want to do good it is something evil that comes to hand. In my inmost self I dearly love God's Law, but I can see that my body follows a different law that battles against the law which my reason dictates. This is what makes me a prisoner of that law of sin which lives inside my body.

What a wretched man I am! Who will rescue me from this body doomed to death? Thanks be to God through Jesus Christ our Lord!

In short, it is I who with my reason serve the Law of God, and no less I who serve in my unspiritual self the law of sin.

The life of the spirit
The reason, therefore, why those who are in Christ Jesus are not condemned, is that the law of the spirit of life in Christ Jesus has set you free from the law of sin and death. God has done what the Law, because of our unspiritual nature, was unable to do. God dealt with sin by sending his own Son in a body as physical as any sinful body, and in that body God condemned sin. He did this in order that the Law's just demands might be satisfied in us, who behave not as our unspiritual nature but as the spirit dictates.

The unspiritual are interested only in what is unspiritual, but the spiritual are interested in spiritual things. It is death to limit oneself to what is unspiritual; life and peace can only come with concern for the spiritual. That is because to limit oneself to what is unspiritual is to be at enmity with God: such a limitation never could and never does submit to God's law. People who are interested only in unspiritual things can never be pleasing to God.

*Chapter 9:*
From this it follows that the pagans who were not looking for righteousness found it all the same, a righteousness that comes of faith, while Israel, looking for a righteousness derived from law failed to do what the law required. Why did they fail? Because they relied on good deeds instead of trusting in faith. In other words, they stumbled over the stumbling-stone mentioned in scripture: "See how I lay in Zion a stone to stumble over, a rock to trip men up—only those who believe in him will have no cause for shame."

*Galatians 3:19–25; 5:16–25:*
Then what of the law? It was added to make wrongdoing a legal offence. It was a temporary measure pending the arrival of the "issue" to whom the promise was made. . . .

Does the law, then, contradict the promises? No, never! If a law had been given which had power to bestow life, then indeed righteousness would have come from keeping the law. But Scripture has declared the whole world to be prisoners in subjection to sin, so that faith in Jesus Christ may be the ground on which the promised blessing is given, and given to those who have such faith.

Before this faith came, we were close prisoners in the custody of law, pending the revelation of faith. Thus the law was a kind of tutor in charge of us until Christ should come, when we should be justified through faith; and now that faith has come, the tutor's charge is at an end. . . .

Let me put it like this: if you are guided by the Spirit, you will be in no danger of yielding to self-indulgence, since self-indulgence is the opposite of the Spirit. The Spirit is totally against such a thing, and it is precisely because the two are so opposed that you do not always carry out your good intentions. If you are led by the Spirit, no law can touch you. When self-indulgence is at work, the results are obvious: fornication, gross indecency and sexual irreponsibilty; idolatry and sorcery; feuds and wrangling, jealousy, bad temper and quarrels; disagreements, factions, envy; drunkenness, orgies and similar things. I warn you now, as I warned you before: those who behave like this will not inherit the kingdom of God. What the Spirit brings is very different: love, joy, peace, patience, kindness, goodness, trustfulness, gentleness and self-control. There can be no law against things like that, of course. You cannot belong to Christ Jesus unless you crucify all self-indulgent passions and desires.

Since the Spirit is our life, let us be directed by the Spirit.

*Hebrews* 9 and 10 (New English Bible):
The first covenant indeed has its ordinances of divine service and its sanctuary, but a material sanctuary. For a tent was prepared—the first tent—in which was the lampstand, and the table with the bread of the Presence; this is called the Holy Place. Beyond the second curtain was the tent called the Most Holy Place. Here was a golden altar of incense, and the ark of the convenant plated all over with gold, in which were a golden jar containing the manna, and Aaron's staff which once budded, and the tablets of the convenant; and above it the cherubim of God's glory, overshadowing the place of expiation. On these we cannot now enlarge.

Under this arrangement, the priests are always entering the first tent in the discharge of their duties; but the second is entered only once a year, and by the high priest alone, and even then he must take with him the blood which he offers on his own behalf and for the people's sins of ignorance. By this the Holy Spirit signifies that so long as the earlier tent still stands, the way into the sanctuary remains unrevealed. All this is symbolic, pointing to the present time. The offerings and sacrifices there prescribed cannot give the worshipper inward perfection. It is only a matter of food and drink and various rites of cleansing—outward ordinances in force until the time of reformation.

But now Christ has come, high priest of good things already in being. The tent of his priesthood is a greater and more perfect one, not made by men's hands, that is, not belonging to this created world; the blood of his sacrifice is his own blood, not the blood of goats and calves; and thus he has entered the sanctuary once and for all and secured an eternal deliverance. For if the blood of goats and bulls and the sprinkled ashes of a heifer have power to hallow those who have been defiled and restore their external purity, how much greater is the power of the blood of Christ; he offered himself without blemish to God, a spiritual and eternal sacrifice; and his blood will cleanse out conscience from the deadness of our former ways and fit us for the service of the living God.

And therefore he is the mediator of a new covenant, or testament, under which, now that there has been a death to bring deliverance from sins committed under the former covenant, those whom God has called may receive the promise of the eternal inheritance. For where there is a testament it is necessary for the death of the testator to be established. A testament is operative only after a death: it cannot possibly have force while the testator is alive. Thus we find that the former covenant itself was not inaugurated without blood. For when, as the Law directed, Moses had recited all the commandments to the people, he took the blood of the calves, with water, scarlet wool, and marjoram, and sprinkled the law-book itself and all the people, saying, "This is the blood of the covenant which God has enjoined upon you." In the same way he also sprinkled the tent and all the vessels of divine service with blood. Indeed, according to the Law, it might almost be said, everything is cleansed by blood and without the shedding of blood there is no forgiveness.

If, then, these sacrifices cleanse the copies of heavenly things, those heavenly things themselves require better sacrifices to cleanse them. For Christ has entered, not the sanctuary made by men's hands which is only a symbol of the reality, but heaven itself, to appear now before God on our behalf. Nor is he there to offer himself again and again, as the high priest enters the sanctuary year by year with blood not his own. If that were so, he would have had to suffer many times since the world was made. But as it is, he has appeared once and for all at the climax of history to abolish sin by the sacrifice of himself. And as it is the lot of men to die once, and after death comes judgment, so Christ was offered once to bear the burden of men's sins, and will appear a second time, sin done away, to bring salvation to those who are watching for him.

For the Law contains but a shadow, and not true image, of the good things which were to come; it provides for the same sacrifices year after year, and with these it can never bring the worshippers to perfection for all time. If it could, these sacrifices would surely have ceased to be offered, because the worshippers, cleansed once for all, would no longer have any sense of sin. But instead, in these sacrifices year after

year sins are brought to mind, because sins can never be removed by
the blood of bulls and goats.

That is why, at his coming into the world, he says:

"Sacrifice and offering thou didst not desire, but thou has prepared a
    body for me.
Whole-offerings and sin-offerings thou didst not delight in.
Then I said, 'Here am I: as it is written of me in the scroll, I have
    come, O God, to do thy will.'"

First he says, "Sacrifices and offerings, whole-offerings and sin-offerings, thou didst not desire nor delight in"—although the Law prescribes them—and then he says, "I have come to do thy will." He
thus annuls the former to establish the latter. And it is by the will of
God that we have been consecrated, through the offering of the body
of Jesus Christ once and for all.

Every priest stands performing his service daily and offering time after time the same sacrifices, which can never remove sins. But Christ
offered for all time one sacrifice for sins, and took his seat at the right
hand of God, where he waits henceforth until his enemies are made
his footstool. For by one offering he has perfected for all time those
who are thus consecrated. Here we have also the testimony of the
Holy Spirit: he first says, "This is the covenant which I will make
with them after those days, says the Lord: I will set my laws in their
hearts and write them on their understanding"; then he adds, "and
their sins and wicked deeds I will remember no more at all." And
where these have been forgiven, there are offerings for sin no longer.

So now, my friends, the blood of Jesus makes us free to enter boldly
into the sanctuary by the new, living way which he has opened for us
through the curtain, the way of his flesh. We have, moreover, a great
priest set over the household of God; so let us make our approach in
sincerity of heart and full assurance of faith, our guilty hearts sprinkled clean, our bodies washed with pure water. Let us be firm and
unswerving in the confession of our hope, for the Giver of the promise
may be trusted. We ought to see how each of us may best arouse others to love and active goodness, not staying away from our meeting, as
some do, but rather encouraging one another, all the more because
you see the Day drawing near.

For if we willfully persist in sin after receiving the knowledge of the
truth, no sacrifice for sins remains: only a terrifying expectation of
judgment and a fierce fire which will consume God's enemies. If a
man disregards the Law of Moses, he is put to death without pity on
the evidence of two or three witnesses. Think how much more severe
a penalty that man will deserve who has trampled under foot the Son
of God, profaned the blood of the covenant by which he was conse-

crated, and affronted God's gracious Spirit! For we know who it is that has said, "Justice is mine: I will repay"; and again, "The Lord will judge his people." It is a terrible thing to fall into the hands of the living God.

4. *The Most Significant Opposition Movements.* The materials on Korah and Christianity indicate how much our impression of historical events is shaped by the attitudes of the people who wrote about them—especially of those who emerged triumphant. Since we are interested in the development of Jewish law as we know it today, we shall henceforth follow the history of the rabbinic tradition to modern times. We should note, however, that during the course of this history significant groups have split off from that tradition, some of whom have remained affiliated with the Jewish people, and some not. These include:

a. The *Samaritans*, descendants of the people living in Samaria (who themselves were descendants of the Joseph tribes of Ephraim and Manasseh) and other peoples from the time of the Assyrian conquest of Samaria in 722 B.C.E. They built a rival Temple on Mt. Gerizim, and their relationship with the Jews in Judea was continually one of betrayal and conflict. Their whole Bible is the Pentateuch, with some variations (for example, their version of the Ten Commandments states that God chose Mt. Gerizim for His sanctuary instead of Jerusalem), and they have little legal development of the 613 precepts in the Torah. After Justinian issued a decree against them in 529, their autonomous existence all but ended, and their numbers declined rapidly under Islam since they were not considered "People of the Book." In 1955 there were 246 Samaritans in Nablus and 67 in Jaffa.

b. The *Christians*, followers of Jesus through the writings of Paul and the Church Fathers.

c. The *Hebrew Christians*, people who observed Jewish law but thought that Jesus was the Messiah, a form of Christianity advocated by Peter. The sect died out in the middle of the fifth century.

d. The *Karaites*, a sect of Jews who rejected the Oral Law and rabbinic authority. Beginning in the eighth century in Persia, the Karaites tried to live by the Pentateuch alone. The group had many schisms, as different elements interpreted and applied biblical law in varying ways. In response to Saadia Gaon's blistering attack (tenth century), the Karaites closed ranks and produced polemical works, biblical commentaries, and codes. Karaism flourished for the next 150 years, especially in Israel and Egypt, and Karaite communities have existed in Spain, Asia Minor, the Balkans, Syria, Cyprus, Crimea, and Lithuania since then, but there are now only about 2,000 Karaites left, living in Israel. Their only doctrinal difference with Judaism is their denial of the Oral Law, but in the course of time they have developed their own Oral Law. Differences in the laws of slaughter prevent social intercourse with Jews following rabbinic dietary rules, and they do not use *tefillin* (the boxes and leather straps Jews use for prayer at the weekday morning service) or *mezuzot* (the containers of a parchment with sections of the Bible on it which Jews affix to their doorposts). They also do not observe Hanukkah since it is postbiblical, and they do not permit illumination on the Sabbath.

e. *Sabbetaians*, followers of Shabbetai Zevi, who, after his death in 1676, believed that he would reappear as savior of Israel to consummate the messianic promises that he made during his lifetime. The ideologist of the Sabbetaians was Abraham Miguel Cardozo (d. 1706), who traveled through North Africa preaching belief in Shabbetai Zevi, as the ascetic, Mordecai Mokhiah, disseminated Sabbetaianism in Germany and Italy. The most extreme development of Sabbetaianism was the *Frankists*, followers of Jacob Frank (1726–1791), who declared himself the Messiah and the successor of Shabbetai Zevi. He allegedly used sexual orgies to bring redemption through impurity. The rabbis excommunicated him and his followers in 1756, and he then persuaded an antisemitic Polish bishop to hold public trials of Judaism and Talmud burnings in 1757 and 1759, at the conclusion of which Frank and his followers were baptized. Eventually Hasidism diverted popular attention from Sabbetaianism.

f. *Hasidim*, followers of Israel Baal Shem Tov (1699–1761), spread as a response to the depressed condition of Eastern European Jewry in the eighteenth century. The Chmielnicki massacres and church prosecutions of the seventeenth and eighteenth centuries, coupled with the oligarchic rule of the rabbis and the disillusionment engendered by the Sabbetaian fiasco, led many unlearned Jews to embrace the Baal Shem Tov's teaching. He taught that the unlearned are equal to the learned before God; purity of heart is superior to study; devotion to prayer and the commandments is paramount but is to be done in a spirit of joy, not asceticism; and one should have faith in the *tzadik*, the righteous man, and consult him for guidance. In the eighteenth century they were bitterly opposed by the rabbis and those who followed them (the *Mitnaggedim*) and were subjected to numerous bans of excommunication, but in the nineteenth century opposition abated and their popularity spread. At the same time the inner decline of Hasidism began. Leadership became a matter of inheritance from father to son, and the various dynastic groups fought among themselves for hegemony and influence among the Jewish masses. They also turned increasingly to study and founded rabbinical academies, despite their earlier opposition to this form of Judaism. Now they are identified with rigid practices and a deep antipathy toward the modern world, although the openness to all and the musical tradition of Hasidism continue on in some circles.

g. *Reform Judaism*, a form of Judaism initiated in nineteenth-century Germany in an attempt to "re-form" Judaism to make it possible for modern Jews to participate fully in Enlightenment societies. This included elimination of the dietary laws, circumcision, and Jewish nationalism, as well as shortening worship and using the vernacular in prayer. Talmudic law and its successive developments were explained as being temporary measures for their time, but now, in the Enlightenment's atmosphere of freedom and opportunity, Jews should ignore them and aspire to the ethical tenets of the biblical prophets in any way they found appropriate. Each individual was to interpret and apply the tradition in his or her own way. In recent times Reform Judaism has become more interested in ritual and more nationalistic, but the individualism and denial of authority to Jewish law persist. Its main strength is in the United States, but there are affiliates world wide.

The twentieth century has seen the development of yet more groups of Jews who understand and interpret the tradition in new (or renewed) ways, some of which are part of the Jewish community (for example neo-Orthodoxy, the Conservative Movement, Reconstructionism, secular Zionism), and some not (Jews for Jesus, and so on). In addition, throughout the centuries there have been minority opinions within the rabbinic tradition itself that have been lost along the way—although there have been some which have been given new life in a later age. In any case, we now continue with the rabbinic tradition, aware that its direction of development was by no means the only logical or historic one possible and that the sources we read that describe it are written, by and large, by its inheritors and lovers.

# Topic Six: The Authority and Morality of the Tradition

## A. The Basis for Obedience of the Law

As we have seen in the biblical materials, motivations for obeying the law are manifold. People abide by the law because they want to avoid punishment, but that is only a small part of the story. There are other sources of human motivation, and the Bible taps many of them to produce compliance.

The rabbis rooted themselves in the biblical tradition, restating almost all of its motivations for obedience in one form or another. They also added some considerations of their own.

1. People become *purified* by observing the commandments. This is similar to the biblical challenge to become holy like God, but the rabbis were willing to break the tie to God, at least for the sake of argument. The law is for mankind's benefit, not God's, and therefore each person should want to improve himself by observing the law, even if God could not care less about human behavior.

> *Midrash Tanhuma Buber*, Shemini, 15b:
> What does God care whether a man kills an animal in the proper way and eats it, or whether he strangles the animal and eats it? Will the one benefit Him, or the other injure Him? Or what does God care whether a man eats unclean animals or clean animals? "If you are wise, you are wise for yourself, but if you scorn, you alone shall bear it" (Prov. 9:12). So you learn that the Commandments were given only to purify God's creatures, as it says, "God's word is purified, it is a protection to those who trust in Him" (II Sam. 22:31).

> *Gen.R.*, Lekh Lekha 44:1 and *Lev.R.*, Shemini, 13:3:
> Rav said: The commandments were given to Israel only in order that people should be purified through them. For what can it matter to God whether a beast is slain at the throat or at the neck?

2. On the other hand, the rabbis asserted the exact opposite claim, too: You should obey the law *as a favor to God*, for He cares very much that you observe it:

*Deut. R.*, Nitzavim, 8:5:

God said, "If you read the Law, you do a kindness, for you help to preserve My world, since if it were not for the Law, the world would again become 'without form and void'" (as before creation, Gen. 1:2). . . . The matter is like a king who had a precious stone, and he entrusted it to his friend, and said to him, "I pray you, pay attention to it and guard it, as is fitting, for if you lose it, you cannot pay me its worth, and I have no other jewel like it, and so you would sin against yourself and against me; therefore, do your duty by both of us, and guard the jewel as is fitting." So Moses said to the Israelites, "If you keep the Law, not only upon yourselves do you confer a benefit, but also upon God," as it is said, "And it shall be a benefit for us" (Deut. 6:25). [The Midrash takes "us" to mean God and Israel, and the word *tzedakah*—"righteousness"—it takes to mean benefit, which led to its later signification of "alms."]

3. Observing the law gives Israel *a separate identity.* This became an increasingly important function of the law from rabbinic times on, as significant numbers of Jews were scattered all over the globe and thus could not depend on a geographic center to unite them.

*Sifra* 112c:

"Yet for all that, in spite of their sins, when they have been in the lands of their enemies, I have not rejected them utterly" (Lev. 26:44). All the goodly gifts that were given them were taken from them. And if it had not been for the Book of the Law which was left to them, they would not have differed at all from the nations of the world.

*Berakhot,* 61b:

Our Rabbis have taught: Once the wicked government decreed that Israel should no longer occupy themselves with Torah. Then came Pappos b. Judah and found R. Akiba holding great assemblies and studying Torah. He said to him, "Akiba, are you not afraid of the wicked government?" He replied, "I will tell you a parable. To what should the matter be compared? To a fox who was walking along the bank of the stream, and saw some fishes gathering together to move from one place to another. He said to them, 'From what are you fleeing?' They answered, 'From nets which men are bringing against us.' He said to them, 'Let it be your pleasure to come up on the dry land, and let us, me and you, dwell together, even as my fathers dwelt with your fathers.' They replied, 'Are you he of whom they tell that you are the shrewdest of animals? You are not clever, but a fool! For if we are afraid in the place which is our life-element, how much more so in a place which is our death-element!' So also is it with us: If now, while we sit and study Torah, in which it is written, 'For that is your life, and the length of your days' (Deut. 30:20), we are in such a plight, how much more so, if we neglect it."

*Ex. R.*, Ki Tissa, 47:3:
If it were not for My Law which you accepted, I should not recognize you, and I should not regard you more than any of the idolatrous nations of the world.

### 4. The law makes Israel *beautiful*.

*Songs Rabbah* I, 15 on Song of Songs 1:15:
"You are beautiful, my love" (Song of Songs 1:15). You are beautiful through the commandments, both positive and negative, beautiful through loving deeds, beautiful in your house with the heave-offerings and the tithes, beautiful in the field by the commands about gleaning, the forgotten sheaf and the second tithe; beautiful in the law about mixed seeds and about fringes, and about first fruits, and the fourth year planting; beautiful in the law of circumcision, beautiful in prayer, in the reading of the *Shema,* in the law of doorposts and the phylacteries, in the law of the *Lulav* and the *Etrog;* beautiful too, in repentance and in good works; beautiful in this world and beautiful in the world to come.

### 5. God's children should see the law as a *blessing,* as an enrichment of life.

*Menahot* 99b:
R. Jonathan said that the famous words in Joshua 1:8, "You shall meditate therein (the Law) day and night," were not a command or obligation, but a blessing. They meant that because Joshua loved the words of the Law so much, therefore they should never depart out of his mouth. In the school of R. Ishmael it was taught that the words of the Law are not to be unto you a burden, but, on the other hand, you are not free to dispense yourself from them.

### 6. But, as the last line of the previous excerpt indicates, the Jew is obligated to observe the law whether or not he understands the reasons why.

*Yoma* 67b; cp. *Sifra* 86a
You shall observe my judgments and execute my statutes (Lev. 18:4). The Rabbis teach: "My judgments": these are the things which, if they had not been written, would have had to be written, such as idolatry, unchastity, bloodshed, robbery, blasphemy. "My statutes": these are the things to which Satan and the Gentiles raise objections, such as not eating pig meat, not wearing linen and wool together, the law of *halizah* (Deut. 25: 5–10), the scapegoat. Should you say, "These are empty things," the Scripture adds, "I am the Lord," i.e., I have made decrees; you are not at liberty to criticize them.

Jews throughout the ages have sought to justify specific laws on a variety of grounds. Such discussion may provide additional motivations to obey because the law is right, wise, efficient, or beautiful. But in the end, the primary insistence is that such reasons are secondary and the Jews must obey the law because it is the law, commanded by the sovereign. In requiring the Jew to obey the law simply because it is the law, Judaism resembles the dominant modern theory of secular jurisprudence, legal positivism. In Jewish law the sovereign is God (and the rabbis are the human beings designated to interpret and apply the revelation of His will in the Torah); in secular law the sovereign is a government of one type or another. In either case the law's authority cannot be undermined by invoking other factors.

> The most pernicious laws, and therefore those which are most opposed to the will of God, have been and are continually enforced as laws by judicial tribunals. Suppose an act innocuous, or positively beneficial, be prohibited by the sovereign under the penalty of death; if I commit this act, I shall be tried and condemned, and if I object to the sentence, that it is contrary to the law of God . . . the court of justice will demonstrate the inconclusiveness of my reasoning by hanging me up, in pursuance of the law of which I have impugned the validity. An exception, demurrer, or plea, founded on the law of God was never heard in a Court of Justice, from the creation of the world down to the present moment (John Austin, *The Providence of Jurisprudence Determined* [London: Weidenfeld and Nicolson Library of Ideas, 1954], 185).

The starkness of such a statement is, of course, mitigated by the assumption that, in general, the sovereign intends to accomplish the right and the good through the law, an assumption that we will investigate in detail in the next section. Judges are therefore given some latitude in applying the sovereign's rules to cases involving special circumstances, for it is assumed that if the sovereign were judge, he would do likewise. Moreover, in Jewish law the sovereign, God, is not available for further, direct consultation through prophecy, and so in practice judges have broad power to limit the application of rules that they do not like. Despite the caveats, rabbinic sources explicitly declare that God's law is binding whether or not we understand or like it.

## B. LAW AND MORALITY

The Bible assumes that God's law is right and good and that humans are moral to the extent that they obey it. In Topic Five we saw that Paul attacks that assumption forcefully: the law itself may be good, but its effect on people is morally destructive. By distinguishing between good acts and bad, the law teaches people how to carry out their sinful inclinations and thus contributes to their degeneracy. Furthermore, emphasis on obedience to the law can lead to obsession with it: people may get so caught up with the details of the law that they forget its original purpose and, in fact, act contrary to its spirit. The Gospels and the Book of Acts in the New Testament portray the Pharisees as being guilty of such legalism.

Paul raises questions that apply not only to Jewish law but to law in general. In the broadest sense, the issues are nothing less than the essence of religion, law, and morality and the relationships among the three. This book cannot treat all of the questions involved adequately, but we will focus on two aspects of this cluster of issues that have affected the nature and development of Jewish law from the rabbinic period on and which have distinguished Judaism's approach to law from those of Christianity and American positivism. The first question is philosophical: is the law the sum total of right and good behavior, or is there some other guide which supplements it and may sometimes conflict with it? In other words, is obeying the law enough in order to be moral? The second issue is psychological and educational: what is the role of law in a person's moral development? If it is a help, how so, and is it effective? If it is a hindrance, how?

There are at least five responses to the first question that have enjoyed a degree of popularity in human history. On one end of the spectrum is the position that the law is identical with the right. Obeying the law, according to this position, is the sum total of what morality requires because the law completely and perfectly articulates the dictates of morality. The most extreme form of this position holds that the law delineates not only what is right and wrong, but also what is good and bad—that is, not only the minimal moral rules which are necessary for a society to function, but also the ideals toward which people should aspire and the abhorrent forms of behavior which they should shun.

In the Western world, Islam is one example of this position. Despite some of the rhetoric of contemporary fundamentalists, Muslims generally have not adopted the most extreme form of this position, for the life of the Prophet Mohammed represents an ideal for Muslims beyond the requirements of his specific utterances. Islam does claim, however, that the Koran perfectly articulates the minimum of moral behavior. The very word "Islam" means "submission" (to the will of Allah), and those who surrender to God's will in accordance with the Koran are "truly rightly guided" (*Koran*, Sura III. 19–20). All people, in fact, are required to do this "willingly or unwillingly" (ibid., 83–85). The early military exploits of Islam, and some of the contemporary ones as well, have been fueled, at least in part, by this assurance that a person's sole duty in life is to submit his or her will to God, with inner conviction or without, as defined by the law of Islam.

The Islamic position represents one end of the spectrum in the sense that it is the most conservative legally. A second position, somewhat to the left of Islam, is held by two segments of contemporary American Judaism as a reflection of their understanding of the Jewish tradition. We shall examine the ideology of the four modern movements at length in Topic Eight, Section D. For now, suffice it to say that the Orthodox and some elements of the Conservative Movement hold that by and large there is an identity between the law and the right, although the law can be misused. It is possible, as the medieval Hebrew expression phrases it, to be a *naval b'reshut ha'Torah*, "a scoundrel within the boundaries of the Torah." Put another way, it is not sufficient to observe the law alone. God Himself requires that we "do the right and the good" over and beyond the requirements of the law. Thus Nahmanides (1194–c.1270), in his commentary on the Torah, explains the verse, "and you shall do the right and the good in the eyes of the Lord" (Deuteronomy 6:18) as follows:

> This refers to compromise [rather than judgment according to strict law] and conduct beyond the requirements of the Law. The intent of this is that initially [in Deuteronomy 6:17] He had said that you should observe the laws and statutes which He commanded you. Now, He says that, with respect to what He has not commanded, you should likewise take heed to do the right and the good in His eyes, for He loves the good and the right. This is a great matter, for it is impossible to mention in the Torah all of a person's actions toward his neighbors and acquaintances, all of his commercial activity, and all social and political institutions. So, after He had mentioned many of them . . . He continues to say generally that one should do the right and the good in all matters through compromise and conduct beyond the requirements of the Law.

God's will is identified with the right, but the law does not completely succeed in defining either one. Consequently, there is need for a general, covering clause to indicate that one must do the right even if it is not part of the law. Nahmanides, following the rabbinic tradition, finds that clause in Deuteronomy 6:18. Nevertheless the law is generally to be trusted as a definition of God's will ( = the right), very much along the lines of these biblical and rabbinic sources.

*Deuteronomy* 30:15–16:
See, I set before you this day life and good, death and evil, in that I command you this day to love the Lord your God, to walk in His ways, and to keep His commandments, His laws, and His norms.

*Genesis Rabbah* 44:1:
Rav taught: The commandments were given only for the purpose of refining men to distinguish them from the animals.

There is another element to this position. Philosophers differ as to the role that intention plays in defining the morality of a person or action, but most assign it some role, and hence the different ways in which Islam and Judaism handle it are important factors in identifying the distinctions between them. Like Islam, Judaism emphasizes action, but Judaism gives intention a greater role. Liability for violation of one of the law's prohibitions generally does not require the intention to commit the violation. That principle is derived from the laws of personal injuries:

*Mishnah Bava Kamma* 2:6 (26a):
A man is considered forewarned, whether he committed the act unintentionally or intentionally, while awake or sleeping.

*Gamara Bava Kamma* 26b:
On the basis of what do we derive that ruling? . . . Scripture says, "wound for wound" (Ex. 21:25) to make him liable for unintentional acts just as he is for intentional ones, for acts done under duress as much as acts done willingly.

The exceptions to that rule are cases involving criminal punishment (see Maimonides, *M.T., Laws of Murder* 6:1–4; *Laws of the Sabbath* 1:1) and situations in which the essence of the act requires intention (for example, cursing God, see *Keritot* 3b–4a and Rashi thereon and *Sanhedrin* 65a); otherwise liability for violations is independent of intention. To acquire the merit for fulfilling a positive command, however, some sources do require the proper intention.

*Rabbi Yonah's Comment on the Rif (Alfasi) to Berakhot* 6a:
Even those who think that fulfilling the commandments does not require the proper intention apply that ruling only to matters which involve an action so that the action can come in place of the intention . . . but an obligation that consists of speech alone certainly requires the proper intention because speech depends upon the heart. Thus if a person does not attend to what he is saying and does not perform an action, he is to be considered as one who has not fulfilled any

of his obligations. . . . And Rabbi Samuel, may his memory be blessed, thinks that even though fulfilling the commandments does not require proper intention so that (one who acts properly) fulfills them retroactively, that is only when he performs the action with no specific intention, but if he knowingly intends not to fulfill an obligation thereby, he clearly does not do so.

> *Sefer HaHashlamah of R. Meshullam, Berakhot* 13a:
> Recognize that there are three separate types of intention involved in reciting the *Shema:* the intention of the heart, and the intention of reading, and the intention to fulfill one's obligation. We do not require intention of the heart (i.e., full attention to what one is doing) except for the first sentence. We do require intention to read in all three paragraphs of the *Shema*, because if he intended instead to proof-read (a manuscript of the *Shema*), he has not fulfilled his obligation. The intention to fulfill one's obligation we do not require even for the first sentence.

Thus while it is true that Judaism, like Islam, lays primary stress on action, Judaism pays considerably more attention to the element of intention. In doing so, it creates a new relationship between law and morality: acting as the law requires involves not only physical motions, but, at least in certain circumstances, a specific mental state as well. Both the law and morality are thus defined in terms of the combination of movement and intention. The primary defining characteristic for both law and morality is still physical action within Judaism because that element affects human society directly and visibly. However, the element of intention is so important that the following tannaitic dictim (*Tosefta Peah* 1:4) is repeated in varying forms in several places in both the Babylonian and Palestinian Talmuds.

> *Kiddushin* 40a:
> R. Assi said: Even if a person intended to do what God's commandment requires and was prevented from doing so, Scripture ascribes to him the merit as if he did it; but if a person has an evil intention, the Holy One, blessed be He, does not join it to an action (to count it as if the person had done it), as Scripture says, "If I intended to do a sin, God does not listen" (Psalms 66:18).

A third position on this issue is another interpretation of rabbinic Judaism common to Reform, Reconstructionist, and some segments of Conservative Judaism, contemporary American Jewish movements. Its view of the role of intention is the same as that of the last position described, but it differs in its understanding of the moral content of the law. For this third position, the law is an accumulation of partial fixes on right behavior. Because the law is understood to derive at least as much from human efforts as from God, there are situations in which its particular form may be challenged and revised on a variety of grounds, the most important of which is a new moral sensitivity. The Reform Movement claims that the law was always intended to be temporary since its form must change continually if it is to embody the highest moral aims of succeeding generations. Hence the law becomes secondary and morals primary in Reform and Reconstructionist thought and practice. Conservative Judaism also claims that the law can be changed on moral grounds, but only by the community's rabbinic leaders and only after serious deliberation. Moreover, Conservative spokesmen maintain that the rabbis of the Talmud did precisely the same thing, and they adduce numerous examples from Jewish civil and marital law to show how the rabbis consciously modified the law out of moral concerns. Thus Conservative Jews who take this position emphasize the fact that generally the law does formulate moral norms, and it is only occasionally that there are moral problems with the law as we have it. Reform and Conservative leaders would agree, however, that the law articulates morals, at least in part, because it reflects human attempts to do so. They also would agree that there are situations where we have recourse to other, extralegal norms by which we live and sometimes change the law itself. The law is therefore not always sufficient as a definition of morality, but for the Conservative Movement it usually is. The Reform Movement is less convinced of that, but is showing increased interest of late in the law as a repository of moral insight.

A fourth position is that law and morality are largely independent phenomena. The law's authority derives from some nonmoral source—custom, agreement, mutual interest or utility, a habit of obedience, or, most commonly, the government's might—and therefore the fact that it sometimes enunciates moral norms is only a matter of coincidence. That might is right was the position taken by much of Greek religion, and it is probably best known through Plato's efforts to refute it as articulated by Thrasymachus in the *Republic* (Book I, pars. 338ff) and by Callicles in the *Gorgias* (pars. 488ff). The separation of law and morality is also the thrust of modern legal positivism (Bentham, Austin, and so on), and it is the position that is commonly asserted in Anglo-American legal practice as well. The following is a good example of that:

> First, Acts of Parliament, it has been asserted, are invalid if they are opposed to the principles of morality or to the doctrines of international law. Parliament, it is in effect asserted, cannot make a law op-

posed to the dictates of private or public morality. Thus Blackstone lays down in so many words that the "law of nature being coeval with mankind, and dictated by God himself, is of course superior in obligation to any other. It is binding over all the globe, in all countries, and at all times: no human laws are of any validity if contrary to this; and such of them as are valid derive all their force and all their authority, mediately or immediately, from this original"; and expressions are sometimes used by modern judges which imply that the courts might refuse to enforce statutes going beyond the proper limits (internationally speaking) of Parliamentary authority. But to words such as those of Blackstone, and to the *obiter dicta* of the Bench, we must give a very qualified interpretation. There is no legal basis for the theory that judges, as exponents of morality, may overrule Acts of Parliament. Language which might seem to imply this amounts in reality to nothing more than the assertion that the judges, when attempting to ascertain what is the meaning to be affixed to an Act of Parliament, will presume that Parliament did not intend to violate the ordinary rules of morality, or the principles of international law, and will therefore, whenever possible, give such an interpretation to a statutory enactment as may be consistent with the doctrines both of private and of international morality. A modern judge would never listen to a barrister who argued that an Act of Parliament was invalid because it was immoral, or because it went beyond the limits of Parliamentary authority. The plain truth is that our tribunals uniformly act on the principle that a law alleged to be a bad law is *ex hypothesi* a law, and therefore entitled to obedience by the courts [A. Dicey, *Introduction to the Study of the Law of the Constitution*, 9th ed. (1939), 62–63].

This is an extreme view; there certainly are other nonreligious conceptions of the relationship between law and morality. Yet it is interesting to note that such an interpretation (or a softened version of it) is not only possible, but remains popular among Anglo-American jurists and theorists. Jews differ among themselves as to the extent to which moral concerns can be used straightforwardly to alter the law, but they would be virtually unanimous in claiming that one of the major tasks of the law is to embody and articulate morality. That is one result of the religious context of Jewish law: God is good, and His law must be also. The tie of Anglo-American law to morality is, at best, more indirect. One practical result of these considerations is that moral concerns are rather naturally introduced into Jewish legal proceedings (both legislative and judicial) and are given substantial weight, while they always seem to be imported from the outside when they appear in Anglo-American legal materials—and Dicey provides us with the reason why.

And finally, the fifth position is that of Paul: law is actually a hindrance to moral knowledge and sensitivity. Because of its emphasis on physical behavior, law leads us in the wrong direction. What is really important is the inner state of grace, and law misleads us into concentrating on the externals. Sometimes it does even worse: it engenders pride in those who keep the law and condescension toward those who do not. For all these reasons, Paul, Luther, and Calvin all claimed that one cannot be saved by works alone. They assume that one who achieves the proper inner state (in Paul's language, one who "lives by the Spirit") will automatically act morally and altruistically, but observing the law is neither a substitute for that inner state nor even a path to it.

These five positions on the relationship between law and morality have immediate and profound implications for the psychological-educational question that we have posed: what is the role of law in a person's moral and spiritual development? For Islam, God's law *is* morality, and obedience to it is a person's prime task in life. For Christianity, the law is spiritually and morally dangerous: the path to salvation is therefore not through law but rather through being born again into faith. Judaism, which recognizes a moral realm other than the law but claims that the law articulates morality by and large, also sees the law as the primary educational tool to inculcate moral knowledge, intention, and action.

The most obvious way in which law contributes to morality is simply by defining what is good and what is bad behavior. It is easy to affirm allegiance to the good, but it is quite another matter to know what that entails. The law provides specific directives for action so that we can know what we should and should not do.

The law also aids in forming and maintaining good moral intentions. By requiring that we act in specified ways, it forces us to test the nature and seriousness of our intentions so that we may avoid hypocrisy. It also graphically shows us the effects of our intentions so that we will alter those that are knowingly or unknowingly destructive. Law's insistence on compliance serves to bring our intentions out into the arena of action, where we can see them clearly and, if necessary, strive to change them.

And finally, the law helps us not only to know and intend what is moral, but to act morally as well. Theories of education are many and diverse, but the Jewish tradition has a clear methodology for moral education.

*Pesahim* 50b, et. al:
Rav Judah said in Rav's name: A man should always occupy himself with Torah and good deeds, though it is not for their own sake, for out

of (doing good) with an ulterior motive he will come to (do good) for its own sake.

This largely behavioristic approach to moral education is not totally so: study of the tradition is also an integral part of Jewish moral education. But, in the end, the emphasis is on action.

> *Avot* 2:1:
> An excellent thing is the study of Torah combined with some worldly occupation, for the labor demanded by both of them causes sinful inclinations to be forgotten. All study of Torah without work must, in the end, be futile and become the cause of sin.

The same educational theory is applied to moral degeneracy and repentance.

> *Yoma* 86b:
> Once a man has committed a sin and repeated it, it appears to him as if it were permitted.

> *Avot* 4:2:
> Run to fulfill even a minor precept and flee from the slightest transgression, for precept draws precept in its train, and transgression draws transgression.

If one accepts this approach to moral education in whole or in part, the formulation of moral norms in terms of law is very important educationally: people are legally required to act in accord with moral rules as a step in teaching them how to do the right thing for the right reason.

In sum, then, Judaism regards the law as both the embodiment of the good—at least, by and large—and the primary method to inculcate it. What emerges within Judaism is a view of the law that gives it a central role in both defining the content of morality and infusing it into human behavior. It is no wonder, then, that the rabbis maintained that God wrote the Torah before He created the world. For them the Torah is the sum and substance of morality, and the world's existence is no less dependent on that than it is on the physical laws of nature.

> *Shabbat* 88a:
> What is the meaning of the words, "The earth feared and was still" (Ps. 76:9)? . . . Before Israel accepted the Torah, the earth was afraid; after they accepted the Torah, it was still . . . For the Holy One, blessed be He, stipulated a condition with the earth: If Israel accepts the Torah, you may exist, but if not, I will return you to the state of being unformed and void.

# Topic Seven: Rabbinic Court Procedures

## A. The Structure and Jurisdiction of Courts

### 1. The Original Structure

The Mishnah describes a well-defined system of courts and judges, including local courts, both professional and lay, to deal with civil matters; larger district courts to handle criminal cases; and an appellate structure centered in the Supreme Court of Jerusalem, as required in Deuteronomy 17. The authority of the judges derived from the fact that they were community leaders, as it had been in biblical times. The stated basis for that authority, however, was the line of personal succession extending from Moses. Another claim for the court's authority was its site at Jerusalem, "the place which the Lord your God has chosen."

> *Mishnah, Avot 1:1:*
> Moses received the Law from Sinai and handed it down to Joshua, and Joshua to the elders, and the elders to the prophets, and the prophets handed it down to the men of the Great Assembly. They said three things: Be deliberate in judgment, raise up many disciples, and make a fence around the Law.

> *Deuteronomy 17:8–13:*
> If a case is too baffling for you to decide, be it a controversy over homicide, civil law, or assault—matters of dispute in your courts—you shall promptly repair to the place which the Lord your God has chosen, and appear before the levitical priests, or the magistrate in charge at the time, and present your problem. When they have announced to you the verdict in the case, you shall carry out the verdict that is announced to you from that place which the Lord chose, observing scrupulously all their instructions to you. You shall act in accordance with the instructions given you and the ruling handed down to you; you must not deviate from the verdict that they announce to you either to the right or to the left. Should a man act presumptuously and disregard the priest charged with serving there the Lord your God, or the magistrate, that man shall die. Thus you will sweep out evil from

Israel: all the people will hear and be afraid and will not act presumptuously again.

The core of the rabbinic system of court jurisdiction is set forth in the tractate *Sanhedrin* of the Mishnah, which also provides some detailed indications of the mode of trial. Chapters three and four are concerned with the rules of evidence and show a tension between rabbinic preference for proof by the testimony of witnesses that have directly perceived the events to which they testify (for example, 3:6, 4:5) and more formal rules of proof by oath and the competency of witnesses (for example, 3:3–5). These tensions are not in themselves unique; they can be found in many developing legal systems. More remarkable is the emphasis rabbinic law places on relatively rational, testimonial examination practices. They will be discussed in more detail later on.

*Mishnah Sanhedrin, Chs. 1; 3; 4; 11:2:*

Chapter One

1. Cases concerning property are decided by three judges; cases concerning theft or personal injury, by three; claims for full damages or half-damages, twofold restitution, or fourfold or fivefold restitution, and the rapist, the seducer, and the defamer (of a bride for not being a virgin) are decided by three judges. So Rabbi Meir. But the Sages say: The defamer must be judged by twenty-three judges, for a capital conviction may result from such a case.

2. Cases concerning offences punishable by lashes are decided by three. In the name of Rabbi Ishmael they said: by twenty-three. Declaring the month to be 30 days (instead of the usual 29) and declaring the year a leap year (of thirteen months instead of the usual twelve) are decided upon by three judges. So Rabbi Meir. But Rabban Simeon ben Gamliel says: The matter is begun by three, discussed by five, and decided upon by seven; but if it is decided upon by three the intercalation is valid. . . .

4. Cases concerning capital offences are decided by twenty-three judges. . . .

5. A tribe, a false prophet, or the High Priest may only be tried by a court of seventy-one judges. The people may be sent forth to wage an optional war (i.e., one not commanded by the Torah) only by a court of seventy-one judges. Additions to the City (of Jerusalem) or the Temple Courts may be made only upon the decision of a court of seventy-one judges. Courts of twenty-three judges for the several tribes may be appointed only by a court of seventy-one judges. A city may be proclaimed an apostate city only by the decree of a court of seventy-one

judges. No city on the frontier should be proclaimed an apostate city, nor three together, but only one or two.

6. The Supreme Court (the "Great Sanhedrin") consisted of seventy-one judges, and the lower courts (the "small Sanhedrin") of twenty-three. On what biblical basis do we know that the Supreme Court consisted of seventy-one? Because it is written, "Gather for Me seventy men of the elders of Israel" (Numbers 11:16), and Moses was added to them for a total of seventy-one. Rabbi Judah says: (The Supreme Court should consist of) seventy. And on what biblical basis do we know that the lower courts should consist of twenty-three? Because it is written, "The congregation shall judge" (Numbers 35:24) and also "The congregation shall deliver" (ibid., v. 25), for a total of twenty. And how do we know that a "congregation" (in each of those verses) consists of ten? Because it is written, "How long shall I bear with this evil congregation?" (Numbers 14:27) in the incident of the twelve spies, but Joshua and Caleb were not included (in the "evil congregation" since they gave a positive report). And on what biblical basis do we know that we should add three to the twenty? By inference from what is written: "You shall not follow after the many to do evil" (Exodus 23:2), from which I deduce that I must be with them to do well. Then why is it written in the same verse, "to follow after the many to determine judgment" (ibid.)? (Is that not superfluous since I already know from the previous words in that verse that judgment is to be by the majority? That phrase comes to tell you that) your verdict for acquittal is not to be like your verdict for condemnation: your verdict for acquittal is reached by a majority of one, but your verdict for condemnation must be reached by a majority of two. But the court must not be divisible equally (lest there be an equal split among the judges and therefore no verdict), and consequently they add one more, for a total of twenty-three. And how many should there be in a city fit to have a lower court? One hundred twenty. Rabbi Nehemiah says: Two hundred thirty, so that the court of twenty-three shall correspond to the officers over the groups of ten (Exodus 18:21).

## Chapter Three

1. Cases concerning property are decided by three judges. Each litigant chooses one and together they choose yet another. So R. Meir. But the Sages say: The two judges choose yet another. Each may refuse to accept the judge chosen by the other. So R. Meir. But the Sages say: This applies only if they can bring proof against them that they are relatives or otherwise ineligible; but if they are not ineligible or are authorized judges, none may refuse to accept them. Each may refuse to admit the other's witnesses. So R. Meir. But the Sages say: This applies only if they can bring proof against them that they are relatives or otherwise ineligible; but if they are eligible, none may refuse to admit them.

2. If one litigant said to the other, "I accept my father as trustworthy" (as a judge or witness even though he is my relative) or "I accept three herdsmen as trustworthy" (even though they do not know the law), Rabbi Meir says that he may later retract. But the Sages say he cannot retract. . . .

3. And these are the ones not eligible (to be judges or witnesses): a dice player, a usurer, pigeon-flyers, and traffickers in Seventh Year produce. Rabbi Simeon said: they used to call them "gatherers of Seventh Year produce," but after the oppressors grew many, they changed this and called them "traffickers in Seventh Year produce" (since people had to gather it to pay the heavy taxes). Rabbi Judah said: When (are all these people ineligible)? When they have no other trade, but if they have some other trade than that, they are not disqualified.

4. These are the relatives who are ineligible to be judges or witnesses: a litigant's father, brother, father's brother, mother's brother, sister's husband, father's sister's husband, mother's sister's husband, mother's husband, father-in-law, or wife's sister's husband, together with their sons and their sons-in-law; also the litigant's stepson, but not the stepson's offspring. Rabbi Jose said: Such was the Mishnah of Rabbi Akiba, but the First Mishnah included also a litigant's uncle, first cousin and all that are qualified to be his heirs. Moreover all who were relatives at the time are ineligible; but relatives who have ceased to be relatives become eligible (e.g., a son-in-law whose wife died before witnessing an incident). Rabbi Judah says: If a man's daughter dies and leaves children, her husband still counts as a relative.

5. A friend or an enemy (of either litigant) is ineligible. "A friend" here means a man's groomsman, and "an enemy" means anyone who out of enmity has not spoken with him for three days. They replied (to Rabbi Judah): Israelites are not suspected for that (i.e., to give false judgment or testimony on this basis).

6. How did they check (the truthfulness of) witnesses? They brought them in and admonished them. Then they removed them all except for the chief among them, and they said to him: "Explain how you know that A is in debt to B." If he said, "A said to me that I am in debt to B," or "So-and-so said to me that A is in debt to B," he has not said anything. He must be able to say, "In our presence A acknowledged to B that he owes him two hundred *zuz.*" Afterward they bring in the second witness and examine him. If their words agreed, the judges discuss the matter. If two (judges) say that A is innocent and one says he is guilty, he is innocent. If two say A is guilty and one says he is not, he is guilty. If one says A is innocent, one says he is guilty, and one says, "I do not know," they must add judges.

7. When the judges reached their decision, they bring in the litigants. The chief judge says: "Mr. A, you are innocent," or "Mr. A, you

are guilty." After one of the judges leaves, he may not say, "I declared him innocent, and my colleagues declared him guilty, but what could I do since my colleagues outvoted me?" For of such a person it is written, "You shall not go about as a talebearer among your people" (Leviticus 19:16), and it also says, "He who goes about as a talebearer reveals secrets, but he who is of a faithful spirit conceals the matter" (Proverbs 11:13).

8. So long as a suitor can produce any proof the court may reverse the verdict. If they had said, "Bring all the proofs that you have within thirty days," and he brought them within the thirty days, the court may reverse the verdict; but if he brought any proof after the thirty days, the court cannot reverse the verdict. Rabban Simeon b. Gamaliel said: What should one do who did not find it within thirty days but found it after thirty days? If they had said to him, "Bring witnesses," and he said, "I have no witnesses," or if they said, "Bring proof," and he said, "I have no proof," and he later found proof or found witnesses, then they are not at all valid. Rabban Simeon b. Gamaliel said: What should one do who did not know that he had witnesses, then found witnesses, or who did not know that he had proof, then found proof? If they had said to him, "Bring witnesses," and he said, "I have no witnesses," or, "Bring proof," and he said, "I have no proof," but, when he saw that he would be accounted guilty, he said, "Come near, such-a-one and such-a-one, and bear witness for me!"; or if he brought forth some proof from his wallet, then it is not at all valid.

Chapter Four

1. Non-capital and capital cases are alike in examination and inquiry, for it is written, "You shall have one manner of law" (Leviticus 24:22). In what do non-capital cases differ from capital cases? Non-capital cases are decided by three and capital cases are decided by twenty-three judges. Non-capital cases may begin either with reasons for acquittal or for conviction, but capital cases must begin with reasons for acquittal and may not begin with reasons for conviction. In non-capital cases they may reach a verdict either of acquittal or of conviction by the decision of a majority of one; but in capital cases they may reach a verdict of acquittal by the decision of a majority of one, but a verdict of conviction only by the decision of a majority of two. In non-capital cases they may reverse a verdict either from conviction to acquittal or from acquittal to conviction; but in capital cases they may reverse a verdict from conviction to acquittal but not from acquittal to conviction. In non-capital cases all may argue either in favor of conviction or of acquittal; but in capital cases all may argue in favor of acquittal but not in favor of conviction. In non-capital cases he that had argued in favor of conviction may afterward argue in favor of acquittal, or he that had argued in favor of acquittal may afterward argue in favor of conviction; in capital cases he that had argued

in favor of conviction may afterward argue in favor of acquittal, but he that had argued in favor of acquittal cannot afterward change and argue in favor of conviction. In non-capital cases the verdict, whether of acquittal or of conviction, may be reached the same day; in capital cases a verdict of acquittal may be reached on the same day, but a verdict of conviction not until the following day. Therefore trials may not be held on the eve of a Sabbath or on the eve of a Festival-day (when court procedures were forbidden).

2. In non-capital cases concerning impurity and purity the judges declare their opinion beginning from the eldest, but in capital cases they begin from them that sit at the side (to prevent the younger judges from being swayed by the more experienced judges). All of the family stocks are qualified to try non-capital cases; but all are not qualified to try capital cases, but only priests, levites, and Israelites who may give their daughters in marriage into the priestly stock.

3. The Sanhedrin was arranged like the half of a round threshing-floor so that they all might see one another. Before them stood the two court scribes, one to the right and one to the left, and they wrote down the words of both those who favored acquittal and those who favored conviction. Rabbi Judah says: There were three: one wrote down the words of those who favored acquittal, one the words of those who favored conviction, and the third wrote down the words of both those who favored acquittal and those who favored conviction.

4. Before them sat three rows of disciples of the Sages, and each knew his proper place. If they needed to appoint another as a judge, they appointed him from the first row, and one from the second row came into the first row, and one from the third row came into the second; and they chose yet another from the congregation and set him in the third row. He did not sit in the place of the former, but he sat in the place that was proper for him.

5. How do they admonish the witnesses in capital cases? They would bring them in and admonish them thus: "Lest you say what is but supposition, or hearsay, or what you learned from another witness or from a reliable person, or lest you do not know that we intend to check your testimony through the processes of examination and inquiry, know that capital cases are not like cases concerning property: in the latter a man may pay money and thereby make atonement (for incorrect testimony), but in capital cases the witness is answerable for the blood of the one wrongfully condemned and his posterity to the end of the world. For so we have found in regard to Cain who killed his brother, where it says, "The bloods of your brother cry out" (Genesis 4:10). It does not say, "The blood of your brother," but rather, "The bloods of your brother," implying his blood and the blood of his descendants. . . . Therefore Adam was created alone to teach you that

anyone who destroys a single life of the people Israel is described by Scripture as if he had destroyed the entire world, and anyone who sustains one life of the people Israel is described by Scripture as if he had kept an entire world alive. (Some manuscripts leave out "of the people Israel" in that sentence.) Again, only a single man was created to promote peace among mankind, so that nodoby could say to his fellow, "My father is greater than yours"; also, so that the heretics should not say, "There are many ruling powers in heaven." Again, only a single man was created to proclaim the greatness of the Holy One, blessed is He; for man stamps many coins with one seal and they are all like one another; but the King of kings, the Holy One, blessed is He, has stamped every man with the seal of the first man, yet not one of them is like his fellow. Therefore (since each person is created in a unique form) everyone must say, "For my sake was the world created." And lest you (witnesses) say, "Why should we take on this burden?" — was it not written, "If he is able to testify as one who has either seen or learned of the matter but does not tell, he will be subject to punishment" (Leviticus 5:1). And lest you say, "Why should we be responsible for the blood of this man?" — was it not once written, "When the wicked perish, there is rejoicing" (Proverbs 11:10).

## Chapter Eleven

2. There were three courts in Jerusalem; one used to sit at the gate of the Temple Mount, one used to sit at the gate of the Temple Court, and one used to sit in the Chamber of Hewn Stone. They (judges of a lower court who disagreed) used to come first to the court that was at the gate of the Temple Mount, and the one would say, "In this way have I interpreted the law, and in that way have my colleagues interpreted it"; "In this way have I taught, and in that way have my colleagues taught." If the members of that court had heard a tradition, they would tell them. If not, the members of both courts would go to the court at the gate of the Temple Court, and one would say, "In this way have I interpreted the law, and in that way have my colleagues interpreted it"; "In this way have I taught, and in that way have my colleagues taught." If the members of that court had heard a tradition, they would tell them. If not, the members of all three courts would go to the Supreme Court ("the Great Sanhedrin") which sat in the Chamber of Hewn Stone, from which the Torah goes forth to all Israel, as it says, "From the place which the Lord shall choose" (Deuteronomy 17:10). If any of the elders who went up to Jerusalem to inquire returned to his own city and again taught as he was wont to teach, he is not yet culpable; but if he rendered a decision concerning what should be done, he is culpable, for it is written, "And the man who acts presumptuously" (Deuteronomy 17:12), implying that he is not culpable until he renders a decision concerning what should be done. A student who rendered a decision concerning what should be done is not culpa-

ble; thus the greater stringency which applies to him on the one hand (i.e., that he rendered a decision when he was not authorized to do so) turns out to be a leniency on the other (since he is not liable for the death penalty for disobeying the Supreme Court).

The Mishnah requires a minimum of three judges to constitute a court, but the Gemara reports a Baraita according to which one judge is sufficient if he is a *mumheh*, an expert. "Our Rabbis taught: Monetary cases are decided by three; but one who is a recognized *mumheh* may judge alone" (*Sanhedrin* 4b–5a). This tannaitic source does not specify whether the *mumheh* needed to have official authorization in addition to his expertise in order to judge alone without being monetarily responsible for his errors of judgment, and that issue will arise in the later discussion of the scope of authority of judges outside of Israel.

## 2. *The Shattering of that Structure*

The Romans physically destroyed Jerusalem in 70 C.E.; they killed or enslaved many of the communal leaders; and they forbade the remaining ones to teach Jewish law or to judge cases on pain of death, thus seriously threatening the line of succession. Thus, all three sources of judicial authority were crumbling in the last decade of the first century and the first decades of the second century.

Under these circumstances, the community first struggled to maintain as much of the original structure as possible. It had to insure the legitimacy of the remaining institutions when divorced from Jerusalem, and it sought to insure the chain of judicial ordination and to define its relationship to the judges of the growing diaspora community in Persia, to which many Israeli Jews were fleeing. This was a trying time, and many of the decisions made at this point were crucial to the survival of Jewish law as an operative system.

The next source is a graphic account of the situation in Israel at the end of the first century and at the beginning of the second. Note how concerned the Romans were to curtail the study and practice of Jewish law. They recognized that Jewish law gave Jews the cohesiveness and inner strength to resist Roman rule, and, consequently, Jewish law was seen as the enemy of Rome as much as were the Jews themselves.

*Gemara, Avodah Zarah, 17b–18a:*
They then brought up R. Hanina b. Teradion and asked him, "Why have you occupied yourself with the Torah?" He replied, "Thus the Lord my God commanded me." At once they sentenced him to be

burned, his wife to be slain, and his daughter to be consigned to a brothel.

It was said that within but a few days R. Jose b. Kisma died and all the great men of Rome went to his burial and made great lamentation for him. On their return, they found R. Hanina b. Teradion sitting and occupying himself with the Torah, publicly gathering assemblies, and keeping a scroll of the Law in his bosom. They immediately took hold of him, wrapped him in the Scroll of the Law, placed bundles of branches around him and set them on fire. They then brought tufts of wool, which they had soaked in water, and placed them over his heart, so that he should not expire quickly. His daughter exlaimed, "Father, that I should see you in this state!" He replied, "If I were alone being burned, it would have been a hard thing to bear; but now that I am burning together with the Scroll of the Law, He who will have regard for the plight of the Torah will also have regard for my plight."

Blowing the shofar (a ram's horn) is not in itself a form of work prohibited on the sabbath, but the rabbis declared that it should not be blown when Rosh Hashanah falls on the sabbath lest someone unlearned in the law carry the horn in the public domain, which is prohibited on the sabbath. That concern did not apply to the Temple itself, however, where everyone involved knew the law. Consequently, blowing the shofar on a Rosh Hashanah which is also the sabbath became the sole prerogative, and hence the distinguishing mark, of the Temple in Jerusalem. The dispute that is recorded next depicts a crucial incident in the legal history of the Jewish people in that R. Johanan b. Zakkai, in ruling that the shofar should be blown on the sabbath of Rosh Hashanah wherever the Sanhedrin sits, was asserting that the authority for making decisions in Jewish law rests in the Sanhedrin and not in the place where it had sat, Jerusalem. That was important because it enabled Jewish law to continue to be an effective governing legal system even when its authority could no longer be connected with possession of the Temple in Jerusalem. This became even more important in later centuries, when Jews were largely outside the land of Israel and were forced to move from place to place.

Even so, one can imagine good arguments against Rabbi Johanan's position. The Torah, after all, had specified clearly that questions of law should be taken "to the place which the Lord your God will have chosen," and the verdict "is announced to you from that place which the Lord chose" (Deuteronomy 17:8, 10). Previous Jewish law and practice had left no doubt that that place was understood to be the Temple in Jerusalem. If the Sanhedrin was no longer to sit there, how did it have any authority at all? Moreover, moving the seat of judicial authority from Jerusalem might well reduce the Jews' resolve to recapture it. Rabbi Johanan, sensing the urgency of the hour, does not even permit such arguments to be raised. In retrospect, his act was both brave and beneficial, but his contemporaries might well have considered it unfounded and presumptuous. Such ambiguity commonly characterizes major departures from previous practice, for what is a necessary and timely change in the eyes of some is a reckless and detrimental upheaval in the eyes of others.

*Mishnah Rosh Hashanah*, 4:1 and *Gemara Rosh Hashanah*, 29b:
MISHNAH. If the festive day of New Year fell on a Sabbath, they used to blow the shofar in the Temple but not in the country. After the destruction of the Temple, Rabban Johanan ben Zakkai ordained that it should be blown on Sabbath in every place where there was a court. R. Eliezer said: Rabban Johanan ben Zakkai laid down this rule for Jabneh only. They said to him: it applies equally to Jabneh and to any place where the Court sits.

GEMARA. "After the destruction of the Temple, Rabban Johanan ben Zakkai ordained etc." Our Rabbis taught: Once New Year fell on a Sabbath and all the towns assembled, and Rabban Johanan said to the Bene Betayra, "Let us blow the shofar." They said to him, "Let us discuss the matter." He said to them, "Let us blow and afterwards discuss." After they had blown, they said to him, "Let us now discuss the question." He replied: "The horn has already been heard in Jabneh, and what has been done is no longer open to discussion."

One source of authority for Jewish judges was the line of ordination, beginning with Moses. In the following story, Rabbi Judah b. Baba insures the continuation of that line by teaching and ordaining other rabbis despite the Roman decree making that a capital crime. The Romans sought to curtail the hold of Jewish law over Jews by eliminating the class of people who knew it, taught it, and applied it. By maintaining the line of rabbinic succession, Rabbi Judah was thwarting the Romans' plans and retaining an important source of authority for Jewish law. (Note: a *kenas* is a case involving a fine or penalty, as distinct from one resulting in simple compensation for the actual monetary loss incurred.)

*Sanhedrin* 13b–14a:
Abbaye asked Rabbi Joseph: On the basis of what Biblical verse do we deduce that three are required for the ordination of Elders? Shall we say, from the verse, "And he [Moses] laid his hand upon him [Joshua]" (Numbers 27:23)? If so, one should be sufficient! And should you say, Moses stood in place of seventy-one, then seventy-one should be the right number!—The difficulty remained unanswered.

R. Aha the son of Raba asked R. Ashi: "Is ordination effected by the literal laying on of hands?"—"No," he answered, "it is by the conferring of the degree: he is designated by the title of Rabbi and granted the authority to adjudicate cases of *kenas.*"

Cannot one man alone ordain? Did not Rab Judah say in Rab's name, "May this man indeed be remembered for blessing—his name is R. Judah b. Baba; were it not for him, the laws of *kenas* would have been forgotten in Israel."—Forgotten? Then they could have been learned.—He meant to say that these laws might have been abolished. For once the wicked Government, as an act of religious persecution, decreed that whoever performed an ordination should be put to death, and whoever received ordination should be put to death, the city in which the ordination took place demolished, and the boundaries wherein it had been performed, uprooted. What did R. Judah b. Baba do? He went and sat between two great mountains, that lay between two large cities, between the Sabbath boundaries of the cities of Usha and Shafaram, and there ordained five elders, viz., R. Meir, R. Judah, R. Simeon, R. Jose, and R. Eliezer b. Shamua. R. Awia adds also R. Nehemiah in the list. As soon as their enemies discovered them, Rabbi Judah b. Baba urged them: "My children, flee." They said to him, "What will become of you, Rabbi?" "I will lie before them like a stone which none is concerned to overturn," he replied. It was said that the enemy did not stir from the spot until they had driven three hundred iron spear-heads into his body, making it like a sieve.—With R. Judah b. Baba were in fact some others, but in honor to him, they were not mentioned.

While R. Johanan b. Zakkai had been able to preserve the authority of the Sanhedrin despite its displacement from Jerusalem, the sanctity of Israel was such that no ordination was possible outside of Israel. The insistence on restricting ordination to the land of Israel was based partially on historical precedent, but the major factors were undoubtedly legal and theological. As we have seen, Deuteronomy 17 situates the Supreme Court specifically in the Temple, and thus judicial authority was associated with Jerusalem and, secondarily, with Israel. Underlying this feature of the law was the belief that God resided in the Temple, and consequently it was only there that one could accurately receive revelation. (Remember that the rabbis understood judicial interpretation as the new form of God's revelation once prophecy ceased.) In other words, authority did not come from knowledge alone; one had to be in the place where revelation was possible. This may well be a remnant of the ancient notion that a god's authority ends at the borders. Rabbinic Judaism did not hold that, but it did maintain the positive converse of that, which is, that God's revelation was available with most fidelity "in the place which the Lord your God has chosen" (Deuteronomy 17:8). Without ordination one could only function as a law clerk.

> *Sanhedrin* 14a:
> R. Joshua b. Levi said: "There is no ordination outside Palestine." What is to be understood by, "There is no ordination"? Shall we assert that they have no authority at all to adjudicate cases of *kenas* outside Palestine? But have we not learned, "The Sanhedrin has competence both within and without Palestine"!—This must therefore mean that ordination cannot be conferred outside Palestine.
>
> It is obvious, that if the ordainers are outside Palestine and those to be ordained in Palestine, then surely as has been said, they cannot be ordained. But what if the ordainers are in Palestine, and those to be ordained outside?—Come and hear: It is related of R. Johanan that he was grieved when R. Shaman b. Abba was not with them in Palestine to receive his ordination. Again it is related of R. Simeon b. Zirud and another who was with him, *viz.*, R. Jonathan b. Akmai, or according to others who invert the order, R. Jonathan b. Akmai and another who was with him, *viz.*, R. Simeon b. Zirud, that the one who was with them was ordained, and the other, who was not, was not ordained.

## 3. *The Reconstitution of Jewish Courts in the Diaspora*

Ultimately the Jewish people were dispersed throughout the world, communication was difficult, and no clear, centralized authority existed. Under these circumstances, the need to maintain the community demanded some way to keep the courts functioning, despite the loss of the Supreme Court.

The following selection from the Gemara records the first attempts to determine the extent of the jurisdiction of judges that had not been ordained in Israel and the rationale for that authority. Rav and Samuel were among the first generation of Jewish leaders to live in Persia after the editing of the Mishnah, when many Jews were emigrating from Israel. They do not claim that full ordination could be conferred outside of Israel, but they do institute a procedure whereby a judge could share the immunity of fully ordained judges if he received authorization to judge from the Resh Galuta (Exilarch), the Persian official appointed as Head of the diaspora community in Persia. As the Gemara selection indicates, in later centuries the Babylonian Jews maintained that such authorization stretched over a greater domain than Palestinian ordination. That was probably dictated by the shifting balance of power from the Israeli Jewish community to the Babylonian, which is reflected in Rabbi Hiyya's ruling, but the Gemara also provides a textual source to support the changing judicial practice.

Note that much of the dialogue centers around Rabbi Judah, the president of the Sanhedrin under whom the Mishnah was edited. Because of the Mishnah's influence, he is called simply "Rabbi." It was in the third century, the generations immediately after him, that the issue of authorization came to a head.

*Sanhedrin* 4b–5b:
Our Rabbis taught: Monetary cases are decided by three; but one who is a recognized *Mumheh* may judge alone.

R. Nahman said: One like myself may adjudicate monetary cases alone. And so said R. Hiyya.

The following problem was consequently propounded: Does the statement "one like myself" mean that as I have learned traditions and am able to reason them out, and have also obtained authorization, so must he who wishes to render a legal decision alone, but that if he has not obtained authorization, his judgment is invalid; or is his judgment valid without such authorization? Come and hear! Mar Zutra, the son of R. Nahman, judged a case alone and gave an erroneous decision. On appearing before R. Joseph, he was told: If both parties accepted you as their judge, you are not liable to make restitution. Otherwise, go and indemnify the injured party. Hence it can be inferred that the judgment of one, though not authorized, is valid.

Rav said: Whosoever wishes to decide monetary cases by himself and be free from liability in case of an erroneous decision, should obtain authorization from the Resh Galuta. And Samuel said the same thing.

It is clear that an authorization held from the Resh Galuta here in Babylonia holds good here. And one from the Palestinian authority there [in Palestine] is valid there. Likewise, the authorization received here is valid there, because the authority in Babylon is designated "scepter," but that of Palestine "lawgiver" (denoting a lower rank), as it has been taught: "The scepter shall not depart from Judah" (Genesis 49:10), this refers to the Exilarchs of Babylon who rule over Israel with scepters (since they were appointed by the Government); "and a lawgiver" (ibid.), this refers to the descendants of Hillel who teach the Torah in public (but who have no governmental authority). Is, however, a permission given there valid here? Come and hear! Rabbah b. Hana gave an erroneous judgment in Babylonia. He then came before R. Hiyya, who said to him: If both parties accepted you as their judge, you are not liable to make restitution; otherwise you must indemnify them. Now, Rabbah b. Hana did hold permission (but from the Palestinian authority). Hence we infer that the Palestinian authorization does not hold good for Babylon.

But is it really not valid in Babylon? Did not Rabbah, son of R. Huna, when quarrelling with the members of the household of the Resh Galuta, maintain: "I do not hold my authorization from you. I hold it from my father who received it from Rav, and he from R. Hiyya, who received it from Rabbi (Judah, the President) in Palestine"?—He was only trying to put them in their place with mere words (and did not seriously think that his authorization was valid in Babylonia).

Well, then, if such authorization is invalid in Babylon, what good was it to Rabbah, son of R. Huna (who had to compensate the litigant he erroneously ruled against)?—(None in Babylonia proper, but) it held good for cities that were situated on the Babylonian border which were under the jurisdiction of Palestine.

Now, what is the content of an authorization?—When Rabbah b. Hana was about to go to Babylon, R. Hiyya said to Rabbi: "My brother's son is going to Babylon. May he decide in matters of ritual law?" Rabbi answered: "He may." "May he decide monetary cases"—"He may." "May he declare firstborn animals permissible for slaughter?"—"He may."

We were told above that Rabbi authorized Rabbah and Rav respectively to decide in matters of ritual law. Since he was learned in the law, what need had he to obtain permission? Because of the following incident, for it has been taught: Once Rabbi went to a certain place and saw its inhabitants kneading the dough without the necessary precaution against levitical impurity. Upon inquiry, they told him that a certain scholar on a visit taught them: Water of *bizeim* (ponds) does not render food liable to become impure. In reality, he referred to *bezim* (eggs), but they thought he said *bizeim* (ponds). They further erred in the application of another Mishnah. . . . There and then it was decreed that a disciple must not give decisions unless he was granted permission by his teacher.

In the previous selection, the Babylonians assert their exclusive authority to appoint judges for the Jewish courts in Babylonia independent of the Israelis. The Babylonians recognized, however, that the topics that they could adjudicate were limited. According to the following sources, there were certain criteria for cases which could be adjudicated only by ordained judges as against those that did not require ordained judges. These criteria restrict the role of Babylonian judges to that of court agents or clerks, authorized to adjudicate only the most common cases in which no special legal expertise is necessary. The Babylonians might well have known as much about the law and its application as the Israelis, but they lacked the formal act of authorization that could only be conferred in Israel. On the other hand, the criteria do give the Babylonians the power to act in a judicial capacity in matters where money is at stake, for incapacity to deal with such cases would be an intolerable obstruction to the normal functioning of the Babylonian Jewish community. The issue of ordination was not simply the political question of who gets to appoint judges or the educational question of who determines the academic qualifications for judges: it was nothing less than the question of whether Jewish law was going to be fully functional outside of Israel.

(Note: "admissions" in these sources refers to claims supported by witnesses attesting to the defendant's admission of his civil liability, despite his present denial. Such cases, together with the more common type in which there were witnesses present during the transaction of the loan itself, were the first that the Amoraim determined to be within the jurisdiction of judges who were not ordained, based on a rather complicated discussion in *Sanhedrin* 2b in the name of R. Abbahu, a third-century Palestinian Amora. The following sources are in the names of Abbaye and Rava, who were fourth-century Babylonian Amoraim, and they consequently based their rulings on an analogy to R. Abbahu's earlier ruling concerning admissions and loans.)

*Gittin* 88b:
Abbaye once found R. Joseph sitting in court and compelling certain men to give a bill of divorce. He said to him: Surely we are only laymen, and it has been taught: R. Tarfon used to say: In any place where you find heathen law courts, even though their law is the same as the Israelite law, you must not resort to them since it says, "These are the judgments which you shall set before them" (Exodus 21:1), that is to say, before them and not before heathens. Another explanation, however, is that it means "before them" and not before laymen?—He replied: We are carrying out their commission, just as in the case of admissions and transactions of loans. If that is the case, he rejoined, we should do the same with robberies and injuries.—We carry out their commission in matters which are of frequent occurence, but not in matters which occur infrequently.

*Bava Kamma* 84a–84b:
Rava said: Payment for damage done to chattel by cattle or for damage done to chattel by man can be collected even in Babylon, whereas payment for injuries done to man by man or for injuries done to man by cattle cannot be collected in Babylon. Now what special reason is there why payment for injuries done to man by cattle cannot be collected in Babylon if not because it is requisite in these cases that the judges be termed *Elohim* (literally, "gods," the word used in Exodus 21:6 and 22:7–8 for judges, connoting expert judges), a designation which is lacking in Babylon? Why then should the same not be also

regarding payment for damage done to chattel by cattle or to chattel by man, where there is similarly required the designation of *Elohim* which is lacking in Babylon? But if on the other hand the difference in the case of chattel damaged by cattle or chattel damaged by man is because we in Babylon are acting merely as the agents of the *mumhin* (expert) judges in the land of Israel as is the practice with matters of admissions and loans, why then in the case of man injured by man or man injured by cattle should we similarly not act as their agents as is indeed the practice with matters of admissions and loans?

It may, however, be said that we act as their agents only in regard to a matter of payment which we can fix definitely, whereas in a matter of payment which we are not able to fix definitely but which requires valuation we do not act as their agents. —But I might object that payment for damage done to chattel by cattle or to chattel by man we are similarly not able to fix definitely, but we have to say, "Go out and see at what price an ox is sold on the market place." Why then in the case of man injured by man, or man injured by cattle should you not similarly say, "Go out and see at what price slaves are sold on the market place"? Moreover, why in the case of double payment (for theft, see Exodus 22:3) and four-fold or five-fold payment (for stealing and slaughtering, see Exodus 21:37), which can be fixed precisely, should we not act as their agents?

It may, however, be said that we may act as their agents only in matters of civil liability, whereas in matters of a penal nature we cannot act as their agents. —We can act as their agents only in a matter of frequent occurrence, whereas in the case of man injured by man, which is not of frequent occurrence, we cannot act as their agents. — But why regarding degradation, which is of frequent occurrence, should we not act as their agents?—It may indeed be said that this is really the case, for R. Papa ordered four hundred *zuz* to be paid for degradation. But this order of R. Papa is no precedent, for when R. Hisda sent to consult R. Nahman in a certain case, did not the latter send word, "Hisda, Hisda, are you really prepared to order payment of fines in Babylon?"

It must therefore be said that we can act as their agents only in a matter which is of frequent occurrence and where actual monetary loss is involved, whereas in a matter of frequent occurrence but where no actual monetary loss is involved, or again in a matter not of frequent occurrence though where monetary loss is involved we cannot act as their agents. It thus follows that in the case of man injured by man, though there is there actual monetary loss, yet since it is not of frequent occurrence we cannot act as their agents, and similarly in respect of degradation, though it is of frequent occurrence, since it involves no actual monetary loss, we cannot act as their agents.

In the period between the editing of the Mishnah (c. 200 c.e.) and the extinction of the patriarchate (that is, the chain of presidents of the Sanhedrin, lasting until 425 c.e.), the Palestinian and Babylonian Jewish communities developed parallel, and not always similar, legal practices. After the extinction of the patriarchate, the unquestioned source of Jewish legal authority became the leaders of the Babylonian Jewish community until its demise in the eleventh century. During that time these leaders received questions from Jews all over the world, and the responsa literature developed consisting of their written responses to those questions.

The only challenge to their centralized authority occurred in 921 c.e., in the time of Saadia, when the Palestinian Jewish community attempted unsuccessfully to reassert its authority. During the decades preceding the incident, schools of higher learning were revived in Palestine, and their leaders, like the heads of the Babylonian schools, assumed the title "Gaon." Prompted by their real achievements and their new mood of vigor, the Palestinians then sought to wrest world leadership of the Jewish community from the Babylonians. To do this they needed to reassert their authority over some institution of Jewish law that was clearly tied to Jerusalem before its demise. The Temple was one such institution, but they did not feel qualified to rebuild it. Consequently, they chose the other legal institution directly connected to Jerusalem, the fixing of the calendar.

Aaron Ben Meir, a Palestinian gaon, conceived a small improvement in the calendar. He then built political support for his innovation. He secured the adherence of the Babylonian master of Pumbeditha, Megasser, by lending him support against his rival for the gaonate, Cohen-Zedek. He also elicited the concurrence of the Egyptian Jewish leaders. With this legal and political preparation, in the autumn of the year 921, Ben Meir proclaimed the rectified calendar from the Mount of Olives in Jerusalem, where the new months had been announced in mishnaic times.

Saadia, a Babylonian rabbi, immediately understood the political dimensions of the act. He resolved the internal quarrel among the contenders for the position of gaon in Pumbeditha, and then managed to coordinate the writing of a joint letter to Ben Meir by all of the authorities of Babylonia, asking him to withdraw his proclamation that the coming Passover would fall on Sunday instead of Tuesday. Ben Meir refused, and increasingly sharp letters passed between Babylonia and Palestine. The holidays were actually celebrated on different days in the spring of 922, and the confusion created thereby was noticed even by non-Jews. Palestine kept insisting on its time-honored prerogative, and Babylonia urged the danger of disunion at a time when the rabbinites in both countries had all they could do to fight the Karaite schismatics.

Saadia ultimately won the battle for the Babylonians by a combination of political and legal skills. He mobilized the Babylonian Jewish leaders to join him in a series of letters to the Palestinians. He also gained the support of the Exilarch, who urged him to write a definitive legal argument against Ben Meir's innovations. Saadia did that in his *Book of Seasons*. The book was written in biblical diction with vowel and accent marks similar to those of the Bible to give it the air of biblical authority. Promulgated throughout the Jewish world, it was to be recited annually in the month preceding the New Year. Ultimately, the Babylonians won the support of the vast majority of the world's Jews, and Saadia was elevated to the Sura gaonate as the reward for his efforts. The authority of diaspora judges, however, was destined to be a recurring issue in Jewish law, and we shall return to it in Topic Eight.

## B. SYSTEMS OF PROOF AND RULES OF EVIDENCE

We stand in the twentieth century, and from our perspective it is natural to assume that legal disputes will be resolved in a courtroom trial by the presentation of evidence and the assessment of its credibility and weight. This expectation reflects our post-Enlightenment, rationalistic optimism concerning the ability to discover historic truth by proof. It understates the very real indeterminacy of many factual issues. Jewish law, like many older legal systems, did not share these rationalistic assumptions, and the process of trial and proof, therefore, takes a somewhat different form.

Until the eighteenth and nineteenth centuries very different systems of proof were used at common law and throughout Europe. These systems relied heavily on modes of decision other than proof by credible testimonial evidence. In particular, champions would battle to demonstrate the justice of their cause, parties would be subjected to ordeals through which truth would be made manifest, oracles would be consulted to find the truth, or persons would prove the justice of their cause by their own oath or that of oath takers. These forms of trial were familiar alternatives to a trial based on the testimony of percipient witnesses. The modern student must understand that in the common law trial by compurgation the party able to produce the requisite number of oath takers was deemed credible and won the suit. In other words, if the plaintiff did everything according to the requisite regimen, he established a fact for the court, against which there was no defense. To establish such a fact, witnesses, whose eligibility was defined in very special ways, had to recite a formula in a consistent manner; this is the "formal" nature of formal proof. They could do this even if they had no personal knowledge about the transaction from which the claim arose because their function was to establish that the plaintiff was a person to be believed. The content of their testimony and of the plaintiff's claim are thus not tested by the trial; what is tested is the credibility of the plaintiff. Since it is the moral trustworthiness of people that is being held up for scrutiny and not their testimony, the tight rules governing the competence of witnesses and the inferences that can be made from testimony make good sense. Formal proof of this sort works as long as people have faith in oaths. In that case all contracts will be authenticated before official witnesses who can testify to the act, to the point that even marriage contracts are signed by witnesses and not by the parties who are being married. It is only when people are no longer convinced of others' respect for oaths that they insist that testimony must be evaluated for its inherent persuasiveness, as we do in American law today.

In the material that follows several terms are used in a connotation quite different from American law. The first is the oath. Note that witnesses are not sworn. The heavy sanction in Jewish law for false testimony is not for violating an oath to tell the truth but rather follows because witnesses are warned of the consequences. The oath is primarily a means of trial, not a testimony. When the party takes his oath, that is the end of the case. As in early common law, the issue is under what circumstances a party may be required to undergo this form of ritual trial.

The term "warning" has two distinct connotations. The first implies the caution that must be given to a witness before he testifies in court. The second connotation refers to the fact that the potential malefactor had (at least in some circumstances) to be adequately aware of the consequences of his actions if he were to be held criminally liable for them.

Finally, the term "witness" describes both a person who testifies to what he has perceived in the modern sense, and, more importantly, the person called on to be the formal observer and witness of a transaction. In the two settings there are different rules concerning the witness and his testimony, but note that in both situations formal requirements as to competence, number of witnesses, and form of testimony are central.

The following excerpts from Maimonides' *Mishneh Torah* were written many centuries after the rabbinic court structure was shattered. As is often the case, Maimonides sets out the classical law with unique clarity and simplicity. These excerpts provide a particularly useful overview of the system. Note how frequently the general statement of a principle—for example, the duty to testify, the necessity of testimonial proof of a claim, the requirement of two witnesses—is followed by important exceptions and limitations which reduce the applicability of the basic principle to a few, unusual cases. Note particularly the extent to which relaxed standards of proof are permitted in cases of civil obligations, which rabbinic courts continued to hear frequently, while the stringent standards are retained for capital cases, which the exilic rabbinic courts generally lacked power to hear after 70 C.E. If the system that Maimonides describes was a real system, it could not have worked well. As we shall see, rabbinic literature itself reports problems with the court system and provides measures to limit the liability of the decision makers. Moreover, arbitration was encouraged as a way of avoiding the judicial system entirely. One would expect that a very high percentage of civil cases was not handled by the formal court procedures outlined; that would be parallel to the situation in American society, where the very structure of the courts encourages people to settle disputes outside of court by other methods.

Maimonides, *Mishneh Torah*, Laws of Evidence, Chaps. 1:1–2; 3:1–6, 11; 4:1, 2; 5:1–3; 17:1–2; 22:5:

### Chapter I

1. A witness is commanded to testify in court regarding any and all testimony which he knows, whether it is testimony which will condemn the defendant or acquit him, as it says, "If he is able to testify as one who has either seen or learned of the matter but does not give information, then he is subject to punishment" (Leviticus 5:1). In money matters this duty devolves upon him only if the claimant asks him to testify.

2. If the witness is a great sage and the judges of the court were inferior to him in wisdom, since it is beneath his dignity to appear before them, he may refrain from testifying because the positive command to pay respect to the Torah (and its teachers) takes precedence over the negative command (of not withholding evidence). This applies only in monetary cases; but in cases in which his testimony would avert the transgression of a prohibition, or in cases involving either capital or corporeal punishment, he must go and testify, for it says, "No wisdom and no understanding can prevail against the Lord" (Proverbs 21:30), that is, wherever there would be a desecration of the Divine Name, the honor due a teacher is disregarded.

### Chapter III

1. Both civil and capital cases require inquiry and query, as it is said: "You shall have one manner of law" (Lev. 24:22). The Rabbis, how-

ever, said that in order not to shut the door to borrowers, witnesses who testify in monetary suits are not subjected to inquiry and query. How so? If the witnesses say, "So-and-so lent So-and-so one hundred *zuz* in our presence in such-and-such a year," although they do not specify the month (when the loan was made), or the place where it was made or the coinage of the *maneh* loaned, their evidence is valid.

2. That applies only to cases of admission and transaction of loans, gifts and sales, and the like. But in cases involving fines inquiry and query are required, and all the more so in cases involving flogging or banishment. Also, if the judge perceives or suspects that the case before him involves fraudulent claims, the witnesses must undergo inquiry and query.

3. Even though witnesses in civil cases are not subject to inquiries and queries, if they contradict each other in their answer to any of the inquiries and queries, their evidence is void. But if they contradict each other in their answer to questions put to them in the course of the cross-examination, their evidence is valid. How so? If one says, "He borrowed from him in the month of Nisan," and the other says, "No, it was in the month of Iyyar," or one says, "(He borrowed from him) in Jerusalem," and the other says, "No, we were in Lod," their testimony is void (since they contradict each other in answering one of the queries). Similarly, if one says, "He lent him a barrel of wine," and the other says, "It was a barrel of oil," their testimony is void, since they contradicted each other in answering one of the inquiries. But if one said, "The *maneh* (which the borrower received from the lender) was black (old)," and the other said, "It was a white (new) *maneh* coin," or if one says, "They were in the upper story when he lent him money," and the other says, "They were in the lower story," their testimony is valid. Even if one said, "He lent him a *maneh* (= 100 *zuz*)," and the other said, "Two hundred *zuz*," the borrower must pay one *maneh* because one hundred is included in the two hundred (and the witnesses agree that he owes him at least one hundred). Similarly, if one said, "He owes him the value of a barrel of wine," and the other says, "The value of a barrel of oil," the borrower pays the lesser sum. This applies to all similar cases.

4. According to Scriptural law, we only accept the oral testimony of the witnesses, both in civil and capital cases, as Scripture says, "By the mouth of two witnesses shall the matter be established" (Deut. 19:15), implying that it must come from their mouths and not from their handwriting. But the Scribes ruled that we may decide civil cases on the basis of documentary evidence, even if the witnesses are no longer living, in order not to shut the door to future borrowers. We do not, however, decide on the basis of documentary evidence in cases which involve fines; and in cases involving lashes or banishment it is even clearer that we require oral testimony and refuse to rely on written evidence.

5. Whether in monetary or capital cases, a witness whose evidence was examined by the court cannot retract. How so? If the witness says, "I was misled," (or) "I erred and later I was reminded that the matter was not that way," (or) "I testified that way because I was afraid of him (one of the litigants)," we do not pay attention to him even if he gives a reason for what he says. Similarly, he may not add to his testimony mention of a verbal condition which was attached to the transaction. The general principle is: once the evidence of a witness has been probed, no attention is paid to any further statement by him, whether the statement would have the effect of nullifying his testimony or of adding a rider to it.

6. If witnesses have signed a document, their signed evidence is as valid as evidence that has been examined by the court, and therefore they cannot retract any of it. That rule applies when it is possible to verify the signatures on the document without resorting to their further testimony—for example, if there are other witnesses who can identify the signatures on the document, or if the identity can be determined by comparison with other documents which they have signed. But if it is impossible to verify their signatures except through their further testimony, and they say, "These are our signatures, but we were compelled to sign," or "We were minors," or "We were relatives," or "We were misled," they are believed, and the document is invalidated.

.　.　.

11. Even in monetary suits, evidence is accepted only in the presence of the defendant. If the defendant was ill, or the witnesses were preparing to go abroad and the court sent for the defendant but he did not appear, we accept evidence in his absence. That applies, however, only to testimony given orally; documentary evidence we confirm even in the absence of the defendant. Even if he protests vehemently, saying, "This document is a forgery," (or) "They are false witnesses," (or) "They are ineligible witnesses," we pay no attention to him and confirm the document. But if he has proof to invalidate it, the document is invalidated.

### Chapter IV

1. In capital cases the two witnesses must simultaneously see the culprit commit the crime, and they must testify at the same time and in the same court; but in monetary cases we do not require that. How so? If one witness saw the culprit from one window when he was committing the crime, and the other witness saw him from another window, their testimony is combined if the two witnesses saw each other; if not, their testimony is not combined (and therefore the two witness rule is not satisfied). (The culprit is guilty only if warned before committing the crime, and) if the admonitor saw the witnesses and the witnesses saw him, then even if the witnesses did not see each other, the admonitor links their testimony together. If both wit-

nesses were in the same house and one of them stuck his head out of the window, saw the offender doing work on the Sabbath (a capital crime) while the admonitor was giving him warning, then withdrew his head from the window, and the second stuck his head out of that window and saw him working, their testimony is not combined—unless both saw him simultaneously. . . .

2. In monetary cases, however, even if the witnesses did not see each other, their testimony is combined. How so? If one says, "The claimant made a loan to the defendant in my presence on such-and-such a day," or "The defendant admitted in my presence the loan made to him," and the second witness says, "I too declare that the loan was transacted in my presence," or "that the defendant admitted in my presence the loan made to him," but he states that it (the loan or admission) was made on another day, their evidence is combined.

.   .   .

### Chapter V

1. Neither in monetary cases nor in capital cases do we decide on a judgment on the basis of one witness, as it says, "A single witness may not confirm against a person any guilt or blame that may be committed" (Deuteronomy 19:15). By tradition, however, we have learned that one witness may confirm enough to force the defendant to take an oath (to contradict the testimony of the one witness), as we have explained in "The Laws of Claims."

2. In two instances the Torah accepts the testimony of one witness: a woman suspected of marital infidelity is not made to drink of the water of bitterness; and the neck of a heifer is not broken, as we have already explained. Moreover, on the authority of the Rabbis, a woman is permitted to remarry on the evidence that her husband is dead.

3. Whenever one witness fulfills the legal requirement, a woman or a person who is generally ineligible to testify may act as witnesses, except for the cases in which the testimony of one witness forces the defendant to take an oath. For we only impose an oath on the basis of the testimony of a competent witness whose testimony can be combined with that of another person such that the defendant who is now ordered to take an oath could be made liable to pay compensation.

"On the testimony of two or three witnesses" (Deuteronomy 19:15), implies that three witnesses are to be treated like two: if one witness of a pair is found to be a relative (of the other witness or either litigant) or is ineligible, that invalidates the testimony (of both); similarly, if one witness in a group of three or, for that matter, a group of one hundred witnesses is found to be a relative or ineligible, the testimony is invalidated, whether the case is a capital one or a civil one.

.   .   .

## Chapter XVII

1. If many people inform a person that they saw someone commit a certain crime or borrow money from someone else, even if the informers are great in wisdom and piety and even if he believes them in his heart to the point that it is as if he himself saw the act, nevertheless he may not testify unless he saw it with his own eyes or the borrower himself admits the loan to him, saying, "Be a witness against me that So-and-so loaned me a *maneh*;" for Scripture says, "He is able to testify as one who has either seen or learned of the matter" (Leviticus 5:1). Moreover, we accept testimony of seeing (without knowing) or knowing (without seeing) only in monetary matters (but in capital cases both are required). Anyone who bases his testimony on what others have told him is a false witness and transgresses a negative command, as it is said: "You shall not bear false witness against your neighbor" (Exodus 20:13).

2. Therefore we admonish witnesses even in civil cases. How do we do that? They are admonished in front of all (who are in court). We inform them of the far-reaching consequences of false testimony and the degradation both in this world and in the world to come of one who testifies falsely. After that we remove all of the witnesses from court except for the oldest of them. Then we say to him, "Tell us how you know that So-and-so is in debt to So-and-so?" If his reply is "He himself told me that he is in debt to the claimant," or "So-and-so informed me that the defendant is in debt to So-and-so," his evidence is of no account. His evidence is considered only if he declares, "The defendant admitted in our presence that he is in debt to the claimant." Then we call in the second witness and examine him in a similar manner. If their statements tally, the judges discuss the case and render a decision.

## Chapter XXII

5. If a man produces witnesses whose testimony is examined and refuted, and then brings other witnesses who testify to the same effect and their evidence is refuted—even if this happens to a hundred sets —and afterward he produces witnesses who testify to the same effect and their testimony is found to be correct, the case is decided on their testimony. For even though the man who makes this claim (on the basis of all these refuted witnesses) is presumed to produce false witnesses, these last witnesses cannot be presumed to be lying. But if a document is contested, that is, two witnesses come and say, "He asked us to forge this document," no claim can ever be collected on it even if the signatures on it are independently confirmed (the assumption being that the signatures are well-executed forgeries by two other people whom the claimant persuaded to sign). It seems to me, however, that if the witnesses of the document themselves come and confirm their signatures, then we (enable the claimant to) collect on it.

Maimonides, *Mishneh Torah*, Laws of Claims, 1:1:

If one makes a claim against his neighbor regarding moveable property, and the defendant admits part of the claim, then the defendant must pay the claimant what he admits he owes and take an oath on the rest [i.e., that he does not owe him that amount]. This is an oath imposed by the Torah, as it says, "in regard to which he says that *this is it*" (Exod. 21:8) [implying that he owes nothing else]. Similarly, if he denies the entire claim and says that the transaction never took place, then if there is one witness who testifies that the defendant owes the claimant money or an object, the Torah imposes an oath on the defendant to establish his claim. On the basis of Tradition the Sages learned that wherever two witnesses would make one liable for paying money, one makes him liable to take an oath. And similarly they learned on the basis of Tradition that one witness does not suffice to establish guilt for any crime or sin, but one witness does suffice in order to impose an oath on the defendant.

Maimonides, *Mishneh Torah*, Laws of Courts (Sanhedrin) 20:1, 4, 5; 21:1–3, 10, 11; 24:3–7, 10:

### Chapter XX

1. The court does not impose the death penalty on the basis of conjecture but only on the testimony of witnesses who have seen the matter clearly. Even if the witnesses saw him (the assailant) chasing the other, gave him warning, and then lost sight of him, or the assailant followed the victim into a ruin and they (the witnesses) followed after him and found the victim writhing in death agony, while the sword dripping with blood was in the hands of the slayer, since they did not see him at the time of the slaying, the court cannot impose capital punishment on the basis of this testimony. Concerning this and similar cases, Scripture says: "Do not bring death on the innocent and the righteous" (Exodus 23:7).

Similarly, if two witnesses testify that the accused committed idolatry but one of them saw him worship the sun and gave him warning (that that was a capital crime), while the other saw him worship the moon and gave him warning (that that was a capital crime), their testimony is not combined, as Scripture says, "Do not bring death on the innocent and the righteous," i.e., since there is a possibility of declaring him innocent such that he would still be righteous, do not condemn him to death.

．　．　．

4. The court is forbidden to have pity on a murderer. It should not say, "This one is already slain; what good will it do to execute the other?" and thus prove lax in the duty of putting the murderer to death. For Scripture says, "You must show him no pity. Thus you will

purge Israel of the blood of the innocent, and it will go well with you" (Deuteronomy 19:13).

Similarly, the court is forbidden to have pity on someone who is liable for a fine. It should not say, "This man is poor, he did it unintentionally." Rather, we collect from him to the limit of his ability without pity, as Scripture says, "You must not show pity: (life for life, eye for eye, tooth for tooth, hand for hand, foot for foot]" *(Deuteronomy 19:21).*

Similarly, in civil cases we do not have pity on the poor. You should not say, "This man is poor, and the claimant against him is rich. Since both the claimant and I are obligated to support him, I will give judgment in his favor and he will be able to support himself honorably." It is against such reasoning that the Torah warns, "Nor must you show deference to a poor man in his dispute" (Exodus 23:3), and it also says, "Do not favor the poor (or show deference to the rich; judge your neighbor fairly)" (Leviticus 19:15).

It is forbidden (at a trial) to show deference to a great man. How so? If two people come before you for trial, one of whom is a great scholar, and the other is an ordinary man, do not greet the great man first, showing him friendliness and esteem, such that the other litigant will find it impossible to marshal his arguments. Rather, the judge should not show partiality to either one of them until the case is concluded, as Scripture says, "Nor show deference to the rich" (ibid.). The Sages said, "Do not say, 'This man is rich, (or) this man is well-connected. How can I put him to shame and see him humiliated?' Therefore Scripture says, 'Nor show deference to the rich'" (*Sifra Leviticus* 19:15).

5. If two people come before you, one of whom is a worthy person, and the other wicked, do not say, "Since this one is wicked, and the presumption is that he is lying, while the presumption is that the other does not lie, therefore I will turn the verdict against the wicked man." Against such reasoning Scripture says, "You shall not subvert the rights of the needy in their disputes" (Exodus 23:6) (implying that) even if a man is needy (lacking) in observing the commandments, do not subvert his judgment.

. . .

## Chapter XXI
1. It is a positive commandment for the judge to judge fairly, as Scripture says, "Judge your neighbor fairly" (Leviticus 19:15). What is fair judgment? It is equalizing the two litigants in every respect. One should not let one litigant speak as long as he wants and tell the other to be brief; and one should not be friendly to one litigant, speaking to him softly, while frowning upon the other and speaking to him harshly.

2. If one of the litigants is richly dressed and the other poorly dressed, the judge must say to the former, "Either dress him like yourself before you come to trial against him, or dress like him such that you are equal; then the two of you may stand in judgment."

3. It must not be that one litigant sits and the other stands, but rather both should stand. If the court wanted to permit both to be seated, it may do so. However, one must not sit on a seat higher than the other; they must be seated side by side. The court may permit the litigants to be seated during the discussion period in the trial, but when the judgment is completed, both litigants must stand, as Scripture says "(Next day Moses sat as magistrate among the people), while the people stood about Moses (from morning until evening)" (Exodus 18:13). And what constitutes the completion of judgment? When the judges announce their decision saying, "So-and-so, you are innocent; So-and-so, you are guilty." This applies only to the litigants, but the witnesses must stand, as it is said: "Then both the men . . . shall stand" (Deuteronomy 19:17).

. . .

10. How do we know that the judge should not express approval of the arguments of a litigant? It is said: "Keep yourself far from a false matter" (Exodus 23:7). Rather, the litigant should say what he thinks, and the judge should keep silent. Nor should he suggest to either suitor a line of argument. Even if he (the plantiff) brought but one witness, the judge should not say to him, "We do not accept the testimony of one man." Rather, he should say to the defendant, "This man has testified against you." Perhaps the defendant would then admit the claim, saying, "He has testified truthfully." The judge must therefore wait until the defendant himself says, "He is only one witness, and he is not to be trusted against me." This applies to all similar situations.

11. If the judge sees a point in favor of a litigant and finds that the litigant is trying to say it but he cannot articulate it, or he sees that a litigant is desperately trying to defend himself with a truthful claim but he loses the point due to his fierce anger, or he finds that the litigant is confused because of an inferior intellect, then he is permitted to assist him a little by giving him a lead on the basis of "Speak up for the dumb" (Proverbs 31:8). But the judge must do this carefully so that he does not play the part of an advocate.

. . .

## Chapter XXIV
3. A judge who knows that a case is full of deceit must not say, "I will decide it (on the basis of the evidence presented), and let the collar (of responsibility) fall on the necks of the witnesses." What biblical

verse tells us that? "Keep yourself far from a false matter" (Exodus 23:7). What should he do? He should persevere in questioning the witnesses, applying the methods of inquiry and query used in capital cases. Then if it seems to him that there indeed is no deceit, he should decide the case on the basis of the evidence. But if his heart tells him that there is deceit, or if he does not trust the witnesses even though he cannot find sufficient reason to disqualify them, or if he suspects that one litigant is deceitful and full of cunning and that he misled the honest men who are witnesses in this case to testify falsely in all innocence, or if it seems to him from the general tone of the case that some information is being withheld which they do not want to reveal, then in all these cases and in all similar ones the judge is forbidden to render a decision. He must rather withdraw from the case and let someone judge it who can do so with a complete heart. These are matters of the heart, and Scripture says, "For judgment is God's" (Deuteronomy 1:17).

4. The court can flog him who is not liable for flagellation and can execute him who is not liable for capital punishment, not in order to transgress the words of the Torah but rather to build a hedge around it. If the court sees that the people disregard a law, it can protect and strengthen the law in whatever way seems fitting to them. All such measures are the instruction of the hour, and the court should not fix the law in this way for all generations to come.

Thus there was a (talmudic) case in which a man was lashed for having intercourse with his wife (in public) under a tree (*Sanhedrin* 46a), and there was a (talmudic) case in which a man rode a horse on the Sabbath during the days of the Greeks and they brought him before the court and they stoned him (ibid.). And there was another (talmudic) case in which Simeon ben Shetah hanged eighty women (who were practicing witchcraft) on one day in Ashkelon without applying all of the methods of inquiry and query, without due warning, and without conclusive testimony, but it was a ruling for the hour according to what he perceived to be necessary (ibid., 45b).

5. Similarly courts in all places and at all times can inflict lashes on anyone whose reputation is unsavory and about whom people are talking, accusing him of violating the rules of sexual morality, on condition that the rumor about him is unceasing, as we have explained, and that those who spread these bad things about him are not known to be his enemies. Similarly, a person of ill repute may be shamed, and she who bore him may be reviled in his presence.

6. Similarly, a judge always has the power to expropriate money from its owner, destroy it, or give it away, disposing of it in any way which in his judgment will halt the breakdown of religion, repair its breaches, or bring to terms the defier of the Law. Thus it is written in

the Book of Ezra (10:8), "Anyone who did not come in three days would, by decisions of the officers and elders, have his property confiscated." From this we learn that whatever the court expropriates is (legally) confiscated.

7. Similarly, when the hour requires such measures, a judge may impose the ban or the more stringent form of excommunication as he sees fit upon him who is not liable for those penalties in order to check the breakdown of religion. . . .

10. All of these disciplinary measures shall be carried out as the judge sees fit and according to the emergency of the hour. In all such cases let his acts be for the sake of Heaven. Let not the honor due to fellow human beings be light in his eyes, for if he does so he is pushing aside a negative Rabbinic command. In regard to the descendants of Abraham, Isaac, and Jacob who uphold the Torah of truth he must be all the more careful not to destroy the honor due them, but must rather act exclusively to enhance the honor of God. For anyone who dishonors the Torah is himself dishonored by his fellow men (*Avot* 4:6), and whoever honors the Torah is himself honored by his fellow men, and the honor of the Torah consists in obeying its statutes and judgments.

## C. Problems with Using Courts

One reason why the preceding materials may have a fairly archaic air about them is that, with certain exceptions (matters of divorce and the conversion of proselytes), the formal rabbinic court system has fallen into disuse in most Jewish communities. In large part, it has been replaced by a reliance on secular courts in Israel and in the diaspora. Within the Jewish community dispute resolution has taken the form of conciliation, mediation, and, perhaps most importantly, arbitration. Certainly historical and political factors were primarily responsible for the decline of litigation, but it is interesting to examine the reasons the tradition itself has given for deeming court trial undesirable and for preferring other modes of dispute settlement.

### 1. The Time, Expense, and Bother of Taking a Case to Court

When American law students think about the problems inherent in the court system, the first thing that comes to mind is the time, bother, and expense involved. Those issues were not nearly as troublesome in the operation of Jewish courts because there were many more courts per capita than in the American system. The Talmud claims that there were 78,000 judges for the 600,000 people who left Egypt

(*Sanhedrin.* 18a)! That may be fanciful, but, more realistically, the Talmud does require civil courts of 3 judges in every village in Israel and a court of 23 judges for the judgment of capital cases in every town of 120 inhabitants or more (*Sanhedrin* 2b, 16b, 17b). Outside the land of Israel courts were first established in every district but not in every town (*Mak.* 7a). By the Middle Ages, however, each city had its own court. Until recent times, a major metropolis consisted of 10,000 people, and most Jews lived in far smaller communities. Since each community possessed its own court, it is unlikely that it was difficult, time consuming, or costly to have one's case heard.

Moreover, most of the cases presumably were not complex and the law was easy to apply. The Mishnah notes that civil courts might render a decision on the very day that the case came before them, while capital cases had to extend over at least two days (Mishnah *Sanhedrin* 4:1). Finally, the judges were paid only for the time lost from their work (Maimonides, Mishneh Torah, *Sanhedrin.* 23:5), they acted in lieu of attorneys for both the prosecution and defense, and there were limits on a litigant's rights to have a written transcript of the verdict (Shulhan Arukh, *Hoshen Hamishpat*, Sects. 14:4; 79). Court costs, therefore, were minimal. In sum, much of the time, bother, and cost of American litigation probably did not exist in the Jewish legal system.

The one occasion where cost factors do affect litigation in the Jewish legal structure is when one litigant wants to force the other to go to a higher or wiser court rather than the local one. In such instances, Jewish law was well aware of the time, expense, and bother involved, as the next reading indicates.

*Sanhedrin* 31b:
When R. Dimi came from Palestine, he said in R. Johanan's name: If a man, known as a difficult adversary in court, has a trial, and one of the litigants says, "Let us be tried here," while the other says, "Let us go to the place of Assembly (i.e., a higher court)," he is compelled to go to the place of Assembly. R. Eleazar, however, said in his presence: Rabbi, if a man claims a *maneh* from his fellow, must he spend another *maneh* on top of the first? No, the other litigant is compelled to attend the local court. It has been stated likewise: R. Safra said in R. Johanan's name: If two litigants are in obstinate disagreement with respect to the venue of a lawsuit, and one says, "Let us be tried here," and the other says, "Let us go to the place of Assembly," he (the defendant) must attend the court in his home town. And if it is necessary to consult the Assembly, the matter is written down and forwarded to them. And if the litigant says, "Write down the grounds on which you made your decision and give them to me," they must write them down and give him the document.

Amemar said: The law is that he is compelled to go to the place of the Assembly. R. Ashi said to him: Did not R. Eleazar say, He is compelled to attend court in his opponent's town? — That is only where the debtor demands it of the creditor; but if the creditor demands it, the debtor must submit, for "The borrower is servant to the lender."

Maimonides, *Mishneh Torah*, Sanhedrin 23:5.

If a judge takes payment for acting as a judge, his decisions are null and void, provided that it is evident that the payment is for his judicial services. But if he was engaged in his work and two people came before him for judgment, and he says to them, "Either get me someone who will work in my place while I am judging your case or give me compensation for my loss of time," that is permitted, provided that it is obvious that that is remuneration for his loss of time and nothing more. And he must take payment equally from each of them and in the presence of both. Payment under those conditions is permissible.

*Shulhan Arukh*, Hoshen Hamishpat, 13:3; 14:2:

Note: the italicized sections are the notes by Rabbi Moses Isserles, whose comments reflect the customs of Franco-German Jewry at variance with, or in addition to, those of Mediterranean Jewry, as reflected by Rabbi Joseph Caro in the body of the text (which is not italicized).

### Chapter 13

3. We do not use means of coercion against a man that he submit his arguments in writing, nor may a judge receive the arguments of the litigants in writing, but the members of the court of law should hear the arguments orally and instruct the scribe to set the arguments down in writing, and they should not write save with the approval of both parties, and both pay the scribe's fee. *However, if both litigants desire to present their pleas in writing, they have a right to do so, and whatever they set down in writing, they cannot retract.*

### Chapter 14

2. If one of the litigants is a scholar and knows how to set down his evidence in writing and his opponent is an illiterate person, the law is that the scholar should not write himself when they send on the case to seek advice from the Supreme Court of Law, but the judges should make a copy of the arguments. *And both litigants pay the scribe's fee.*

## 2. The Cumbersome Procedures of Court Trial Have Bad Social Effects

Note that (a) witnesses in a civil case are not questioned extensively by the judges despite the Torah's command to do so; (b) written testimony is accepted in civil cases despite the Torah's requirement of oral testimony; and (c) expert judges are not required in civil cases. In each of these instances, Jewish law has deviated from the norm to reduce the difficulty of litigating cases in court (remember that creditors may not charge interest in Jewish law, and, therefore, loaning money to someone is a real act of kindness). Are there elements of the American system of justice which attempt to deal with this problem? Consider the role of the small claims court and the problems described in the Rothschild excerpt.

(See Maimonides, *Mishneh Torah, Laws of Evidence*, 3:1, 4, in section B).

> *Gemara, Sanhedrin* 2b–3a:
> And what is the point in excluding cases of indebtedness (from the first clause of the Mishnah requiring three judges in monetary cases)? Shall I say it is to show that three judges are not required for them? But did not R. Abbahu himself say that all agree that no judgment given by two in monetary cases is valid?—It is to teach that cases of indebtedness require no *Mumhin* (ordained judges) for their adjudication: in accordance with the strict application of the law, in cases of indebtedness the Tanna would require (three) *Mumhin*, nevertheless they have become exempted from this regulation for the reason advanced by R. Hanina. For R. Hanina said: In accordance with the Biblical law, the judicial procedure in regard to the investigation and examination of witnesses applies to monetary as well as to capital cases, for it is written, (3a) "One manner of judgment shall you have" (Lev. 24:22). Why then did they (the Sages) declare that monetary cases are not subject to this exacting procedure? In order not to "bolt the door" against borrowers. (Similarly, the requirement for certified judges was dropped for that reason.) But if non-*Mumhin* are competent to adjudicate in monetary cases, ought they not to be protected against any claim of compensation in case of their having given an erroneous decision?—All the more then would you be "bolting the door" against borrowers.

> C. Rothschild, "A New Deal On Costs," 39 *Commercial Law Journal* 43 (1934):
> You have sold merchandise to a customer for which he has agreed to pay in sixty days. The bill becomes due, but he not only fails to pay but ignores entirely your requests for settlement. When finally you are forced to threaten suit, he tells you coolly, that if you sue, instead of being satisfied to wait until he gets good and ready to pay, it will take you six months or more to get your money. Every credit man knows that in a great many jurisdictions your customer will have no trouble at all in carrying out his threat. He puts in a general denial,

claims that your merchandise had some latent defect, seeks refuge behind some mythical oral agreement with your salesman, or brings up
some other equally trumped-up objections and legal technicalities. Of
course you can prove him wrong. But he is hundreds of miles away —
which means depositions, appearances of witnesses, and other expensive and highly troublesome legal procedures. What is the result? You
make the best compromise you can—and so not only give up money
to which you are fully entitled but promote deliberate crookedness.

Perhaps, however, you are among the fortunate people able to afford
the spending of money for the sake of principle, and enough of a be-
liever in principle to fight for it if there is any chance of success. Let
us assume too that the debtor is in your own town, so that expense for
such things as depositions will be avoided; and further that after every
conceivable obstacle has been put in your way, such as application for
jury trial on a crowded calendar, you finally after many months win
your case completely and obtain judgment for the full amount of your
claim. Does that mean that you will receive 100 cents on the dollar?
Not at all. You will be lucky if your expense does not amount to more
than 25%. In other words, you are compelled to accept 75¢ on the dollar from a solvent debtor, and this in spite of the fact that you have
beaten him on every count and are able to prove, from his own written
statement, that his objections were frivolous and that he had acted in
bad faith in every respect.

## 3. The Possibility of Making Mistakes in Law

Under certain circumstances, a judge who erred in judgment must
pay from his own pocket for losses sustained by the aggrieved litigant
as a result of the judicial error (see *Bekhorot* 28b; *Sanhedrin* 5a, 6a,
33a; M. T. *Laws of Courts (Sanhedrin)* 6:1–4; S. A. *Hoshen Mishpat*
25). Amoraic and medieval rulings narrowed the applicability of that liability, but the fear of making a mistake in judgment persisted. Even if
the judge is exempted from civil penalties for his error, he clearly does
not want to hazard God's wrath for misapplying His law. The remaining civil liability and the risk of divine punishment for error together
made arbitration a very attractive alternative to decisions rendered according to strict law.

> *Jerusalem Talmud, Sanhedrin* 1:1 (18a):
> Two people once came to be tried before R. Jose b. Halafta. They
> said to him, "on the condition that you try us in accordance with
> strict law." He answered, I do not know the strict law, and in any
> event, only He who knows man's thoughts (God) is able to punish
> those people who make false statements." When a person would
> come to R. Akiba with a lawsuit, he used to say to them (the litigants),

"Know before whom you stand; before Him who spoke and the world came into being, as it is written, 'the case of both parties shall come before God' (Exodus 22:8) (implying) but not before Akiba b. Joseph." It was taught: Forty years prior to the destruction of the Temple capital punishment was abolished and in the days of Simeon b. Shetah civil suits were abolished. Said R. Simeon b. Yohai, "Blessed be the Lord that I am not wise enough to act as judge."

## 4. The Need to Reach a Conclusion

*Sanhedrin* 6b:

The view of Resh Lakish is as follows: When two men bring a case before you, one of small influence, the other of great influence, before you have heard their case, or even after, so long as you are in doubt in whose favor judgment is inclining, you may tell them, "I am not bound to decide in your case" lest the man of great influence should be found guilty and use his influence to harass the judge. But if you have heard their case and know in whose favor the judgment inclines, you cannot withdraw and say, "I am not bound to decide in your case" because it is written, "Fear no man (for judgment is God's)" (Deuteronomy 1:17). . . .

Judges should also know whom it is they are judging, before whom they are judging, and who will call them to account if they pervert justice, as it is written, "God stands in the Congregation of God, in the midst of judges does He judge" (Psalms 82:1). And thus it is said concerning Jehoshaphat, "He charged the judges: 'Consider what you are doing, for you judge not on behalf of man, but on behalf of the Lord' " (II Chronicles 19:6). And lest the judge should say, "Why have all this trouble and responsibility?" it is further said, "He is with you when you pass judgment" (ibid.). The judge is to be concerned only with what he actually sees with his own eyes.

*Shulhan Arukh*, Hoshen Hamishpat, Laws of Judges, 12:5:

The judge has the power to adjudicate a lawsuit in a manner similar to a settlement where the matter cannot be otherwise determined according to strict law and he is not permitted to allow the verdict to pass out of his hand only in part without bringing the proceedings to a complete close.

## 5. The Desire to Avoid an Oath

*Shulhan Arukh*, Hoshen Hamishpat, Laws of Judges, 12:2:

Every court of law that always brings about a settlement is considered praiseworthy. When does this apply? Before the conclusion of the trial, even though one has heard their pleas and knows which way the judgment will incline, it is a religious duty to attempt a settlement.

But after the judge concludes the trial and makes the pronouncement, "so-and-so, you are innocent, so-and-so, you are guilty," he is not permitted to attempt a settlement between them. . . . If the court of law imposes an oath upon one of the parties, the court is permitted to bring about a settlement between them even after the conclusion of the trial so that the one who is bound to take an oath should be exempt from the responsibility for a false oath.

## 6. The Desire to Produce Peace

In the following sources, arbitration is thought to be more likely to produce peace than litigation is. What are the reasons for such a view? If arbitration is thought to be superior, why do Jewish and American societies bother to maintain a court system?

*Gemara, Sanhedrin* 6b:
R. Judah b. Korha says: Settlement by arbitration is a meritorious act, for it is written, "Render judgment of truth and peace in your gates" (Zekhariah 8:16). Surely where there is strict justice there is no peace, and where there is peace, there is no strict justice! But what is that kind of justice with which peace abides?—We must say: Arbitration. So it was in the case of David, as we read, "And David executed justice and righteousness (charity) towards all his people" (II Samuel 8:15). Surely where there is strict justice there is no charity, and where there is charity, there is no justice! But what kind of justice is compatible with charity?—We must say: Arbitration.

Maimonides, *Mishneh Torah*, Sanhedrin 22:4:
It is a commandment to say to the litigants at the outset of the trial, "Do you want a judgment in law or a settlement by arbitration?" If they wanted arbitration, we arbitrate a compromise between them. Every court which constantly effects arbitration is to be praised, and it is of such a court that the verse says, "Render a judgment of peace in your gates" (Zekhariah 8:16). Which judgment contains peace? Surely it is arbitration. And similarly with reference to David it is said: "And David executed justice and charity unto all his people" (II Sam. 8:15). What is the kind of justice which carries charity with it? Undoubtedly, it is arbitration, i.e., compromise.

The possibility of arbitrating a dispute holds only before the verdict has been announced. In that situation, even if the judge heard their arguments and determined the side in whose favor the verdict will be, it is still a commandment to try to arbitrate the dispute. But after he has handed down the verdict, saying, "So-and-so, you are innocent; So-and-so, you are guilty," he may not arrange a compromise between them, but rather let the law split the mountain (i.e., let the law take its course).

## D. ALTERNATIVES TO COURTS

### 1. *Jewish Law on Arbitration*

The selections that follow are brief and rarely discussed in Jewish legal literature or in the course of seminary training. Instead, the student of Jewish law gets the impression from the popularity and the sheer number of passages dealing with the formal court system that it is the view of the Jewish tradition that disputes should normally be handled by courts in accordance with the procedures that Jewish law meticulously works out. As we have seen, that impression is not correct. Nevertheless, much attention is paid to the formal court system because arbitration is not always possible. It is inapplicable to ritual, family, and criminal matters, and in civil suits the parties are not always willing to arbitrate. Moreover, little attention is paid to the form of arbitration because imposing many rules would be counterproductive to the goal of arbitration to effect an amicable settlement between the parties. The paucity of material about arbitration is thus not an indication of lack of interest in the procedure, but rather an appreciation of the flexibility that must be allowed if it is to work effectively in the cases that can be arbitrated. In such cases it is the preferred mode.

> *Sanhedrin* 5b–6a:
> R. Simeon b. Gamaliel says: Legal judgment is by three; arbitration is valid if made by two. And the force of arbitration is greater than that of legal judgment, for if two judges decide a case, the litigants can repudiate their decision, but if two judges arbitrate, the parties cannot repudiate their decision. . . .
>
> Arbitration is by three, so says R. Meir. The Sages say that one is sufficient. Now the Schoolmen presumed that all agree that the force of arbitration is equal to that of legal decision; their point of difference would accordingly resolve itself into one holding that three are required for legal decision and the other holding that two are enough. — No, all (both R. Meir and the Sages) agree that legal decision is by three, and the point in which they differ is this: One (R. Meir) holds that the force of arbitration should be regarded as equal to that of legal decision, while the other disputes it.
>
> May it be assumed then that there are three views held by the Tannaim with regard to arbitration, viz., one (R. Meir) holds that three are needed; another (R. Simeon b. Gamaliel) holds that two are sufficient, while the Sages hold that one is enough? — R. Aha the son of R. Ika, or according to others R. Yemar b. Salomi, said: The Tanna who says two are necessary is really of the opinion that a single one is sufficient.

And the reason he requires two is that they might act as witnesses in the case, if required.

*Shulhan Arukh,* Hoshen Hamishpat, 12:2, 5–7:

2. It is a religious duty to say to the litigants at the outset, "Do you wish to resort to law or to submit to arbitration?" If they consented to submit to arbitration, they bring about a settlement between them. And just as the judge is cautioned not to pervert judgment, so too, is he cautioned not to direct the arbitration in favor of one party more than the other. Every court of law that always brings about a settlement is considered praiseworthy. When does this apply?—Before the conclusion of the trial—even though one has heard their pleas and knows which way the judgment will incline—it is a religious duty to attempt a settlement; but after the judge concluded the trial and made the pronouncement, "So-and-so, you are innocent, So-and-so, you are guilty," he is not permitted to attempt a settlement between them. However, another person who is not a judge is permitted to attempt a settlement between them, provided that this is not attempted in a court sitting that is appointed for the purpose of holding legal sessions. If the court of law imposed an oath upon one of them, the court of law is permitted to bring about a settlement between them even after the conclusion of the trial, so that the one who is bound to take an oath should be exempt from the responsibility thereof. *The court of law cannot compel one to fall in with the principle of equity, i.e., acting beyond the requirements of the line of justice, although that would appear to them to be the proper thing to do. However, some differ with this opinion.*

5. The judge has the power to adjudicate a lawsuit in a manner similar to a settlement where the matter cannot be otherwise determined according to strict law and he is not permitted to allow the verdict to pass out of his hand only in part without bringing the proceedings to a complete close.

6. One against whom there is a monetary claim regarding something which the defendant possesses is forbidden to seek means to evade the claim in order that the plaintiff should consent to make a settlement with him and forgo the balance of the claim. *And if he violated this law and employed evasive means, he does not comply with the requirements of Heaven until he restores to him (the plaintiff) what rightfully belongs to him.*

7. Although the litigants consented to submit their case to arbitration before the court of law, they can retract so long as a formal agreement was not made with them by means of a Kinyan, for the law is that arbitration requires a Kinyan, even if made before three. However, if a formal agreement was made with them by means of a Kinyan, they cannot retract even if made before one. And some say

that they cannot retract only if made at least before two. *And this has reference not only to a formal agreement made by means of a Kinyan, but likewise, if he (the defendant) gave a note of indebtedness thus obligating himself to carry out the settlement, or by any one of the other modes of transference of rights. Some say that when he assumes liability by means of a Kinyan relative to the arbitration, he must give him acquisition rights in the article so that it should not be a mere verbal agreement as will be explained infra §203.*

Arbitration was more than a theoretical alternative to Jewish courts; the available sources indicate it was heavily used. The following documents show how the process worked in pre-Enlightenment societies. The following excerpts from Gulak's book do not include all of the documents to which he refers in his introduction, but some representative documents will suffice to indicate the nature and varying contexts of Jewish arbitration agreements.

H. Gulak, *Treasury of Documents* [Jerusalem: D'fus Ha'Poalim, 1926], 281–86 [our translation from the Hebrew].

### Chapter 36—Arbitration Documents:
Arbitration documents are mentioned in the Mishnah (*Bava Metzia* 20, *Moed Katan* 18). They would be written at a time in which the litigants chose judges for themselves to adjudicate or arbitrate between them. In periods in which the Jewish court did not have legal power, the litigants would also choose judges who would adjudicate their case on the basis of strict Jewish law, and they would write documents in which the litigants imposed upon themselves the responsibility to carry out their decision. In Documents #302 and #308 below, the arbiters are apparently acting as judges, and the litigants have written a document announcing their choice of judges in order to give greater authority to their decision.

In most of the copies of documents that we have, the litigants chose two judges or arbiters; in Document #307 one side chose one arbiter and the second chose another arbiter according to the established order in the Mishnah (*Sanhedrin* 23a). For fear that the two arbiters would not agree with each other, the litigants chose a third in order to make the decision (cf. #306); or the two arbiters would themselves choose a third who would form the majority (cf. #307 below). In Document #308 it appears that arbiters who did not agree would often ask the advice of another rabbi and act according to his opinion.

A document in which arbiters were chosen was executed with witnesses as was the case with all other documents. Document #308, however, was executed through the signatures of the litigants them-

selves, i.e., witnesses did not sign the document but rather the litigants themselves did so. In most of the documents on arbitration the
litigants would empower the arbiters to judge according to law or
through compromise (#302, #306, and #308), and in Document #304
permission is granted them to judge according to law, compromise, or
"something close to law." Apparently at times it was customary to
stipulate that the arbiters had to rule according to law or something
close to law and not through compromise (#307).

There were times in which the litigants established a specific time
for the arbitration. In Document #307 a time for arbitration was established, but the arbiters were granted permission to lengthen that
time if they so desired. In order to give legal authority to a document
of arbitration, witnesses would receive a movable object from the litigants through the formal act of acquisition (*Kinyan*), indicating that
they accepted the responsibility to carry out the decision, and in Document #306 the document is confirmed by basing the acquisition on
real estate (which was an even stronger form of acquisition). Generally in documents of arbitration the litigants would also establish a
fine that would be imposed upon either party that violated the agreement. Half the fine would be given to the leaders of the Jewish community and half to the party that abided by the agreement (#304), or
to charity (#308); or they would give half to the court and half to the
party that abided by the agreement (#307). They would add further
authority to the document of arbitration by oath or by invoking a ban
on those who violated it (#306, #308), or through the signatures of
the litigants in those documents which were executed with such signatures (#308).

Document #304 (*from Libri norarili, Roma*):
Before us, the witnesses signed below, during this day which is
Monday, the twenty-third of the month of Kislev in the year 5303
(1543 C.E.) there came before us, the witnesses signed below, the litigants who are the honorable Mr. Moshe, son of Joseph Mareneno, may
his Rock and Redeemer guard over him, on the one side, and Mrs.
Alegaretza, the widow of Mr. Solomon Mekameou, may his rest be in
the Garden of Eden, and her sons on the other side. And so, the two
parties said to us who are named below: "Write and sign a document
for us in clear and unmistakable language indicating that we with
total free will and without any force whatsoever, hand over all our
claims and disputes and arguments in regard to a certain house that
stands on Martenello Street, to honorable men, namely the honorable
Mr. Benjamin, son of Joseph from Arishani, may his Rock and Redeemer guard over him, and the honorable Mr. Moshe, son of Yiheal.
And we, the two sides mentioned above, give them permission, sovereignty, and power to judge and decide or to form a compromise
whether through the dictates of justice or through compromise or

through something close to justice. And neither one of the two parties may refuse to abide by all of what they decree on pain of a fine of fifty scudi, half going to the community treasury and half to the party that abides by the agreement."

And with permission of the parties mentioned above, we wrote and signed in the day and month and year mentioned above. Everything is firmly established.

(the signatures of the two witnesses)

*Document #306 (from the Manual for Scribes [Tikkun Soferim] of Rabbi Samuel ben Isaac Jaffe, sixteenth century):*
Since there were and there are matters of dispute and counterclaims between Mr. A on the one side and between Mr. B on the other side in regard to a certain issue and in regard to other claims that each has against the other, and since the number of arguments and disputes between them has multiplied beyond reason, in order to remove all such controversy between them the two parties mentioned above agreed to appoint judges and arbiters for them, i.e., the Sages C and D. A and B give them sufficient power and complete permission based on the act of acquisition on four cubits of land, and sign, and give to each one of us (a document of appointing arbitrators), so that a copy will be in the hands of each one of us and in the hands of our representatives as testimony and proof and a basis for future claims. The document should stipulate how, out of complete free will, without any compulsion or force but rather with a complete heart and total desire and with clear and calm minds, we, the parties mentioned above, have chosen for us the arbiters that we shall name, i.e., "E" and "F." One side chose for itself Mr. "E" and afterward the other side chose for itself Mr. "F," both in the presence of the witnesses below, so that the arbiters might decide and judge between us whatever is good and proper, whether by law or something close to law, according to the best of their judgment, but not by a compromise in regard to the claims and disputes. Everything that the arbiters mentioned above will decree on us, whether by law or by something close to law, according to the best of their judgment, we will do. And, if the two arbiters mentioned above do not agree, from this time on we accept upon ourselves that if the arbiters mentioned above agree to appoint a third arbiter, we shall abide by whatever the majority of the three arbiters decide without any protest or doubt, and everything will be established by their combined authority. And whoever rebels against their decision will be subject to such-and-such a fine, half going to the party that abides by the agreement and half to the Board of Arbiters.

The time of arbitration should extend to such-and-such a month, but from this point on we, the parties mentioned above, give power and permission and authority to the arbiters mentioned above to extend the time of arbitration according to their will and their best judgment.

And so the parties mentioned above said to us, the witnesses signed below, and they wrote this document of arbitration in the market place, and signed it clearly so that it would not be a secret thing but rather revealed and public to everyone. They wrote it then a hundred times over so that one document may be written by their hands which would be executed according to all of the requirements of the Sages, with the specific nullification of any sort of protest whatsoever. And afterwards the ceremony of kinyan was performed between the two parties before two witnesses with a movable object fit for such ceremony to establish everything that is written and specified above in this document, and everything in it is firmly established.

*Document #308 (from Nahalat Shiva, by Rabbi Samuel ben David Moses Halevi of Mezhirech'ya, 1625):*

We, the litigants signed below, announce and testify through our signatures below, and that should testify about us like 100 fit and faithful witnesses, that we, the people signed below, have together chosen two judges, i.e., A and B, and we have accepted them over us to judge between us according to the best of their judgment or to make a compromise between us, whichever they find appropriate. And if the two aforementioned judges cannot agree, they may choose a third judge.

Whatever they decide in regard to our claims, or whatever compromise they arrange according to the best of their judgment, we are hereby obligated to obey. Each one of us who are signed below will not turn either to the right or to the left from their instructions, and no part of the directions that they will give us will fall to the ground, whether it be according to law or according to compromise, as if we were standing before the court of Ravina and Rav Ashi. If either one of us signed below rebels against the dictates of the judges mentioned above in any respect, whether they rule by law or by compromise, whether they rule by themselves or whether they ask the advice of another rabbi, then that party will be fined with such-and-such a fine, half to be given to the leaders of the Jewish community and half to charity. All of this we have accepted upon ourselves on the pain of a stringent ban of excommunication, and with an oath of biblical authority, and with shaking of hands, in order to strengthen and establish everything that has been mentioned above and to indicate that it has not been said with exaggeration or with countervailing documents.

In testimony and witness thereto, we have written and signed on this day (date) (Signatures of the litigants).

## 2. *Arbitration in American Law*

Arbitration at common law did not receive the sympathetic treatment given it by the rabbis. Its early history is traced by Judge Jerome Frank in *Kulukundis Shipping Co.* v. *Amtorg Trading Co.*, 126 F. 2d 978, 982–85 (2d Cir. 1942) (footnotes omitted).

In considering these contentions in the light of the precedents, it is necessary to take into account the history of the judicial attitude towards arbitration: the English courts, while giving full effect to agreements to submit controversies to arbitration after they had ripened into arbitrators' awards, would—over a long period beginning at the end of the 17th century—do little or nothing to prevent or make irksome the breach of such agreements when they were still executory. Prior to 1687, such a breach could be made costly: a penal bond given to abide the result of an arbitration had a real bite, since a breach of the bond's condition led to a judgment for the amount of the penalty. It was so held in 1609 in Vynior's Case, 8 Coke Rep. 81b. To be sure, Coke there, in a dictum, citing precedents, dilated on the inherent revocability of the authority given to an arbitrator; such a revocation was not too important, however, if it resulted in a stiff judgment on a penal bond. But the Statute of Fines and Penalties (8 & 9 Wm. III c. 11, s. 8), enacted in 1687, provided that, in an action on any bond given for performance of agreements, while judgment would be entered for the penalty, execution should issue only for the damages actually sustained. Coke's dictum as to revocability, uttered seventy-eight years earlier, now took on a new significance, as it was now held that for breach of an undertaking to arbitrate the damages were only nominal. Recognizing the effect of the impact of this statute on executory arbitration agreements, Parliament, eleven years later, enacted a statute, 9 Wm. III c. 15 (1698), designed to remedy the situation by providing that, if an agreement to arbitrate so provided, it could be made a "rule of court" (i.e., a court order), in which event it became irrevocable, and one who revoked it would be subject to punishment for contempt of court; but the submission was revocable until such a rule of court had been obtained. This statute, limited in scope, was narrowly construed and was of little help. The ordinary executory arbitration agreement thus lost all real efficacy since it was not specifically enforceable in equity, and was held not to constitute the basis of a plea in bar in, or a stay of, a suit on the original cause of action. In admiralty, the rulings were much the same.

It has been well said that "the legal mind must assign some reason in order to decide anything with spiritual quiet." And so, by way of rationalization, it became fashionable in the middle of the 18th century to say that such agreements were against public policy because they "oust the jurisdiction" of the courts. But that was a quaint explanation, inasmuch as an award, under an arbitration agreement, enforced both at law and in equity, was no less an ouster; and the same was true of releases and covenants not to sue, which were given full effect. However, the agreement to arbitrate was not illegal, since suit could be maintained for its breach. Here was a clear instance of what Holmes called a "right" to break a contract and to substitute payment of damages for non-performance; as, in this type of case, the damages were only nominal, that "right" was indeed meaningful.

An effort has been made to justify this judicial hostility to the executory arbitration agreement on the ground that arbitrations, if unsupervised by the courts, are undesirable, and that legislation was needed to make possible such supervision. But if that was the reason for unfriendliness to such executory agreements, then the courts should also have refused to aid arbitrations when they ripened into awards. And what the English courts, especially the equity courts, did in other contexts, shows that, if they had had the will, they could have devised means of protecting parties to arbitrations. Instead, they restrictively interpreted successive statutes intended to give effect to executory arbitrations. No similar hostility was displayed by the Scotch courts. Lord Campbell explained the English attitude as due to the desire of the judges, at a time when their salaries came largely from fees, to avoid loss of income. Indignation has been voiced at this suggestion; perhaps it is unjustified. Perhaps the true explanation is the hypnotic power of the phrase, "oust the jurisdiction." Give a bad dogma a good name and its bite may become as bad as its bark.

In 1855, in *Scott v. Avery*, 5 H.C.L 811, the tide seemed to have turned. There it was held that if a policy made an award of damages by arbitrators a condition precedent to a suit on the policy, a failure to submit to arbitration would preclude such a suit, even if the policy left to the arbitrators the consideration of all the elements of liability. But, despite later legislation, the hostility of the English courts to executory arbitrations resumed somewhat after *Scott v. Avery*, and seems never to have been entirely dissipated.

That English attitude was largely taken over in the 19th century by most courts in this country. Indeed, in general, they would not go as far as *Scott v. Avery*, supra, and continued to sue the "ouster of jurisdiction" concept. An executory agreement to arbitrate would not be given specific performance or furnish the basis of a stay of proceedings on the original cause of action. Nor would it be given effect as a plea in bar, except in limited instances, i.e., in the case of an agreement expressly or impliedly making it a condition precedent to litigation that there be an award determining some preliminary question of subsidiary fact upon which any liability was to be contingent. *Hamilton v. Liverpool*, 1890, etc., Ins. Co., 136 U.S. 242, 255, 10 S.Ct. 945, 34 L.Ed. 419. In the case of broader executory agreements, no more than nominal damages would be given for a breach.

Generally speaking, then, the courts of this country were unfriendly to executory arbitration agreements. The lower federal courts, feeling bound to comply with the precedents, nevertheless became critical of this judicial hostility. There were intimations in the Supreme Court that perhaps the old view might be abandoned, but in the cases hinting at that newer attitude the issue was not raised. Effective state arbitration statutes were enacted beginning with the New York Statute of 1920.

The United States Arbitration Act of 1925 was sustained as constitutional in its application to cases arising in admiralty. *Marine Transit Corp. v. Dreyfus*, 1932, 284. U.S. 263, 52 S.Ct. 166, 76 L.Ed. 516. The purpose of that Act was deliberately to alter the judicial atmosphere previously existing. The report of the House Committee stated, in part: "Arbitration agreements are purely matters of contract, and the effect of the bill is simply to make the contracting party live up to his agreement. He can no longer refuse to perform his contract when it becomes disadvantageous to him. An arbitration agreement is placed upon the same footing as other contracts, where it belongs. . . . The need for the law arises from an anachronism of our American law. Some centuries ago, because of the jealousy of the English courts for their own jurisdiction, they refused to enforce specific agreements to arbitrate upon the ground that the courts were thereby ousted from their jurisdiction. This jealousy survived for so long a period that the principle became firmly embedded in the English common law and was adopted with it by the American courts. The courts have felt that the precedent was too strongly fixed to be overturned without legislative enactment, although they have frequently criticized the rule and recognized its illogical nature and the injustice which results from it. The bill declares simply that such agreements for arbitration shall be enforced, and provides a procedure in the Federal courts for their enforcement. . . . It is particularly appropriate that the action should be taken at this time when there is so much agitation against the costliness and delays of litigation. These matters can be largely eliminated by agreements for arbitration if arbitration agreements are made valid and enforceable."

During the past half century, a number of American states have followed the lead of New York in enacting arbitration statutes. The Uniform Arbitration Act, promulgated in 1955 by the National Commissioners of Uniform State Laws, has served as a model for some of them, but great variation persists from state to state. This is just one indication of the difficulty which the legal community has had in adjusting to arbitration. Until the 1970s, in fact, a majority of the states did not give full effect to an executory agreement to arbitrate. Moreover, judicial hostility to arbitration still exerts a strong influence in many jurisdictions. The United States has acceded to the United

Nations Convention on the Enforcement of Foreign Arbital Awards, and domestic legislation has been enacted to effectuate its provisions. Thus arbitration awards from most foreign nations are enforceable in federal district court, frequently with less difficulty than would be encountered enforcing the judgment of a foreign court. The net result is that arbitration is given great scope in the federal courts in labor contracts, and interstate and foreign commercial transactions. It also is favored in most of the more populous commercial states (New York, California). But hostility persists.

In addition to arbitration, American law, like rabbinic law, has long depended on a number of other alternative methods for resolving disputes. Conciliation and mediation of labor disputes and family controversies have become very important adjuncts to court litigation, supported by substantial federal mediation agencies and conciliation services that are part of metropolitan family courts. In Los Angeles Superior Court attempts at conciliation of child custody and related controversies have for a number of years been a mandatory precondition of court litigation of such issues. General dissatisfaction with the processes of litigation, the slowness and expense of lawsuits, and the counterproductive, adversary posture that American lawyers introduce into a dispute have all led the business community increasingly to use alternative methods of dispute resolution. These include mediation, conciliation, minitrials, private court systems, and a number of similar techniques. It is unnecessary here to describe these mechanisms in detail beyond noting that in general they share with the rabbinic materials presented in this topic a high degree of scepticism about whether litigation by formal trial applying rigid rules of law is the best way to resolve contentious human situations between persons who must continue to live together in the same community.

# Topic Eight: The Responsa Literature

## A. THE TALMUDIC AND GEONIC PERIODS: HESITANT BEGINNINGS

The rabbinic legal system emphasized in a variety of ways that it was a tradition. It insisted the law was derived from a divine source and was transmitted by a chain of teachers whose central functions were to recall, to apply, to explain, and to argue. Argument, debate, and painstaking exploration of cases in a dialogue between teacher and student were cherished literary forms preserved in the Mishnah, Gemara, and Midrash. Deuteronomy clearly contemplates that law would be preserved by having people ask teachers questions regarding proper practice in novel or difficult situations. The accumulation of questions and answers over the generations became part of the Oral Law passed on in turn by its rememberers. In a real sense, the literary style we examine in this topic, legal authority in the form of questions asked and opinions given in response, is a central and continuous strand that runs through the history of the Jews from the biblical period to the present. While the literary forms studied in previous topics in this unit are tied closely to a single historic period, a review of the responsa literature must range over time from the ancient to the modern.

Unlike statutes, responsa arise out of specific cases. They differ from case decisions issued by a court, however, in that the questioner is often a rabbi seeking advice from another rabbi, and the question is asked to help the questioner decide what to do rather than decide the matter for him. On the other hand, in contrast to many discussions in the Talmud, responsa are intended for immediate practical use. As such, they must be published in some way, but not necessarily in written form. To this day many responses are given orally, often for reasons of convenience and sometimes out of a reluctance to commit the answer to writing.

Responsa are authoritative teaching or persuasive advice accepted because of the prestige of the respondent or the intrinsic power of the answer given. In contrast, modern Americans are used to attributing authority to people on the basis of the official positions they hold, and most secular legal opinions are issued by a judge when deciding a specific lawsuit in an official, rather than an individual, capacity. The issuance by courts of advisory opinions is generally frowned on, although the practice is used in a few states and by several administrative agencies.

Perhaps the closest parallel in American law to a responsum is an opinion of counsel, typified by the Opinions of a State Attorney General on an open question of law. Such opinions are collected and published in a number of states and often are relied on later by courts seeking an interpretation of the legal question at issue. Such opinions are official acts of a governmental agency, although not of the judiciary.

A less analogous, but more common source of legal advice for a judge is the opinion of an expert. In Europe, much weight is given to authoritative treatises by renowned scholars, which are a favored source for interpretation of the law. In some European legal systems, judges regularly rely on the written opinion of experts, known as *gutachten*, in deciding technical issues. These include some legal questions, particularly the state of foreign law. Similarly, in the United States, members of the judiciary and press regularly consult experts in deciding cases and in reporting about them (for example, Nimmer on Copyright). Even so, in the American, European, and rabbinic systems, the theoretical basis for obeying a given response is not as important a measure of its authority as the fact of its acceptance by the community for which it is intended.

The early rabbis might have preferred to maintain the tradition in oral form, but events during the first two centuries of the Common Era forced them to organize the common law material and commit it to writing. (See Topics Four and Five.) Rabbi Johanan and Rabbi Simeon b. Lakish, who lived at that time, admitted that writing the law down constituted a violation, but they justified writing both the *halakhah* and the *aggadah* on the basis of the need to preserve them in the emergency at hand.

> *Temurrah* 14b:
> "It is time for the Lord to work, they have made Your law void" (Ps. 119:126). R. Johanan and R. Simeon b. Lakish explained that as follows: It is better than one letter of the Torah (that is, the prohibition against committing the Law to writing) should be uprooted than that the whole Torah should be forgotten.

Once the Mishnah was edited, the prohibition effectively lapsed, and the Gemara records a number of instances in which Babylonian rabbis sent questions in written form to the authorities in Israel and received written responses. This correspondence is called *She'elot u' Teshuvot* ("questions and answers") in Hebrew, or *responsa* in Latin.

There are almost no recorded responsa from the middle of the fourth to the middle of the eighth centuries. This may have been due to a vacuum of leadership in the Jewish community at the time so there was no clearly recognized authority to whom scholarly questions could be addressed. That situation changed, however, by about 750 c.e., when a period of prolific responsa writing begins, primarily in Babylonia. By that time the Islamic Arabs had established their rule from Spain to India. The Babylonian Jewish community was the largest at the time, and it had the economic resources to support two major institutions of higher Jewish learning, one in Sura and one in Pumbeditha. The Babylonian academies were situated at the center of the Arab realm, and were in the best position to influence the Arab government through its Minister for Jewish Affairs, the *Resh Galuta* (the Jewish exilarch, or literally, "the head of the diaspora community"). Their proximity to the center of government also gave the Babylonian rabbis the best access to lines of communication. Hence their responsa were well publicized among Jewish communities throughout the world. These external factors, coupled with the inherent quality of the legal work being done in the Babylonian schools, lent them great renown and prestige—more, in fact, than that ascribed to the rabbis remaining in Israel. The Babylonians buttressed their supremacy by creating a theory based on the claim that the head of the exile community was a successor to the Davidic monarchy. While Israel may be the sole place where the rabbinic authority of Hillel could be passed on from generation to generation, that chain of authority lapsed in 361 c.e. Meanwhile, the place where the Jewish head of state resided inherited the power of the monarchical line of David—or so the Babylonians claimed—and that power was more ancient and more far-reaching than whatever was left of Israel's rabbinic authority.

Because of the power and reputation of the Babylonian schools and the theory that legitimated their authority, the heads of these academies, called "Geonim" (singular, "Gaon"), were regularly consulted by other Jewish communities when questions arose. The Geonim were especially interested in standardizing Jewish worship in the face of increasingly diversified practices. Jews living far from the major Babylonian centers of Jewish learning often were ignorant of the nonlegal aspects of the tradition as well, and so many geonic responsa consist of interpretations of biblical or talmudic passages and explanations of theology, history, science, and medicine. The responsum thus was used as an educational device as well as a legal one. Hundreds of questions were discussed by the entire academy during two, month-long, conventions (Hebrew, *kallot;* singular, *kallah*) that were held each year, and the answers were signed by the Gaon and by all those attending.

The preservation of many geonic responsa is an accident since the Geonim themselves did not keep copies of their responsa. We know about them only through later codes and responsa, particularly through the few collections of responsa that students in the geonic academies edited, and, most especially, those found in the *genizah*. The *genizah* is a storage room attached to the ancient synagogue of Cairo. It was used for centuries to store books and ritual objects that contained the name of God and that therefore could not be destroyed. The dry climate preserved much of the written material, and some 200,000 pages of fragments were unearthed by S. A. Wertheimer and Solomon Schechter at the beginning of the twentieth century. Cairo was the major postal junction on the road from North Africa and Western Europe to Babylonia, and Jews there copied every question and geonic answer that passed their way. The material in the *genizah* is therefore a rich collection. The vast majority of geonic responsa found in the *genizah* remain unpublished to this day, but Benjamin Lewin (1879–1944) collected and published many geonic responsa found in manuscripts all over the world in a book called *Otzar Ha-Geonim*, arranged according to the order of the Talmud. This work brings some order into the chaos that is geonic literature and makes at least some of these responsa readily available.

Geonic responsa are often brief, sometimes just a "yes" or a "no." The brevity and anonymity of many geonic responsa and the disregard for preserving them may be the result of a lingering discomfort with committing the tradition to writing. In any case, more than half of the extant geonic responsa were written by the last two Geonim, Sherira Gaon and Hai Gaon. The longer responsa are almost always those written in the late period.

The following responsa from the geonic period gave a sense of how two kinds of issues were then approached. The first is jurisprudential. It examines the authority of the rabbinic judge, which was cast into doubt when the chain of ordination was broken toward the end of the fourth century. The issue had special implications for the rabbis of the ninth century, for they not only had to defend their personal authority, but also that of their talmudic predecessors from the challenge of the Karaites. Karaism was a powerful, dissenting movement that arose in Persia in the eighth century. It sanctioned and encouraged personal interpretation of the Torah as the sole authoritative source of Jewish law. It dismissed the Talmud as man-made law that had been substituted for God-given Torah. The Karaites were known for their asceticism and their emphasis on the return to Palestine as a precondition of the Messiah's arrival. Although small in numbers, they remained an influential, dissenting voice for centuries; indeed, several thousand survivors can still be found in Israel. The responsum of Rav Sherira Gaon is important for its jurisprudential response to the Karaites and also as the single most important historical source on the chain of authority within the rabbinic tradition.

The second issue is also jurisdictional in a sense, but it directly affects personal injury litigation. The problem is how courts whose judges are not ordained and who operate outside of Palestine can impose the traditional penalties on those who injure their fellows. The responsum by Rav Tzemah Tzedek, Gaon of Sura from 988–997 C.E., indicates that the Geonim had decided to circumvent the limits on their power to impose penalties in cases of personal injuries as early as the days of Rav Tzadok, Gaon of Sura from 816–818 C.E. Rav Sherira Gaon's responsum on the same issue spells out even more clearly the clever method which the Geonim used while still remaining within the theoretical bounds of their authority.

These responsa seem to be directed to different audiences. Rav Sherira Gaon, in the first responsum, speaks to a general audience, arguing the existence of divine sanction for the Oral Law. Rav Sherira deals with an external threat from those outside the tradition who would deny its legitimacy. Rav Tzemah Tzedek Gaon and Rav Sherira, in the second of the latter's excerpted responsa, are speaking to a more parochial audience, which already accepts rabbinic authority, including the limits the Talmud places on diaspora judges. For them the point is not to convince the reader to respect received authority, but to encourage the reader to accept the exercise of Babylonian judicial power in personal injury matters despite the Talmud's denial of such authority. Rav Sherira's first responsum is answering the attacks of outsiders; Rav Tzemah Tzedek and Rav Sherira in his second responsum are responding to the doubts of insiders.

S. Freehof, *A Treasury of Responsa* (Philadelphia: Jewish Publication Society of America, 1962), chap. 1: The History of Tradition. [The following note and the parenthetical notes within the text are Rabbi Freehof's.]

## 1. *The Letter of Rav Sherira Gaon*

> Rabbi Sherira ben Hanina, Gaon of the Pumpeditha academy during the second half of the 10th century, died at an advanced age about the year 1000. Famous throughout the Diaspora, he attracted many questions, none more important than that which elicited his letter to the Jews of Kairawan.
>
> The Gaon Sherira declares in his responsum that the *entire* talmudic material in its complete bulk was an ancient tradition (i.e., not

a gradual accumulation, which would make it of doubtful authenticity) and that all Rabbi Judah the Prince did was to rearrange the material and clarify it. The essence of his answer is that the total material constituted an unbroken tradition going back to antiquity, and that all the various men whom we might think of as authors were not that at all, but merely interpreters and transmitters of this ancient tradition. While explaining this basic principle, namely, that the Oral Law as found in the Mishna, Talmud, and their accompanying books, is virtually of equal antiquity with the Written Law, and therefore of equal authenticity, he also lists the rabbis of the various generations who worked, expounded and transmitted this ancient oral material. Thus his responsum is the chief source for all the later study of the history of talmudic literature, and is itself a great monument of Jewish literary creativity. In fact, it is one of the two, among the thousands of Geonic responsa which we now possess, which are basic to Jewish studies down to our day: one being the responsum of the Gaon Amram which gives the history of the development of the synagogue liturgy (*Siddur Rav Amram*), and the other this justly famous responsum of Sherira Gaon on the history and nature of rabbinic texts.

TEXT OF RESPONSUM

*(Heading from the Oxford Manuscript):*
Isaac, son of Nissim, son of Josiah, turned with a question to our lord Sherira, head of the Yeshiva; he asked in the name of the sacred congregation of Kairawan; and he (that is, Sherira) ordered that the response be written here, in the year one thousand two hundred and ninety-eight of the documentary (that is, the Seleucidan) dating, and the documentary dating is before four thousand five hundred and fifty-two (that is, 986 of the Christian era).

Question:
As for your question, namely: How was the Mishna written? Did the men of the Great Synagogue begin to write it and the sages of the succeeding generations write part of it until Rabbi Judah the Prince came and completed it? But if this is so, and since most of its text is anonymous, why are we taught that the anonymous parts of the Mishna were written by Rabbi Meir (*Sanhedrin* 86a)? Besides, most of the rabbis who are mentioned in the Mishna—Rabbi Meir, Rabbi Judah, Rabbi Yose and Rabbi Simeon—all of them were pupils of Rabbi Akiba, and the rules of decision that the rabbis of the Talmud taught us mention the same generation saying that the law is according to Rabbi Akiba when he disagrees with his colleagues, and according to Rabbi Judah the Prince in preference to his colleagues. All of these lived at the end of the time of the Second Commonwealth. If so (if all the authors mentioned lived so late), why did the more ancient rabbis

leave so much to the later rabbis; and all the more is it significant if nothing of the Mishna was written until the days of Rabbi Judah the Prince. (The question implies that since the rabbis mentioned in the Mishna are all late and since the Mishna was not written down until the days of Rabbi Judah the Prince, it would be difficult indeed to answer the charge of the Karaites that the Mishna is not ancient tradition at all.)

Furthermore, the question continues, although the arrangement of the six main Orders of the Mishna are logical, what reason is there for the seemingly illogical arrangement of the tractates within these six Orders? Why, for example, was the tractate *Yoma* (dealing with the Day of Atonement) placed before the tractate *Shekalim* which should precede discussion of the Passover? And why does *Sukkah* come before the tractate *Yom Tov*? And why do both of them precede *Rosh Hashanah*? Thus our question covers all the tractates which are not in sequential relationship with the other tractates according to content. Furthermore, as to the Tosefta, which we have heard was written by Rabbi Hiyyah, was it written after the sealing of the Mishna or was it written at the same time as the Mishna? And why did Rabbi Hiyyah write it (since it contains, though generally in a fuller form, the same material as the Mishna)? If he merely added material which expounds the material in the Mishna, why did Rabbi Judah himself omit it and fail to include it in the Mishna? Is not all of this material in the Tosefta quoted in the names of the same rabbis who are mentioned in the Mishna? And similarly, how were the *baraitot* (material similar to Mishna and Tosefta, but quoted only in the Talmud) written? And also, how did the Talmud come to be written? And so the *saboraim*? What was their order after Rabina? (Saboraim were the first post-talmudic rabbis, and Rabina was among the last talmudic rabbis.) And who bore authority after them? And how many years was each of them in authority from that time up to today? (In other words, the community of Kairawan asked for a complete history of the development of the talmudic literature from its beginning and also, by implication, for the proper defense of its antiquity and its authenticity.)

### Answer:
Our view is as follows: The saintly Rabbi Judah certainly arranged the six Orders of the Mishna so that we might study the laws one after the other, without intending to add or to diminish. For thus it is said in the Talmud (*Yeb.* 64b): "When was the Mishna fixed? In the days of Rabbi (Judah the saintly Prince)." As for your question: Why did the earlier rabbis leave so much to the later rabbis? (As is evidenced by the fact that the rabbis mentioned in the Mishna were all contemporaries or pupils of Rabbi Akiba, which might imply that the Mishna is not ancient at all.) The earlier rabbis did not leave much for the later rabbis to do (i.e., to innovate), but all of the later rabbis studied and inter-

preted the words of the earlier rabbis (i.e., they merely expounded; they did not create the tradition). For when Hillel the Elder was appointed by the B'nai Bathera as prince over them, he said to them (*Pes.* 66a): "What led to my being chosen prince over you? It was your own laziness, in that you did not serve sufficiently under the two great men of your generation, Shemaya and Abtalyon" (i.e., the knowledge had already been available in an earlier generation, but they did not take advantage of it).

The reason that the older rabbis are not mentioned by name, except for their prince and the head of the court, was that there never was any controversy among them. They knew thoroughly all the reasons for the teachings of the Torah and they knew the whole Talmud completely, and all the arguments, and they were careful in their study of every subject; for we see (*B.B.* 134a) that there were eighty disciples of Hillel the Elder, thirty of them were worthy that the Divine Presence should rest upon them as it did upon Moses our teacher; and thirty of them were worthy that the sun should stand still for them as it did for Joshua; and twenty were average. The greatest of them was Jonathan the son of Uziel and the least of them was Yohanan ben Zakkai. And they said about Yohanan ben Zakkai (the least of them all) that there was not a single text of Scripture that he did not know, nor Mishna, nor Talmud, nor laws, nor narratives, nor text details of the Torah or of the scribes, of all the arguments *a fortiori* and analogies and proverbs, etc., all matters great and small, and even the arguments of Abbaye and Rava (who lived four hundred years after his time). This tells us that even the arguments of Abbaye and Rava were not original with them, but were all well known to the ancients. (Thus Sherira indicates that the total tradition recorded now in the rabbinic books was all known to the ancients; and the tradition, therefore, is authentic. If their names are not mentioned, it was because there was no need to record their names. In later times the names of various rabbis were recorded in order to explain who took one side of a controversy and who took the other. But among the ancients there was no controversy; they all possessed full knowledge. Now Sherira goes on to explain why it was necessary for Rabbi Judah the Prince to reorganize this vast material which presumably was perfect from the very beginning. He proceeds as follows:)

When the Temple was in existence, each one of the great teachers would explain to his disciples the reasons for the laws of the Torah, Mishna, and Talmud. Each teacher would put it in the words that appealed to him at the time, and thus taught it to his disciples so that they could understand. Abundant wisdom was then available and they needed no other effort (than just to explain the law, each in his own words). The dispute as to the laying on of hands was the only dispute among them (i.e., hands laid upon the sacrifice on the holidays, whether such action was permitted on the holidays or not, that is, whether or not it was a violation of the requirements of rest on the festivals). When Shammai and Hillel arose there were only three matters that they disagreed on (*Shab.* 14b). Then came the time of Bethar (i.e., the Bar Kokhba revolt) and Bethar was destroyed and the rabbis were scattered in every direction. Because of these disturbances and persecutions and confusions, there were many disciples who never studied long enough with their teachers. Hence controversies arose among them. (Sherira then proceeds to mention other controversies due to other persecutions and confusions, resulting in lack of time for sufficient study, and hence the increase of disputes. He continues down to the destruction of the thousands of pupils of Rabbi Akiba and continues from there, as follows:)

Rabbi Meir was more learned and more keen than all of them and Rabbi Akiba ordained him even though he was still young. . . . (He continues with the generation of Rabbi Meir and the following one, coming down to Rabbi Judah the Prince; and he writes:)

After the great calamity of the destruction of the Temple and the doubts that arose due to all the confusions of the time and all the divisions that arose in those three generations when the law was not settled among the rabbis, there became known among the rabbis the words of individuals and the words of the majority. The rabbis went to great trouble to gather the exact wording of the Mishna but they did not add anything to the words of men of the Great Synagogue. They toiled and searched to bring to light what those ancients had said and what they had done, until all those doubts (which had arisen in the three generations of confusion) were finally cleared up for them. Not one of the ancients had written down his own original opinion, until the end of the days of Rabbi Judah when it was recorded. Nor had they all taught in the same phraseology, but they all gave the reasons for the laws which were well known to them and all were unanimous as to the meaning. They knew what was the word of the majority and what were the opinions of the individuals, but the wording was not fixed so that all might study in the same language. It was the meanings and the explanations that were known to them. (He proceeds to show how each rabbi taught in his own words and how much greater was the mentality of the ancients than that of their successors. Since they all knew all of the matrial, there was no real controversy among them. And then he continues:)

The rabbis found peace in the days of Rabbi Judah, the Prince, because of the friendship between Antoninus (Pius, the Roman emperor) and Rabbi Judah, and he decided to arrange the laws so that thereafter all the rabbis would use the same phraseology and no longer teach each in his own phrasing. The ancient rabbis did not need this uniformity of phrasing since it was all Oral Law, and its explanations were not given to them in fixed language, as was the Written Law. They knew the reasons of the Oral Law by heart, and each taught them to his disciples in any language he wished to use, as a man converses with his neighbor. In the days of Rabbi, help came from Heaven and they arranged and wrote down these words of the Mishna just as Moses had done at the dictation of God as a sign and a miracle. Not of his own invention did he (Rabbi) compose it; for the words that had been taught by the ancients were all before him. (The rest of the responsum goes on to discuss the development of the other rabbinic books, leading to the development of the Talmud and to the post-talmudic era of the geonim. And he concludes with a benediction extended to the congregation of Kairawan for its deliverance and blessing.)

## 2. The Responsa of Rav Tzemah Tzedek, Gaon of Sura (988–997) and Rav Sherira, Gaon of Pumbeditha (968–998): Making Jewish Tort Law Viable

Exodus 21:6 and 22:7–8 refer to judges as *Elohim*, literally "gods." Exactly why the Bible used that term is a matter of dispute among biblical scholars, as we have seen, but the rabbis of the Talmud interpreted that to mean that only experts (with knowledge like gods) could be full-fledged judges with the broad jurisdiction and immunities pertaining to that title. The certification of judges, though, was through the chain of authority known as *semikhah* ("laying on of hands"), and that could only be granted in Israel. Babylonian rabbis could therefore justify their judicial authority only through the claim that they were acting as the agents of their Palestinian counterparts, but that meant that their jurisdiction was limited to the types of cases that junior law clerks could be expected to handle—specifically those of a purely civil nature and of frequent occurrence. As we have seen, Rava, teacher of the third century, spelled this out to mean that "payment of damage done to chattel by animals (lit., 'an ox') or for damage done to chattel by man can be collected even in Babylonia, whereas payment for injuries done to man by another man or for injuries done to a man by animals cannot be collected in Babylonia" (*Bava Kamma* 84a). "It thus follows," the Gemara concludes after some discussion, "that in the case of a man injured by another man, though there is actual monetary loss in such a case, yet we cannot act as their agents since this (personal injuries to one man by another) does not occur frequently; and similarly, in regard to (fines for) degradation, though it occurs frequently, we cannot act as their agents since no actual monetary loss is involved" (*Bava Kamma* 84b). Similarly, when R. Hisda in Babylonia thought that he could impose a fine in a case before him because the amount of the fine was fixed, he was chided by R. Nahman of Israel,

"Hisda, Hisda! Is it your practice in Babylonia to impose fines?" (*Bava Kamma* 27b, 84b).

This, of course, meant that all of the remedies for personal injury which the Mishnah had developed were inoperative in Babylonia. If the early Babylonian teachers were prepared to acquiesce to that situation for fear of stepping beyond the bounds of their legitimate authority, later Babylonian authorities were not willing to remain so inactive. By the time of the Geonim, the Sanhedrin had ceased to exist, and the Palestinian Jewish community had lost much of its prestige. Babylonian academies had become centers of Jewish learning. The Moslems left it to the Jewish community to govern itself, and so the Geonim had to find some way to reactivate the laws of personal injuries in the diaspora. They also needed to find some way to impose fines and deal with criminal cases. This authority had been restricted to Palestinian judges in the Talmud, but the Babylonians needed to find some talmudic support, however slight. They found it in the following passage:

> *Bava Kamma* 15b:
> Were the plaintiff to plead "fix me a definite time for bringing my case to be heard in the land of Israel," we would have to fix it for him; were the other party to refuse to obey that order, we would have to excommunicate him. But in any case, we have to excommunicate him until he abates the nuisance, in accordance with the dictum of R. Nathan. For it was taught: R. Nathan says, Whence is it derived that nobody should breed a bad dog in his house or keep an impaired ladder in his house? From the text, "do not bring blood upon your house" (Deuteronomy 22:8).

On the basis of this, the Geonim used excommunication as the sanction for all cases that had been ruled beyond their jurisdiction in the Talmud. In so doing, they maintained the letter of talmudic law while effectively reinstituting the remedies for personal injuries. The following responsa show how the scope of excommunication was gradually increased in order to accomplish that. The use of excommunication and exclusion from the community as a basis for jurisdiction becomes widespread in later historic periods. The Jewish community often lacked the physical force to compel its members to appear and to comply with court orders directly, but the rabbis could exclude those who did not obey, and hence their power was largely respected. They said in effect to the reluctant, "We cannot make you pay, but we can make you wish you had!"

> *The Responsum of Rav Tzemah Tzedek, Gaon of Sura* (988–997)
> (from *Otzar Hageonim, Bava Kamma* #182, p. 60):
> Rav Tzemah Gaon, may his memory be blessed: In regard to what

you asked, i.e., can we collect fines so that the sinner is not rewarded
[for his sin through our powerlessness to fine him, I answer this]: The
Rabbis announced this rule, that fines are not collected in Babylonia,
for R. Nahman sent a responsum to R. Hisda, saying: "Hisda, do you
collect fines in Babylonia?" Therefore it is a widespread law that we
do not collect fines except in Jerusalem through a small court of 23,
and moreover we rule according to Rava, who said, "Payment for
damage done to chattel by animals (lit., 'an ox') or for damage done to
chattel by man can be collected even in Babylonia, whereas payment
for injuries done to a man by another man or for injuries done to a
man by animals cannot be collected in Babylonia." But so that a sinner will not be rewarded, and so that the Children of Israel will not be
dissolute in causing injuries (for since they know that we do not impose fines in Babylonia, they may strike one another), the latest authorities have become accustomed to excommunicate the culprit until he satisfies the injured party through money or until many of his
(the tortfeasor's) friends come to him and pacify him with words. And
there is a precedent in regard to someone who knocked out someone
else's tooth, and the tortfeasor came before Rav Tzadok Gaon (of Sura,
816–818), may his memory be blessed, who said to him: "I am not de-
creeing a specific amount that you must pay him, but go and satisfy
him with either money or words." And now that all of the laws of
fines are null and void, the custom which our master, Rav Tzadok
Gaon, established (may his memory be for life) is what we do too.

*The Responsum of Rav Sherira, Gaon of Pumbeditha (968–998)*
*(from Otzar Hageonim, Bava Kamma #188, pp. 58–59):*
Our Rabbi, Sherira, may his memory be blessed: In regard to what
you asked concerning the laws of fines, which our Rabbis have ruled
to be uncollectable in Babylonia, and, all the more so, in other lands:
(1) if someone injures another and is excommunicated until he satisfies the injured party, and he says, "I do not want to be excommunicated (lit., I do not accept the ban on me), and so I will satisfy him,"
and he (seeks to) satisfy him by paying the fullest extent of the fines
that the Rabbis would have imposed, but the injured party did not
want to be satisfied; or (2) the injured party.demanded a lot of money
and the tortfeasor was willing to give him only the money for his injury; or (3) if the injured party was a scholar or rich or important, and
the tortfeasor was from the masses and therefore the injured party is
entitled to payment for embarrassment according to the Mishnah; or
(4) if someone pulled out someone else's beard or the hair on his head,
or if he spat in his face, and the injured party then poked out the
tortfeasor's eye, so that both of them are liable for excommunication,
and the embarrassed party says to the other, "I will not forgo payment
for my embarrassment until you forgo payment for the injury to your
eye," then is the injury of the one considered to be payment for the
embarrassment of the other or not?

This is what we have seen fit to answer: According to the principles of the law, location determines the collectability of fines. Therefore they may not be imposed either in Babylonia or in other lands. Moreover, what you are asking about is not a set amount, but rather everything depends upon the person of the embarrassing and embarrassed parties and upon the nature of the specific pain, injury, medical expense, loss of time, and embarrassment in this case.

The Talmud only allows us to excommunicate the culprit until he pays for the damage, based upon what R. Nathan says; but the latest authorities and the heads of the academies, since they saw a great loss because fines were not being imposed, used that as the basis for making a revision (*takkanah*) in the law such that the tortfeasor is to be excommunicated until he satisfies the injured party. They did not make their revision in order to impose more stringent penalties than the law provides and not even the exact amount, but rather less than what the law specifies such that the law is considerably more demanding than the settlement. Therefore if the injured party says, "I will not be satisfied except with a large sum of money," we do not accept his plea or even pay attention to him. Instead, the court on its own estimates, using its own opinion: if there was only embarrassment in the case at hand, then it assesses the payment according to the person of each of the parties involved, and if all five of the elements of torts occurred, then each one is assessed according to its law.

And we say specifically in giving judgment that the Torah says in such a matter that "the conflict between them must come before the judges (*elohim*)," and we are not worthy to be called *elohim* in this matter and we cannot judge in such a case; but, in accordance with the revision of the sages we have estimated the damages according to our own opinion and have set them approximately, as our reasoning dictates. If you do not accept our decision, we will release the tortfeasor from the ban of excommunication. And even in the case where one party claims, "let his eye be payment for my embarrassment," we do not listen to him, and his words are regarded as being of no substance. Instead, when the party who caused the embarrassment offers a sum close to what the judges estimated in their hearts, they take it from him and release him from the ban, and they obligate the tortfeasor to pay approximately the amounts for the five elements (injury, pain, healing, loss of time and embarrassment) because they have no way of being specific since it is assumed that they are not expert since they are not certified through *semikhah*.

They do not say to him (the tortfeasor) "we have decided that you must give so-and-so much money," and they do not say to him (the injured party) "we have decided that you should get so-and-so much money," because that would be enforcing the laws of fines which we do not have the authority to do. Instead, they estimate in their hearts

an amount close to that which the law provides, and they do not reveal it to either litigant; they then excommunicate the tortfeasor until he satisfies the injured party, and they say nothing to him. They
see how much he offers to give the injured party: if it is close to the
amount that they had fixed in their hearts, and if the injured party refuses to accept it, they say to him (the injured party), "we do not have
the power to impose a ban on him for more than that amount," and
they release him (the tortfeasor) from the ban; and if the amount
which the tortfeasor offers to pay is far from what is in their hearts,
they excommunicate him and remain silent until he comes close to
that amount.

Note that the goal in all three of the previous responsa is to enable
contemporary judges to make Jewish law operative in their own time.
The reader will recognize this as a familiar theme in Jewish law, originating in the biblical use of prophecy and judges for this purpose and
continuing in rabbinic exegesis and the rabbis' theory of the Oral Law
in order to legitimate broad judicial powers. In each case those seeking
to change the law from within were not interested in undermining its
authority or abandoning it altogether; on the contrary, they expended
great effort to link changes to the previous tradition in order to preserve its integrity, continuity, and authority.

But the recurrence of this theme in the Middle Ages comes with a
new twist. In biblical and Second Temple times a significant percentage of Jews lived in Israel. That was a strong uniting and identifying
factor, enabling Jews to differ broadly in their interpretation of Jewish
law and yet see themselves as all inheritors of the tradition of Sinai.
There were distinct groups, and there undoubtedly was rivalry and recrimination between them; but, except for the Samaritans, all were
considered Jews. Thus Josephus describes the Pharisees, Sadducees,
and Essenes as simply three Jewish parties, none of which held a monopoly on what it meant to be Jewish. By the Middle Ages, however,
Jews were scattered all over the map, and they lacked the organizing
and identifying influences of an autonomous state of their own. Under
these circumstances the law functioned as the mark of the Jews wherever they were, and those who differed radically from the rabbis' interpretation of it threatened the survival and identity of world Jewry. Rav
Sherira Gaon therefore argues against the populous Karaite group for
the continuity and authority of the rabbinic tradition with a sense of
urgency and a clear understanding of the political dimensions of his
writing. This was no longer one sect among many defending its way of
doing things in a setting that could tolerate them all; this was the
group that had become the definitive interpreters of the tradition protecting it and its adherents against defection from within in a context

where the success of that defense meant the difference between the tradition's life or death.

On the other hand, the need to adapt the law to new circumstances continued unabated, and so new ways to interpret and apply it had to be found. What looks like a fixed, long-standing tradition in Rav Sherira's defense of the rabbinites against the Karaites therefore becomes a flexible legal system that can be molded to a new situation when he and Rav Tzemah Tzedek address a problem within the community of the faithful. Thus authority, continuity, and change all continue to be indispensable elements of Jewish law, but they are balanced and justified in new ways in order to meet new challenges.

After these responsa, rabbis outside of Israel broadened their assertion of jurisdiction over personal injuries. The *Shulhan Arukh*, an important code completed in 1565, provides a classical statement of the full flowering of this expanded view of court jurisdiction. (Sections in italics are the glosses of Rabbi Moses Isserles to Rabbi Joseph Caro's original manuscript.)

> *Shulhan Arukh*, Hoshen Hamishpat, 1; 2:1:
>
> Chapter 1: The Appointment of the Judges In and Outside the Land of Israel:
> 1. Nowadays the judges may adjudicate cases of admissions and transaction of loans, marriage contracts, inheritances, gifts and damage done to another person's chattel, which are matters that are of frequent occurrence and involve a monetary loss; but matters that are not of frequent occurrence although they involve a monetary loss, e.g., cattle that injured other chattel, or matters that do not involve a monetary loss although they are of frequent occurrence, e.g., the repayment of a double amount, and likewise, all fines that were imposed by the Sages, as in the case of one who boxes his neighbor's ear— *The meaning of Toke'a should be understood as "he shouts in a loud voice into his neighbor's ear and frightens him"*—or as in the case of one who slaps his neighbor— *I.e., He strikes him with his hand on the cheek*—and thus also whosoever pays more than the actual damage done, or one who pays half-damages,—the law is that only authoritative judges duly ordained in the Land of Israel may judge it save in the case of the liability for half-damages done by pebbles, which is regarded as civil and not as penal.
>
> 2. In the case of a man who injured his fellow-man— the law is that judges who are not duly ordained in the Land of Israel cannot order the payment for injury, pain, blemish, indignity, and indemnity, but they may order the payment for loss of time and healing. *Gloss: And some say that also cases of healing and loss of time they do not adjudicate. However, I have not seen them adopt this practice, (viz.,) to be strict*

in this matter, save that they coerce the injurer to appease the injured with money and to penalize him according to that which appears reasonable to them, as will be explained.

3. With respect to cattle that injured man,—the law is that judges who are not duly ordained in the Land of Israel may not collect payment for his injury because it is a matter that is not of frequent occurrence. However, a man who caused damage to his fellow-man's cattle pays full damages everywhere. Likewise, cattle that caused damage by means of Tooth and Foot, since, with respect to the latter, it is regarded as warned from the outset, this is considered a matter of frequent occurrence, and judges who are not duly ordained in the Land of Israel may order the payment thereof. Thus also, with respect to one who stole or robbed an object, they may collect from him the principal only. *Gloss: And some say that this applies only to cases of larceny that are of frequent occurrence, e.g., a guardian who denies having received a deposit and the like, but actual larceny is not considered of frequent occurrence and they do not adjudicate this unless the robbed object is still intact, in which case they order him to return it.*

4. With respect to the laws of damage caused indirectly, and likewise, regarding the law of the informer,—judges who are not duly ordained in the Land of Israel may adjudicate them. *Gloss: Witnesses who offered false evidence and were found Zomemim (plotters), and they (the judges) had already collected payment on the strength of their testimony, and it is impossible to recover the payment now, the law is that they judge them and order them to pay.*

5. Although the law is that judges that are not duly ordained in the Land of Israel cannot order the payment of fines, nevertheless, they may place him under the ban until he appeases his litigant with money, and as soon as he gives him an amount which appears reasonable for the injurer to give him, they release him (the injurer) from the ban, whether his litigant was appeased thereby or whether he was not appeased. And likewise, if the injured person seized an amount, [viz.] whatever is proper for him to take, they do not reclaim it from him. *Gloss: And if the injured person should say, "Assess for me my damage so that I should know up to how much I should seize," he is not obeyed, save that if he had already seized, they assess for him his damage and instruct him, "So much you may keep as your own and so much you must return to the injurer." And all this applies only to fines stated in Biblical law, but as to fines which the Sages from time to time impose of their own accord with respect to one who does not observe their ordinances, they may collect everywhere as will be explained in Chapter 2.*

6. One who insults his fellow-man merely in words is placed under the ban until he appeases him as is becoming his dignity.

Chapter 2: The Court of Law May Administer Flogging and Impose
Death Penalties Because of the Exigencies of the Hour:
1. Every Court of Law, even one whose members are not duly ordained in the Land of Israel,—if they see that the people are unre-
strained in committing sins, *and provided that the exigencies of the
hour demand it,*—may pass judgment both with respect to death and
monetary penalties as well as administer all laws of punishment, even
if in the case in question there is no valid evidence available. And if he
is a stern individual, they may flog him by means of heathen authorities. *And they have authority to expropriate his property and to forfeit it according to whatever they see fit in order to fence in the lawlessness of the generation.* All their acts, however, should be done for
the sake of Heaven. And this should be executed only by a great per-
sonage of the generation or by the representative of the town whom
they (i.e., the people) have recognized as the Court of Law over them.
*Gloss: And this is the accepted practice everywhere, [viz.,] that the
representatives of the town are regarded in their own town as authoritative as the former Great Sanhedrin. They may administer flogging
and impose death penalties and their expropriation (of one's property) is considered valid according to the adopted custom, although
there are some who differ and are of the opinion that the representatives of the town have no power in these matters save that they have
the authority to compel the community in observing whatever was
an adopted practice heretofore, or a new measure which they accepted upon themselves with the consent of all the townspeople, but
they may change naught in any matter that would involve a gain for
one person and a loss for another or to declare a debt cancelled without the consent of all the townspeople. Nevertheless, in these matters
we follow the adopted custom of the town, especially if the townspeople accepted them to render decisions in every matter. This seems
to me to be the correct view. The later authorities state in the
responsa that one who has been sentenced to flogging may give forty
gold coins instead of the flogging. This is, however, not stated as a
law, only that they decided thus because of the needs of the hour, but
in reality the Court of Law has the authority to flog him or to confis-
cate his property as they see fit according to the matter in hand in order to safeguard a cause.*

## B. The Eleventh to Fifteenth Centuries: Franco-Germany and Spain-North Africa

By the end of the geonic period (c. 650–1050 c.e.), the level of Jewish knowledge in the Western communities had risen, and in those
communities, local rabbis were increasingly asked to respond to new
questions.

In the centuries that followed, there were two major centers of Jewish scholarly activity: Spain and North Africa (called the "Sephardic," or Spanish, community) on the one hand, and northern France and Germany (called the "Ashkenazic," or German, community) on the other. In the eleventh and twelfth centuries, Spanish scholars manifested the effects of the "The Golden Age in Spain," and their responsa reveal a wide-ranging, scientific spirit, invoking knowledge from many areas of inquiry. They are written in a lucid, logical, and usually brief form. In contrast, the Ashkenazic responsa are longer, more closely tied to the Talmud, and more dialectical in nature. The distinctions in style and content reflect the generally self-confident spirit of the Spaniards and the free-flowing social and commercial interactions between Jews and non-Jews in their lands, while the Ashkenazic responsa reflect the more diffident, insecure self-image of Jews in France and Germany as they faced the problems of living as Jews in a closed, hostile environment. These differences disappear in the responsa of the thirteenth, fourteenth, and fifteenth centuries. Spanish Jews underwent the trials and tribulations of the Crusades, the Inquisition, and expulsion, and so the circumstances under which they lived more closely paralleled those of Ashkenazic Jewry. Moreover, the respondents of each community learned of the responsa of the other, and this contact blurred distinctions in style.

As noted, early geonic responsa were not considered a separate genre of legal literature: they were short answers to legal questions or explanations of talmudic passages written in the vernacular to people who were assumed not to know very much. The respondents generally did not even think enough of their work to preserve their answers; their real intellectual efforts were preserved for other kinds of literature. As the general level of learning rose, however, responsa came into their own. Now responsa were written by scholars for other scholars, who could not be answered without an explanation of the grounds of decision. Beginning in France with Rabbenu Tam (1100–1177) and in Spain with Solomon ben Adret (1235–1310), respondents began to preserve their responsa, which increasingly became full essays, written in Hebrew, almost exclusively on legal questions. Two great masters of this style of responsa were Rabbi Meir of Rothenburg and Rabbi Asher ben Yehiel.

## 1. A Responsum of Rabbi Meir of Rothenburg: Introduction

Rabbi Meir of Rothenburg (c. 1220–1293) was recognized everywhere by the Jews of his generation as the chief rabbi of Germany. He was a prolific writer of talmudic commentary and liturgical poetry (nineteen of his poems are still part of the High Holy Day prayerbook), but he is most well known for his extensive and influential responsa, especially on issues relating to the financial conditions and physical safety of the communities of Germany. For example, he decided that no member of a community should be permitted to negotiate his own tax deal with the secular authorities since that might be detrimental to the community, and he ruled that ransomed Jews must reimburse the community in every case and that the community may seize the prisoner's property in order to ransom him, even if he prefers prison to poverty. Ironically, Rabbi Meir himself died in captivity after trying to emigrate to Israel.

The rabbis of the Talmud had interpreted "eye for an eye" to be a general rule of compensation in cases of tort. In the following responsum, Rabbi Meir expands the scope of the principle of compensation to cover damages incurred by a Jewish defendant who was sued in a Gentile court by another Jew. This capacity for creative growth is the mark of a really useful legal idea. That capacity often depends on the basic ambiguity of the concept and therefore allows room for its expansion.

The development of an "eye for an eye" in this respect is comparable to the way the originally limited notion of the common law writ of trespass grew to become a major foundation for the modern law of personal injuries, contracts, and much criminal law. The jurisdiction of the king's courts in England, soon after the Norman Conquest, was very limited. It depended largely on a connection between the lawsuit and the king's twin responsibilities to keep the military peace and to maintain the feudal pattern of land-tenure. The writ of trespass initially was a basis to invoke the king's court on a claim that the defendant had done damage by violent injury or by unlawful entry onto the land. By the thirteenth century the writ had broadened to include all claims of suffered damage, including those in which there was no violence. Several centuries later it had grown to include injury based on the failure to keep a promise, forming the foundation for the modern law of contract. One reason why the writ of trespass was more popular than competing sources of legal authority is that it provided for trial by jury, which came to be seen as a more rational and useful approach to factfinding than trial by ordeal or oath. In criminal cases the older form of action, known as appeal of felony, carried the possibility of a defendant demanding trial by battle, and so trial by jury had attractions in these cases as well. Moreover, as the nation state grew and feudalism weakened, the king's courts using the jurisdictional basis of the writ of trespass displaced the local, feudal, and church courts in both civil and criminal matters.

Notice that, on the one hand, Rabbi Meir is careful to link his answer to talmudic precedents in order to maintain the continuity of the law, but, on the other hand, he is prepared to apply talmudic rules in completely new ways. He could, of course, simply have ruled that he had no authority to impose penalties on the plaintiff who took the defendant to a Gentile court. He clearly chose to interpret the talmudic precedents broadly rather than narrowly in order to meet the Jewish community's need for self-discipline and cohesion in the face of the increasingly violent attacks on the Jews of Germany in his time. He felt no compunctions about expanding the scope of the precedents when warranted by the circumstances of his time.

Notice also the varying degrees of authority that he ascribes to the Talmud, secular courts, and the local Jewish community. One might anticipate the unquestioned authority that the Talmud carries for him and his refusal to attach any legitimacy whatsoever to the acts of the Gentile courts. The attention that he pays to local custom may, however, be rather surprising. As will be seen, custom played an expanding role in Jewish law once it became clear that the central authority of the Babylonian geonim was not going to be replaced by an equivalent authority in Europe. Rabbi Meir bases his reliance on local custom on a talmudic rule dealing with property, but late sources will simply accept the rule set by custom because it *is* the custom—sometimes even when it conflicts with previous law. In this case, Rabbi Meir thinks that the custom of considering anger as an excuse for causing injury is in error, and he therefore seeks to restrict the custom's exemption to the criminal penalties involved. However, if there is evidence that the community exempted a person who injures in anger even from civil penalties, then he acquiesces to that as well. In his mind, custom clearly carries great authority.

The responsum involves two cases: Reuben bit Simon's finger, and Reuben sues Simon for informing. Rabbi Meir rules on the basis of the principle of comparative negligence, which is the law in about three-fourths of American states. That is, if one of the litigants is 47 percent wrong and the other is 53 percent wrong, the damages are divided accordingly. The common alternative to comparative negligence is contributory negligence, which, until quite recently, had been the law in most American states. Under the terms of contributory negligence, if a party is partially at fault, he cannot collect any damages. Rabbi Meir's method of calculating damages is considered the newer, more progressive method, but, as this responsum reveals, it is not very new at all.

One bibliographical note: Rabbi Meir and Rabbi Asher identify their references in the Talmud by citing the name of the chapter in the Talmud where the reference occurs. We have supplied the exact page references in parentheses, but Rabbis Meir and Asher could not have done so since the standard pagination of the Talmud was not established until the first printing of the Talmud in 1520–1523, two centuries after they lived. They therefore identify the source of their references as closely as they can by citing the chapter in which the sources appear.

2. *Responsum of Rabbi Meir of Rothenburg #777: Text:*

QUAERE: We have received the claim that Reuben complained against Simon saying "You said about me that I bit your finger until blood spurted from it, and you took me to the secular court, and you made me lose 20 sculda, and concerning this I have witnesses." Simon retorted: "That is in fact what happened, that is, that you bit my finger, and this happened 15 years ago; but I never brought you before the secular courts, and I never made you lose anything. If the matter did come before the secular courts, it was in the heat of anger, but I did not bring the suit. Moreover, I have witnesses that you forgave me and freed me of responsibility for all loss that you claimed of me." My teacher, tell me whether Simon is responsible or not.

RESPONSE: I will respond briefly. As to the claim which is commonly heard that one who acts in the heat of anger is not liable, I reply in general that if he handed him over to the secular courts and caused him to lose money, then even though it was in the heat of anger, the defendant is responsible for the loss. This is because the obligation is not less binding than when two men injure one another where they each have to pay complete damages (*Bava Kamma* 33a). Even though Reuben injured Simon at the outset, Simon retaliated and caused an even greater injury to Reuben, and therefore Simon must pay. He is not free to say that it was in the heat of anger and that no man is responsible for what he does in anger. I frankly do not know where that line of reasoning comes from. As to the claim that the community has a practice to excuse him, perhaps the intent of the practice was that he should not suffer penal sanctions such as flogging or be fined as an informer. But he remains liable for damages for the injury. Consequently it seems to be that we should estimate the amount of damages for the five elements, whether he is responsible for all of them or for part of them, because there are times when one is responsible for all five and there are times when one is responsible for only some of them, as we learn in the chapter "The Tortfeasor" (*Bava Kamma* 83b).

If it seems that the amount of damages for his injury is equivalent to the damages he caused the victim to lose by turning him over to the government, then we may relieve him of all further liability. If the amount for the injury is less than what he caused the other party to lose by informing on him, then we deduct the amount of the injury and he must pay the rest even though it was in the heat of anger. However, if the community has instituted the practice of excusing him completely if he acted in the heat of anger . . . , then I will not take exception to that practice because the Talmudic rule is that property which the court makes ownerless is ownerless (i.e., such interests are locally defined). Finally, if in fact it is the case, as Simon claims, that he never handed Reuben over to the secular court and did not make him lose any money or that Reuben forgave him, then we do not need to be concerned with the remedies in this response, provided Simon will swear to Reuben in court that he did not cause Reuben to lose any money or will swear that Reuben forgave him.

### 3. A Responsum of Rabbi Asher ben Yehiel: Introduction

Rabbi Asher ben Yehiel (called the "Rosh," c. 1250–1327), a student of Rabbi Meir of Rothenburg in Worms, became the acknowledged leader of German Jewry after the imprisonment of Rabbi Meir. He led the unsuccessful efforts to free Rabbi Meir, and he distinguished himself during the *Rindfleisch* massacres of 1298 for his political activities in trying to save as many Jews as possible and for his decisions on matters arising from the resulting disruption of family and communal life. Fearing the same fate as Rabbi Meir, Asher left Germany in 1303. He reached Spain, where he was welcomed with great honor and was appointed the rabbi of Toledo. Because of his background in Germany and his long career in Spain, he is famous for combining the method of study and the customs of German Jewry with the legal decisions and methodology of Spanish Jewry. He was not afraid to challenge decisions of the geonim or rishonim before him when he thought that they were not based on a proper understanding of the Talmud. His desire to draw from both German and Spanish Jewish culture did not carry over to non-Jewish culture. He supported a ban against the study of philosophy until age twenty-five because young Jews were devoting too much time to it and not enough to the study of Torah, and he fought customs which Jews had learned from the Christians, e.g., granting equal rights of inheritance to husband and wife, bequeathing the whole estate to the oldest son, chaining of debtors, and compelling a husband to grant his wife a divorce on her declaration of her unwillingness to live with him. On the other hand, despite his reservations as to the right of the rabbis to impose capital punishment, he nonetheless permitted them to do that in accordance with the custom prevalent in Spain, and he consented to sentences of mutilation, particularly in the case of informers.

The following responsum is interesting from a number of perspectives. Its subject matter is wrestling, and Rabbi Asher demonstrates that he understands it well. He must have seen much of it. Jews thought of sports in rather negative terms since, in the mind of the Jew, they were connected to the Greek worship of the body against which the Maccabees fought in the Hanukkah story and since athletics took time away from other pursuits which were more important, especially learning. Some sports were completely prohibited because of their cruelty, e.g., hunting and cock fights. Ball games and horseback riding were popular, and, as we see in this responsum, so was wrestling.

Contrary to the explicit rulings of the Torah and the Mishnah in the sections which we have studied on personal injuries, Rabbi Asher does not impose eye for an eye on the wrestler who blinds the eye of his fellow, nor does he impose the Mishnah's five monetary remedies. He is too great a legal mind to just read the law out of the code without thinking of all of the relevant features of the case before him. In this case, he draws on other sections of the Talmud to determine that even though a man is always considered to be forewarned and therefore responsible for his actions, this does not apply when his actions are forced. This is surprising since other tannaitic sources explicitly say that people are responsible for their actions even if forced, but Rabbi Asher draws a distinction between being partially forced and completely so. Since, says Rabbi Asher, the wrestlers do not have sufficient control over their actions during the bout to prevent physical injury, and since they do not intend to injure each other in the first place, they should not be held responsible for any injuries which they inflict on each other. This adds a major new restriction to the laws of personal injury, especially since, in Rabbi Asher's ruling, the case is one in which the two wrestlers voluntarily put themselves into the wrestling situation, knowing that injury could result.

4. *Responsum of Rabbi Asher ben Yehiel* 101:6: *Text:*

> The case concerns two men who wrestled together, and one threw the other to the ground and fell upon him. When he fell upon him, he blinded the eye of the one on the bottom.
>
> It seems to me that the injurer is exempt from the five remedies (for assault in the Mishnah). For even though we learn (in the Talmud) that "a man is always forewarned (and therefore liable), whether he acts by mistake or intentionally, whether forced or voluntarily, whether asleep or awake" (*Bava Kamma* 2:6, 26a; *Sanhedrin* 72a), where there is complete compulsion he is exempt, as we learn at the beginning of the chapter entitled "One Who Deposits a Pitcher": "If one (Reuben) deposits a pitcher in the public thoroughfare and an-

other (Shimon) comes along and trips over it and breaks it, the latter is exempt (from paying damages for the pitcher)" (*Bava Kamma* 3:1). The Gemara on that Mishnah asks: "Why is he exempt? He should have looked where he was going!" And it answers:

> The School of Rav said in the name of Rav: (The Mishnah refers to a case) where he (Reuben) had filled the entire thoroughfare with barrels (and therefore Shimon could not possibly have avoided tripping over Reuben's property). And Samuel said: (The case is one in which) the thoroughfare was dark (thus diminishing Shimon's culpability). . . . And Rabbi Ulla said that it (the exemption) is because people are not in the habit of looking down at the streets (while they walk) (*Bava Kamma* 27b).

Therefore if a man does damage through compulsion, like that man (Shimon), he is exempt.

And we say in the Jerusalem Talmud: "If one was sleeping in bed, and another came and fell asleep next to him, the first is exempt for any injury he causes the second man" (P.T. *Bava Kamma* 2:8[3a]). . . .

And we say in the chapter entitled, "One Who Deposits" (*Bava Kamma* 3:5, 32a), "If one who is carrying a barrel is walking in front of one who is carrying a beam, and the barrel broke by collision with the beam, he (the carrier of the beam) is liable. If, however, the carrier of the barrel suddenly stopped, he (the carrier of the beam) is exempt. . . ."

And it is also taught in a Baraita in the chapter entitled, "One Who Deposits" (*Bava Kamma* 32a), "Issi ben Judah maintains that one who runs (in the public thoroughfare) is liable (for any injuries or damages he causes) because his conduct is unusual; but Issi ben Judah agrees that if it were on the eve of the Sabbath (when everybody would be rushing to make last minute preparations for the Sabbath), then the runner would be exempt because running at that time is permissible." Also, "If two people were running and they injured each other unintentionally, both are exempt" (*Bava Kamma* 3:6, 32a).

Similarly in our case, the two men wrestled with each other with their common consent, and they injured each other unintentionally, for it is a well-known fact that when they both wrestled the primary intention of each was to throw the other (to the ground). Now, when one exerts himself against the other, it is impossible for him so to control his strength that the other shall fall gently and not be hurt; for they wrestle with all their strength and each tries to make the other fall.

C. THE SIXTEENTH TO TWENTIETH CENTURIES: THE AHARONIM OF THE
EASTERN MEDITERRANEAN AND EASTERN EUROPE

During the fourteenth and fifteenth centuries, Jews were expelled
from Western European countries. The Ashkenazic community moved
from France and Germany eastward to Poland and other countries in
Eastern Europe, where the rulers of these undeveloped lands welcomed
Jews for their commercial talents. Almost as soon as the Jews arrived,
they found themselves in a particularly uncomfortable position. The
rulers used them to collect taxes from the peasants and supervise estates as agents for absentee landlords. The Jews were therefore seen as
the visible enemy by the lower economic classes. Jews were also subject to everchanging restrictions on their personal and professional
lives, discrimination, libel, extortion, and expulsion at a moment's notice. They were caught in the middle between oppressive Christian
rulers and the oppressed Christian masses. This situation is reflected
in responsa that attempt to respond to the taxation, ransom, bribery,
and forced conversion that the princes perpetrated and the butchery
that the masses inflicted.

During the nineteenth and twentieth centuries, Ashkenazic responsa from those Jewish communities affected by the Enlightenment
and Emancipation (especially in Germany) deal with problems of assimilation, Jewish nationalism, the innovations of the Reform Movement, and the legal status of Reform marriages and divorces. They
were concerned, too, with the use of new inventions on the sabbath
and festivals, the closer ties to Gentiles, and new modes of business.
The Jewish community lost judicial autonomy in the countries affected by Emancipation as Jews came out of the ghetto and were
granted freer legal status in the larger community they now joined.
Responsa dealing with civil matters decreased as Jews took to the state
courts.

Jews expelled from Spain and Portugal in the late fifteenth century
also moved eastward. Most settled in the Moslem countries of North
Africa and the Eastern Mediterranean (especially Turkey, Egypt, and
Palestine), but some found refuge in Italy. The popes, who controlled
much of Italy, were more tolerant of Jews than were most secular rulers. Eastern Europe, to which the Ashkenazic Jews fled, did not have a
large, preexisting Jewish community, but the places to which Sephardic Jews fled had long-established Jewish communities. Conflicts of jurisdiction and practice inevitably arose between the newcomers and
the old settlers, and responsa were written on acrimonious questions
of communal organization. Turkey, in particular, became a center of a

flourishing literature of responsa from the fifteenth through the seventeenth centuries.

These four centuries are the most prolific period of responsa writing: there are more than 250,000 known responsa from the times and places that we are now considering. They deal primarily with legal matters, not theological or other issues. Apparently the Jews of this period were challenged less on issues of faith than their ancestors of the Middle Ages had been. Both the legal and nonlegal responsa exhibit less creativity than those of previous times. Jews had faced the problems of persecution before. On the other hand, both the questioner and the respondent often knew Jewish law well, and the responsa reflect this erudition: they often involve "pilpul," that is, complex reasoning on a highly theoretical point of law or talmudic exposition.

From the sixteenth century on, the decisions of the scholars before the *Shulhan Arukh* (that is, the *Rishonim*) were considered binding, and from the seventeenth century on the *Shulhan Arukh* itself, together with Moses Isserles' notes to it, was considered authoritative. Despite that, the rulings issued contradicted each other more and more. The increasingly disparate decisions solidified the differences between the Ashkenazic and Sephardic communities. As access to a broader world opened for more Jews, their attention turned away from the fine points and the technical quibbles that occupied so much of the rabbinic literature of this time.

By the middle of the nineteenth century traditional Ashkenazic life had been ripped apart in the Jewish communities of Western and Central Europe. The Jews came out into the receptive commercial and intellectual climate of an increasingly progressive, nationalistic, egalitarian, modern world. Given their small numbers, Jews contributed remarkably to the economic development of the Western world and even more significantly to its new ideological framework. Major intellectual movements of the past century in the arts, music, literature, economics, physics, philosophy, and medicine have, to a grossly disproportionate degree, been the product of persons of Jewish background. It would be a distortion to refer to Marx, Freud, Einstein, Kafka, or Mahler as Jewish thinkers. Each of them had largely abandoned traditional practices and assimilated into the larger secular community (as had Theodore Herzl, who provided impetus for Zionist Jewish nationalism). But none of these thinkers can be understood in total isolation from the tradition from which they came, for its influences persist in their work.

Jews had suffered persecution before, but their experience did not prepare them for the Holocaust of World War II. Undoubtedly the most anguished responsa in the literature were those rendered during the war by rabbis in the concentration camps. Among the questions they treat are: whether a Jew forced by a Nazi to tear a scroll of the Torah or die should do one or the other; whether a coffin containing soap made from the bodies of Jews may be reinterred in Israel; whether a Jew may save his life by purchasing a certificate of conversion; whether inducing abortion is permitted in view of the Nazi directive that any Jewish woman found to be pregnant should be killed with her fetus; the status of sites where Jews killed by the Nazis were buried in a common grave; and the case of a woman taken to a brothel where her arm was tatooed, "a harlot for Hitler's troops." Earlier generations of rabbis had demonstrated that the law can be stretched like a tent to provide a backdrop for all the glories of the heavens. The responsa of the Holocaust teach that the law can also be stretched to provide a veil over the mouth of hell.

The capacity for jurisprudence to grow out of the Holocaust also can be seen in the legal sequels to the agony of Spanish Jewry in the fifteenth and sixteenth centuries. The introduction of Rabbi Freehof to the following responsa indicates the experience these Jews passed through, from suffering, shame, and forced conversion to the felt need to find a legal mechanism to atone for whatever guilt they incurred. To find that legal mechanism the rabbis again confronted the problems of rabbinic ordination and the jurisdiction of courts.

S. Freehof, *A Treasury of Responsa*, [Philadelphia: Jewish Publication Society of America, 1962], Chapter 18: Restoring the Sanhedrin.

> Jacob Berab (born in Moqueda, near Toledo, 1474; died in Safed, Palestine, 1546) fled from Spain to Tlemcen, in North Africa; and though he was a youth of eighteen, this large community chose him as their rabbi. He moved to Jerusalem and finally settled in Safed, which was the great Jewish center, Jerusalem being then only a minor community.
>
> Levi ibn Habib (born in Zamora, Spain, 1480; died in Jerusalem, ca. 1545) was compelled at the age of seventeen, in Portugal, to undergo baptism. He fled to Salonika, where he could return to the Jewish faith. His responsa are often quoted; and fortunately for us, the correspondence with Jacob Berab is preserved at the back of the book of his collected responsa.
>
> As the exiles from Spain and Portugal sought new homes, chiefly in the lands of the eastern Mediterranean, they were concerned, first of all, with physical safety. Having found a fairly secure residence, they began to think of strengthening their personal religious life and rehabilitating and reconstructing the Jewish community. The inner mood

of that vast exile was never adequately described by historians of that day; it was, after all, before the age of socio-psychological studies. Yet we can get an insight into some of their prevailing ideas and attitudes from the problems presented and the proposals discussed in the responsa of that day.

Tradition taught that the messianic time would be preceded by a period of general agony. On the one hand, the exiles naturally believed that their widespread sorrows were the sufferings preliminary to the coming of the Messiah. But on the other hand, if the Messiah was to come, the people of Israel had to be worthy of his advent. Now these tragic exiles felt deeply unworthy. Many of them had been forced to adopt Christianity. How could they do adequate penance for their apostasy?

Apart from this personal problem of the individual and his sense of guilt, there were new problems for the Jewish community. The refugees settled in the communities in the east, where they encountered *minhagim* (customs) different from their own. The new settlements were therefore disunited, disorderly, and quarrelsome. Was there no central source of authority that could bring order into Jewish life?

The desire for personal atonement in preparation for the Messiah and the hope for an overall authority to bring order into the communities were united in the plan evolved by a group of Spanish exiles in the city of Safed to re-establish the ancient Sanhedrin.

The ancient Sanhedrin, which had ceased with the destruction of the Temple by the Romans, was held to have been the last in an unbroken sequence of authoritative bodies going back to the seventy men assembled by Moses. It had enjoyed supreme authority. If such a Sanhedrin could possibly be revived, order and system could easily be restored to all the Jewish communities. But this restoration seemed impossible because membership in the Sanhedrin needed a special type of ordination: Just as the Sanhedrin as a body had been in unbroken sequence from the days of Moses, so the individual members of the Sanhedrin had received special ordination, each pupil from his teacher, back to the days of Moses. Though the Sanhedrin had been dispersed at the time of the destruction of the Temple, its ordained members still retained their individual authority. They continued to ordain their disciples. Thus continuous ordination had existed down to the time of Hillel II (4th century), when the chain of ordination broke.

What we call "ordination" today is not the classic, unbroken, spiritual ordination of the past. It is merely *hatarat hora'ah*, a certificate permitting a disciple to teach independently of his teacher. It is a scholar's license and not a spiritual ordination.

Now, since the true ordination had ceased finally in the 4th century, and since no one could be ordained unless his teacher himself had been ordained, there seemed no way of reviving ordination, and hence no way of re-establishing the old Sanhedrin.

In spite of this seemingly insuperable difficulty, the emotional need to re-establish the Sanhedrin persisted. It was rooted in the sense of personal guilt borne by the refugees, so many of whom had been converts. The punishment for apostasy was *karet*, literally, a cutting-off, a shortening of life, as a punishment from God. For a sin which involves *karet*, repentance seemed an insufficient atonement. From their Catholic life they had observed that atonement was made for certain serious offenses by physical penance, as well as by repentance. Was there not some physical penance in Judaism which could save them from the punishment of *karet?* Yes, there was: The Law (M. *Mak.* III.15) says that those who are flogged are freed from the punishment of *karet.* But no judge could inflict flogging unless he were duly ordained. Thus the yearning for such expiation was, perhaps, the chief motive for the attempt to restore the old ordination.

But how could ordination be established? Only a man, himself ordained, could ordain others; and there had been nobody for centuries who had been duly ordained. A way was found out of the impasse by one of the great exiles from Spain, Jacob Berab, the Rabbi of Safed.

Jacob Berab noted that Maimonides (whose authority was, of course, supreme for the Spanish Jews) had made clear (in his commentary to the Mishna, *Sanh.* I.3, and in his Code, *Hilkhot Sanhedrin* IV.11) that there must surely be a method for restoring ordination, for God had promised: "I will restore thy judges as of yore" (Isa. 1:26). Since, according to the Law, the Messiah will not innovate anything, the restoration must occur by human means before the Messiah comes. Hence there must be a practical method provided by Law for re-establishing ordination. Such a method is available, said Maimonides: If the scholars of Palestine (the classic ordination could take place only in Palestine) would agree to ordain one of their number, that man would thus be duly ordained in the ancient, classical sense. He, in turn, could then ordain others, and so the old Sanhedrin would be re-established.

Thereupon the scholars of Safed issued a public statement through which they ordained their teacher, Jacob Berab. Jacob Berab ordained his famous disciple, Joseph Caro, and three others. But a difficulty arose. At that time, Jerusalem was a small community compared to Safed. Yet it had the sanctity of its name and was led by another famous Spanish exile, Levi ibn Habib.

Berab sent an ordination by messenger to Levi ibn Habib, and the sages of Safed sent him a copy of their proclamation. Ibn Habib, however, declared the whole procedure invalid and explained that Maimonides in this case was not properly understood. The famous dispute between the two men followed.

We cite the chief letter of Jacob Berab defending the new ordination, and then the preliminary part of the pamphlet in which Levi ibn Habib sums up all his arguments against the ordination.

TEXT OF RESPONSUM

*Statement in Letter of Jacob Berab:*
Our sins have brought it about that ordination ceased at the end of the days of the sages of the Mishnah, when the alien government decreed that both the ordained and the ordainer shall be put to death. No regular court of ordained judges was therefore left in the Land of Israel. This was about three hundred years after the destruction of the Temple. At that time the sages of Israel and the elders of that generation gathered and agreed upon a sound plan to remove disputes and disagreements that had existed until then on the method of settling the dates for the New Year, the Day of Atonement, and the other holidays. The dispute was whether to continue the old method of witnesses who see the new moon or to adopt the newer method of settling the calendar by calculation. With great wisdom, and by using the calendar tradition that they had possessed since the days of the prophets and ancient sages of Israel, they then agreed to establish for us the proper calculation which they bequeathed to us: namely, how to intercalate the years (i.e., how to determine which is a leap year) and to fix the months of the festivals, etc. This they did so that the children of Israel, who from then on would be scattered to all the ends of the earth, might be able to follow these rules for the years and the months and the festivals every year.

(Berab begins with a discussion of the question of calendation because Levi ibn Habib, in a previous responsum objecting to the new ordination, expressed the fear that if men were newly ordained, they might restore the ancient method of determining the calendar by witnesses and thus throw the whole calendar into confusion. Berab indicates that this will not occur because the patriarch, Hillel II, and his court, who fixed the mathematical determination, were themselves ordained with the old ordination and that, therefore, their mathematical determination would remain sacred until the time of the Messiah. There is no fear, then, that the restoration of ordination would upset the calendar. Then Berab, having disposed of this objection, goes into the central problem: whether it is legally possible to restore the old ordination after the lapse of all those centuries, when there is no longer an ordained rabbi. He proceeds to examine the texts of Maimonides upon which his plan is based.)

I found that Maimonides wrote in his "Laws of Sanhedrin," ch. IV.11, as follows: "It seems to me that if all the sages in Israel agree to appoint judges and to ordain them, these will be ordained (truly ordained with the ancient ordination); and they will have the authority to judge laws of fines (only ordained judges of the ancient ordination could impose fines and such punishments as flogging, etc.). They will have the right to ordain others. If so, why were the rabbis (in the Talmud) worried lest the ordination disappear? Because Israel was scattered and it was impossible to obtain unanimity. Of course, if there were one man ordained by a teacher who had been previously ordained (i.e., by an unbroken ordination back to Moses), such a person would not need unanimous consent but could judge laws of fines for all. But the matter needs further consideration."

(The closing phrase in the statement of Maimonides is the crucial one — "the matter needs further consideration." Levi ibn Habib, as we shall see, bases his chief objection to the new plan for ordination on this phrase. He says that Maimonides, in his commentary to the Mishnah, gives his plan for renewing ordination, but he wrote his commentary in his youth. When, however, he wrote his great Code, he ended with the words "the matter needs further consideration." According to Ibn Habib, this cautionary statement is, in effect, a retraction of the entire plan. He takes it to mean that when Maimonides was mature and wrote his Code, he no longer believed in the possibility of restoring ordination by the agreement of the sages in the Land of Israel. Therefore, Berab now tries to prove that the phrase, "the matter needs further consideration," was not to be understand as applying to the whole paragraph, but only to the last sentence. That is to say, what needs further consideration is only the concluding statement, whether or not an individual scholar who is ordained can judge alone without needing other ordained judges. Berab then reverts to the question of the calendar and adds further proof that there will be no possibility of upsetting the calendar if ordination is restored.

He concludes his long responsum with a discussion of the personal motives which impelled many of the exiles, namely, the need of having an ordained court which should have the right to impose flogging as a complete penance for the sin of apostasy. He continues as follows:)

Now there remains for me to explain the matter of flogging. If a penitent comes before an ordained court and he had not been warned previously as to his sin and there are no witnesses that the sin occurred, are they able to impose the flogging prescribed by the Torah or not? (In other words, can a man demand such a penance when his sin is not even legally proved?) We are not speaking here of compelling the man (against his will) to be flogged, for under those circumstances (compulsion), we may not flog a man unless there are witnesses and previous warning. The question before us is, however, this: If a man comes as a penitent to the court and says, "I have committed a sin that incurs *karet*, and I wish to receive flogging to be freed from *karet*, as the Mishnah says in Sanhedrin" (can the court order the flogging?).

(Then the question is, can an ordained court inflict flogging when there is no other proof except the statement of the repentant sinner? He cites and refutes a number of opinions to the effect that the court cannot allow a man on his own statement to declare himself a wicked man; and he continues:)

Nevertheless, if he wishes to do penance, we flog him and thus give him atonement; for this is the atonement, namely, that the flogging takes the place of death (*karet*). As for the maxim of Rava (*Yeb.* 25b) that a man may not declare himself wicked, that maxim applies only to the death penalties inflicted by the human court, but not to *karet* (shortening of life at the hands of Heaven). . . . Thus, if a repentant man comes before a court and asks to be put to death, they may not put him to death. But in the matter of flogging in place of *karet*, a man may of his own choice accept the punishment of flogging. (Having thus disposed of the various objections, he concludes his responsum as follows:)

This is what seems to me to be the case with regard to ordination in our time. In the year 5298 (that is, 1583) the Lord aroused the spirit of the sages of Israel. There were one or two exceptions, who can be ignored because they were so few, who were in doubt and confused by the phrase of Maimonides, "the matter needs careful consideration." They (the minority) believed that this referred to the whole matter of ordination. Therefore they thought that we have no power to re-establish ordination in these days. They also feared that it would enter our minds to tamper with the calendar, with the result that we will consume leaven on Passover and eat on the Day of Atonement. But, thank God, we have disposed of all these doubts and have explained to what the phrase of Maimonides refers. Also we have written above that, even if we have many newly ordained men, we will not have the power to fix the calendar until the Messiah comes, for only then will there be a court equal in standing to the court of Rabbi Hillel (Hillel II who fixed the calendar in the 4th century). So they (the scholars) came to an agreement and they ordained me, the humble one among the tribes of Jacob, Jacob Berab. After two or three months, there almost happened to me what had happened to Rabbi Judah ben Baba (*Sanh.* 14a), whom the Romans put to death for ordaining his disciples. Two informers rose up against me for no sin of mine—may God punish them for their evil work—and forced me to leave Palestine (he went for a time to Damascus). Then I thought that perhaps, God forbid, the opportunity would be lost when I leave Palestine; for no one can ordain anybody outside of Palestine (*Sanh.* 14a), and so the result would be that all our labors would have been in vain; for it had already become clear how difficult it is to weld a multitude of opinions into a joint agreement. Therefore I ordained four elders, the best of the colleagues there at the time.

God knows that my intention was only for the sake of Heaven, and not to lord it over anybody. I saw Maimonides wrote in his commentary to the Mishnah, as I mentioned above, namely, that when God shall prepare the hearts of men and their intentions become pure, the children of the land of Israel will agree to appoint over them the head of a yeshiva; and he (Maimonides) came to this conviction because of what the prophets said: "I shall restore thy sages as of old" (Isa. 1:26). May God fulfill among us the verses which the prophets spoke: "And the redeemed of the Lord will return and come to Zion with joy (Isa. 51:11). Amen. May this be God's will.

Jacob Berab

Levi ibn Habib's objections to the plan are clearly stated in the correspondence published at the end of his responsa. At the beginning of that section, he summarizes all his arguments in answer to those of Jacob Berab. It is from this summary that we cite relevant excerpts. He begins as follows:

*Statement in Correspondence of Levi ibn Habib:*
A short booklet on the dispute and the legalistic discussion of law leading to action (*halakhah l'ma'aseh:* the rabbinic literature makes a distinction between Halakhah which is merely the clarification of the law and *ma'aseh,* the definite direction to act on the matter. The phrase implies that there is no further doubt) passed between the sages of Safed and the sages of Jerusalem in our day. The sages of Safed saw fit to take action on the basis of the teaching which our teacher, Moses ben Maimon, of blessed memory, made in his commentary to the Mishnah, *Sanhedrin* I:3, and in his law book, chapter 4 (Yad, *Sanh.* IV:11), namely, that the sages of the Land of Israel have the power to ordain even if there is no teacher left who had himself been ordained. So they (the sages of Safed) ordained the greatest among them, the sage, Jacob Berab. Then they sent to us who dwell in Jerusalem a letter describing their decision which began with the words: "Behold, one people!" (Farther along in his epistle Levi ibn Habib gives the full text of the letter.) Also they ordained me, the humble one, Levi ben Jacob ibn Habib, and this by the hand of the messenger who brought the above-mentioned letter; through him they sent the document of ordination, signed by all of them.

When I saw, after careful thought, that there is no legal validity in the ordination, I answered them with a long pamphlet (the Hebrew word is *kuntrus* from Latin *commentarius*) to stop them. It begins with the words: "I have seen what is written." Also the above mentioned sage who is responsible for all this action, before he saw my pamphlet, himself composed a pamphlet in support of the ordination. It begins: "Inasmuch as." (This is the legal opinion which we have just cited.) This too came into my hands and I composed a second pamphlet against it. Meanwhile, the sage received my first pamphlet and composed one against it . . . may the God of justice not judge us harshly for the unfair inclusion of other matters. May He soon redeem Zion in justice and establish the throne of David. Amen.

(After some general considerations and after citing the proclamation of the rabbis of Safed, he continues as follows:)

It was clear to them that this agreed proclamation of theirs cannot stand without our agreement, namely, ours the humble ones of the flock in Jerusalem. For though we are few in number compared to them, nevertheless, we are not mere reed-cutters (a phrase from the Talmud, *Sanh.* 33a, here meaning ignoramuses). Besides the sanctity of this place (Jerusalem), there is an added consideration, in that the matter of ordination is in the hands of *all* the sages of the holy land, as Maimonides has written. That is why they sent to us their agreement, sealed by their hand through the messenger, the sage Solomon Chasan, in order that we should uphold their hands by signing our name too. But with all due respect to their learning, it seems that in this matter they have veered off the road of decency and right. The proper procedure would have been for them not to sign this agreement until they had learned what we thought, after they had told us their arguments.

It entered my mind to forgive them for this and to say that their intention was a worthy one. They meant to hasten and achieve the desired end. For that reason they did not wish to prolong the matter. So they decided on action, since they thought that I also would agree with them. But this excuse (for their procedure) is not sufficient. With due apologies, I would say that even if this was their intention, they made a mistake. On the contrary, through their very desire to hasten the matter, they have pushed it off. Certainly they should have sensed that perhaps I could not agree to their plan as long as I did not know their arguments. Then, if we had any doubt as to their arguments, we would have let them know. After that, if they persisted in their opinions and their arguments, and then took action contrary to our opinions, it might have been possible to say that their agreement would have validity since they gave us a chance to express our opinion, and since they are a majority, and it is a commandment of the Torah to follow the majority, as long as the agreement of the majority follows discussion by *all*.

This is clear in the prelude to what Maimonides wrote in his commentary to the Mishnah and in his decision on this new law when he said: "It seems to me that if all the sages agreed, etc." Of course, that does not mean that they must be unanimous. It means the majority of them, for the majority has the authority over all of them, as is explained in many places in the Talmud. I shall discuss this matter later. But when the agreement of the majority takes place without the chance being given to everybody to debate it, it is not a valid agreement at all. For if the majority had had a chance to hear the arguments of the minority, they might have agreed with them and changed their minds. For thus wrote Solomon ben Adret in his responsum. (Ibn Habib cites this responsum to prove that the validity of the majority decision depends upon the participation of the entire assembly.)

Therefore, not only is that agreement of theirs invalid as to a majority, but now even though they wish to debate it with us and hear our arguments and let us know their arguments, if it seems to us that their arguments are invalid, they are not going to change their minds. Therefore their agreement has no validity.

This is the essence of Ibn Habib's objection. He later goes into additional objections, but the heart of it is that the sages of Jerusalem were not consulted before the action was taken. Jacob Berab ordained four disciples. These four ordained another generation, and these still another. Then this new ordination lapsed completely.

The subject of ordination and Sanhedrin has come up since. At the turn of this century, Rabbi Mendel Cohen of the Ashkenazi congregation in Cairo attempted to organize a society whose aim would be to re-establish ordination in Palestine. Recently the subject has come up once more. In all modern discussions, as probably in all future discussions, the debate rests on the arguments advanced pro and con by Jacob Berab and Levi ibn Habib in the days when the exiles from Spain and Portugal sought to recover their own spiritual self-respect and to re-establish Jewish religious life.

D. World War II–Present: America: Four Movements, Four Conceptions of Jewish Law

To understand relatively recent developments of the responsa literature it is necessary to take into account the particular tendency of contemporary American Judaism to be dominated by four distinct movements: Orthodox, Conservative, Reform, and Reconstructionist. The movements we are discussing are peculiar to the American community. The attitudes that typify these groups can be found in every community, but only in America have the differences been sharpened by competing organizational structures of synagogues and rabbis. Only in the tolerant climate of American society have Jews been able to afford the luxury of division, a luxury permitting the benefits of diversity balanced by the costs of divisiveness, organizational competition, and duplication of expensive resources.

Jews first arrived in America in 1654, but the largest waves of Jewish immigration to the New World occurred between 1881 and 1923. Few responsa of note were written in America for the first two and a half centuries because the rabbis here deferred to the learning of Eastern European scholars. After the destruction of the great European centers of Jewish population and learning during World War II, the American Jewish community became the largest Jewish community in the world. It could no longer depend on Europe to train its scholars and answer its questions. American rabbis of all movements in American Judaism therefore adopted the practice of issuing rulings on legal questions. Sometimes the answers are written in Hebrew, and sometimes in English; sometimes the responsa are written in the name of one rabbi only, and sometimes (especially in the Conservative Movement) in the name of a committee of rabbis appointed for the purpose. In all cases the respondents are consciously continuing the responsa tradition.

None of the four movements in Judaism is a monolith; each includes a spectrum of belief and practice. They are identifiably different movements, however, because they affirm four differing conceptions of what Jewish law is and what it should be.

For the Orthodox, the Written and Oral Torahs are the exact words of God revealed to the People Israel at Sinai. Orthodox belief depends on the twin doctrines that God articulated His will verbally and that we have the *verbatim* record of that revelation in the Written Torah and in the unbroken chain of tradition that continues to our own day. Since the Torah is the word of God, no human being has the right to modify it. The self-perceived needs and values of the contemporary Jewish community are not an acceptable, alternative source of value. We must obey the word of God as it has come down to us in the texts of the tradition, and when we apply them to new circumstances, we must hew to received authority as closely as possible.

This rhetorical stand has the virtue of simplicity: people should do what God's text tells them to do. Moreover, the authority of Orthodoxy's demands seems unquestionable since it is that of God Himself. Furthermore, Orthodox spokesmen claim that their ideology is not new at all, that it is simply a continuation of the age-old tradition. These factors of apparent simplicity, authority, and traditionalism enable Orthodoxy to inspire devotion in its adherents.

All three claims, however, are open to serious question. As for simplicity, Orthodox rhetoric makes Orthodoxy seem much neater and cleaner than it actually is. While Orthodox theory demands adherence to the texts of Jewish law, there are many different texts of Jewish law and varying interpretations of those texts. Moreover, the customs that surround the law vary widely. Consequently, Orthodoxy itself is splintered into many groups. These groups are often as hostile to each other as they are to other denominations of Judaism, and intergroup marriages within the Orthodox communities are uncommon. Not only are the groups diverse; in significant areas they do not recognize the legitimacy of each other's acts. Some, for example, will not eat the meat slaughtered under the supervision of others. Following the text is not always as simple as it seems.

Christian fundamentalists claim to live by the literal meaning of both the Hebrew and Christian Bibles, and that is the basis for their claim to the divine authority of their religion. Orthodox Jews sometimes claim to be "Torah-true," but they are not taking the same stance. For all of its literalism, Orthodoxy depends crucially on the rabbinic understanding of Jewish law which has always interpreted the texts. Christians should not, therefore, equate Jewish Orthodoxy with Protestant fundamentalism.

At the same time, Orthodox Jews want to make the same claim to authority as do Christian fundamentalists. Instead of restricting themselves to the text of the Hebrew Bible, however, they assert, along with rabbinic Judaism, that the full expression of God's will is contained in the sum of the Written and Oral Torahs, the latter articulated in the Mishnah, Talmud, responsa, and codes. Orthodox Jews claim to adhere to that total embodiment of God's will by interpreting and applying it literally.

The appealing authority of both Christian fundamentalism and Jewish Orthodoxy is compromised, however, when one recognizes that *human beings* must interpret and apply the texts taken to be divine before one can live by them. Even if one wanted to follow the literal word of God, the need for people first to understand that word necessitates human interpretation. Through that process human fallibility is inextricably mixed into the very meaning of the divine word. As a result, it is impossible to follow the indubitable word of God; one can only achieve a human understanding of God's will.

Orthodoxy's claim to traditionalism is as tangled as its claims to simplicity and authority. In light of its emphasis on retaining traditional practices, one can understand why many Orthodox Jews claim to be the sole legitimate heirs of the tradition. It is important to realize, however, that all four of the modern movements could well make the same claim. Each chooses different parts of the tradition to emphasize and others to downplay or ignore. Each claims that its response to modernity is the appropriate one.

Subgroups within the Orthodox community disagree among themselves regarding the extent to which it is permissible for contemporary Jews to incorporate elements of modernity into their lives. Some, the "neo-Orthodox" or "modern Orthodox," wear contemporary styles of clothing (except that males commonly cover their heads throughout the day), study the liberal arts on all levels of education, engage in a full range of vocations and occupations, and participate in most forms of modern culture. Other Orthodox Jews wear the black coats and hats common to Polish gentry of several centuries ago and as a matter of principle shun almost every facet of life they deem modern.

Moreover, many Orthodox quietly have made a number of changes during the last century in both their thought (such as, their stance toward Zionism and the State of Israel) and practice (such as, permitting themselves to be photographed; participating in an Israeli government headed by a woman). Clearly Orthodoxy's claim to be guided by tradition alone is neither as uniform nor as pure as its rhetoric makes it seem.

The easiest place for the English reader to find examples of Orthodox responsa is in the quarterly journal *Tradition*. Rabbi Moses Feinstein of New York and Rabbi Dov Soloveitchik of Boston are probably the two most quoted American Orthodox respondents of our day, although decisions of the latter are often communicated by word of mouth because a family tradition makes him reluctant to write down rulings.

Within the Conservative Movement, Jewish law is understood to be divine in origin, but human in application. The connection of the law to God is understood in various ways by members of the Conservative Movement. Conservative rabbis and laymen are uncomfortable with this issue and prefer not to talk about it. Their assertion of a divine character to the law, however, bespeaks their commitment to Torah, their belief that the areas of life which religion addresses are important, and their conviction that Jewish law is crucial for the expression of religious sensitivities.

The Conservative Movement begins with the methodological principle that the Jewish tradition must be studied in historical context, using the same intellectual tools that researchers employ in investigating other aspects of life. The upshot of such an investigation is that Judaism is based primarily on how the rabbis of the Talmud and Midrash interpreted the Bible (in contrast to the ways in which it has been interpreted by other Jewish sects, Moslems, Christians, and secularists). The rabbis saw decisions of Jewish law as matters for human courts to decide in each generation, and Jews over the centuries have modified Jewish law and ideology considerably, adding some ideas and practices, dropping others, and changing the form of yet others. Often this has occurred when Jews came into contact with other cultures. The Conservative Movement seeks to continue this process of conserving the tradition while incorporating its openness to new ideas and practices.

Individual Conservative rabbis may answer legal questions posed to them, or they may refer questions to the Committee on Jewish Law and Standards of the Rabbinical Assembly. Summaries of the committee's decisions appear in the *Proceedings of the Rabbinical Assembly* each year, and discussion of the most important issues is aired in the quarterly journal *Conservative Judaism.* The Conservative rabbi whose individual decisions are most often cited is Rabbi Isaac Klein (1905–1979) from his *Responsa and Halakhic Studies* (New York: KTAV, 1975) and, especially, *A Guide to Jewish Religious Practice* (New York: The Jewish Theological Seminary of America and KTAV, 1979). A collection of articles dealing with the theory and practice of Conservative Jewish law can be found in Seymour Siegel and Elliot Gertel, eds., *Conservative Judaism and Jewish Law* (New York: Rabbinical Assembly and KTAV, 1977).

The dual commitment to the conservation and development of Jewish law has made it difficult for the Conservative Movement to take a stand on many issues. The decisions of the Committee on Jewish Law and Standards often appear in a form that endorses a given practice as one legitimate option within the Conservative Movement, but does not require it. This has led to complaints about a perceived lack of decisiveness on the committee's part and to protests that the committee seems always to permit behavior and never forbids anything. Growing dissatisfaction by Conservative Movement traditionalists grew louder in 1983 after the Jewish Theological Seminary of America, the only North American seminary for training Conservative rabbis, voted to admit and ordain women rabbis. A vocal, dissident group formed the Union for Traditional Conservative Judaism, hired a professional director, and formed a Board of Halakhic Inquiry to answer questions on Jewish law. Similar dissatisfaction on the other end of the Conservative Movement led to the formation of the Reconstructionist Rabbinical College in 1968. This formalized the break between the Conservative Movement and what had until then been simply a Reconstructionist group within its midst. There is a real question whether the Conservative Movement can continue to embrace so many different theologies and practices while retaining coherence—

although the broad center within the movement continues to advocate tolerance for the unsettling effect of diversity in order that Jewish law can be both maintained and developed.

A candid Conservative spokesman would admit that the most troubling and widespread legal problem of the Conservative Movement is not its theory of law or its mechanism for decision making, but rather its practice. The fact is that, despite the repeated statements of commitment to Jewish law by individual synagogues and by the United Synagogue of America as a group, the large majority of Conservative lay people do not adhere to Jewish law. Conservative leaders have not communicated either the depth of their commitment to Jewish law or the reasons why one can and should observe it. Creation of an observant laity is increasingly being recognized as *the* major problem for the Conservative Movement in general and for its approach to Jewish law in particular.

The Reconstructionist Movement claims that Jewish law can no longer be treated as law, but instead must be regarded as an evolving, cultural artifact, part of the folkways that underlie Jewish civilization. Jewish norms always included a substantial number of customs, but the Reconstructionists maintain that even the positive law of the tradition is in reality only custom. They claim that for two reasons. First, they deny a supernatural lawgiver. Therefore, the only source for Jewish norms is the people themselves. Second, Jews live in societies in which observance of Jewish law is totally voluntary and unenforceable, and that, according to the Reconstructionists, precludes its characterization as law.

The second, legal, claim is clearly based on an unjustifiably narrow definition of law. Customs have power to bind no less than legislation. In both the Jewish and Anglo-American legal systems, courts have often enforced customs, sometimes in preference to legislation. Moreover, the binding power of law is not limited to formal enforcement procedures. Social, moral, historical, and even aesthetic factors all contribute to the binding character of norms, and, in fact, are responsible for the success or failure of enforcement procedures when they are invoked. The failure of the prohibition of alcohol by a constitutional amendment demonstrates that legislation and law enforcement are not alone sufficient to make effective laws. Conversely, the lessening social tolerance for smoking illustrates that formal enforcement procedures are not always necessary to give a norm binding authority. Consequently, even if Jewish law were only the collected folkways of the people, that would not necessarily deprive it of the status of law.

Reconstructionists, however, have been concerned to provide

guidance in matters of Jewish moral and ritual practice so that they can be a means to express and enhance Jewish identification. An ongoing discussion of issues from a Reconstructionist perspective appears in the quarterly journal *The Reconstructionist*. Probably the easiest way to get a sense of Reconstructionist responsa is by consulting the collection of responsa by Reconstructionism's founder, Rabbi Mordecai M. Kaplan, entitled *Questions Jews Ask: Reconstructionist Answers* (1956).

The founders of Reform Judaism embraced a fourth understanding of Jewish law. They interpreted the Books of Isaiah, Jeremiah, and Amos to mean that God is primarily interested in the moral norms of the Bible; ritual laws had become a hindrance to moral development. Rabbis of the Talmud and the Middle Ages had added to the ritual legislation of the Bible to maintain the Jewish people in times of persecution. But in the Enlightenment Germany of the 1830s and in the America of the latter part of the nineteenth century when the major figures of classical Reform Judaism wrote, Jews no longer suffered such discrimination. The rituals were no longer needed to maintain cultural and national identity. On the contrary, such laws isolated Jews from the general world and were counterproductive because they prevented Jews from fulfilling their mission as "a light unto the nations" (Isaiah 42:7; 49:6; 51:4). These writers urged Jews to return to the Judaism of the prophets (as the Reformers interpreted them), that is, an ethical monotheism devoid of rituals and nationalism and aspiring toward a universal, messianic age. These views were combined with the nineteenth century progressive and rationalistic emphasis on individual conscience and choice to form a largely antinomian version of Judaism.

It is a monument to the resilience of Jewish law that the Reform Movement has taken a decided turn toward a more observant stance in the last decade aided, no doubt, by the renaissance of ethnic consciousness in the United States and the national development of Israel. Solomon Freehof's books on Reform practices were regarded by many in the Reform Movement until recently as the idiosyncratic interests of one rabbi, but his writings have gained greater attention as the Reform Movement turns toward more traditional practices. Simeon J. Maslin's book, *Shaarei Mitzvah*, published in 1978 by the Reform rabbinical organization (New York: Central Conference of American Rabbis), is described in its introduction as the "first guide to Jewish practice ever issued under the auspices of Reform Judaism." The same organization published even more recently a collection of 172 responsa ranging in subject matter over the entire scope of Jewish law (Walter Jacob [ed.], *American Reform Responsa: Jewish Questions, Rabbinic Answers,*

*1889–1983* [New York: Central Conference of American Rabbis, 1983]). As Rabbi Arnold Jacob Wolf, a Reform rabbi, said, the most important parts of that book "are the seven pages of the table of contents. They prove that Reform Jews are intensely interested in Jewish law, in having standards, and in obeying some persons or some official body of scholars" (*Sh'ma* 14:275 [May 25, 1984], p. 114).

Wolf does not think that Reform responsa have matured sufficiently in their underlying ideology and methodology to provide a serious form of liberal Jewish legal practice as yet, but the very attempt to formulate responsa indicates that even the Reform community is seeking to strike roots in Jewish law. One Reform seminary professor, Steven Passamanek, has pointed out that this is perfectly in keeping with the origins of Reform Judaism, that indeed if the Reform Movement is to fulfill its original ideological commitments of realizing the ethical message of Judaism, it must pay more attention to the responsa literature, for it is in the responsa that Jews have dealt with the specific moral problems of each age ("A Motion for Discovery," Los Angeles: Hebrew Union College, 1977). Consequently, in years to come one can look forward to an increasing number of responsa not only in the Orthodox and Conservative Movements, which have been committed to Jewish law from their inception, but also in the Reconstructionist and Reform Movements, which have a relatively new interest in Jewish law.

At the same time, the Reform Movement has made major departures from traditional Jewish law. In 1975 the convention of Reform rabbis took a stronger stance against the intermarriage of Jews and non-Jews than many observers had expected; but it failed to prohibit Reform rabbis from performing such wedding ceremonies, and a significant percentage of them still do so. For at least eighteen hundred years Jewish law has defined a Jew as a person born to a Jewish mother or converted to Judaism. In 1985 the Reform Movement endorsed the principle of patrilineal descent, so that a child of a Jewish father, but not of a Jewish mother, would also be considered Jewish if the parents reared the youngster as a Jew. In light of the large numbers of intermarriages, one can understand the sociological motivation for this decision. This decision, however, would treat a significant number of people as Jewish who do not have that status under rabbinic law, and so most traditional Jews and some Reform leaders see this change as a threat to the identity of the Jewish people.

Perhaps more significant than these specific departures from Jewish law is the Reform Movement's continued insistence that it is the individual who decides what segments of Jewish law he or she will observe. This tenet is the ideological reason why some developments in recent years in the Reform Movement have brought it closer to the tradition while others have moved it further away; individuals have simply wanted different things. Reform Jews are encouraged to study the tradition and to incorporate elements of it into their lives, but the Reform Movement's most recent platform, entitled "Reform Judaism: A Centenary Perspective" adopted in June, 1976, asserts. "Within each area of Jewish observance Reform Jews are called upon to confront the claims of Jewish tradition, however differently perceived, and to exercise their individual autonomy, choosing and creating on the basis of commitment and knowledge." One may wonder how a legal system can survive if each individual has the right to pick and choose which laws to obey.

The ideological stances of the four movements have not developed in a sociological vacuum. The influx into the United States of Eastern European Jews in the late nineteenth century and the early twentieth century and the sizable number of Jews who have come from Russia, Iran, and Israel since then have all experienced the pressures common to any immigrant group. Urbanization, modernization, public education, and the desire to be part of the new environment have raised significant questions for such people about whether to retain their Jewish identity and, if so, how to balance that with their new identity as Americans. People who were used to identifying as Jews because the larger community gave them no other choice were faced with new, hard questions about their understanding of themselves. The freedom of American society, a major factor in attracting Jews to come here, ironically became a primary factor in the decision of large numbers of Jews not to affiliate with synagogues and other Jewish institutions. On the other hand, that very freedom has also fed a new creativity in Jewish rituals and culture, the proliferation of courses in Jewish studies on America's college campuses, and an increasing number of children studying in Jewish parochial schools. America's open society provides a radically new context for Jewish life that is both a threat to the authority of Jewish law and an opportunity for new expressions of Jewish culture and law. The four movements in American Judaism each attempt to enable Jews to retain and enhance their religious identification in that environment.

Throughout Part One we have used the topic of personal injuries to illustrate the genres of Jewish legal literature. The following, contemporary responsa on smoking are an extension of that topic because in Jewish law it is forbidden to injure yourself just as it is forbidden to injure someone else. Judaism assumes that each human body belongs to God, and that limits the rights that any person has over his or her body. That assumption also creates positive obligations to take care of the body through proper exercise, diet, hygiene, and medical attention since our bodies are really God's property which He has given us on loan. Both the prohibition against injuring oneself and the obligation to take care of oneself are the bases of these responsa.

In some respects the following responsa are unusual, and in others they are exemplary of the responsa of the movements from which they come. They are most obviously unusual in that the Orthodox responsum is ultimately permissive on the issue while the Conservative and Reform take the stringent position. While that may seem surprising at first, an examination of the methodology of the three responsa will explain this result.

Rabbi Bleich, a leading Orthodox scholar, rules that smoking cannot be prohibited by Jewish law because it has not been so prohibited in the past, and contemporary authorities lack the power to institute a new *takkanah*. He therefore opts to stick to the rules and objects to the Orthodox rabbis before him who expanded the scope of the law. He is reluctant to assert contemporary rabbinic authority to alter previous decisions, and that is typical of Orthodox responsa, although the Orthodox generally do not have difficulty in instituting new restrictions. Note that he cites Rabbi Moshe Feinstein, a contemporary rabbi whom the American Orthodox group respects highly, and that the other responsa and principles that he cites are largely from the last several centuries. "The law is according to the latter authorities" is a procedural rule that was developed during the geonic period, and the Orthodox follow that extensively in making their legal decisions. In contrast, both the Conservative and Reform responsa cite texts from the entirety of Jewish legal literature in keeping with the larger scope of responsibility and authority that they accord to contemporary judges and the greater measure of confidence that they have in them. The modern judge is to weigh the legal considerations involved in the case from beginning to end and is not to be restricted to the way in which a previous judge rules.

Rabbi Freehof's responsum is unusual for the Reform Movement only in that it includes a thorough review of the previous legal literature on the topic. Most Reform respondents do not pay as much attention to the legal materials as Rabbi Freehof does because, according to Reform ideology, they can at best serve only as a guide. Rabbi Freehof has no compunctions about extending the sources to cover the case at hand. Citing the chapter of Mishnah on our sample topic for this unit, personal injuries, he claims that if it is proved to be a fact that tobacco is harmful to health, "the Jewish traditional law would have a clear attitude toward its use."

In Rabbi Siegel's responsum note the variety of sources quoted: Bible, Talmud, Maimonides' code, and the comment of Isserles to a section of the *Shulhan Arukh.* This is certainly a clear reflection of the Conservative Movement's commitment to see Jewish law in its historical context. Because this is a decision in Jewish law, the texts are treated as they were interpreted historically within the Jewish tradition, whether that was their original meaning or not. Thus Deuteronomy 4:9 and 4:15 are taken to be a divine command to preserve one's health. This is consistent with how the rabbinic tradition has long understood those verses, although it appears that the original intent of the biblical passage was that people should be careful to teach their children the law and refrain from making images of God, as a reading of those verses in context will reveal:

> *Deuteronomy* 4:9–20:
> [9] But take utmost care and watch yourselves scrupulously, so that you do not forget the things that you saw with your own eyes and so that they do not fade from your mind as long as you live. And make them known to your children and to your children's children: The day you stood before the LORD your God at Horeb, when the LORD said to me, "Gather the people to Me that I may let them hear My words, in order that they may learn to revere Me as long as they live on earth, and may so teach their children." You came forward and stood at the foot of the mountain. The mountain was ablaze with flames to the very skies, dark with densest clouds. The LORD spoke to you out of the fire; you heard the sound of words but perceived no shape—nothing but a voice. He declared to you the covenant which He commanded you to observe, the Ten Commandments; and He inscribed them on two tablets of stone. At the same time the LORD commanded me to import to you laws and norms for you to observe in the land which you are about to cross into and occupy.
>
> [15] For your own sake, therefore, be most careful—since you saw no shape when the LORD your God spoke to you at Horeb out of the fire—not to act wickedly and make for yourselves a sculptured image in any likeness whatever, having the form of a man or a woman, the form of any beast on earth, the form of any winged bird that flies in the sky, the form of anything that creeps on the ground, the form of any fish that is in the waters below the earth. And when you look up to the sky and behold the sun and the moon and the stars, the whole heavenly host, you must not be lured into bowing down to them or serving them. These the LORD your God allotted to the other peoples everywhere under heaven, but you the LORD took and brought out of Egypt, that iron blast furnace, to be His very own people, as is now the case.

The Talmud interpreted verses 9 and 15 of this text out of context and read into them a general duty to preserve the health and safety of one's body. In Jewish law, as in any other legal system, the meaning of a law is determined more by how courts interpret the statute than by either the dictionary meaning or the narrow, contextual sense of its words. Thus Rabbi Siegel, in citing the traditional gloss on these verses, is acting properly as a jurist, although a biblical scholar would explain the verses differently. He also is giving expression to the Conservative Movement's commitment to traditional Judaism, that is, to the whole body of Jewish law that has developed over the centuries and not to its form at any particular time, even if that form is found in the Bible.

The rabbis not only established the directive to preserve one's health; they claimed that "one should be more concerned about a possible danger to life than about a possible [ritual] prohibition." Rabbi Siegel uses that statement to justify his injunction against smoking. The Conservative Movement regularly tries to root its decisions in principles embedded in the law, especially where the decision represents an extension or a change in the law. The movement prefers interpretation and extension of traditional principles to innovation by legislating new law. In so doing it seeks to preserve the law's continuity. American jurists do the same thing for the same reason, and they are particularly careful to note the elements of continuity when their decisions are most revolutionary.

The style of Rabbi Siegel's decision is also noteworthy. He does not confine himself to legal considerations alone, but phrases the decision in moral and theological categories concerning the whole of life. This indicates the Conservative view that ethics and theology are part of the law and may be invoked to influence its development.

In this regard the Conservative Movement is considerably less positivistic than the Orthodox. Orthodox jurists use moral and theological principles only if they are already embodied in a legal text, and even then it is the text that carries the legal weight, not the moral or theological concept. In our particular case, some of the relevant precedents deal with the question of relying on miracles, and so Rabbi Bleich talks about what constitutes "an unseemly demand for Divine protection." His interest, however, is purely legal; he wants to distinguish the case of smoking from that of relying on miracles. By contrast, Rabbi Siegel speaks freely about what constitutes an affront to God, the community's stake in the well-being of its members, the preciousness of life, and the tenet that life is given to us as a trust. He also draws on the personal experiences of smokers who have been able to abstain from smoking on the sabbath—including Rabbi Siegel himself.

The outcomes of these responsa at first may be surprising. The permissive Reform and Conservative authorities prohibit smoking, while the more rigorous Orthodox authority declines to prohibit the practice. This apparent paradox may reflect the different attitudes of the audiences to whom these responsa are addressed. The Conservative and Reform communities are more open to contemporary values and sensitivities, including the recent concern about smoking in secular society. A responsum prohibiting smoking, which is what Jewish law would seem to require in light of what we now know about its health effects, would therefore gain a more sympathetic hearing in those communities. Moreover, Conservative and Reform laypeople view Jewish law and rabbinic pronouncements as advisory guides, not mandatory rules for conduct. Those Reform or Conservative Jews who are inveterate smokers will either never hear of the responsum or will ignore it. This is less likely to happen in the Orthodox community, where the law and rabbinic expositions of it are taken more seriously, and violation engenders more guilt. Knowing this, in 1982 a number of Conservative rabbis proposed a resolution on smoking at the national convention of the Rabbinical Assembly, the organization of Conservative rabbis. Through a resolution, which is circulated by mail to all of the members several weeks before the convention and which must be discussed in an open meeting of the convention, they hoped to publicize concern about the matter more effectively than a responsum alone would afford. The resolution gained the approval of the convention, but few rabbis have discussed it with their congregations. In any case, these responsa and the resolution illustrate that in Jewish law, as in American law, a good judicial ruling is at least as much a function of the social context in which it is to be applied as it is the result of strong, logical connections between the ruling and its precedents.

    1. J. David Bleich, "Smoking," *Tradition*, Vol. 16, No. 4 (Summer, 1977), pp. 130–133.

    A pronouncement by the Sephardic Chief Rabbi of Tel Aviv, Rabbi David Halevy, declaring cigarette smoking to be a violation of Jewish Law has received much publicity in the press and was reported in the *JTA Daily News Bulletin*, November 28, 1976, and *The NEW YORK TIMES*, December 11, 1976, page 2. Rabbi Halevy is reported to have ruled that the risk posed by cigarette smoking renders this act a violation of Deuteronomy 4:15 which bids man to preserve his health and that offering a cigarette to a friend is tantamount to "placing a stumbling block before the blind" (Leviticus 19:14). The same opinion was expressed a number of years ago by Rabbi Moses Aberbach, "Smoking and the Halakhah," *TRADITION*, Spring, 1969, and by Dr. Fred Rosner in "Cigarette Smoking and Jewish Law," included in his book, *Modern Medicine and Jewish Law* (New York, 1972). A similar view was advanced by Rabbi Nathan Drazin, "Halakhic Attitudes and Conclusions to the Drug Problem and its Relationship to Cigarette Smoking," *Judaism and Drugs*, ed. Leo Landman (New York, 1973).

In the opinion of this writer, it is not possible to sustain the argument that smoking, in addition to being foolhardy and dangerous, involves an infraction of Halakhah as well.

Halakhic strictures against placing oneself in danger are not applicable to the case at hand for two reasons. The first argument is stated by Rabbi Moses Feinstein, *Iggrot Mosheh, Yoreh De'ah*, II, no. 49. In a responsum which is but seven and a half lines in length Rabbi Feinstein preemptorily dismisses the contention that smoking constitutes a violation of Jewish law. The answer serves to delineate the nature of risk which is halakhically acceptable.

There is an obvious tension between the pertinent Talmudic dicta bearing upon actions which pose a hazard to life or health. *Shabbat* 32b declares, "A man should not place himself in a place of danger." Yet elsewhere, (*Shabbat* 129b and *Niddah* 31a as well as other places), the Talmud cites the verse "The Lord preserves the simple" (Psalms 116:6) as granting sanction to man to place his trust in Divine providence and to ignore possible danger. The Gemara itself dispels what would otherwise be an obvious contradiction by stating that certain actions which contain an element of danger are permitted since "the multitude has trodden thereupon."

The concept embodied in this dictum is not difficult to fathom. Willfully to commit a daredevil act while relying upon God's mercy in order to be preserved from misfortune is an act of hubris. It is sheer audacity for man to call upon God to preserve him from calamity which man can himself avoid. Therefore, one may not place oneself in a position of recognized danger even if one deems oneself to be a worthy and deserving beneficiary of Divine guardianship. Nevertheless, it is universally recognized that life is fraught with danger. Crossing the street, riding in an automobile, or even in a horsedrawn carriage for that matter, all involve a statistically significant danger. It is, of course, inconceivable that such ordinary activities be denied to man. Such actions are indeed permissible since "the multitude has trodden thereupon," i.e., since the attendant dangers are accepted with equanimity by society at large. Since society is quite willing to accept the element of risk involved, any individual is granted dispensation to rely upon God who "preserves the simple." Under such circumstances the person who ignores the risk is not deemed to be presumptuous in demanding an inordinate degree of Divine protection; on the contrary, he acts in the manner of the "simple" who pose no questions. An act which is not ostentatious, which does not flaunt societally accepted norms of behavior and does not draw attention to itself, is not regarded by Halakhah as an unseemly demand for Divine protection. The risk involved may be assumed with impunity, if the individual desires to do so. Rabbi Feinstein states simply that cigarette smoking falls within the category of permissible activity. There is little doubt that although the road is fraught with danger it is—at least for the present—indeed a path well trodden by the multitude.

In the opinion of this writer, another argument permitting cigarette smoking in terms of Jewish law may be drawn from the discussion of R. Ya'akov Etlinger, *Binyan Zion*, no. 137. Jewish law provides that those who return safely from a sea journey or from a trip across the desert must offer a *korban todah*, a thanksgiving sacrifice. This offering is brought in gratitude for having been delivered from danger. In our day, in the absence of the sacrificial order, this deliverance is acknowledged in the public recitation of *ha-gomel* which is a *birkat hoda'ah*, or blessing of thanksgiving. In light of the recognized danger inherent in such travel, *Binyan Zion* questions the permissibility of taking such journeys in the first place. He responds by drawing a distinction between an immediate danger and a potential or future danger. Immediate danger must be eschewed under all circumstances; future danger may be assumed if, in the majority of cases, no harm will occur. One who embarks upon a sea voyage or caravan journey is in no immediate danger, although at some point in his travel danger may arise. Since, in the majority of cases, no harm will befall the traveler, the risk of future danger may be hazarded. It is for this reason, asserts *Binyan Zion*, that the sages, invoking the verse "The Lord preserves the simple" rule that a woman whose life may be endangered by pregnancy is permitted to engage in normal coital relations without any restrictions whatsoever. Justification for assuming the risks involved follows an identical line of reasoning: Intercourse itself poses no hazard. The jeopardies of pregnancy lie in the future and may be assumed since, in the majority of cases posing such risks, no harm will actually result. Cigarette smoking would appear to be analogous to the cases ruled upon by *Binyan Zion*. No danger is present at the time the act is performed. The health hazards posed by smoking lie in the future. To be sure, certain physiological changes occur immediately upon inhalation of cigarette smoke, but such changes assume clinical significance only when they develop into symptoms of smoking related illnesses. Since even in light of presently available evidence it appears that the majority of smokers do not compromise their health and do not face premature death as a result of cigarette smoking there is, according to *Binyan Zion's* thesis, no halakhic reason to ban this activity.

To be sure, no one can conceivably argue that smoking is a *mitzvah* or worthy of encouragement on any other ground. In earlier periods of Jewish history, the Sages promulgated decrees against specific hazardous actions which they did not regard as Biblically proscribed. For example, Tosafot, *Beitzah* 6a, describes the prohibition against drinking uncovered water lest a snake had previously partaken of the water and deposited poisonous venom therein as a *davar she-be-minyan*, a specific rabbinic promulgation. The hazards of cigarette smoking are quite probably greater than those of drinking uncovered water. Had tobacco been known and had smoking been prevalent in days gone by, the Sages of the Talmud might well have deemed it wise to ban smoking. In the absence of such a rabbinical decree, either in the past or in the present, it cannot be maintained that smoking constitutes a violation of Halakhah. Despite the technical inability of contemporary rabbinic authorities to promulgate formal *takkannot*, binding in nature upon all of Israel, the extensive rabbinic powers of moral persuasion and exhortation might well be harnessed in urging the eradication of this pernicious and damaging habit.

2. Solomon B. Freehof, "The Use of Tobacco," *Reform Responsa for Our Time* (New York: Hebrew Union College Press, 1977), Ch. 11.

QUESTION: Should not the use of tobacco be prohibited by Jewish law on the basis of the growing consensus of physicians that it is injurious to health? Also, what are the chief responsa which deal with the question of the use of tobacco? (Asked by Dr. S. Z. Hulman, Leeds, England.)

ANSWER: Tobacco was introduced into Europe in the sixteenth century (in England, in 1565). The use of it in various forms spread immediately all over Europe. Both Church and State expressed strong opposition to its use. At times the Church threatened excommunication, and the State imposed fines, imprisonment, and even capital punishment.

Naturally the Jewish legal authorities, likewise, reacted to the sudden spread of this new habit. But the attitude of Jewish law was not entirely prohibitive. It could more properly be described as deprecatory and, to some extent, restrictive. The first full discussion of the use of tobacco was by Chaim Benvenisti of Constantinople (1603–1673) in his long supercommentary to the *Tur* (*K'nesses Hagdola*, #567, sec. 3). He gives a description of how smokers have become so deeply addicted that they cannot wait for the Sabbath to end. They watch eagerly for the stars to appear so that they can begin to smoke. He tells how smokers crowd the streetcorners, puffing clouds of smoke. Specifically, he deals with the legal question of whether tobacco may be smoked on fast days (on personal fast days, on semi-strict fast days, such as the fast of Esther, etc., and on the strict fast day of the Ninth of Av). In general he is opposed to smoking on any of the fast days because, he says, it brings Judaism to shame in the eyes of the Moslems, who strictly refrain from smoking on their fast days.

He also discusses the fact that smokers claim that tobacco calms their nerves, making them forget their poverty and their troubles. He responds to that claim by saying that is the very reason why it should be prohibited on the Ninth of Av, when it is our duty to mourn and weep over the destruction of Jerusalem.

The next early authority to discuss smoking was Abraham Gumbiner, in his classic commentary to the *Shulchan Aruch* (*Mogen Avraham* to *Orah Hayyim* 210, par. 9). The question is whether smoking requires a blessing before its use, as all foods do. His opinion is given in commenting on the law in the *Shulchan Aruch* which says that when a person is a mere taster, not an eater (as a woman at the stove who takes a small amount into her mouth and then spits it out), such tasting requires no blessing. Since tobacco is inhaled and then exhaled, is it not similar to mere tasting and, therefore, requires no blessing? But perhaps it is like incense, which does require a blessing. He leaves the matter undecided.

The next important discussion is by Isaac Lampronti of Ferrara (1679–1756). Isaac Lampronti was both the physician and the rabbi of Ferrara. His scientific alphabetical encyclopedia of Jewish law contains a number of articles on tobacco. First he has an article under the heading "Apalto," in which he discusses the question of a license granted to a Jew to have a monopoly in the tobacco trade. The article reveals the fact that the Jews were active, and perhaps leaders, in the tobacco business.

Under the heading "Tobacco," Lampronti has a whole series of articles on the matter. Perhaps the most significant of them is the one in which he describes the prevalence of the use of tobacco in the synagogue. He describes the conviviality this arouses and how it destroys the whole mood of sanctity of the synagogue, and he declares that if he had the authority, he would abolish its use in the synagogue.

Elijah of Lublin (d. 1735), in his responsa *Yad Eliahu,* #65 refers to the spread of the tobacco habit among women. He discusses a rather curious question. Since a husband must avoid any contact with his wife during her menstrual period (for example, he may not drink from the same cup), may they both take puffs from the same tobacco pipe?

There is an interesting statement about smoking by Moses Hagiz (b. 1671). Hagiz was an emissary from Jerusalem to collect funds, and so visited many Jewish communities. He finally settled in Amsterdam, where he compiled his work *Leket ha-Kemach,* which is composed chiefly of an epitome of the responsa literature. At the end of the volume, he speaks of the fact that many scholars have prohibited the use of tobacco on Yom Kippur, but he says the prohibition is not sound and that it is really permitted. Of course, he adds, those who are strict with themselves should remain strict. Naturally he refers not to pipes or cigarettes, which would require lighting, or to chewing tobacco, which might be swallowed; he refers to snuff. This statement is found on the last page of the original edition. The new edition is not yet complete and therefore does not contain this statement.

Another full discussion of the matter of smoking is given by Chaim Mordecai Margolis (d. 1818), the author of the index commentary to the *Schulchan Aruch, Shaarey Teshuva*. He has two lengthy discussions of the question, one to *Orah Hayyim* 210 and the other to *Orah Hayyim* 511. To *Orah Hayim* 210, he mentions that no blessing is needed before the use of tobacco. He mentions the discussion of whether it is permitted to light a cigarette or pipe at the flame of a tallow candle, since tallow is prohibited food. By the way, Isaac Lampronti, in his discussion of this question, describes a scientific experiment he conducted to prove that the smoke of the prohibited tallow actually enters into the tobacco, and so such a lighting should not be permitted. To return to *Shaarey Teshuva*, Margolis discusses the question frequently dealt with, whether tobacco may be smoked on the holidays. In 511, he discusses the relationship or a comparison of the use of tobacco with the use of incense. He tends to permit that use.

A more recent responsum is one by Abraham Sofer, the son of Moses Sofer of Pressburg and his father's successor. In his responsum (*K'sav Sofer*, #66) he discusses smoking on the holiday. He must have been a pipe smoker himself, because he describes precisely the question of extinguishing the fire in the pipe (which would be prohibited on the holidays if the pipe has a cover which is not perforated).

The above include most of the important responsa on the various questions involved in smoking, namely whether a blessing is needed; whether it may be lighted from a candle made of prohibited tallow; whether it may be indulged in on holidays or on fast days; and whether it can be used in the synagogue at all. But as to the second question raised by the inquirer, whether it should be prohibited because of the increasing medical opinion that it is dangerous to health, the fact is that the healthfulness or harmfulness of the use of tobacco was not especially discussed in the past. The opposition of Church and State to its use was based upon a general conservatism and a superstition that it was "burning incense to the devil." But, understandably, the users of tobacco in the early days praised it as beneficial. In fact it was called *herba panacea*, an all-healing herb; thus the only references to its effect on the body seemed to be, rather, in favor of its use. We mentioned above that smokers would tell Chaim Benvenisti that tobacco calmed their nerves; moreover, Abraham Sofer, in his responsum, speaks of the fact that smokers would tell him that the smoking was good for their health, especially for their digestion after a heavy meal. But the idea that tobacco could be harmful to health is a modern one, and if it is proved to be fact, then certainly the Jewish traditional law would have a clear attitude toward its use.

It is distinctly a duty incumbent upon every person to protect his health. The Mishnah, in *Baba Kamma* 8:6 (and the Talmud in 91b), states that a person may not injure himself. The law continues that if one does what he is forbidden, he is not punished for it. The statement means that if a man injures someone else, the courts punish him, but the courts will not punish a man who injures himself, even though it is a sin. So, too, the law is that a man may not even live in a city that has no physician (*Sanhedrin* 17b). The Talmud is full of laws which speak of what to do to prevent sickness and protect health. Maimonides, the great legalist and physician, said (*Yad*, Hil. Rotzeach 11:5): "Our sages have prohibited many things because they involve bodily danger, and everyone who transgresses against and says, 'I am only harming myself and it is nobody else's affair,' or if he says, 'I do not pay attention to such things,' such a person deserves to be flogged." This statement of Maimonides is repeated at the very end of the *Shulchan Aruch*, which adds, after Maimonides' statement, that such a person deserves to be flogged: "he who is careful about such matters will receive the blessing of happiness." Isaac Fifkes, in his commentary *Be'er Hagola*, explains this statement as follows: "The Torah warns us to be careful of our health because God, blessed be He, created the world in kindness, to do good to His creatures." In other words, he says that to neglect one's health would be a denial of God's merciful intention to us.

Therefore, if, for example, a man has had a heart attack or has some lung infection or some other bodily ailment, because of which his physician orders him to stop smoking, it is not only ordinary caution for this man to obey his physician but it may be considered a mandate of Jewish law that he should do so.

As for other people who smoke, whether Jewish law would have them give up the habit would depend upon the degree of conviction that the medical profession has come to with regard to it. If ever the medical profession definitely agrees that the use of tobacco is of danger to every human being, then, of course, it could well be argued that Jewish law, which commands self-preservation, would prohibit its use. Until such time, we can only say that those for whom it is surely harmful would be carrying out, not only the recommendation of their doctor, but the mandate of Jewish law if they give up their use of tobacco.

3. Seymour Siegel, "Smoking—A Jewish Perspective," in Tom McDevitt, ed., *Smoking: Is It A Sin?* (Pocatello, Idaho: Little Red Hen, Inc., 1980), pp. 50–56.

"The Surgeon General Has Determined that Cigarette Smoking is Dangerous to Your Health." This sentence confronts us wherever we go. It is prominently displayed on all advertisements for cigarettes. It is printed on every package of cigarettes. It is repeated on radio and television. Nevertheless, smoking of cigarettes continues here and abroad.

Judaism, an ancient source of religious and ethical wisdom, expresses attitudes and values which are relevant to the question of cigarette smoking. There are definite directives about substances which are "dangerous to health."

It is important, first of all, to explain the Biblical attitude toward maintenance of our own health. The basic attitude is expressed in the verses (Deut. 4:9) "Take heed to thyself, and take care of thy life." and (Deut. 4:15) "take good care of your lives." These passages reflect the understanding, basic to all Biblical faiths, that life is a gift, a privilege given to us by the Creator. This means that we are bidden to guard, preserve, and enhance our lives and the lives of others. To neglect our health, to willfully do something which can harm our lives, is not only to court disaster for ourselves, but is also an affront to the One Who gave it to us. Therefore, the preservation of health is a *mitzvah* (a commandment).

This idea is expressed most concisely by Moses Maimonides (1135–1204), who is considered one of history's greatest physicians. Maimonides is accepted by Jewry as one of the greatest scholars in Jewish history. Maimonides' code is called *Yad ha-Chazakah* (the strong hand). In the section dealing with "Murder and the Guarding of Life," he writes:

> It is a positive commandment to remove any stumbling block which constitutes a danger and to be on guard against it. The Sages have prohibited many things because they are dangerous to life. If one disregards any of them and says, "I am only endangering myself, what business do others have with me," or "I don't care (if they are dangerous); I will use them (that is, harmful things), anyway," he can be subjected to disciplinary flogging (Chapter 11:4–5).

Maimonides reflects the Judaic ethos which sees life as not being the sole possession of the individual. A person must avoid harm to himself and avoid being a source of harm to others. He should not feel that since the harm is only to himself, there is nothing that can be done by the community. We are all part of each other. The community has a stake in the well-being of all of its members, as the individual has a stake in the well-being of the community. Both the community and the individual have responsibilities to the Creator. Life is too precious to deliberately expose it to dangerous and harmful effects.

The Talmud (*Bava Kamma* 80a) states that a person is not permit-ted to wound himself. The Rabbis derive this law from the Biblical ad-monition which sees the Nazarite who voluntarily deprives himself of the legitimate goods of the world as a sinner. They reason: if a per-son who deprives himself of wine is considered in a bad light, cer-tainly one who causes himself to suffer (by bodily harm) is culpable in God's eyes.

Another classical writer, Rabbi Moses Isserles (1525–1572), whose notes on the *Shulhan Arukh* (The Set Table, the authoritative code of Jewish Law) are seen as binding, writes:

> . . . one should avoid all things that might lead to danger because a danger to life is stricter than a prohibition. One should be more con-cerned about a possible danger to life than a possible prohibition. . . . And it is prohibited to rely on a miracle or to put one's life in danger.

The concept that Rabbi Isserles expounds—"a danger to life is stricter than a prohibition . . . One should be more concerned about a possible danger to life than about a possible prohibition"—is of spe-cial importance. Judaism exhorts the Jew to be careful in avoiding anything that might be prohibited according to ancient Jewish pre-scription. Therefore, an observant Jewish person would make sure that he does not eat anything that involves the slightest suspicion of containing something forbidden, for example, swine's flesh. Rabbi Isserles says that he should be even more careful about eating or tak-ing into his body anything that might be dangerous. The application of this exhortation to the problem of cigarette smoking seems obvi-ous.

It is also interesting to note that Rabbi Isserles says: "In these mat-ters it is forbidden to rely on miracles." This means that an individ-ual should not deceive himself in thinking that although others are harmed, he might escape the consequences since he possesses special merit or because he is entitled to special, divine providence. The sources are clear: avoid danger to your health; do not assume God will help you avoid dangerous consequences; it is a divine commandment to preserve the heatlh of your body and spirit.

These exhortations apply even when the risk appears to be mini-mal. This is illustrated in the following way. In ancient times, people were warned not to drink water that had been left uncovered for a pe-riod of time. The water might become contaminated in some way. The rabbis prohibited the drinking of "uncovered water." What if the risk is minimal? The rabbis ruled: "If a jar was uncovered, even though nine persons drank of its contents without any fatal conse-quences, the tenth person is also forbidden to drink from it."

Even a minimal risk should not be taken. Life is too precious; health is too important; well-being is too vital to be risked.

The attitude of Judaism toward possible risk to health can be summed up:

1. Life is precious. It is given to us as a trust. We may, therefore, not do anything which would possibly impair our health, shorten our lives, or cause us harm and pain.

2. We may not do this to ourselves. We can, of course, not do harm to others. All human lives are precious in God's sight.

3. The responsibility to avoid danger to ourselves or others applies even when it is not certain that harm will ensue. We are forbidden even to take the risk.

4. The harm is to be avoided even if the bad effects are not immediately evident—but will show up in the long run.

There is little difficulty in applying these principles to the question of smoking. Scientific evidence has now established beyond doubt that smoking, especially cigarette smoking, is injurious to our health. It is now evident, too, that the non-smoker can be harmed when he has to suffer the smoke of those who use tobacco. The smoking habit is dirty, harmful, and anti-social. It would therefore follow that Jewish ethics and Jewish law would prohibit the use of cigarettes. Smoking should, at least, be banned in synagogues, Jewish schools, and in Jewish gathering places. The rabbinate and the community leaders should discourage smoking. This would help us live longer and healthier. In doing so, we would be fulfilling our responsibilities to God and man.

There is one aspect of this question which is of special interest.

According to Jewish law, the observance of the Sabbath is of paramount importance. One of the Ten Commandments exhorts us to cease from labor every seventh day. The rabbis have long and complicated discussions of what is "work." The kindling of fire and the extinction of fire is forbidden on the Sabbath. Thus from sundown Friday to sundown Saturday, Jewish law forbids smoking. I have personally known many people who were heavy smokers who did not touch tobacco the entire Sabbath day. What is remarkable is that in most of these cases all smoke hunger ceases during the Sabbath day. It is only as the sun begins to wane and the end of the Sabbath day approaches that the yearning for tobacco returns. I myself experienced this phenomenon when I was an habitual smoker. As far as I know, scientists have not fully investigated the fact that the religious prohibition against smoking on the Sabbath seems to distract habitual smokers from their addiction. This points to the fact that there is no real physical addiction to tobacco, at least in most cases. It means that determination and commitment can overcome the desire to smoke.

Surely, religious people seek to do God's will. When they accept the idea that it is forbidden to smoke on the Sabbath day, they are freed of the compulsion. We fervently hope that the considerations of health, risk, and danger to health by smoking might become internalized so that those who now shorten their lives by the use of cigarettes will hear God's command to stop shortening their lives through cigarettes.

4. Resolution of the Rabbinical Assembly, 1982 (from *Proceedings of the Rabbinical Assembly* 44:182 [1983]).

SMOKING

Whereas the latest report of the Surgeon General of the United States has reiterated the potential harm to smokers and non-smokers through inhalation in smoke-filled rooms and other areas in which people congregate, and

Whereas smoking poses serious and proved dangers to health in violation of Jewish law that exhorts us to "be very careful about your lives" (Deuteronomy 4:15) and urges us "to choose life, if you and your offspring would live" (Deuteronomy 30:19), and

Whereas the pollution of the public domain is a breach of a principle of Halakhah (*Baba Kama* 30a) and cigarette, cigar, and pipe smoke are serious pollutants that endanger the health of smokers and non-smokers alike, therefore

Be it resolved that The Rabbinical Assembly expresses alarm over the increasingly documented danger to health posed by smoking and urges its members to make every effort to sensitize their congregations to this problem with a view toward significantly decreasing the practice of smoking along with other proven addictions and substance abuse, such as narcotics and alcohol, and

Be it resolved that we advocate and support local legislation that bans smoking in public places, and

Be it further resolved that smoking be banned at public sessions and in dining areas at this and at future Rabbinical Assembly Conventions.

The development of the modern movements and these illustrative responsa also replay themes that we have seen throughout our treatment of Jewish law to this point. One continuing theme has been the theoretical and social bases for the authority of the law. Maimonides was still part of the same club even if you disagreed with him, but in significant ways that is no longer true for the members of the modern religious movements because they do not share the same assumptions

about the origins, methods, and authority of Jewish law. For the Orthodox, the law is the word of God at Sinai as literally recorded in the Torah. Therefore all decisions should be based on legal reasoning alone;
socioeconomic considerations, if adduced at all, must be introduced
under cover of textual precedent. That is a simple and straightforward
theory that motivates obedience, but Conservative Jews cannot accept
it because of what we know today about the history of the text that we
have in hand. Even if God spoke in words at Sinai, we do not have the
only record of those words, as we learn from the history of canoniza-
tion. Moreover, we know that there are direct parallels in the language
and history of other contemporaneous societies to many parts of the
Bible, and that makes one wonder whether it is the unique word of
God that it claims to be. Then, too, there is ample evidence of changes
that were introduced into Jewish law on the basis of the legal institutions of the people among whom the Jews lived and the socioeconomic
conditions that they faced. Conservative Jews accept these results of
historical analysis, but they then face the difficulty of explaining why
one should obey the law if the Torah is not the literal word of God.
Many Conservative spokesmen suggest nonverbal theories of revelation. Although such theories have precedent within the tradition, in
the eyes of the Orthodox they constitute denial of a fundamental principle of the faith. For that reason many Orthodox rabbis will not even
join a communal Board of Rabbis for fear of being associated with such
heresy. The problem becomes even worse when we come to the Reconstructionist and Reform movements, who accept historical analysis
and, partially on that basis, abandon claims for the authority of the
law as law. They hold that one may adopt some Jewish rituals if one
chooses to express one's Jewishness in that way, but there is no obligation to do so. The entire theoretical structure of the origins, methods,
and authority of the law are thus questioned in modern times in ways
far more radical than Jews of earlier periods ever contemplated.

These theoretical issues, in justifying the authority of the law, are
complicated yet further by social factors. There have always been Jewish communities that did not fully recognize the legal acts of other
Jewish communities, but generally they were differentiated by geogra-
phy and the extent of nonrecognition was not great. Jews of all four
modern movements, however, live in the same neighborhoods, making their differing ideologies and practices the source of constant irrita-
tion to each other, and they differ considerably more widely than Jews
ever have before. Thus members of one movement will rarely recognize the authority of responsa by spokesmen of another movement.
Conservative and Reform rabbis accept Orthodox legal practices such
as supervision of kosher slaughter and catering, and the conversion of

proselytes, but the recognition is not reciprocal. That asymmetry increasingly is being challenged as the non-Orthodox movements gain greater confidence in their own abilities to determine proper Jewish practice.

These social realities, internal to the Jewish community, are exacerbated by the external social context in which Jews live. Since Jews move at least as much as other Americans, most do not feel ties to old neighbors and friends or to old ways of doing things. Moreover, they mix freely with other types of Jews and, more importantly, with non-Jews. This social mobility wreaks havoc with the stability and continuity that a more settled society affords its legal system. Even those who accept Jewish law as binding may generally follow the decisions of a given rabbi, but they can and do ignore him if they disagree with what he says on a particular issue. If sufficiently provoked they simply change their loyalties to another rabbi down the block. This milieu hardly provides the social basis for a cohesive, stable, authoritative legal system.

Another theme that recurs in a new guise in contemporary Jewish law is the relationship between law and morality. The tradition assumed that by and large the law articulated the substance of morality, although it recognized norms "beyond the letter of the law." Because of a combination of factors—Protestantism's distaste for law, the Enlightenment conviction that law is a public thing and morality a private one, the experiences of Vietnam and Watergate, and so on—contemporary Americans draw a sharp distinction between the demands of law and those of morality. American Jews cannot help but be influenced by that attitude. In religious circles Orthodox spokesmen maintain that the law takes precedence over any moral concerns, both because the author of the law is God while moral notions are human, and also because the Orthodox presume that God already has built proper moral considerations into the law. Conservative writers maintain the traditional belief that the law generally articulates the substance of morality, but they assert that that is because whenever the letter of the law was seen to be immoral, the rabbis adjusted the law, and contemporary rabbis should do likewise. Reconstructionist and Reform writers assert that morality is binding and the law is not. They thus accept the American dichotomy between law and morality. In sum, the modern American forms of Judaism vary widely in their views of the ties between law and morality, with only the Orthodox and Conservative maintaining some form of the tradition's confidence in the morality and the moral efficacy of the law.

Similar remarks apply to another one of our themes, the relationship between law and religion. The Jewish tradition identified the law as the creation of God and asserted that law is the chief expression of religion. Traditional Jewish and Christian sources recognized state-made law, but they assumed that the king ultimately had to answer to the King of Kings, and that human law therefore was subject to divine veto. In contrast, Enlightenment philosophy provided a justification for the separation of church and state, and that principle pervades the governmental structure and ideology of Americans. As a result, in modern times the state asserts jurisdiction over religious property (and so, for example, religious institutions provide no sanctuary from the police). The state even asserts authority over marriage and divorce, which used to be unquestionably and exclusively the domain of religion. American Jews have largely adopted these beliefs and values with regard to governmental structure, and many have extended them to their understanding of religion as well. Orthodox Jews still define Jewish religious commitment primarily as obedience to Jewish law. Law is a major component of Judaism for Conservative Jews also, although they devote considerable effort to promoting aspects of Judaism as a civilization. But law has little to do with piety or ethnicity for Reconstructionist and especially Reform Jews. Despite the growth of concern for law described earlier, very few rabbis or laypersons in the Reform Movement articulate their religious beliefs and values in legal terms. Thus law is no longer understood religiously by many Jews, and religion is no longer primarily a legal phenomenon.

These theoretical stances on the relationship between religion and law have direct consequences for our case. In each of the responsa, smoking is considered a matter properly within the purview of law. Is it appropriately treated as such? Americans might think of Prohibition as a prime example of the ineffectiveness of law to determine social habits. Western liberals like John Stuart Mill would question whether it is proper for any legal system to protect a person against himself. As we have seen in earlier topics, however, the specifically religious character of Jewish law enables it to assert competence over every aspect of life. Since God governs everything, there can be no Bill of Rights protecting the individual's autonomy in personal matters from the law. This underlying faith in God's rule leads even the Reform spokesman to treat the issue of smoking in the context of Jewish law. As a Reform Jew, Rabbi Freehof does not consider the law to be binding, but it nevertheless is an appropriate expression of the religious values and the ideology which enables religion to make demands in these areas.

As one contemplates the changes that have occurred in each of these jurisprudential areas, one wonders how Jewish law in any recognizable sense can survive in any form. These responsa illustrate amply that it can and does.

## E. World War II–Present: Israel

The establishment of a Jewish state in Israel in 1948 produced a spate of responsa dealing with the new circumstances such as: What measures may and should be taken to maintain civilian services and insure civilian and military security on the sabbaths and festivals? Do the biblical laws dealing with agriculture in Israel and the holiness of the Temple site apply despite the fact that the Temple has not been rebuilt? Under what conditions should a Jewish state permit autopsies, abortions, and other medical procedures that raise moral and halakhic questions? How can an observant Jew do business in a Jewish state where the civil law is based on British common law and the legislation of the Knesset (parliament) rather than the Talmud, responsa, and codes?

Many of these questions arise now for the first time for reasons of both substance and form. Jews in the diaspora could depend on Gentiles to perform many services for them on sabbath and festival days that Jews were forbidden to do. But such avoidance of sabbath laws is impractical and hard to justify legally when the majority of the inhabitants are Jewish. New procedures must be found based on the assumption that it will be Jews carrying them out. Similarly, Jews in the diaspora learned to do business according to the rules of the realm for the simple reason that they had no choice, but in a Jewish state Jews must take responsibility for what the law is. Reverting to talmudic business law would not be easy after the centuries in which international business practices have changed radically and Jews themselves have gotten used to doing business by other rules.

Some issues are even more serious because they involve the procedures by which binding law and decisions are made and the determination of who is entrusted to make them. When Israel was founded, the division of legal authority used under the Ottoman Turks and the British mandate was retained. Under this system the religious authorities of the various religious groups exercise jurisdiction in matters of personal status (marriage, divorce, adoption), and the state, by statute enacted by the Knesset, is empowered to deal with all other matters. Judges are to use those elements of British common law and Turkish law that were in common practice in Israel from the time of Ottoman and British rule to supplement the legislation of the Knesset.

This allocation of power between the rabbinate and the Knesset was largely a political compromise, but it also expressed two conflicting features of Israeli society. On the one hand, some 85 percent of Israelis define themselves as nonreligious and would be loathe to expand the power of the Orthodox rabbinate. The Orthodox rabbinate has managed to antagonize virtually every non-Orthodox element in the society through the way it has interpreted, applied, and explained Jewish law on matters of personal status. In fact, a political majority of Israelis increasingly calls for an end to the Orthodox monopoly over issues of personal status. At the same time, Israelis feel a conflicting wish that their Jewish state have a Jewish character, and Jewish law has historically been the primary defining element of what it means to be Jewish. As a result, conscientious Jews in Israel—rabbis, civil judges, legislators, and laypeople—are trying to deal with the new realities of the Jewish state and the conflicts between modern Israeli law and traditional Jewish law.

A variety of legal authorities are thus involved in deciding issues treated by Jewish law in modern Israel, including the people who first created the Israeli system of giving authority on matters other than personal status to the Knesset and British common law. Until then Jewish law had allowed diaspora Jewish communities to rely on a secular government for civil and criminal law ("*Dina de malkhuta dina*," "the law of the land is the law"—a principle that we shall discuss at length in Topic Fourteen). The decision of Israel's founders significantly expanded the scope of that rule such that even Jews living in a Jewish state in Israel would rely on nonrabbinic law.

The list of important participants must also include the legislators and judges who have made the many decisions defining the ways in which the sabbath and festivals would be observed (or not observed) in the cities and towns of Israel, the type of Jewish education the Jewish state would provide for its inhabitants, and issues in medical ethics, court procedures, and family law. All of these were decisions which will determine the future nature and viability of Jewish law in Israel, even if they were often made by people who were not consciously trying to continue the tradition. In addition, of course, several of the Orthodox rabbis of Israel have issued important responsa on modern Israeli life, including especially several former chief rabbis of either the Ashkenazic or Sephardic communities in Israel, that is, Abraham Isaac Kook (1865–1935); Ben Zion Ouziel (1880–1953); and Isaac ha-Levi Herzog (1888–1959).

Perhaps even more significant than any of the new responsa coming out of Israel are two new developments that have taken place there, one legal and the other technical. In 1980, the Knesset passed the Foundations of Law Act. According to that legislation, in the absence of specific precedent or law, Jewish law is to serve as a source of guidance for the court. This raises the possibility that responsa literature will become increasingly significant in the determination of Israeli legal practice. Moreover, as lawyers, legislators, and judges are increasingly involved in interpreting that literature and deciding when to apply it, the responsa themselves may well become broader in scope and more flexible in responding to new circumstances.

These possibilities make the new, technical advance all the more important. In 1963 the Institute for Research in Jewish Law at the Hebrew University and Bar Ilan University began to classify the responsa from all times and places in a variety of ways (subject, sources, and so on) and put them in machine-readable form. Soon a scholar will be able to know quickly whether there are responsa on a question he is considering, no matter whether those responsa come from the ninth century or the nineteenth, from Morocco or Poland. The lack of accessibility and organization that has plagued responsa literature from the beginning will finally be alleviated. That undoubtedly will mean that the use of responsa in making legal decisions will increase. This would be a welcome change that would occur none too soon: codes tend to become hard and fast, and the ever-changing facts of contemporary Jewish life demand the greater flexibility and the wealth of human experience that the responsa provide.

# Topic Nine: Codes

## A. The Types of Codes and Their Use

The Talmud and responsa are loose and disorganized styles of legal literature. The rabbinic mind loves discursive argumentation and emphasizes case-based law; its literature therefore tends to be quite disorganized. Yet, periodically throughout its history, the rabbinic tradition has felt the need for a coherent exposition of its content, a clear and single code that makes the law accessible to everyone. The greatest periods of code making were during the medieval and Renaissance centuries, extending from Maimonides' *Mishneh Torah* in the twelfth century to Joseph Caro's *Shulhan Arukh* in the sixteenth century.

Before examining classical medieval Jewish codes and the biblical and mishnaic codes that preceded them, it will be helpful to explore the concept of a legal code, for the term is ambiguous. In the folds of its uncertainties are found significant controversies regarding the creation and use of codes. The medium is at least part of the message. Codal form implies, but does not demand, certain ideological views about the nature of legal authority and reasoning. To see that, consider that the term "code" is used to describe at least five distinct types of legal literature.

1. *Compilation.* Most legal systems feel from time to time the need to gather together all the rules and statutes that have been enacted piecemeal over time. Then the laws that are obsolete or have been repealed can be weeded out, and the laws that remain can be organized by subject. Revised statutes or compiled statutes found in England and many American states follow this pattern. These are codes that merely attempt to give some logical format to laws adopted episodically.

2. *Encyclopedias.* Some compilations go further and seek to provide a coherent statement of the entire corpus juris. The whole body of law, statutes, rules, decisions, and interpretations are organized and indexed with plentiful cross-references. An attempt is made to describe all the legal authority on a given point.

3. *Educational handbook.* A very different type of legal code is designed to be an easy reference source, a guide for the uninitiated. The original aim of such a code is probably not to be a source of positive law at all, but rather a teaching book, a student's outline. In time, as generations of students use it, the handbook that has provided such reliable guidance becomes an authoritative statement. Coke's and Blackstone's commentaries are English examples of this phenomenon. Although scholars disagree about this, the Mishnah may have gained its authority in precisely this way—first as an educational handbook and only later as a definitive statement of the law.

4. *Restatements of the law.* The foregoing types of codes are all attempts to compile and explain existing law. The process goes one step further as the compiler takes more strenuous steps to make the law coherent by filling in gaps in received law and reconciling or choosing between conflicting lines of authority. A restatement of the law is presumably more complete and clearer than the law was when first formulated. The codifier now has definitely produced something new and different. Since the first quarter of this century the American Law Institute has been engaged in a systematic effort to restate American common law, organizing, reconciling, and rationalizing the legal rules of the various states. Some of these restatements have been very influential in bringing a high degree of uniformity to state laws. The restatements also have contributed to the growth of the law by suggesting a coherent approach to areas of confusion. Although the Restatement of Contracts, for example, is not the law in any state, some rules and concepts that originated in the restatement have become generally accepted as the law in most states. It is not unusual to find a state court opinion on a fine point of contract law that discusses and adopts the restatement rule in preference to a theoretically binding older or dubious precedent from its own state.

5. *The Code as the Law.* Codification in some periods and cultures connotes more than collecting, reconciling, and organizing the law. In the centuries since the French Revolution nations all over the world have emulated the example of the Napoleonic and German codes. These codes are more than statutory compilations. Like restatements, they reorganize the law rationally, providing a complete statement of its logical principles. Restatements, however, are in the end, only one statement of the law. They may be more organized and complete than previous statements, but they do not supplant or annul them. Lawyers and judges will be attracted by the virtues of a restatement to use its version of the law, but they may use other versions as well. In contrast, codes like the Napoleonic and German codes replace prior piecemeal legislation and interpretation and become the first and primary source

of law. No other statement of the law is authoritative once such a code has been enacted.

Adoption of such a code affects the operation of the law as well as its base of authority. Interpretation and supplementation are not foreclosed, but their character is profoundly changed. When an interpreter deals with case law that is based on specific experience, he reasons inductively from the example contained in the law to the situation under consideration. In contrast, the reasoning of an interpreter of a code is, in a sense, deductive. The code is the axiomatic repository of all needed principles and logic. From those premises the right answer to a specific problem can be deduced.

The distinctions in function between these five types of codes are not always clear in practice. Shifts in usage are especially noticeable over time. The Covenant Code in Exodus appears to be a compilation of decisions, but it later becomes Holy Writ and part of the ultimate, authoritative text of Jewish law. It is hard for the modern reader to tell whether R. Judah intended the Mishnah to be a compilation, an education book for judges, or a restatement, but it does not seem likely that it was intended as a positive command (if it were, why include minority opinions?). In time, however, its reputation bestowed an authority on the text that probably went beyond the author's intention. Similar fates befell Maimonides' *Mishneh Torah*, the *Shulhan Arukh*, and Blackstone's *Commentaries*.

These distinctions should also help to illustrate an important fact about Jewish and Anglo-American law in contrast to continental law. The major legal systems of continental Europe treat law codes as the final and highest forms of legal expression. In European countries the law is what the code says because the code contains the command of the sovereign: it was promulgated by those empowered to rule. It is for that reason that the code supersedes the authority of all previous legal sources. From that command, proper conduct can be ascertained deductively. In Anglo-American and Jewish law, that is not possible. Even when the law is codified in statute, it continues to be tempered with common law and custom. In other words, the Jewish and Anglo-American systems use codes more selectively and contextually, balancing them with interstitial, uncodified legislation, judicial decisions, responsa, and customs. In Anglo-American law this concern for custom and judicial decisions stems from a highly developed sense of popular sovereignty: common law and custom reflect what people do more closely than legislated codes do. In Jewish law the emphasis on judicial decisions and custom is based, in part, on the historical fact that Jews were seldom ruled by a universal, authoritative body that could produce a binding code. Moreover, no human body could legislate a code that would replace the body of rules that was based on God's revelation. Thus the reasons are different, but the methodological result is the same: one cannot reason deductively from a code in the Anglo-American and Jewish systems of law. Instead, it is necessary to consider all of the sources of the law and draw conclusions based on one's judgment of which applies most fittingly to the case at hand. The Internal Revenue Code is the primary authority for an American tax lawyer, but it must be read with government regulations and court cases. Orthodox Jews, for all their citations of the *Shulhan Arukh*, do not use that code directly or exclusively; they see it through the lens of the numerous commentaries on it and the codes and responsa that preceded and followed it.

The point should not be carried too far. Codes and common law are not polar opposites. Most legal systems use both forms of law, and they interact. But the deductive style of legal reasoning that is associated with codes has for two centuries been dominant on the continent, while inductive, casuistic, or case-based thinking characterizes most Anglo-American and Jewish legal thought and practice.

The preference in Jewish law for judicial rulings in specific cases over the use of the broad provisions of codes was by no means undisputed. In section C, the most important arguments on both sides of that issue will be considered. Moreover, it would be erroneous to conclude from this discussion that Jewish law either has no codes or effectively ignores them. There are a number of Jewish law codes, and those that have attained wide distribution and popularity are afforded great respect and are regularly quoted. What follows is a description of the most important codes.

## B. The Literature of Jewish Codification

1. *The Bible.* The urge to codify appears in the Bible, which contains several distinct codes. In addition to the Covenant Code in Exodus that we have already considered, the Bible embodies a comprehensive Deuteronomic Code; the Holiness Code (Leviticus, chapters 17–26); the Priestly Code (chapters 1–17 of Leviticus, the legal sections of Numbers, some portions of Exodus, the section on circumcision in Genesis); and the Temple Code in Ezekiel, chapters 40–48. Because of conflicts in their rules (for example, Exodus 20:24 versus Deuteronomy 12:13; Exodus 22:19 versus Deuteronomy 17:5) and due to linguistic and historical considerations, modern biblical scholars see these as distinct codes from different time periods. The traditional view is that they are all one code coming from God at Sinai, and the in-

consistencies are to be reconciled by differentiating the cases to which the conflicting verses apply.

Both traditional Jews and modern scholars commonly think of these biblical materials as legal codes. These passages certainly include many laws, and the later Jewish tradition based its wide-ranging legal corpus on this biblical base. There are, however, several features of biblical laws that make them different from modern legal codes. The Bible does not specify laws governing common human situations like marriage and divorce except in the most accidental of ways; it omits penalties for some of its prohibitions; and it adds moral and religious rationales for a number of its commandments. Moreover, some of its legal clauses are phrased in a casuistic form ("If somebody does X, then the judgment shall be Y"), suggesting a compilation of earlier case decisions; and some are written in apodictic form ("Do X!"), suggesting legislative commands. If this is a law code, then, it involves two different understandings of the nature of law. In a casuistic system you decide what is right in one case and then use it to compare to other specific cases, but there are no stated basic principles from which correct results are derived. In an apodictic system there is a known set of fundamental principles which you apply through syllogistic deduction.

These features of biblical law have led one modern biblical scholar, Umberto Cassuto, to suggest that until the time of Ezra, biblical laws were not used as a complete legal system; they functioned instead as religious and moral bounds for the royal statutes and customs that constituted the body of the law. Consequently, what we have in the Bible is not codes or even compilations of precedents or statutes, but rather religious and ethical instructions in particular cases and thus "notes on the existing laws":

U. Cassuto, *A Commentary on the Book of Exodus* [Jerusalem: Magnes Press (Hebrew University), 1967], 260–64.

> Now it is possible to show that also among the Israelites, during the whole period preceding the destruction of the First Temple, the sources of the official law were the secular statutes of the ruling authorities and accepted usage; whereas the Torah laws were regarded as religious and ethical requirements directed to the collective and individual conscience. Although Israelite governmental codes, like those of the Mesopotamian kings, have not come down to us, yet we are permitted to posit that such codes existed at the time. Clear indications of the existence of secular law among the Israelites are to be found in the Bible. . . .
>
> Similarly there are references in the Bible to the existence of recognized legal usage. . . .

It may also be assumed that the law of Israel was an offshoot of the general legal tradition that was current, as we have stated, throughout the ancient East. But the statutes of the Torah are not to be identified with Israel's secular legislation. Only in the time of Ezra were the laws of the Torah accepted as the laws of the country, by the consent of the people and its leaders. When we come to compare the Pentateuchal statutes with those of the neighbouring peoples, we must not forget, as the scholars engaged in this field of study usually do, the difference in character between them: the laws of the neighbouring peoples were not decreed on behalf of the gods, but on behalf of the kings; whereas the laws of the Torah were not promulgated in the name of the monarchy, nor even in the name of Moses as the leader of Israel, but are religious and ethical instructions in judicial matters ordained in the name of the God of Israel. . . .

These directions are based, therefore, on the premise that there are already in existence legal usages and secular statutes, and that the rulers have the right to enact more laws, only the Torah sets bounds to this right from a religious viewpoint.

Hence, the legal sections of the Pentateuch should not be regarded as a code of laws, or even as a number of different codes, but only as separate instructions on given matters. This fact explains why the Torah does not deal at all with several subjects that constitute basic legal themes: for example the laws of marriage, apart from forbidden relations and the reference to the marriage-price of virgins, which occurs incidentally; or with the laws of divorce, which are also mentioned only incidentally in order to forbid, on moral grounds, that a divorced woman who has married another man should return to her first husband. Although the codes of the Eastern kings are also incomplete and do not include every branch of law, yet, when they deal with a given subject, they enter into all of its details, and are not content with a few chance, unrelated notes. . . .

Another important distinction between state legislation and the Torah laws is to be seen in the fact that the form of the latter is not always that of a complete statute. They do not always state the penalty to be imposed on the transgressor; sometimes only an absolute command or prohibition is enjoined as an expression of the absolute will of the Lord. Alt already has rightly recognized that the absolute apodictic form of statutes is of Israelite origin, in contradistinction to the casuistic form, which is common also to the other peoples. . . .

Contrariwise, sometimes the Torah adds the reason for the law, from the religious or ethical point of view, unlike the codes mentioned above, which give no reasons. It would be superfluous to state further that in the Pentateuch are to be found, as is well known, religious and ritual regulations alongside legal ordinances without differentiation, which is not the case, as we have seen, in codes of the neighbouring nations.

The Torah's ethical intent creates further disparity. The entire concern of the aforementioned codes is to determine what is due to a person according to the letter of the law, according to abstract justice, whereas the Torah seeks on many an occasion, to go beyond strictly legal requirements and to grant a man what is due to him from the ethical viewpoint and from the aspect of the love a man should bear his fellow, who is his brother, since both have One Heavenly Father.

In view of the fact that the Torah statutes are only notes on the existing laws, we should feel no surprise at the fact that their style and usual phraseology resemble those of the prevailing legal traditions. One of the similarities, recognized already some time ago, is to be found in the casuistic formulation, which begins by setting out a given case (if such-and-such an instance [casus] occurs), and thereafter states what the law is in that particular case.

The Bible thus clearly includes substantial collections of important legal and ethical traditions of the ancient Israelites, although it is not clear that these collections served a function parallel to the modern conception of a full law code.

2. *The Mishnah.* The first authoritative Jewish code organized by subject was the *Mishnah*, compiled by Judah ha-Nasi about 220 c.e. Because he often cites minority opinions, some scholars do not regard the Mishnah as a code at all but simply as a compilation of sources. There is, however, stylistic evidence that Judah intended to write a code designed to regulate practice. Judah used a style that does not attribute rules to a particular author (*stam*) to state the law, thus harkening back to the centuries before the destruction of the Second Temple when the Sanhedrin's prestige made its majority opinion the undisputed law. This anonymous style gives the impression that the law is fixed and agreed on in the way that Judah wanted it to be determined. Judah nevertheless included minority opinions in order to preserve the sense of continuity in the law, the feeling that the chain of transmission from scholar to scholar had been maintained. A thousand years later Maimonides failed to mention the names of the authors of rulings and ignored contrary opinions, and those were major reasons why his code was so severely criticized. Most other major codifiers followed Judah's example.

3. *The Mishneh Torah.* Rabbi and Seminary Professor Louis Ginzberg called the *Mishneh Torah* by Maimonides "not only the most brilliant work of codification, but also the greatest product of (all genres of) rabbinical literature" (*On Jewish Law and Lore* [Philadelphia: Jew-

ish Publication Society of America, 1955], 170); Professor and Justice of the Israeli Supreme Court Menachem Elon describes it as "the greatest and most comprehensive halakhic code of all" ("Codification," *Encyclopedia Judaica*, 5:630). Maimonides' code delineates Jewish law in the clearest literary style and in a masterfully well-organized way. Most other Jewish codifiers had followed the lead of Yehudai Gaon, who, in his *Halakhot Pesukot* (c. 750 c.e.) omitted sections of the law that were not applicable to his diaspora community, for example, laws relating to the Temple and agricultural production in Israel. Maimonides, however, includes all sections of the law in his code, motivated, no doubt, by a sense of loyalty to the law's history, a faithful anticipation of the return of the Jewish people to Israel together with the restoration of the Temple, and a philosopher's passion for completeness. His training in Greek philosophy enabled him to recast the Jewish tradition in a clear, systematic style. Neither Jewish law nor Jewish thought has been the same since.

The title, *Mishneh Torah*, is a clever epigram which can mean "second to the Torah," "the teaching of the Torah," or "repetition of the Torah." It also calls to mind the use of the same phrase in Deuteronomy 17:18, where the king is commanded to write "a copy of this Torah (*Mishneh ha-Torah*) in a book." The first translation, "second to the Torah," reflects the purpose that Maimonides had in writing the code, that is, that the reader could study the Torah and the *Mishneh Torah* and would thereby know every detail of Jewish law without needing any other book. This purpose, articulated in his introduction to the code, reflects the changing circumstances which prompted him to write. The classical materials (the Midrash Halakhah, the Mishnah, the Gemara) assume that the user has the skills of legal reasoning, a familiarity with the entire literature, and the time and educational institutions to gain both. As the Middle Ages progressed, however, those assumptions were undermined. The large centers of learning that existed in Babylonia were dispersed, and most Jews lived in much smaller and poorer communities. Both Islamic and Christian cultures became increasingly intolerant of the Jews and made it much harder to study. There was, therefore, a need for a legal cookbook for the unlearned, a "Guide for the Perplexed" not only in matters of ideology, but in issues of law, too.

Maimonides' own life reflects the increasingly difficult times in which he lived. Moses ben Maimon was born in 1135 in Spain, but during early adolescence he and his family were driven from that country by a sect of Muslim fundamentalists, the Almohades. He wandered to Jerusalem, where he was subject to the rigors of Christian Crusader rule. Finally, he settled in Egypt, where he wrote the *Mishneh Torah* between 1177 and 1187 and *The Guide for the Perplexed* (a philosophic work) in 1190.

The *Mishneh Torah* is divided into fourteen books and is therefore sometimes called *Ha-Yad Ha-Hazakah*, "The Strong Hand" or "The Strong Fourteen." The name is a play on the fact that the Hebrew letters spelling *"Yad"* ("hand") have the numerical value of fourteen. Each book is in turn divided into several parts, called "Laws" (for example, "Laws of Business"), totalling 83, and each of the laws is divided into chapters and paragraphs. References to the *Mishneh Torah* usually omit the name of the book in which a citation is found and go directly to the name of the section within that book, such as *M.T.* Laws of Business 3:7; *Yad*, Laws of Business 3:7.

4. *Arba'ah Turim* ("The Four Rows") or, for short, the *Tur*. Jacob ben Asher's code, compiled during the first half of the fourteenth century, is important for several reasons. First of all, he included a rich collection of responsa from the Ashkenazic (French-German) communities in his rulings as well as summaries of the decisions appearing in the comments of the Tosafot on the Talmud. This served to organize and preserve that material which otherwise would surely have been lost.

The *Tur* is also important to this discussion because a later code, the *Shulhan Arukh*, is based on its pattern of organization. The *Tur* is divided into four sections (hence the name, "Four Rows," although it is also a play on Exodus 39:10). *Orah Hayyim* ("The Path of Life") includes all of the rules relating to daily activities, such as prayer, blessings, and so on, as well as the laws of sabbaths and festivals. *Yoreh Deah* ("It Shall Teach Knowledge") deals at length with the dietary laws and also includes the laws of purity, mourning, circumcision, interest, and visiting the sick. *Even Ha-Ezer* ("The Rock of the Helpmate") covers all matters of family law, including marriage, divorce, and the monetary arrangements between spouses. *Hoshen Hamishpat* ("The Breastplate of Judgment") covers civil law, criminal law, and court procedures. Reference to the *Tur* will therefore say *"Tur,"* followed by an abbreviation for one of its four books, the chapter and paragraph, for example, *Tur*, O.H. 22:3.

5. *Shulhan Arukh*. When one versed in Jewish law hears the word "code," probably the first thing that comes to mind is Joseph Caro's *Shulhan Arukh* ("Prepared Table"). Like Maimonides, Caro sought to make the essentials of Jewish law simple for both the professional judge and the layman; he attempted to lay out the major institutions of Jewish law so that the reader need only sit at the table and eat. Caro would, as it were, spoonfeed him. In fact, Caro hoped that even "the lesser students shall constantly have reference" to his book, and hence

he divided it into thirty parts, one to be read each day of the month (*Hoshen Mishpat*, introduction).

The importance of Caro's work is derived less from its clarity than from an historical accident. Caro (1488–1575), a Sephardic Jew, was born in Spain just before all Jews there were exiled. His family moved to Turkey, where Caro lived for forty years before migrating to Safed, Israel, where he spent the rest of his life. At the same time that Caro was writing, Moses Isserles, an Ashkenazic Jew in Poland, was also writing a summary of the laws found in the *Tur*, entitled *Darkhei Moshe*. But Caro finished his book first. Caro had largely ignored Ashkenazic scholars in his study. When the *Shulhan Arukh* appeared, Isserles wrote his *Mappah* ("Tablecloth"), a gloss on the "prepared table" of the *Shulhan Arukh*, in which Isserles cited Ashkenazic opinions and customs when they differed from the Sephardic interpretations Caro listed. As a result, the combined volume is a code that summarizes Jewish law as it was observed by Jews all over the known world. This was the last time that such a volume was produced. It is for that reason that the *Shulhan Arukh* has become the most authoritative code in Jewish law.

Isserles continued writing his *Darkhei Moshe* for another reason, which is crucial to our understanding of the role of the *Shulhan Arukh*. In his book Caro had used a novel way of coming to a decision. Wherever Alfasi, Maimonides, and Asher b. Jehiel had considered a particular matter, Caro decided the law according to the majority of the three. If the matter had been discussed by only two of the three and their opinions differed, then five additional authorities were considered. Isserles objected to this procedure because it ignored the rule that "the law was to be decided according to the latest authorities." Moreover, according to the Talmud every judge was to act "only according to what he sees with his own eyes," even when that requires him to differ from the latest authorities. Isserles was worried that the code would deprive the judge of the right to exercise his own discretion in the concrete case before him and would thus prevent him from carrying out his judicial obligations. The different contributions of Caro and Isserles to the finished product are indicative of the Sephardic and Ashkenazic traditions from which they came. Ashkenazic attitudes were more receptive to the authority of contemporary community authorities to expand on the law, while Sephardic attitudes were more restrictive. Sephardim tended to be more attracted by set, general formulas for determining the law, while Ashkenazim gave more weight to the special circumstantial nature of situations and the discretion of the authority called on to decide a specific case.

It is an ironic trick of fate that Isserles' comments to the *Shulhan*

*Arukh* were the major reason why that code gained the degree of authority that it has. Isserles cherished the judge's discretion, yet his work has intimidated rabbis in the last four hundred years from making their own decisions. There have been many commentaries on the *Shulhan Arukh*, but Orthodox rabbis have come to treat that work as the articulation of God's will at Sinai, fearing to differ from it in any way. They also have presented the *Shulhan Arukh* as the final articulation of Jewish law to their students. That is indeed unfortunate because it has frozen Jewish law in a way contrary to the Jewish tradition itself—and contrary to the expressed will of one of its two authors.

Because Caro intended the *Shulhan Arukh* to be a summary of the laws of the *Tur*, it follows the divisions and order of the *Tur*. Consequently references to the *Shulhan Arukh* begin with "S.A." (for *Shulhan Arukh*) and will then list which of its four books contains the citation, followed by the chapter and law number, for example, *S.A.*, H.M. 22:1.

## C. Pros and Cons of Codification

1. *Pros.* Jewish codes were created to answer specific internal needs of Jewish law and to respond to several external threats to its existence and authority. The internal factors include problems of accessibility, style, and the avoidance of contradiction. The proliferation of norms scattered in statutes, decisions, and other literary sources calls for compilation and organization so that the norms will be known and easily accessible. The differing styles of the various literary sources of the law are a potential source of confusion and dispute; the uniform style of a code eliminates that. Moreover, some genres of the legal literature are difficult to follow; codifiers try to articulate legal norms in a concise, direct way which is clear to the layman as well as the lawyer.

When laws are made by a variety of different authorities over the course of years, conflicts inevitably result. In Jewish law this issue was especially troublesome since Jews were scattered all over the world and there was no single body to reconcile the conflicting decisions and interpretations that were made by rabbis in widely varying places and times. This problem was already felt by the rabbis after the destruction of the Second Temple in 70 c.e. (see Tosefta *Eduyot* 1:1ff), but it was even more prevalent in the Middle Ages, when, as Jacob ben Asher said, "there remains no decision in Jewish law which is not subject to disputing opinions so that many will search in vain to find the word of the Lord" (*Tur*, Yoreh Deah, Introduction). Codifiers sought to resolve that situation by creating a clear, well-known list of laws that effectively made a final decision in the many disputed areas.

External challenges to rabbinic authority also contributed to the creation of Jewish codes. The Karaites, a group that denied the legitimacy of the Oral Law, were a particular threat. The geonic codes, produced between 750 and 950 C.E., were largely an attempt to formulate the Oral Law clearly and succinctly in order to demonstrate its ties to the Written Law. This was also one of Maimonides' goals in writing his code in the late twelfth century. Maimonides justified omission of the names of the scholars whose rulings he used as a response to the Karaite claim that the rabbis "rely on the statements of individuals." He took note of the chain of tradition in the introduction of his code but simply stated the halakhic rule in the body of the work to communicate that "the law was transmitted by way of the many to the many and not from a single individual to another individual" (Letter to R. Phinehas, judge of Alexandria, in *Kovetz Teshuvot*, Pt. 1, 250–270, No. 140).

In later years there were challenges to the very existence of Jewish law. Beginning with the decree of Pope Gregory IX in 1242, Christian authorities burned the Talmud and forbade its study during the thirteenth, fourteenth, and fifteenth centuries. Codes were a way of keeping the practices and study of Jewish law alive during those years.

Maimonides (1140–1204) lived before the Talmud burnings, but the introduction to his code is a classic statement of the motivations for writing codes. As you read it now, take note of the following:

1. The reasons Maimonides gives for thinking that a code is necessary.

2. Maimonides' rationale for regarding the authority of the Talmud pre-eminent over the decisions of the geonim and later authorities.

3. The extent to which contemporary judges have authority to overturn post-talmudic ordinances according to Maimonides.

4. Maimonides' use of the Letter of Rav Sherira Gaon in Topic Eight. Note that he has shifted its focus. For Maimonides, the survey of the history of Jewish law not only demonstrates the continuity of the law in the face of Karaite claims, but also justifies deviations from post-talmudic rulings. By Maimonides' time the Karaite challenge was not as great, but Jews needed to adapt their law to the new circumstances in which they lived.

5. The conflict between the flexibility that Maimonides gives the law by limiting the authority of post-talmudic rulings, and the rigidity imposed on the law by codifying and claiming that the Torah and his book embody everything anyone needs to know about Jewish law.

6. Maimonides' transmission of Aristotle to Jewish culture. This partially explains his comfort with codification in contrast to other Jews of his time and later: systematics (if not dogmatics) was not foreign to him. One wonders how much of the fierce opposition to his code was motivated simply by the strangeness of the codal form to Jews and by their recognition that that form was a foreign, largely Greek, invention. On the other hand, one also wonders how much the content of Maimonides' code was affected by the need to fit Jewish law into a neat system.

Isidore Twersky, *A Maimonides Reader*, (New York: Behrman House, 1972), pp. 35–41, Introduction to Mishneh Torah.

All the precepts which Moses received on Sinai were given together with their interpretation, as it is said, "And I will give to you the tables of stone, and the law, and the commandment" (Ex.24:12). "The law" refers to the Written Law; "the commandment" to its interpretation. God bade us fulfill the Law in accordance with "the commandment." This commandment refers to that which is called the Oral Law. The whole of the Law was written by Moses our Teacher before his death, in his own hand. . . . "The commandment," which is the interpretation of the Law, he did not write down but gave a charge concerning it to the Elders, to Joshua, and to the rest of Israel, as it is said, "All this which I command you, that shall you do; you shall not add to, nor diminish from it" (ibid. 4:2). Hence, it is styled the Oral Law.

Although the Oral Law was not committed to writing, Moses taught the whole of it, in his court, to the seventy elders as well as to Eleazar, Phineas, and Joshua—all three of whom received it from Moses. To Joshua, his disciple, our teacher Moses delivered the Oral Law and charged him concerning it. So too, Joshua, throughout his life, taught orally. Many elders received the Oral Law from Joshua. Eli received it from the elders and from Phineas. Samuel, from Eli and his court. David, from Samuel and his court. . . .

R. Judah, our teacher, the saint, compiled the Mishnah. From the time of Moses to that of our teacher, the saint, no work had been composed from which the Oral Law was publicly taught. But in each generation, the head of the then existing court or the prophet of that time wrote down for his private use a memorandum of the traditions which he had heard from his teachers, and which he taught orally in public.

So too, every student wrote down, according to his ability, the exposition of the Torah and of its laws, as he heard them, as well as the new matter evolved in each generation, which had not been received by tradition but had been deduced by application of the thirteen hermeneutical rules and had been adopted by the Supreme Court. This was the method in vogue till the time of our teacher, the saint.

He gathered together all the traditions, enactments, interpretations, and expositions of every portion of the Torah, that had either come down from Moses our Teacher or had been deduced by the courts in successive generations. All this material he redacted in the Mishnah, which was diligently taught in public, and thus became universally known among the Jewish people. Copies of it were made and widely disseminated, so that the Oral Law might not be forgotten in Israel.

Why did our teacher, the saint, act so and not leave things as they were? Because he observed that the number of disciples was diminishing, fresh calamities were continually happening, the wicked government was extending its domain and increasing in power, and Israelites were wandering and emigrating to distant countries. He therefore composed a work to serve as a handbook for all, the contents of which could be rapidly studied and not be forgotten. Throughout his life, he and his colleagues were engaged in giving public instruction in the Mishnah. . . .

All these sages . . . were the great men of the successive generations; some of them were presidents of colleges, some Exilarchs, and some were members of the great Sanhedrin; besides them were thousands and myriads of disciples and fellow-students. Ravina and Rav Ashi closed the list of the sages of the Talmud. It was Rav Ashi who compiled the Babylonian Talmud in the land of Shinar (Babylon), about a century after Rabbi Johanan had compiled the Palestinian Talmud. These two Talmuds contain an exposition of the text of the Mishnah and an elucidation of its abstruse points and of the new subject matter that had been added by the various courts from the days of our teacher, the saint, till the compilation of the Talmud. The two Talmuds, the Tosefta, the Sifra and the Sifre, and the Toseftot are the sources, from all of which is elucidated what is forbidden and what is permitted, what is unclean and what is clean, what is a penal violation and what involves no penalty, what is fit to be used and what is unfit for use, all in accordance with the traditions received by the sages from their predecessors in unbroken succession up to the teachings of Moses as he received them on Sinai. From these sources too, are ascertained the decrees, instituted by the sages and prophets, in each generation, to serve as a protecting fence about the Law, in accordance with Moses' express injunction, "You shall keep My charge" (Lev. 18:30), that is, "Ordain a charge to preserve My charge." From these sources a clear conception is also obtained of the customs and ordinances, either formally introduced in various generations by their respective authorities or that came into use with their sanction; from these it is forbidden to depart, as it is said, "You shall not turn aside from the sentence which they shall declare to you, to the right hand, nor to the left" (Deut. 17:11). So too these works contain the clearly established judgments and rules not received from Moses, but which the Supreme Court of each generation deduced by applying the hermeneutical principles for the interpretation of the Law, and which were decided by those venerable authorities to be the law—all of which, accumulated from the days of Moses to his own time, Rav Ashi put together in the Gemara.

After the Court of Rav Ashi, who compiled the Gemara which was finally completed in the days of his son, an extraordinarily great dispersion of Israel throughout the world took place. The people emigrated to remote parts and distant isles. The prevalence of wars and the march of armies made travel insecure. The study of the Torah declined. The Jewish people did not flock to the colleges in their thousands and tens of thousands as heretofore; but in each city and country, individuals who felt the divine call gathered together and occupied themselves with the Torah; studied all the works of the sages; and from these learned the method of legal interpretation.

If a court established in any country after the time of the Talmud made decrees and ordinances or introduced customs for those residing in its particular country or for residents of other countries, its enactments did not obtain the acceptance of all Israel because of the remoteness of the Jewish settlements and the difficulties of travel. And as the court of any particular country consisted of individuals (whose authority was not universally recognized), while the Supreme Court of seventy-one members had, several years before the compilation of the Talmud, ceased to exist, no compulsion is exercised on those living in one country to observe the customs of another country; nor is any court directed to issue a decree that had been issued by another court in the same country. So too, if one of the Geonim taught that a certain way of judgment was correct, and it became clear to a court at a later date that this was not in accordance with the view of the Gemara, the earlier authority is not necessarily followed but that view is adopted which seems more reasonable, whether it be that of an earlier or later authority.

The foregoing observations refer to rules, decrees, ordinances, and customs that originated after the Talmud had been compiled. But whatever is already mentioned in the Babylonian Talmud is binding on all Israel. And every city and country is bound to observe all the customs observed by the sages of the Gemara, promulgate their decrees, and uphold their institutions, on the ground that all the customs, decrees, and institutions mentioned in the Talmud received the assent of all Israel, and those sages who instituted the ordinances, issued the decrees, introduced the customs, gave the decisions, and taught that a certain ruling was correct, constituted the total body of the majority of Israel's wise men. They were the leaders who received from each other the traditions concerning the fundamentals of Judaism in unbroken succession back to Moses our Teacher, upon whom be peace.

The sages, however, who arose after the compilation of the Talmud, studied it deeply and became famous for their wisdom, are called Geonim. All these Geonim who flourished in the land of Israel, Babylon, Spain, and France, taught the method of the Talmud, elucidated its obscurities, and expounded the various topics with which it deals, for its method is exceedingly profound. Furthermore, the work is composed in Aramaic mixed with other languages—this having been the vernacular of the Babylonian Jews at the time when it was compiled. In other countries, however, as also in Babylon in the days of the Geonim, no one, unless specially taught, understood that dialect. Many applications were made to the Gaon of the day by residents of different cities, asking for explanations of difficulties in the Talmud. These the Geonim answered according to their ability. Those who had put the questions collected the responses which they made into books for study. The Geonim also, at different periods, composed commentaries on the Talmud. Some of them explained specific laws; others, particular chapters that presented difficulties to their contemporaries; others again expounded complete treatises and entire orders of the Talmud. They also made compilations of settled rules as to things permitted or forbidden, as to infractions which were penal or were not liable to a penalty. All these dealt with matters in regard to which compendia were needed, that could be studied by one not capable of penetrating to the depths of the Talmud. This is the godly work in which all the Geonim of Israel engaged, from the completion of the Talmud to the present date which is the eighth year of the eleventh century after the destruction of the Second Temple [1177 c.e.].

In our days, severe vicissitudes prevail, and all feel the pressure of hard times. The wisdom of our wise men has disappeared; the understanding of our prudent men is hidden. Hence, the commentaries of the Geonim and their compilations of laws and responses, which they took care to make clear, have in our times become hard to understand so that only a few individuals properly comprehend them. Needless to add that such is the case in regard to the Talmud itself—the Babylonian as well as the Palestinian—the Sifra, the Sifre and the Tosefta, all of which works require, for their comprehension, a broad mind, a wise soul, and considerable study, and then one can learn from them the correct practice as to what is forbidden or permitted, and the other rules of the Torah.

On these grounds, I, Moses the son of Maimon the Sefardi, bestirred myself, and, relying on the help of God, blessed be He, intently studied all these works, with the view of putting together the results obtained from them in regard to what is forbidden or permitted, clean or unclean, and the other rules of the Torah—all in plain language and terse style, so that thus the entire Oral Law might become systematically known to all, without citing difficulties and solutions or differences of view, one person saying so, and another something else—but consisting of statements, clear and convincing, and in accordance with the conclusions drawn from all these compilations and commentaries that have appeared from the time of Moses to the present, so that all the rules shall be accessible to young and old, whether these appertain to the (Pentateuchal) precepts or to the institutions established by the sages and prophets, so that no other work should be needed for ascertaining any of the laws of Israel, but that this work might serve as a compendium of the entire Oral Law, including the ordinances, customs, and decrees instituted from the days of our teacher Moses till the compilation of the Talmud, as expounded for us by the Geonim in all the works composed by them since the completion of the Talmud. Hence, I have entitled this work *Mishneh Torah* (Repetition of the Law), for the reason that a person who first reads the Written Law and then this compilation, will know from it the whole of the Oral Law, without having occasion to consult any other book between them.

I have seen fit to arrange this compendium in large divisions of the laws according to their various topics. These divisions are distributed in chapters grouped according to subject matter. Each chapter is subdivided into smaller paragraphs so that they may be systematically memorized. Among the laws in the various topics, some consist of rules in reference to a single Biblical precept. This would be the case when such a precept is rich in traditional matter and forms a single topic. Other sections include rules referring to several precepts when these all belong to one topic. For the work follows the order of topics and is not planned according to the number of precepts, as will be explained to the reader.

The total number of precepts that are obligatory for all generations is 613. Of these, 248 are affirmative; their mnemonic is the number of bones in the human body. 365 precepts are negative and their mnemonic is the number of days in the solar year.

Blessed be the all-merciful who has aided us.

These are the 613 precepts which were orally imparted to Moses on Sinai, together with their general principles, detailed applications, and minute particulars. All these principles, details, particulars, and the exposition of every precept constitute the Oral Law, which each court received from its predecessor. There are other precepts which originated after the Sinaitic Revelation, were instituted by prophets and sages, and were universally accepted by all Israel. Such are the reading of the Scroll of Esther (on Purim), the kindling of the Hanukkah lights, fasting on the Ninth of Av. . . . Each of these precepts has its special interpretations and details, all of which will be expounded in this work.

All these newly established precepts, we are duty bound to accept and observe, as it is said, "You shall not turn aside from the sentence which they shall declare to you, to the right hand, nor to the left" (Deut. 17:11). They are not an addition to the precepts of the Torah. In regard to what, then, did the Torah warn us, "You shall not add thereto, nor diminish from it" (ibid. 13:1)? The purpose of this text is to teach us that a prophet is not permitted to make an innovation and declare that the Holy One, blessed be He, had commanded him to add it to the precepts of the Torah or had bidden him to abrogate one of these 613 precepts. But if the Court, together with the prophet living at the time, institute an additional precept as an ordinance, judicial decision, or decree, this is not an addition (to the precepts of the Torah).

For they did not assert that the Holy One, blessed be He . . . ordered the reading of the Scroll of Esther at the appointed time. Had they said this, they would have been adding to the Torah. We hold, however, that the prophets, in conjunction with the Court, enacted these ordinances, and commanded that the Scroll of Esther be read at the appointed time so as to proclaim the praises of the Holy One, blessed be He, recount the salvations that He wrought for us, and that He was ever near when we cried to Him, and that we should therefore bless and laud Him and inform future generations how true is the reassurance of the Torah in the text, "For what great nation is there that has God so near to them, as the Lord our God is [to us], whensoever we call upon him (ibid. 4:7). In this way every precept, affirmative or negative, instituted by the Scribes, is to be understood.

I have seen fit to divide this work into fourteen books.

2. *Cons.* By now it is clear that Jews produced authoritative codes at various points in history. As we now turn to the opposition to codification, it is important to realize that the opponents were not on the fringes of the Jewish community. On the contrary, some of the very rabbis who wrote codes also wrote responsa warning of the dangers of codes. These responsa, however, are seldom read, and that helps to explain why their authors' worst fears about codification were indeed realized.

One continuing argument against the development of codes is that they promote ignorance. Since the code pretends to give the authoritative statement of the law, some will mistakenly conclude that there is no longer any need to study the sources of the law and the history of its development. That in itself is a problem from a Jewish point of view because study of the Bible and Talmud is viewed as a sacred activity in its own right. Thus Paltoi Abbaye Gaon, responding in the middle of the ninth century to one of the earliest codes, complains that "The majority of the people follow *Halakhot Ketu'ot*, saying, 'Why should we be occupied with the complexity of the Talmud?'" Paltoi condemns this attitude because it will lead to the law being forgotten, and he declares that "*Halakhot Ketu'ot* have been compiled not in order to be studied intensively, but rather so that they may be referred to by those who have studied the whole of the Talmud and experience doubt as to the proper interpretation of anything in it" (*Hemdah Genuzah* [Jerusalem, 1863], #110; S. Assaf, *Teshuvot Ha-Geonom* [Jerusalem, 1928], 81]. Centuries later, Yom Tov Zahalon (1559–after 1638) flatly asserts that the *Shulhan Arukh* was compiled by Caro "for children and ignoramuses" (Responsum #67]) and R. Hayyim bar Bezalel (1520–1588) says:

> *Vikkuah Mayyim Hayyim*, Introduction:
> (Codes) produce laziness in regard to the studying of the ancient texts. . . . The easier they make learning, the more they add to the laziness . . . and, in fact, there are now many more ignoramuses than there used to be in days past. . . . Anyone who gives instructions on the basis of the recent compilations alone is like a poor man who received a great deal of charity from many rich people, crops from one, wine from another, fruit from another, clothes from another, and money from another, until he obtained enough to fill his needs. Another poor man comes and sees all of these goods that the various rich people gave him and he (the second poor man) considers him richer than all of the other (rich people), and he seeks his sustenance from him. That fool does not know that the first man's bread is the bread of poverty and that he has only what the other, rich people gave him! That is the essential nature of the wisdom of the people of our age: it is only what they glean from the earlier books, a little from here and a little from there, so that they have a few (pieces of information) in hand.

In addition to the religious problems involved in the neglect of the classical texts, ignorance of those texts has the pragmatic consequence that provisions of the code may well be misunderstood and misapplied. Asher ben Yehiel (1250–1327) wrote a caustic responsum in reply to one instance of that:

*Responsum #31:9:*
Thus do all of those people err who try to base their decision on the words of Maimonides, of blessed memory, when they are not themselves sufficiently adept in the Talmud to know whence he drew his words. They err, and permit the forbidden and forbid the permitted; for he (Maimonides) did not do as other authors do who quote proofs for their words and refer to the sources of their opinions in the Talmud. When they do this, one can (review the sources and) arrive at the essence and at the truth. But he, Maimonides, wrote his book as one prophesies at the dictation of God, without arguments and without proof. Whoever reads it (the Code of the Maimonides) might *imagine* he understands him but it is really not so. For if he (the student) is not adept in the Talmud, he does not understand the matter correctly and may therefore stumble both in the law and (in his own) decision. Therefore a man should not rely merely upon what he reads in his (Maimonides') book in judging and making decisions, as long as he himself is unable to find the proofs in the Talmud.

Later authorities applied the same reasoning to the *Shulhan Arukh.* Meir b. Gedaliah (the Maharam of Lublin, 1558[?]−1616), says:

*Responsum #135:*
I will base no decision of mine on the *Shulhan Arukh* or the *Levushim* (a code by Mordecai b. Abraham Jaffe) since they are like headnotes and are unclear, and many are led astray by their statements to wrongly permit what is prohibited or exempt from liability.

Rabbi Shelomo b. Yitzhak (Rashi, 1035−1104), author of the most widely quoted commentary to the Talmud, says that even the earliest authorities are not to be spared from this objection to the use of codes. Only those who demonstrated that they could carry on legal reasoning are to be heeded, not those who could only quote precedents, no matter how venerable they were.

Rashi's comment on *Niddah* 7b:
We do not derive the law from a Mishnah or Baraita that teaches "the law is according to so-and-so" because the late Amoraim carefully examined the rationales of the Tannaim and analyzed the law thoroughly, but the earlier rabbis did not carefully examine each other's opinions: whatever one heard from his teacher he taught to his pupil just as he heard it, and that is what constitutes the Mishnah and Baraitot.

Another major concern was that codes might mislead people about the nature of law itself. After reading the codes one might well think that the law is a set of rules. That ignores the dynamics of the law and seriously distorts its purpose and process. A set of rules, especially one in which no differences of opinion are recorded, may be easy to comprehend, but the law is more complex than that, and for good reason. The task of building and maintaining a just and good society in the ever-changing circumstances of life demands much more than a set of rules. It requires powers of sound judgment, keen intellect, and good will. Without those a collection of rules can actually be a detriment to the proper functioning of the law, an obstacle in its attempt to create a good and just society. The rule that was just yesterday may well be a travesty on justice today. Consequently, opposition to the codes is often grounded in the fear that they would lead to a decreasing knowledge of the content, process, and aims of the law.

In commenting on the section in the introduction to the *Mishneh Torah* in which Maimonides announces his intention to write a book that would make it unnecessary for a Jew to read any other book except the Torah in order to know the law, R. Abraham b. David of Posquieres (1120–1198) calls the whole enterprise of codification into question on these grounds:

> Comment on *Mishneh Torah*, Introduction:
> He (Maimonides) intended to improve matters, but he did not do so because he abandoned the method of all authors before him. They provided evidence for their statements and quoted the words (of others) in the name of those who said them. He (the contemporary judge) gained much from that because many times he might think that he should forbid or permit something based on evidence from one source, and if he knew that there was a greater rabbi who disputed that decision, he would change his mind. Now (that Maimondes has left out the names of the rabbis whose decisions he used) I will not know why I should retract from a decision that I learned (literally, "received") and a proof-text that I have, simply because of the compilation by this compiler (Maimonides). If the one who disagrees with me is greater than I, fine; but if I am greater than he, why should I give up my opinion for his? Furthermore, there are matters on which the Geonim disagreed with each other, and this compiler chose the opinion of one of them and wrote it in his compilation, but why should I rely on his choice if it does not seem right to me? And I will not know who it is who disagrees with him (because of Maimonides' failure to cite names of judges) and whether he is worthy of disputing (the opinion that Maimonides uses) or not. This is nothing but a product of his overweening conceit.

But probably the clearest, most forceful statement on this issue was made by R. Hayyim bar Bezalel (1520–1588):

*Vikkuah Mayyim Hayyim,* Introduction, sections 6 and 7:
Not by his (the codifier's) work alone should a man live, but by all of what comes out of the mouth of the other books should a man live (a play on Deuteronomy 8:3). . . . Just as Nature still today makes the face of every man different from his fellow's, so we have reason to believe that wisdom is still apportioned to the heart of every man in a way that is different in this (man) from (what it is in) that (man). . . . Therefore everyone who seeks instructions should not depend firmly and confidently on contemporary compilers alone, but should rather see fit to glean from their books so that they can be a guide in exploring the opinion of their rabbi, *for he too is a man among men.* After he (the inquirer) has taken note of the variant rulings in regard to that law, he should quickly run to the sea of wisdom, that is, the early judges (*posekim*), to draw water in joy from there, the springs of salvation (a play on Isaiah 12:3), the place from which those worthy compilers also drew. . . . And if (the rabbi's own) instruction of yesterday is that such-and-such is the law, then he should deal with the present case just as he dealt with the former case: he should be deliberate (that is, he should not apply the precedent mechanically) because a small change (in the facts) may reverse the ruling, as I have already written. Moreover, one's opinion is not the same at all times, and he may not be inclined to rule in that case now as he ruled in it yesterday. There is no change or lack in this, as if his action were making the Torah like two Torahs, God forbid; on the contrary, *that is the way of the Torah,* and "both (conflicting) rulings are the words of the living God" (*Eruvin* 13b). . . . Therefore they (judges) would rely on the comments (written by a number of rabbis on sections of the codes), for they (the authors of the comments) wrote to teach us how they acted; and if sometimes conflicting rulings appeared in the comments such that it was impossible that both would be according to the law, that was better in their (the judges') opinion than choosing between the great mountains (that is, authorities) and suppressing the opinion of one of the holy, former rabbis. So they saw fit to place the two opinions before the rabbi who was asked to rule, and he would choose as Heaven taught him, for the Torah gave him authority to rule.

These objections go to the very heart of the codification process. Since codifiers try to make things as simple and coherent as possible, they often presume to make decisions where, in fact, the law has not been determined. They also tend to provide only one version of the law on any given topic, ignoring contrary opinions. While the tendencies are understandable, the inevitable result is that codes dampen the vitality and pluralism of the law. Concern about that prompted the rabbis of the Talmud and Midrash to make extensive use of exegesis and the oral tradition, as we have discussed (Topic Five, sections A-4 and D); they even depicted God as refusing Moses' request to know the final decision on each matter of law "so that the situation would not become intolerable" (*Num R.* 14:4). The heavy reliance on codes in the Middle Ages and the modern period raises these concerns once again and with more force than ever.

The remarks of R. Hayyim bar Bezalel that were just quoted point to another, related problem with codification: it undercuts the authority of contemporary judges to interpret the law. The rabbis of the Talmud carefully and definitely established both that right and that obligation based on Deuteronomy 17. A number of the talmudic passages in which they explain and justify that policy have been examined in Topic Five. Rabbis during the Middle Ages and the early modern period often referred to those passages to reaffirm that the right was not only theoretical, but one that was to be used in practice.

Moreover, the right and obligation of the judge in each generation to rule on matters of Jewish law were extended further during the geonic period. At that time the rule became that *hilkhata ke-vatraei*, "the law is according to the latter ones." That is, while Jewish judges continued to have great respect for those who preceded them, it was assumed that rabbis living in later times took into account everything that the earlier judges had, and more. Therefore, if the latter judges differed from the former, it was the latter judges' ruling that was to determine practice. This obviously expanded the authority of judges considerably. Not only did they have the authority to apply the law in their times and to rule in new cases; they even could overrule a precedent. The most important exposition of this right is the following comment of R. Asher ben Yehiel on a section of the talmudic tractate *Sanhedrin*:

> *Piskei Ha-Rosh, Sanhedrin* 4:6:
> If the words (of the Geonim or later rabbis) do not seem right to the (contemporary) judge, and if he adduces proofs for his opinion which are accepted by the people of his generation, then "Jepthah in his generation is (to be considered) as Samuel in his" (*Rosh Hashanah* 25b), that is, we have no judge except the one that lives in our own times. He may contradict their words (that is, of his predecessors) because one may tear down and rebuild (rulings on) all matters that are not decided (literally, "explained") in the Talmud which Ravina and Rav Ashi edited. One may even disagree with rulings of the Geonim . . . for the later Amoraim sometimes disagree with the former ones. Indeed, we rule that the words of the later authorities are determinative because they knew the reasoning of the former authorities and their own thinking and they decided between these two lines of thought and identified the essence of the matter. And so we find (P.T. *Peah* 2:6) that we do not learn the law from the Mishnah; rather it is on the basis of the rulings of the Amoraim that we determine the law, even

though the Tannaim were greater than the Amoraim. Where two great authorities dispute the law, the judge must not say, "I will rule according to whomever I want," and if he did so, that is a lying judgment. Instead, if he is very wise, learned, and intelligent, and if he can decide according to one of them with clear and cogent proofs, he has the authority to do so. And even if another wise man ruled (on the same matter) on another case, this wise man can contradict his words through proofs and dispute his ruling as long as he has support from one of the former disputants on the matter.

This tension between ascribing greater authority to early sources or to late ones should be familiar to students of American law. On the one hand, the Constitution is the most authoritative law in the land, but, on the other, lawyers learn quickly that it is the Supreme Court's latest interpretation of that document that is the most authoritative.

Most Jewish codes, however, do not distinguish between those rulings which have a talmudic source and those which are made by post-talmudic rabbis (for example, the codifier), and that effectively deprives later judges of authority and prevents them from carrying out their full responsibility to judge. Even Moses Isserles (1525–1572), whose comments to the *Shulhan Arukh* made that book the authoritative code it is, was keenly aware of this responsibility and of the dangers involved in rendering any decision, let alone making all the decisions involved in writing a code. In Responsum #25 he writes:

And so I have learned as a precedent to be practiced from my master, my teacher, my father (in learning), the genius, the master and teacher of all of the people of the Diaspora, Rabbi Shalom Shakhna, may the holy memory of the saint be blessed, the great eagle, may I bear the repayment (for his sins) after his death, who trained many students from one end of the world to the other, from his words they live and from his water they drink. I swear that many of his students and I asked that he render a decision numerous times, but because of his great saintliness and humility (he was more humble than any other man on earth) his answer was this: "I know that (if I render a decision) nobody will rule except as I write because the law is according to the latest authorities, and I do not want the world to rely on me." That is, where there is a dispute between authorities, if he decides between them or disagrees with them at times (none of his students will decide the matter on his own); but "the judge must act only according to what he sees with his own eyes" (*Bava Batra* 131a). Therefore each one should act (decide) according to the present exigencies and the dictates of his own heart. And for the same reason, his teacher, the genius, our teacher, Rabbi Jacob Pollak, never wrote a single book. Furthermore, these geniuses (R.Shalom Shakhna and his teacher,

R. Jacob Pollak) never kept a copy of any of their responsa to far-away communities in their homes because it seemed to them to be a haughty thing to do.

And in the introduction to *Darkhei Moshe*, one of his books on Jewish law, Isserles goes to great lengths to prevent his book from becoming a substitute for the ruling of a contemporary judge:

> I was careful not to write without citing names so that people later on will not think that my words are God's and consequently be afraid to say that this matter is difficult as if they were disputing the Torah of Moses. I furthermore wrote my name on my work so that from now on anyone who wishes may disagree with what I have said, and any-one who wants to rely on me, may do so. There is no sin except for the one who relies on me because the choice is in the hands of each man, whether he chooses correctly or erroneously. In either case, a judge must act only according to what he sees with his own eyes, and he must put the Worker of Marvels (God) before him at all times (as he makes his decision) for God's faithfulness is eternal and He will teach us to go in the paths of Moses, His servant. Therefore I have called this short composition "The Paths of Moses," for I drew it out of the waters of the Torah.

While Isserles laid the groundwork for subsequent rabbis to disagree with him, he himself was reluctant to disagree with acknowledged, earlier authorities, and he objected strongly when Rabbi Solomon Luria (1510–1573) did so. Luria, however, saw the duplicity in this and responded sharply:

> You wonder by what warrant I am empowered to bring certainty into the law. You impugn my authority to disagree with the codifiers. It is the knowledge of the law which invests me with the prerogative to take issue with the halakhists and expose their errors (Quoted in the Responsa of M. Isserles, #6).

And in his large work, *Yam Shel Shelomo*, Luria carefully delineates the authority of contemporary judges, and the consequences of failing to exercise that authority, as follows:

> *Yam Shel Shelomo, Bava Kama* 2:5:
> It is definitely beyond the province of the rabbis to adjudicate con-troversies in which the question involved has been sealed with the Talmudic *teku* (let the matter stand undecided). For on such questions the Talmud ventured no opinion. However, in the event the rabbi is confronted with a conflict of authority which resulted in a declared *safeka*, a talmudic draw, leaving the law in doubt and unsettled, it is mandatory upon him to elect and adopt one of the varying views in or-der to conclude the litigation before him; and with even greater rea-

son is the rabbi obligated to reach a determination which necessitates a choice between the conflicting opinions of post-talmudic authorities. For in such cases it is the plain duty of the rabbi to explore and review the sources of the law with the view towards clearing the indicated doubt. The incompetence of the rabbi cannot prescribe or curtail the function of the rabbinic court. "Jepthah in his generation is (to be considered) as Samuel in his" (*Rosh Hashanah* 25b)—that is, the incumbent neither transcends nor submerges the office. In the event the decision is withheld in such a mandatory case the claimant may rely upon the authority which favors him and, in self-help, seize and legally retain the disputed chattel.

Recent American experience suggests that these medieval rabbis were wise to avoid excessive proliferation of written opinions. The past generation has witnessed an explosive increase in the number of reported court decisions. To some extent this increase is the inevitable consequence of the growth in the number of lawsuits, their increased complexity, and the greater likelihood of an appeal from a court that announces its decision by a written opinion. To some degree the increase may reflect the availability of commercial reporters, who earn good profits by publishing the courts' decisions. The technology of indexes, finding aids, and computer systems add to the capacity to find and use massive numbers of cases. The increase also reflects changing professional expectations of appeals judges. Formerly, the tradition was for appellate courts to hear the arguments of the counsels at length, then retire to the robing room adjoining the courtroom, decide the case, and immediately announce the decision orally in open court. This tradition was common in English appeals courts until recent years. Decision was reserved pending a written opinion only in the most complex and difficult cases. In most American states and the federal appeals courts today, the assumption is that an appeals judge will prepare a written opinion in almost every case. In some states this expectation is embodied in a law requiring an opinion. In California there has been a lively controversy over when it is proper for a court to order that its opinion *not* be published.

Everyone (except perhaps a few publishers and booksellers) would agree that the system would be improved if there were fewer case opinions as precedents. There is now such a mass of opinions for the researching lawyer or judge to dig through on even simple points of law that the import of any single opinion is inevitably diminished. Perhaps the time is approaching for American lawyers to take Isserles' advice seriously and drastically curb the temptation to write their opinions and add them to the mountain of precedent. Then future judges will be led to consider less what the mass of prior authority has written on a problem and to consider more what the problem says directly to the judge.

And finally, perhaps the meanest cut of all against Jewish codes was that they failed to achieve their purpose of providing a simple, organized, authoritative rendition of the law. Often they do just the opposite, making the law more diverse and complex. As Menahem Elon ("Codification," *Encyclopedia Judaica* [1972], 5:642–43) has noted in regard to Maimonides' *Mishneh Torah*, probably the clearest and most organized Jewish code of all:

> It would be difficult to find in all of halakhic literature another instance of a work that produced results so contrary to the avowed purpose of its author. Far from restoring to the *halakhah* its uniformity and anonymity, "without polemics or dissection . . . but in clear and accurate statements" (*Mishneh Torah*, Introduction), Maimonides' pursuit of that very aim became the reason for the compilation of hundreds of books on his work, all of them dissecting, complicating and increasing halakhic problems, resulting in a lack of uniformity far greater than before.

These arguments pro and con the acceptance of codes led to conflicting evaluations of their worth as a basis for judicial decisions. Were codes or responsa more authoritative? The Talmud regularly invokes both the rules and precedents of the Tannaim in order to make a decision or object to one; but it restricts the use of rules and verdicts to those rendered with the intention of being precedents for action (and not just tentative conclusions reached in the course of study or argument), and it raises doubts about using even those as automatic prescriptions. Decisions must be made by contemporary judges who know the various sources of the law and have the skill to apply them appropriately to the case at hand.

Medieval sources confronted the reality that most judges lacked the qualifications that the Talmud specified, but they came to differing conclusions as to whether Jewish law fared better when contemporary judges used codes or responsa. Rabbi Joseph ben Meir Halevi Ibn Megash (1077–1141) was more sanguine than many toward the use of codes, as this responsum (#114) indicates:

> QUESTION: What would our master say in regard to a man who never read law (that is, the Talmud) with a rabbi and does not know the way of the law, its interpretation, or its language, but he saw many of the responsa of the Geonim, may their memory be blessed, and the books of laws: may such a person, who neither understands the essence of the law nor its source in the Talmud, teach, and is it fitting to rely on his opinion in any matter?

ANSWER: Know that it is more fitting that this man teach than many who have appointed themselves to give instruction in our time, most of whom possess neither of these two things, that is, an understanding of the law [as it develops in the Talmud] and a knowledge of the rulings of the Geonim, may their memory be blessed. Indeed, those who pretend to teach on the basis of a careful analysis of the law are precisely the ones who should be prevented from doing so because in our time there is nobody who is fit to do that, nobody who knows enough Talmud such that he can rule on the basis of it without consulting the rulings of the Geonim, may their memory be blessed. On the other hand, one who rules on the basis of the Geonic responsa and relies on them, even if he cannot understand the Talmud, is more fitting and praiseworthy than the one who thinks that he knows the Talmud and relies on himself: the latter, even if he misapplies the rules of the Geonim, may their memory be blessed, nevertheless does not err in basing his ruling on their decisions since they are a supreme court for the masses; but one who rules on the basis of his own examination of the law (in the Talmud) may wrongly think that the law requires something which it does not, and he may err in his examination of the law or in its interpretation.

On the other hand, Rabbi Jacob Moedlin (c. 1360–1427) was among the many that favored responsa, as he writes in Responsum #72:

As for your statement that one should not rely upon responsa, I say, on the contrary, that they are practical law and we should learn from them more than from the codifiers who, after all, were not present at the time when the decision was made.

Some claimed that decisions should be based neither on the codes nor on the responsa, but only on a careful application of the relevant material in the Talmud, the source of all Jewish law. These included none other than Maimonides and Joseph Caro, authors of the two most important codes in Jewish law. For both, the Talmud's authority is based on its universal acceptance by the Jewish community, an acceptance which makes its conclusions indisputable:

Maimonides, *Mishneh Torah*, Introduction.

If one of the Geonim ruled that the law is so-and-so, and it became clear to another, later court that that is not the way the law is written in the Talmud, then we do not [necessarily] obey the former but rather follow what seems most reasonable, whether that be the opinion of an earlier or later authority . . . but all Israel must follow all of the laws in the Babylonian Talmud.

Joseph Caro, *Kesef Mishnah*, on Maimonides, *Mishneh Torah*, Hilkhot Mamrim (Laws of Rebels) 2:1:

> Even though we find in the Talmud that a Mishnah by the Tannaim
> is [regularly] used as an objection to [conflicting] words of Amoraim,
> as if the Amoraim do not have the authority to disagree with them
> [the earlier Tannaim], it is possible to say [that the reason for that is
> that] from the day of the final editing of the Mishnah they [the Amor-
> aim] accepted upon themselves [the rule] that later generations will
> not dispute the earlier ones, and so they did also after the Talmud was
> edited, that from the day that it was completed nobody had the au-
> thority to dispute it.

The unquestioned authority of the Talmud, however, existed side-
by-side with the assumption that recent rabbis would surely have
taken it and all relevant, subsequent considerations into account, and
so de facto it was the codes and responsa which carried legal authority,
along with popular custom. Which of those three sources of the law
was the most authoritative depended on the time, place, judge, and issue. Nevertheless one can generalize to this extent:

1. There was opposition to writing the law down in any form, but
once that practice was accepted, the forms that developed naturally
were debates (as in the Gemara), responsa, and interpretations of the
Bible or Talmud. None of those types of legal literature engendered opposition to the genre itself. It was only the codes that did so.

2. Responsa and glosses on the Talmud were much more popular
genres of legal literature than codes throughout the history of post-talmudic Jewish law. This has been especially true in the modern period.
While responsa have been issued almost daily, there have been only
one or two important codes of Jewish law created in the last four hundred years. Jewish law and Anglo-American law are thus quite similar
in the extent to which they rely on precedent in preference to promulgated codes.

3. The movement to create Jewish codes tied Jewish law to general
medieval thought in its heavy emphasis on systematics (see Aquinas'
*Summa Theologica* or Dante's *Divine Comedy*)—a feature especially
evident in the most comprehensive and systematic of Jewish codes,
the *Mishneh Torah.* The codes marked a turning point for Jewish law
because of their tendency to freeze case law in rigid, conceptual frame-
works. The *Shulhan Arukh* is especially important in this regard.
Codes have had the same affect on American law. In recent years, in
states such as California and in the federal courts, the rules of evidence
that had previously been matters of unwritten practice were reduced to
codes and formal rules of evidence. Heretofore vague but useful doctrines, such as best evidence, privilege, or hearsay rules, have become
unjustifiable and often absurd when employed rigidly as a matter of
principle, rather than flexibly in those situations where they make
sense. Because the codes harden law in that way, the development of

Jewish codes was an important step toward the emergence of Orthodoxy.

## D. EXAMPLE OF CODIFICATION: MAIMONIDES ON PERSONAL INJURIES

As you read the following selection, note the following:
1. *Use of Multiple Sources.* Almost all of the Gemara's discussion on the elements of depreciation and humiliation for personal injury is found in Topic Four. It is shown there as it appears in *Bava Kamma*, chapter eight, the *locus classicus* for the talmudic laws of damages. Yet Maimonides writes a code that includes laws about a number of cases that are not treated there, but come from elsewhere in the Babylonian Talmud. He even includes some laws from the Palestinian Talmud. To insure that this feature of Maimonides' work is observed, here is a list of the sources of Maimonides' rules, other than Chapter Eight of *Bava Kamma*:

| | Chapter and Law in Maimonides | Rabbinic Source |
|---|---|---|
| 1. | 1:11, last clause | *Bava Kamma*, ch. 1 |
| 2. | 1:3 | *Sifra* on Lev. 24:20 |
| 3. | 1:7 | *Ketubbot*, ch. III, 32b (In *Bava Kamma* 26b and 85b, this ruling is based on a different source, i.e., Ex. 21:25) |
| 4. | 1:8, 9 | *Bava Kamma*, ch. II, 27a |
| 5. | 1:11, first paragraph | *Bava Kamma*, ch. II, 26a–26b |
| 6. | 1:11, second paragraph | P.T. *Bava Kamma*, ch. II, 3a |
| 7. | 1:12 | *Bava Kamma*, ch. II, 27a and Rashi there |
| 8. | 1:15 | *Bava Kamma*, ch. II, 26b |
| 9. | 1:16 | *Bava Kamma*, ch. V, 48 |
| 10. | 1:17 | *Bava Kamma*, ch. III, 32 |
| 11. | 1:19, first clause | *Sanhedrin*, ch. IX, 76b |
| 12. | 1:19, second clause | *Bava Kamma*, ch. III, 33 |
| 13. | 2:2, last two clauses | P.T. *Bava Kamma*, ch. VIII, 6b |
| 14. | 3:5, middle clause | P.T. *Bava Kamma*, ch. VIII, 6c |

In addition, Maimonides includes some rulings of post-talmudic origin. For example, the first and last clauses of Chapter Three, Law Five, are based on the geonic ruling discussed in Topic Eight, Section A-2, above, and Law Six of that chapter reflects Jewish practice in twelfth century Spain. Maimonides thus brings together material on a given topic from many different sources. Inevitably he is selective in his choices.

2. *No Citation of Sources.* Maimonides does not list the sources of his rulings since that would only complicate matters for his intended reader, that is, someone who simply wants to know what the law is. His failure to cite his sources, however, was the reason behind much of the criticism levelled against his code—and codes in general. We know his sources only because his defenders wrote commentaries to his code which list the probable sources for his rulings. If you lacked such commentaries, how would you react to his neat, undocumented code? Many of his readers found his code to be presumptuous in the extreme: his failure to cite sources made it seem as if Maimonides was creating all of Jewish law on his own authority.

3. *Deciding Disputes Without Mentioning Them.* The learned among Maimonides' readers objected to another facet of his work. In a number of instances he chooses one side of a talmudic dispute as the law, even if the matter was left undecided in the Talmud and later literature. Since he was presumably not writing for the learned, he never mentions where there is a disagreement, let alone explains why he chose as he did. Understandably, this raised the ire of many rabbis who chose differently. Even those who agreed with him often objected to his audacity in presenting his own opinion as the only possible one— as Jewish law, plain and simple. One example of this in the following selections is Chapter Two, Law Two, where he rules according to Rava over Abbaye in their dispute about temporary injuries in *Bava Kamma* 85b (see Topic Four, Section E).

4. *Presenting His Own Decisions as Established Law.* Once in a while Maimonides goes even further: he rules in a case not previously treated. When he does this, he sometimes indicates what he is doing, but he often does not. In Chapter One, Law Eighteen of our selections, for example, Maimonides rules in the case where the object used in the injury was lost. Vidal of Tolosa, a fourteenth century Spanish scholar who was one of Maimonides' chief defenders through his commentary on the *Mishneh Torah* entitled *Maggid Mishneh*, admits that the ruling is not found in the Gemara, but he quickly adds that the ruling is a correct one. In this case he does not have to argue very much on Maimonides' behalf because even R. Abraham b. David of Posquieres, one of Maimonides' sharpest detractors, agrees with his ruling. Regardless

of whether the ruling is a good one, Maimonides' presentation of it gives the reader no clue whatsoever that the ruling is his own and not based on previous authorities. In many cases, of course, other rabbis did not agree with Maimonides' interpretations of the Talmud or his rulings, and then he was roundly criticized both for his lack of candor in presenting his own opinion as law and for the substance of the ruling itself.

5. *Clarity.* Maimonides' code is clearer in both language and organization than any other Jewish code, and yet there are some passages where explanation is necessary. So, for example, Vidal finds it necessary to explain each clause in Chapter Two, Law Two.

The selections that follow are taken from Chapters One, Two, and Three of "The Laws Concerning Wounding and Damaging" in Maimonides' *Mishneh Torah.* They cover the assessment of damages and humiliation. In the paragraphs that have been omitted in those chapters, Maimonides explains the laws in regard to the other three elements involved in personal injuries (pain, medical expenses, involuntary idleness) in addition to a number of other, specific rulings on damages and humiliation.

MAIMONIDES, *MISHNEH TORAH*, LAWS CONCERNING WOUNDING AND DAMAGING (*HILKHOT HOVEL U'MAZIK*), CHAPS. I–III:

### Chapter One

1. A person who wounds another must pay him for five effects of the injury: damages, pain, medical expenses, involuntary idleness, and humiliation. These five effects must all be paid from the best of the injurer's property, as is the law for all who do wrongful damage.

2. How are the damages assessed? If someone cut off the hand or foot of another, we view him (the injured party) as if he were a slave being sold in the market: how much was he worth then (before the injury) and how much is he worth now? The tortfeasor must then pay the amount by which he diminished the victim's value, for it says, "Eye for an eye," and from tradition the Rabbis learned that the word translated "for" signifies monetary compensation.

3. When Scripture says, "If anyone maims his fellow, as he has done so shall it be done to him" (Leviticus 24:19), it does not mean that the injurer is actually to be wounded as he wounded the victim, but rather that he *deserves* to be deprived of a limb or wounded as he did, and therefore he must pay damages. For Scripture says, "You may not accept a ransom for the life of a murderer" (Numbers 35:31), implying that it is for the murderer alone that ransom may not be accepted, but it may be accepted for causing the loss of limbs or for inflicting wounds.

4. Similarly where Scripture says of one who wounds and injures another, "You must not show pity" (Deuteronomy 19:21), it means that you must not show pity in exacting payment: lest you say, "He is a poor man and did not injure the victim intentionally, and therefore I will pardon him," Scripture says, "You must not show pity."

5. How do we know that when Scripture says of limbs, "Eye for an eye" (Exodus 21:24), it means compensation? Because it says (in the verse immediately following), "bruise for bruise," and it also says explicitly, "When a man strikes another with stone or fist . . . he shall only pay for his idleness and his cure" (Exodus 21:18–19). You thus learn that the word "for" (*tahat*) in the case of a bruise (in Ex. 21:24) refers to monetary compensation, and the same must be true in regard to the use of "for" (*tahat*) in the case of the eye and the other limbs (in the same verse).

6. Even though these conclusions seem plausible from the context of the Written Torah and were all interpreted as such by Moses, our teacher, from Mount Sinai, they all have come down to us as practical law (and therefore their authority does not depend on our reasoning alone or on a tradition of interpretation). For so our ancestors have ruled in the court of Joshua and in the court of Samuel of Ramah, and in every court ever established from the time of Moses, our teacher, until the present day.

7. How do we know that one who injures another must pay separately for the pain he caused? Because Scripture says in regard to a man guilty of rape, "Because he has afflicted her" (Deuteronomy 22:19), and the same applies to anyone who subjects another to bodily pain: he must pay money in compensation for the pain caused.

8. How do we know that the tortfeasor is liable separately for the involuntary idleness and for the medical treatment? Because Scripture says, "But he must pay for the victim's loss of time and his cure" (Exodus 21:19).

9. How do we know that he is liable separately for humiliation? Because Scripture says, "And she puts out her hand and seizes him by his genitals, then you shall cut off her hand" (Deuteronomy 25:11–12). Included in this law is anyone who causes humiliation.

10. One who causes humiliation is liable only if he does so intentionally, as Scripture says, "And she puts out her hand" (ibid.); but one who humiliates another unintentionally is exempt. Therefore a person asleep or in a similar state is exempt if he humiliates somebody.

11. A person is always considered forewarned: (therefore) whether he acts by mistake or deliberately, whether he is awake, asleep, or drunk, if he injures someone or damages property, he must pay from the best of his possessions.

The rule that a sleeping person is liable to pay compensation applies only to the case where two lie down at the same time and one of them rolls over and injures the other or tears his clothes. However if a person was sleeping and another came and lay down beside him, the one who came last is considered the forewarned one, and if the sleeping person injured him, he is free of liability. Similarly, if someone left an article at the side of a sleeping man, and the latter breaks it, he is free of liability because the one who left it is considered forewarned and negligent.

12. If someone is blown off a roof by an ordinary wind and causes damage, he is liable for four effects but not for humiliation. If he is blown off the roof by an unusual wind, he is liable for damages alone, not for the other four effects. But if he turns over (to break his fall), he is liable for all five effects, including humiliation, because anyone who intends to cause damage is liable for humiliation even if he did not intend to humiliate.

·  ·  ·

16. One who injures another intentionally is liable for the five effects wherever the injury occurs. Even if one enters another person's property without permission and the owner injures him, the owner is liable because he has the right to expel him but not the right to injure him. However if the trespasser is injured by the owner accidentally, the owner is free from liability. If, on the other hand, the owner is injured by the trespasser accidentally, the trespasser is liable because he entered the premises without permission. If both have authority to enter the premises or neither has, and each is accidentally injured by the other, both are free from liability.

17. If one is chopping wood in a public domain and a piece of wood flies off and injures someone within a private domain, or if one is chopping in a private domain and injures someone within the public domain, or if one is chopping in a private domain and injures someone in another private domain, or if one enters a carpenter's shop, with or without permission, and a chip flies up and strikes him in the face, in each of these cases the one causing the injury is liable for four effects but free from paying for humiliation.

18. Just as we make an appraisal of the capacity to harm in the case of death, so we make such an appraisal in cases of injury. How so? If one struck another with a small pebble which is not large enough to cause injury, or with a small chip of wood, and it inflicts an injury which that object would not normally be expected to inflict, then the injuring party is free from liability, as it says, "with stone or fist" (Exodus 21:28), that is, with an object capable of causing injury. He is, however, liable for the humiliation alone, for even if he only spits on another person he would be liable for humiliation. Therefore witnesses must know by what means the injury was caused, and the

wounding instrument must be brought to court so that the court can appraise it and judge with it in mind. If the object is lost and the defendant says, "It was not large enough to cause injury, and therefore it is as if my hand was coerced," and the wounded man says, "It was large enough to inflict injury," then the latter may take an oath and receive compensation, as will be explained.

19. No appraisal is made in the case of iron because even a small needle can potentially kill, let alone injure a person.

### Chapter Two

1. One who inflicts a wound on another which involves culpability for all five effects must pay for all five. If the injury only involves four effects, then he must pay for the four; if it involves three, he must pay for the three; if two, he must pay for the two; if one, he must pay for the one.

2. How so? If someone cut off another's hand, foot, or finger, or if he made him blind in one eye, he must pay for all five effects, that is, damages, pain, medical expenses, involuntary idleness, and humiliation. If he struck him on the hand so that it swelled up but will eventually return to normal size, or in the eye such that it became inflamed but will eventually heal, he must pay for four effects, that is, pain, medical expenses, involuntary idleness, and humiliation. If he struck him on his head such that it swelled, he must pay for three effects, that is, pain, medical expenses, and humiliation. If he struck him in a place which is not seen—for example, if he struck him on his legs or back—he must pay for two effects, that is, pain and medical expenses. If he struck him with his handkerchief or with a document or something else, he must pay for only one effect, that is, humiliation.

### Chapter Three

1. How do we assess humiliation? Everything depends upon the relative status of the one who causes the humiliation and the one who is humiliated. The humiliation caused by an insignificant person is not the same as the humiliation caused by a great and respected individual: there is greater humiliation if the offender is a commoner.

2. If one humiliates a naked person or someone in a bath-house, he is free of liability. If the wind blows the hem of one's garment over his face such that he is exposed, and someone else uncovers him still more, the offender is liable for humiliation, but the humiliation of someone who is already exposed is not the same as the humiliation of someone who is not exposed at all. Similarly, if one lifts up his clothes to go down into a river or is coming up from a river and someone humiliates him, the offender is liable, but the humiliation of such a

person is not the same as the humiliation of someone who is fully clothed.

3. One who humiliates a sleeping person is liable for humiliation. If the person dies without waking up from his sleep and without feeling that someone humiliated him, we do not exact compensation for this humiliation from the offender. However, if the heirs seize money for the compensation [from the offender's property] we do not require them to give it back.

4. One who humiliates an imbecile is free of liability, but one who humiliates a deaf-mute is liable. One who humiliates a convert or a slave is held liable. If one humiliates a minor, he is liable if the minor feels ashamed when insulted, but if not, he is exempt. In any case, humiliation of a minor is not the same as humiliation of an adult; humiliation of a slave is not the same as humiliation of a free man, and humiliation of a deaf-mute is not the same as humiliation of a person with normal hearing and speech.

5. One who humiliates another through speech or by spitting on his clothing is exempt from paying compensation, but courts everywhere and at all times should institute preventive measures in this matter as they see fit. One who humiliates a scholar must pay him full compensation for humiliation, even if he does so only through speech. The law has already been determined that anyone who humiliates a scholar, even in speech, is to be fined and made to pay thirty-five *denar* in gold, which is equal in weight to nine *sela* less a quarter; and we have a tradition that this fine may be enforced everywhere, both inside and outside the land of Israel.

6. Cases of this kind occurred regularly in Spain. Some scholars would forgo their right to this money, and that was commendable of them, but some would make the claim and a compromise would be reached. The judges, however, would say to the offender, "You really owe him a pound of gold."

7. Even though one who humiliates an ordinary person through speech is not required to pay compensation, it is a great sin. Only a foolish scoundrel blasphemes and curses people. The Sages of old have said, "One who makes an honorable Israelite blanch by his words will have no share in the world to come."

. . .

11. The payments delineated above apply only to a respectable person, but a common person who is indifferent to these and other insults receives only an amount commensurate to his status, as the court determines, because there are contemptible people who do not care about being humiliated and degrade themselves all day long in every possible way out of mere sport and frivolity or to earn a penny from idle people seeking amusement.

# Topic Ten: Legislation (Takkanot)

## A. The Nature, Development, and Justification of Legislation in Jewish Law

Jewish law developed primarily through the judicial interpretations that were embodied in Midrash and responsa and summarized in the codes. The Bible specifically prohibits adding laws or deleting them (Deuteronomy 4:2 and 13:1). From a very early period, however, legislative revision of existing rules has existed in Jewish law in a form known as *takkanot* (singular, *takkanah*).

Despite the questions about the propriety of legislation as a source for legal development in Jewish law, the history of *takkanot* goes back almost to the beginning of Jewish law. The rabbis of the Talmud even ascribed *takkanot* to the patriarchs (their institution of prayers three times a day—*Ber.* 26b) as well as to Moses and Joshua (*B.K.* 80b–81b) and other biblical figures. Other *takkanot* are ascribed to Ezra and the men of the Great Assembly, but it is during the tannaitic period (70 C.E.–220 C.E.) that *takkanot* seem to have been accepted as a normal source for the development of Jewish law. Many *takkanot* were issued by the Sanhedrin, which effectively functioned as a legislative body as well as a Supreme Court. Rabbis continued promulgating *takkanot* throughout the Middle Ages and in the modern period as well, and the practice continues today.

The subjects covered by *takkanot* range the entire gamut of law, civil, criminal, family, ritual, and public. *Takkanot* issued by the Chief Rabbinate Council of Israel in 1943 and 1944, for example, provide for the payment of court fees, the introduction of adoption as a legal institution, the legal duty of a father to maintain his children until they reach the age of fifteen (rather than six, as prescribed by the Talmud), and the decision to hold spouses and children equal in their rights of intestate succession, regardless of sex. Talmudic and medieval *takkanot* provide for the transfer of property in new ways; they decree the punishment of flogging and even death for offenses not proscribed in the Torah; they institute the punishment of incarceration; they relax the procedural rules in criminal cases to allow circumstantial evidence; and they dispense with the requirement of prior warning when necessary to preserve public order in community emergencies.

The distinction between legislation and interpretive adjudication is not always clear, nor should we expect that other legal cultures share the American preference for a sharp separation between those officials who make the law and those who interpret the law in deciding cases. The English House of Lords combines lawmaking and appellate court functions in a single institution. Similar experiments were tried by New York and several other states early in the nineteenth century. Every year Congress and most state legislatures continue to pass large numbers of private bills, which are essentially legislative acts granting private relief in individual cases.

*Takkanot* are used either to fill a lacuna in the law that cannot be treated through interpretation or precedents, or to amend an existing law. Revision of the law through legislation is banned in the Torah, and, consequently, the rabbis used legislation sparingly in those subject areas which the Torah treats extensively, such as bodily injury and unlawful possession. On those topics interpretation was always the preferred mode of development. On the other hand, there are many *takkanot* on issues of property and communal obligations (such as, taxation) since the Torah is largely silent about those subjects. Moreover, those legal topics were particularly subject to change as Jews moved from one secular legal system to another, specifically from the Middle East and North Africa to France and Germany in the tenth and eleventh centuries, and from Western Europe to Eastern Europe in the fifteenth and sixteenth centuries.

Scholars spent considerable effort in justifying the use of legislation in the face of Deuteronomy 4:2 and 13:1. We will see in section B that Maimonides says that the Torah prohibits only legislation that presumes to share the primary authority of the Torah. The Torah is binding eternally, and no human legislation can alter it or attain its degree of authority. Rabbis may, however, enact supplementary laws by virtue of their powers in Deuteronomy 17 as long as they specify that these laws originate with them, and then all Israel must obey. R. Abraham b. David of Posquieres disagreed with Maimonides' theory:

Ra'avad's comment on *M.T.* Rebels 2:9:
All of this is a lot of hot air, for everything that they (contemporary rabbis) prohibited and proscribed in order to create a hedge around the Torah and guard it does not constitute a violation of the Torah's law against adding to it, even if they established it for all generations to come and made it seem like a law from the Torah by supporting it

with a Scriptural reference, as we find in a number of places [in the Talmud] where the verse quoted is only a general support for the Rabbinic law. . . . Violations of the law against adding to the Torah occur only in positive commandments like [adding to the four prescribed species for] the palm branch [on the Feast of Tabernacles], [the compartments of the] phylacteries, [the knots of] the fringes, or similar commandments, whether that be temporary or permanent and whether it be in a matter prescribed by the Torah or not.

Another, more popular, approach understood Deuteronomy 17 to refer to the identity of the legislators rather than the method of legislation. Thus R. Solomon b. Abraham Adret claimed that those verses only prohibit legislation by those acting without due authority. The rabbis of each generation, however, not only may, but must, enact new laws if that is necessary to fulfill their mandate under Deuteronomy 17:8–11 to solve the problems of their age (Novellae, Rashba, R.H. 16a).

Takkanot may be issued by the legal authorities of the day, in which case they are referred to as takkanot with no qualifying phrase, or they may be adopted by the lay leaders of a community or profession, in which case they are called takkanot ha-kahal, or "revisions of the community."

Takkanot ha-kahal do not become important until the tenth century, but they too have talmudic roots in a few cases of legislation by the townspeople (benei ha-ir) or their representatives in matters such as the prices of commodities, weights and measures, laborers' wages, and fines. The communities that produced most takkanot were those of Spain in the eleventh through the fifteenth centuries, France in the twelfth century, Germany in the thirteenth century, and the Eastern European countries in the sixteenth through the eighteenth centuries. As the Enlightenment spread throughout Central and Western Europe in the eighteenth and nineteenth centuries, the concomitant dissolution of the religious community's autonomy and the decrease in observance of Jewish law led to a gradual cessation of the enactment of takkanot ha-kahal. Only rabbinic takkanot have been promulgated in the twentieth century, and their number has been relatively small. The genre of responsa has been more popular in this age of decentralized communities and uncertain halakhic authority.

The use of takkanot ha-kahal as a source of the law and their acceptance by the rabbis may seem surprising in light of the emphasis in the Bible and Talmud on the authority of legal officials. How can those without rabbinic training be permitted to participate in so sensitive a task as lawmaking? Lay people were appointed by communal authorities to act as judges from early biblical times, and we have to assume that only a small minority of them had legal training. Rabbinic law clearly prefers schooled and authorized judges (*Mumhin*), but it recognizes that many civil cases will be decided by untrained people, whom the litigants choose on the spot, and it gives the verdicts of such courts its reluctant approval (Mishnah *Sanhedrin* 1:1, 3:1; Gemara *Sanhedrin* 4b–5a). Consequently our image of a professional judiciary is probably exaggerated: there was a legal oligarchy, but many legal proceedings were not carried on under its auspices. The law, in other words, was not the sole province of the officials: from earliest times lay people were heavily involved in the administration of the law.

The involvement of the laity in the development of Jewish law was consonant with feudal customs of the Christian nations in which Jews lived during the Middle Ages. Under feudalism the king did not rule as an absolute monarch, but consulted with his vassals on major governmental acts. In most times and places the king had to act with and through the other estates (nobility, ecclesiastics, commons). This was the king's "court of suitors," or the *"curia regis"* (king's court). Although this system was hardly democratic, it supported the idea that laws should be made by a deliberative, representative body. It was precisely in these centuries that *takkanot ha-kahal* were most widespread, consistent with the model of government that the Jews saw around them at the time.

It was both easier and harder to justify the authority of communal enactments (*takkanot ha-kahal*) than it was to justify rabbinic *takkanot*. It was easier because the rabbis limited communal enactments to matters governing human relations, and those are temporal and changeable. In contrast, ritual regulations, which only rabbinic *takkanot* could change, invoke the relationship between man and God, and that was eternal and immutable. On the other hand, the Torah never recognizes the authority of the community in any area of law. Those arguing for its power to legislate therefore had to expand the meaning of two biblical sources in order to justify that power.

The specifications of the king's powers in Deuteronomy 17:14–20 and I Samuel 8, and the specific examples of royal decrees in Former Prophets and in Chapter Ten of Ezra, were such sources. The community council was understood by later rabbis as a replacement for the king, especially since the king's powers from the very beginning were based on the people's demand to have a king (I Samuel 8). The other biblical source that was used to justify the community's lawmaking powers was the command in Exodus 23:2 to follow the majority of the court in judgment, which was expanded to enjoin following the majority in legislation too:

Rosh, *Responsa* 6:5, 7:
In regard to a matter concerning the public, the Torah enjoined following the majority, and . . . individuals must obey all that is assented to by the majority . . . because if it were not so, and the minority had the power to set aside the assent of the majority, the community would never agree on anything . . . for where would the community ever be in unanimous agreement?

These arguments are obviously analogies to other institutions established in the Bible; the power of the community has no clear biblical foundation. In light of that, the rabbis sought to buttress the community's authority by integrating its enactments into the corpus of Jewish law. While they recognized most communal *takkanot*, they used several devices to avoid those they did not like. They required, first, that *takkanot ha-kahal* be confirmed by a distinguished person living within the community, "distinguished person" being defined as a scholar who also was recognized by the community as its governor. The approval of that person would serve to link the community's action with rabbinic authority, even though the rabbi did not initiate the action. This explains why many of the *takkanot ha-kahal* are known by the names of the rabbis who approved them, so much so that it is often difficult to determine whether a given piece of legislation is a rabbinic *takkanah* or a communal *takkanah* that was later confirmed by a rabbi.

The rabbis sometimes invalidated a communal enactment on the ground that it was not just or equitable. This restriction could completely undermine the community's power to legislate, but in fact it was rarely invoked. Yet Solomon b. Abraham Adret said that if a communal enactment "does not protect the law or produce a real good, then even if it was instituted by the representatives and leaders of the public, the public need not act in accordance with their wishes" (*Responsa*, vol.7, no. 108). *Takkanot* falling under this rubic have included those that encourage moral laxity, prove to be too onerous for the community to sustain, apply retroactively to an earlier period, infringe on the rights of a minority or an individual, or do not apply equally to all.

A third restriction on communal enactments was that the rabbis reserved the authority to interpret and apply them. As a result, communal legislation gradually was integrated into Jewish law not only in subject matter but in literary form as rabbis increasingly cited it in their responsa.

These restrictions allayed rabbinic anxiety about *takkanot ha-kahal*; indeed the rabbis repeatedly confirmed the community's right to legislate. So, for example, R. Solomon b. Abraham Adret (thirteenth century) stated:

*Responsa*, vol. 3, no. 411:
No man is entitled to withdraw and disregard a communal ordinance by saying, "I shall not take part in the promulgation of the statutes," and the like, because the individual is subject to the majority will. . . . They [the majority] stand in the same relationship to the people of their town as the people of Israel to the Supreme Court or the king.

In fact, the rabbis expanded the power of the majority of the community to bind future generations and temporary residents by their enactments. They also approved of vesting the majority's authority in elected representatives, thus facilitating democratic government.

These developments produce a tension within Jewish law that we have seen before, and the next topic, on custom, will demonstrate yet another manifestation of it: that is the tension between the imposed will of God, as mediated by the rabbis, and the will of the people. Biblical leaders (kings, priests, prophets, judges) were not popularly elected, and neither were the kings and judges in Second Temple and rabbinic times. Nevertheless, their authority was partially dependent on the acquiescence of the people, and some lost not only their positions, but their lives, when they did not have public support. Democracy was apparently the rule among the members of the Sanhedrin, but that was only in the context of making a decision, not in choosing the membership. Medieval synods seem to have been a bit closer to majoritarian rule, but it is important to see that they are not that. The delegates to the synods were not necessarily rabbis, and that represents a step in the democratic direction; but the need for rabbinic approval of *takkanot ha-kahal* indicates that authority in Jewish law still does not rest with the people. On the other hand, as the following sources will demonstrate, it does not rest solely with the rabbis either.

## B. MAIMONIDES ON LEGISLATION: MISHNEH TORAH, LAWS OF REBELS (MAMRIM)

Maimonides' treatment of the power of courts in the following passage is probably the most systematic statement on the issue in Jewish law. Skill in organizing diverse materials is typical of Maimonides. Another common characteristic of his writings is also illustrated here. He records his interpretation and application of the law with no hint that others understand or apply it differently. Thus the *Sifre* establishes that the rabbis have the authority to interpret the Torah's laws, and violation of their interpretations constitutes a violation of two of the Torah's laws ("Act according to the instruction which they give you," "You must not deviate from the verdict that they announce to you," both parts of Deut. 17:11). Maimonides, however, extends this duty of strict obedience to the "ordinances, decrees, and customs which they instruct the masses to observe." R. Moses b. Nahman (Nahmanides, 1195–1270), in his comments on Maimonides' *Book of Commandments* (Root One, Number Four), objects to this strongly. If Maimonides is correct, argues Nahmanides, then all of the words of the scribes (rabbis) become negative and positive commandments of the Torah, and we should be stringent in enforcing all of the words of the rabbis because they are derived from the Torah since the Torah commanded "Do not deviate, and so on" and similarly enjoined "Act according to the instruction which they give you." Maimonides' extension of the *Sifre* passage is inconsistent not only with the Talmud but also with what he himself says in another place in the following passage (1:5).

Maimonides' interpretation of Deuteronomy 17:11, at the end of Chapter One, Law Two, in this selection, is also his own invention, but you would never know it from the text. He presents his exegesis of that verse as if it were the obvious and commonly accepted meaning. Similarly, his interpretation of the mishnaic rule concerning the qualifications of courts that may overturn precedents (2:2) is by no means obvious or unanimous. The Mishnah (*Eduyot* 1:5) says that the later court must be of a "greater number" than its predecessor. Since all supreme courts consisted of seventy-one judges, Maimonides understands that phrase to refer to the number of contemporary sages who agree with the later court's decision (*Mishneh Torah, Hilkhot Mamrim*, 2:1–2). In contrast, R. Abraham b. David of Posquieres, in his commentary on this Mishnah, follows the Jerusalem Talmud in understanding "number" to refer to the number of years, or age, of the jurists. A modern commentator on the Mishnah, Hanokh Albeck, claims that *takkanot* could be instituted by courts of all sizes and not just the Supreme Court of seventy-one. He consequently interprets "number" in that same Mishnah in terms of the number of jurists who belonged to the court which instituted the decree in contrast to the number of judges on the court which now wants to change it. Since the context of the Mishnah speaks of judges of the court and not their age or respected rabbis outside the court, Albeck is probably closest to the original meaning of the text.

None of the sources disagree regarding the authority of courts to instruct the masses to observe "ordinances, decrees, and customs," even though they disagree as to the source of that authority. The power is so broad that it enables later courts to suspend precedents and even the laws of the Torah itself in an emergency situation, "just as a physician may amputate a man's hand or foot to save his life." Although Maimonides is the first to use that analogy, his ruling is based on the following talmudic precedent:

> *Sanhedrin* 46a:
> It has been taught: R. Eliezer b. Jacob said: I have heard [from my teachers] that the court may impose flagellation and pronounce [capital] sentences even where not warranted by the Torah, yet not with the intention of disregarding the Torah but, on the contrary, in order to safeguard it. It once happened that a man rode a horse on the Sabbath in the Greek period and he was brought before the court and stoned, not because he was liable for that but because it was required by the times. Again, it happened that a man once had intercourse with his wife under a fig tree [that is, in public]. He was brought before the court and flogged, not because he merited it, but because the times required it.

There is always the danger, of course, that the emergency power will be abused, as in the case of many South American countries where "emergencies" justifying martial law have lasted for decades. It nevertheless is necessary for societies to provide for such situations, and even the United States Constitution contemplates the suspension of habeus corpus. What makes such a provision noteworthy in Jewish law is that despite the belief that the Torah is the eternally valid word of God, temporal legal authorities are empowered to suspend its rules when necessary.

Similarly, Maimonides insists that before instituting a decree, the court must determine whether the majority of the community can and will live up to it, and if the court legislates but the majority disobeys, the law should be abrogated. This concern for the acceptability of the law is readily understandable when a legislature considers a new law and must weigh the prospect of pervasive disobedience. Massive communal disobedience may also prompt a legislature to abrogate a law. Prohibition of alcohol and laws forbidding the smoking of marijuana, gambling, and private sexual acts between consenting adults are recent examples in American law. These common law analogies would lead us to expect Jewish synods to be concerned about public reaction in legislating revisions in the law, and so they are. The extent to which this is the case, however, is surprising in light of the fact that the ultimate authority behind *takkanot* is God. Since religions are supposed to be challenging and normative, one would expect that the religious context of Jewish legislation would enable legal authorities to legislate more freely against the public will, but that is decidedly not the case.

The second clause of Maimonides' ruling is even more remarkable. It deals with the enforcement of legislation in a specific case. If a law is enacted but the majority continues to disobey, the law is unenforceable. Secular courts face similar situations, but they do not invalidate laws on this ground. Courts commonly dismiss charges based on unpopular laws so that the law is not challenged, but not enforced either. More dramatic examples occur when judges or juries hear a case but hand down a verdict of acquittal despite overwhelming evidence for conviction. The common law provides no appellate review of such verdicts, and that leaves effective power in the jury to nullify criminal laws, although legal scholars are divided as to the legitimacy of this method of circumventing an unpopular law. When a court does annul a law, it is not on the stated ground that the law is widely disobeyed; it is always for some purported constitutional reason, such as, that widespread disobedience makes enforcement "unusual punishment" or deprives the defendant of "equal protection of the laws."

Jewish courts act in all of these ways too, but, as Maimonides says, they also may annul a law on grounds of widespread disobedience. Moreover, legislators are duty-bound to insure social acceptance before they legislate. Once again, the religious context of Jewish legislation makes this especially surprising. If secular courts generally lack the power to rescind human legislation, how can Jewish courts abrogate what is theoretically God's law? Moreover, how can they construe public disobedience as sufficient grounds for nullification?

Maimonides does not explain why the community's level of disobedience is so important in determining the authority of a *takkanah*, but several factors are clearly involved. A *takkanah* is enforceable only within communities whose rabbinic or lay leaders have enacted it. It is thus closely tied to a specific community, and hence widespread disobedience within that community effectively undermines it in practice. Maimonides probably also wanted to avoid having laws on the books that were not obeyed lest that lead to a general disrespect for the law. Rabbinic theology reenforces the importance of the community's support. The tradition claims that while the people are not prophets, they are at least children of prophets (*Pesahim* 66a). Communal disobedience therefore suggests that the objectionable *takkanah* is a mistake in the transmission of God's word.

While we may surmise that some or all of these factors motivated Maimonides' statement, it still is troubling. One wonders whether it was ever applied in practice, and, if so, how. These analogies suggest some possibilities, but both the rationales for Maimonides' statement and its mode of operation remain unclear. Whatever our difficulties with this, however, the fact that Jewish courts can revoke *takkanot* for such a reason illustrate graphically how much the authority of Jewish law depends on social acquiescence to its demands. God and His rabbinic representatives may lay down the law, but its effective authority depends crucially on the practices of the people. For just that reason Maimonides announces in the introduction to the *Mishneh Torah* that the Talmud is more authoritative than the decrees of the geonim, in part because the latter were not practiced by all the People Israel while the Talmud was. Social acceptance determines the authority of *takkanot* and it plays an even more direct role in shaping the content and authority of Jewish law through its manifestation as custom, the subject of the next topic.

MAIMONIDES, *Mishneh Torah*, LAWS OF REBELS:

Chapter One

1. The Supreme Court (*Sanhedrin*) in Jerusalem is the root of the Oral Law. Its members are the pillars of instruction, the source of statutes and judgments for all Israel, and it is they that the Torah authorized to rule, as it says, "Act according to the instruction which they give you" (Deut. 17:11). That is a positive commandment. . . .

2. Anyone who does not obey their instruction violates a negative commandment, as it says, "You must not deviate from the verdict that they announce to you either to the right or to the left" (ibid.). . . . Whether they derived their rulings from an oral tradition (that is, the Oral Law), or deduced them through their own application of any of the hermeneutical rules by which the Torah is interpreted (such that it seemed to them that the matter is to be decided in such-and-such a way), or made a hedge around the law according to the needs of the hour through decrees, ordinances, or (the strengthening of new) customs, it is a positive commandment to obey them in each of these three categories [of decision], and anyone who disobeys any of those transgresses a negative commandment. For Scripture says: "You shall act in accordance with the instructions given you" (Deuteronomy 17:11), which refers to the ordinances, decrees, and customs which they instruct the masses to observe in order to strengthen religion and improve the world; "and the ruling handed down to you" (ibid.), which refers to rulings which they derive through reasoning, using one of the hermeneutic principles by which the Torah is interpreted; "you must not deviate from the verdict that they announce to you" (ibid.), which refers to the chain of oral traditions that they received.

3. . . . If some [members of the Supreme Court] saw a need to institute a decree, enact an ordinance, or confirm a custom, and some saw no need to do that, they discussed the matter, decided according to the majority, and acted accordingly.

4. . . . After the Supreme Court ceased to exist, controversies multiplied among the Jewish people: one person declared something pure, another impure, each giving a reason for his ruling; one forbade something while another permitted it.

5. If two scholars or courts disagree with each other when there is no Supreme Court in existence or before the Supreme Court had clarified the matter, whether they rule simultaneously or consecutively, one declaring something pure and the other impure, one forbidding something and the other permitting it, and you do not know which is the law, then act according to the more stringent opinion if a Scriptural law is involved and according to the more lenient opinion if a Rabbinic law is at issue.

### Chapter Two

1. If the Supreme Court used one of the hermeneutic principles to deduce a ruling which, in its judgment, expressed the law, and it rendered a decision to that effect, but a later court found a reason to set aside the ruling, then the later court may indeed set it aside and rule according to its own judgment, as the Torah says: "[appear before] . . . the judge in charge in those days" (Deuteronomy 17:9), that is, you are bound to obey the court in your generation.

2. If a [Supreme] Court issued a decree, enacted an ordinance, or introduced a custom, and their action was universally accepted in the Jewish community, but another, later court sought to rescind the former action by abrogating the ordinance, decree, or custom, then it may do so only if it is greater than the first in wisdom and number. If it was greater in wisdom but not in number, or in number but not in wisdom, it cannot invalidate the former court's ruling, even if the reason which prompted the earlier court to enact its decree or ordinance no longer holds. How is it possible for the later court to be greater in number in light of the fact that every [Supreme] Court consists of 71 judges? The "number" referred to is the number of sages of the age who agree with the Supreme Court's decision and accept it without demur.

3. The last clause applies only to prohibitive measures which were not instituted to create a hedge around the Torah; decrees and prohibitions which were instituted for that purpose and which were universally accepted by the Jewish community may not be abrogated or dissolved by any later court, even if it was greater than the first court [that enacted the measure].

4. However, even such things may be abrogated temporarily, even if the court that does so is inferior to the original court that instituted the decree. For such decrees cannot be more stringent than the commands of the Torah itself, which any court may suspend as an emer-

gency measure. How so? If a court finds it necessary to strengthen religion and create a hedge so that the people will not transgress the Torah's commands, then it may inflict flagellation and other punishments which are not warranted by the law, but it may not establish the measure for all generations, proclaiming that this is the law. Similarly, if it sees fit to abolish a positive commandment or transgress a negative commandment as an emergency measure to bring the masses back to religion or save them from being corrupted, then it may do so according to the needs of the hour. Just as a physician may amputate a man's hand or foot to save his life, so the court may occasionally instruct people to disobey some of the commandments so that the commandments as a whole may be preserved, just as the early Sages said: "Desecrate one Sabbath for him [a sick person] so that he may be able to observe many Sabbaths" (*Yoma* 85b).

5. A court that sees fit to institute a decree, enact an ordinance, or introduce a custom must first determine whether the majority of the community can live up to it. At no time may a decree be imposed on a community unless the majority of its members can bear it.

6. If the court issued a decree that seemed bearable for the majority, but after its issuance the people made light of it and its observance did not spread to most of the community, then that decree is null and void, and the court may not force people to obey it.

7. If a court issued a decree which seemed to spread to the whole Jewish community, and that was the state of things for many years, but after a long time another court investigated and found that observance of the decree was not widespread, then the later court may abrogate it, even if the later court was lesser than the former one in wisdom and number.

8. Any court that permitted two things [that had been declared forbidden] should not rush to permit a third thing.

9. Since a court can issue decrees prohibiting what is permitted and its prohibition can endure for generations, and since it can similarly permit matters which the Torah forbids for a period of time, what is the import of the Torah's warning, "You shall not add anything to what I command you or take anything away from it" (Deuteronomy 13:1)? It is that we not add to the words of the Torah or subtract from them and establish such a measure forever as if it were from the Torah itself, whether the Written Torah or the Oral Torah. For example, it is written in the Torah, "Do not seethe a kid in its mother's milk" (Exodus 23:19). The traditional understanding of this verse is that it forbids cooking and eating milk with meat, whether it be the flesh of a domestic animal or that of a wild animal, but the flesh of fowl may be eaten with milk according to Biblical law. If a court permits [eating or cooking] the meat of a wild animal with milk, it would be eliminating

one of the commandments of the Torah; and if it forbids [the eating or cooking] of the flesh of fowl [with milk], claiming that that is within the category of a kid and is therefore forbidden by Biblical law, that would constitute adding to the commandments of the Torah. But the court may say this: "[Eating or cooking] the flesh of fowl [with milk] is permitted by the Torah, but we forbid it." It then must inform the people that the decree has been made in order to prevent violations of the law. For some would argue that the flesh of fowl [with milk] is permitted because it is not expressly forbidden [in the verse], and therefore the flesh of wild animals [with milk] is also permitted since it too is not expressly forbidden [in the verse]. Others would say that even the meat of domesticated animals may be [eaten and cooked with milk] except for that of a goat. Others might claim that even the flesh of a goat may be eaten with the milk of a cow or a sheep because the verse states, "its mother's milk," thereby forbidding only the milk of the same species. And some might argue that [eating a kid's meat] even in the milk of a goat other than its mother is permitted since the verse says, "its mother." Therefore we will forbid [eating and cooking] all flesh with milk, even the flesh of fowl. That would not constitute adding to the Torah but would rather be making a hedge around it. And the status of all similar legislation is the same [that is, not a violation of Deuteronomy 13:1].

## C. Takkanot of Rabbenu Tam (R. Jacob b. Meir), c. 1100–1171

Rabbenu Tam was probably the leading French scholar of the twelfth century. On a standard page of Talmud text, the only commentaries that invariably appear are those of Rashi, his grandfather, and the *Tosafot* ("additions"), many of which are based on R. Tam's explanations, glosses, and decisions. He was recognized by all contemporary scholars, even those in remote places, as the greatest scholar of his generation, and he used his reputation to assert his authority over the Jewish communities of Provence and Germany in addition to those of northern France, where he lived.

In both his exegesis of talmudic texts and his legal decisions R. Tam was generally very conservative, but the respect he enjoyed enabled him to introduce important legal permissions dictated by the times. For example, the Mishnah clearly forbids Jews to engage in business with Gentiles on the day of their holidays, three days before, and three days after, lest Jews be enticed into their worship. That ruling was both sensible and practical for the rabbis of the Mishnah, who were referring to the yearly Saturnalia of the Romans, but it was totally unworkable for Jews living among Christians, who have a holiday every Sunday. Despite the clarity of the language of the Mishnah, R.

Tam managed to interpret the text in a rather forced way in order to permit Jews to engage in business with Christians, and that was absolutely essential since the Christians forbade Jews from engaging in agriculture and many crafts.

R. Tam himself was a moneylender and winemaker, and he became rather well-to-do. His business affairs brought him into contact with the nobility and the authorities, who caused him much trouble. To a great extent, his attitude toward non-Jews in various halakhic questions, as reflected in the first set of *takkanot* which follow, was conditioned by his direct contact with them and his knowledge of their attitudes toward Jews. Because the Christians forced Jews to engage in business, Jewish men often had to be away from home, and the second set of *takkanot* which follows sought to regulate such business trips in order to preserve family life (a remarkably modern problem for men and women). The third group is the "Code of R. Tam," which was preserved in that form by later authorities and includes his responsa on a number of questions.

These *takkanot* provide clear evidence of the process, power, and background assumptions of medieval *takkanot*. The *takkanot* were instituted "with a scroll of the Torah" in hand, but they "will stand effective if approved by our masters." The process, in other words, invoked the sanction of the Torah, but it was not through an assertion of revelation; it was clearly by vote of the representatives of the districts involved. Several types of representatives are mentioned: sages, leaders, inhabitants, and elders. The body that enacted *takkanot* was thus not restricted to rabbis alone. It included a broad representation of the laity. Nevertheless the *takkanot* are issued in the name of Rabbenu Tam in order to give them added authority.

The sanction that is mentioned most often is that of *herem*, excommunication, since that was a powerful penalty that the communities could effectively impose. Its power was broadened by the expectation of mutual reciprocity, that is, that each community would recognize and enforce bans of excommunication imposed by another community. Nevertheless excommunication was not the only method for ensuring obedience. Others included the association of these *takkanot* with the laws of the Torah and with the words of the Creator Himself through the ceremony of enactment; respect for the famous rabbis and leaders involved; the assertion that the *takkanot* are internally "good and upright"; the confidence that they will ultimately produce peace; and the claim, at least in some cases, that they are "in accordance with ancient custom." We shall investigate the ties between customs and *takkanot* in the next topic, but for now note that *takkanot* are rationalized by the broadest possible spectrum of rationales and that among those are assertions that they represent the ongoing tradition of revelation, law, and custom, even though their very name and form declare that they are revisions of the law.

These sources illustrate the ambivalent relationship of the Jewish communities of twelfth century France with the Christian government. On the one hand, the whole thrust of the first group of *takkanot* is to prevent Jews from bringing their lawsuits to the gentile courts, and the one exemption from those provisions is for the Jew who acts under the government's duress. These rules bespeak a suspicious and sometimes hostile relationship. On the other hand, the gentile courts are to be used if a defendant refuses to appear before the Jewish courts, and they are even to be used to enforce these rulings preventing Jews from trying cases before them.

Finally, note that these *takkanot* considerably expand the law regarding personal injuries. A person who strikes another in the synagogue is to be fined double the amount that he would have to pay if the incident occurred elsewhere. Since this is a *takkanah*, one would expect that this double fine is an innovation unknown in previous sources. This is surprising, since the Babylonian Talmud specifically denies the right of authorities outside of Israel who have not been ordained to impose any fines. As we have seen, the geonim circumvented that restriction by inventing ways to assess and require compensation in cases of personal injuries, but this *takkanah* goes further. The court outside of Israel may impose a fine on the culprit beyond compensation for the injury itself. Moreover, women and relatives are accepted as witnesses in such cases "and in any matter of contention where it is not usual that witnesses should be present." The legal authorities of the time were clearly determined to enable Jewish law to settle all types of dispute within the community, and they were willing to alter longstanding, restrictive, procedural rules to accomplish that. Above all, Jewish law would not be allowed to petrify; *takkanot* were adopted to provide whatever was necessary to insure its viability.

A *Takkanah* of Rabbenu Tam and Others on Relationships with the Gentile Courts and Governments, in Louis Finkelstein, *Jewish Self-Government in the Middle Ages* (New York: The Jewish Theological Seminary of America, 1924), pp. 155–158.

[The introduction, which is in the usual style of the French rabbis of the period, recites the serious troubles that had come upon the Jews because of denunciations. Some had defamed their fellows in secret, other had committed the crime in public, with equally dire results. The ordinance continues thus:]

Therefore have we taken counsel together, the elders of Troyes and her Sages, and those of her vicinity, the Sages of Dijon and its vicinity, the leaders of Auxerre, and of Sens and its suburbs, the elders of Orleans (?), and the vicinity, our brothers, the inhabitants of Chalon-sur-Saone, the Sages of the Rhine country, and our masters of Paris, and their neighbors, the scholars of Melun and Etampes, and the inhabitants of Normandy, and the shore of the sea, and Anjou and Poitiers, the greatest of our generation, the inhabitants of the land of Lorraine; of those mentioned here, some have already agreed and from some we have not yet heard, but since the matter was pressing, we were confident (in their agreement) knowing that they are great men who listen to their inferiors, and knowing that the decision is a correct one, which if it were not written down, ought to be written down.

1. We have voted, decreed, ordained and declared under the *herem*, that no man or woman may bring a fellow-Jew before Gentile courts or exert compulsion on him through Gentiles, whether by a prince or a common man, a ruler or an inferior official, except by mutual agreement made in the presence of proper witnesses.

2. If the matter accidentally reaches the Government or other Gentiles, and in that manner pressure is exerted on a Jew, we have decreed that the man who is aided by the Gentiles shall save his fellow from their hands, and shall secure him against the Gentiles who are aiding him so that the Jew may not be harmed or even be in apprehension because of the Gentiles, nor shall he lose his claim or his property. He shall see to it that his fellow shall be in no fear of them, and he shall make satisfaction to him and secure him in such manner as the seven elders of the city will ordain. If there is no such board in his town, he shall act on the order of those of the nearest city in which such are to be found.

3. He shall not intimidate the "seven elders" through the power of Gentiles. And because the masters of wicked tongue and informers do their deeds in darkness, we have decreed also excommunication for indirect action unless he satisfy him in accordance with the decision of the "seven elders" of the city.

4. It was further decreed that he should apply to them (to the "seven elders") on the first possible day, and that he should return the damage in accordance with all that they decree to him.

5. No man shall try to gain control over his neighbor through a king, prince or judge, in order to punish or fine or coerce him, either in secular or religious matters, for there are some who play the part of saints and do not live up to ordinary standards.

6. He who transgresses these three decrees of ours [that is, (1), (2)–(4), and (5), which forbids a Jew to accept a Jewish communal office at the hands of Gentiles] shall be excommunicated, all Israel shall keep apart from him, those who sign (this decree) as well as those who do not sign, their pupils, and the pupils of their pupils, their comrades, great and small.

7. As for him who transgresses our decree, his bread is [prohibited like] that of a Samaritan, his wine is that of [idolatrous] libations, his books are as those of the magicians, and whoever converses with him is like him, and he shall be in excommunication like him. But he who takes these matters to heart, and is apprehensive of the words of our Creator and our words, will find our words good and upright. There is an old ordinance against informers, *malshinim*, and those who tell tales in secret; if a man sin against man, let him be judged by proper judges, but let not the hand of a stranger pass among them, and let them behave themselves with sanctity and purity, separating themselves from the peoples of the land, then shall each come to his destination in peace.

8. If because of the fear of the Government, a man speak to the informer occasionally, this excommunication shall not fall on that man, provided he does not use this pretext to multiply words with him. This is an application of the principle given in regard to the fasting of pregnant and nursing women on fastdays other than Yom Kippur and Tisha B'Av, — "they need not fast, but yet they must not indulge in delicacies; they may only eat and drink for the sake of the child."

9. If one refuses to come to Court and there are proper witnesses in regard to the matter and the plaintiff collects a claim through the power of Gentiles, our excommunication will not apply.

10. We, the undersigned, request all those that are in touch with the Government to coerce through the power of Gentiles anyone who transgresses our commandments, in order that the Scriptural injunction, "to observe very much and to carry out" what they are commanded, may be fulfilled. And righteous action leads to peace.

Samuel b. Meir
Jacob b. Meir (Rabbenu Tam)
Samuel b. Jacob
Isaac b. Solomon Troyes.

*On Absentee Husbands:*
[Omitting the first paragraph, the text may be rendered as follows:[

1. We have decreed in consonance with a letter which we have received from Dreux that no one shall be permitted to leave his wife for more than eighteen months without permission of the Court of the nearest city, unless he receive the consent of his wife in the presence of proper witnesses.

2. We have permitted the absence of eighteen months only to such as leave out of necessity to earn and provided the husband is at peace with his wife.

3. No one may remain away from his wife against her will unless the Court of Seven Elders before whom the matter is taken permit the continuance of his stay. The Court may give the husband permission to remain absent according to the circumstances, for example, if he must collect his debts or if he is engaged in study or learning to write or he is engaged in business.

4. When the husband returns from his journey he must remain at home for no less than six months before undertaking a second journey.

5. But in no case may one forsake his wife as the result of a quarrel or with bitter feelings, but only with the consent of the Court in the manner described. Each man must send his wife the means for her livelihood every six months. He must make payment through the Court for whatever debts were contracted in his absence in order to maintain his family and give his children their education in accordance with the law of the Talmud (*Ketubbot* 50a).

6. One who is able to do so must before leaving on a journey give his wife sufficient means for the support of the family.

7. We have decreed that no one shall evade the law and leave unless he is sincerely attached to his wife, and no one may refuse to return home after being summoned by the Court of the city in which his wife resides, or the Court of the nearest city, if there is none in that city. He must return within six months from the time of the call.

8. Anyone transgressing this ordinance shall be refused hospitality and shall be excommunicated.

This decree was enacted "with a scroll of the Torah and the 613 commandments" and it will stand effective if approved by our masters.

R. Tam wrote that is a proper decree and in accordance with ancient custom and "we agree to it in accordance with the view of our masters in France."

The Code of Takkanot of R. Tam (Finkelstein, *Jewish Self-Government*, 179–91):
These are the Takkanot of R. Jacob who is called R. Tam.
1. Not to mention his sin to a repentant.
2. Not to rent for a whole year the house of a Gentile in which a Jew has lived (after the removal of the Jew).
3. In a place where a great Rabbi lived in former times we may assume the existence of a *herem Beth Din* (court power to excommunicate) and one must stand trial there.
4. If a man divorces his wife against her will and she marries thereafter, he is free and is not called a "transgressor." If he

gave her a writ of divorce with her consent and it is found to
be invalid, he may divorce her against her will.

5. If a man apprehends that he will be defamed to the government, he may interrupt the prayers of the afternoon or the
morning, even on the Sabbath, until they do him justice;
one may announce a *herem* (ban of excommunication) compelling the defamer to reveal to him what he said to the
ruler.

6. If one transgresses a *herem Beth Din* (a court-imposed ban
of excommunication), he should be compelled to make
amends.

7. To come under the *herem* to "bring the tithe to the treasure
house" one must be but one month in the city. Members of
a community who cannot give charity may compel others
who can afford to give, provided they (those who cannot
give) are not appointed treasurers of the funds.

8. Not to take a *Tallit* (prayer shawl) or *Mahzor* (High Holiday
prayerbook) from a Synagogue without the permission of
the owner.

9. Not to strike one's neighbor. If one did strike another, no release is to be granted him until he performs or agrees to perform the decree of the Court. The fine of one who strikes
another shall be twenty-five dinars, and if the quarrel occurred in the Synagogue, fifty dinars. If the assailed turned
and struck the assailant, he loses his rights. Women and relatives are accepted as witnesses in this case and in any matter of contention where it is not usual that witnesses should
be present. Similarly for one accused of defamation they are
accepted, even though they give only circumstantial evidence since there could not possibly be a witness present
when the denunciation was made.

10. Not to tear the margin of a book even in order to write on it.

11. Not to accept Church vessels as security for debt.

12. Not to read another's letters.

13. One need not go to a distant city to a great Rabbi, but in
the city which is nearest the complainant. The summons
should call one to go to one of the three nearest cities which
have a *herem Beth Din*. If there is a great Rabbi in the vicinity he may not refuse to issue the summons. The summons
should call upon the defendant to appear before the Court of
one of the three nearest cities. If the defendant is (not?) in a
settled community, the statement of the agent of the Court
that he delivered the summons is to be accepted as final.

14. If a man is not in the city (or even if he is in the city) and his
wife demands her maintenance, a *herem* may be announced
against all who know aught of his property, and even bailments are to be reported.

# Topic Eleven: Custom (Minhag)

A. THE RECOGNITION OF BINDING CUSTOMS IN JEWISH AND COMMON LAW

A survey of the institutions of Jewish law would be seriously deficient without some examination of the place of custom in the structure. The distinction between law and custom often appears artificial and has been a fertile source of scholarly disagreement among lawyers, anthropologists, and philosophers. When law and custom are contrasted, the distinction which is often drawn is that custom arises from habitual, longstanding, communal practice, while law is created by a conscious, legislative act. This distinction does not work out perfectly, for many laws are the result of accumulated social practice, custom is one form of law in many societies, and law greatly influences customary practices. These uncertainties are not a sign that the basic distinction is sloppy or unserviceable; they reflect the practical reality that most legal norms have a variety of sources that overlap and cannot be untangled without distortion. Accepting these limits, this topic will examine the role of customary practices in the system of Jewish law.

The attitudes of common law and rabbinic law toward custom are quite similar in important respects. Both systems are notable for their appreciation of traditional rules and for their acceptance of norms that are not based on, or embodied in, an explicit provision of positive law. In both systems, much, if not most, law develops unconsciously and informally as the group carries out and repeats the patterns of its activity. One of the root meanings of "common law" is the body of norms based on the common practices of Englishmen. Both Jewish law and modern, secular law recognize that custom influences law, contributes to its development, and sometimes may even displace it. Just what is meant by custom, how it arises, and how it gains normative force are not totally clear in either system. Despite these important similarities, three major differences between the two legal systems in their attitudes regarding custom should be delineated at the outset to prepare the reader for some of the uncertainties that must follow.

421

## 1. *The Stability and Homogeneity of Society.*

As a group of people live together for a long time, they develop expectations of what is proper social behavior and what sorts of deviance from these patterns are tolerable. Two prime expectations are likely to be that members of the group will conform to conventional patterns of behavior and that problems will be dealt with next time the way they were handled last time. If the society is stable, these expectations will become increasingly fixed over time, and the range of tolerable deviance will become clear. Members of the group eventually will consider themselves bound by customary practices, which will thereby become the law of the group. Only later will the practices be collected, written down, and codified in some orderly set of positive laws. This would appear to describe the essential process of legal growth which resulted in the Pentateuch. Custom has continued to develop in stable Jewish communities since ancient times, and these practices supplement, give meaning to, and sometimes modify the law as written.

In contrast, the current generation in most Western societies has lost the homogeneity and stability upon which customary law rests. Change, not stability, the novel and the unexpected, not the familiar, predominate. The homogeneity of locality, family, class, and ethnicity have been weakened as a community of strangers tries to live together as autonomous individuals, each one forced to confront the conflicting values, practices, and expectations of others. Contemporary secular society finds it difficult to define traditional offenses against community tranquility, such as disorderly conduct, disturbing the peace, or obscenity, precisely because it lacks those shared expectations and a recognition of the limits of tolerance for deviance. In a more stable situation it would be much easier to define the point at which the behavior of a group of young people coming home from a party late at night would be a disturbance of the peace. Some communities might be very tolerant, others quite repressive, but the custom would be easily recognized by everyone. Similarly, one could identify the obscene, which American law now recognizes as a matter of communal standards. Without a stable referent these lines are obscured, and we cannot describe customs with certainty even if we are aware of the wrongness of the behavior. As one justice of the Supreme Court has said about obscenity, we may not be able to define it, but we still know it when we see it.

## 2. *The Scope of Law.*

The Jewish tradition sees heaven and earth as filled by law. The natural world obeys its laws without question, but people have the gift of choice, the knowledge of good and evil. Each of myriad choices carries a moral value: there is a right thing to do, a correct way to perform every ordinary act. The sum of all right choices is the halakhah. People are guided in making their choices by instruction embodied in the tradition. Sometimes this guidance is in the form of a positive or negative commandment from Sinai, sometimes in a rule of a rabbinic court authoritatively announced, sometimes in advice from a particular rabbi, and sometimes this guidance can be seen only in the accepted ways people behave, the communal habits that are custom. You can tell the laws of birds by watching their flight; you can tell the laws of people by watching their journey. In such a system, law and custom are two components of a single stream that defines correct behavior.

Modern secular society usually holds a more limited view of normative law. People must do that which they are commanded by positive law, but there is not a law governing every matter, and outside the area of positive law the individual may do as he or she pleases. Customary usage is less likely to become comprehensive and normative when there is no expectation that there is a law for every situation.

### 3. Legislative Jurisdiction.

Modern societies have clear rules defining the authority to make rules. Subject matter and territorial limits on lawmaking are embedded in constitutions. Some matters are the exclusive concern of a federal legislature, while others are reserved for the city council. Power to make rules is regulated among competing legislative, judicial, and executive authorities within government, each of which defines and limits the authority of the others. Practices and customs determine much official behavior, but the modern society's preoccupation with jurisdiction limits the likelihood that such custom will be perceived as law. It is more likely that such practices initially will be seen as illegitimate usurpers of the law.

For example, by constitution, statute, and decision each state has defined a procedure for trial of criminal charges in court, but this procedure is not exclusive, and in most states only a modest portion of all serious criminal charges are disposed of by the procedures of the formal law. In many American communities as many as nine out of ten cases are disposed of by customary practices, sometimes labelled "guilty plea bargaining" or "prosecutorial discretion" by which the accused is persuaded to admit his guilt and acquiesce in punishment. The official reaction to these customary practices has followed an interesting course. The predominant initial reaction was to ignore customary practices, act as if the formal rules were being followed, and even deny the existence of deviance. When the evidence of deviation became too great to deny or ignore, the next reaction was indignation and insistence that custom be abandoned and the rules obeyed. Only in 1970 did the United States Supreme Court unambiguously recognize the customary practices of plea bargaining as legitimate. Since then the reaction has been to incorporate the custom into law, to embody it in written rules, and to try to police its operation.

The Jewish tradition has not been as concerned with jurisdiction. Its rules were long ago separated from the territorial limits of sovereignty over land and the personal authority of kings, ordained priests, or rabbis. Consequently, no clear geographic, jurisdictional hierarchy of authority defines the power to speak. The literary forms of the law reinforce these uncertainties. The Torah speaks with binding force but in ancient words that can be understood only with the help of customary interpretation. The classic bodies of rabbinic laws (Midrash Halakhah, Mishnah, Gemara) are discursive, argumentative, and frequently not dispositive. They, too, can be understood and obeyed only with the help of traditions that tell which argument won the decision. Only with the help of custom does Jewish practice gain coherence. Today different rabbis hold conflicting views, but the practice of the community (or of the subcommunities into which the Jews have split) can be observed. Instead of initial hostility and opposition to custom as binding rule, the rabbinic tradition depends on custom to define the law and is less likely to see it in opposition to the law.

Nonetheless, Jewish law, especially in the systematic, medieval codifications, continued to be reluctant to admit publicly that large parts of the law, particularly that governing civil matters, are the product of custom, although that was the case. This reticence may reflect a fear that the product of a particular community will lack persuasive authority in other communities. The result can be conflict among communities with different customs and a denial of the universality of the law.

Custom also is suspect because it is discontinuous with the tradition tracing back to Sinai and the legal authorities who claim guardianship of that tradition. When a rule is based on the reinterpretation of a received text, no matter how strained the interpretation may be and how novel its result, some connection is maintained with undoubtedly legitimate, ancient authority. Moreover, the declaration of the new rule rests in the hands of legal authorities, while custom arises out of the practice of ordinary people. Toward the end of this topic are texts in which rabbis seek to overlay custom with a dose of rabbinic legitimation by requiring rabbinic approval before the recognition of a binding custom.

## B. The Interactions Between Custom and Law

One of the most important connections between custom and law is historical: custom is the source of rules later embodied in positive law. Custom often operates as law in a simple or traditional society in which the law is primarily a collection of received group practices. These customary laws eventually may be written down and become part of the positive law. Even in sophisticated societies custom can be a preliminary form of law. The conventions of vehicular traffic, for example, developed largely as custom, but when the advent of the automobile created a new need for legal control of these practices, they were adopted into positive law as the core of the vehicle code. When a formal legal structure is in place, custom continues to grow up interstitially to explain, expand, and reconcile the law. These interstitial customs are soon recognized as binding by legal authorities.

This historical connection is clearly in evidence in the development of Jewish law. The rabbis even claim that "custom always precedes law" (*Soferim* 14:18). The validity of this statement is doubtful, but it is certainly true that many biblical and rabbinic laws had their origins in the customs of the people. Laws such as those requiring circumcision or prohibiting the eating of blood may well have originated in patriarchal days, as the Bible records, before the formalization of Jewish practice in a legal code. Many of the stories in Genesis assume rules of custom that are only later given legal articulation. Abraham's purchase of the cave of Makhpelah (Gen. 23) is later relied on by the rabbis as the basis for legal rules, including laws which require identifying marks of the property to be sold, define what a buyer and seller can legitimately understand to be included in a sale, and determine the forms of transaction which constitute a legally binding sale. Much of rabbinic law on the methods of transfer of property comes from that story and from the usages recorded in Chapter Four of Ruth—usages that were clearly customary, as the text explicitly says: "Now this was the custom in former times in Israel concerning redeeming and exchanging: to confirm all things a man drew off his shoe and gave it to his neighbor. This was the attestation in Israel" (Ruth 4:7). Sometimes the Torah itself records a law that was earlier followed as a matter of custom. Thus when Jacob and Laban argue over the responsibilities of a paid bailee, Jacob indicates that he took responsibility not only for theft but also for unavoidable damages, in this case, if the animal was torn to pieces by an attacker (Gen. 31:39). His behavior foreshadows the law in Exodus 22:9–12, according to which the bailee is responsible for theft, but not for unavoidable damage. His plea to Laban thus makes sense: Jacob served Laban beyond the requirements of the prevailing custom, and so Laban should show him consideration.

The historical connection between custom and law depends on the ability of custom to operate as a source of rules in the absence of law in the first place. The Jerusalem Talmud explicitly recognizes that custom can do this. When it discusses whether it is necessary to set aside tithes from fruit trees in their fourth year, a point on which the Written Law is silent, it says: "When there is no clearly established law on any matter before the court and you do not know what its true nature is, go and ascertain the custom of the people and act accordingly, and we see that the public does not set aside tithes in this case" (P.T. *Peah* 7:6, 20c). Later Jewish law codes applied this principle broadly, often by simply recording the common practice. As a result, customs govern much of Jewish civil and ritual practice, either on their own authority or by virtue of being subsequently incorporated into codes or responsa.

Customs also serve to decide what the law is when the legal authorities differ. This in effect is another way of acting in the absence of law, because in some areas of Jewish law, when the jurists disagree, there effectively is no law. Both the Babylonian and Jerusalem Talmuds record conflicts between laws settled by the rule, "Go check the practice of the people." Some Babylonian rabbis did not permit custom to determine the law in matters concerning ritual law (see *R.H.* 15b), but Palestinian and some Babylonian rabbis accorded custom that power, even when the result was contrary to the previously accepted rules of decision. Thus while the general rule was that the majority of a rabbinic court was to be followed, there are several cases in which an individual opinion becomes the law in preference to the majority because the custom supported the individual opinion. In post-talmudic times, most rabbis followed the rule that in disputes about biblical law the more stringent view was to be followed, but if the dispute concerned rabbinic legislation, the more lenient rule prevailed. That rule, however, was set aside when there existed a clear customary pattern to the contrary, as Rabbi Meir of Rothenburg stated in the thirteenth century: "In all matters on which the great legal scholars are in dispute I hold that a stringent approach must be followed except when the permissibility of a matter has spread in accordance with the custom of the scholars by whom we have been preceded" (Responsum #386).

The connections between law and custom do not all run in one direction; law becomes custom as surely as custom becomes law. As Topic Three discusses, no effective legal system can hope to rely exclusively or even primarily on force and the fear of punishment to enforce its norms. Group and individual adherence to the commands of the law must be gained, and lawful behavior must be assimilated into communal expectations. The reason why most people do not rob banks, cheat their neighbors, or walk down the street naked, is not primarily because we are afraid of being sent to prison. We do not do those things because they are not right and because that is not the way people in our society behave. Law can be a powerful teacher. It operates most efficiently when its demands are assimilated into public morality and public expectations.

If a legal norm exists, there may be no need for the added authority of custom, but laws and judicial decisions sometimes do affect custom by establishing new usages and abrogating old ones. The Supreme Court's racial integration decisions have uprooted longstanding usages and customs in many areas of the United States, in addition to overturning a variety of laws. It no longer is common usage among advertisers to picture white people exclusively, and the unwritten customs restricting social dealings between blacks and whites increasingly have been set aside.

In Jewish law, the ability of law to influence the content and authority of custom is probably most in evidence when law abrogates custom. As one might expect, the rabbis strongly asserted the authority of the law over those customs that were based on a misunderstanding of the law. The Jerusalem Talmud specifically decrees (in the name of R. Abun) that when a custom prohibits what is legally permitted, the custom is authoritative if it is well known that the law itself would permit the action, but the custom is invalidated if it is based on the erroneous assumption that the law is the source of the prohibition (P.T. *Pesahim* 4:1, 30d). There are a few talmudic instances in which the rabbis overruled a custom based on error, but many more such cases occurred in post-talmudic times. So, for example, Rabbenu Tam, responding to the custom of counting a minor in a *minyan* (quorum for prayer) if he holds a Pentateuch in his hand, exclaimed: "This is a nonsensical custom. . . . Is a Pentateuch to be regarded as a man?" (Tosafot to *Berakhot* 48a). Similarly, R. Asher b. Yehiel overruled a custom concerning the testamentary disposition of property by a woman since it was "erroneous" (*Responsa, Rosh* 55:10); Mordecai Jaffe attacked the custom of not reciting Grace after Meals in the home of a Gentile because "this nonsensical custom" originated from a mistaken understanding of a talmudic statement on a completely different subject (*Levush ha-Takhelet*, 193:6); and Simeon Duran strongly condemned a custom that imposed the status of marriage on a woman in circumstances where all scholars agreed that there was no marriage at all: "This is a custom born in ignorance which the public must not be compelled to obey" (*Tashbez*, 1:154).

Rabbis reacted with even more zeal in combating customs that they perceived to be contrary to important principles of Jewish law. So, for example, R. Solomon ibn Adret strongly condemned a custom that permitted joint owners of a courtyard not to partition off the sections of the courtyard in which each dwelled, because the customary practice was contrary to the legal principle that "the injury of being observed is a real injury" (M.T. *Shekhein* 2:14–15, based on *B.B.* 3a, 4a).

> *Resp. Rashba,* vol. 2, no. 268:
> If it has been the custom, as regards houses and courtyards, not to pay heed at all to the injury of observing one's neighbor, the custom is a bad one and no custom at all; for waiver may only be made in matters of civil law, in which event a person may give of his own or tolerate damage to his property, but he is not free to breach the fences of Israel and to act immodestly in a manner causing the Divine Presence (*Shekhinah*) to depart from this people, as it is said, "a person shall not make his windows to open onto his joint owner's courtyard" (*B.B.* 3:7).

Similarly, Moses Rothenburg rejects a tax custom that fails to distinguish between rich and poor because it violates Jewish principles of justice and equity.

> *Pithei Teshuvah,* H.M. 163, no. 16
> The contention of the rich has no justification, for certainly according to the law of the Torah taxes must be shared according to financial means, and there can be no greater injustice than to make the rich and the poor bear the tax burden in virtually equal measure. Even if the custom has been in existence for some years, it must not be upheld.

One can understand why rabbis act against customs based on error or injustice, but the motive did not have to be that strong. The Jerusalem Talmud records a decision to invalidate the custom of fishermen of Tiberias not to work during the intermediate days of the Feast of Tabernacles and Passover because it was impossible to prepare fresh fish for the festival in advance, and the absence of it would detract from the joy of the festival. On the other hand, the same custom was affirmed in the case of those who crushed wheat and prepared wheat because those products could be prepared beforehand (T.J. *Pes.* 4:1, 30d; *Ta'an* 1:6, 64c). While rabbis did invalidate customs on the grounds of the community's general welfare, they did so sparingly, holding that in general "all is in accordance with custom." They were especially reticent to act with regard to civil matters where the offensive custom was locally accepted.

The ability of the law to abrogate customs varies, of course, according to the power and prestige that rabbis have enjoyed in various times and places. For example, modern rabbis have difficulty convincing Jews to observe the dietary and Sabbath laws, even though the practice of most Jews is in clear violation of Jewish constitutional law. Whether successful or not, however, rabbinical legal authorities attempt to implant new practices and customs and annul those that they consider offensive. In doing so rabbis enable law to influence custom just as custom affects law.

## C. Justifying the Authority of Custom

The rabbis raised objections to the content of some customs, but they had no compunctions about the authority of custom in general. On the contrary, they even maintained that "custom can nullify the law," at least in civil areas (P.T. *B.M.* 7:1, 11b; P.T. *Yev.* 12:1, 12c). For example, deeds that are not signed as required by Jewish law are valid if prepared in accordance with local custom. Similarly, debts may be recovered by levying against movable property if local custom permits that even though talmudic law does not; and custom may override laws regulating the financial arrangements between husband and wife. The legislative authority of custom was complemented by enforcement procedures. The rabbis imposed fines for violations of customs, enunciating the rule that "just as a fine is imposed in matters of law (*halakhah*), so a fine is imposed in matters of custom (*minhag*) (P.T. *Pes.* 4:3, 30d). R. Abbahu even sought to have a person flogged for transgressing a prohibition decreed by custom.

The authority of custom is based on concerns quite similar to those that lead to obedience of the law. When the family, clan, or village are coextensive with society and government, their rules, embodied in customary practice, are the law. Tradition is the repository of accumulated wisdom; doing things the way they have been done for a long time enhances the security of social transactions and increases the likelihood that they will be done sensibly.

Both rabbinic and secular law required that the law follow the will of the majority, although majoritarian practice is quite differently defined in the two systems. The majority does not make its will known only through momentary acts of voting directly in a general election or indirectly in an assembly of elders. Majority will also is shown by how people choose to behave over time, by the persistent choice of one alternative over another in a specific and concrete situation.

While these factors underlie the authority of custom in any legal system, Jewish sources offer two principal theories to substantiate the authority of custom in Jewish law. One is that customs are merely laws that were enacted long ago but are no longer recognized as such.

> *P.T. Shabbat* 19:1, 17a:
> They asked Hillel the Elder: "What should people do if they forgot to bring their knives with them (to slaughter the Passover offering if Passover falls on the Sabbath, a day on which it is forbidden to carry objects from one's private domain to the public domain)?" He said to them: "I have heard the law, but I forgot it. But leave it to the People Israel: if they are not prophets, they are children of prophets." Everyone whose Passover sacrifice was a lamb automatically stuck it (the knife) in its wool, and he whose Passover sacrifice was a goat stuck it between its horns so that the animals themselves would carry the knives with them. Once he saw the practice, he remembered the law and said to them: "So I have received the tradition from the mouth(s) of Shemayah and Avtalyon." R. Zeara said in the name of R. Eliezer: "Any instruction (custom) which does not have a legal source is not a (valid) instruction."

This view is also shared by a few post-talmudic writers. It gives custom latent judicial authority and ultimately, as Hillel the Elder says, divine authority. That accords considerable legal weight to custom and closely connects custom with other kinds of Jewish law, especially communal legislation (*takkanot ha-kahal*). However, this theory also restricts the scope and creative power of custom. Nahmanides, a proponent of this position, understood that clearly.

> Nahmanides, *Novellae on Bava Batra* 144b:
> We say that custom is legally binding (lit. "a legal matter") only when the people of the city or the seven city representatives made an agreement in accord with it, but other customs do not have the power to annul a law but only to decide in matters where the law is not clear.

Most Jewish legal authorities hold the second view. They agree that some customs may have arisen as the result of a previously approved statute or decision, as in the case of Hillel the Elder, but they do not take that as being paradigmatic. They instead explain the authority of most customs as deriving from the power of individuals—and even more, the community—to agree to their own conditions in secular matters. The first three generations of Tannaim, and Rabbi Meir and Rabbi Simeon b. Gamliel after them, held that people are not free to make stipulations contrary to the Torah's laws even in civil matters, but from the fourth generation on, Jewish law followed the opinion associated with R. Yehudah, which is that people are not free to stipulate contrary to Jewish law in ritual and family matters, but they are free to do so in monetary issues. There is some ambiguity as to exactly what is included in "monetary issues": because the law in Mishnah *Bava Batra* 8:5 was established before this distinction, a father does not have the right to withhold a double portion of his estate from his eldest son or a single portion from any other son even though that clearly seems to be a monetary matter. Some sources extend the right to stipulate to cover conjugal obligations in marriage, while others see that as a matter regarding one's body and not one's money and therefore beyond one's jurisdiction to govern. Despite such disputes, the general principle is clear enough and widely accepted: individuals have the right to create conditions in monetary matters. Jewish law in those areas is binding only if the parties do not disclose their preference for an alternative arrangement. Such reasoning holds all the more strongly when an entire community wants to adopt practices at variance with existing legislation, and hence the power of custom is often justified by reference to the right of individuals to stipulate.

This second explanation of the authority of custom does not root it as firmly in the corpus of Jewish law as the first theory does. Two factors mitigate that, however. First, customs, like communal legislation, are subject to rabbinic review, and many of them eventually find their way into codes and responsa. Through that process many customs gain official recognition. Beyond that, both theories, but especially the second, can and do depend on the scriptural authorization that the Talmud and Midrash confer on custom. The rabbis link the validity of custom to scriptural passages in two different ways. "Do not change the custom of your ancestors," R. Simeon b. Yohai says, supporting his words with a verse from Proverbs (22:28), "Do not remove the ancient landmark which your ancestors have set." R. Yohanon bases the authority of custom on another verse in the Book of Proverbs (1:8), "Hear, my son, the instruction of your father, and do not forsake the teaching of your mother." Sherira Gaon later supported the authority of custom with yet another verse, Deuteronomy 19:14, "Do not remove your neighbor's landmark, which they have set of old": as landmarks that have been set may not be removed, so communal norms that have long been practiced may not be trespassed.

If one result of the second theory is that greater attention must be paid to strengthening the authority of custom, another consequence is that custom is given authority in broad areas of Jewish civil law. Since many of the topics that are considered part of criminal law in the Anglo-American system are treated as civil matters in Jewish law, the effect of custom is even greater than the talmudic phrase, "money matters," connotes. We have already seen a responsum by R. Meir of Rothenburg about personal injuries in which he is faced with a custom that he does not like. He nevertheless says that "if the community has instituted the practice of excusing him (the tortfeasor) if he acted in the heat of anger, . . . then I will not take exception to that practice because the talmudic rule is that property which the court makes ownerless is ownerless."

The authority of custom is much weaker, however, in family and ritual law because in those areas individuals do not have a voice in determining the law. Custom may prohibit what the law permits, but it cannot allow what the law forbids. Only an express revision of the law by the rabbis can alter Jewish ritual law to make it more lenient. This principle is stated clearly in the Talmud by the rhetorical question, "Does the matter then depend upon custom?" (*Hullin* 63a; *B.M.* 69b–70a). Some borderline areas, such as liturgical issues, are not clearly matters of money or matters in which the Torah announces prohibitions and permissions. In those borderline areas some rabbis recognize the authority of custom to abrogate laws and some do not. All agree, however, that custom has no such power in matters that are clearly governed by the Torah's rules of what is prohibited. Communal enactments (*takkanot ha-kahal*) are similarly restricted to civil and criminal matters, and for the same reason. It is easier to justify human legislative activity in matters governing the relationships between individuals than it is to substantiate human authority in the more sensitive ritual areas expressing the relationship between an individual and God.

Despite that restriction, the authority of custom is both broad and deep. The general principle is the one stated in the Talmud several times: "We may not make a decree upon the community unless the majority is able to abide by it" (*B.K.* 79b; *B.B.* 60b; *A.Z.* 36a; *Hor.* 3b). That effectively tailors the law to the practices of the people. In a source that we have seen in another context, Maimonides spells out the far-reaching implications of this rule:

> *Mishneh Torah*, Laws of Rebels 2:7:
> If a court issued a decree which seemed to spread to the whole community, and that was the state of things for many years, but after a long time another court investigated and found that observance of the decree was not widespread, then the later court may abrogate it, even if the later court was lesser than the former one in wisdom and number.

The power of custom continues to this day, even when rabbis would prefer it to be otherwise. One interesting example occurred recently when Yeshiva University of Los Angeles announced that it was moderating its stringent stance in order to attract a broader spectrum of the Orthodox community to its high school. One facet of that moderation is a greater tolerance for boy-girl relationships as long as they "remain within the bounds of propriety and do not flaunt Halakhah." Elaborating on that change in policy, Rabbi Sholom Tendler, dean of the high school, said:

*Israel Today* 12:73 [May 18, 1984], pt. II, p. 2.

> The study of Torah will force anyone to draw negative conclusions about teenage boy-girl social relationships. Our policy to treat these social relationships as a non-issue does not reflect a Halakhic decision in *Even Ha'Ezer* (the laws about relationships between men and women), but rather a Halakhah in the laws of education: "As it is a mitzvah (commandment) to speak words which will be accepted, so it is a mitzvah to be quiet when your words will be rejected." Our students are taught the true Torah philosophy in all areas without any "watering down," but it is the responsibility of an educator to know his constituency and to know which issues to focus upon in order to achieve his real goals.

One can hear in Rabbi Tendler's words both his reluctance to adopt the position that he is being forced to espouse and his recognition that he has no choice. Even among the right-wing Orthodox, the customs of the community play a crucial role in determining the application and effectiveness of segments of the law; and, for the sake of the integrity of the law itself, "We may not make a decree upon the community unless the majority is able to abide by it."

Custom thus affects the formation of the law, its content, the degree of its authority, and the conditions under which it is annulled, either de facto or de jure. It consequently is a major source of law and a crucial factor in understanding the context of its operation.

American law also recognizes the role of custom as a source of binding rules in commercial matters. As in rabbinic law this is understood to be closely linked to the right of parties to a transaction to agree on their own rules within broad limits. The Uniform Commercial Code portions that follow have been adopted in forty-nine states. From its origins commercial law in the common law courts has been heavily influenced by the practice of merchants. This deference to custom was somewhat weakened during the nineteenth century period of legal conceptualism. A major aspect of the twentieth century reforms embodied in the Uniform Commercial Code is renewed emphasis in the law on the primacy of commercial practice. Custom again has been a major influence in creating law.

§ 1–205 *Course of Dealing and Usage of Trade*
(1) A course of dealing is a sequence of previous conduct between the parties to a particular transaction which is fairly to be regarded as establishing a common basis of understanding for interpreting their expressions and other conduct.

(2) A usage of trade is any practice or method of dealing having such regularity of observance in a place, vocation or trade as to justify an expectation that it will be observed with respect to the transaction in question. The existence and scope of such a usage are to be proved as facts. If it is established that such a usage is embodied in a written trade code or similar writing, the interpretation of the writing is for the court.

(3) A course of dealing between parties and any usage of trade in the vocation or trade in which they are engaged or of which they are or should be aware give particular meaning to and supplement or qualify terms of an agreement.

(4) The express terms of an agreement and an applicable course of dealing or usage of trade shall be construed wherever reasonable as consistent with each other; but when such construction is unreasonable express terms control both course of dealing and usage of trade and course of dealing controls usage of trade.

(5) An applicable usage of trade in the place where any part of performance is to occur shall be used in interpreting the agreement as to that part of the performance.

(6) Evidence of a relevant usage of trade offered by one party is not admissible unless and until he has given the other party such notice as the court finds sufficient to prevent unfair surprise to the latter.

# Topic Twelve: The Interaction Between Jewish Law and Common Law

I t is dangerous to draw superficial comparisons between legal systems. Legal institutions that look alike when viewed from the outside have very different meanings in the context of a particular historical tradition or in a specific social or political setting. Nonetheless, there are several striking points of similarity between Jewish law and the common-law tradition in England and America.

The two systems share certain preferences of legal style. Both are primarily case-law systems in which legislation typically addresses specific problems rather than general principles. Neither system has been attracted to legal codes in the sense that codes are used in Roman and many European systems. The dominant stream of legal reasoning in both systems grows from the resolution of concrete disputes to the accretion of more general policies and principles, rather than the deduction of specific issues from general principles. In short, both systems carry the strong flavor of judge-made law (although both systems speak in the name of a law giver).

Moreover, in comparison to their contemporaries and neighbors, both systems assign law a relatively important role in human affairs. The common law has developed a grand constitutional doctrine under which even the king and the state are seen as subordinate to the law. The rabbis saw law as an essential characteristic of the universe, and Jews have speculated since biblical times whether God himself is bound by His law (see Topic Three, Section E).

Both systems are especially concerned with jurisprudential questions of legitimacy, jurisdiction, and legal authority. Perhaps this reflects the relatively individualistic orientation of the two cultures. In both, authority is dispersed within society and therefore must be justified and defined. Neither is a monolithic society in which all power is centralized and the individual is without recourse or resource. In American constitutional theory, government is limited and possesses only delegated powers. Similarly, rabbinic legal authority was limited by a hostile and alien secular hegemony. Both situations have led to a heightened awareness of the limits of authority. They also lead to great concern for individual and residual rights.

Beyond these similarities of style and value, there are a few ways in which Jewish law has directly influenced common law. Some of the clearest of these influences can be traced back to the period immediately following the Norman Conquest of England in 1066, when Jews arrived in large numbers after toleration was extended to them. Jews achieved an important role as bankers and moneylenders and influenced the economic life of England for about two centuries before being expelled from the realm at the end of the thirteenth century. Although some Jews returned to England as early as the seventeenth century, they did not attain full legal rights until the nineteenth century, and so the direct influences of Jewish law on common law are either very old or very new.

Available legal materials on twelfth and thirteenth century England are more extensive than might be thought, but the story of how new legal institutions developed during that period is necessarily incomplete. The conquerors imposed a layer of Norman and Roman Church law on pre-existing Anglo-Saxon law, which itself was an amalgam of Danish, Germanic, and Celtic customs. The major form of wealth was the ownership of land, which was not freely alienable; that is, land could not be transferred by its holder without permission from the feudal overlord.

Jews were active in creating the legal tools that enabled them as moneylenders to secure the interest of the creditor in the debtor's land without disturbing the title to the land. The success of these devices led to the freer alienability of land and contributed to the ultimate decline of the social and economic bases of medieval feudalism. Jacob J. Rabinowitz ("The Influence of Jewish Law on the Development of the Common Law," in Louis Finkelstein, ed., *The Jews: Their History, Culture, and Religion*, Third Edition [New York: Harper, 1960], Vol. I, pp. 823–853) has traced the evolution from Jewish law sources of common law security interests, including the recognizance, the common law mortgage, the warranty of title, the distinction between suretyship and guaranty, the general release, penal bonds, and the dower interest. The general pattern was for Jews to adopt traditional transaction forms with talmudic roots for use in loans to their Christian debtors. The transactions were enforced in both rabbinic and royal courts. The legal devices proved so successful that Christians began to use them among themselves and gradually they were absorbed as part of the common law.

In addition to these direct adoptions, biblical law exerts a continuing influence on common law through its role as a sacred text of the

Christian community. After the Reformation, Protestant attention to the Old Testament led to renewed interest in biblical laws. One example is the evidence rules requiring two witnesses and corroboration of testimony. Some American colonies, notably in New England, saw themselves as latter-day Israelites living in the wilderness under divine providence. They sought guidance in the Mosaic Codes for their new society.

The Supreme Court of the United States has several times in recent years referred to Jewish law as a source of guidance on moral issues relevant to constitutional issues before the court, including the admissibility of confessions from criminal suspects and the permissibility of abortion.

There is also clear evidence of the influence of common law on Jewish law. Throughout the Jewish experience in the Greek, Roman, Persian, Muslim, and Christian worlds, non-Jewish commercial practices had a direct effect on the ways that Jews did business, and Jewish law incorporated and enforced the outside rules in disputes among Jews. Criminal law within the Jewish community was also heavily dependent on the rules of the realm. With the rise of the modern national state and the admission of Jews to the status of citizens, the influence of secular law was felt even more directly. Before the modern period secular law was filtered through Jewish courts; now Jews turned directly to secular courts for adjudication of their disputes. When the State of Israel was established, traditional rabbinic courts were given jurisdiction in limited areas, but in constitutional law, commercial law, and criminal law the courts of the state apply essentially common law principles. These Jewish courts draw on the decisions of American and English courts as highly persuasive authority.

These connections exist between Jewish law and common law, but their limitations demonstrate the distinct nature of the two systems. Rather than overdraw parallels and comparisons, the student is better advised to try to understand each system on its own ground and to use comparisons to highlight the differing ways in which legal systems deal with similar problems.

# PART II:

## *Marriage*

The content of Jewish marriage law tells important things about the substance of Jewish life and culture. It also casts into an interesting perspective some pressing problems of American law. Marriage has always been the backbone of social stability and acculturation, and it remains the style of life that most of the world's population adopts. Even those who choose other living arrangements usually see marriage as the norm by which they measure the alternative they have chosen. But the Jewish conception of marriage is very different from the Christian concept that was the basis for the marital laws in most American states until the late 1960s and early 1970s. Recent developments in a number of states appear to have moved American law somewhat closer to the Jewish model. Hence, our study of this body of law may contribute to shaping the evolving American law.

The sections that follow analyze the content of marriage as the fusion of three distinct factors: the contractual, the social, and the sacred. To some extent marriage is a private, personal relationship between two people that is ordered primarily by their consensual agreement. *Consensus non concubitus facit matrimonium*, "It is the agreement, not the coition that makes it a marriage," declares the ancient maxim.

Yet marriage is more than an individualistic agreement; it is a social status, part of the structure that defines family, clan, and society. The marriage bond is the source of social strength. The parties may voluntarily choose to enter the status, but its important incidents and content are defined by society, not by the parties.

In addition to these consensual and social factors, marriage is a sacred bond, entry into which fulfills a divine commandment and plan for humans. The biblical injunction to be fruitful and multiply is a crucial aspect of God's work of creation. An essential human obligation is to bring the next generation into the world and to prepare it to carry on history and culture. In celebration of their union men and women perpetuate the goodness of life and love. To fulfill its divine purposes marriage must follow certain patterns.

The following sections will consider these three aspects separately to see how they interact and combine in forming the Jewish law of marriage. The categories are neither watertight nor exclusive, and a number of the items might fit under more than one heading. Separating the elements of Jewish marriage in this way will, however, help explain the legal concept of Jewish marriage and demonstrate its richness.

This analysis should also help illuminate at least two jurisprudential issues:

## 1. *The Extent to Which Law Governs All Relationships*

Judaism announces rules to govern the intimate aspects of the lives of its adherents to a much greater extent than does American law. This is not just a matter of taste or social convention. Embedded in this distinction are two significantly different conceptions of law and its role in society. Judaism tends to see law as filling life and expects that there is a correct way to do even the most minor act. We have seen indications of this special Jewish view in the psalmist's claim that God's law orders human society and all of nature (Psalm 19). While the scope of law has grown tremendously in America in the past generation, Americans do not expect there to be a law about everything. Law is a set of interstitial rules to fill pressing needs. No topic illustrates the differing conceptions of the ambit of law more clearly than does family law.

## 2. *Conflicts of Jurisdiction*

Until the revolutions of the eighteenth and nineteenth centuries, marriage was considered a religious function that the state did not regulate by law. This has changed: the secular state has occupied the field. Consequently marital issues represent a prime example of conflict of jurisdiction between religious and civil authorities both in the United States and in Israel. The ways in which the conflicting jurisdictions accommodate each other are significant facets of the operation of both legal systems.

# Topic Thirteen: The Nature of Marriage in Jewish and American Law

## A. The Contractual Element in Jewish Marriage

The earliest records that we have of marriage in the ancient Near East indicate that marriage was an agreement not between two individuals, but between two families. The newly married man usually did not make a new home for himself; he and his bride took up residence in his father's house. The family of the groom gained, and the family of the bride lost, a valuable member to tend the flock, draw water from the well, grind flour, bake bread, and assist in household tasks. It is not surprising, therefore, that marriage was viewed as the acquisition of the woman by the groom and his family from the family of the bride.

Originally the acquisition was instantaneous. The father of the groom paid the father of the bride a bride price, called a *mohar*. In biblical times the usual bride price seems to have been fifty shekels of silver (see Ex. 22:15–16 and Deut. 22:28–29), but the story of Shekhem indicates that sometimes a woman's father could set an extraordinarily high *mohar* in order to discourage a groom. Shekhem, after raping Dinah, says to Jacob, her father, and to her brother: "Ask me a bride price (*mohar*) ever so high, as well as gifts, and I will pay what you tell me; only give me the maiden for a wife" (Gen. 34:12). The *mohar* might be paid in kind or service. Thus after Laban agrees to give Rebekah in marriage to Isaac, Abraham's servant "brought out objects of silver and gold, and garments, and gave them to Rebekah; and he gave presents to her brother and her mother" (Gen. 24:53). In the next generation Jacob paid the *mohar* to Laban by working for him for twenty years, seven years for Leah, seven for Rachel, and six for a salary (Gen. 30:26; 31:41). Saul demanded valiant deeds from David in place of a *mohar* for his daughter Mikhal (I Sam. 18:25), and Caleb demanded the same for his daughter Akhsah (Josh. 15:16–17; Judges 1:12–13).

In addition to the *mohar*, the groom gave the bride gifts at the time of the marriage, as illustrated by the verses from the stories of Dinah and Rebekah. Moreover, a bride expected that a significant portion of

442

the *mohar* her father received from the groom's father would be passed on to her as a wedding gift (and as compensation for the rights of inheritance from her clan which a married woman gave up). When Laban refused to do this, Leah and Rebekah complained bitterly: "Have we still a share in the inheritance of our father's house? Surely he regards us as outsiders now that he has sold us and used up our purchase price" (Gen. 31:14–15).

The Bible does not specify what is to be done with the *mohar* if either of the two parties breaks the marriage agreement after it has been paid. The Code of Hammurabi does provide for that situation, and the law of the early Hebrews was probably similar. According to Hammurabi's Code (pars. 159–160), a groom who changes his mind forfeits both the *mohar* and the gifts that he gave the woman that was to be his bride. If the girl's father broke the agreement, he had to return double of everything given by the groom to him and his daughter.

During the biblical period the consent of the woman to the marriage was sought, but only in a perfunctory way. Her father negotiated the marriage with the groom and his father, and it was difficult for the woman to withhold her consent after her father and her whole family had agreed to the match. Thus Laban and Betuel first tell Abraham's servant, "Here is Rebekah before you; take her and go, and let her be a wife to you master's son" (Gen. 24:51), and only afterwards do they seek Rebekah's consent (Gen. 24:57–58).

As time went on, Jewish marriage increasingly took the character of a contract, a betrothal or engagement for *future* cohabitation rather than *present* acquisition. Greater emphasis inevitably was put on the two elements that characterize a contract in contrast to an acquisition: futurity and consent.

During the difficult economic circumstances of the late second century and early first century B.C.E., many Jewish men did not marry because they simply could not afford to. Simeon ben Shetah, head of the Pharisees at that time, devised an ingenious scheme which simultaneously encouraged marriage and discouraged divorce. By application of a lawyer's sleight-of-hand he transformed the *mohar* from a cash price into a lien against the husband's property that would have to be paid to the woman (not her father) in the event he divorced or predeceased her. This meant that a man did not have to raise the bride price in order to get married, thus making marriage easier. It also meant that divorce would be harder, because the lien would become due if the husband subsequently decided to divorce his wife (Tosefta *Ketubbot* 12:1; B.T. *Ketubbot* 82b; P.T. *Ketubbot* 8:11). In time the *mattan*, the gifts that the groom gave the bride at the time of marriage, were also transformed into a lien against the groom's property.

At the same time, the biblical custom of fathers giving their daughters gifts at marriage hardened into an obligatory expectation. Bachelorhood had become more common as economic conditions in Israel worsened during the first two centuries C.E. The fathers of girls no longer expected suitors to pay a bride price, a portion of which they could then turn over to their daughters as gifts. Now fathers had to promise large dowries from their own resources to attract suitors. So desperate were some fathers that they promised dowries beyond their means and then reneged on them after the betrothal. The Mishnah records court cases arising from such situations as early as the days preceding the destruction of the Second Temple in 70 C.E. (see Mishnah *Ketubbot* 13:5; B.T. *Ket.* 52b–53a, *B.M.* 75b). In time the expectation of a dowry became so fixed that even an orphaned girl received a dowry from the community's charity fund. Since dowries were expected and varied widely in sum, bachelors were frequently warned against choosing a wife on the basis of the size of her dowry (see *Kiddushin* 70a)— an indication that many men did just that.

In any case, by the time of the Mishnah there were three sums of money that entered into the common marriage contract (the contract is called a *ketubbah*): the *ketubbah* money proper (the equivalent of the old *mohar*, or bride price), the *tosefet* ("the additional sum," the old *mattan*, or gifts), and the *nedunyah* (dowry). The first two were liens against the husband's property to be paid to the woman if he divorced or predeceased her; the third was money or property that the bride's father promised the groom, to be paid either immediately after betrothal or according to the schedule established in the *ketubbah.* These changes in the monetary arrangements of Jewish marriage gave the transaction futurity.

The second element of a contract, consent, took a longer time to be built into the institution of Jewish marriage. At least the formal consent of the woman was always required. Even though a woman was consulted in the process of choosing a mate and often negotiated the conditions of the marriage herself, in most communities it was ultimately the parents rather than the children who chose the spouse. That was the case in many Sephardic and Eastern European Jewish communities down to the twentieth century. The extent to which the woman's consent to marriage was real rather than pro forma varied with time and place, as well as with the normal age of marriage. During some periods and in some communities the betrothal of preadolescents was common, but the girl could release herself from the marriage without obtaining a writ of divorce from her husband once she reached thirteen years of age (Mishnah *Yevamot* 13:1). This preserves at least the formal requirement for a woman's consent at an age of maturity.

## 1. *Divorce—Dissolving the Contract*

One corollary of the view that marriage is the product of contractual agreement is that the parties should be free to modify or terminate the arrangement by consent. Jewish law has recognized divorce by a personal act of the husband since biblical times. Deuteronomy 24:1–4 makes it clear that the husband can effect a divorce by simply giving his wife a writ.

> *Deuteronomy 24:1–4*
> A man takes a wife and possesses her. She fails to please him because he finds something obnoxious about her, and he writes her a bill of divorce, hands it to her, sends her away from his house; she leaves his household and becomes the wife of another man; then the second man rejects her, writes her a bill of divorce, hands it to her, and sends her away from his house; or the man who married her last dies, then the husband who divorced her first shall not take her to wife again, since she has been defiled—for that would be abhorrent to the Lord. You must not bring sin upon the land which the Lord your God is giving you as a heritage.

The rabbis later used these verses to protect the parties from public interference. Divorce is effected by the husband's writ, not by a court decree. No court has power to dissolve the relationship without the husband's act. Unfortunately, as we shall discuss in detail later, this has left the wife in a disadvantageous position.

These biblical verses were also used as the basis for requiring a formal, public document of divorce. This was designed to protect the economic and social status of the wife in that she would have written proof of her status and could thereby sue for the financial rights accruing with that status. By contrast, Muslim law still allows secret divorces in which the husband sends a stranger to throw his wife out of the house without ceremony or financial settlement.

While early Jewish law required a writ, it did not demand the wife's consent. A man could even effect a divorce by throwing the writ into the woman's property. It was only after the decree of Rabbenu Gershom (c. 1000 C.E.) that Jewish law required a woman's consent to a divorce.

The issue of consent is tied to the question of grounds for divorce. In the following Mishnah, the School of Shammai wanted to require the husband to show grounds for divorce, but the law followed the School of Hillel, which made no such demands. Nevertheless, divorce was not taken lightly, and the paragraphs by Maimonides which follow reflect the caution necessary.

The resulting law after Rabbenu Gershom can be summarized as follows: If both parties agree to the divorce, Jewish law does not require them to show grounds. In such a case the court only acts in a supervisory role as the husband hands his wife the writ, thereby dissolving the marriage contract. If a woman refuses to accept a writ of divorce, the court determines whether she has grounds to refuse. If, for example, the woman has been taken captive, the man cannot avoid his duty to redeem her by divorcing her while she is in captivity. Similarly if the writ of divorce indicates that the man does not intend to fulfill his financial obligations under the marriage contract toward the woman and her children, the court will enforce compliance. But since the man ultimately has the power to divorce in Jewish law, once the court is satisifed that he has fulfilled his obligations under the marriage contract and under Jewish law, it urges the wife to accept the writ. If she refuses, the court accepts the writ on her behalf, freeing the man to marry someone else.

The man's consent to the divorce is assumed since he initiates the action. A court might use force to persuade a man to divorce his wife, as we shall read, but even then the court "exerted pressure on him until he says 'I want to.'" That pressure could be social, economic, or penal (including even flogging or imprisonment), but ultimately the man's consent is required, even if it is obtained under duress.

*Mishnah Gittin* 9:10

The School of Shammai says, A man may not divorce his wife unless he has found something improper in her, as it is said, "because he finds something obnoxious about her" (Deut. 24:1). But the School of Hillel says, Even if she spoiled a dish for him, as it is said, "because he finds something obnoxious about her." R. Akiba says, Even if he found another more beautiful than she is, as it is said, "She fails to please him."

*Maimonides, Mishneh Torah, Laws of Divorce* 10:21–23:

21. A man should not marry a woman with the intention of divorcing her, nor should she live with him and serve him while he intends to divorce her.

A man should not divorce his first wife unless he found her guilty of misconduct, as Scripture says, "because he finds something obnoxious about her" (Deuteronomy 24:1). It is not proper for a man to be hasty in divorcing his first wife, but his second wife he may send away if he comes to hate her.

22. It is a religious duty to divorce a woman who is wicked in her ways or who is not modest like proper daughters of Israel, as Scripture

says, "Cast out a scoffer, and contention will depart" (Proverbs 22:10). It is not proper for a man to marry a woman who was divorced because of licentiousness lest people say, "This one dismissed a wicked woman from his house, and that one took her in."

23. If a man's wife became a deaf-mute, he may divorce her with a writ, but if she becomes an imbecile, he may not divorce her until she recovers. The Sages instituted that rule so that she would not be free for licentious men to have their way with her, for she cannot take care of herself. Therefore her husband may leave her and marry another woman, but he must continue to provide food and drink for her out of her own possessions. He is not, however, obligated to provide her with food, clothing, and conjugal rights because it is unbearable for a sane person to live in the same house with an insane person. He also is not liable for her medical expenses or for her ransom. If he nevertheless divorces her, the divorce is valid: he may force her to leave his house, and he is not liable to take care of her any longer.

In contrast to the Jewish, contractual view, in the common law, marriage was construed as an ontological act in which the wife became part of the husband's being and hence inseparable from him. Once the couple married, the wife lost her separate legal status, and her husband alone had legal standing (he was *sui juris*). That metaphysical view in the common law derives at least in part from Christianity's understanding of Genesis 2:24, "Hence a man leaves his father and mother and clings to his wife so that they become one flesh." Based on this long, common-law tradition of reticence to recognize divorce, general civil divorce laws were unusual in early American law, and dissolution of marriage required an ecclesiastical court decree or a special legislative act.

Today every state permits divorce, and in some of the more populous states more divorces have been recorded in recent years than marriages. In most states in the past ten or fifteen years there has been substantial easing of legal grounds for divorce and of the procedural complications. The California statute is typical of the recent pattern of no-fault divorce laws while the Oklahoma law follows the older pattern which presumed fault. As no-fault divorce becomes indistinguishable from divorce on application of either party, there is less point in requiring a complicated court process for divorce. Some states now allow couples without minor children or property disputes to dissolve their marriage without either partner personally appearing in court. These changes represent a radical transformation in the conception of both marriage and divorce on the part of Americans: what used to be a fact of nature that could only be undone in the direst of circumstances has now become a contractual arrangement which can be dissolved by the consent of the parties like other contractual agreements. In this respect American law has become remarkably similar to Jewish law.

*California Civil Code* 4506:
A court may decree a dissolution of the marriage or legal separation on either of the following grounds, which shall be pleaded generally:

(1) Irreconcilable differences, which have caused the irremediable breakdown of the marriage.

(2) Incurable insanity.

12 *Oklahoma Stas. Ann.* 1271:
1271. Grounds for divorce

The district court may grant a divorce for any of the following causes:

First. Abandonment for one (1) year.

Second. Adultery.

Third. Impotency.

Fourth. When the wife at the time of her marriage, was pregnant by another than her husband.

Fifth. Extreme cruelty.

Sixth. Fraudulent contract.

Seventh. Incompatibility.

Eighth. Habitual drunkenness.

Ninth. Gross neglect of duty.

Tenth. Imprisonment of the other party in a State or Federal penal institution under sentence thereto for the commission of a felony at the time the petition is filed.

Eleventh. The procurement of a final divorce decree without this State by a husband or wife which does not in this State release the other party from the obligations of the marriage.

Twelfth. Insanity for a period of five years, the insane person having been an inmate of a State institution for the insane in the State of Oklahoma, or inmate of a State institution for the insane in some other state for such period, or of a private sanitarium, and affected with a type of insanity with a poor prognosis for recovery; . . .

## 2. *Acquisition of the Wife*

The Mishnah which follows is a classical statement of the contractual character of Jewish marriage. Note that through the contract of marriage a woman is "acquired" from her father for sums of money, whether the amount be the substantial *denar* or the minimal amount for legal consideration, a *perutah.*

### *Mishnah Kiddushin* 1:1:

The woman is acquired by three means, and she regains her freedom by two methods. She is acquired by money, or by document, or by sexual intercourse. By money—the School of Shammai says, By a *denar* or by a *denar's* worth; but the School of Hillel says, By a *perutah* or by a *perutah's* worth. And how much is a *perutah*?—One eighth part of an Italian *issar.* And she recovers her freedom by a writ of divorce or on the death of the husband. The widowed sister-in-law is acquired by sexual intercourse, and she obtains her release by the ceremony of removing the shoe (Deuteronomy 25:9) or on the death of the brother-in-law.

Betrothal and divorce documents are different from other contracts in that only one of the two parties to the contract, the husband, has the power to initiate the act. This is based, no doubt, on custom and also on Deuteronomy 24, which records a case in which a man gave a writ of divorce to his wife. The rabbis took that as being paradigmatic for all other marriages and divorces (whether or not it was originally meant that way).

### *Gemara Kiddushin* 5b:

Our Rabbis taught: "How is a woman acquired by money? If a man gives her money or its equivalent and declares to her, 'You are herewith consecrated unto me, 'or' You are herewith betrothed unto me,' or 'You are herewith my wife'—then she is betrothed. But if she gives him money or its equivalent and says 'I am herewith consecrated unto you,' 'I am herewith betrothed unto you.' I am herewith your wife,' she is not betrothed." R. Papa demurred: Thus it is only when he both gives the money and makes the declaration that the betrothal is valid, but if he gives it and she speaks, she is not betrothed? Then consider the second clause of the Tannaitic statement: "But if she gives it to him and she makes the declaration, the betrothal is not valid." Hence, it is only when she both gives the money and she speaks that the betrothal is not valid, but if he gives the money and she speaks the betrothal should be valid!—The first clause is exact, while the second is mentioned incidentally. But may a statement be made in the second clause (at least by inference which is) contradictory to the first? — But this is its meaning: If he gives the money and he speaks, the betrothal is obviously valid; but if he gives, and she speaks, it is accounted as though she both gives and speaks, so that the betrothal is not valid. Alternatively, if he gives and speaks, she is betrothed; if she gives and speaks, she is certainly not betrothed; but if he gives and she speaks, it is doubtful, and as a Rabbinical measure we fear that the betrothal may be valid (and therefore require a writ of divorce to dissolve it).

Samuel said: "In respect to betrothal, if he gave her money or its equivalent and declares, 'You are herewith consecrated,' 'You are herewith betrothed,' or 'You are herewith a wife,'—then she is betrothed. If he declares, 'I am herewith you husband,' 'I am herewith your master,' 'I am herewith your betrothed'—there are no grounds for fear (that is, no grounds to suspect that his act is legally valid). The same applies to divorce: If he gives her the document of divorce and declares, 'You are herewith sent forth,' 'You are herewith divorced,' or 'You are henceforth permitted to any man,'—then she is divorced. But if he declares, 'I am not your husband,' 'I am not your master,' 'I am not your betrothed,' there are no grounds for fear (that his act is valid)."

## 3. Binding the Contract by Money

Note the flimsiness of the reasoning in the following paragraph of Gemara as to why money effects a betrothal. The rabbis probably went out of their way to justify that form of betrothal because money was used to bind other contracts (at least morally) and therefore it should be applicable to the contract of betrothal too. Moreover, Jewish custom at the time of the Mishnah no doubt recognized the validity of betrothal by money, and so the rabbis felt obligated to find biblical justification for it, however forced.

Gemara Kiddushin 2a:
"A woman is acquired." Why does the Tanna state here, "A woman is acquired," while elsewhere he teaches "A man may betroth," etc.? [They seem redundant.]—Because here he wishes to state (the availability of betrohal by means of) "money." And how do we know that money effects betrothal? By deriving the meaning of "taking" from the field of Ephron: Here (Deut. 24:1) it is written, "If any man take a wife," while there (Gen. 23:13) it is written, "I will give you money for the field: take it from me." Moreover, "taking" is designated acquisition, for it is written, "the field which Abraham acquired" (Gen. 23:18); alternatively, "men shall acquire fields for money" (Jer. 32:44), and therefore he teaches "a woman is acquired."

## 4. *The Standard Marriage Contract*

Americans raised on a romantic view of marriage might expect a marriage contract to emphasize the mutual love and hopes of the couple, with only cursory references, if any, to their economic and legal obligations. The Jewish wedding contract, the *ketubbah*, contains remarkably little on the emotional aspects of marriage, and when it does talk about them, it speaks of the "honor" due to each partner rather than the love. Jewish marriages, like those in any other group, obviously include love, passion, hopes, and all of the other emotional components of marriage, but Judaism assumes that those will follow if the material conditions are straightened out first. That certainly is the assumption underlying the custom common in the Jewish community by which parents arranged marriages for their children: the bride and groom often hardly knew each other, but the marriage took place if the financial arrangements were set.

The *ketubbah* also concentrates on the detailed obligations incurred by both parties because that is the specific task of the contract. Jewish law deals in extraordinary detail with every aspect of marriage, but the role of the marriage contract is to spell out the financial responsibilities of each party. This was especially important for the woman since the *ketubbah* was the major instrument by which the rabbis expanded her rights in marriage and provided for her security. Consequently the man gives the *ketubbah* to the woman as part of the wedding ceremony, and she is enjoined to preserve the deed and to take care not to misplace it.

The terms of the contract are open to negotiation in those areas which were not fixed by Jewish law, but since the days of Maimonides (twelfth century) *ketubbot* commonly follow a more or less standard formula. The *ketubbah* is written in Aramaic and is signed by two competent witnesses, not by the couple. Even when it includes an English translation, the English translation is often only a paraphrase of the Aramaic, and in any case most rabbis consider the Aramaic version to be the authoritative one. Moreover, *ketubbot* are often decorated, thus adding to the impression that they are really religious symbols rather than legal documents. These features raise substantive questions about their power to bind under secular law. Nevertheless, the *ketubbah* functioned as a binding contract in most periods of Jewish law, and some American and Israeli courts want to use it as such today.

Following is a translation of the standard, Aramaic *ketubbah* for a woman's first marriage (the form changes somewhat for a widow or divorcee):

On _____ (day of the week), the _____ day of the _____
month _____, in the year _____ since the creation of the
world, the era according to which we are accustomed to reckon here
in the city of _____, _____ son of _____ said to this virgin
_____ daughter of _____ "Be my wife according to the law of
Moses and Israel, and I will work for you, honor, support, and maintain you in accordance with the custom of Jewish husbands who work
for their wives, honor, support, and maintain them in truth. And I will
set aside for you 200 *zuz*, in lieu of your virginity, which belong to you
(according to the law of Moses), and your food, clothing, and necessar-
ies, and live with you in conjugal relations according to universal
custom." And _____, this virgin, consented and became his wife.
The dowry that she brought from her father's house, in silver, gold,
valuables, dresses and bedclothes, amounts to _____ (100 silver
pieces), and the bridegroom consented to increase this amount from
his own property with the sum of _____ (100 silver pieces), making in all _____ (200 silver pieces). And thus said _____ the
bridegroom, "I take upon myself and my heirs after me the responsibility of this marriage contract, of the dowry, and of the additional
sum, so that all this shall be paid from the best part of my property,
real and personal, that I now possess or may hereafter acquire. All my
property, even the mantle on my shoulders, shall be mortgaged for the
security of the contract and of the dowry and of the addition made
thereto." _____ the bridegroom has taken upon himself the responsibility for all the obligations of this ketubbah, as is customary
with other ketubbot made for the daughters of Israel in accordance
with the institution of our sages—may their memory be for a blessing! It is not to be regarded as an illusory obligation or as a mere sym-
bolical delivery ("kinyan") between _____ son of _____, the
bridegroom, and _____ daughter of _____, this virgin, and we
have employed an instrument legally fit for the purpose to strengthen
all that is stated above, and everything is valid.

) Witnesses.

## 5. *Adding Conditions to the Standard, Traditional Contract*

The sums that a man has to promise his wife in the event of divorce or his death are set by Jewish law, but because marriage is contractual, the husband can add to the minimum. Moreover, the couple
can agree to a whole host of other conditions, and Maimonides spells
out the rules for making such conditions legally binding. Note that the
rules for imposing conditions on a marriage contract are exactly the
same as those that apply to any other contract. Note also that the

woman may agree to forfeit her rights to food and clothing because those are money matters which may be altered by the two parties if they so desire, but she cannot forfeit her rights to sex because that is understood to be part of the very fiber of marriage such that it is not a "marriage contract" without it. Moreover, the Torah imposes sexual obligations on the man in marriage, and neither party can abrogate those, just as no two parties in American law can stipulate in a contract between them that they will not abide by state law (for example, that they will not support children born of their union). The parties may determine by contract only those elements of the relationship which the law permits them to decide.

*Mishnah Ketubbot* 5:1:

Though they said that a virgin claims two hundred *zuz* and a widow one *maneh* (100 *zuz*), if one be minded to add to it, even a hundred *manehs*, he may add thereto. If she became a widow or were divorced, whether after betrothal or after marriage, she receives the whole. R. Elazar ben Azariah says, If after marriage, she receives the whole, but if after betrothal a virgin receives two hundred and a widow one *maneh* because he assigned to her only on the stipulation that he wed her. R. Judah says, If a man so desired, he may write out a bond for two hundred for a virgin and she may write, "I have received from you one *maneh*," for a widow one *maneh* and she may write, "I have received from you fifty *zuz*." R. Meir says, Anyone who assigns less than two hundred to a virgin or one *maneh* to a widow is as if he committed fornication.

Maimonides, *Mishneh Torah*, Laws of Marriage 6:1, 2, 8–10:

### Chapter Six

1. If a man betroths a woman on condition, then if the condition is fulfilled, she is betrothed, and if the condition is not fulfilled, she is not betrothed, and it makes no difference whether the condition favors the man or the woman. Any condition whatsoever, whether it applies to marriage or divorce, buying or selling, or any other money matter, must satisfy four requirements.

2. These are the four requirements for any condition: it must specify both alternatives; the positive alternative must precede the negative one; the condition must precede the action; and the condition must be possible to fulfill. If the condition lacks any one of those elements, the condition is void, and it is as if there were no condition at all. The woman is thus betrothed or divorced immediately and the purchase or gift takes effect immediately as if no condition had been made, since the condition lacks one of the four elements.

8. If he stipulated a condition which is possible to fulfill but forbidden by the Torah as, for example, if he said to the woman, "If you eat (forbidden) fat or blood, you are betrothed to me with this *denar,* and if you do not eat that, you are not betrothed"; "If you eat pig meat, here is your writ of divorce, and if you do not eat it, it will not constitute a writ of divorce," and after enunciating the stipulation he hands her the *denar* or the writ of divorce, the condition is valid. If she sins and eats, she is betrothed or divorced; if she does not eat, she is not betrothed or divorced. We do not say in such a case, "He has made a condition which is contrary to what is written in the Torah" because she can choose not to eat and not to be betrothed or divorced.

9. To what did the Sages apply the principle, "A condition contrary to what is written in the Torah is void, except for money matters, where it is valid"? To a case like this: a man betrothed, divorced, gave a gift, or sold something on condition that he thereby acquired title to something to which the Torah did not entitle him but, on the contrary, denied him; or he exempts himself through his condition from something which the Torah requires of him. In such cases we say to him: "Your condition is void, and your actions are now fully valid, and you are not exempt from anything which the Torah requires of you, and you do not have title to anything which the Torah denied you."

10. How so? If, for example, a man betrothed a woman on condition that he is to be free from the obligations of providing her with food, clothing, and sex, we say to him, "Your conditions on food and clothing are valid because they are conditions on money matters, but your condition on sex is void because the Torah obligated you to provide sex. She is therefore betrothed, and you have conjugal obligations which you cannot avoid through your stipulation." And the same holds true in all similar cases.

Similarly, if a man betroths a beautiful, captive woman on condition that he may treat her as a bondswoman, she is betrothed, but he may not treat her as a bondswoman because the Torah has denied him the right to enslave her after he has had intercourse with her. He may not acquire through his stipulation anything which the Torah denies him; rather, his condition is void. And the same holds true in all similar cases.

## B. The Contractual Element of Marriage in Civil Law

### 1. *Balfour* v. *Balfour*

The following opinion by the English Court of Appeals states the traditional common law views toward economic agreements between spouses during a marriage. Despite the fact that Mr. and Mrs. Balfour in fact lived at opposite ends of the earth and ultimately divorced, at the time of the agreement in question they were legally residing together as husband and wife.

Each of the three judges delivered an individual opinion in this case, as is the custom in English appellate courts. The attitudes and reasons expressed for reaching the unanimous decision, that Mr. Balfour's agreement is not legally enforceable, differ significantly. To some extent this agreement was not enforceable because it was not a bargain meeting legal requirements, to some extent because courts should not disturb marriages by interfering, and to some extent because it would injure the court system if judges were saddled with these disputes. Notice how these three themes are drawn on in different ways by each of the judges.

BALFOUR V. BALFOUR
In the Court of Appeal, 1919
[1919] 2 K.B. 571

Appeal from a decision of Sargant, J., sitting as an additional judge of the King's Bench Division.

The plaintiff sued the defendant (her husband) for money which she claimed to be due in respect of an agreed allowance of 30 *l*. a month. The alleged agreement was entered into under the following circumstances. The parties were married in August, 1900. The husband, a civil engineer, had a post under the Government of Ceylon as Director of Irrigation, and after the marriage he and his wife went to Ceylon, and lived there together until the year 1915, except that in 1906 they paid a short visit to this country, and in 1908 the wife came to England in order to undergo an operation, after which she returned to Ceylon. In November, 1915, she came to this country with her husband, who was on leave. They remained in England until August, 1916, when the husband's leave was up and he had to return. The wife however on the doctor's advice remained in England.

On August 8, 1916, the husband being about to sail, the alleged parol agreement sued upon was made. The plaintiff, as appeared from the judge's note, gave the following evidence of what took place: "In August, 1916, defendant's leave was up. I was suffering from rheumatic arthritis. The doctor advised my staying in England for some months, not to go out till November 4. On August 8 my husband sailed. He gave me a cheque from 8th to 31st for 24 *l*., and promised to give me 30 *l*. per month till I returned." Later on she said: "My husband and I wrote the figures together on August 8; 34 *l*. shown. Afterwards he said 30 *l*."

In cross-examination she said that they had not agreed to live apart until subsequent differences arose between them, and that the agreement of August, 1916, was one which might be made by a couple in amity. Her husband in consultation with her assessed her needs, and said he would send 30 *1.* per month for her maintenance. She further said that she then understood that the defendant would be returning to England in a few months, but that he afterwards wrote to her suggesting that they had better remain apart. In March, 1918, she commenced proceedings for restitution of conjugal rights, and on July 30 she obtained a decree nisi. On December 16, 1918, she obtained an order for alimony.

Sargant, J. held that the husband was under an obligation to support his wife, and the parties had contracted that the extent of that obligation should be defined in terms of so much a month. The consent of the wife to that arrangement was a sufficient consideration to constitute a contract which could be sued upon.

He accordingly gave judgment for the plaintiff.

The husband appealed.

WARRINGTON, L. J. (after stating the facts). Those being the facts we have to say whether there is a legal contract between the parties, in other words, whether what took place between them was in the domain of a contract or whether it was merely a domestic arrangement such as may be made every day between a husband and wife who are living together in friendly intercourse. It may be, and I do not for a moment say that it is not, possible for such a contract as is alleged in the present case to be made between husband and wife. The question is whether such a contract was made. That can only be determined either by proving that it was made in express terms, or that there is a necessary implication from the circumstances of the parties, and the transaction generally, that such a contract was made.

It is quite plain that no such contract was made in express terms, and there was no bargain on the part of the wife at all. All that took place was this: The husband and wife met in a friendly way and discussed what would be necessary for her support while she was detained in England, the husband being in Ceylon, and they came to the conclusion that 30 *1.* a month would be about right, but there is no evidence of any express bargain by the wife that she would in all the circumstances treat that as in satisfaction of the obligation of the husband to maintain her.

Can we find a contract from the position of the parties? It seems to me it is quite impossible. If we were to imply such a contract in this case we should be implying on the part of the wife that whatever happened and whatever might be the change of circumstances while the husband was away she should be content with this 30 *l.* a month, and bind herself by an obligation in law not to require him to pay anything more; and on the other hand we should be implying on the part of the husband a bargain to pay 30 *l.* a month for some indefinite period whatever might be his circumstances.

Then again it seems to me that it would be impossible to make any such implication. The matter really reduces itself to an absurdity when one considers it, because if we were to hold that there was a contract in this case we should have to hold that with regard to all the more or less trivial concerns of life where a wife, at the request of her husband, makes a promise to him, that is a promise which can be enforced in law.

All I can say is that there is no such contract here. These two people never intended to make a bargain which could be enforced in law. The husband expressed his intention to make this payment, and he promised to make it, and was bound in honour to continue it so long as he was in a position to do so. The wife on the other hand, so far as I can see, made no bargain at all. That is in my opinion sufficient to dispose of the case. . .

DUKE, L. J. I agree. This is in some respects an important case, and as we differ from the judgment of the Court below I propose to state concisely my views and the ground which have led me to the conclusion at which I have arrived. . . .

It is impossible to say that where the relationship of husband and wife exists, and promises are exchanged, they must be deemed to be promises of a contractual nature. In order to establish a contract there ought to be something more than mere mutual promises having regard to the domestic relations of the parties. It is required that the obligations arising out of that relationship shall be displaced before either of the parties can found a contract upon such promises. . . .

The proposition that the mutual promises made in the ordinary domestic relationship of husband and wife of necessity give cause for action on a contract seems to me to go to the very root of the relationship, and to be a possible fruitful source of dissension and quarrelling. I cannot see that any benefit would result from it to either of the parties, but on the other hand it would lead to unlimited litigation in a relationship which should be obviously as far as possible protected from possibilities of that kind.

I think, therefore, that in point of principle there is no foundation for the claim which is made here, and I am satisfied that there was no consideration moving from the wife to the husband or promise by the husband to the wife which was sufficient to sustain this action founded on contract. I think, therefore, that the appeal must be allowed.

ATKIN, L. J. The defence to this action on the alleged contract is that the defendant, the husband, entered into no contract with his wife, and for the determination of that it is necessary to remember that there are agreements between parties which do not result in contract within the meaning of that term in our law. The ordinary example is where two parties agree to take a walk together, or where there is an offer and an acceptance of hospitality. Nobody would suggest in ordinary circumstances that those agreements result in what we know as a contract, and one of the most usual forms of agreement which does not constitute a contract appears to me to be the arrangements which are made between husband and wife.

It is quite common, and it is the natural and inevitable result of the relationship of husband and wife, that the two spouses should make arrangements between themselves—agreements such as are in dispute in this action—agreements for allowances, by which the husband agrees that he will pay to his wife a certain sum of money, per week, or per month, or per year, to cover either her own expenses or the necessary expenses of the household and of the children of the marriage, and in which the wife promises either expressly or impliedly to apply the allowance for the purpose for which it is given. To my mind those agreements, or many of them, do not result in contract at all, and they do not result in contracts even though there may be what as between other parties would constitute consideration for the agreement.

The consideration, as we know, may consist either in some right, interest, profit or benefit accruing to one party, or some forbearance, detriment, loss or responsibility given, suffered or undertaken by the other. That is a well-known definition, and it constantly happens, I think, that such arrangements made between husband and wife are arrangements in which there are mutual promises, or in which there is consideration in form within the definition that I have mentioned. Nevertheless they are not contracts, and they are not contracts because the parties did not intend that they should be attended by legal consequences.

To my mind it would be of the worst possible example to hold that agreements such as this resulted in legal obligations which could be enforced in the Courts. It would mean this, that when the husband makes his wife a promise to give her an allowance of 30 s. or 2 1. a week, whatever he can afford to give her, for the maintenance of the household and children, and she promises so to apply it, not only could she sue him for his failure in any week to supply the allowance, but he could sue her for non-performance of the obligation, express or implied, which she had undertaken upon her part. All I can say is that the small Courts of this country would have to be multiplied one hundredfold if these arrangements were held to result in legal obligations.

They are not sued upon, not because the parties are reluctant to enforce their legal rights when the agreement is broken, but because the parties, in the inception of the arrangement, never intended that they should be sued upon. Agreements such as these are outside the realm of contracts altogether. The common law does not regulate the form of agreements between spouses. Their promises are not sealed with seals and sealing wax. The consideration that really obtains for them is that natural love and affection which counts for so little in these cold Courts. The terms may be repudiated, varied or renewed as performance proceeds or as disagreements develop, and the principles of the common law as to exoneration and discharge and accord and satisfaction are such as find no place in the domestic code. The parties themselves are advocates, judges, Courts, sheriff's officer and reporter. In respect of these promises each house is a domain into which the King's writ does not seek to run, and to which his officers do not seek to be admitted.

The only question in this case is whether or not this promise was of such a class or not. For the reasons given by my brethren it appears to me to be plainly established that the promise here was not intended by either party to be attended by legal consequences. I think the onus was upon the plaintiff, and the plaintiff has not established any contract. The parties were living together, the wife intending to return. The suggestion is that the husband bound himself to pay 30 *l*. a month under all circumstances, and, although she was in ill-health and alone in this country, that out of that sum she undertook to defray the whole of the medical expenses that might fall upon her, whatever might be the development of her illness, and in whatever expenses it might involve her. To my mind neither party contemplated such a result. I think that the parol evidence upon which the case turns does not establish a contract. I think that the letters do not evidence such a contract, or amplify the oral evidence which was given by the wife, which is not in dispute. For these reasons I think the judgment of the Court below was wrong and that this appeal should be allowed.

Appeal allowed.

## 2. *Riesenfeld* v. *Jacobson*

A somewhat different view of the contract element of marriage is expressed by Justice Haim Cohn in the following excerpt from a decision of the Supreme Court of Israel.

RIESENFELD V. JACOBSON
Supreme Court of Israel
17 Piskei Din 1009 (1963)

The appellant, a married man, agreed with the respondent that upon the dissolution of his marriage they would become husband and wife. Meanwhile, they lived together in a flat purchased by the appellant, but registered in the respondent's name. It had expressly been agreed between them that in the event of their separation (either before or after their marriage), the flat should belong and be restored to the appellant. In fact, appellant and respondent were never married to each other, and they separated, the flat remaining occupied by the respondent. An action brought by the appellant for a declaration that the flat was his property and for an order to have the registration in the name of the respondent cancelled, was dismissed by the District Court on the ground that the contract between the parties had been repugnant to public policy and morals and no action could be founded thereon. On appeal, Held, reversed by majority decision.

PER COHN, J.: Assuming the illegality or immorality of a contract by a married man to marry another woman after dissolution of his marriage—or of a contract by a married man to live with another woman as husband and wife—the question arises whether this action was founded upon any such contract. . . . The only contract which has to be pleaded as the cause of the present action is the respondent's promise to return the flat to the appellant in the event (*inter alia*) of their not being married to each other. If there was anything illegal or immoral in their contract to become married to each other after the dissolution of the appellant's marriage, then legality and morals have prevailed when the respondent refused to perform that contract; and in so letting legality and morals prevail, she has herself fulfilled the condition stipulated by her to return the flat to the appellant: why should the courts not enforce that stipulation? . . .

However, be that as it may, while the common law of England always regarded contracts by married men in contemplation of a dissolution of their marriage as repugnant to public policy and hence unenforceable, this was not the law of Israel. . . . The English rule originated in the conception of marriage as a sacrament and its purpose is the protection of this sacred institution from any harm or interference which may be caused to it by the performance of adverse contractual obligations. But as distinguished from the law of England, Jewish law—which applies in Israel to marriages of Jews—does not impose any "status" of marriage of which, once they entered into it, the parties cannot rid themselves except by legislation or judicial act. The marriage in Jewish law is a contract, albeit a very solemn one, between husband and wife; as they entered into it from their own free will, so they may, at any time and for any reason, terminate and rescind it from their own free will. Where spouses agree to have their marriage dissolved, the function of the courts is a purely supervisory and executory one; they do not, as in other systems, "decree" a divorce, but they only see to it that the divorce, agreed upn by the parties, is properly executed. It is in this divergence from other systems that the distinction—you may even say the modernity—of Jewish law lies; no imposition of a status, whether you like it or not, but your own and your spouse's right to determine yourselves when and whether to marry, and when and whether to dissolve your marriage. It follows that an agreement cannot be said to be repugnant to public policy or morals for the reason alone that it presupposes, or stipulates, the prior consent of a third party to have a marriage dissolved; parties are bound to their contracts only so long as they do not agree to terminate them, and there is nothing wrong in entering into agreement which is to come into force only when it can be performed so that a previously made contract should not be broken.

## 3. Antenuptial Agreements

Antenuptial agreements, in which partners on the threshold of marriage provide for the property, services, and social incidents of their union, have long been recognized by most legal systems, including the common law. The traditional *ketubbah* is itself a marriage settlement, assigning property and other interests. In the 1970s, when the feminist movement challenged traditional gender roles, antenuptial agreements became a popular vehicle for couples to spell out their new expectations of each other in marriage and in the event of divorce. The excerpt from *Time*, written at the height of that period, describes the intent, extent, and content of such contracts. The paper by Professor Grace Blumberg, written six years later, indicates some of the unexpected pitfalls of such agreements—to the point that in many cases these agreements act to the detriment of the very women they originally sought to protect. Both articles also raise substantial questions regarding the legal enforceability of such agreements and the capacity of two humans at the outset of their relationship to provide rationally for the contingencies the agreements contemplate.

TIES THAT BIND
*Time*, September 1, 1975, 62

Jackie and Aristotle Onassis reportedly drew up a 170-point marriage contract covering every possible detail of their married life. In 1969, Kleenex heir James Kimberly, then 63, and his third wife, Jacqueline Trezise, then 19, signed a prenuptial contract limiting any possible alimony payments to $18,000 for every year of marriage. Her divorce lawyer is now seeking a larger settlement on the grounds that she was "a mere schoolgirl" when she signed.

The well-to-do have long used marriage contracts to protect their wealth from the caprices of divorce courts. But now contracts are increasingly popular among educated, middle-class couples who have their own misgivings about traditional marriage. Feminism is playing a driving role. So is the rising divorce rate. Torn between the need for companionship and the notion that marriage is a trap, many of the young want their expectations and rules for married life clearly laid out in a contract.

*Petty Issues.* One student of such agreements, Cleveland Sociologist Marvin B. Sussman of Case Western Reserve University, has made a comprehensive study of marriage contracts. He has compiled more than 1,500 such documents. Typically, the contracts shuttle between large and petty issues. Some provisions in one: "Ralph agrees not to pick, nag or comment about Wanda's skin blemishes," "Wanda will refrain from yelling about undone chores until Sunday afternoon," and both parties agree to avoid using the words "married to, married, husband, wife . . . and other derogatory terms." More seriously, the couple agreed to allow extramarital affairs, keep separate bank accounts, and not have children—at least until the five-year contract comes up for renewal.

The gut issues in most contracts are money, sex and responsibilities in the home. Economic provisions generally aim at equality—sometimes by pooling income and assets and agreeing to divide them evenly in case of divorce. If the wife works, partners usually keep resources separate and share expenses.

Husbands commonly waive their legal right to determine where the couple will live, and agree to do half of the household chores. Many provisions emphasize privacy and freedom, calling for separate rooms and nights out. Extramarital affairs, says Sussman, bring "the greatest amount of inconsistency and confusion." Some contracts permit affairs, though there are often rules about how long an affair can go on without one's married partner being informed.

Some couples agree to turn over important unresolved disputes to an impartial arbitrator. In fact, some of Sussman's contracts, which he calls "therapeutic," were written in mid-marriage with the help of a therapist or counselor, mainly to "get the most obvious kinds of annoying behavior out on the table." Two representative provisions: "Wife will not say she does not believe her husband loves her" and "husband will lift the toilet seat before urinating."

Private marriage contracts are legally ambiguous, even when they are drawn up by lawyers, signed by witnesses and properly notarized.

Contracts or no, courts will usually not intervene in a marriage or enforce any private contract law. Thus a wife whose marriage contract waives alimony and grants her husband the right to have extramarital affairs could conceivably win a divorce on the grounds of adultery and get her alimony too. But contracts between unmarried lovers are not limited by established marriage law. If a couple wants to make sure that their agreement has legal force, advises New York Feminist Lawyer Brenda Feigen Fasteau, "They should stay unmarried," in which case their contract is like any other private agreement between individuals.

## 4. The Dangers of Contract

Grace Ganz Blumberg, "Cohabitation Without Marriage: A Different Perspective," 28 *UCLA L.Rev.* (1981), pp. 1125, 1160–65, 1168–70 (footnotes omitted).

Maine described the movement in our law from status to contract. More recently, commentators have recounted the public disillusion with contract and the return to publicly created status relationships between, for example, employers and employees, landlords and tenants, and manufacturers and consumers. Freedom of contract has not proven to be the key to human mobility that Maine and other nineteenth-century political economists envisaged. Instead, contract theory has often been an intensifier of human disadvantage by which the wealthy and powerful exploit the poor and weak.

Yet, in domestic relations, contract is heralded as a harbinger of freedom of choice, mobility, and economic well-being. This is because domestic relations is a developmentally retarded field. The status disabilities of married women were abandoned centuries after those of serfs. Formal legal economic equality between the sexes has been attained only in the last two decades. (Actual economic and social equality is a distant and perhaps unrealizable goal.) Domestic relations law still restricts the rights of spouses and cohabitants to contract freely. Freedom of contract is a significant expression of equality of legal capacity. Believing that freedom of contract is also likely to achieve substantive equality between the sexes, some commentators advocate destruction of these remaining status fetters. This approach is manifest in recent judicial treatment of cohabitation under the contract rubric, and judicial and legislative expansion of the capacity of spouses to alter or destroy the status incidents of marriage. These developments are, however, conceptually inconsistent with the dominant tendency in domestic relations law to recast status constructs to take into account gender-related differences in wealth and power. This tendency is manifest in the dramatic development of equitable property distribution at divorce, the movement to consider homemakers' services in calculating support, property distribution, and social benefits, and the rise of rehabilitative alimony. That some commentators argue for both goals, freedom of contract and fortified status constructs, and that legislatures pass laws embodying both concepts, should not obscure the essential inconsistency of these two positions. I will argue that publicly created status is a much more suitable vehicle for handling support and property claims of unmarried and married cohabitants than is contract theory.

We know more than Maine did. We have had our romance with freedom of contract, epitomized in the notorious *Lochner* case. The inequality between the baker and his employer was greater in scale but was not significantly different in kind from the inequality between the sexes. In general, the essence of a cohabitation or marriage contract between heterosexual cohabitants is that the man gives up wealth that would otherwise accrue to him in order to insure the woman some semblance of economic dignity. Self-interest would lead the man to give up as little as possible. The woman has scant leverage with which to persuade him otherwise. She lacks economic power. She needs a stable relationship more than he does: it is vital to the comfortable exercise of her reproductive potential, and it is a means of enhancing her wealth and standard of living. For a male, on the other hand, marriage or stable cohabitation is likely to diminish both his personal wealth and his standard of living. Even a feminist must agree that there is ample economic and biological basis for Midge Decter's assertion that "marriage is something asked by women and agreed to by men." Thus, the cohabitants' unequal bargaining power leads to unjust results under contract theory.

Moreover, the market model fails to take into account emotional factors. The most notable characteristic of western love is its particularity. That another suitor offers better terms, such as marriage and its concomitant property rights—does not enhance a woman's bargaining power vis-a-vis the desired suitor. The relative infrequency of market opportunity also tends to limit her capacity to turn down the desired suitor's offer. Who knows when, if ever, love will come again? And, by the time contract negotiation is expected to begin, on the eve of cohabitation or marriage, she has already made substantial emotional and time investment in the relationship.

Furthermore, it may not be desirable for couples to contract on the eve of cohabitation about future circumstances that can be only dimly forseen. A contract is binding even when matters turn out very differently than the parties expected. Domesticity and maternity surprise and alarm even the most astute women. The life of economic achievement and independence which a woman may anticipate is often severely disrupted. Additionally, the economic and social integration that will take place during the relationship has not yet begun on the eve of cohabitation or marriage. The fixing of individualistic rights and duties at this point is premature and may well impede the process of economic and social integration. The interest of the parties in the success of their relationship may best be served by postponing their recognition of their conflicting interests until they are firmly established as a couple. Recognition of unequal contribution to material wealth, for example, is likely to pass with little effect after the birth of a child, but might pose a serious stumbling block to negotiation of a cohabitation contract. The provisions that fix rights for married cohabitants—equitable distribution and elective share laws—are written, as they should be, from the vantage point of an ongoing mature marriage. This is the perspective of a majority of the public and the legislators.

Finally, unmarried cohabitating couples simply do not make formal cohabitation contracts. Trost, in his sample of 250 Swedish couples, found only one contract. American case law does not reveal one formally executed contract. Instead, plaintiffs allege vague oral pooling agreements, protestations of love and respect accompanied by assurances that "everything I have is yours" or "I'll always take care of you." Absent even such loving words, some courts will imply a contract from the behavior of the parties. Since the issue is the "intent" of both parties, however, the consciously selfish behavior of one may defeat the clearly expressed community intent of the other. An implied pooling contract could conceivably rest on no more than cohabitation and some degree of economic cooperation, such as division of labor. A serious impediment, however, to the growth of implied contract (and constructive trust) is the unavoidable result that a prevailing cohabitant might enjoy a better property settlement in many states than would a lawfully married spouse. . . .

Most discussions of "intent" refer to "intent of the couple" or "intent of the parties" as though cohabitants operate with one heart and one mind despite their conflicting interests. This view of the cohabiting couple is belied by reported cases, sociological studies and gender-related social and economic conditions. In most reported cases, the woman wanted to marry and was economically powerless. The man was domineering and economically powerful. The relationship was long and traditional in terms of sex stereotyped role assumption. The woman took the man's name and often bore his children. When sociologists have asked the question (and they have not asked it frequently or pointedly enough), they have found that female cohabitants tend to want to marry while male cohabitants do not. Moreover, cohabitants assume traditional sex roles as frequently as do married persons. This finding undercuts the primary argument of proponents of nonmarital arrangements, that is, that marriage is the villain and nonmarital "experimentation" will free women from their traditional roles. That marriage-like conditions perpetuate traditional roles is indisputable, but marriage-like conditions without the protection of legal marriage further retard the position of women.

Much contract analysis refers not only to the parties' "intent," but also to their "reasonable expectations." The courts, we are told, should enforce such expectations through the vehicles of contract and quasi-contract. Without reference to state support and marital property law, however, there is nothing "reasonable" about the expectation that property owned and funds earned by one party will be judicially awarded to another. In most situations, the predicate for such "reasonable expectations" is the homemaker's provision of ephemeral and evanescent services for herself and her cohabitant. Unlike labor contributed to a business, which would support a claim in implied partnership or constructive trust, the cohabitant's services have been completely consumed. For most Americans, her service contribution did not eliminate expenditures which her cohabitant would otherwise have incurred. He would have taken care of his own homemaking needs, albeit in a less elaborate manner. Her services simply enhanced the quality of their relationship and of their individual lives. Thus, it is not reasonable for her to expect a future accounting unless her expectation is formed, as it seems to be, by knowledge of the way divorcing homemakers are treated under state support and marital property law. The present contract scheme recognizes this expectation, but only indirectly: state marital property law = basis for reasonable expectations of some recompense for homemaking contributions = quantum meruit recovery of value of services less value of support. Since marital property law informs the cohabitant's expectations, it makes more sense to apply it directly than it does to give her an unsatisfactory panoply of contract remedies which are once removed from the source of her expectations.

Some commentators suggest that the party's/(ies') choice between marriage and cohabitation should be read as acceptance or rejection of the economic incidents of marriage. This suggestion is based on three untenable assumptions: that people who marry realize what marriage entails; that people get married for the purpose of acquiring the legal incidents of marriage; and that people who marry would generally think the incidents of marriage appropriate to the estate they have assumed. Cohabitants, both married and unmarried, are notoriously ignorant of the economic incidents that their relationship entails. Moreover, when cohabitation becomes a well-established institution, cohabitants who marry do so for reasons other than to acquire the legal incidents of marriage. Finally, few people think, during or after marriage, that it is appropriate that their personal income and assets are subject to the support claims of another *after* dissolution of the relationship by divorce. Thus, an obligation few would voluntarily undertake is legally imposed because of our knowledge of the economic dynamics of marriage and concern about avoidable public expense. In view of this, it seems inappropriate to require that unmarried cohabitants demonstrate affirmative assumption of these economic incidents before they attach to their relationship.

## C. THE SOCIAL ELEMENT IN JEWISH MARRIAGE

Marriage is a social institution in several quite different connotations of the word "social." Marriage is social in that it is especially vital to the group self-perpetuation of Jews. Their society is defined by common descent, and the family is the place where education and acculturation occur. Lacking common land or political sovereignty, Jews gain identity primarily through being born to a Jewish mother and through their membership in a Jewish family. Endogamy and related practices are a crucial element of Jewish group survival. If Americans were to stop getting married, the nation could still persist through births out of marriage, immigration, and, perhaps, by conquest of childbearing people. Any such children would be Americans. But without the family identity dependent on marriage, Jewish identity would soon disappear.

Another social connotation of marriage is that marriage defines social status. Entitlements and obligations regarding the distribution of goods and services are established. Spouses, parents and children, siblings and collaterals have claims for maintenance and support, distribution and inheritance, management and control of property. As has already been mentioned, Jewish marriage itself traditionally was seen as an acquisition, a property transfer affecting relationships between the families of husband and wife and the redistribution of their wealth. The parties and their families have had great flexibility in establishing these property relationships by contract, but Jewish law has long insisted that these are more than private agreements. Their social dimension will be apparent in the discussion later in this section on the imposition by the rabbis of economic conditions on the parties and the refusal to allow couples to avoid their obligations by agreement. Noneconomic forms of social status such as honor, respect, and position are also defined at least in part through marriage.

A marriage creates a new social unit of husband and wife, and this is a third social dimension of marriage. The preceding discussion of clan and enlarged family entitlements should not obscure the unusually heavy emphasis Jewish tradition places on spouses as a crucial social unit. Without marriage a person is incomplete, and through marriage people can deal with the trials of the world. The myths of Genesis from Adam and Eve through the patriarchs and matriarchs are remarkable in this respect. It is hard to find a parallel in other peoples' literatures that approaches the warmth and fine delineation of marital interaction captured in the sparse tales of Abraham and Sarah. Law imperfectly captures the essence of the union of two bodies in one flesh; nevertheless, the legal structure of marriage is seriously deficient if it does not promote the potential of marriage to become such a union.

Finally, everyone knows that weddings are social occasions in yet another sense: the whole community is likely to participate. The laws that structure the ceremony reflect the group values attached to the event itself. Jewish marriage is a public occasion. Betrothal can occur in front of two witnesses alone, but recitation of the seven blessings that constitute the core of the wedding ceremony requires a quorum of ten (a *minyan*). Moreover, accompanying the bride to the wedding canopy is one of only two reasons recognized in Jewish law for interrupting study, the other being participation in a funeral. The following tannaitic source suggests that God likes to attend weddings too.

> *Avot D'Rabbi Natan*, chap. 4:
> If two scholars sit and study Torah and before them passes a bridal procession or the bier of a dead man, then if there are enough in the procession, they ought not neglect their study; but if not, let them get up and cheer and hail the bride, or accompany the dead.
>
> Once as Rabbi Judah bar Il'ai sat teaching his disciples, a bride passed by. So he took myrtle twigs in his hand and cheered her until the bride passed out of his sight.
>
> Another time as Rabbi Judah bar Il'ai sat teaching his disciples, a bride passed by. "What was that?" he asked them.
>
> "A bride passing by," they replied.
>
> "My sons," he said to them, "get up and attend upon the bride. For thus we find concerning the Holy One, blessed be He, that He attended upon a bride, as it is said, 'And the Lord God built the rib' (Genesis 2:22). If He attended upon a bride, how much more so we!"
>
> And where do we find that the Holy One, blessed be He, attended upon a bride? For it is said, "And the Lord God built (*banah*) the rib." Now, in the sea towns they call plaiting *binyata*. Hence we learn that the Holy One, blessed be He, fixed Eve's hair and outfitted her as a bride and brought her to Adam, as it is said, "And He brought her unto the man" (ibid.). The first time the Holy One, blessed be He, acted as best man for Adam; henceforth one must get a best man for himself.

In this section we shall explore some of the legal manifestations of the social element in marriage in all four senses of the word "social."

## 1. *Endogamy*

From the very beginning of Jewish group identity, Jewish marriage has been endogamous: Jews are allowed to marry only other Jews. This insistence on marrying within the clan is not a common feature of other cultures, ancient or modern. Undoubtedly the practice has contributed both to the persistence of the culture and to the hostility of other people toward this group, which insists on standing apart.

Abraham was content only after his servant swore to him that he would take a wife for Isaac from among Abraham's own relatives (Genesis 24), and Rebekah and Isaac saw to it that Jacob did likewise (Gen. 27:46–28:5). The Bible records the great displeasure of Rebekah and Isaac when Esau marries Hittite women (Gen. 26:34–35)—so great that Esau takes an additional wife from Ishmael's daughters to placate his parents (Gen. 28:6–9). Part of the ruse by which the children of Jacob revenge the rape of their sister Dinah is their feigned promise that "we will give our daughters to you, and we will take your daughters to us, and we will dwell with you, and we will become one people" (Gen. 34:16).

Biblical law contains no general affirmative requirement of marriage within the group although it clearly assumes the practice and both Moses (Exodus 34:16; Deuteronomy 7:3–4) and Joshua (Josh. 23:12) declare God's commandment not to marry Canaanite women. Despite the merit ascribed to endogamy, the Bible records a number of cases when Hebrews married foreign women. Several of Jacob's sons married outside their clan (Genesis 38:1–2; 41:45), and Moses himself found his wife from among the Midianites (Exodus 2:21). Some of the leaders and kings of Israel married princesses and other important women from other nations for political reasons (Judges 3:6; Ruth 1:4; II Samuel 3:3; 11:3; I Kings 3:1; 7:14; 9:1; I Chronicles 2:17). Nevertheless, endogamous marriages were clearly preferred during the early biblical period, and centuries later Ezra and Nehemiah prohibited Jews from marrying any foreigners and forced those returning to Jerusalem from the Babylonian exile to divorce their foreign wives (Ezra, chap. 9 and 10; Nehemiah 13:13–30).

During most of the last two millenia Jews were kept apart by external forces limiting their social intercourse with their neighbors, as well as by their own customs. No Jewish marriage could be contracted with a non-Jew under either Jewish or non-Jewish law, so it must be assumed that the Jewish partner either left the community, the non-Jew converted, or their relationship was something other than marriage. The emancipation of the Jews during the Enlightenment was contemporaneous with the assertion of jurisdiction over marriage by most European secular governments, which theretofore had deferred to church authorities on matters of marriage and divorce. Civil marriage and civil divorce created challenges to Catholic canon law and to Jewish endogamous law. Jews living in a secular state have no choice but to conform to the requirements of the government, but compliance with secular law is only a necessary, and not a sufficient, condition of Jewish marriage. Jews may not contract a Jewish marriage without a license from the state, nor will a rabbinic court grant Jews a divorce until the state courts have entered their decree. But rabbinic law, like cannon law, accords only very limited legal recognition to a civil marriage and none to a civil divorce. Specifically, when a state marries two Jews who could have lawfully married under Jewish law, their marriage will generally be retroactively, albeit reluctantly, recognized by rabbinic authorities. That means all legal rights and obligations of spouses would be enforced by rabbinic courts. Moreover, children of a Jewish woman are Jews from birth whether she is lawfully married or not, and so her secular marriage (even to a non-Jewish man) does not affect the children's status. But if two persons marry under civil law who could not marry under Jewish law (including a Jew and a non-Jew), only Reform rabbis recognize the union; for all others, the marriage is not legally recognized, and the civil act has no consequences.

## 2. *"Conditions of the Court"*

The connections between the contractual and the social themes in Jewish marriage are especially visible in those situations where the rabbis placed limits on what the parties could establish by agreement as the law of their marriage. Marriage itself is an acquisition in which money changes hands. Stipulating a settlement of property on behalf of the bride in case she is divorced or widowed safeguards her economic security. The parties are given wide latitude in fixing the maximum settlement for the wife, but no husband can avoid basic financial obligations by clever draftsmanship. If the contract fails to contain the minimum amounts considered decent, the court will construct the needed condition and read it into the document. Similarly, the husband could not by inserting a clause in the contract avoid obligations to support, ransom, and care for his wife in the event of kidnapping, illness, or insanity. Nor could he by agreement deprive his children of support.

Asserting their authority to shape the institutions of Jewish law, the rabbis built such conditions into the very definition of "Jewish marriage." In doing so they effectively annulled the husband's privileges under biblical law to determine important aspects of the marital agreement. Every Jewish man who sought to be married was understood to have agreed to these conditions, whether explicitly or implicitly, and he could not avoid them by specific contractual agreement to the contrary. These implied, constructive conditions are therefore part of the obligatory, social fabric of Jewish marriage which supersedes the voluntary, contractual element.

Through these conditions, the rabbis expanded the wife's rights and protections considerably beyond those in the Bible. The examples that follow do not exhaust the constructive conditions which the rabbis read into every marriage contract, but they are typical.

*Mishnah Ketubbot* 4:7–12; 5:1–2:

### Chapter 4
### Mishnah 7

If one had not provided for a marriage settlement for her in the marriage contract, then if she is a virgin at the time of marriage she may claim two hundred *zuz*, and if she is a widow one hundred, for that is a condition of the Court. If he assigned her in writing a field of value of one hundred *zuz* instead of two hundred and did not stipulate, "Everything which I possess is surety for your marriage settlement," he is nevertheless liable (for the full two hundred *zuz*) since that is a condition instituted by the Court.

### Mishnah 8

If he had not written for her, "If you are taken captive, I will ransom you and I will take you back as my wife," . . . he is nevertheless liable because that is a condition enjoined by the Court.

### Mishnah 9

If she were taken captive, he must ransom her; and if he said, "Here is her bill of divorce and her marriage settlement, let her redeem herself," he has no such power. If she came to harm, he must heal her. If he said, "Here is her bill of divorce and her marriage settlement, let her cure herself," he is entitled to do so.

### Mishnah 10

If he did not stipulate in writing for her, "Your male children by me shall inherit the money of your marriage settlement above the share (of my property) which they are to receive with their (half-) brothers (that is, my sons by other marriages)," he is nevertheless liable for that, since this is a condition laid down by the Court.

### Mishnah 11
(If he did not stipulate in writing for her), "Your female children by me shall stay in my house and be maintained from my possessions until they are wed to husbands," he is nevertheless liable, as this is a condition instituted by the Court.

### Mishnah 12
(If he did not stipulate in writing for her), "You shall dwell in my house and you shall be supported from my goods as long as you stay a widow in my house," he is nevertheless liable, for this is a condition established by the Court. The people of Jerusalem used to write ". . . . until the heirs are willing to give you your marriage settlement." Therefore if the heirs were so minded, they would give her her marriage settlement and send her away.

### Chapter 5
### Mishnah 1
. . . Rabbi Judah says, If a man so desires, he may write out a bond for two hundred *zuz* for a virgin, and she may write, "I have received from you one hundred," or for a widow (he may write a bond for) one hundred *zuz* and she may write, "I have received from you fifty." Rabbi Meir says, Anyone who assigns less than two hundred to a virgin or one hundred to a widow is as if he committed fornication.

### Mishnah 2
They grant a virgin twelve months, after her betrothal, to provide herself [with an outfit], and just as they grant to a woman so they grant the man to provide himself [with an outfit]. And to a widow, thirty days. If the time has arrived, and they (the virgin and widow) were not taken into marriage, she is to be maintained out of his property.

## 3. *Obligations of Spouses to Each Other*

The rabbis spelled out the obligations of partners in marriage more explicitly than the Bible. The Mishnah establishes the obligations in detail as positive law creating a basis for court intervention on the wife's behalf to enforce the husband's obligations. The selections from the *Shulhan Arukh* indicate the situations when a court may act to force a husband to divorce his wife. These provisions, therefore, retrospectively spell out the man's obligations in marriage by indicating when the court has such grounds to intervene in the matter of divorce, which in Jewish law is the prerogative of the husband. The last of the mishnayot (7:6) which follows indicates when a woman has failed in her duties sufficiently to deprive her of her *ketubbah* payments if her husband divorces her. This situation also illuminates the legal expectations of performance by indicating what kinds of breach are total and excusing conditions of the husband's monetary obligations.

Students of American law may be surprised by the confidence these laws express in the power of the law to regulate highly personal matters. The Mishnah seems to assume society so closely knit that everything is everybody else's business, including what the spouses have for dinner, whether they eat together, and how frequently they have sexual intercourse.

Moderns may find the lack of privacy embedded in these laws objectionable. From stories about specific couples recorded in the Talmud we know that, for all the pervasiveness of these laws, each couple had its own unique way of doing things, just as one would expect. Note that there are no third-party rights here to claim failure of performance against either the man or the woman. In fact, that would be considered *lashon hara*, defamation. This limits these laws as measures of social control, in contrast to the Puritans, for example, among whom a husband could be sued for not sleeping next to his wife.

On the other hand, these laws create a social framework within which each couple can define its relationship. In other words, through these laws Jewish law establishes a public norm, even if it is not a norm that would often be entered into legal judgment. This implies an attitude toward marriage different from that in American law, one in which marriage is much more clearly a social institution open to social expectations in even the most personal of matters.

We do not know how often rabbinic courts intervened in the ongoing relationships between spouses to ensure that the wife received her due, but such suits undoubtedly did occur. They still occur today in the State of Israel, where the jurisdiction of rabbinic courts over family relations among Jews is recognized. The following story from the *San Diego Evening Tribune*, December 20, 1979, indicates the continuing vitality of this body of law.

ISRAELI COURT ORDERS MAN TO PERFORM SEXUAL "DUTIES"

Tel Aviv, Israel (UPI)—A rabbinical court has handed down a landmark judgment ordering a 32-year-old man to perform his conjugal duties or pay 36 grains of silver a week until he does so, an Israeli news report said.

Ruling the man "rebellious" against religious law for refusing to have sexual relations with his wife, the three rabbis decreed the countdown start with the handing down of the judgment Tuesday, the *Maariv* newspaper said.

If the husband disobeys the rabbinical court, the woman will be eligible for a divorce, with the silver accruing over the period added to the alimony settlement. There are 43.5 grains of silver in an ounce.

The court summoned the couple to a hearing based on the wife's complaint. The woman described her husband's behavior toward her in every other way as "exemplary."

But the husband was quoted as having told the rabbis "I am fed up with her" when he was asked to explain why he refused to have relations with his wife.

Rabbinical courts have sole jurisdiction over marriages and divorces in Israel.

### Mishnah Ketubbot 5:5–7, 9:

#### Mishnah 5
These are the tasks that a wife must carry out for her husband: she must grind corn, bake, and do washing, cook, suckle her child, make his bed for him, and work in wool. If she brought him one bondwoman, she need not grind nor bake nor wash; if two, she does not have to cook, nor give suck to her child; if three, she is not required to make his bed for him, nor work in wool; if four, she may sit on a raised seat. R. Eliezer says, Even if she brought him a hundred bondwomen, he can compel her to work in wool, since idleness leads to lewdness. Rabban Simeon ben Gamaliel says, Even though one place his wife under a vow not to perform any task, he should divorce her and give her her marriage settlement, as idleness leads to lightmindedness.

#### Mishnah 6
If one put his wife under a vow to have no connubial intercourse, the School of Shammai says (He may continue to maintain the vow) for two weeks; but the School of Hillel says, For one week only. Students may leave their wives at home to study the Torah without their wives' permission for thirty days; laborers for one week. The time for marital duties enjoined in the Law are: for men of independent means every day, for workmen twice weekly, for ass-drivers once a week, for camel-drivers once every thirty days, for sailors once every six months. This is the opinion of R. Eliezer.

#### Mishnah 7
If a woman be refractory against her husband (in not letting him have sex with her), he may reduce her marriage settlement by seven *denars* every week. R. Judah says, Seven half-*denars*. How long is the reduction to be continued? Until it reaches the full amount of her marriage settlement. R. Jose says, He may continue to diminish it, in

case an inheritance may fall to her from some source and he can then claim (the amount beyond her marriage settlement) from her. Similarly, if a man rebels against his wife (by not offering to have sex with her), they (the Rabbis) may add to her marriage settlement three *denars.* . . .

### Mishnah 9
He must give her a silver *maah* for her requirements, and she should take her meal with him every Sabbath night. And if he does not give her a silver *maah* for her needs, then the earnings of her own hands are hers. And how much does she have to work for him? — She must weave five *selas* weight of warp in Judaea, which are equal to ten *selas* in Galilee, or ten *selas'* weight of woof in Judaea, which are equal to twenty *selas* in Galilee. And if she were suckling, the quantity of her labor is to be diminished and that of her maintenance increased. When does this apply? — In the case of a poor man in Israel; but in the case of a man of the better class all should be in accordance with his respectability.

### *Mishnah Ketubbot* 7:3–6, 9–10:

### Mishnah 3
If one accepted the vow of his wife [rather than annulling it in accordance with Numbers 30] that she would not put on some kind of adornment, he must divorce her and give her her marriage settlement. R. Jose says, In the case of poor women (this applies) if he set no fixed period, and in the case of well-to-do women thirty days.

### Mishnah 4
If one placed a vow upon his wife that she was not to go to her father's house, if he lived with her in the same town and the vow was for one month, he may continue to keep her as his wife, but if for two months, he must divorce her and give her her marriage settlement; but if he lived in another town, and the vow was for one Holyday, he may continue to keep her as his wife, but if for three he must divorce her and grant her her marriage settlement.

### Mishnah 5
If one set a vow upon his wife that she was not to go to a house of mourning or to a house of feasting, he must divorce her and grant her her marriage settlement because he closes all doors to her. But if he would urge that there is another motive [for his insistence on the vow, such as, that licentious people live there], it is permitted. If he said to her, "I impose upon you an oath that you shall say to so-and-so [the foul language] which you said to me," or, "which I said to you," or "that you draw water and empty it on a dunghill" [Talmud: this either means that she do that literally, appearing like a lunatic; or this is a

euphemism for accepting his resolve to interrupt coitus and mastur-bate], then he must divorce her and give her her marriage settlement.

### Mishnah 6
And these are the women who are divorced without their marriage settlement: she who transgresses the Law of Moses and [she who transgresses] Jewish custom. And what constitutes "transgressing the Law of Moses"? If she gives him food which has not been tithed, or if she has sexual intercourse with him when she is a menstruant, or if she does not separate the priest's share of the dough, or if she makes a vow and does not fulfill it. And what constitutes "transgressing Jew-ish custom"? If she goes out with her hair uncovered, or if she spins wool in the marketplace, or if she converses with every man. Abba Saul says, Also if she curses his parents to his face. Rabbi Tarfon says, Also if she is a loud-voiced woman. And what constitutes "a loud-voice woman"? One who speaks in her house such that her neighbors hear her voice. . . .

### Mishnah 9
If physical defects form in a man, the court may not compel him to divorce his wife. Rabbi Simeon ben Gamaliel said, When is this the case? In regard to small defects, but when there are large defects, the court compels him to divorce her.

### Mishnah 10
And these are the men whom the court forces to give a divorce: one afflicted with a skin-disease, or one who has a polypus, or one who collects [the dung of dogs for tanning hides], or one who mines copper-ore, or a tanner, whether these defects were part of them before they were married or whether they were formed after they were married. And regarding all of them R. Meir said, Even though he made it a con-dition with her [at the time of marriage to accept this defect], she can say, "I thought that I would be able to endure it but now I can not bear it." But the Sages say, She must put up with it against her will, except in the case of a skin disease because she enervates him [through inter-course]. It once happened in Sidon that a certain tanner died and he had a brother who was also a tanner; the Sages said, she can say, "Your brother I could bear, but you I cannot."

*Shulhan Arukh, Even Haezer* #154:
1) These are the sorts of men whom we force to divorce their wives and pay the *ketubbah* settlement: (i) A man who develops bad breath or nasal odor, or who turns to collecting dog droppings, tanning hides, or mining copper. But if the wife is willing to stay with him, she may do so. (ii) A man who is stricken with boils is compelled to dismiss his

wife and pay her her *ketubbah*. Even if she is willing to stay with him, we pay no attention to her. They should be separated against their wishes because she is bound to aggravate his condition. If, however, she says, "Let me stay with him in the presence of witnesses" so that he can not have intercourse with her, her wish may be honored.

(Gloss by Isserles) (iii) There are some authorities who rule that we force an apostate to divorce his Jewish wife through the Gentile courts, on condition that (we can get him to) cancel his apostasy for the time he gives the divorce [for only a Jew can give a Jewish divorce], and there are some who disagree, maintaining that we force an apostate or another transgressor of Judaism to divorce his wife only if his sins affect her, for example if he feeds her forbidden food. . . . (iv) If a man is a pander (lit. "a shepherd of prostitutes") and his wife complains about it, there are some authorities who say that we force him to divorce his wife . . . if there are witnesses that saw him with seducers or if he admits to it.

2) (v) Suppose a woman's husband is afflicted with bad breath or nasal odor, or collects dog droppings, or has a similar defect but he dies. The widow then becomes subject to levirate marriage with his brother who is afflicted with the same defect. She may say "From your brother I could take it, but from you I cannot," whereupon he must submit to the ceremony of removing the shoe (Deuteronomy 25:9) and pay her her *ketubbah*.

3) (vi) If a man says, "I will not feed or support my wife," we force him to feed her. If the court cannot force him to feed her, if, for example, he has no money to support her and he does not want to get work to earn money to feed her, then, if she desires, we force him to divorce her immediately and to pay her *ketubbah*. (vii) The law is the same for a man who does not want to have sexual relations with his wife.

(Gloss by Isserles) (viii) Similarly, a man who often flies into a rage and continually drives his wife from his house may be forced to divorce her because through such behavior he occasionally fails to sustain her and separates himself from her sexually more than he may under her conjugal rights. He is like one who vows not to feed her or have sex with her [whose vows are invalid]. (ix) A man who strikes his wife commits a sin, just as if he were to strike anyone else; if he does this often, the court may punish him, excommunicate him, and flog him using every manner of punishment and force. The court also may make him swear that he will no longer do it. If he does not obey the court's decree, there are some authorities who say that we force him to divorce her, if he has been warned once or twice, because it is not the way of Jews to strike their wives: that is a Gentile form of behavior. The above applies when the husband starts the dispute, but if the wife curses him without cause or shows contempt for his father or

mother, then if he verbally warned her and she was not careful [to re-
strain herself], then there are those who say that he has (legal) permission to hit her. Some say it is forbidden to strike even an evil woman,
but the first opinion is the correct one. If it is not certain who causes
the fights, the husband is not trusted when he says that she starts
them, because all women are assumed to be proper. In that case we appoint others to observe them to find out who is at fault. If she curses
him, she is divorced and forfeits her *ketubbah* if she repeatedly does
so and has been warned. . . .

4) (x) If after his marriage, a man has his arm or leg amputated or is
blinded, and his wife refuses to stay with him, he may not be compelled to dismiss her and pay her her *ketubbah*. If she consents to stay
with him, she may do so; if not, she must be dismissed without her
*ketubbah*, like any other rebellious wife.

(Gloss by Isserles): Some authorities say that this applies only if he
lost one hand, foot, or eye, but if he lost both of his hands, feet, or
eyes, we force him to divorce her.

5) A man becomes wildly insane from time to time. His wife claims
"My father married me off to him because of his (her father's) economic difficulties. I thought I could live with him, but I cannot. I am
afraid lest he kill me in his anger." In such a case we do not force him
to divorce her because we only force him in those areas which the
Sages decreed.

(Gloss by Isserles): (xi) If he is an epileptic, some authorities say that
is not a blemish and we do not force him to divorce her, nor do we
force her to stay with him. Some rule that that is a blemish and we
force him to divorce her.

6) (xii) A woman who seeks a divorce on the grounds that she cannot conceive by her husband is not listened to. But she may claim she
wants to bear a son who will support her, that her husband is at fault
because he "does not eject semen with the force of an arrow." If she
has lived with him for ten years and has not become pregnant, we
force him to divorce her, if she does not claim her *ketubbah* [such that
we would suspect that she is seeking a divorce only to collect her
*ketubbah*] and if there does not seem to be any other ulterior motive
on her part. That is the law even if he has children by another woman,
for he might have become impotent afterward. In such cases he must
pay the 100 or 200 *zuz* of the *ketubbah* itself and the dowry but not
the additional sum that he promised her. . . . If he said, "I will marry a
second woman to check myself," we accept his proposal. If the second
woman gives birth, the first may be divorced without her *ketubbah*. If
the second woman does not conceive, he must divorce both and pay
the *ketubbah* sum to each. If it is known that he is at fault, and she
comes to court seeking a divorce, then he is forced to divorce her immediately [without waiting the ten years].

7) (xiii) If a wife claims that her husband cannot have an erection in order to have intercourse with her and she seeks a divorce, but he denies her claim, some authorities say she is to be believed and we force him to divorce her immediately, but he need not pay her the *ketubbah* sum. If he divorces her on his own without force, he must pay her the *ketubbah* sum. This applies only when she does not claim her *ketubbah*. If she does, she is not to be believed, and we do not force him to divorce her.

(Gloss by Isserles): There are those authorities who say that in our time, when woman are impudent, she is not to be believed.

8) (xiv) A man who is known to want to travel to another country is required to swear not to go or is forced to divorce his wife temporarily before he goes.

9) (xv) If a man is not permitted on threat of death by the secular authorities to stay in the place where he married her, we force him to divorce her. [Note: This was especially common in the Middle Ages when governments would only allow a fixed number of people to live in the Jewish ghetto of a town, and the Jewish community was forced to establish priorities regarding the right to take up residence.]

10) (xvi) If a man marries a woman, and she lives with him for ten years without bearing children, then he must divorce her and pay her the *ketubbah* sum or marry another woman who is fit to give birth. We force him to divorce her even if he does not want to [so that he will fulfill his obligation of procreation.] . . .

20) (xvii) Any man whose marriage to a woman involves a transgression, even of a Rabbinic injunction (for example, against marrying relatives of the second degree), is forced to divorce her.

Compare the much sparser California statutes on the obligations of the spouses in both property and other aspects of marriage.

## THE CALIFORNIA CIVIL CODE

5100. Husband and wife contract toward each other obligations of mutual respect, fidelity, and support.

5102. Neither husband nor wife has any interest in the separate property of the other, but neither can be excluded from the other's dwelling except . . . a court may order the temporary exclusion of either party from the family dwelling or from the dwelling of the other upon a showing that physical or emotional harm would otherwise result, until the final determination of the proceeding.

5103. Either husband or wife may enter into any engagement or transaction with the other, or with any other person, respecting property, which either might if unmarried; subject, in transactions between themselves, to the general rules which control the actions of persons occupying confidential relations with each other. . . .

5104. A husband and wife may hold property as joint tenants, tenants in common, or as community property.

5105. The respective interests of the husband and wife in community property during continuance of the marriage relation are present, existing and equal interests. This section shall be construed as defining the respective interests and rights of husband and wife in community property.

5131. A spouse is not liable for the support of the other spouse when the other spouse is living separate from the spouse by agreement unless such support is stipulated in the agreement.

5132. A spouse must support the other spouse while they are living together out of the separate property of the spouse when there is no community property or quasi-community property. . . .

5133. The property rights of husband and wife are governed by this title, unless there is a marriage settlement containing stipulations contrary thereto.

5134. All contracts for marriage settlements must be in writing, and executed and acknowledged or proved in like manner as a grant of land is required to be executed and acknowledged or proved.

### 4. Support and Maintenance

Jewish law, like many other legal systems, permits the property arrangements inherent in marriage to be altered in most respects by consent of the parties. But the law establishes expectations regarding support that are binding in the absence of an explicit agreement as well as irreducible minimal levels of support that are constructive conditions of the contract irrespective of agreement to the contrary.

Property law is rarely a simple matter, and Jewish property law is no different. A brief description of the rudiments of Jewish marital property law may serve to illustrate the social dimensions of Jewish marriage. A man's possessions, whether acquired before or after marriage, are his alone. Upon his death they pass to his sons. Two of the constructive conditions of the *ketubbah* cited previously in section 2, however, provide that the woman and her daughters shall be maintained by the man's possessions if he predeceases her (*Mishnah Ketubbot* 4:11–12), and Jewish law requires him to provide for her food and clothing and that of her children during his lifetime as well.

*Mishnah Ketubbot* 5:8–6:1:

## Chapter 5
### Mishnah 8
If one supported his wife through a third person, he must not give her less than two *kab* of wheat or four *kab* of barley. R. Jose said, Only R. Ishmael who lived close to Edom granted her this double allowance of barley. And he must give her also half a *kab* of peas and half a *log* of oil and a *kab* of dried figs or a *maneh* of fig-cake; and if he does not have these; he must supply her with other produce in their stead. And he must give her a bed, a mat, and cover. And he must give her a cap for her head and a girdle for her loins, and shoes at every Holyday, and clothing worth fifty *zuz* every year. And he may not give her new garments for summer nor threadbare clothes for winter; but he must give her clothing worth fifty *zuz* for winter, and she may cover herself with the worn-out ones in summer; and the threadbare ones belong to her.

## Chapter 6
### Mishnah 1
That which a woman finds and the work of her hands belong to her husband, and he enjoys the usufruct of whatever she inherits during her lifetime. Compensation for indignity to her and for injury to her belong to her. R. Judah ben Bathyra says, When in an unexposed part, two parts go to her and one part falls to him; but when in an exposed part, two parts are his and one part is hers. His parts must be given to him immediately; but with her parts land must be purchased and he enjoys the usufruct of it.

Maimonides, *Mishneh Torah*, Laws of Marriage 12:10, 11, 14, 15; 13:3–6:

## Chapter 12
10. How much food is the wife entitled to? She is entitled to bread for two meals daily, each being the average meal of the normal person in that city (that is, one who is neither ill nor gluttonous) and made from the same grain used by the people of the city: if wheat, wheat, if barley, barley, and similarly rice, millet, or any other kind of cereal customarily used by the people. She is also entitled to a side dish to eat with the bread, such as pulse, vegetables, or the like; oil for eating and for lighting a lamp; fruit; and a little wine to drink if it was the local custom for women to drink wine. On the Sabbath she is entitled to three meals, with meat or fish, according to the local custom. The husband must also give her a silver *maah* every week for her other needs, such as a perutah for laundry, the bathhouse, and the like.

11. To whom does this apply? To a poor man among Jews, but if he is rich, everything is determined according to his wealth. If he is rich enough to afford her several meat meals each day, we force him to pro-

vide her with food according to his wealth. If he is exceedingly poor, such that he is not even able to provide her with the bread that she needs to live, we force him to divorce her, and her *ketubbah* becomes a debt that he owes until such time that he is able to pay it. . . .

14. Just as a man is liable for food for his wife (according to the Torah), so he is obligated to provide food for his young sons and daughters until they reach the age of six; from that time on he must feed them until they grow up according to the enactment of the Sages. If he refuses, we threaten him, shame him, and beg him; if he still refuses, we make a public announcement about him as follows: "So-and-so is a cruel man since he refuses to feed his children; he is therefore worse than an impure bird (of prey), who does feed its young." After the age of six, however, we do not force him (legally) to feed them.

15. To whom does this apply? To a man whose wealth has not been assessed and it is not known whether or not he has enough to give to charity, but if an assessment was made that he does have enough money to give charity in an amount sufficient to cover their needs, then we take the money from him even against his will as a required act of charity and we feed them from it until they grow up. . . .

Chapter 13
3. House furnishings and a dwelling to live in are included within the garments that he is obligated to give her. What house furnishings are involved? A bed, a mattress or mat to sit on, and utensils for eating and drinking, such as a pot, a bowl, a cup, a bottle, and the like. As for the dwelling, he must rent her a house of at least four cubits by four cubits, and there must be a yard outside for her use, and it must have a lavatory in addition to the living space.

4. We also obligate him to give her ornaments, such as colored fabrics to wind around her head and forehead, as well as eye shadow, rouge, and the like so that she is not unattractive to him.

5. To whom does this apply? To the poor man in Israel, but for the rich man, everything depends upon the extent of his riches. Even if he is able to buy her clothes of silk and embroidery and jewelry of gold, we force him to give that to her. Similarly, the nature of the dwelling, ornaments, and house furnishings depends upon the extent of his wealth. And if he was so poor that he could not provide her with even the amount set for the poor man in Israel, we force him to divorce her, and her *ketubbah* is a liability against him until he earns enough to pay it.

6. This obligation does not only apply to the wife; the man must also supply his sons and daughters six years of age or younger with clothing sufficient for them, utensils, and a dwelling to live in. But to them he gives not according to his wealth, but only according to their

needs. This is the general rule: if the man is obligated to give food to someone, whether during the man's life or after his death, he is also obligated to supply that person with clothing, house furnishings, and a dwelling; and just as the court may sell the man's property to provide food for that person, so it may sell his property to fulfill his obligations to supply clothing, house furnishings, and a dwelling.

A woman's property rights are a little more complicated. At the time of the marriage she can designate her property either *nikhsei tzon barzel* ("property of iron sheep") or *nikhsei melog* ("property of plucking"). When sheep raising was the major occupation, wool was the safest and most permanent (iron) source of profit. Similarly, if the woman designates all or part of her property "property of iron sheep," and if the husband accepts the responsibility, he guarantees to return to her the value of that property, as stipulated in the *ketubbah*, in the event of divorce or his death, and his property is mortgaged to protect the condition and value of the wife's property. In return for that guarantee, any increase in value of the property belongs to him, but any decrease is his loss. The property becomes, in effect, his investment. On the other hand, if she designates all or part of her property "property of plucking," the responsibility for the principal remains hers, and she gains any increase in value and suffers any loss. It is called "property of plucking" because the husband nevertheless has title to the usufruct (fruits of income) in return for his responsibility to redeem her from captivity. Even if she sells her "property of plucking," he still owns the usufruct. He has title to the usufruct of "property of iron sheep" too, and for the same reason, but in "property of plucking" that is all that he gains. In both cases, he inherits all of her property listed in the *ketubbah* if she predeceases him since he has a prior claim on the property, dating from the time of betrothal. The only way that she can alienate the usufruct from him is by giving her property away as a gift before the betrothal; if she does that, and he predeceases her, she can still reclaim her property because it is assumed that she did that only to deprive her husband of the usufruct since "no person abandons himself by giving away his property to others" (*Ketubbot* 79a).

*Mishnah Ketubbot* 8:1:
If property falls to a woman before she is betrothed, whether by inheritance, find, or gift, the School of Shammai and the School of Hillel agree that she may sell it or give it away and that her act is valid. If she inherited it after she was betrothed, the School of Shammai says, She may sell it; but the School of Hillel says, She may not sell it. But they both admit that if she did sell or give it away her act is valid. R. Judah said, The Sages argued before Rabban Gamaliel that since one has

come into the possession of the woman, does it not follow that he should come into the possession of her property too?—He replied to them, We feel ashamed at the rights conceded to the husband on her new property, and you wish to impose on us the task of conceding similar rights on her old property? If she inherited property after she was wedded, both concur that if she sold it or gave it away the husband may take it away from the purchasers. If [property fell to her] before she wed and she then married, Rabban Gamliel says, If she sold it [after she was married] or gave it away her act is valid. R. Hanina ben Akabia said, They inquired before Rabban Gamliel, Since he has acquired the woman, should he not acquire also her property? He replied to them, We are embarrassed [by the husband's rights over] her new property, and you would also burden us with the old?

Maimonides, *Mishneh Torah*, Laws of Marriage 16:1–2; 22:7–9:

### Chapter 16
1. The property that a woman adds to her husband's estate, whether real estate, chattels, or slaves, is not considered part of her *ketubbah* even if it is listed in the *ketubbah* contract but is rather her dowry (*nedunyah*). If the husband took the responsibility of the dowry upon himself such that it became part of his property, then if the principal loses value, he suffers the loss, and if it gains in value, he acquires the gain. Such property is called "property of iron sheep." If he did not accept the responsibility of the dowry upon himself and the property remained the woman's possession, then if it loses value, she suffers the loss, and if it gains in value, she acquires the gain. Such property is called "property of plucking."

2. Similarly, all of a woman's property which she did not assign to her husband and which they did not record in the *ketubbah* but rather remained her possession, or which fell to her as an inheritance after she was betrothed, or which was given to her as a gift—all such property is considered "property of plucking" because it all belongs to her. The "*ketubbah*" is only the base sum of the *ketubbah* which is 100 or 200 *zuz* plus the standard additional sum (*tosefet*). . . .

### Chapter 22
7. The husband is entitled to usufruct of all of his wife's property during her lifetime, whether it is "property of iron sheep" or "property of plucking," and if she dies during her husband's lifetime, he inherits everything. Therefore, if the woman sells "property of plucking" after she is married, the husband can, as long as she is living, recover the income from it from the purchasers, even if that property became hers before she was betrothed; he cannot, however, recover the land itself because he has no claim on the property of plucking itself until she dies. [Note: If the husband dies during her lifetime, then

the purchasers are entitled to both the land and its income.] If she dies during his lifetime, the husband can recover the land itself from the purchasers without payment. However, if the money which the wife had received from the purchasers is still on hand, then he must return it to them and may not say, "perhaps this is money that she found."

8. . . . If a betrothed woman sold property before marriage, the sale is valid because the husband has no title to the property of his betrothed until he marries her.

9. If a woman assigns all her property in writing to another person before marriage, whether a relative or a stranger, the husband is not entitled to the income from it, even though her gift would be annulled if she were to be divorced or widowed, as will be explained in the Laws Concerning Gifts; and if she dies during his lifetime, he does not inherit her property because she gave it away before marriage; at her death the recipient of the gift acquires full possession of his gift. Moreover, even if she gave away all or part of her property before marriage and stipulated that the recipient would acquire title to the property as of that day provided that she confirm the gift at some future date such that the recipient would not acquire full title until she confirms it, the husband is likewise not entitled to the usufruct of that gift, and if she dies, he does not inherit it.

## 5. *The Marital Society*

The discussion of marriage as an aspect of a people's national, clan, or tribal survival and its impact on the distribution of family wealth and status should not obscure the fact that the heart of the social unit of marriage is two people. Human potential is extended when a person has the physical and emotional support of a helpmate. The Bible does not require monogamous, lifelong union; polygamy and divorce are permissible. But the model of human life in the Bible and later sources is grounded on a life shared with a spouse. These ideas are difficult to reconcile with a modern, individualistic ideology that emphasizes personal autonomy, growth, and change, but it is undeniably the preference of the Jewish tradition.

*Genesis* 1:27–28;
And God created man in His image, in the image of God He created him; male and female He created them. God blessed them and God said to them, "Be fertile and increase, fill the earth and master it."

*Genesis* 2:18, 21, 22, 24:
The Lord God said, "It is not good for man to be alone; I will make a fitting helper for him." . . .

So the Lord God cast a deep sleep upon the man and he slept; and He took one of his ribs and closed up the flesh at that spot. And the Lord God fashioned into a woman the rib that He had taken from the man, and He brought her to the man. . . . Hence a man leaves his father and mother and clings to his wife so that they become one flesh.

Marriage is to serve the purposes of procreation and companionship, and God Himself endorses marriage. The commandment to procreate is the first of the biblical demands, and the rabbis treated it as a legal command which one fulfills by having two children, one male and one female, in imitation of God's creation as described in the first passage from Genesis. According to the second account of creation, however, Eve is created to be Adam's helpmate before any mention is made of their becoming one flesh. Using Exodus 21:10, the rabbis expanded this theme and made sexual contact one of the rights and duties of marriage, regardless of its potential for procreation. Jews therefore used contraceptive devices from at least mishnaic times, and as R. Nahman said in the name of Samuel, "A man is forbidden to remain single even if he has children from a previous marriage" (*Yevamot* 61b). Procreation and companionship are independent goals in the Jewish view of marriage, and both are not only legitimate, but the preferred—indeed, the commanded—option: "Whoever finds a wife finds a great good and obtains the favor of the Lord" (Proverbs 18:22).

This attitude has several legal implications. Since marriage is a command, bachelorhood is a sin.

*Midrash on Psalms 59:2:*
Our Rabbis taught: A man without a wife lives without blessing, without life, without joy, without help, and without peace: Without blessing, for it is said, "And God blessed them" (Genesis 1:28), that is, blessed them when they were two; without joyful life, for it is said, "Enjoy life with the wife that you love" (Ecclesiastes 9:9); without joy, for it is said, "Have joy with the wife of your youth" (Proverbs 5:18); without help, for it is said, "I will make him a helpmate for him" (Genesis 2:18); without good, for it is said, "Whoever finds a wife finds a great good" (Proverbs 18:22); without peace, for it is said, "And you will know that your tent is in peace" (Job 5:24), "tent" plainly meaning wife as in the verse, "Go say to them, 'Return to your tents'" (Deuteronomy 5:27). Some say that a man without a wife also lives without Torah, for it is said, "If I have no help with me, then sound wisdom is driven from me" (Job 6:13).

*Kiddushin 29b–30a:*
R. Hisda praised R. Hamnuna before R. Huna as a great man. Said he to him, "When he visits you, bring him to me." When he arrived, he

saw that he wore no head covering [a sudarium with which married men used to cover their heads]. "Why have you no headdress?" asked he. "Because I am not married," was the reply. Thereupon R. Huna turned his face away from him. "See to it that you do not appear before me again before you are married," said he. R. Huna was thus in accordance with his views. For he said, "He who is twenty years of age and is not married spends all his days in sin." "In sin"—can you really think so?—But say, spends all his days in sinful thoughts.

*Zohar Hadash* 4.50b:
The divine presence can rest only upon a married man because an unmarried man is but half a man and the divine presence does not rest upon that which is imperfect.

Contrast those sources with the following from Paul's letters in the New Testament. Paul's coolness toward marriage is traceable to his apocalyptic expectations. If the end of time is near, the significance of long-term relationships pales.

*I Corinthians* 7:25–40:
About remaining celibate, I have no directions from the Lord but give my own opinion as one who, by the Lord's mercy, has stayed faithful. Well then, I believe that in these present times of stress this is right: that it is good for a man to stay as he is. If you are tied to a wife, do not look for freedom; if you are free of a wife, do not look for one. But if you marry, it is no sin, and it is not a sin for a young girl to get married. They will have their troubles, though, in their married life, and I should like to spare you that.

Brothers, this is what I mean: our time is growing short. Those who have wives should live as though they had none, and those who mourn should live as though they had nothing to mourn for; those who are enjoying life should live as though there were nothing to laugh about; those whose life is buying things should live as though they had nothing of their own; and those who have to deal with the world should not become engrossed in it. I say this because the world as we know it is passing away.

I would like to see you free from all worry. An unmarried man can devote himself to the Lord's affairs, all he need worry about is pleasing the Lord; but a married man has to bother about the world's affairs and devote himself to pleasing his wife: he is torn two ways. In the same way an unmarried woman, like a young girl, can devote herself to the Lord's affairs; all she need worry about is being holy in body and spirit. The married woman, on the other hand, has to worry about the world's affairs and devote herself to pleasing her husband. I say this only to help you, not to put a halter around your necks, but simply to make sure that everything is as it should be, and that you give your undivided attention to the Lord.

Still, if there is anyone who feels that it would not be fair to his daughter, to let her grow too old for marriage, and that he should do something about it, he is free to do as he likes: he is not sinning if there is a marriage. On the other hand, if someone has firmly made his mind up, without any compulsion and in complete freedom of choice, to keep his daughter as she is, he will be doing a good thing. In other words, the man who sees that his daughter is married has done a good thing but the man who keeps his daughter unmarried has done something even better.

A wife is tied as long as her husband is alive. But if the husband dies, she is free to marry anybody she likes, only it must be in the Lord. She would be happier, in my opinion, if she stayed as she is—and I do have the Spirit of God, I think.

Unlike a number of other faiths in the Occident and in the Orient, which at times regard marriage as a concession to mortal weakness, Judaism sees no conflict between the duties to family and to God. On the contrary, to fulfill one's duty to God one must get married. For that and other reasons, Jewish congregations shy away from engaging unmarried rabbis, in marked contrast to the practice of Roman Catholics and others of having a celibate clergy.

Parents have the initial obligation to insure that their children get married, but when the parents cannot, it becomes the community's responsibility:

Ketubbot 67b:
Our Rabbis taught: If an orphan applies for assistance to marry, a house must be rented for him and he must also be supplied with all household furnishings required for his use and then he is given a wife in marriage, for it is said in Scripture ["If there is a needy person among you . . . you must open your hand and lend] him sufficient for whatever he needs" (Deuteronomy 15:7–8): "sufficient" refers to the house, "whatever he needs" refers to a bed and table; "him" refers to a wife, for Scripture says, "I will make a helpmate for him" (Genesis 2:18).

The community is also responsible to insure that a newly married couple has the opportunity to work out the problems that inevitably surround the first year of marriage—even during a community emergency:

*Deuteronomy* 24:5:
When a man has taken a bride, he shall not go out with the army or be assigned to it for any purpose; he shall be exempt one year for the sake of his household to give happiness to the woman he has married.

In the 1970s and 1980s, many Americans have questioned the value of the marital society. Some have decided not to get married at all in order to avoid the obligations of marriage; others have wed but with the clear intention of subordinating the marital relationship to the pursuit of a career. Some have engaged in a number of serial marriages. These developments are at least partially the result of the contemporary American ethic of self-fulfillment. That ethic has had its advantages, especially in the liberation of both men and women to be active parents and to hold jobs that were formerly closed to people of one gender or the other. Its price, however, may be our failure to attain the goal of a life-long, stable marriage, the goal that the Jewish tradition prized so highly.

NOTES AND COMMENT
*The New Yorker*, August 30, 1976, pp. 21–22

A friend of ours has written us as follows:

One afternoon this spring, on the upper East Side of Manhattan, about eighty people sat in pews in a low-ceilinged, rectangular room that had been converted into a chapel. The chapel was an annex of the main church, and, though it was expensively fitted out, had an impersonal, functional character that made one think of the word "service" not in the sense of a religious ritual but in the sense in which the word is linked to "commodity." The presiding minister went well with this impression. The commodity he was providing that afternoon was a funeral, and he delivered the psalms and led the hymns with a professional sincerity that resonated through voids of lost faith. The mood of the congregation, however, was strikingly intent. I would not describe it as either religious or secular; it seemed, rather, to be a sharply focused mood, bearing witness to a life and death. This focus of feeling cohered within the boundaries of the ceremony like a liquid contained by a centripetal force of its own within a broken, leaky vessel.

I had not been close to the woman whose funeral this was. Let's call her Mary Jones. She and her husband, Robert, had spent their summers in the community in which I, two generations younger, was growing up, and this meant that I had seen her often during my life but did not mean, as far as I could remember, that I had ever had a substantial conversation with her. She was, however, part of a privately held image; and it was in honor of this image that I was there, and with it that I contributed to the centripetal force in the room. Every summer for as far back as I could remember, I had watched Robert and Mary Jones walking down the beach to the water for a swim: she a tall, big-boned woman, clearly beautiful when young, a person with a languorous, faintly ironic style suggesting both character and humor; he a small man, distinguished (although not as glamorous as she), upright (in spirit and body), cheerfully earnest, energetic. A slightly comical couple because of their difference in size, they would walk at a leisurely pace, several feet apart, conversing. I never overheard much of what they said, but it was apparent that the conversation ranged from serious discussion to banter. Often it was punctuated with laughter; I remember the laughter most vividly. When they reached the water, they would wade in, still talking, losing their balance somewhat on the rocks underfoot, talk more, and, finally, sink in and swim around a little—in a semi-upright position that allowed them to continue talking. Their enjoyment of each other was arresting— sharp as pepper, golden. I have seen other happy old couples, but this picture of the Joneses, renewed many times, came to represent to me an essence of human exchange—something indescribably moving and precious, which comes to fruition only toward the end of a life-long marriage. Whatever that essence is, I find it dazzling. It has always struck me as one of the great possibilities life has to offer.

All through the successive movements of personal emancipation which have been washing across our world in the last century, and particularly in the last decade—drawing power from the most profound intellectual currents of the century, but for the first time forming the values and governing the lives of most of a generation—I have held on to this image of the Joneses. That was not because I disagreed with the principles: the spirit of emancipation has also touched deep nerves of truth, has also opened windows on life's great possibilities. I kept hold of the image not as a refutation of my generation's values but because it reminded me of their limitations: of the blind side of our age, and the cost of the blindness; of a perhaps fatal stupidity intertwined with our enlightenment. The idea of emancipation, after all, has to do with an escape from bonds, not a strengthening of bonds. Emancipation has to do with power, not love; and a view of life in terms of emancipation—or liberation—will tend to be a political view, or, at least, it will interpret life with the political metaphor. Finally, the object of emancipation is the individual, not the connection between individuals; the doctrines of this emancipation stress terms like "self-awareness," "self-fulfillment," "self-discovery," "self-determination," and "self-sufficiency"—terms that crowd anybody other than the "self" right out of one's imagination. The doctrines claim that the relationships between people will be better, on the whole, for the participants' having been emancipated, but even if this is sometimes true, it is fairly plain that the better relationship is not a goal in itself; what is considered worth working for is the individual self-fulfillment possible within the better relationship. (When the relationship—no matter how good—gets in the way of self-fulfillment, it is clear which one has to go.) This may seem to be a purely academic difference of emphasis, but I don't think it is. I don't think that it's a coincidence, for example, that more and more people are living alone these days, that more are getting divorced, that fewer are getting married; it's no coincidence, in other words, that in the age of emancipation—all the talk about "healthier" relationships notwithstanding—there are going to be fewer and fewer Robert and Mary Joneses.

During Mary Jones's funeral, I basked in the thought of her marriage, hoarding the warmth against the astral chill of an unknown future. The future chilled me not because I think it promises to eradicate long, happy marriages from the face of the earth; only the most tyrannical social system could accomplish that. What chilled me was a more general sense of the transformation of our society from one that strengthens the bonds between people to one that is, at best, indifferent to them; a sense of an inevitable fraying of the net of connections between people at many critical intersections, of which the marital knot is only one. Each fraying accelerates others. A break in one connection, such as attachment to a stable community, puts pressure on other connections: marriage, the relationship between parents and children, religious affiliation, a feeling of connection with the past— even citizenship, that sense of membership in a large community which grows best when it is grounded in membership in a small one. If one examines these points of disintegration separately, one finds they have a common cause—the overriding value placed on the idea of individual emancipation and fulfillment, in the light of which, more and more, the old bonds are seen not as enriching but as confining. We are coming to look upon life as a lone adventure, a great personal odyssey, and there is much in this view which is exhilarating and strengthening, but we seem to be carrying it to such an extreme that if each of us is an Odysseus, he is an Odysseus with no Telemachus to pursue him, with no Ithaca to long for, with no Penelope to return to—an Odysseus on a journey that has been rendered pointless by becoming limitless. The pointlessness of unlimited dispersal: that was the chill against which I hoarded a small, indirect warmth, against which all the people in the room seemed to be exercising, through sheer power of attention, a centripetal, connective force. Death, as always, had reminded me, and perhaps all of us there of the passionate loneliness at the center of each destiny, and this has no doubt always been a side of human awareness. But the other side— that we give form and meaning to those solitary destinies through our associations with others—has been allowed to fade away, leaving us exposed to a new kind of cold; leaving us to be bound occasionally by the fleeting miracle of coinciding emotions—as in that chapel this spring—but otherwise to hold together through the sheer quixotic effort of individual will alone.

## D. THE SACRED ELEMENT IN JEWISH MARRIAGE

### 1. Marriage as a Divine Command

Marriage is understood as a divine commandment in the Jewish tradition. The insistence that God is concerned that people marry might be passed off either as sentimentalism or as just a metaphor for the instrumental importance of marriage for society, but that would ignore salient features of Jewish marriage. It is certainly true that marriage imitates divine activity in the world. Marriage advances the work of creation and the fulfillment of the covenant as each couple participates in making new lives and in passing on to their seed the promise and responsibility received from their ancestors. Moreover, love as well as creation are divine activities. God works in the world through love, by which humans are bound to the divine. Through their experience of love humans learn about the nature of God. The Book of Hosea draws the direct parallel between the love that binds men and women and the love that binds God to people. The rabbis and Church fathers understood the Song of Songs that way as well.

God is first introduced in the Bible as Creator, and the rabbis considered man God's partner in creation (*Shabbat* 118). The rabbis went as far as to say that there are three partners in the conception of every human being: the mother, father, and God (*Niddah* 31a). The theological point is deep-seated: marriage, and the sexual relations and procreation that accompany it, are nothing short of divine activities since they aid God in His continuing acts of creation and fulfill His commandments for us to help Him in that way. The *Zohar*, the primary source for medieval Jewish mysticism, put it this way: "God creates new worlds constantly. In what way? By causing marriages to take place" (*Zohar* 1.89a).

God is most often encountered in the Bible as lawgiver: He prescribes an entire way of life. For Torah to be transmitted from one generation to another requires a massive educational effort, and parents have primary responsibility for that. "Teach it to your children" (Deuteronomy 6:7) is a commandment uppermost in the consciousness of the Jew and recited twice daily as part of the *Shema*, a central prayer. Thus marriage is a divine act for both its creativity and its educational import.

*Yevamot* 62b:
Our Rabbis taught: Concerning a man who loves his wife as himself, who honors her more than himself, who guides his sons and daughters in the right path and arranges for them to be married near the period of their puberty, Scripture says, "And you shall know that your tent is in peace" (Job 5:24).

Marriage also has legal consequences, for marriage annuls all sins. God not only pardons sins in celebration of a marriage: He joins couples together and participates in the ceremony itself. The point of the following fanciful sources is serious: marriage is sacred because God desires it—so much so that He personally involves Himself in making it happen.

*Genesis Rabbah* 68:4:
Once a Roman matron asked Rabbi Jose bar Halafta: "How long did it take the Holy One, blessed be He, to create the world?"

He said to her: "Six days."

"And from then until now what has He been doing?"

"The Holy One, blessed be He, is occupied in making marriages."

"And is that His occupation?" the woman asked. "Even I can do that. I have many men slaves and women slaves, and in one short hour I can marry them off."

"Though it may appear easy in your eyes," he said, "yet every marriage is as difficult for the Holy One, blessed be He, as the dividing of the Red Sea." Then Rabbi Jose left her and went on his way.

What did the matron do? She took a thousand male slaves and a thousand female slaves, placed them in two rows and said: "This one should wed that one, and this one should wed that one." In one night she married them all. The next day they came before her—one with a wounded head, another with a bruised eye, another with a fractured arm, and another with a broken foot.

"What is the matter with you?" she asked.

Each one said, "I do not want the one you gave me."

Immediately the woman sent for Rabbi Jose bar Halafta and said to him: "Rabbi, your Torah is true, beautiful and praiseworthy."

"Indeed a suitable match may seem easy to make, yet God considers it as difficult a task as dividing the Red Sea," Rabbi Jose acknowledged.

*Pirke de Rabbi Eliezer* 12:
The wedding of the first couple was celebrated with pomp never repeated in the whole course of history since. God Himself, before presenting Eve to Adam, attired and adorned her as a bride. Indeed, He
appealed to the angels, saying: "Come, let us perform services of
friendship for Adam and his helpmate, for the world rests upon
friendly services, and they are more pleasing in My sight than the sacrifices Israel will offer upon the altar." The angels accordingly sur-
rounded the marriage canopy, and God pronounced the blessings upon
the bridal couple, as the cantor does under the wedding canopy.
The angels then danced and played upon musical instruments before
Adam and Eve in their ten bridal chambers of gold, pearls, and precious stones, which God had prepared for them.

## 2. Forbidden Relationships

One connotation of the statement that marriage and sexual union
are sacred matters is that they are governed by rules that may not be
set aside either by private agreement or by community permission.
Holiness is closely linked in the Hebrew language with marriage since
the same root is used for both words. The source of the linguistic link
probably is that spouses are set apart, made special and unique to the
exclusion of all others, just as a priest or shrine is set apart or holy because of its connection with God.

In the biblical readings that follow, notice the categorical nature of
the rules respecting forbidden sexual unions and the link that is established between avoiding such behavior and maintaining holiness. In
Leviticus 20, for instance, after categorizing the sexual prohibitions,
the text concludes:

*Leviticus* 20:22–26:
You shall faithfully observe all My laws and all My regulations, lest
the land to which I bring you to settle in spew you out. You shall not
follow the practices of the nation that I am driving out before you. For
it is because they did all these things that I abhorred them and said to
you: You shall possess their land, for I will give it to you to possess, a
land flowing with milk and honey. I the Lord am your God who has
set you apart from other peoples. So you shall set apart the clean beast
from the unclean, the unclean bird from the clean. You shall not draw
abomination upon yourselves through beast or bird or anything with
which the ground is alive, which I have set apart for you to treat as unclean. You shall be holy to Me, for I the Lord am holy, and I have set
you apart from other peoples to be Mine.

Living in an age in which law is seen primarily as the embodiment
of majoritarian policy, a modern liberal may find it hard to accept rules

that have no apparent reason and that punish people whose behavior does not obviously harm themselves or others. But the rational views people proclaim often diverge from how they feel and behave. Modern secular people do not usually see sexual behavior as the subject of divine categorical imperatives, but they do tend to hold very stong views regarding the behavior they will engage in themselves, what they find acceptable for their friends, relatives, and others close to them, and what acts they believe society should condemn even when strangers engage in it. Such views are not rationally coherent, but they are frequently seen as key parts of a person's sense of what is right and what is wrong. They are not understood simply as matters of aesthetic taste or idiosyncratic, personal preference.

The provisions of biblical law are quite permissive regarding sexual behavior. Sex is an important, affirmative part of life. It is not inherently dirty or sinful. Within marriage all is permissible, including some behavior that is still felonious in many American states. But sexual activity is understood to be at the root of how nature operates, and some kinds of contact undermine that basic order. God not only wants certain sexual practices and forbids others; He is seen as being particularly insistent on His will in these matters.

Many societies have laws against incest and adultery. The rationales for such laws vary. The prohibition against adultery is often explained as a measure to strengthen the family unit and thereby strengthen society as a whole, but there are also considerations of honor and even property involved. Thus when David arranges Uriah's death in battle so that he can marry Batsheva, Uriah's wife, God sends Nathan, the prophet, to David. Nathan likens David's act to that of a rich man with many sheep who steals the lone ewe lamb belonging to a poor man (II Samuel 11:27–12:4). He also declares God's punishment in terms that reflect the property element in adultery: "I gave you your master's house and possession of your master's wives. . . . Why then have you flouted the command of the Lord and done what displeases Him: . . . Therefore . . . I will take your wives and give them to another man before your very eyes and he shall sleep with your wives under this very sun" (II Samuel 12:8, 11). The prohibition against adultery (Ex. 20:13) and the prohibition against covetousness (Ex. 20:14) appear close to each other in the Ten Commandments, and the text of the last of the ten ties adultery to property considerations further: "You shall not covet your neighbor's house. You shall not covet your neighbor's wife, or his male or female slave, or his ox or his ass, or anything that is your neighbor's." Taking their cue from these juxtapositions in the text, the rabbis later said, "One who has adulterous relations with his neighbor's wife craves all that belongs to him" (*Numbers Rabbah* 9:8).

The prohibition against incest is often justified in modern times in terms of genetic danger to the offspring, but ancient rationales included an aesthetic sense that it is not proper and an assertion of moral principle to the effect that it is a violation of natural law or that it is wrong on some other ground. Saadia Gaon (892–942), who was convinced that all principles of Judaism are rational, combined a number of elements in his explanation of the prohibitions against adultery and incest.

> Saadia Gaon, *Book of Doctrines and Beliefs*, chap. III, sect. 2:
> Wisdom imposes the prohibition of adultery, for otherwise human beings would become similar to the animals. No person would be able to know and honor his father in return for the education he received at his hands. Nor would a father be able to bequeath to his son his means of livelihood though the son inherited his existence from him; nor would one know one's other relatives such as paternal and maternal uncles; nor would one be able to show them the kindness due to relatives. . . .
>
> The prohibition of sexual intercourse with . . . one's mother, sister, and daughter has this reason: the necessities of life foster intimacy between the members of a family. Consequently, if marriage between them were permitted, they would indulge in sexual license. Another purpose is to prevent men from being attracted only by those women who are of beautiful appearance and rejecting those who are not, when they see that their own relatives do not desire them.

While Judaism certainly has expressed such aesthetic and social concerns in reference to its proscriptions of adultery and incest, they have never been primary. What rings in the head of every knowledgeable Jew on this issue are the following selections from the Torah, which make it clear that the main reason for the prohibitions is that God proscribes incest and adultery in no uncertain terms and punishes such behavior severely.

> *Leviticus* 18:1–30:
> The Lord spoke to Moses, saying: Speak to the Israelite people and say to them:
>
> I the Lord am your God. You shall not copy the practices of the land of Egypt where you dwelt, or of the land of Canaan to which I am taking you; nor shall you follow their customs. My norms alone shall you observe, and faithfully follow My laws: I the Lord am your God.
>
> You shall keep My laws and My norms, by the pursuit of which man shall live: I am the Lord.

None of you shall come near anyone of his own flesh to uncover nakedness: I am the Lord.

Your father's nakedness, that is, the nakedness of your mother, you shall not uncover; she is your mother—you shall not uncover her nakedness.

Do not uncover the nakedness of your father's wife; it is the nakedness of your father.

The nakedness of your sister—your father's daughter or your mother's, whether born into the household or outside—do not uncover their nakedness.

The nakedness of your son's daughter, or of your daughter's daughter—do not uncover their nakedness; for their nakedness is yours.

The nakedness of your father's wife's daughter, who was born into your father's household—she is your sister; do not uncover her nakedness.

Do not uncover the nakedness of your father's sister; she is your father's flesh.

Do not uncover the nakedness of your mother's sister; for she is your mother's flesh.

Do not uncover the nakedness of your father's brother: do not approach his wife; she is your aunt.

Do not uncover the nakedness of your daughter-in-law: she is your son's wife; you shall not uncover her nakedness.

Do not uncover the nakedness of your brother's wife; it is the nakedness of your brother.

Do not uncover the nakedness of your wife's daughter, nor shall you marry her son's daughter or her daughter's daughter and uncover her nakedness: they are kindred; it is depravity.

Do not marry a woman as a rival to her sister and uncover her nakedness in the other's lifetime.

Do not come near a woman during her period of uncleanness to uncover her nakedness.

Do not have carnal relations with your neighbor's wife and defile yourself with her.

Do not allow any of your offspring to be offered up to Molech, and do not profane the name of your God: I am the Lord.

Do not lie with a male as one lies with a woman; it is an abhorrence.

Do not have carnal relations with any beast and defile yourself thereby; and let no woman lend herself to a beast to mate with it; it is perversion.

Do not defile yourselves in any of those ways, for it is by such that the nations which I am casting out before you defiled themselves. Thus the land became defiled; and I called it to account for its iniquity, and the land spewed out its inhabitants. But you must keep My laws and My norms, and you must not do any of those abhorrent things, neither the citizen nor the stranger who resides among you; for all those abhorrent things were done by the people who were in the land before you and the land became defiled. So let not the land spew you out for defiling it, as it spewed out the nation that came before you. All who do any of those abhorrent things—such persons shall be cut off from their people. You shall keep My charge not to engage in any of the abhorrent practices that were carried on before you, lest you defile yourselves through them: I the Lord am your God.

Leviticus describes forbidden sex, not just forbidden marriage. These rules are not simply a matter of protecting family interests from improvident marriage, nor are they reconcilable with an eugenic theory of appropriate human breeding to avoid defects. The rabbis recognized from an early date that these rules cannot be rationalized socially, and Saadia's rationales are both late and atypical in the history of Judaism. Certainly prohibitions of incest and adultery have strong social justifications, but in Leviticus incest is defined to include unions which do not present genetic risk. A man's sexual intercourse with a menstruating woman or another male is treated as an offense as serious as child sacrifice, bestiality, and sex with parents. The rabbis were certainly right in seeing these rules as *hukkim*, absolute commands of God which were to be obeyed simply because they were His commands.

The regulations of Leviticus 18 may sound like something out of Puritan New England, but they are only part of the Jewish tradition's strong affirmation of sexuality in the context of marriage. Maimonides and other medieval rabbis wrote manuals to instruct husbands in the art of sexually engaging their wives. The Talmud permits virtually all private, sexual practices of husband and wife (*Nedarim* 20b; *Sanhedrin* 58b); although medieval rabbis sought to limit this liberality in various ways (for example, *M.T.* Sexual Prohibitions 21:9; *Tosafot* to *Yevamot* 34b and *Sanhedrin* 58b).

The Talmud (*Ketubbot* 48a) also permits each partner to insist that neither be clothed during intercourse since naked coitus is the form of sex that each could properly have in mind as one's right when one gets married. The Bible strictly forbids nonmarital sex without any explanation; marital sex is not only permitted and encouraged, but commanded.

### 3. The Prohibition Against Betrothal by Intercourse

Human beings mated for many centuries without benefit of ceremony. The Torah records instances in which a man simply had intercourse with a woman in order to marry her, and that is the basis for the Mishnah's acceptance of intercourse as a form of betrothal. By the time of the Gemara, however, that was no longer considered consonant with the holiness of the marital state, and so Rav, a third century Amora, sought to abolish it. Since betrothal by intercourse had both a biblical and mishnaic base, he upheld the validity of such betrothals after the fact, but he imposed lashes upon men who betrothed women in this way (*Kiddushin* 12b). In light of the biblical and mishnaic provision for betrothal by copulation, this was a major departure from precedent, but his ruling was accepted.

Maimonides gives eloquent expression to the fact that this change in practice was motivated by concern for the sacred element of marriage. He notes that betrothal by intercourse has a strong base in the Torah itself; betrothal by money, on the other hand, is only an institution of the Scribes since it does not appear explicitly in the Torah but is only derived from it by reasoning. Nevertheless it is the latter which is the preferred mode, and the former which is actually punished.

Maimonides, *Mishneh Torah*, Laws of Marriage, 1:1, 2, 4; 3:20–22:

#### Chapter One

1. Before the revelation of the Torah, when a man would encounter a woman in the street, if both consented to marriage, he would bring her into his house and would have intercourse with her in privacy, and she would thereby become his wife.

Once the Torah was given, the people of Israel were commanded that if a man wants to marry a woman, he must first acquire her in the presence of witnesses, and after that she becomes his wife, as the Torah says, "If a man take a woman and goes in unto her . . ." [and thus "taking" precedes intercourse] (Deuteronomy 22:13).

2. This acquisition is a positive commandment of the Torah, and a woman may be acquired in one of the following three ways: with money, by a writ, or by an act of sexual intercourse. Intercourse and writ are based on the Torah, while money is derived from the words of the Scribes. . . .

4. Before the revelation of the Torah, when a man would encounter
a woman in the street, if both were willing, he would pay her her fee,
have intercourse with her right there at the crossroads, and go his
way. Such a woman is called a harlot.

After the Torah was given, harlots were forbidden, as the Torah
says, "There shall be no harlot of the daughters of Israel" (Deuteronomy 23:18). Therefore anyone who has intercourse with a woman for
the purpose of harlotry, without betrothal, is liable to a flogging on
the authority of the Torah because he had intercourse with a harlot.
. . .

Chapter Three
20. One who betroths through intercourse has fulfilled the Torah's
requirements for betrothal, and similarly one who betroths through a
document. Just as [a document] can fulfill the act of divorce (as Scripture says, "And he writes her a writ of divorce" (Deut. 24:1), so too [a
document] can complete the act of betrothal. But the use of money (as
an instrument of betrothal) is only authorized by the Rabbis: Scripture says, "When a man takes a woman" (Deut. 24:1), and the Rabbis
said, "This form of taking must be by money, as it says, 'I have given
the money for the field, take it from me' (Gen. 23:13)."

21. Even though that is the essence of the matter, all Israel has already adopted the custom to betroth by money or its equivalent, but if
he wants to betroth through a document, he may. But *ab initio* we do
not betroth through intercourse, and if he did betroth through intercourse, we flog him with lashes for rebellion so that Israelites will not
be licentious in this matter, even though such betrothal is fully valid.

22. Similarly, if a man betroths a woman without prior negotiation,
or if he betroths her in the market, even though the betrothal is perfectly valid, he is liable to a flogging for disobeying the Rabbis, so that
this procedure should not become a habit leading to harlotry, for it
makes the woman resemble a harlot who was common in the time
preceding the giving of the Torah.

## 4. The Jewish Wedding Ceremony

Jewish marriage is, on one level, a contractual transaction involving the acquisition of property, but it is also a sacred ceremony in
which divine sanction is invoked.

Jewish marriage is a two-stage process: the act of betrothal, and
the wedding itself. Until the Middle Ages the two ceremonies were
separated by a year so that the couple could make the necessary preparations for marriage and the wedding. Medieval rabbis combined the
two ceremonies into one, to save poor families from the expense of two

feasts. Beyond that, the times were very unsettled then, and people doubtless worried that they might not be around to complete the wedding process a year later. Consequently the traditional wedding ceremony now used in Conservative, Orthodox, and many Reform synagogues combines the betrothal and the wedding ceremonies into a single event separated by the reading of the *ketubbah*. Other elements are often added (songs, sermonettes, dancing, and extravagant feasting), but they are woven around that basic rubric.

Jewish law requires that ceremonies be publicly solemnized by the presence of two witnesses at a betrothal and a quorum of ten men (a *minyan*) at a wedding. Jewish law has the same problems with non-ceremonial marriages that civil law has; nevertheless, like most legal systems, Jewish law retroactively recognizes the validity of such marriages.

The "document of betrothal" spoken of in the sources which follow is *not* the wedding contract (*ketubbah*): it is a written statement that the man sanctifies the woman in betrothal. The *ketubbah* is a separate document that is required regardless of the form of betrothal. The "money" is most commonly given to her in the form of a ring, and, as Maimonides indicates, it is the usual form of betrothal. Hence the betrothal formula is: "By this ring I betroth you according to the laws of Moses and Israel."

Both the man's and woman's consent are necessary for marriage, and both must be publicly declared: the man's, by saying so verbally or in writing, and the woman's by accepting the instrument of betrothal. The reading from Maimonides which follows reflects a time when the man's consent was not formally required because he has initiated the act of betrothal and that indicates his consent, even when he later verbally protests.

The Jewish wedding ceremony need not be performed by a rabbi, except when secular law requires one! Any Jewish man who knows how to fill out the *ketubbah* and say the blessings may do so—including the groom himself. The religious element is thus not the officiant, but rather the text of the betrothal and wedding ceremonies.

The betrothal liturgy is remarkably short—especially in comparison to Jewish daily or festival prayers—and yet it conveys several religious messages. In addition to the blessing over wine, the symbol of joy, the betrothal ceremony includes one other blessing in which God is praised for distinguishing legitimate marital partners from illicit ones and for ordaining a ceremony by which people may be married in a consecrated way. The groom places a ring on the finger of the bride, betrothing her according to the laws of Moses and Israel.

The wedding ceremony consists of seven blessings, which are recited at the wedding itself, at the feast thereafter, and as part of Grace After Meals for the first week of marriage. The initial blessing is over wine: two cups are used—one for the betrothal and one for the wedding. God is then praised for creating the world, humanity as a whole, men and women separately, and this couple in particular, and His blessings are invoked upon them. God as Creator is linked to God as Redeemer: the couple comes to symbolize Jewish hopes for the future, when all Jews will be reunited in Jerusalem and rejoice in the same way that this couple rejoices today. The blessings thus place this wedding in the broader framework of the covenant of Israel, and link this couple to God's promises of creation and redemption.

MARRIAGE SERVICE
P. Birnbaum, *The Daily Prayerbook* [New York: Hebrew Publishing Company, 1949], pp. 753–756.

*Rabbi*:
He who is supremely mighty,
He who is supremely blessed,
He who is supremely sublime,
May he bless the groom and the bride.

Blessed art thou, Lord our God, King of the universe, who createst the fruit of the vine.

Blessed art thou, Lord our God, King of the universe, who hast sanctified us with thy commandments, and commanded us concerning illicit relations; thou hast forbidden us those who are merely betrothed, and permitted us those who are married to us through consecrated wedlock. Blessed art thou, O Lord, who sanctifiest thy people Israel by consecrated wedlock.

*The groom, placing the ring on the forefinger of the bride's right hand:*

With this ring, you are wedded to me in accordance with the law of Moses and Israel.

*After the reading of the ketubbah the seven blessings are chanted:*

Blessed art thou, Lord our God, King of the universe, who createst the fruit of the vine.

Blessed art thou, Lord our God, King of the universe, who hast created everything for thy glory.

Blessed art thou, Lord our God, King of the universe, Creator of men.

Blessed art thou, Lord our God, King of the universe, who hast created man in thy image, and didst forever form woman out of his frame to be beside him. Blessed art thou, O Lord, Creator of man.

May Zion exult at the joyful reunion of her children in Jerusalem. Blessed art thou, O Lord, who causest Zion to rejoice in her children.

O give abundant joy to these loved companions, even as thou didst gladden thy creation of old in the Garden of Eden. Blessed art thou, O Lord, who givest joy to groom and bride.

Blessed art thou, O Lord, King of the universe, who hast created groom and bride, joy and gladness, delight and cheer, love and harmony, peace and companionship. Lord our God, may there soon be heard in the cities of Judah, in the streets of Jerusalem, the sound of joy and gladness, the sound of joyous wedding celebrations, the sound of young people feasting and singing. Blessed art thou, O Lord, who makest the groom rejoice with the bride.

Maimonides, *Mishneh Torah* Laws of Marriage 3:1, 3–5, 8, 19, 23, 24; 4:1; 10:3–5, 7, 11, 12:

### Chapter 3
1) How is a woman betrothed? If the man betroths her with money, he must use no less than a *perutah* or its equivalent. He says to her: "With this you are sanctified to me," or "With this you are betrothed to me," or "With this you are my wife," and he gives it to her before witnesses. It must be the man who speaks, saying words whose import is that he thereby acquires her as a wife, and it must be he that gives the money. . . .

3) If he betroths her through document, he writes on paper, earthenware, a leaf, or anything he wants: "You are sanctified to me," or "You are betrothed to me," or the like, and he gives it to her before witnesses.

4) He must write it for the specific woman to be betrothed, as is the rule in regard to a writ of divorce, and he may only write it with her knowledge. If he wrote it but not in her name, or if he wrote it in her name but without her knowledge, then she is not betrothed, even if he gave it to her with her knowledge in front of witnesses.

5) If he betroths her through intercourse, he says to her: "By this act of coitus you are sanctified to me (you are betrothed to me, you are my wife, etc.)," and he enters a room together with her before two witnesses and has intercourse with her. . . .

8) A man may betroth a woman in any language that she understands as long as the import of his words in that language is that he acquires her, as we have explained. If he was speaking with the woman

about matters of betrothal and she indicated agreement, and if he then stood and betrothed her without specifying that he was doing that— in fact, without saying anything—but he gave it (the money or document) to her or had intercourse with her, since they were occupied with the matter, that is sufficient, and he need not be specific. Similarly, he need not specifically designate the witnesses for a betrothal or divorce, saying, "You are my witnesses;" as long as he divorced or betrothed in front of them, she is betrothed or divorced. [Comment of *Maggid Mishneh*: The last clause holds true only if the witnesses are near her, she saw them, and she is aware of them. But if he hid witnesses behind a fence, she is not betrothed, because if she were aware of them, she may not have accepted the betrothal.] . . .

19) It is a better fulfillment of the commandment if a man betroths his wife by himself rather than by his agent, and it is similarly better for a woman to be betrothed in person rather than through her agent. Even though the father has the authority to give his minor daughter in betrothal to whomever he wants, it is not fitting to do that; it is rather the command of the Sages that he not give his daughter in betrothal while she is a minor but rather wait until she attains majority and says, "I want to be betrothed to so-and-so." Similarly it is not proper for a man to betroth a minor girl, and he should not betroth a woman until he sees her and she is pleasing to him, lest she not be and he ultimately divorces her or lies with her while he hates her [and the Torah said, "You shall love your neighbor as yourself" (Lev. 19:18)—*Kiddushin* 41a]. . . .

23) Whether a man betroths a woman himself or through an agent, either he or his agent must pronounce a blessing before the betrothal, just as a blessing is recited before fulfilling all commandments, and after that he may betroth her. If, however, he betroths her without first reciting the blessing, he should not recite it after the betrothal, for that would be a blessing for no purpose since that which has been done is already done.

24) How should he bless? "Blessed are You, O Lord, our God, King of the universe, who has sanctified us through His commandments and separated us from forbidden relations, who has prohibited to us those who are only betrothed but has permitted us those who are married through the bridal canopy and betrothal. Blessed are You, O Lord, who sanctifies Israel." That is the blessing of betrothal, and it is customary among the people to perform this blessing over a cup of wine or liquor. If wine is available, the blessing over wine should be pronounced first, then the blessing of betrothal, and then the betrothal should be performed [by giving her the money or ring and pronouncing the formula of betrothal]. If no wine or liquor is available, the benediction of betrothal is the only one to be recited.

## Chapter 4

1) A woman may not be betrothed except with her consent, and if a man betroths a woman against her will, she is not betrothed. But if a man was forced to betroth a woman against his will, she is betrothed. [*Maggid Mishneh's* comment: Even if he did not say in the end, "I want to," the fact of his act of betrothal testifies to his will, and it is as if he said, "I want to." In this case the Sages did not rule that the betrothal would be annulled because he can divorce her against her will (before the *takkanah* of Rabenu Gershom). But if he betroths against her will, she cannot extricate herself from it except with his consent. Therefore the Sages decreed a retroactive annullment of the betrothal so that she is not betrothed at all and consequently does not need a writ of divorce.]

## Chapter 10

3) One must bless the wedding blessings in the house of the groom before the wedding, and they are six in number, and these are they: . . .

4) And if there is wine available, then a cup of wine is brought and one recites the blessing over the wine first and arranges all the other blessings around the cup, so that he says seven blessings in all. And there are places where myrtle leaves are used (for their sweet fragrance) along with the wine, and then they bless over the myrtle after the blessing over the wine, followed by the other six blessings.

5) We only recite the wedding blessings in the presence of a quorum of ten adult, free males, with the groom counted as one of their number. . . .

7) And the man must write a marriage contract (*ketubbah*) before entering the wedding canopy, and afterward his wife is permitted to him. The groom pays the scribe's fees. How much does he write for her? If she is a virgin, he may not write less than 200 *denarim*; if she was formerly married, he may not write less than 100 *denarim* for her. That sum is what is called "the core of the *ketubbah*." If he wants to add to that amount, even to a brick of gold, he may. . . . It was the Sages who established the *ketubbah* for a woman so that divorcing her will not seem to him to be a light matter. . . .

11) One who betroths a woman and writes a *ketubbah* for her is only betrothed and not married to her until she enters the wedding canopy, for the *ketubbah* does not by itself effect marriage. . . .

12) Thus the Sages established: any man who marries a virgin must rejoice with her for seven days. He may not engage in his work and may not do business in the market. He must eat, drink, and be merry with her, whether he was previously a bachelor, or a widower. And if she was previously married, he must rejoice with her for not less than three days.

## 5. The Secular Wedding Ceremony

Due to the separation of church and state, American law specifically rules out any requirement for a religious ceremony. The California law on this is typical.

*California Civil Code, pars. 4206, 4206.5:*

4206. No particular form for the ceremony of marriage is required, but parties must declare in the presence of the person solemnizing the marriage, that they take each other as husband and wife.

4206.5. No contract of marriage, if otherwise duly made, shall be invalidated for want of conformity to the requirements of any religious sect.

On the other hand, American law does permit members of the clergy to act as the state's representative in solemnizing a marriage—along with others acting in a nonreligious capacity:

*California Civil Code, pars. 4205, 4205.1, 4205.5:*

4205. Marriage may be solemnized by any judge or retired judge, commissioner, or assistant commissioner of a court of record or justice court in this state or by any priest, minister, or rabbi of any religious denomination, of the age of 18 years or over or by a person authorized to do so under Section 4205.1.

A marriage may also be solemnized by a judge who has resigned from office.

4205.1. In any county with a population of 60,000 or more as determined by the last federal decennial census the board of supervisors of the county may designate the country clerk as a commissioner of civil marriages. The commissioner of civil marriages may appoint deputy commissioners of civil marriage who may solemnize marriages in his county under the direction of the commissioner of civil marriages and shall perform such other duties as the commissioner may direct. The commissioner of civil marriages and his deputy commissioners shall solemnize marriages only within their county and only during regular hours established by the board.

4205.5. In addition to those persons permitted to solemnize marriages under the provisions of Section 4205, a county may license officials of a nonprofit religious institution, whose articles of incorporation are registered with the Secretary of State, to solemnize the marriages of persons who are affiliated with or are members of the religious institution. The licensee shall possess the degree of doctor of philosophy and must perform religious services or rites for the institution on a regular basis. Such marriages shall be performed without fee to the parties.

To be valid in California law, specific procedures must be followed, but the marriage is not invalidated by the failure of the state's representatives to fulfill their role properly.

> *California Civil Code, pars.* 4100, 4200, 4201, 4202, 4207–4215:
> 4100. Marriage is a personal relation arising out of a civil contract, to which the consent of the parties capable of making that contract is necessary. Consent alone will not constitute marriage; it must be followed by the issuance of a license and a solemnization as authorized by this code, except as provided by Section 4213.
>
> 4200. Marriage must be licensed, solemnized, authenticated, and the certificate of registry of marriage filed as provided in this article; but noncompliance with its provisions by others than a party to a marriage does not invalidate it.
>
> 4201. All persons about to be joined in marriage must first obtain a license therefor, from a county clerk, which license must show all of the following:
>
> (1) The identity of the parties.
>
> (2) Their real and full names, and places of residence.
>
> (3) Their ages.
>
> No license shall be granted when either of the parties, applicants therefor, is an imbecile, or insane, or is at the time of making the application for the license, under the influence of any intoxicating liquor, or narcotic drug. If the person is under the age of 18 years, no license may be issued by the county clerk unless both parties are capable of consenting to and consummating marriage as provided for in Section 4101 and such consent or consents or court orders, provided for in Section 4102, must be filed by the clerk. . . .
>
> 4207. The person solemnizing a marriage must first require the presentation of the marriage license; and if he has any reason to doubt the correctness of its statement of facts, he must first satisfy himself of its correctness, and for that purpose he may administer oaths and examine the parties and witnesses in like manner as the county clerk does before issuing the license.
>
> 4208. The person solemnizing a marriage must make, sign and endorse upon or attach to the license a statement, in the form prescribed by the State Department of Public Health showing all of the following:
>
> (1) The fact, time and place of solemnization.
>
> (2) The names and places of residence of one or more witnesses to the ceremony.

(3) A statement of the official position of the person solemnizing the marriage, or of the denomination of which such person is a priest, minister or clergyman. The person solemnizing the marriage shall also type or print his name and address.

The marriage license, thus endorsed, shall be returned to the county recorder of the county in which the license was issued within four days after the ceremony.

4210. If no record of the solemnization of a marriage heretofore contracted, be known to exist, the parties may join in a written declaration of such marriage, substantially showing all of the following:

(1) The names, ages, and residences of the parties.

(2) The fact of marriage.

(3) That no record of such marriage is known to exist.

Such declaration shall be subscribed by the parties and attested by at least three witnesses.

4211. Declarations of marriage must be acknowledged and recorded in like manner as grants of real property.

4213. When unmarried persons, not minors, have been living together as man and wife, they may, without a license, be married by any clergyman, without the necessity of first obtaining health certificates. A certificate of marriage shall be filled out by the parties to the marriage and authenticated by the clergyman performing the ceremony. The certificate shall be filed by the clergyman with the office of the county clerk in the county in which the ceremony was performed within four days after the performance of the ceremony. The county clerk shall maintain this certificate as a permanent record which shall not be open to public inspection except upon order of the superior court issued upon a showing of good cause.

4215. The provisions of this article, so far as they relate to the solemnizing of marriages, are not applicable to members of any particular religious denomination having, as such, any peculiar mode of entering the marriage relation; but such marriages must be declared, as provided in Section 4210, and be acknowledged and recorded, as provided in Section 4211. Where a marriage is declared as provided in Section 4210 the husband must file said declaration with the county recorder within 30 days after such marriage, and upon receiving the same the county recorder must record the same; and if the husband fails to make such declaration and file the same for record, as herein provided, he is liable to the same penalties as any person authorized to solemnize marriages, who fails to make the return of such solemnization as provided by law.

The only two substantive requirements for marriage relate to age and health.

*California Civil Code, pars.* 4101, 4300:

4101. (a) Any unmarried person of the age of 18 years or upwards, and not otherwise disqualified, is capable of consenting to and consummating marriage.

(b) Any person under the age of 18 years is capable of consenting to and consummating marriage if each of the following documents is filed with the clerk issuing the marriage license as provided in Section 4201:

(1) The consent in writing of the parents of each person who is underage, or of one of such parents, or of his or her guardian.

(2) After such showing as the superior court may require, an order of such court granting permission to such underage person to marry.

(c) As part of the order under subdivision (b), the court shall require the parties to such prospective marriage of a person under the age of 18 years to participate in premarital counseling concerning social, economic, and personal responsibilities incident to marriage, if it deems such counseling necessary. Such parties shall not be required, without their consent, to confer with counselors provided by religious organizations of any denomination. In determining whether to order the parties to participate in such premarital counseling, the court shall consider, among other factors, the ability of the parties to pay for such counseling.

4300. (a) Before any person, who is or may hereafter be authorized by law to issue marriage licenses, shall issue any such license, each applicant therefor shall file with him a certificate from a duly licensed physician which certificate shall state that the applicant has been given such examination, including a standard serological test, as may be necessary for the discovery of syphilis, made not more than 30 days prior to the date of issuance of such license, and that, in the opinion of such physician, the person either is not infected with syphilis, or if so infected, is not in a stage of that disease which is or may become communicable to the marital partner.

(b) Such certificate shall also state whether the female applicant has laboratory evidence of immunological response to rubella (German measles). Such certificate shall not contain such evidence of response to rubella where the female applicant (1) is over 50 years of age, or (2) has had a surgical sterilization or (3) presents laboratory evidence of a prior test declaring her immunity to rubella.

These provisions reflect the relatively narrow purview of the state's interest in marriage. The availability of civil marriage is an important element of American freedom of religion, but it comes at the price of impoverishing the American conception of marriage. For the state, marriage is a civil procedure; for Judaism, it is a sacred act, rooted in the structure of the universe.

### 6. Creative Wedding Ceremonies vs. Traditional Ones

It is not just in the literal meaning of the words that the traditional wedding ceremony expresses communal and religious commitments. That has become especially clear in recent years after considerable experimentation with using new, specially created ceremonies. The following editorial essay articulates some of the new meanings that are captured in the new forms and some of the old ones that are lost.

"THE HAZARDS OF HOMEMADE VOWS,"
Lance Morrow, *Time*, June 27, 1983, p. 78.

The 60's and the 70's were the great epoch of the improvisational, personalized wedding ceremony. . . . The logic behind writing one's own vows is not all bad. It is very American: the kids going into business for themselves and wanting to define precisely what the terms of the enterprise are to be. Good luck. The self-made ceremony expresses a kind of romantic individualism (not to say, sometimes, narcissism) that wants to reclaim the event from its bloodless institutional routine and make it mean something wondrous and memorable. Marriage is, one thinks at the start, a long journey. The couple want a bright send-off at the station to think about during those interminable stretches later on, when the landscape becomes as featureless and wearying as the steppe. To write one's own vows is to think about marriage, what it is, what one wants it to be. It is, at best, an act of self-awareness.

This nuptial theater is also meant as a gesture against anonymity and mass production: our love is special in the universe. Unfortunately, the event usually becomes the rhetorical equivalent of those incredible pastel, ruffled-and-piped rent-a-tux outfits that are becoming the uniform for American grooms and their groomsmen.

Beyond the aesthetics of the thing, writing one's own ceremony may reflect a basic misunderstanding about the event. If bride and groom repeat the same vows their parents repeated, the vows they may expect their children to repeat, and if the same tears are shed now that were shed five generations before at the same rite, then the ceremony has its continuity and resonances. The formality may be boring, but it is not meaningless.

If the bride and groom have intimacies to whisper, there are private places for that. A wedding is public business. That is the point of it.

The couple are not merely marrying one another. They are joining the enterprise of the human race. They are, at least in part, submitting themselves to the larger logics of life, to the survival of the community, to life itself. They enter into a contract with processes deeper than they can know. At the moment of their binding, they should subsume their egos into that larger business within which their small lyricisms become tinny and exhibitionistic. The ceremony dignifies the couple precisely to the degree that they lose themselves therein. The mystery of what they do is more interesting than they can ever be.

# Topic Fourteen: Conflicts and Choice of Law I: Jewish Recognition of Civil Marriage and Divorce

## A. CHOICE OF LAW IN THE COMMON LAW

In a world ruled by a multitude of diverse legal regimes and divided court jurisdictions, judges often are called on to decide cases that might be governed by two or more different sets of legal rules. Two Jews marry with a traditional *ketubbah* in Morocco, move to New York where they acquire substantial property, then move to California where the marriage breaks down and a judge is called on to settle the property rights of the spouses. The problem is not that there is no relevant set of legal rules to govern the situation, but that there are too many: rabbinic law, Moroccan national law, New York law, and California law. The choice of rabbinic law may require the judge to choose between the Sephardic practices of the Moroccan community and the Ashkenazic practices of the American community where the couple now resides.

Choice of law problems can be analytically complex in the abstract, but courts usually arrive at sensible, practical choices by applying the legal rules that appear to have the strongest contacts with the transaction before it becomes a lawsuit. Choice of law problems are sometimes simplified because the choice is inconsequential in that both possible choices lead to the same legal result. It is only when there is a truly consequential conflict in legal rules that choice of law becomes a troubling matter.

In most Anglo-American jurisdictions rules governing choice of law develop as common law decided by judges rather than through statutes passed by legislatures. The common law rules have been collected, rationalized, and filled in by the American Law Institute in its *Restatement, Second, of Conflict of Laws*, excerpts from which follow. The general principles stated are subject to exceptions, but they are a useful summary of the rules applied not only in most American states but in most advanced nations of the world.

American Law Institute, *Restatement, Second, Conflict of Laws Sections 6, 283, 285, 222, and 233* (1969):

§ 6. Choice-of-Law Principles

(1) A court, subject to constitutional restrictions, will follow a statutory directive of its own state on choice of law.

(2) When there is no such directive, the factors relevant to the choice of the applicable rule of law include:

a. The needs of the interstate and international systems,
b. the relevant policies of the forum,
c. the relevant policies of other interested states and the relative interests of those states in the determination of the particular issue,
d. the protection of justified expectations,
e. the basic policies underlying the particular field of law,
f. certainty, predictability and uniformity of result, and
g. ease in the determination and application of the law to be applied.

## Marriage

§ 283. Validity of Marriage

(1) The validity of a marriage will be determined by the local law of the state which, with respect to the particular issue, has the most significant relationship to the spouses and the marriage under the principles stated in § 6.

(2) A marriage which satisfies the requirements of the state where the marriage was contracted will everywhere be recognized as valid unless it violates the strong public policy of another state which had the most significant relationship to the spouses and the marriage at the time of the marriage.

§ 285. Law Governing Right to Divorce

The local law of the domiciliary state in which the action is brought will be applied to determine the right to divorce.

## Property

§ 222. The General Principle

The interests of the parties in a thing are determined, depending upon the circumstances, either by the "law" or by the "local law" of the state which, with respect to the particular issue, has the most significant relationship to the thing and the parties under the principles stated in § 6.

§ 233. Effect of Marriage on Existing Interest in Land
(1) The effect of marriage upon an interest in land owned by a spouse at the time of marriage is determined by the law that would be applied by the courts of the situs.

(2) These courts would usually apply their own local law in determining such questions.

## B. Rabbinic Choice of Law

The Talmud (*Ketubbot* 54a) records a case involving a woman from Mahoza who married a man from Nehardea. It was decided that the rights of the widow were governed by the customs of Nehardea. Later rabbis followed that precedent in assuming that the laws of the husband's place of residence should govern all rights and obligations of marriage because normally the couple resided there. So, for example, Solomon b. Abraham Adret in the thirteenth century ruled that the law of the couple's place of residence was binding, and if they had not decided on a place of residence, then the husband's home was determinative "for he marries in accordance with the conditions of his own home, to which he takes her" (*Responsa Rashba*, vol. 1, no. 662). Other scholars ruled similarly on the basis of the talmudic precedent, and Moses Isserles codifies the law that way: "If a man marries with the intention that his wife live with him at his place of residence, the custom of his place is to be followed" (*Rema* to E.H. 66:12).

As Jews became more mobile, however, another opinion began to predominate. The husband's domicile and, for that matter, the couple's place of residence were no longer as permanent as they once were, and so some authorities determined questions about the financial obligations of the marriage according to the laws of the place where the wedding took place "for the husband undertakes liability only in accordance with that place" (*Responsa Ribash*, no. 105). Isserles himself adopts that view (*Rema* to E.H. 118:19), restricting the talmudic preference for the husband's domicile to cases in which that was explicitly stated to be determinative at the time of marriage. The results are the same in the famous sixteenth century case of Hannah Gracia Mendes, one of the Marranos from Portugal who reached Turkey and there reembraced Judaism. She sued for half of her husband's estate in accordance with the customs of Portuguese Jewry. The scholars were all in agreement that the customs to be followed were those in practice in Portugal, where the wedding was held, even if they were not the same as those of Turkey, where the hearing took place; they differed only on whether Jewish marriage law applied to her at all since her wedding was not celebrated in accordance with Jewish law (*Avkat Rakhel*, nos. 80–81; *Resp. Makarashdam*, H.M. No. 327; *Resp. Maharibal* 2:23). In modern Israel, the rabbinical courts have held that the law of the place of celebration must be upheld, even if the marriage was not valid in Jewish law. The case concerned a Jewish couple married in a Russian civil marriage in 1942. In their divorce suit, the court decided that their common property should be divided in accordance with the law in practice in Russia in 1942 (PDR 5:124ff.). Thus the law of the place where the obligation was established has come to be the determining factor in Jewish marital law.

## C. DINA DE-MALKHUTA DINA AND THE TRADITIONAL REFUSAL TO RECOGNIZE CIVIL DIVORCE

As we have learned from extensive archaeological evidence, the Israelites of biblical times used many of the legal institutions of the surrounding cultures, especially in commercial matters. When Jeremiah buys a field, for example, he says that he took "the book of purchase, both that which was sealed, containing the terms and conditions, and that which was open," and he gave it to Barukh, his secretary, to deposit in earthen jars so that it would last a long time (Jeremiah 32:6–14). As Rabbi J. H. Hertz (*The Pentateuch and Hafturahs*, 2nd ed. [London: Soncino, 1960, p. 540], notes;

> The Jews had been vassals of Assyria and Babylon for about a century; and, it seems, transference of land was now performed according to the legal procedure of the Sovereign Power. As in all Babylonian documents of that nature, the deed was written on clay, and enclosed in a clay envelope, which was sealed up. A copy of the contract was inscribed on the envelope: this is referred to in verse 14 as the "open" deed. Only in case of the writing on the envelope becoming obliterated, or of suspicion that it had been tampered with, was the envelope broken and the text itself examined.

While such borrowings were common, in some cases the Jews adopted the foreign institution as their own, and in others they acquiesced to it because they had no choice but to comply with the demands of a foreign government in power. It was only in the third century C.E.

that the first generation Amora, Samuel, proclaims the legitimacy of obeying the laws of non-Jewish governments as a principle of Jewish law. The principle announced in his name is *dina de-malkhuta dina,* "the law of the government is the law." The Talmud cites it explicitly only four times (*Ned.* 28a; *Git.* 10b; *B.K.* 113a; *B.B.* 54b–55a), in cases recognizing Persian laws dealing with transfer of land ownership, presumptive ownership, documents, the sale of land confiscated for nonpayment of the land tax, and the prohibition against cheating tax collectors or hiding assets from them unless the taxes are illegal for reasons that the Talmud states. Although it is not explicitly invoked, it is also applied in the talmudic rule affirming the right of the king to enslave a person who evades payment of the poll tax and the propriety of a Jew buying the debtor from the government and keeping him as a slave (*Yev.* 64a, *B.M.* 73b).

Since Samuel's principle effectively abrogates Jewish law in the areas to which it is applied, it may seem surprising that Samuel does not offer a justification for his ruling. Indeed it was not until the Middle Ages that justifications were attempted. Jews accepted his principle as simply expressing the reality of power: it was inevitable that Jews recognize secular law when the power of the government gave them little choice. The first extant rationale for the principle reflects the resignation Jews felt in acting according to the principle. The gaon (cited in S. Assaf, *Teshuvot Ha Geonim,* no. 66) writes that it is the will of God that Jews should obey the laws of their rulers, and he quotes Nehemiah 9:36–37 in support of that contention:

> Behold we are slaves this day; in the land You gave to our fathers to enjoy its fruit and its good gifts, behold, we are slaves. Its rich yield goes to the kings whom You have set over us because of our sins; they have power also over our bodies and over our cattle at their pleasure, and we are in great distress.

Later rabbis offered more positive explanations for the principle's authority. Rashi (*Gittin* 9b) suggests that Jews may follow non-Jewish law in certain cases because non-Jews are subject to the seven Noahide laws according to Jewish law and one of those is the obligation to enact laws to preserve orderly social life. Rashbam (c. 1080–1158) propounds a third, contractual reason: Jews have accepted the king's statutes along with all other citizens "of their own free will" (Rashbam on *B.B.* 54b). Maimonides agrees with that rationale (M.T. *Laws of Theft* 5:18). Another, somewhat different version of that theory emphasizes that the land belongs to the king, and therefore if Jews want to reside on it, they are obliged to abide by the conditions he lays down (Ran, *Ned.*

28a; *Or Zarua, B.K.* no. 447). There is still the element of mutual agreement here, but it is clearly the king who determines the nature of the relationship; it is less a matter of the Jews' own free will. Later rabbis base the authority of Samuel's principle on the right of a Jewish court to expropriate a person's property and to redistribute it as it will. Others justify Jewish enforcement of the state's civil law on the basis of custom: it is simply the custom of the people to abide by the king's rules, and that custom, like any other, has legal authority in Jewish law because it refers to monetary issues which the parties to an agreement have the right to determine (*Aliyyot de Rabbenu Yonah, B.B.* 552).

Whatever justification is used, Samuel's principle had far-reaching implications in Jewish law, but not as extensive as one might first expect. It did enable Jews to adopt the rule of the realm when they had to without too many pangs of conscience, but Jews wanted their own law to operate in as many areas as possible. Consequently Samuel's principle was treated in two contrary ways. On the one hand, the initial restrictions imposed on its application were weakened or dropped as the principle was invoked in new situations. On the other, Jews used it as little as possible. Thus the theoretical groundwork for expanding the use of foreign law was laid at the same time that its application was constricted.

There are three primary ways in which use of the principle was expanded. Most early rabbis, influenced by the medieval jurisprudential tenet that only ancient laws were valid, held that Samuel's rule does not apply to laws introduced by incumbent kings but only to the longstanding laws of the realm. Maimonides and Asher b. Jehiel disagreed, however, and Joseph Caro decided the law according to their stance, making no mention of this restriction (see also Sh. Ar., *H.M.* 369:8–10). As the medieval system waned beginning in the fifteenth century, legislation not based on ancient practices became more common in many countries. The removal of that restriction was important for Jews living under changing circumstances.

Second, while the Talmud recognized the king's right to collect taxes and classified tax evasion as robbery, it established criteria to distinguish between justified and unjustified taxes. It declares unjustified taxes illegal, and a Jew would not be duty-bound to pay them under Samuel's principle. In the course of time, however, the definition of talmudically illegal taxes became ever more narrow, such that sometimes even unlimited taxes or wicked and cruel taxes were recognized by rabbinic authorities as binding on Jews to pay under Samuel's principle.

Finally, as we shall see in the reading which follows, from the

Mishnah through Maimonides Jewish law limited the acceptability of certain documents issued by non-Jewish courts. After Maimonides however, the tendency was to ignore the earlier restrictions. For example, communities which accepted Maimonides' *Mishneh Torah* as their code commonly made three exceptions to his decisions, one of which was to accept benefactions executed by non-Jewish courts. Similarly, the Geonim had permitted the collection of bills issued by non-Jewish courts from free assets only, but later authorities permitted seizure of the debtor's real property as well, just as they could in the case of any note of indebtedness affirmed by a Jewish court. Maimonides and other early authorities require that the honesty of the non-Jewish court be established before its documents would be recognized, but later authorities assumed the legitimacy of courts unless the contrary were proved. Moreover, they recognized not only the acts of judges but also those of administrative officers of the court.

The adoption of Samuel's principle and the weakening of the restrictions on its application did not mean that Jewish law effectively became inoperative. Until the end of the eighteenth century most countries in which Jews lived placed the authority for governing the Jews and for settling their disputes in the hands of Jewish institutions. Romans, Persians, Muslims, and Christians all governed the Jews and other minority groups through their ethnic leaders rather than directly as subjects of the state. Ethnic leaders then imposed rules on community members with the backing of the government. As a result, Jewish communities, like others, legislated, judged, and executed sanctions, including the attachment of property, monetary fines, corporal punishment, imprisonment, death (in some locales), and, most effectively, excommunication (*herem*) in varying degrees of severity.

As a result of the overlords' administrative organization Jews enjoyed judicial autonomy. Jews actively sought the requisite charters of privileges from heads of government to enable them to govern themselves. Because Jews understood Jewish law to be God's law, every effort was made to make it operative on as many topics and in as many regions of the world as possible.

Moreover, rabbis took steps to insure that *dina de-malkhuta dina* did not undermine Jewish law. Jewish choice of law, like modern conflict of law principles, was understood to incorporate only substantive laws from foreign legal systems into Jewish practice, but not the procedural parts of foreign law. For example, a non-Jewish law about the disposition of debts might be used in a Jewish court, but proof of the relevant facts had to satisfy Jewish rules of evidence. More broadly, Jews were prohibited from taking their disputes to the Gentile courts: the law of the land may be the law, but Jews were expressly forbidden from going to the king's courts to have it applied. This rule is recorded first in the name of R. Tarfon, who writes soon after the destruction of the Temple (and with it Jewish political autonomy) in 70 C.E.:

> *Gittin* 88b:
> Rabbi Tarfon used to say: Wherever you find Gentile law courts, even if their law is the same as the law of Israel, you may not resort to them since it is written, "These are the judgments that you shall set before them" (Ex. 21:1)—"before them" and not before the Gentiles.

Resort to a Gentile court of law was equated with denial of God and the Torah and with outright profanation of the Divine Name. Thus litigants in a monetary dispute may stipulate all kinds of things, even contrary to scriptural rules, but they may not mutually agree to submit their case to a non-Jewish court.

There were also substantive restrictions on the use of *dina de-malkhuta dina*. The foreign law could not violate fundamental Jewish principles of law and equity. So, for example, it must apply to everyone equally; a directive that discriminates against one group of citizens is not law but "robbery." Similarly, imposition of a fine on a whole group for the transgression of a few individuals was seen as "absolute robbery" because such a rule inflicts vicarious punishment which is in clear violation of Jewish law.

Samuel's principle was also limited substantively by the understanding that it did not govern ritual, family, or criminal law. Some Jewish communities possessed jurisdiction over criminal matters (notably in thirteenth and fourteenth century Spain and in Eastern Europe under the Council of the Four Lands from the mid-sixteenth century to 1764), but most lacked that authority and were forced to apply the criminal law of the realm. They did so because they had no choice, not because they saw that law as effectively part of Jewish law under the principle of *dina de-malkhuta dina*. Because it was so widely accepted that Samuel's principle does not apply to ritual matters and family law, this restriction is expressly mentioned only in a few sources.

As a result of these limitations on the use of *dina de-malkhuta dina*, Samuel's principle was largely restricted in practice to the areas governing the relations between the government and the Jews, such as taxation and expropriation of property for governmental purposes, and Isserles ultimately embodied that limitation in law (*Rema* to *H.M.* 369:11). The rationale for this severe limitation was fear that extension of the doctrine to all matters of civil law would lead to "nullification of all the laws of Israel." Consequently, Menahem Elon characterizes the doctrine of *dina de-malkhuta dina* as "only a marginal aspect of the Jewish legal system"—despite its revolutionary implications in theory.

For our purposes, the most important limitation on the use of Samuel's principle is the refusal of Jewish law to apply it to divorces executed in non-Jewish courts. The basis for that refusal is the following talmudic section. Writs of divorce and emancipation executed by Gentile courts are unacceptable in Jewish law, according to the Talmud, because the law requires such acts to be those of the husband or master, not the court. In other words, the court's role is to supervise the divorce or manumission; it does not effect the act by decree. Since Jewish courts do not have authority to act in such matters, you can understand why Jewish law would deny such power to non-Jewish courts. Note that in Roman law also divorce was a personal matter, not a judicial one.

Rafram requires that to be recognized under Samuel's rule the forum must be an official judicial body. American and international rules of reciprocity are similar: jurisdictions limit the recognition of foreign acts to the legal effects they would have where executed.

Rava is ruling in a case in which *Jewish* courts are dealing with a document written in a foreign language. In interpreting his ruling, the Gemara stipulates that the witnesses be able to understand the foreign tongue, that the document be ineradicable, and that the gist of the document be summarized in the last line. Maimonides adds to those restrictions when it is a matter of recognizing instruments signed by Gentile witnesses and executed in Gentile courts. The direction of the sources is clear: the rabbis have no choice but to recognize the validity of the acts of non-Jewish courts, but they insure the legal integrity of those acts as much as possible.

> *Gittin* 10b–11a:
> MISHNAH. All documents which are accepted in heathen courts, even if they that signed them were Gentiles, are valid for Jewish courts except writs of divorce and of emancipation. R. Simeon says: these also are valid; they were only pronounced to be invalid when drawn up by unauthorized persons.
>
> GEMARA. Our Mishnah lays down a comprehensive rule in which no distinction is made between a sale and a gift. We can understand that the rule should apply to a sale, because the purchaser acquires the object of sale from the moment when he hands over the money in their presence, and the document is a mere corroboration; for if he did not hand over the money in their presence, they would not take the risk of drawing up a document of sale for him. But with a gift it is different. Through what does the recipient obtain possession? Through

this document, is it not? And this document is a mere piece of clay! —Said Samuel: The law of the government is law. Or if you prefer, I can reply: instead of "except writs of divorce" in the Mishnah, read, "except documents like writs of divorce."

"R. Simeon says: these also are valid etc." How can this be, seeing that to heathens the act of "severance" is not applicable?

Said R. Zera: R. Simeon here accepts the view of R. Eleazar, who said that the separation is actually effected by the witnesses to the delivery of the document.—But has not R. Abba said that R. Eleazar used to admit that a writ of divorce which in itself contained a flaw was invalid?—We are dealing here with signatures which are obviously those of heathens. Can you give some examples of names which are obviously those of heathens? Said R. Papa: for instance, Hannez and Abudina, Bar Shibthai, Bar Kidri, Batti and Nakim and Una.— What then if the signatures are not obviously those of heathens? The document, you will say, is invalid? If so, instead of going on to say, "they were only pronounced to be invalid when drawn up by unauthorized persons," R. Simeon should draw a distinction between the signatures themselves, and should continue thus: "when I say they are valid, I mean when the names are obviously heathen, but otherwise they are invalid!"—This in fact is what he does mean, viz: "when I say they are valid I mean when the names are obviously heathen, but where they are not so, the document is on a par with one drawn up by unauthorized persons and is invalid." Or if you like I can reply that the last clause of the Mishnah refers to monetary documents, and the meaning is as follows: "Monetary documents were not pronounced to be invalid save when they were drawn up by unauthorized persons."

It has been taught: R. Eleazar said in the name of R. Jose: Thus did R. Simeon say to the Rabbis in Sidon: R. Akiba and the Sages were agreed in reference to all documents entered in heathen courts that even if those that signed them were heathens they were valid, including also writs of divorce and of emancipation. They differed only in the case where they were drawn up by unauthorized persons, R. Akiba declaring all such documents to be valid and the Sages declaring them all invalid, save only writs of divorce and of emancipation. Rabban Simeon b. Gamliel says that these too are valid only in places where Jews are not allowed to sign documents, but where Jews are allowed to sign documents they are not valid. Why does not Rabban Simeon b. Gamliel declare them invalid even in places where Jews are allowed to sign, for fear lest they should come to be deemed valid even in places where they are not?—Names may be confused but not places.

Ravina had a mind to declare valid a document which had been drawn up in a gathering of Arameans. Said Rafram to him: "We learned distinctly 'Courts.'"

Rava said: A document drawn up in Persian which has been handed over in the presence of Jewish witnesses is sufficient warrant for recovering from property on which there is no previous lien.—But the witnesses to the transfer cannot read it!—We speak of the case where they can.—But we require writing which cannot be erased!—We speak of a case where the sheet has been dressed with gall-nut juice. —But we require the rule to be observed that the gist of the document must be summarized in the last line.—We speak of a case where this has been done.—If so, why not recover from mortgaged property also? —The contents of a document of this kind do not become generally known.

Maimonides, *Mishneh Torah*, Laws of Slaves 6:5:
In six respects writs of manumission for slaves are the same as writs of divorce, and in all other respects they are like all other documents. These are the six respects:

i. They are invalid (if executed) by Gentile courts.
ii. They are valid if a Gentile serves as a witness.
iii. They need to be written specifically on behalf of the emancipator.
iv. They may not be written on anything attached to the ground.
v. And the witnesses (for both types of document) must sign each in the presence of the other. . . .
vi. They are subject to the same rules (of confirmation) when taken (from the land of Israel to foreign parts) or *vice versa* (specifically, they may be confirmed either by witnesses who recognize the signatures or by the messenger attesting that he witnessed the writing and signing of the document—cf. 6:7).

All documents of the Gentile courts are valid, assuming that they satisfy all the requirements that we explain in "The Laws of Creditor and Debtor," except for writs of divorce and manumission.

Maimonides, *Mishneh Torah*, Laws of Creditor and Debtor 27:1:
An instrument that is written in any language and in any script, if it was prepared in accordance with the formal requirements of instruments used in Israel which cannot be forged or added to or diminished from, and the witnesses thereto are Israelites who know how to read it, is valid and collection may be made thereon even from alienated property.

But instruments which are signed by heathens as witnesses are invalid. An exception, however, is made in the case of instruments of purchase and sale and of indebtedness, provided the money was handed over in their presence and the instrument recites, "In our presence such a one counted to such a one so much, being the amount of the purchase price or of the debt," and provided further that the instrument was made in their courts. But if the instrument was made in the place of assembly of their courts, without the judge's confirmation, it is of no avail. It is also necessary that Israelite witnesses testify that the heathen who attested the instrument, and the judge who confirmed their attestation, are not known as bribe-takers.

If an instrument prepared by the heathen lacks any one of these requisites, it is deemed like a potsherd. Similarly, instruments of recognizance, gift, compromise, or release which are attested by their witnesses, even though the instruments possess all the requisites we have enumerated, are deemed like potsherds.

My teachers have taught that even an instrument of indebtedness, which was prepared by them after the money loaned was handed by the creditor to the debtor in their presence, is invalid, my teachers having ruled valid only an instrument of purchase and sale which was prepared after the purchase money was handed by the vendee to the vendor in their presence. However, I do not agree with them.

If the Israelite judges do not know how to read an instrument which was prepared in the courts of the heathen, they give it to two heathens who read it, each in the absence of the other, so that each one of them may be considered like a witness who speaks in the integrity of his mind, without being aware that his statement will be used as testimony.

Collection on such an instrument prepared by the heathen may be made only out of free property, seizure not being allowable thereon, since it is not accompanied by publicity and the obligor's vendees are not presumed to have known what was done by the heathen.

D. THE OPERATION OF JEWISH MARITAL LAW WITHIN THE CONTEXT OF BINDING, CIVIL MARITAL LAW

As we have seen, Jewish law does not recognize the validity of civil divorce. No serious conflict of jurisdiction arose until the Enlightenment because most nations delegated authority over marriages and divorces to the religious authorities of the various communities in their realms. A central principle of the Enlightenment, however, was that all people should be treated alike, as *individual* citizens of the state rather than as members of a particular group within the nation. That philosophy served to liberate Jews from many of the restrictions they had endured in education, government, and commerce, but it also created major conflicts of jurisdiction for Jewish family law.

In civil and criminal matters, post-Enlightenment Jewish communities in Central and Western Europe and the United States generally deferred to the authority of the state, based on clear precedents in Jewish law. Jurisdiction over family law, however, was another matter, for there Jewish law specifically did not recognize civil divorce actions, and states increasingly asserted their right to govern all questions of family law. Consequently, Jews found themselves in the awkward situation of being subject to both civil and Jewish law in matters of marriage and divorce.

While most states of the United States provide a means of getting married without religious trappings, they also empower religious authorities to act as agents of the state in performing marriages. The requirements of both the civil and Jewish legal systems can be met simultaneously without much trouble. Since most people consider a wedding a religious event, they usually take advantage of this possibility. In any case, rabbis will not officiate at marriages unless the civil requirements are met. On the other hand, while Jewish law imposes an obligation on Jews to marry in a Jewish ceremony with a *ketubbah*, the law recognizes, after the fact, the validity of a nonceremonial marriage between Jews who could have married according to its rules. Civil marriage of people who may not be married in Jewish law (such as a Jew and a non-Jew) are simply not recognized: it is as if nothing happened from the point of view of Jewish law. Consequently, since in practice there can never be a Jewish marriage without a civil marriage, and since post factum Jewish law will recognize a civil marriage as valid even though it is not happy with that form of marriage, there are no serious conflicts of jurisdiction in regard to marriage.

Divorce, however, presents serious jurisdictional issues. Civil law may recognize some stipulations of Jewish divorces as a supplement to the agreement entered into in civil court, as we shall see in Topic Fifteen, but it certainly does not recognize Jewish divorce proceedings in lieu of civil action. Similarly, Jewish law does not recognize civil divorces, as we have seen. If a Jewish couple is civilly divorced and the woman remarries in a civil ceremony, she has committed adultery in terms of Jewish law because the first marriage was never dissolved in Jewish law. She is not only not married to her second husband; she can never marry him because he is her guilty, adulterous partner. Moreover, her children of the second marriage are considered illegitimate (*mamzerim*) and may not marry Jews for ten generations (Deut. 23:3). (A man who remarries without a Jewish divorce has violated the decree of Rabbenu Gershom requiring monogamy, but he is simply considered as having taken a second wife, and his children are legitimate. A man is guilty of adultery in Jewish law only if he has intercourse with a woman married to someone else.) More commonly, and hence more tragically, Jewish couples often simply neglect to go through the Jewish procedures when they are civilly divorced. When one of the parties wants to remarry, it sometimes is difficult to arrange for the Jewish divorce, either because the whereabouts of the former spouse is unknown or because that spouse refuses out of spite to issue or accept a Jewish divorce.

Conservative and Reform rabbis have taken different measures, described in the readings which follow, in an attempt to resolve these difficulties. To understand those readings, the reader should be aware of several features of Jewish divorce law.

First, in Jewish law only the man can issue a divorce, based on Deuteronomy 24:1–4 (see also Gemara, *Kiddushin* 5b, cited in Topic Thirteen, Section A-2). In talmudic law, the woman need not accept the divorce for it to be effective. The husband can simply throw the writ into her domain, and it is binding on her. Rabbenu Gershom, however, decreed (c.1000 C.E.) that the wife's consent must be obtained for the divorce to be valid.

If both spouses consent to the divorce, then no grounds need be supplied; the court simply supervises the procedure. If, however, the woman refuses to consent to the divorce, then the rabbinic court determines whether the man has grounds to divorce her based on the Mishnah, *Ketubbot* 5:5, 5:7, 7:6 (See also Topic Thirteen, Section C3), and the legal developments of those passages. If he does, he may divorce her against her will despite Rabbenu Gershom's decree. A typical case nowadays is one in which the woman has obtained a civil divorce from her husband. In that case, the rabbinic court will be inclined to rule that her act constitutes a consent to the divorce, no matter what she says now. Moreover, since they are living apart, his conjugal rights have been violated, and hence he has legal grounds to divorce her against her will.

If the court finds that the husband has grounds to divorce the wife or that she has consented in action if not in words, then it will try to convince her to accept the writ of divorce. If she refuses, then the court will accept the writ of divorce from the husband on her behalf, and he is free to remarry at once. The writ that the rabbinic court issues is called a *get zikkui* (lit. "a writ of imparting a privilege") because the court is acting on the principle that "one may act for the benefit of a person even though that person is not present" (*Ketubbot* 11a). Since the wife has lost all social, sexual, and economic benefits of marriage through her civil divorce, it is now to her advantage to have a Jewish writ of divorce so she can remarry Jewishly if she so desires. If she does not realize this, the rabbinic court will act for her in accepting the writ of divorce from her husband. She may take advantage of that writ of divorce and remarry at any subsequent time.

If a man refuses to issue a Jewish writ of divorce (get), then the situation is more troublesome because only he has the power to do so. The court cannot act on the husband's behalf without his express permission since it is not considered a benefit to be divorced. Once again the rabbinic court will determine whether the woman has grounds to insist on a divorce in terms of her rights as specified in the Mishnah *Ketubbot* 5:5–6:1 (see Topic Thirteen, Section C-3) and the later legal developments summarized in the section of *Shulhan Arukh* in Topic Thirteen, Section C3. If the couple has been civilly divorced, then her conjugal rights have no doubt been violated, thus constituting grounds. In any case, if the court determines that such grounds exist and the husband nevertheless refuses to grant the divorce, the court's first recourse is to exert social and economic pressure on the husband. As the rabbinic sources which follow indicate, they may also apply corporal punishment in that "we force him until he says, 'I want to'!" In Israel, where rabbinic courts have sole jurisdiction over Jews in matters of personal status, this even includes imprisonment. There are cases of husbands held in jail for lengthy periods for refusing to give their wives a *get*. In the United States the pressure is usually moral, social, and economic.

There are two other resources existing in Jewish law that Conservative rabbis may use if necessary. The first, which is described in a following article, is to insert an explicit condition in the marriage agreement that makes the marriage null and void if there is a civil divorce and no Jewish divorce within six months thereafter. The second is to rely on the rabbinic dictum that "everyone who betroths does so at the pleasure of the Rabbis" (*Gittin* 36b), and hence a rabbinic court can annul a marriage if they deem it necessary to do so in the interests of justice. In other words, there is an implicit condition in every Jewish marriage that the marriage is subject to annulment by Jewish legal authorities. This view gains strength from the fact that the betrothal formula used at every Jewish wedding and included in the wedding contract itself says that the betrothal and marriage are "according to the laws of Moses and Israel," thus invoking all of the constructive conditions of Jewish marriage.

Despite the legitimacy of these methods, they are used sparingly for several reasons. In the case of the explicit condition, some have argued that a couple cannot possibly understand this condition concerning divorce while their minds are bent on thoughts of marriage, even if the clause is in English and is explained to them some time before the wedding. Annulment without divorce threatens the institution of divorce. Consequently, rabbinic courts that use these methods will insist that the recalcitrant husband issue a get (called a *get humrah*, "a writ of stringency") before they will allow him to remarry. They do this "so that the sinner may not be rewarded (by the technicalities of the law)" (*Ketubbot* 11a). The *get* will be insisted on even though the first marriage has been annulled judicially and the first wife has been allowed to remarry.

There are also two more radical approaches to these problems. The Conservative Movement has been increasingly extending the rights of women in various areas of Jewish law in recognition of their changing social and educational status in our society. There has been some discussion—but at this point only preliminary discussion—of allowing a woman to issue a writ of divorce. That would be a much more efficient solution than any of those mentioned, but it would represent a major departure from traditional Jewish law from its very beginning.

The Reform Movement has used a different method. As Freehof explains, in practice Reform rabbis simply recognize the validity of civil marriage and divorce proceedings, thus extending the traditional Jewish recognition of other civil actions in the state courts. He discusses the justification and ramifications of this method. Once again, it is an efficient solution to the problem, but it seriously calls into question the authority of any part of Jewish law in the modern period. This was an acceptable result to the classical Reform Movement, which was not very interested in the continuity of Jewish law. It is hard for Jews of other groups to accept, and second thoughts have developed in recent years within the Reform Movement itself as its approach to Judaism incorporates greater appreciation of Jewish law.

*Bava Batra* 47b–48a:
R. Huna said: If a man consents to sell something through fear of physical violence, the sale is valid. Why so? Because whenever a man sells, it is under compulsion, and even so his sale is valid.—But should we not differentiate internal from external compulsion—We must therefore give another reason, as it has been taught: (48a) From the superfluous words "he shall offer it" (Lev. 1:3), we learn that a man can be forced to bring an offering which he has vowed. Does this mean even against his will? This cannot be because it says, "of his own free will" (Lev. 1:3). What, then, are we to say? Force is applied to him until he says, "I consent."—But perhaps there is a special reason in this case, viz. that he may be well satisfied to do so retrospectively, so as to have atonement made for his sins?—We must therefore look for the reason in the next passage of the Baraita quoted: "Similarly in the case of divorces, where the Rabbis have said that the husband can be forced to give a divorce, we say that what is meant is that force is

applied to him until he says, 'I consent.'"—But there too perhaps
there is a special reason, viz. that it is a religious duty to listen to the
word of the Sages.—What we must say therefore is that it is reasonable to suppose that under the pressure he really made up his mind to
sell.

Rav Judah questioned this on the ground of the following Mishnah:
"A get (bill of divorce) extorted by pressure applied by an Israelite is
valid, but if the pressure is applied by a non-Jew it is invalid. A non-
Jew also, however, may be commissioned by the court to flog the husband and say to him, 'Do what the Israelite bids you.'" Now why
should the get be invalid if extorted by the non-Jew? Cannot we say
that in that case also the man makes up his mind under pressure to
grant the divorce?—This rule must be understood in the light of the
statement made by R. Mesharsheya regarding it: According to the Torah itself, the get is valid even if extorted by a non-Jew, and the reason
why the Rabbis on their own authority declared it invalid was so as
not to give an opportunity to any Jewish woman to keep company
with a non-Jew and so release herself from her husband (by inducing
the non-Jew to go and extort a get from him).

Gittin 88b:
MISHNAH: A get given under compulsion exercised by an Israelite
court is valid, but by a heathen court is invalid. A heathen court however, may flog a man and say to him, "Do what the Israelite authorities command you," and it is valid.

GEMARA: R. Nahman said in the name of Samuel: "A get given
under compulsion exercised by an Israelite court with good legal
ground is valid, but if without sufficient legal ground, it is invalid, but
it still disqualifies the woman for marrying a priest (kohen). If enforced by a heathen court on good legal grounds, it is invalid, but
disqualifies; if without sufficient legal ground, in no sense is it a
get—How can you have it both ways? If the heathens are competent
to apply compulsion, then it should actually be valid. If they are not
competent to apply compulsion, it should not disqualify!—R. Mesharsheya explained: According to the strict rule of the Torah, a get
enforced by a heathen court is valid, and the reason why the Rabbis
declared it invalid was to prevent any Jewish woman from attaching
herself to a heathen and so releasing herself from her husband.—If
that is so, why did Samuel say that if it is enforced by a heathen court
without sufficient legal ground, it has not even the tincture of a get?
Let it at least be on a par with the similar get exacted by an Israelite
court, and disqualify the woman for marrying a priest?—The truth
is that R. Mesharsheya's explanation is erroneous (and the heathen
court is in fact not competent to enforce the giving of a get). And what
is the reason? A get enforced by a heathen court on legal grounds is li-

able to be confused with a *get* enforced by an Israelite court on legal grounds, but a *get* enforced by a heathen court without proper grounds will not be confused with a *get* enforced by a Jewish court with legal grounds.

Abbaye once found R. Joseph sitting in court and compelling certain men to give a bill of divorce. He said to him: Surely we (in Babylonia) are only laymen, and it has been taught: R. Tarfon used to say: In any place where you find heathen law courts, even though their law is the same as the Israelite law, you must not resort to them since it says, "These are the judgments which you shall set before them" (Ex. 21:1) that is to say, "before them" and not before heathens. Another explanation, however, is that it means "before them" and not before laymen?—He replied: We are carrying out their commission, just as in the case of admissions and transaction of loans.—If that is the case, he rejoined, we should do the same with robberies and injuries?—We carry out their commission in matters which are of frequent occurrence, but not in matters which occur infrequently.

(Note: The last paragraph assumes that divorces were given frequently, and that is certainly at odds with what many people assume about the low divorce rate among Jews before modern times. Our impression may be true of some Jewish societies, but certainly not all, as this text indicates.)

"T'NAI B'KIDDUSHIN (A CONDITION OF BETROTHAL),"
Committee on Jewish Law and Standards, *Proceedings of the Rabbincal Assembly* [1968], 229–41.

QUESTION: One of the vexing problems in *halachah* today involves the woman, divorced from her husband by a civil court, who cannot persuade him to give her a *get* which would permit her to remarry according to Jewish law. Moral suasion is often insufficient to induce a man to give a *get* under these conditions, and we are powerless to enforce upon him what we believe to be a proper and moral course of action. The Rabbinical Assembly *ketubbah* has been of much help, but many problems remain. Are there any further steps which might be taken to safeguard against *iggun* of this type? (Note: *iggun* = the status of being an *agunah* = "a chained woman," i.e., one who is chained to her husband because he either cannot or will not issue her a writ of divorce even though he no longer lives with her in marriage.)

ANSWER: The subject of the *agunah* has held the attention of more rabbis for more time than probably any other single problem, and for those who tried to find solutions that would remain within the framework of *halachah* it has proved almost insurmountable. The inherent difficulties caused by the nature of *halachah* in this area have been complicated by the obduracy of much of the rabbinate in rejecting solutions which, while operating within the framework of the tradition, have taken different approaches from those used in the past. This committee has undertaken to take up the matter again. We understand full well the asperity of the problem, and we do not expect to be able to solve the problem completely, or to the satisfaction of everyone, but we will offer what may be a solution to at least one aspect of it, in the hope that this may be a step in the direction of alleviating this very grievous situation.

The *agunah*, the woman who is unable to live with her husband because of his disappearance, insanity or abandonment while refusing to give her a *get*, and yet is declared by Jewish law to be still married, has been known for ages. Her plight has evoked much sympathy. Many steps have been taken by the rabbinate to alleviate the condition of such women. Within the context of previous ages, they had a certain amount of success. But with the coming of the modern era, the rise of modern nationalism and the civil emancipation of the Jews of Western Europe and America, a new version of the problem arose. The Jews obtained civil emancipation in the form of full and equal citizenship only at the cost of relinquishing their autonomous communities, and subjecting themselves to the full range of civil law, including family law. This meant that Jewish laws of marriage and divorce would be applied only as supplementary to the civil law of the state. In the area of divorce it meant that, for all intents and purposes, the real act of divorce was thrown completely into the jurisdiction of the civil courts. Only after the civil authorities had taken action to terminate the marriage would the Jews add the religious requirement of a *get*. The *get* has become an appendage to the civil divorce, and one which a great many Jews have chosen to dispense with, whether through ignorance, apathy or deliberate rejection. The dimensions of this situation are well known to every rabbi who works within the Jewish community, and a not insignificant number of rabbis, even those of a traditional bent, have reluctantly resigned themselves to considering the situation hopeless and the trend irreversible.

It is the intention of this committee to at least begin to reverse this tide. We have done so by concentrating our efforts on what we consider to be the most compatible with the requirements of *halachah*. In doing so we do not repudiate previous attempts to meet the problem, nor do we rule out any further discussion or other approaches.

The problem that concerns us here is the following: All too often a Jewish couple obtains a civil divorce and then the husband refuses to give his "wife" (according to Jewish law) a *get*. The wife is then usually helpless, and unless she can put extraordinary persuasive pressure upon her husband, she is faced with the alternatives of either obeying *halachah* and living out her days as a woman barred from remarriage, or marrying in defiance of *halachah* in a civil ceremony or before a rabbi who chooses to ignore *halachah* in this very serious matter. It is technically possible for a husband also to find himself in such a situation, when a wife refuses to or cannot accept a *get* after a civil divorce, but there is available to him the relief offered by *get zikkui* or *heter me'ah rabbanim*. But the most pressing problem is that of a woman who cannot obtain a *get* after a civil divorce, and who may be subject to the whims of a vindictive husband.

The result of this situation is not that there is a large number of Jewish women whose lives are destroyed by such husbands, numerous *agunot* suffering from their miserable condition. Quite the contrary; there are hardly any *agunot* in America. Rather there are great numbers of women who, according to *halachah*, should be *agunot* but instead have remarried without the benefit of a *get*, and who are now living in a state of technical adultery and whose children are *mamzerim* (bastards). It is ironic that, of those rabbis who oppose any attempt to change this situation, some take comfort in the fact that the existence of *agunot* has been in fact practically eliminated by the convenient solution of widespread recourse to adultery and bastardy. The problem of the actual *agunah*, which is basically a humanitarian problem, has been solved by resorting to what should be considered the most abhorrent sin known to *halachah*, on the same level with idolatry and murder. Thus the problem of the *agunah* is quite different now from what it was thirty years ago. There is still the humanitarian problem of alleviating the condition of some Jewish women who would not marry without obtaining a *get* and whose husbands maliciously refuse to cooperate. However, the widespread disregard of Jewish divorce laws by Jews has reached the stage where a major part of the American Jewish community will live under the shadow of technical *mamzerut* (bastardy) or *safek mamzerut* (possible bastardy). Time is not on our side in this problem; the longer action is delayed, the more entangled the situation becomes.

The solution here proposed is to create the possibility of the annulment of a marriage when a husband refuses to give a *get* after a civil divorce. The annulment of marriage in Jewish law is a very complex subject, and much has been written about it. Although annulment has always been a possibility in Jewish law and occasionally used, it has generally been avoided. The basic reason is that, since divorce has always been permitted, and since in Jewish law it is (from the point of view of a husband) very easy, marriage has been made correspondingly easy; that is, the ready availability of divorce made it possible to make marriage binding with the minimum of formalities and legal requirements. In ancient times the fact that a husband could easily initiate a *get* was balanced by the Rabbis' enabling a wife to sue for divorce on numerous grounds, and the Rabbinical Courts would exert pressure upon a husband to comply. However, the radical change of the social and political condition of the Jews in the modern era in Western Europe and America has created a new context for the rules of divorce and annulment. Jewish courts no longer exist in the old sense; hence, Jewish divorce is now entirely a matter of consent between the parties, and this puts the wife at a very great disadvantage.

In recent years the possible use of annulment has been suggested with increasing frequency. It is the opinion of this committee that it can effectively be put into operation by means of introducing a "resolutive" condition at the time of a wedding which possibly could be invoked to annul the marriage in the event of certain circumstances. The main problems involved will be discussed below.

The matter of conditional marriages has been thoroughly investigated by various authors, and a further restatement of all the details of the sources and their interpretations is not necessary here; a summary of the most important points in the discussions should suffice.

A very full historical survey of the evolution of post-talmudic marriage *halachah*, including conditional marriage, is to be found in A. Freimann, *Seder Kidushin ve'Nissuin* (Jerusalem, 1945, reprinted 1964). Of special interest is Freimann's Appendix on "Proposals for Reforms" (385–397). He lists a long series of attempts at introducing various forms of marriage annulment, including the use of conditional marriages, up to his own time (Cf. Boaz Cohen, *Law and Tradition in Judaism*, p. 94, n. 70; pp. 95–96, 112f.). Recently, Mosad Harav Kook in Jerusalem published a book by Rabbi Eliezer Berkowitz entitled *Tnai be'Nissuin uv'Get* (1966), containing a most searching analysis of the various arguments and a very strong case for the *halachic* validity of conditional marriage with a view to annulment of the marriage to prevent *iggun*. Most recently (January, 1968) the Supreme Court of Israel handed down a judgment in the case of a man who had been imprisoned for six years because of his refusal to give a *get* to his wife, and whose appeal for release the Court rejected. In the course of his lengthy judgment, Justice Moshe Silberg made a detailed review of the history of attempts within the *halachic* tradition to create annulment of marriage by means of conditional marriages, found that the *halachic* basis was very sound and, although it is obviously not in the competence of the Supreme Court to enact rabbinic law, he was joined by other Justices of the Court in urging the Israeli Rabbinate to consider the use of such an arrangement in order to prevent wretched situations such as that which faced the Court.

Basically, the cases of conditional marriage in the Talmud make it clear that it was possible for a marriage to be made conditional if both *kiddushin* (betrothal) and *nissuin* (marriage) were made conditional.

If, however, the condition made at the *kiddushin* was not repeated at the *nissuin*, there was ground for thinking that the husband intended to make his marriage unconditional (*Ketubbot* 7:7, 72b ff.). It becomes obvious, however, when all the Talmudic discussion is analyzed, that the conditions mentioned are always with reference to existing situations, e.g., ". . . on condition that you do not have certain physical blemishes." Even the condition ". . . on condition that my father will be willing" refers to his present satisfaction with the marriage, a fact which will be ascertained later (a case of *bereirah*), but which refers to his consent at the time of marriage. That a condition to a marriage refer to a *future event* does not come into consideration.

In modern terms, the problem can be clarified quite easily. Basically there are two types of conditions. In one type, the contemplated agreement does not take effect unless a specified fact is true or becomes true; this is a "suspensive" condition or "condition precedent" to the agreement. Thus, the contemplated agreement is "suspended" until it is ascertained that the condition is fulfilled. This is the type of condition discussed in the Talmud. The other type of condition is the "resolutive" condition or "condition subsequent" by which the contemplated agreement takes effect when it is made, but subject to being nullified if a specified fact becomes true at some time in the future. This sort of condition is the one which is not mentioned in the Talmud with respect to marriage, but was in certain circumstances resorted to in medieval times to prevent *iggun*.

The first use of a "condition subsequent" to annul a marriage was made by Rabbi Israel of Brunn (1400–1480), who introduced a condition into marriage whereby if a husband died childless and left a widow who required *chalitzah* from his brother, who was an apostate, the marriage was null and void (cited by *Rama* in *Shulchan Aruch, Even Ha'ezer* 157:4). There was some dispute among the commentators concerning the validity of this condition, but it was accepted by many of the greatest authorities (fully documented in Berkowitz, 29–56). There is a distinction to be made between the condition of Rabbi Israel of Brunn and further extensions. In the case of Brunn the fulfillment of the condition was relegated to a time after the death of the husband. Could such a condition be used to refer to an event which would occur during the lifetime of a husband? Berkowitz (51–56) argues very cogently that the conditions which would depend on a husband's giving a *get* would be preferable to Brunn's condition, for now it would be possible for a husband to make his marriage retroactively unconditionally valid by giving the *get*.

In 1907 the French rabbinate, faced with the difficulties arising out of the existence of civil divorce and the inability of the Jewish rabbinic courts to pressure a recalcitrant husband into giving a *get*, decided to make a general *takkanah* that all marriages henceforth would carry the following condition:

"You are betrothed to me on condition that you not be left an *agu-nah* on account of me; and if the civil court dissolves our marriage, my betrothal shall not be valid, and (you) my wife will be able lawfully to re-marry with *chuppah* (wedding canopy) and *kiddushin* (betrothal)" (following the version in Freimann's appendix). The objections of numerous rabbis were collected and printed in a book, *En Tnai be-Nissuin* (Vilna, 1930). Basically, the objections rested on the contention that the conditions threw the determination of Jewish divorce directly into the hands of the civil courts, which was against the principles of Jewish law. There were numerous other specific objections, but fundamentally this was the crux of the argument.

In 1924 the Turkish rabbinate issued a proposal calling for a conditional form of marriage that was considerably wider in scope than the French proposal. It called for the annulment of the marriage in case a husband refused to give a *get*, or disappeared for a certain length of time, or refused to give his wife her maintenance due her according to Jewish law. The proposal was largely ignored by the European rabbinate, and with the appearance of the objections to the French proposal it was generally thought that the same objections would hold against the Turkish one. The matter was given some consideration in Palestine, and was rejected, although it was not given the same attention as the French *tnai* [condition]. It is difficult to evaluate it, as it can be examined only through references in the writings of its opponents; however, it seems that the proposal ought to be given more consideration in light of the much wider range of possibilities which it offers. Berkowitz proposes that the objections raised in the collection *En Tnai be'Nissuin* could be met if the condition were made to depend not on the action of the civil courts but on the will of the husband after the civil courts have taken their action. This has the effect of averting the argument that the French *tnai* was *matneh la'akor davar min hatorah*, making it possible to abolish a principle of the Torah, since it is in the power of the husband to give a *get* and to affirm his *kiddushin* (p. 64 f.).

Furthermore, if the *tnai* stated that it is the husband's will that if in certain circumstances in the future he should not give a *get*, the *kiddushin* will be null and void, it would follow that upon the fulfillment of the condition the marriage would be *automatically* dissolved, without any further act by either the husband or any Beth Din [rabbinic court], and only the facts of the case would have to be verified in order to permit the wife to be remarried. This has an enormous advantage over any method of annulling marriage through the declaration of a Beth Din (*hafka'at kiddushin*) without prior agreement between the parties, since mere verification of fact is very simple, while annulment by declaration or decree of a Beth Din is difficult, though not impossible. The argument is not that the *tnai* is the only means of annulling a marriage, or that other possibilities are hereby excluded, but that the *tnai* method is much neater in operation. To use a legal phrase, it is a more "elegant" solution.

One objection to the French *tnai* was that since it would be brought into operation automatically upon the dissolution of the marriage by the civil courts, and since according to the laws of the French Republic a wife may initiate action to obtain a divorce, it would have the effect of permitting a wife to take the initiative in taking action that would either force the husband to give a *get*, or to make the marriage annulled and so permit her to remarry; in effect it would give a wife the power to put herself out of the marriage, which is against the principle of Jewish law. This is answered very well by Berkowitz (64 f.). A distinction is to be made between a *tnai* based on the will of a husband and one on which the objectors base their argument: that if a man stipulates he betroths a woman on condition that he be free of the obligation of *sh'er k'sut ve'onah* (food, clothing, and conjugal rights), his condition is void and the betrothal is valid (cf. *Teshuvot Beit Meir*, 38). In the latter case the husband intends to abolish a condition of marriage enjoined by the Torah, for the Torah declares that if marriage is to exist it must exist on the basis of the husband's obligation for *sh'er*, etc. Marriage without it is inconceivable. Hence, the husband in making his condition is either intending to be married *with sh'er* or not married at all; and we assume that he wishes *to be married* and that his condition therefore is meaningless. However, if the husband wishes to enter marriage and undertake *by his own free will* the condition that in certain events his *kiddushin* will not be valid, or that he will give a *get*, such a condition is perfectly valid, for he is not stipulating for any type of marriage not envisaged by the Torah, and the fact that he later may have to act in a specified way is based upon his own will as expressed at the time of marriage. Furthermore, there is good authority in the ruling of the *Rosh* (*Teshuvot, Klal 33*) that if it is not inevitable at the time of making the condition that a principle of the Torah will be uprooted, then the condition is valid. In this case, it is obviously in no way inevitable that the husband will have to give a *get* against his will, for it is not inevitable that there be a divorce at all; therefore, his voluntary action in making the condition at the time of marriage does not have the consequence of *matneh al davar sheba-Torah*.

The objection that the *tnai* may be a form of *bereirah*, which is not permitted *de'oraita* (according to the Torah), is to be rejected. *Bereirah* means that an agreement contains subject matter that is to be ascertained after the act; that is, at the time of making the agreement it is not known what the subject matter of the agreement is, and it is only stated in the form of several alternatives, e.g., "I give this object to whichever of my sons will arrive first at Jerusalem to celebrate the Passover" (a stock example of *bereirah*). It is well known that *bereirah* is to be distinguished from *tnai* in that there are not two alternative subject matters in *tnai* but only one, and the condition makes it either valid or invalid (e.g., *Gittin* 25b). Hence, there is no ground for bringing *bereirah* into our case. The attempt by Rabbi Meir Simcha (in *En Tnai be'Nissuin*) to make the will of the French civil judge a subject of *bereirah* is answered by Berkowitz as follows: the authorities who rule that where an act depends on the *will* of a third party it is a case of *bereirah*, do so only where the act itself (in our case, the *kiddushin*) would depend on it, e.g., "I betroth you on condition that father consents" (*Gittin* 25a). But here the validity of the act (i.e., the *kiddushin*) depends on the will of *the husband himself*, which is clearly a case of *tnai* rather than *bereirah*, for it is within his power to affirm the *kiddushin* should the necessity arise, by giving a *get* (cf. Berkowitz, 66, 165).

The principle *en adam oseh be'ilato be'ilat znut* (a man would not make his acts of sexual intercourse acts of prostitution) would not apply in the case of a conditional marriage, because the principle is used only when the husband at the time of marriage has made a "condition precedent" and is not certain whether the condition is at that moment actually fulfilled (e.g., "on condition that you are not now under any vows"), and we assume that a man would not enter into such a dubious relationship, but rather would want his betrothal to be valid and therefore, if necessary, unconditional. However, when the condition is "subsequent," i.e., related to an event clearly in the future, he has no doubts whatsoever as to the present situation and enters the marriage with the clear intention of making it a valid marriage, but based on a specific condition which may or may not take place in the future, and with the full understanding that with that proviso his marriage will be entirely valid (Berkowitz, 32ff.) and his relationship with his wife will be one of partners to a legitimate marriage.

It should be noted that the children of a marriage which is eventually annulled would be in Jewish law completely legitimate (*k'she-rim*), for in Jewish law an illegitimate child (*mamzer*) is only the issue of an incestuous or adulterous relationship. The children of an annulled marriage would continue to maintain all existing relationships with their parents, and their status in Jewish law would be completely unchanged.

In view of all the foregoing, we suggest that if a rabbi wishes to counsel a prospective bride and groom concerning a way to assure that their marriage should not even theoretically be able to lead to the *agunah* situation described above, he may inform them that they may make a conditional agreement part of their Jewish marriage ceremony. If it be done according to the rules set forth here it will be recognized by The Rabbinical Assembly as binding upon the parties involved and could be invoked should the need arise.

The suggested procedure for preparing and writing the *tnai* is as follows:

1. The rabbi must fully explain the meaning and effect of the *tnai* to the parties. It is important that the parties fully understand the nature of their agreement.

2. Before the wedding ceremony, in the privacy of the rabbi's office or in a similar place (cf. Berkowitz, p. 45) the parties agree to the *tnai* before a Beth Din consisting of the rabbi and the two witnesses who will witness the *chupah* (or, if the rabbi will himself be a witness at the *chupah*, the rabbi, the other witness and a third *dayan* [judge]). The groom should read the *tnai* aloud before the Beth Din in the presence of the bride, and then sign it. The bride should indicate her consent by signing it also. It should then be signed by the Beth Din. The form of the *tnai* should conform to the requirements of all conditions in Jewish law; we propose the formula given at the end of this *teshuvah* (responsum).

3. Under the *chupah*, immediately before the groom makes the statement of the *kiddushin* (*harei at*, etc.) the rabbi should ask bride and groom together, "Do you enter this marriage according to the laws of Moses and the people Israel and the conditions you have undertaken?" Both parties should answer: Yes. The ceremony should then proceed in the usual way.

It is recommended that the Committee on Jewish Law and Standards of the Rabbinical Assembly, or any designated subcommittee thereof, hear petitions for a declaration of nullity of marriage on the ground of the above-mentioned *tnai* to verify the facts of the case and to issue, if justified, a declaration that the marriage is in fact null and void. It is further recommended that the Committee, following its regular rules of procedure, should accept requests for such declarations only when submitted through a member of The Rabbinical Assembly, that the *tnai* be signed in duplicate, and that one copy be given to the wife and the other deposited with the Committee on Jewish Law and Standards.

Finally, it should be clearly understood that the above-mentioned procedure is suggested only in order to prevent an *agunah* situation from arising. It is not intended in any way to weaken the desirability of the termination of marriage by means of *get* rather than by annulment. In all cases the husband will be urged most strongly to comply with the traditional form of the termination of Jewish marriage, the *get*, and it will be impressed upon him that it is most desirable for him that he preserve the validity of his marriage for as long as it existed, by means of giving a *get*. Let it be clearly understood that the decree of nullity will be considered only a last resort to prevent *iggun*. Accordingly, it is recommended that when a decree of nullity is issued to a wife, a similar decree not be issued to the offending husband. Further, he should not be granted any permission to remarry until he gives a *get* to his wife on the ground of *get chumrah*. This should act as a further encouragement to the husband to comply with the wife's request for a *get*.

This responsum was prepared by a sub-committee on *Hilkhot Ishut* (Marriage Law) of the Committee on Jewish Law and Standards of the Rabbinical Assembly. Members of the sub-committee were Rabbis Eli Bohnen, Edward Gershfield, Benjamin Kreitman and Seymour Siegel. The responsum was accepted and affirmed unanimously by the Committee on Jewish Law and Standards at its meeting of March 25, 1968.

### ANTE-NUPTIAL AGREEMENT

On the _____ day of _____ 19_____, corresponding to the _____ day of _____ 57 _____, in _____ (City and State) _____, the groom _____ and the bride _____, of their own free will and accord entered into the following agreement with respect to their intended marriage.

The groom made the following declaration to the bride:

"I will betroth and marry you according to the laws of Moses and the people Israel, subject to the following conditions:

"If our marriage should be terminated by decree of the civil courts and if by expiration of six months after such a decree I give you a divorce according to the laws of Moses and the people Israel (a *get*), then our betrothal (*kiddushin*) and marriage (*nissuin*) will have remained valid and binding;

But if our marriage should be terminated by decree of the civil courts and if by expiration of six months after such a decree I do not give you a divorce according to the laws of Moses and the people Israel (a *get*), then our betrothal (*kiddushin*) and marriage (*nissuin*) will have been null and void."

The bride replied to the groom:

"I consent to the conditions you have made."

Signature of groom _____
Signature of bride _____

We the undersigned, acting as a Beth Din, witnessed the oral statements and signatures of the groom and bride.

_____

(rabbi)

_____

_____

*Ketubbah currently used by rabbis affiliated with the Rabbinical Assembly (Conservative):*

In the name of the Lord, the Eternal God, Amen.

This *ketubbah* witnesseth, before God and Man, that on the _____ day of the week, the _____ of the month _____, in the year 57 _____ corresponding to the _____ day of _____ 19 _____ the holy covenant of marriage was entered into between _____ bridegroom, and _____ his bride, at _____. Duly conscious of the solemn obligations of marriage, the bridegroom made the following declaration to his bride: "Be thou consecrated unto me as my wife according to the laws and traditions of Moses and Israel. I will love, honor and cherish thee; I will protect and support thee, and I will faithfully care for thy needs, as prescribed by Jewish law and tradition." And the bride made the following declaration to the groom: "In accepting the marriage ring, I pledge you all my love and devotion, and I take upon myself the fulfillment of all the duties incumbent upon a Jewish wife."

And both together agreed that if this marriage shall ever be dissolved under civil law, then either husband or wife may invoke the authority of the Beth Din of the Rabbinical Assembly and the Jewish Theological Seminary of America or its duly authorized representatives, to decide what action by either spouse is then appropriate under Jewish matrimonial law; and if either spouse shall fail to honor the demand of the other or to carry out the decision of the Beth Din or its representatives, then the other spouse may invoke any and all remedies available in civil law and equity to enforce compliance with the Beth Din's decision and this solemn obligation.

Bride and groom then together declared before God and man that they have signed their names to this *ketubbah* of their own free will without reservation or restraint, and that they intend to be bound by this holy covenant so long as they shall live.
_____ Bridegroom _____ Bride
_____ Rabbi _____ Witness _____ Witness

Solomon B. Freehof, "Civil Divorce," *Reform Jewish Practice* (New York: Union of American Hebrew Congregations, 1974), pp. 99–110.

CIVIL DIVORCE . . . Reform congregations recognize Civil Divorce as completely dissolving the marriage and permit remarriage of the divorced persons.

While this statement describes the actual practice in Reform congregations as it has developed during the last fifty years, the principle of the absolute validity of the Civil Divorce has never been formally adopted by the Central Conference of American Rabbis. While no doubt is cast upon the validity of the remarriage of individuals who have only a civil divorce, the whole subject is recognized as both delicate and complicated and one, therefore, which will need further discussion and elucidation.

The Jewish divorce, the Get, never seemed satisfactory to the pioneers of Reform Judaism and is equally unsatisfactory to their successors. In the early Conferences and synods in Germany and America, the problem involved in the Get occupied a great part of the agenda, and if the discussion has not been so vehement in recent years, it is only because the civil divorce laws have been generally improved and regularized in most of the states of the Union, and the subject is not as urgent as it was. But the relation of Reform Judaism to Orthodoxy and Conservatism with regard to divorce remains unsettled.

Jewish Orthodoxy understands fully that its rabbinical courts no longer have the power to dissolve a marriage as they did in the earlier centuries. Only the civil courts, which gave a license for marriage, have the authority to dissolve marriage. Therefore in America and in other lands where Jewish courts lack authority to dissolve a marriage, the rabbinical court, when it grants a "Get," gives a document (a P'tur) to the parties divorced which reads as follows:

> [To the woman] "The woman [Name] has received a Get from her husband [Name] according to the law of our holy Torah, but this divorce is only according to our holy Torah; but she is not permitted to marry another man until she obtain permission from the law of the state, since according to the law of the state this Get has no validity." [To the man] "The man [Name] has divorced his wife [Name] but the divorce, etc." [See *Otsar Dinim u-Minhagim*, art. "Get."]

Then the Get document itself is torn. However, in actual practice, the average Orthodox rabbi does not give a Jewish Get until after the civil divorce has been granted. Then the caution in this form of the P'tur is not necessary. It has long been the custom to tear the original Get and to give the woman a brief document (a P'tur) saying that she is now permitted to remarry. (Cf. Ba'er Heteb to Eben Haezer 142 Note and Turei Zahav Note 4.) The purpose of the procedure is that no one should cast doubt on the validity of the divorce years later (i.e., that it was improperly written, etc.) and thus cast doubt upon the legitimacy of the children born of the new marriage.

Although it is thus fully realized that Jewish law cannot dissolve marriage in modern times, yet the attitude of Orthodox authorities with regard to the Jewish Get is equivalent to the attitude of all religious authorities on religious marriage. No one may be married without a license from the state, and the state also provides means for being married by secular authorities, registry offices in England, Justices of the Peace in America, etc. Yet from the religious point of view, no marriage is complete unless it be solemnized by a religious authority.

So it is with divorce. The state makes all the legal provisions for divorce, but from the point of view of Orthodox Judaism, the divorce is not complete unless the religious divorce is also provided. This attitude is not exclusively Jewish. The Catholic and Episcopal church, as far as their communicants are concerned, likewise superimpose their own religious concepts of divorce upon that of the state. The church concept of divorce has profoundly affected the civil law of divorce in Europe and in some of the states in the Union (cf. *Encyc. Britannica,* art. "Divorce"). The rabbinic law of divorce has, of course, had no such influence upon civil law.

The analogy that Jewish divorce is an additional requirement to civil divorce as religious marriage is to civil marriage is not a complete one since the state makes provision for Jewish marriage by authorizing rabbis to solemnize marriage, but takes no cognizance of Jewish divorce by authorizing rabbis to arrange Jewish divorces. Yet the analogy is close enough to have motivated the early Reformers to seek to establish some form of Jewish divorce. They did make some such attempt, but they were evidently not too persistent about it and their plans never were fulfilled.

It is evident from the debates in the various Reform synods and conferences that Reform Judaism from the beginning had a general objection to the Orthodox divorce. This objection has various arguments. The first is that the Get contravenes the principle stressed by Reform, of the complete equality in religious status of men and women. The traditional idea of divorce is that the husband could divorce his wife but the wife could not divorce the husband. The basis of the law is the verse in Deuteronomy 24:1:

> When a man taketh a wife, and marrieth her, then it cometh to pass, if she find no favor in his eyes, because he hath found some unseemly thing in her, that he writeth her a bill of divorcement, and giveth it in her hand, and send her out of his house.

The implications of this verse constituted the subject of a famous discussion between the school of Shammai and the school of Hillel (m. Gittin IX, 10). The school of Shammai says that a man may not divorce his wife unless he found her guilty of adultery; and the school of Hillel says, even if she scorch the soup, he may divorce her (i.e., for any cause that he desires). The law is according to the school of Hillel, and Rabbi Akiba, in order to make it absolutely clear, says, even if he found another prettier than she.

This complete dominance of the husband is based upon the theory almost universal in antiquity that the wife is the purchased property of the husband, and, in fact, similar laws of divorce are found among the ancient Arabs and among the ancient Romans (see *Encyc. Judaica* Vol. VI, pp. 259–260, and *Encyc. Britannica,* art. "Divorce").

This supreme right of the husband, so wide-spread in many ancient legal systems, was quickly brought under control by the moral conscience of Judaism. The instituting of the Ketubah, which provided that the wife should receive certain sums of money if divorced, served the purpose of making hasty divorce less likely. Also the gradual development of many formalities with regard to the giving of a divorce made divorce more difficult. The many formalities involved in the giving of the divorce, the examination of witnesses, the careful questioning, the laws safeguarding the appointment of agents to bring the divorce, etc., etc., all these served the same purpose. For all the multifarious details as to the text of the bill of divorce, see particularly Nachlat Shiv'ah (Samuel ben David Halevi, seventeenth century, ed. Warsaw, 1898, pp.91a ff.). See also Seder Ha Get at the end of Sh.A. Eben Haezer at the end of #154. A greater degree of equality for the wife was already known in Mishnaic times, whereby under certain circumstances the husband was compelled by the court to give the wife a divorce (m. Gittin IX, 8). For circumstances under which the wife could ask the court to force the husband to give her a divorce, see Sh. A. Eben Haezer 154. The greatest step forward of all towards equalizing the right of husband and wife was taken in the tenth and eleventh centuries by Rabbenu Gershom ("The Light of the Exile") who summoned a synod which declared: (a) the prohibition of polygamy, and, (b) the necessity of obtaining the consent of both parties to a divorce. In Sh.A.Eben Haezer 119 #6, Joseph Karo gives the old law, that the husband can divorce his wife without her consent, but Isserles in his note cites the Cherem of Rabbenu Gershom against divorcing a wife without her consent. However, in spite of all these many modifications of the ancient law, the basic principle remained that a husband had the right to divorce his wife whereas the wife, except in special cases of hardship where she could appeal to the court to force her husband to divorce her, had no right to divorce a husband.

In this connection it may also be mentioned that Reform Judaism, which emphasizes the religious equality of men and women, also refuses to regard any difference in the religious status between priests, Levites and Israelites. Therefore, the special prohibition of the law forbidding a priest to marry a divorced woman likewise seemed contrary to the modern spirit of equality of status.

Besides the inequality of husband and wife with respect to divorce, there is a tragic hardship involved in Jewish law of divorce which the best rabbinic minds have been unable to remove, namely, the case of the Agunah (the woman "chained" to marriage even though her husband has disappeared). Jewish law has no provision as has the secular law in almost every country, for declaring a man presumably dead if he has not been heard of for a certain specified number of years. In Jewish law there must be actual evidence of witnesses who saw him die. This fact, coupled with the fact that only the husband can give a divorce, has resulted in the tragic state of Agunah in which countless women whose husbands have disappeared have no way of being freed from the bonds of matrimony. This unfortunate situation has engaged the keen attention and evoked the warmest sympathy of rabbinic authorities for centuries. They have tried to mitigate the state of the Agunah. They have liberalized the laws of testimony as to the death of the husband. They have made it easier for a man to send a divorce by messenger from a distant land, but none of these have altered the basic fact that since only the husband can divorce the wife, and since the Jewish court has no way of declaring a presumption of death, there is no real solution under Jewish divorce laws for the unfortunate Agunah.

For these reasons the Reform movement has turned away from the traditional laws on divorce, classifying the divorce laws with all the civil laws governing business relations which were an important part of Jewish law when all of Jewish life, religious and secular, was governed by Jewish law. These civil laws are now under the principle of dina d'Malchusa dina, i.e., the law of the land is the law with regard to civil law. Similarly, divorce (so argued the early Reformers) must no longer be considered a religious matter but a civil matter. Besides, it is the true function of the rabbi to solemnize marriage and not to break it. Divorce should also be under the control of civil law and the rabbi have nothing to do with it. This point of view was first put forth by Holdheim in 1843. He says that since divorce is a civil act only, it is to be entirely submitted to the laws of the country and therefore the ritual Get is now superfluous. This point of view met with considerable opposition on the part of other Reform leaders like Dr. Geiger who desired rather that the forms of the rabbinic Get be modified. However, Holdheim's point of view was accepted by the rabbinical conference in Philadelphia, 1869. Einhorn reaffirmed Holdheim's position. He said:

> Rabbinic Judaism also, though in various cases considering divorce a religious duty, could not remove the civil character of divorce and introduce a religious form for the act. It prescribes no benediction for it as it does for marriage. The concluding words of the bill of divorce "according to the laws of Moses and Israel" confer in no wise a religious character upon the act as indeed some authorities maintain that these very words were anciently in use also in other Jewish documents which had no religious character at all . . . when two persons unite in community for life, it is the function of religion to offer consecration . . . but if the holy bonds are severed, religion can only tolerate the act in sorrow and silence.

The Philadelphia Conference finally decided as follows: "the dissolution of marriage is, on Mosaic and rabbinical grounds, a civil act only which never received religious consecration. It is to be recognized, therefore, as an act emanating altogether from the judicial authorities of the state. The so-called ritual Get is in all cases declared null and void." (See entire discussion in Mielziner, *Jewish Law of Marriage and Divorce*, Chapter 16.) The Central Conference of American Rabbis continued along the same line. See the recommendation in the *Yearbook* of the Central Conference of American Rabbis, Vol. XXIII, p. 154.

This declaration, that divorce is a civil matter and therefore the ritual Get is unnecessary and the civil divorce should be deemed fully valid, is quite understandable as a general principle. But there were many complications involved which made it necessary to have more than merely this general declaration. There was first, the consideration that just as the traditional Jewish laws of divorce were unsatisfactory for modern life, so were many of the civil laws of divorce unsatisfactory. The civil laws of divorce in America, particularly a half century ago, were chaotic, differing widely from state to state and therefore merely to accept civil laws as they were was likewise unsatisfactory. Therefore, from the very beginning, the general principle of accepting civil laws as valid was modified by a plan to have the rabbi or a group of rabbis refuse to remarry a couple civilly divorced until the rabbi study the grounds upon which the divorce was granted. "Judaism recognizes the validity of the divorce then only if the cause assigned is sufficient in conformity with the spirit of the Jewish religion." (The decision of the Philadelphia Conference, 1869; see Mielziner, p. 155.) Kaufmann Kohler, who was asked by the Central Conference of American Rabbis to study the problem of the harmonization of Jewish and civil laws of marriage and divorce, made a similar recommendation. (*Central Conference of American Rabbis Yearbook*, Vo. XXV, pp. 335–378, especially pages 376–378, the recommendations.) He says, page 377 #3: "Inasmuch as the civil courts in many states often grant a divorce in cases where from the religious view of Judaism objections might be raised, a body of three rabbis should attest to the correctness from the Jewish point of view of the findings of the court in matters of divorce, and attach their signature to the bill of divorce issued by the court."

These recommendations were not formally accepted by the Conference, and the whole subject of divorce is still unsettled. The urgency of the subject has been somewhat mitigated by the constant improvement in the divorce laws of the various states. The general principle of the Conference, although not formally adopted, can be described as follows: civil divorce is accepted as of absolute validity and the rabbinic Get deemed no longer necessary. There is, however, a tendency to have the rabbi or a group of rabbis review the civil divorce granted and officiate at the remarriage of only such divorces as are approved.

In other words, instead of having a parallel system of divorce law as Orthodoxy has in relation to civil law, the Reform movement prefers to accept every civil divorce which conforms to the point of view of Jewish ethics. This latter test has not yet developed as a practice. In actual practice, the civil law is simply accepted as final.

Another complication inherent in the decision of Reform Judaism to accept civil divorce comes from the relationship of Reform Judaism to Conservative and Orthodox groups. Conservative rabbis generally and Orthodox rabbis always will refuse to marry a couple if one or both of the parties is divorced in the courts but lacks a Get. Often such couples come to the Reform rabbi to be married. Should he, in accordance with the Reform principle of accepting the validity of civil divorce, marry them? This question has not been decided by the Conference, but it would seem that consideration for the religious scruples of Orthodox and Conservative congregations should impel the Reform rabbi to refuse to marry members of other congregations whose rabbi refuses to marry them. If an unaffiliated couple, one or both parties of which had been civilly divorced (without a Get) comes to a Reform rabbi to be married, he must decide according to his own judgment. If they are children of Orthodox parents to whom such a marriage would seem to be no marriage at all, he should in kindness to the parents, and therefore for the happiness of the couple, refuse to marry them. If however, they have no especial Orthodox affiliations, he can, according to his principle of recognizing the validity of civil divorce, officiate at the marriage.

# Topic Fifteen: Conflicts and Choice of Law II:
## Civil Recognition of Jewish Marriage and Divorce

Anglo-American secular law assumed legislative control over marriage and divorce relatively late, but the occupation of the field by the secular law, once accomplished, has been total. Before general divorce laws were enacted in the middle of the nineteenth century, divorce, if possible at all, was primarily a matter for religious courts. Today it would seem strange to suggest that a couple living in England or in the United States could divorce without a court decree issued under the applicable statute. Before general divorce laws were enacted, a local rabbinic court would issue a *get* to local Jews, which would be recognized by the secular courts. An English court of the eighteenth century presumably would have recognized a *get* issued to English Jews in London, and a California court today probably would recognize a *get* issued by a rabbinic court in Israel or in an Arab country in which local, secular courts recognized religious court decrees dealing with divorce and other questions of personal status. But what significance would an American court today attach to a *ketubbah* or a *get* between two American Jews? Assuming that these documents do not "marry" or "divorce" a couple who has not complied with local requirements (licenses, decrees), will the document be given any effect? A *ketubbah*, for example, might be considered an antenuptial agreement, in which case it might be enforced to the extent the state enforces any agreement reached in the same circumstances. A *get* may not be a divorce, but does it not at least mark the termination of the marital community? After its delivery can it be said that the husband has deserted his wife? By consenting to it does the wife condone the husband's cohabitation with another woman?

These matters arise in a variety of contexts in secular courts. The decision of the New York Court of Appeals in *Avitzur v. Avitzur*, represents the judgment of the highest court of the state with the largest

546

Jewish population. This decision was by a narrowly divided court and came to the Court of Appeals after a large number of lower court decisions in New York that appeared to go in diametrically opposite directions. A number of divergent analyses had been used by the lower courts in deciding these cases, including: (a) the matter is one governed by the law of the state and not subject to private agreement; (b) religious agreements are not really agreements because the parties did not negotiate the terms, which are archaic (such as, 200 *zuzim*) and may not have been understood by the parties; (c) these agreements look very much like antenuptial agreements or arbitration clauses and should be given as much enforcement; (d) the law that the court is being asked to enforce, after all is said and done, is religious, and the constitutional separation of church and state precludes the court from interfering; (e) enforcement will require the secular court to order a party to submit to a religious authority, and that also is precluded by the First Amendment; (f) the court is being asked to direct specific performance of an act that religious law says must be a matter of consent, and consequently such an action by the court would be ineffective even if it were legal; (g) unless the secular court lends its weight to the parties' religious agreements, great hardship will occur to the wife, who cannot remarry, or to the adopted child, who will be left without support, and therefore the court should take action, for this is really not a religious matter at all but rather one in which a governmental agency (the court) is legitimately being asked to protect the welfare of its citizens.

Because *Avitzur* was based on a clause that the Conservative Movement wrote into the *ketubbah* and would presumably not apply to other forms of the *ketubbah*, the New York state legislature enacted legislation that effectively extends the *Avitzur* protections to all Jewish marriages without reference to the special Conservative clause or a specific stipulation in the separation agreement. That law, which follows, withholds a civil divorce from a couple until "all barriers to the other party's remarriage" are removed, where "barriers to remarriage" specifically "includes any religious or conscientious restraint or inhibition imposed on a party to a marriage, under the principles of the denomination of the clergyman or minister who has solemnized the marriage, by reason of the other party's commission or withholding of any voluntary act."

There is no express reference to Jews in the statute in an attempt to avoid the appearance of violating the constitutional separation of church and state, but nevertheless it is highly questionable whether the statute is constitutional. New York courts have enforced clauses in separation agreements in which the husband or both parties agree to obtain a religious divorce, even to the extent of imposing fines or with-holding civil economic relief (for example, *Marguilies* v. *Marguilies* 42 A.D.2d 517, 344 N.Y.S.2d 482 (1st Dept. 1973) [husband fined]; *Waxstein* v. *Waxstein*, 90 Misc.2d 784, 395 N.Y.S.2d 877 (Sup. Ct. Kings County 1976) [stock and deed to marital residence not to be turned over to husband until he obtains a *get* pursuant to separation agreement]). They have restricted their enforcement, however, to secular matters, specifically denying the court authority to convene a rabbinic tribunal for purposes of forcing the husband to issue a *get* (*Pal* v. *Pal*, 45 A.D.2d 738, 356 N.Y.S.2d 672 [2d Dept. 1974]). *Avitzur*, a controversial decision issued by a badly split court, extended judiciary action to enforcing an agreement in a religious document (the *ketubbah*), viewing it as a secular, contractual obligation in an antenuptial agreement. The legislation goes further yet in compelling Jewish spouses, especially men, to voluntarily accede to religious divorces or else be denied a civil divorce decree. Since no indication of the husband's agreement to such action exists anywhere, even in a religious document, it seems doubtful that a civil statute can constitutionally coerce a party to engage in a religious act on pain of withholding civil relief. A similar law proposed in California has so far failed in committee largely because of these constitutional issues.

*Brett* v. *Brett* is an attempt by the British Court of Appeals to deal with similar issues. Note particularly the ingenious recognition of the economic consequences to the wife of being unable to remarry and the consequential significance of the husband's refusal to issue a divorce on his obligations to provide support and maintenance. The last two paragraphs of Lord Justice Willmer's opinion and Lord Justice Phillimore's opinion provide powerful incentives for the husband to grant a *get* without actually ordering him to do so.

AVITZUR V. AVITZUR:
New York Court of Appeals
58 N.Y. 2d 108, 459 N.Y.S.2d 572 (1983)

WACHTLER, JUDGE. This appeal presents for our consideration the question of the proper role of the civil courts in deciding a matter touching upon religious concerns. At issue is the enforceability of the terms of a document, known as a Ketubah, which was entered into as part of the religious marriage ceremony in this case. The Appellate Division, 86 A.D.2d 133, 449 N.Y.S.2d 83, held this to be a religious covenant beyond the jurisdiction of the civil courts. However, we find nothing in law or public policy to prevent judicial recognition and enforcement of the secular terms of such an agreement. There should be a reversal.

Plaintiff and defendant were married on May 22, 1966 in a ceremony conducted in accordance with Jewish tradition. Prior to the marriage ceremony, the parties signed both a Hebrew/Aramaic and an English version of the "Ketubah." According to the English translation, the Ketubah evidences both the bridegroom's intention to cherish and provide for his wife as required by religious law and tradition and the bride's willingness to carry out her obligations to her husband in faithfulness and affection according to Jewish law and tradition. By signing the Ketubah, the parties declared their "desire to . . . live in accordance with the Jewish law of the marriage throughout [their] lifetime" and further agreed as follows: "[W]e, the bride and bridegroom . . . hereby agree to recognize the Beth Din of the Rabbinical Assembly and the Jewish Theological Seminary of America or its duly appointed representatives, as having authority to counsel us in the light of Jewish tradition which requires husband and wife to give each other complete love and devotion, and to summon either party at the request of the other, in order to enable the party so requesting to live in accordance with the standards of the Jewish law of marriage throughout his or her lifetime. We authorize the Beth Din to impose such terms of compensation as it may see fit for failure to respond to its summons or to carry out its decision."

Defendant husband was granted a civil divorce upon the ground of cruel and inhuman treatment on May 16, 1978. Notwithstanding this civil divorce, plaintiff wife is not considred divorced and may not remarry pursuant to Jewish law, until such time as a Jewish divorce decree, known as a "Get," is granted. In order that a Get may be obtained plaintiff and defendant must appear before a "Beth Din," a rabbinical tribunal having authority to advise and pass upon matters of traditional Jewish law. Plaintiff sought to summon defendant before the Beth Din pursuant to the provision of the Ketubah recognizing that body as having authority to counsel the couple in the matters concerning their marriage.

Defendant has refused to appear before the Beth Din, thus preventing plaintiff from obtaining a religious divorce. Plaintiff brought this action, alleging that the Ketubah constitutes a marital contract, which defendant has breached by refusing to appear before the Beth Din, and she seeks relief both in the form of a declaration to that effect and an order compelling defendant's specific performance of the Ketubah's requirement that he appear before the Beth Din. Defendant moved to dismiss the complaint upon the grounds that the court lacked subject matter jurisdiction and the complaint failed to state a cause of action, arguing that resolution of the dispute and any grant of relief to plaintiff would involve the civil court in impermissible consideration of a purely religious matter. Plaintiff, in addition to opposing the motion, cross-moved for summary judgment.

Special Term denied defendant's motion to dismiss, noting that plaintiff sought only to compel defendant to submit to the jurisdiction of the Beth Din, an act which plaintiff had alleged defendant bound himself to do. That being the only object of the lawsuit, Special Term was apparently of the view that the relief sought could be granted without impermissible judicial entanglement in any doctrinal issue. The court also denied plaintiff's motion for summary judgment, concluding that issues concerning the translation, meaning and effect of the Ketubah raised factual questions requiring a plenary trial.

The Appellate Division modified, granting defendant's motion to dismiss. Inasmuch as the Ketubah was entered into as part of a religious ceremony and was executed, by its own terms, in accordance with Jewish law, the court concluded that the document constitutes a liturgical agreement. The Appellate Division held such agreements to be unenforceable where the State, having granted a civil divorce to the parties, has no further interest in their marital status.

Accepting plaintiff's allegations as true, as we must in the context of this motion to dismiss, it appears that plaintiff and defendant, in signing the Ketubah, entered into a contract which formed the basis for their marriage. Plaintiff has alleged that pursuant to the terms of this marital contract, defendant promised that he would, at plaintiff's request, appear before the Beth Din for the purpose of allowing that tribunal to advise and counsel the parties in matters concerning their marriage, including the granting of a Get. It should be noted that plaintiff is not attempting to compel defendant to obtain a Get or to enforce a religious practice arising solely out of principles of religious law. She merely seeks to enforce an agreement made by defendant to appear before and accept the decision of a designated tribunal.

Viewed in this manner, the provisions of the Ketubah relied upon by plaintiff constitute nothing more than an agreement to refer the matter of a religious divorce to a nonjudicial forum. Thus, the contractual obligation plaintiff seeks to enforce is closely analogous to an antenuptial agreement to arbitrate a dispute in accordance with the law and tradition chosen by the parties. There can be little doubt that a duly executed antenuptial agreement, by which the parties agree in advance of the marriage to the resolution of disputes that may arise after its termination, is valid and enforceable (e.g., *Matter of Sunshine*, 40 N.Y.2d 875, 389 N.Y.S.2d 344, 357 N.E.2d 999, aff'g 51 A.D.2d 326, 381 N.Y.S.2d 260; *Matter of Davis*, 20 N.Y.2d 70, 281 N.Y.S.2d 767, 228 N.E.2d 768). Similarly, an agreement to refer a matter concerning marriage to arbitration suffers no inherent invalidity (*Hirsch v. Hirsch*, 37 N.Y.2d 312, 372 N.Y.S.2d 71, 333 N.E.2d 371; see *Bowmer v. Bowmer*, 50 N.Y.2d 288, 293, 428 N.Y.S.2d 902, 406 N.E.2d 760). This agreement—the Ketubah—should ordinarily be entitled to no less dignity than any other civil contract to submit a dispute to a nonjudicial forum, so long as its enforcement violates neither the law nor the public policy of this State (*Hirsch v. Hirsch, supra,* at p. 315, 372 N.Y.S.2d 71, 333 N.E.2d 371).

Defendant argues, in this connection, that enforcement of the terms of the Ketubah by a civil court would violate the constitutional prohibition against excessive entanglement between church and State, because the court must necessarily intrude upon matters of religious doctrine and practice. It is urged that the obligations imposed by the Ketubah arise solely from Jewish religious law and can be interpreted only with reference to religious dogma. Granting the religious character of the Ketubah, it does not necessarily follow that any recognition of its obligations is foreclosed to the courts.

It is clear that judicial involvement in matters touching upon religious concerns has been constitutionally limited in analogous situations, and courts should not resolve such controversies in a manner requiring consideration of religious doctrine (*Presbyterian Church v. Hull Church,* 393 U.S. 440, 449, 89 S.Ct. 601, 606, 21 L.Ed.2d 658; *Serbian Orthodox Diocese v. Milivojevich,* 426 U.S. 696, 709, 96 S.Ct. 2372, 2380, 49L.Ed.2d 151; *Jones v. Wolf,* 443 U.S. 595, 603, 99 S.Ct. 3020, 3025, 61 L.Ed.2d 775; see, e.g., *Reardon v. Lemoyne,* H.H., 454 A.2d 428 [1982]). In its most recent pronouncement on this issue, however, the Supreme Court, in holding that a State may adopt any approach to resolving religious disputes which does not entail consideration of doctrinal matters, specifically approved the use of the "neutral principles of law" approach as consistent with constitutional limitations (*Jones v. Wolf, supra,* 443 U.S. at p. 602, 99 S.Ct. at 3024). This approach contemplates the application of objective, well-established principles of secular law to the dispute (*id.,* at p. 603, 99 S.Ct at 3025), thus permitting judicial involvement to the extent that it can be accomplished in purely secular terms.

The present case can be decided solely upon the application of neutral principles of contract law, without reference to any religious principle. Consequently, defendant's objections to enforcement of his promise to appear before the Beth Din, based as they are upon the religious origin of the agreement, pose no constitutional barrier to the relief sought by plaintiff. The fact that the agreement was entered into as part of a religious ceremony does not render it unenforceable. Solemnization of the marital relationship often takes place in accordance with the religious beliefs of the participants, and this State has long recognized this religious aspect by permitting duly authorized pastors, rectors, priests, rabbis and other religious officials to perform the ceremony (Domestic Relations Law, § 11, subds. 1, 7). Similarly, that the obligations undertaken by the parties to the Ketubah are grounded in religious belief and practice does not preclude enforcement of its secular terms. Nor does the fact that all of the Ketubah's provisions may not be judicially recognized prevent the court from enforcing that portion of the agreement by which the parties promised to refer their disputes to a nonjudicial forum (see *Ferro v. Bologna*, 31 N.Y.2d 30, 36, 334 N.Y.S.2d 856, 286 N.E.2d 244). The courts may properly enforce so much of this agreement as is not in contravention of law or public policy.

In short, the relief sought by plaintiff in this action is simply to compel defendant to perform a secular obligation to which he contractually bound himself. In this regard, no doctrinal issue need be passed upon, no implementation of a religious duty is contemplated, and no interference with religious authority will result. Certainly nothing the Beth Din can do would in any way affect the civil divorce. To the extent that an enforceable promise can be found by the application of neutral principles of contract law, plaintiff will have demonstrated entitlement to the relief sought. Consideration of other substantive issues bearing upon plaintiff's entitlement to a religious divorce, however, is appropriately left to the forum the parties chose for revolving the matter.

Accordingly, the order of the Appellate Division should be reversed, with costs, and defendant's motion to dismiss the complaint denied.

JONES, JUDGE (DISSENTING). We are of the opinion that to grant the relief plaintiff seeks in this action, even to the limited extent contemplated by the majority, would necessarily violate the constitutional prohibition against entanglement of our secular courts in matters of religious and ecclesiastical content. Accordingly, we would affirm the order of the Appelate Division.

We start on common ground. Judicial intervention in disputes with respect to religious and ecclesiastical obligation is constitutionally proscribed, save with respect to a narrow class of issues, as to which, under "neutral principles of law," the secular component of the religious and ecclesiastical rights and obligations may be resolved without impermissible trespass on, or even reference to, religious dogma and doctrine (pp. 114–115, 459 N.Y.S.2d 574, 446 N.E.2d 138). We depart from the conclusion of the majority that in this case the courts may discern one or more discretely secular obligations which may be fractured out of the "Ketubah," indisputably in its essence a document prepared and executed under Jewish law and tradition.

We are constrained, as is the majority, by the allegations of the complaint. Plaintiff therein alleges: that the parties were married on May 22, 1966 in a religious ceremony in accordance with Jewish law and tradition; that pursuant to the terms and conditions of the religious ceremony they entered into a contract known as a "Ketubah"; that under the Ketubah the husband declared and contracted with the

wife to be her husband according to the law of Moses and Israel and to
honor and support her, faithfully cherishing her and providing for her
needs as prescribed by Jewish religious law and tradition; that pursuant to the Ketubah the parties agreed to recognize the Beth Din of the
Rabbinical Assembly and the Jewish Theological Seminary of America as having authority to summon either party at the request of the
other and further agreed that in the event of any civil divorce decree
the husband would grant and the wife accept a Jewish divorce ("Get")
in accordance with the authority vested in the Beth Din; that under
the law of Moses should the husband arbitrarily refuse to give a "Get"
the wife, such as plaintiff in this case, is known and referred to as an
"Aguna" which is a state of limbo wherein the wife is considered neither married nor divorced; that a judgment of civil divorce of the parties was entered on May 16, 1978 in the Albany county clerk's office;
that the wife has requested and summoned the husband to appear before the Beth Din of the Rabbinical Assembly pursuant to the terms of
the Ketubah but that he has willfully and intentionally refused to appear before the assembly in violation of his contractual obligations;
that in consequence the wife is consigned to the status of "Aguna"
and is barred from remarrying within the context of a Jewish religious
ceremony. The wife demands judgment against the husband: declaring "the rights and other legal relation of the plaintiff and defendant
in the marriage contract (Ketubah), created by reason of the written
instrument"; declaring that the husband specifically perform pursuant to the terms and conditions of the Ketubah in that he appear before the Beth Din of the Rabbinical Assembly and the Jewish Theological Seminary of America or its duly appointed representatives pursuant to the wife's request; declaring that failure of the husband so to
appear constitutes a breach of contract; and for other incidental relief.

Determination whether judicial relief may be granted the wife
without constitutionally impermissible interjection of the court into
matters of religious and ecclesiastical content requires examination
of the English translation of the Ketubah in the context of the wife's
allegation that this document was made and entered into as part of
the religious ceremony in accordance with Jewish law and tradition:

"On the First Day of the Week, the 3rd Day of the Month Sivan,
5726, corresponding to the 22nd Day of May, 1966, Boaz Avitzur, the
bridegroom, and Susan Rose Wieder, the bride, were united in marriage in Old Westbury, N.Y. The bridegroom made the following declaration to his bride: 'Be thou my wife according to the law of Moses
and Israel. I shall honor and support thee, faithfully I shall cherish
thee and provide for thy needs, even as Jewish husbands are required
to do by our religious law and tradition.'

"In turn, the bride took upon herself the duties of a Jewish wife, to
honor and cherish her husband, and to carry out all her obligations

to him in faithfulness and affection as Jewish law and tradition prescribe.

"And in solemn assent to their mutual responsibilities and love, the bridegroom and bride have declared: As evidence of our desire to enable each other to live in accordance with the Jewish law of marriage throughout our lifetime, we, the bride and bridegroom, attach our signatures to this Ketubah, and hereby agree to recognize the Beth Din of the Rabbinical Assembly and the Jewish Theological Seminary of America, or its duly appointed representatives, as having authority to counsel us in the light of Jewish tradition which requires husband and wife to give each other complete love and devotion, and to summon either party at the request of the other, in order to enable the party so requesting to live in accordance with the standards of the Jewish law of marriage throughout his or her lifetime. We authorize the Beth Din to impose such terms of compensation as it may see fit for failure to respond to its summons or to carry out its decision.

"This Ketubah was executed and witnessed this day in accordance with Jewish law and tradition.

"Boaz Avitzur, bridegroom; Susan Wieder, bride; Melvin Kieffer, rabbi; Abraham Weisman, witness; Melvin Kieffer, witness."

At the outset we observe that the complaint contains no allegation that the parties intended that the Ketubah should manifest secular promises or have any civil or secular status or any legal significance independent of the religious ceremony between them of which it was an integral part. Nor is any such assertion advanced in the papers submitted by the wife in support of her cross motion for summary judgment.

Moreover, it appears evident to us that any determination of the content and particulars of the rights of the wife or the obligations of the husband under this document cannot be made without inquiry into and resolution of questions of Jewish religious law and tradition. We think it inaccurate to identify the relief sought by plaintiff, as does the majority, as "simply to compel defendant to perform a secular obligation to which he contractually bound himself." (At p. 115, 459 N.Y.S.2d 575, 446 N.E.2d 139.)

The complaint's first request for relief paints with a broad brush, asking that the court "declare the rights and other legal relation of the plaintiff and defendant in the marriage contract" created by reason of the Ketubah. That such an all encompassing declaration of rights exceeds the authority of the civil court seems to be implicitly conceded by the majority's attempt to limit its consideration to enforcement of an obligation of the husband to appear before the Beth Din.

The wife's pleading itself, however, not to mention the affidavits submitted by her, makes it clear that even a definition of the purported "secular obligation" requires an examination into the principles and practice of the Jewish religion. Although the English translation of the Ketubah attached to the complaint recites that the parties "recognize the Beth Din . . . as having authority . . . to summon either party at the request of the other," the complaint seeks a declaration that the husband specifically perform "in that he appear before the Beth Din . . . pursuant to the request of the plaintiff." Thus, the wife tenders her construction of the document, which in turn presumably is predicated on what she contends is tradition in the faith, i.e., that there is an obligation imposed by the agreement to appear before the Beth Din at the summons alone of the other party to the marriage despite the facial reference to a summons by the Beth Din. The husband, tendering his own construction of the document, denies that he is under any obligation to appear before the Beth Din because an earlier request by him for convocation of such a body was refused. Thus, it appears evident that any judicial determination whether the husband is obligated to appear before the Beth Din, or what nature of summons is required to call such obligation into play, necessarily involves reference to substantive religious and ecclesiastical law. (The recital in the testimonium clause itself is indicative—"this Ketubah was executed and witnessed this day in accordance with Jewish law and tradition.")

The unsoundness of the position espoused by the majority to justify judicial action to compel the husband to appear before the Beth Din, is revealed by projection of the course the continuing litigation will take in this case. The motion to dismiss and the cross motion for summary judgment having both been denied, the case will be set down for trial. The evidence which the wife may be expected to introduce is revealed by examination of the affidavits she submitted in opposition to the motion to dismiss and in support of her cross motion for summary judgment. Her affidavit conveys information furnished her by Rabbi Mordecai Kieffer who in his accompanying affidavit describes himself as "qualified to render an expert opinion concerning matters of Jewish laws and custom." She relies on his affidavit to support her claim that there was "good and legal consideration" for the Ketubah and that the Beth Din presently has no authority to compel the husband to submit to its jurisdiction. The rabbi, predicated on what he offers as a more accurate translation of the Ketubah into English, expresses the opinion that "good and legal consideration" is to be found in the document itself. Then, describing in detail the procedures incident to the issuance of a "Get," the rabbi concludes that the husband was obligated to submit to the jurisdiction of the Beth Din without the issuance of any summons by it. Accordingly, it is evident that the wife and her counsel are themselves of the view that substantiation of her position will depend on expert opinion with respect to Jewish law and tradition.

The majority's reference to the fact that marriage relationships solemnized within a religious context are recognized by the civil law is not determinative of the question here presented where what is sought to be enforced is an aspect of the relationship peculiar to the religion within which the ceremony creating it took place. No authority is cited in which a civil court has enforced a concomitant undertaking required by the ecclesiastical authority under which the marriage ceremony was solemnized. That no such civil enforcement of the obligation to appear before the Beth Din was contemplated either by the drafter of the Ketubah or by the parties as its signatories is evident from the inclusion of explicit authorization to the Beth Din "to impose such terms of compensation as it may see fit for failure to respond to its summons or to carry out its decision." Nothing in the record suggests that it was the intention of the parties when they signed this religious document that the civil courts of the State of New York were to have jurisdiction to determine the substantive right created thereby or to invoke civil procedures and remedies for the enforcement of such rights. Indeed, any conclusion on the part of our courts that this express provision was not intended by the parties as the exclusive remedy available to them for any breach of their obligations under the Ketubah would itself necessarily entail examination of Jewish law and tradition.

Finally, the evident objective of the present action—as recognized by the majority and irrefutably demonstrated by the complaint—even if procedural jurisdiction were to be assumed, is to obtain a religious divorce, a matter well beyond the authority of any civil court. (Again supplying her own interpretation of the Ketubah, the wife alleges: "That pursuant to the terms of the Ketubah, the plaintiff and defendant agreed that in the event of any civil divorce decree that the husband grant and the wife accept a Jewish divorce decree in accordance with the authority vested in the Beth Din of the Rabbinical Assembly.") As was noted at the Appellate Division, the interest of the civil authorities of the State of New York in the status of the marriage between these parties was concluded when the final judgment of divorce was entered in 1978.

COOKE, C.J., and FUCHSBERG and MEYER, JJ., concur with WACHTLER, J.

JONES, J., dissents and votes to affirm in a separate opinion in which JASEN AND SIMONS, JJ., concur.

Order reversed, etc.

NEW YORK DOMESTIC RELATIONS LAW

§ 253. Removal of barriers to remarriage.

1. This section applies only to a marriage solemnized in this state or in any other jurisdiction by a person specified in subdivision one of section eleven of this chapter.

2. Any party to a marriage defined in subdivision one of this section who commences a proceeding to annul the marriage or for a divorce must allege, in his or her verified complaint, that he or she has taken or will take, prior to the entry of final judgment, all steps solely within his or her power to remove any barrier to the defendant's remarriage following the annulment or divorce.

3. No final judgment of annulment or divorce shall thereafter be entered unless the plaintiff shall have filed and served a verified statement that he or she has, prior to the entry of such final judgment, taken all steps solely within his or her power to remove all barriers to the defendant's remarriage following the annulment or divorce.

4. In any action for divorce based on subdivisions five and six of section one hundred seventy of this chapter in which the defendant enters a general appearance and does not contest the requested relief, no final judgment of annulment or divorce shall be entered unless both parties shall have filed and served verified statements that each has taken all steps solely within his or her power to remove all barriers to the other party's remarriage following the annulment or divorce.

5. As used in the verified statements prescribed by this section "barrier to remarriage" includes any religious or conscientious restraint or inhibition imposed on a party to a marriage, under the principles of the denomination of the clergyman or minister who has solemnized the marriage, by reason of the other party's commission or withholding of any voluntary act. It shall not be deemed a "barrier to remarriage" within the meaning of this section if the restraint or inhibition cannot be removed by the party's voluntary act. Nor shall it be deemed a "barrier to remarriage" if the party must incur expenses in connection with removal of the restraint or inhibition and the other party refuses to provide reasonable reimbursement for such expenses. "All steps solely within his or her power" shall not be construed to include application to a marriage tribunal or other similar organization or agency of a religious denomination which has authority to annul or dissolve a marriage under the rules of such denomination.

6. No final judgment of annulment or divorce shall be entered, notwithstanding the filing of the plaintiff's verified statement prescribed by this section, if the clergyman or minister who has solemnized the marriage certifies, in a verified statement, that he or she has solemnized the marriage and that, to his or her knowledge, the plaintiff has failed to take all steps solely within his or her power to remove all barriers to the defendant's remarriage following to annulment or divorce, provided that the said clergyman or minister is alive and available to testify at the time when final judgment would be entered.

7. Any person who knowingly submits a false verified statement under this section shall be guilty of making an apparently sworn false

statement in the first degree and shall be punished in accordance with section 210.40 of the penal law.
(eff. Aug. 8, 1983)

> BRETT V. BRETT
> Court of Appeals
> [1969] 1 All. E.R. 1007

WILLMER, L.J. We have before us an appeal and cross-appeal from an order made by Baker J. on July 5, 1968, varying a previous order made by the senior registrar on June 14, 1968, awarding to a successful wife petitioner maintenance consisting partly of a lump sum payment and partly of annual payments, including a nominal order for secured maintenance. The case has raised interesting questions as to the considerations affecting the award of a lump sum payment and the proper balance to be maintained between any such lump sum payable and an award of annual payments.

The order appealed from was made in pursuance of section 16 (1) of the Matrimonial Causes Act, 1965, the effect of which was substantially to re-enact section 5 (1) of the Matrimonial Causes Act, 1963. The subsection reads as follows:

> On granting a decree of divorce or at any time thereafter (whether before or after the decree is made absolute), the court may, if it thinks fit . . . make one or more of the following orders—(a) an order requiring the husband to secure to the wife, to the satisfaction of the court, such lump or annual sum for any term not exceeding her life as the court thinks reasonable having regard to her fortune (if any), his ability and the conduct of the parties; (b) an order requiring the husband to pay to the wife during their joint lives such monthly or weekly sum for her maintenance as the court thinks reasonable; (c) an order requiring the husband to pay to the wife such lump sum as the court thinks reasonable.

It has been held by this court in *Davis v. Davis* [1967] P. 185 that the word "reasonable" in paragraphs (b) and (c) is governed by the same considerations as are applicable to paragraph (a); that is to say, "reasonable" means "reasonable having regard to the wife's fortune, the husband's ability and the conduct of the parties."

The history of the marriage, since it lasted only some five-and-a-half months, can be briefly stated. The marriage took place on December 11, 1966. The parties lived together until June 1, 1967, when the wife left the husband. She complained that, during that period of five-and-a-half months' cohabitation, the husband had horrified her by his revolting sexual demands and practices. She obtained leave to file a petition forthwith, notwithstanding that three years had not elapsed since the marriage, obtaining that order on the grounds of exceptional depravity and exceptional hardship. The petition was not defended by the husband, and it resulted in a decree nisi being granted to the wife on the ground of his cruelty on October 10, 1967. On the wife's application leave was granted to expedite the decree absolute, and the decree was in fact made absolute on October 26, 1967.

At the time of the marriage the wife had just been admitted as a solicitor, and she had in fact worked for a month or so for her father but had not taken out a practicing certificate. As a result of the husband's treatment of the wife her health was adversely affected. According to the doctors, whose affidavits we have seen, she was reduced to a severe anxiety state which appeared likely, if she went on, to lead to a complete breakdown in her health. We are informed that even now she is not fully recovered and has not yet been able to resume work as a solicitor. In the meantime, since the breakdown of the marriage, she has lived mostly with her parents.

It is common ground that the husband is an extremely wealthy man. Exactly how wealthy he is is not really known because of his persistent failure to afford proper discovery of documents. The case proceeded before the senior registrar and before the judge on the basis that, in relation to any facts which were in dispute, the court was entitled to draw inferences in favor of the wife and against the husband, as was done in *J. v. J.* [1955] p. 215.

In this court it was at first submitted on behalf of the wife that the husband was not entitled to be heard at all on his appeal, having regard to his contempt in failing to comply with the order of the court, but, when it appeared that the court might be disposed to order an adjournment so as to enable the husband to purge his contempt and give proper discovery, Mr. Eastham, who appears for the wife, on instructions elected to waive his objection so as to enable the court to achieve finality on this hearing. The case, therefore, proceeded before us on the same basis as it had proceeded in the court below.

. . .

The problem which has to be solved is how much, in such circumstances, ought to be awarded to the wife by way of annual maintenance, and what, if any, lump sum payment should be ordered, bearing in mind the husband's relatively small income but very substantial capital assets. The registrar awarded a sum of £15,000 by way of lump sum payment. He also awarded by way of annual maintenance £2,250 per annum, but as an interim measure the annual maintenance was to continue at £3,000—the figure awarded by the interim maintenance order—until such time as the lump sum payment was made. He also awarded £1 per annum to be secured. As to that, no question has arisen in the subsequent proceedings. On appeal, Baker J.

increased the lump sum payment to £25,000, but ordered a decrease of the annual payment to £1,000 per annum less tax. He granted a stay pending appeal on terms that the husband continue for the time being to pay £3,000 per annum as under the interim order.

Both parties now appeal to this court. On behalf of the husband it has been contended that there should, in the circumstances of this case, be no lump sum payment, or, alternatively, that the lump sum payment should be a much lower figure than that ordered by the judge. It is conceded on his behalf that, if the lump sum awarded is set aside or reduced, then the annual payments should be correspondingly increased, but it is also contended that if, on the other hand, the lump sum payment is to stand as ordered, then the annual payments should be decreased. On the other side, on behalf of the wife, it has been contended that both the lump sum payment and the annual payments should be increased.

I turn now to consider the provisions of section 16 (1) of the Act. In the present case the wife's fortune consists substantially of her ability to earn about £1,250 per annum as soon as she is well enough to resume work. The husband's ability is obviously very large indeed. I do not think that I need say more about it than that it is certainly large enough to provide for any payment to the wife that could conceiveably be justified.

With regard to the conduct of the parties, that of the wife does not appear to be open to any criticism whatsoever. In this respect this case is to be contrasted with *Davis v. Davis* [1967] P. 185, to which I have already referred, in which case the wife had been guilty of adultery in respect of which she had had to pray for the exercise of the court's discretion in her favor. As to the conduct of the husband here, perhaps the less said the better. It is, I think, sufficient to remark that the charges made against him by the wife have never been denied. The question has been raised, however, as to the relevance in the circumstances of this case of the husband's conduct when it came to assessing the maintenance due to the wife. It has been conceded on her behalf that an award of maintenance cannot be used as a means of punishing the husband for his misbehavior. It has, however, been submitted—I think rightly—that the husband's conduct is, at any rate, relevant in two ways. First, in view of his conduct, which had the effect of driving the wife out, it is submitted that he can hardly be heard to use the argument that this marriage only lasted a very short time. In this respect also this case is to be contrasted with *Davis v. Davis*, where the marriage had lasted for something over ten years. Secondly, it is said that the conduct of the husband is relevant in relation to his refusal or failure to obtain a gett, thereby precluding the possibility of the wife remarrying and thus finding some other man to support her in the event of her wishing to do so.

. . .

From that statement of principle it has been argued on behalf of the wife that she is entitled, in effect, to compensation for the loss of the position which she would have held as the husband's wife and for the loss of the benefits which would have accrued to her from living with a husband of such wealth and position. On behalf of the husband, on the other hand, it has been contended that maintenance never has been awarded, and ought not to be awarded, on a compensation basis, like an award of damages. For my part, I think that this is largely a battle of words. Whether or not maintenance is called "compensation," I do not propose to depart from Lord Merrivale's test, that is to say, the test of taking into consideration the position in which the wife was entitled to expect herself to be, and would have been, if the husband had discharged his marital obligation—the marital obligation being, of course, an obligation to maintain her on the scale appropriate to his station in life.

It has been argued on behalf of the husband, I think in reliance on what I said in *Davis v. Davis* [1967] P. 185, that the only specific project put forward to justify a lump sum payment in this case is that of purchasing a relatively modest flat, for which purpose, it is said, the £15,000 lump sum payment awarded by the registrar would be amply sufficient. I think, however, that I should make it clear that the illustrations which I gave in *Davis v. Davis*, in the passage which I have already quoted, p. 192, as to the type of case which the legislature must be assumed to have had in mind, were not intended to be exhaustive. By 1963, when the power to award lump sum payments was first introduced, several cases had already arisen in which it had been found advantageous in this day and age for husbands possessed of large capital assets so to arrange their affairs that they had little or no apparent income but were able, by skillful use of their capital assets, to enjoy a high standard of living. I feel little doubt that section 16 (1) is well designed to deal with just that class of case, of which the present case seems to be a conspicuous example. It would be quite absurd, in my view, in the present case to award maintenance merely on the basis that this husband is a man with an income of something just in excess of £4,000 per annum and nothing more. If ever there was a case in which it would be appropriate to order a substantial capital payment in order to make proper provision for the wife, the present case is that case. Moreover I think that there is an additional reason in the present case for ordering a substantial capital sum to be paid, having regard to the risk that the husband may see fit in the future to remove still more of his capital assets out of the jurisdiction, as he has already done to a substantial extent by way of the Bahamas trust, and the further risk that he may even go away himself to live abroad.

Finally, I am disposed to accept the submission put forward on behalf of the wife that, in the circumstances of this case, it would be right to make provision in the award for the possibility of the husband persisting in his refusal to obtain the gett which would make it possible for the wife to remarry if she wants to.

In all the circumstances I have come to the conclusion that the proper award to make in this case is, first, a lump sum award of £30,000, payable in two installments, vis., £25,000 within fourteen days, and the balance of £5,000 three months from today, if by that time the husband has not obtained a gett. With regard to the annual payments, I think that the proper award is one of £2,000 per annum less tax, with this further addition: that: in the event of the husband obtaining a gett, so that the £5,000 lump sum installment does not become payable, then the annual payment should be increased by £250 to £2,250 per annum less tax; that is to say, the sum at which the registrar originally arrived. This, as it seems to me, involves the dismissal of the husband's appeal and allowing the wife's cross-appeal to the extent which I have stated.

DANCKWERTS L.J.: I agree with the judgment which has been delivered by Willmer L.J., and I do not wish to add anything.

. . .

PHILLIMORE L.J.: . . . Mr. Eastham, for the wife, has said that this wife, married to a man with the very large financial resources of this husband, could reasonably have expected to receive presents of jewelry, furs, perhaps a motor car, and to be provided with every domestic convenience, while she would normally have enjoyed, if she had wanted them—holidays abroad, perhaps some capital out of which to provide for her own requirements, and, of course, of great importance to a woman, provision made for her if he pre-deceased her—and he was, after all, 17 years older. Mr. Eastham argued that the rights now afforded by section 26 of the Matrimonial Causes Act, 1965, to apply for maintenance from the estate of the deceased husband were not likely to afford the same result as a wife would normally receive if still living with her husband at the time of his death. He concedes that the only reservation to be applied in considering all these matters is the reservation that this court must not go further than is reasonable.

How are these matters to be translated into the terms of a reasonable award? I confess that at one time I thought that this was a case where there was a good deal to be said for a lump sum award in place of any other form of maintenance, and, in that event, the lump sum would, as I think, have amounted to at least £50,000. It seemed to me that there were two reasons for this. First of all, this husband is a man who has so arranged his affairs that, in substance, he lives on capital. Secondly, and more important, he has on his own admission already transferred what he calls part of his capital to two trust companies in the Bahamas. The wife says that he told her that he was able to direct the use of this money and to get it back into his own hands if he wished to do so. I do not doubt that that is the position. Moreover, according to the wife, he told her that he himself might have to live abroad for tax reasons; and, of course, if he is meditating that, and meditating the transfer of the capital which he retains in this country, and which I have no doubt is at least half a million pounds, then he might be in a position to defeat an order for periodical payments.

I have, however, come to the conclusion that it would not be reasonable in this particular case to make an award in that form, and I find myself convinced by the arguments which have appealed to my Lords and which have been recited by Willmer L.J. So far as the lump sum is concerned, it has to be remembered that this young woman is only 23, and, if she gets the freedom to remarry, and does remarry, and particularly if she remarries a very rich man, or even a rich man, it might be thought that a sum of £50,000 was excessive and that she had acquired far more than in the event was justified. It must be remembered that, once a capital sum has been awarded and paid, the order cannot be varied and the money cannot be recalled. Accordingly, I entirely agree that this is a case for the award of £30,000, to be dealt with in the manner that Willmer L.J. has proposed together with the order for periodical payments as proposed by him.

So far as the £5,000 to be paid if no gett has been granted, it is perhaps material to observe that this man, as we are informed—and I do not think that he has disputed it—is not an orthodox Jew, whereas his wife is an orthodox Jewess. For all practical purposes, therefore, the position at the moment is this: that, since only the husband can apply for the gett, he is in a position to remarry, whereas the wife, being an orthodox Jewess, is not. I have not the slightest doubt that his failure to apply for a gett has been due to the reason to which the judge concluded it was due, namely, the hope that he could use his power to bargain to avoid payment of part of any maintenance award by the court. Apparently, it costs 25 guineas to obtain a gett, and the procedure involved only occupies a few days. By his failure to apply for a gett the husband is preventing this woman from obtaining other support, and in addition, as I have said, I have no doubt that he is seeking to obtain an advantage in bargaining with her.

For these reasons, I entirely agree with the order as proposed by my Lords, and I would dismiss the husband's appeal and allow the wife's cross-appeal accordingly.

Order accordingly.

# Topic Sixteen
## Epilogue: The Future of Jewish Law

In the Introduction, to this book we suggested that if one looks at the tips of the branches of the tree of Jewish law one will see new life and growth. That suggestion leads us at the end of the book to consider briefly the future of Jewish law.

## A. JEWISH LAW IN ISRAEL

In the State of Israel the future of Jewish law is a subset of a broader set of constitutional concerns that have been left unresolved since the establishment of the state in 1948. Zionism is partly a secular, nationalistic movement and partly a messianic, religious one. When the movement triumphed in 1948, its leaders were unable to satisfactorily resolve the constitutional implications of its discordant parts. As a result, there is an ad hoc quality to the organic legal structure as Israelis await the needed consensus on constitutional questions. In the meantime, the legal structure of the Ottoman, Turkish Empire and the successor, British mandate over Palestine has been retained, including Article 46 of the Palestine Order in Council, which the British enacted in 1922. This article provides that the jurisdiction of the civil courts shall be exercised in conformity with the rules of the English Common Law and the doctrines of equity to the extent that circumstances permit. Limited areas of personal status are carved out for decision by religious rather than civil courts. Consequently, Israeli civil courts use British law as a major source of civil decision. In 1980, however, the Knesset (Parliament) passed the Foundations of Law Act, which formally establishes a link between Israeli law and "the principles of freedom, justice, equity and peace of Israel's heritage." In other words, Jewish law is now to be a primary source of legal guidance in the absence of specific precedent or legislation by the Knesset.

Since the enactment of the Foundations of Law Act, several steps have been taken to implement it. An Advisor on Jewish Law has been appointed by the Ministry of Justice. The Advisor on Jewish Law furnishes opinions that explain the position of Jewish law on issues arising before the courts, and he assists state prosecutors to draft pleadings in those cases where the directives of the Foundations of Law Act may be properly invoked.

The Ministry of Justice is also engaged in drafting bills that would apply Jewish law to many civil and criminal issues and to standards of evidence. Commentaries will compare the provisions of the contemplated acts with the sources of Jewish law and suggest how to interpret and apply the new acts in the spirit of Jewish law. At this writing, most work has been done on issues in civil law, including guarantee, unjust enrichment, agency, hire, loans, and copyright.

These activities are intended to set the stage for the extensive use of Jewish law in Israeli Courts. That will not happen, however, until lawyers and judges are widely educated in Jewish law and feel comfortable with it. Toward that end the Ministry of Justice has organized conferences, workshops, lectures, courses and seminars to provide information about Jewish law to lawyers, judges, and legislators, and it has initiated discussions with the law schools and universities in Israel to encourage more emphasis on Jewish law in the curriculum. The sources of Jewish law, including parts of Maimonides' *Mishneh Torah*, are being published in editions rearranged to follow the order of the Israeli Civil Law Code. Supreme and district court decisions since 1948 are being compiled with comparative references to Jewish law. Bar-Ilan University has stored a large body of responsa in a computer file to make this material more readily accessible.

It is clear nonetheless that for some time to come Israeli courts will continue to use the British common law precedents that have informed Israeli legal activity over three decades. People cannot be re-educated quickly, and they resist change. It is also clear that there will be opposition to the use of Jewish law by many Israelis who are afraid that the Orthodox establishment is becoming more entrenched through the implementation of the Foundations of Law Act. Ironically, precisely the reverse may occur. As more and more non-Orthodox Israelis come to know and use Jewish law, people with increasingly wide views will have a role in interpreting and applying it. That will provide a much healthier context for its interpretation and operation, and it may well wrench control of Jewish law from the hands of the Orthodox. As Jewish law comes into more general use, its rules can be expected to converge with those of other modern legal systems. In any case, the process of using Jewish law as a source for modern Israeli law has been set in motion.

## B. THE UNITED STATES

In the United States Jewish law has also enjoyed something of a re-naissance in the last decade. Orthodox groups, partially under the in-fluence of their Israeli counterparts, are attempting to study Jewish law in a more coordinated, topical way than they have in the past. Or-thodox spokesmen have written works that examine, among other subjects, the relevance of Jewish law to several amendments of the United States Constitution. The Conservative Movement has begun publishing the responsa of its Committee on Jewish Law and Standards with the intention of making those responsa more widely available to Conservative rabbis and, through them, to their constituents. More-over, the youth group of the Conservative Movement, United Syna-gogue Youth, has undertaken a project to increase the knowledge and observance of the Sabbath laws to the 25,000 members of that group. Even Reform Judaism has become more seriously interested in Jewish law in recent times. In 1976 the Central Conference of American Rab-bis approved a statement of principle entitled "Reform Judaism: A Centenary Prospective," which included the following section:

> *Our Obligations: Religious Practice.* Judaism emphasizes action rather than creed as the primary expression of a religious life, the means by which we strive to achieve universal justice and peace. Re-form Judaism shares this emphasis on duty and obligation. Our found-ers stressed that the Jew's ethical responsibilities, personal and social, are enjoined by God. The past century has taught us that the claims made upon us may begin with our ethical obligations, but they extend into many other aspects of Jewish living, including: creating a Jewish home centered on family devotion; life-long study; private prayer and public worship; daily religious observance; keeping the Sabbath and the holy days; celebrating the major events of life; involvement with the synagogue and community; and other activities which promote the survival of the Jewish people and enhance its existence. Within each area of Jewish observance Reform Jews are called upon to con-front the claims of Jewish tradition, however differently perceived, and to exercise their individual autonomy, choosing and creating on the basis of commitment and knowledge.

This theoretical statement makes it clear that the Reform Movement also is interested in incorporating aspects of Jewish law into its defini-tion of Judaism and its goals for Jews. Nor is this statement only theo-retical; Reform day schools and adult education programs have begun to create a constituency of Reform Jews who are committed to observing aspects of Jewish law in their lives, even if they do not see the entire corpus of law as a binding structure.

These developments within the Jewish community are no doubt aided by the softening of the all-encompassing quality of secular law in America. The assumption of most moderns has been that all law is to be administered by the state. As we saw in Part Two, the Enlightenment ideology pushed the modern secular state to take control of matters of marriage and divorce so that religious authorities would no longer have primary domain even over matters of personal status. Increasingly, however, American courts and legislatures have permitted groups to create their own rules and tribunals of arbitration and conciliation. The heavy workload of cases that crowd state courts and the greater recognition of the efficacy of nonjudicial means for solving social problems have motivated this acceptance of other means of resolving disputes. These developments have enabled Jewish groups to use Jewish law in a variety of areas. Jewish conciliation boards have been created in some of the major centers of Jewish population in the United States. They deal with landlord-tenant disputes, inheritance problems, and many other issues that would normally go to the courts. Another sign of this reawakening interest in Jewish law in the United States is the publication in English of a number of serious scholarly works on Jewish medical law and Jewish business law. Yet another manifestation of this interest is the offering of courses on Jewish law in some American colleges and law schools, including the course that initiated the writing of this book.

## C. Limits on Jewish Law

Despite this concrete evidence of new study, interpretation, and application of Jewish law in our time, there are limits to its growth. Probably the most fundamental limit is the simple fact that most modern Jews do not accept the divine authority of Jewish law. If God is not the author and enforcer of the law, then, some moderns ask, why obey it? To paraphrase Martin Buber, "I cannot keep as a commandment that which I do not believe was commanded." The result is that approximately 85 percent of Israelis and a comparable percentage of American Jews do not behave according to the requirements of Jewish law.

Another factor that inhibits the use of Jewish law in our time is the need to update it in a number of areas before it can be operative in a modern setting. These new understandings and applications of the law are emerging especially in Israel, but the process will take both wisdom and time.

Jewish law does not exist in a vacuum in the modern world, and most Jews look to the law of the state to resolve their disputes. This is not surprising since the state possesses the means of enforcement which the Jewish community lacks. Moreover, it is only in certain areas that American law allows people to make their own rules by contract or arbitration. Secular law may allow civil claims, personal injuries, and labor disputes to be resolved by the rules that the parties agree on, but it is unlikely to tolerate private criminal law. Thus the existence of a competing, authoritative, secular legal system imposes built-in limitations to the scope of issues that American Jews could legally refer to their own tribunals.

There is another matter: If the state recognizes as binding the rules of one religious community, it will find itself diluting the separation between church and state. The state will also be led to assist in enforcing the rules of all communities, including some that are less attractive than Jewish law. Juvenile authorities in several states have faced the problem of young children being subjected to severe corporal punishment in the name of religion. Judges have had to intervene to insist on life-saving blood transfusions for children whose parents object to such treatment on religious grounds. In the case of the cults, state authorities have had enough difficulty trying to balance the right to freedom of religion against the state's interest in protecting its citizens against kidnapping and involuntary confinement; the state certainly does not want to enter the arena of enforcing the cults' discipline on their members. If religious affiliation and commitment is anything but voluntary, the state would be involved in deciding some very sticky issues.

Obedience to Jewish law may often have been motivated by theological beliefs, but it was prompted by social considerations as well. The authority of Jewish law was always crucially dependent on the sense of community that existed among Jews; and one sad feature of modern Jewish life in the last and the present generation is that many Jews have lost confidence in the Covenant, the sense of communal link with the past and the memory that we stood together at the foot of Sinai to receive the law. The Jewish community is unified by social and political concerns for Soviet Jewry and the maintenance of the Jewish state in Israel, but that communal sense has lost its religious moorings. The Covenant with God to which the governed consented, even though the rules were hard to obey, no longer commands the same respect.

One can understand the whole story that we have recounted in this book as that of a people in search of God through law. The law, for Judaism, is God's chief expression to human beings and the most reliable means for people to know and do God's will. It is an everpresent and all-encompassing manifestation of God's love. If our experience as students and teachers has persuaded us of anything, it is that this search still has meaning and still makes claims on modern minds and souls. The same Oliver Wendell Holmes, Jr., who said that certainty generally is illusion and repose is not the destiny of man also proclaimed that it is possible to live greatly in the law.

> *Psalms* 119:57–64:
> The Lord is my portion;
>   I have resolved to keep Your words. . . .
> I have considered my ways,
>   And have turned back to Your decrees.
> I have hurried and not delayed
>   To keep Your commandments. . . .
> I arise at midnight to praise You
>   For Your just rules.
> I am a companion to all who respect You,
>   To those who keep Your precepts.
> Your steadfast love, O Lord, fills the earth;
>   Teach me Your laws.

The words of the psalmist may seem a bit too certain and confident to reflect our state of mind, but the postmodern world increasingly resonates with them. The new branches on the tree of Jewish law look different from the ones that flourished in times past, but they surely form part of the same living tree.

# Appendix A
## Time-Line on Jewish Law

c. 1700–150 B.C.E.: PERIOD OF THE HEBREW BIBLE

    c. 1700 B.C.E.—Abraham
    c. 1290 B.C.E.—Exodus from Egypt
    c. 1000 B.C.E.—David
       722 B.C.E.—Fall of Northern Kingdom  ⎫  Biblical laws and
                   10 tribes become "lost"  ⎬  Prophets
       586 B.C.E.—Fall of Southern Kingdom,  ⎨  (Isaiah, Jeremiah,
                 exile to Babylonia  ⎭  and others)
       516 B.C.E.—Some return to Israel under Haggai and Zekhariah
       444 B.C.E.—Ezra: A. Institutes synagogue and prayer service.
                          B. Canonizes the Torah by reading it publicly in Jerusalem on Sukkot.
                          C. Sets up the Men of the Great Assembly (who are probably the same people later known by the Greek name "Sanhedrin"); they are scholars, judges, and legislators.
    444 B.C.E.–70 C.E.—Development of the Oral Tradition

70 C.E.–220: PERIOD OF THE TANNAIM (ORGANIZED ORAL LAW)
    A. The decisions of the Tannaim are contained in:
       1. The Mishnah: R. Judah HaNasi (The President): 6 Sedarim, (Orders), 63 Massekhtot, (Tractates), Hebrew.
       2. The Tosefta: R. Hiyya and R. Oshaiah.
       3. Baraitot: known only through their appearance in the Gemara.
    B. Their legal interpretations of biblical verses appear in *Midrashai Halakhah*:
       1. The Mekhilta: on Exodus.

2. The Sifra: on Leviticus.
3. The Sifre: on Numbers and Deuteronomy.

220–500: PERIOD OF THE AMORAIM
    A. The Babylonian Talmud (Gemara) compiled by Ravina
       and Rav Ashi c. 500 C.E. (same order as Mishnah; Baby-
       lonian Aramaic).
    B. The Palestinian (Jerusalem) Talmud (Gemara)—com-
       piled c. 400 C.E. (same order as Mishnah; Palestinian Ar-
       amaic; much shorter than the Babylonian Talmud).

500–650: PERIOD OF THE SABORAIM

650–1050—PERIOD OF THE GEONIM (IN BABYLONIA)
    The responsa literature

c. 1000–1250: PERIOD OF THE COMMENTATORS AND EARLY POSEKIM
           (IN SPAIN, FRANCE, AND NORTH AFRICA)
    1013–1073—R. Isaac of Fez ("Alfasi," "Rif")
    1040–1105—R. Sh'lomo Yitzhaki ("Rashi")
  c. 1100–1275—Tosafot (e.g., Rabbenu Tam, Ri, etc.)
    1135–1204—Maimonides ("Rambam") (*The Mishneh Torah;
        The Guide for the Perplexed*)

c. 1250–1550—PERIOD OF THE RISHONIM (IN SPAIN, FRANCE AND
          NORTH AFRICA)
    1195–1270—R. Moses b. Nahman (Nahmanides, "Ramban")
    1233–1310—R. Solomon b. Abraham ibn Adret ("Rashba")
    1250–1327—R. Asher ben Yehiel ("Rosh," "Asheri")
    1270–1343—R. Jacob ben Asher (*Arbaah Turim* or "The Tur"—
        "4 rows" or parts: *Orah Hayyim, Yoreh Deah,
        Eben-Ha-Ezer, Hoshen Hamishpat*)
      1565—R. Joseph Caro (*The Shulhan Arukh*—the order of
        the *Tur*)

1565–PRESENT—PERIOD OF THE AHARONIM (PRIMARILY IN EASTERN
         EUROPE)
  c. 1650—R. David ben Samuel HaLevy (*Turei Zahav*—"Taz")
  c. 1650—R. Shabb'tai b. Meir Ha Kohen (*Siftei Kohen* =
       "Shakh")
  1720–1797—R. Elijah, the Gaon of Vilna
      1863—R. Solomon Ganzfried (*The Kitzur Shulhan Arukh*)
  c. 1900—R. Yehiel M. Epstein (*Arokh Ha Shulhan*)

# Appendix B
# Books of the Hebrew Bible (Tanakh)

I. The Torah (Pentateuch)
  A. Genesis
  B. Exodus
  C. Leviticus
  D. Numbers
  E. Deuteronomy

II. The Prophets
  A. Former Prophets ("former" in the sense that these historical books come before the literary prophecies in Section B)
    1. Joshua
    2. Judges
    3. I Samuel
    4. II Samuel
    5. I Kings
    6. II Kings
  B. Latter Prophets
    1. The Major Prophets ("major" in the sense that their books are much longer than those of the "minor" prophets)
      a. Isaiah (Chapters 1–39 = First Isaiah, or Isaiah of Jerusalem; Chapters 40–66 = Second Isaiah, or Isaiah of Babylonia)
      b. Jeremiah
      c. Ezekiel
    2. The Twelve Minor Prophets
      a. Hosea
      b. Joel
      c. Amos
      d. Ovadiah (Obadiah)
      e. Jonah
      f. Mikhah (Micah)

g. Nahum
h. Habbakuk
i. Zephaniah
j. Haggai
k. Zekhariah (Zechariah)
l. Malakhi

III. The Writings (Hagiographa)
   A. Psalms
   B. Proverbs
   C. Job
   D. The Five Scrolls (that are read in the synagogue on special occasions during the year)
      1. Song of Songs
      2. Ruth
      3. Lamentations
      4. Ecclesiastes
      5. Esther
   E. Daniel
   F. Ezra
   G. Nehemiah
   I. I Chronicles
   J. II Chronicles

# Appendix C
## The Structure of the Mishnah

| Title | Subject |
|---|---|
| A. Seder Zeraim (Agricultural Law) | |
| 1. Berakhot | Blessings |
| 2. Pe'ah | Gleanings from the harvest (Lev. 19:9–10) |
| 3. Demai | Doubtfully tithed produce |
| 4. Kilayim | Diverse kinds (Deut. 22:9–11) |
| 5. Shevi'it | The Sabbatical Year (Ex. 23:10–11) |
| 6. Terumot | Heave offering (Lev. 22:10–14) |
| 7. Ma'aserot | Tithes (Num. 18:21) |
| 8. Ma'aser Sheni | Second Tithe (Deut. 14:22ff.) |
| 9. Hallah | Dough offering (Num. 15:17–21) |
| 10. Orlah | The fruit of young trees (Lev. 19:23–25) |
| 11. Bikkurim | First fruits (Lev. 26:1–11) |
| B. Seder Mo'ed (Special Days) | |
| 1. Shabbat | The Sabbath |
| 2. Eruvin | Sabbath limits |
| 3. Pesahim | Passover |
| 4. Shekalim | The Shekel dues (Ex. 30:11–16) |
| 5. Yoma | The Day of Atonement |
| 6. Sukkah | The Feast of Tabernacles |
| 7. Betzah | Festival laws |
| 8. Rosh Hashanah | Rosh Hashanah and other new years |
| 9. Ta'anit | Fast days |
| 10. Megillah | Purim |

575

| Title | Subject |
|---|---|
| 11. Mo'ed Katan | The intermediate days of Festivals |
| 12. Hagigah | The Festival offering (Deut. 16:16–17) |

C. Seder Nashim ("Women"—Family Law)

| | |
|---|---|
| 1. Yevamot | Levirate marriage (Deut. 25:5–10) |
| 2. Ketubbot | Marriage contracts |
| 3. Nedarim | Vows (Num. 30) |
| 4. Nazir | The Nazirite (Num. 6) |
| 5. Sotah | The suspected adulteress (Num. 5:11ff.) |
| 6. Gittin | Divorce |
| 7. Kiddushin | Betrothal, marriage |

D. Seder Nezikin ("Damages"—Civil and Criminal Law)

| | |
|---|---|
| 1. Bava Kamma | Torts (e.g., personal injuries, property damages) |
| 2. Bava Metzia | Civil law (e.g., questions of ownership, renting, etc.) |
| 3. Bava Batra | Property law |
| 4. Sanhedrin | Courts (procedures, jurisdiction, remedies) |
| 5. Makkot | Whipping (Deut. 25:2), cities of refuge (Num. 35:9ff.) |
| 6. Shevu'ot | Oaths |
| 7. Eduyyot | Testimonies, hierarchy of courts |
| 8. Avodah Zarah | Idolatry, wine, milk and meat |
| 9. Avot | Moral maxims |
| 10. Horayot | Erroneous rulings of the court (Lev. 4:22ff.) |

E. Seder Kodashim (Sacrifices)

| | |
|---|---|
| 1. Zevahim | Animal offerings |
| 2. Menahot | Meal offerings |
| 3. Hullin | Animals slaughtered for food |
| 4. Bekhorot | Offerings of first-born animals (Deut. 15:19ff.) |
| 5. Arakhin | Vows of valuation (Lev. 27:1–8) |

| Title | Subject |
|---|---|
| 6. Temurah | Substitution of offerings (Lev. 27:10) |
| 7. Keritot | Extirpation (Lev. 18:29) |
| 8. Me'ilah | Sacrileges (Lev. 5:15–16) |
| 9. Tamid | The daily sacrifices (Num. 28:3–4) |
| 10. Middot | Measurements of the Temple |
| 11. Kinnim | The bird offering (Lev. 5:7ff.) |
| F. Seder Tohorot (Purity) | |
| 1. Kelim | Impurity of articles |
| 2. Oholot | Impurity through overshadowing (Num. 19:14–15) |
| 3. Nega'im | Leprosy (Lev. 13; 14) |
| 4. Parah | Red heifer (Num. 19) |
| 5. Tohorot | Ritual purity |
| 6. Mikva'ot | The ritual pool of water for purification |
| 7. Niddah | The menstruant woman |
| 8. Makhshirin | Liquid that predisposes food to becoming impure (Lev. 11:37–38) |
| 9. Zavim | Emissions (Lev. 15) |
| 10. Tevul Yom | Impurity between immersion and sunset (Lev. 22:6–7) |
| 11. Yadayim | The impurity of hands |
| 12. Uktzin | Parts of plants susceptible to impurity |

# Index of Subjects

Aaron, 127; and blood sacrifice, 79–80; clash with Korah, 230–35; compared to Bedan, 226; and dietary laws, 62; and Golden Calf incident, 230; at Mt. Sinai, 36–37; as progenitor of Jewish priesthood, 62

Abba b. Memel, Rav, 176–77

Abbahu, 272, 429

Abbasid Caliphate, 10–11

Abbaye, 168, 310; on compensation for temporary injury, 176; on extortion of a *get*, 529; on Eye for eye, 172, 173; and ordination of rabbis, 267; on relations with non-Jewish courts, 272

Abdimi, R., 189

Abihu, 36–37

Abiram, 230–35

Abraham, 442; buys cave of Makhpelah, 18–19, 425; circumcision of, 84, 88; Convenant Code, and, 84, 86–88; discusses fate of Sodom with God, 110–11; and endogamy, 469; and "measure for measure," 183; settles in Canaan, 17

Abraham b. David of Posquieres, R.: criticism of Maimonides, 386, 396, 408; opposes legislation by rabbinic courts, 403–404

Absalom, 182; as judge, 57, 58

Abun, R., 427

Adam, 468, 486, 494

Adultery: *See* Sexual relations.

Agricultural laws, 35

*Agunah* ("A chained woman"), 529. *See also* Divorce.

Ahab, 8; delayed punishment of, 120

Aharonim, 12

Akiba, 290–91; in clash between Rabbi Gamliel II and Rabbi Joshua b. Hananiah, 229; compared to worker with basket, 152; on divorce, 521, 541;

as editor of oral law, 141, 216, 308–12; on eligibility of witnesses to be judges, 178; Maimonides on, 379–80; and Midrash Halakhah, 146; opposes death penalty, 225; ordains Rabbi Meir, 311; and parable of fox and fishes, 247; rejects status considerations in compensation, 157, 159; on rules of evidence, 179; on uncovering a woman's head, 159–60; visited by Moses, 196

Albeck, Hanokh, 408

Alexander the Great, 135–36

Alfasi, 375

Almohades (Spain), 373

Amariah, 68

*American Reform Responsa: Jewish Questions, Rabbinic Answers, 1889–1983* (Jacob), 343–44

American law: bases of authority and legitimacy in, 49–51, 126; jurisdiction of courts, 65–66; rules of evidence in, 73; *See also* United States.

—compared to Jewish law, 3, 46, 48, 56, 435–37; and arbitration, 299–302; and attaints, 117; attitude toward custom, 422–24, 431, 433–34; attitude toward codification, 368–69; continuity and change in, 186, 199, 204–13, 403; on divorce, 447–48; means of minimizing litigation, 289–90; personal injury awards, 160–65; reason for obedience to, 95; requiring forgiveness, 158; and responsa 304; role of oral materials in, 222, 391–92; role of covenant in, 92–93; similarities of Constitution and Oral Torah, 217, 225–26; and withholding testimony, 70

"American Legal Realism and the Covenantal Myth" (Sturm), 82–83

Isserles, Rabbi Moses, 288, 317;
commentaries on *Shulhan Arukh*, 375–
76; on divorce, 542; on endangering
oneself, 357; influence of, 328; on
marriage laws, 514; on right of judges
to interpret the law, 389–90
Italy, Jewish communities in, 327

Jacob, 425–26, 442, 469
Jacob ben Asher, 12, 374, 376
Jacob b. Meir, R. *See* Rabbenu Tam
Jehoiakim, 131
Jehoshaphat, 67, 68, 291
Jepthah, 226
Jeremiah, 8; buys a field, 515; predicts
death of King Jehoiakim, 131; sabbath
law, and, 128; warns that God may
destroy the Temple, 99, 100
Jerubbaal, 226
Jerusalem Talmud, 143
Jerusalem: Maccabee rebellion, and, 136;
as seat of Jewish cult, 67; welcomes
Alexander the Great, 135–36
Jesus: clash with Pharisees, 135; early
followers of and Jewish law, 235–43; on
Eye for eye, 181; parables on retribution,
183; possible member of Essenes, 140;
rejected by Palestinian Jews, 24
*Jewish Self-Government in the Middle
Ages* (Finkelstein), 416
Jewish Theological Seminary of America,
341
Jewish community: in biblical times, role
of elders, 59, 60–61; legislation by, vis-
a-vis rabbinical courts, 404–407, 415,
432; and nonobservance of rabbinical
decrees, 409–11, 413
Jewish law: in America, 337–62, 566–67;
authority in, 51, 52–53, 248–49; and
biblical law, 13–14; on intention, 252–
53; in Israel, 363–65, 402, 532, 564–65;
and legal positivism, 249–50, 254–55;
legislative rights of community in,
405–407, 432; majority rule in, 195,
222, 336–37, 426; oral tradition in, 141;
present applications, 567–69;
prohibition on injuring self, 346–52,
355–59; prohibition on risking danger,
350–52; prohibition of sculptured
images, 347; teaching proscribed by

Romans, 265–69; transcendental
elements in, 14, 52, 53, 249–57, 361
—continuity and change in, 52, 123–32,
227; after rejection of new prophecy,
129–31; through fuller understanding,
124–25; through judicial interpretation,
131–32, 187–204, 213–35, 424 (*see
also* Rabbinic law: exegesis as means of
change); through revelation, 125–28
—interaction with common law, 435–37;
in divorce, 272, 470, 512–23, 546–63;
jurisdictional base in non-Jewish states,
51; in marriage, 454–67, 470, 506–15,
523–63. (*See Dina de-malkhuta dina*)
—legislation (*takkanot*) in: biblical
prohibition of, 402; community
disapproval, 409–410, 432; history and
justification of, 402–07; Maimonides
on, 407–14; Rabbenu Tam on, 414–20
—*See also*, Codes (Legal), Covenant Code,
Custom, Rabbinic courts, Rabbinic law
Jewish nationalism: initially rejected by
Reform Judaism, 245
Jews for Jesus, 245
Job: on God and nature of evil, 113–15;
and "measure for measure," 182
Job, Book of: problems of dating, 113
Johanan ben Zakkai, Rabbi, 189, 310; as
president of Sanhedrin at Yavneh, 227–
28, 266–67
John the Baptist, 179
Joseph, 182
Josephus: on Alexander's welcome in
Jerusalem, 135; on Eye for eye, 181; on
Pharisees, 140, 216, 316
Joshua (biblical): prohibits marriage to
Canaanite women, 469; receives Oral
Torah, 378
Joshua, Rabbi, 189, 190, 223
Joshua b. Hananiah, 141, 228–29
Joshua b. Levi, R.: on ordination outside
Palestine, 269
Josiah, 8, 67, 120
Book of Jubilees, 180, 183
Judah b. Baba, Rabbi: ordains rabbis, 267–
68
Judah bar Ilai, Rabbi, 468
Judah Ha-Nasi (Rabbi), 178; on Akiba,
152; on compensation for degradation,
176, 177; as editor of the Mishnah,
141–42, 169, 308–12, 368, 378–79; on

# Index of Sources

## Rabbenu Tam

## RESPONSA

## OTHER SOURCES